EUROPE AFTER ROME

Europe after Rome offers an integrated appraisal of the early Middle Ages as a dynamic and formative period in European history. The book overturns traditional narratives, replacing them by an entirely fresh approach to the period *c.*500–1000, and arguing that the post-Roman world was characterized by great diversity of experience and perception. To explain how the men and women who lived in this period ordered their affairs, the author uses an innovative methodology combining cultural history, regional studies, and gender history. Extensive use of original sources introduces all levels of society from slave to emperor, allowing individuals to speak to us in their own words.

Regional variations, the nature of power, and the legacy of Rome are the three central themes of an analysis that ranges comparatively across the length and breadth of Europe—from Ireland to Hungary and from Scotland to Scandinavia to Spain and Italy—leaving little doubt of the complex cultural realities of this period. In the context of debates about the social, religious, and cultural meaning of 'Europe' in the early twenty-first century, we should look to the early Middle Ages for the origins of European pluralism and diversity.

St Andrews sarcophagus (front panel). © Crown copyright. Reproduced courtesy of Historic Scotland.

Europe after Rome

A New Cultural History
500–1000

Julia M. H. Smith

OXFORD

UNIVERSITY PRESS

OXFORD
UNIVERSITY PRESS

Great Clarendon Street, Oxford OX2 6DP

Oxford University Press is a department of the University of Oxford.
It furthers the University's objective of excellence in research, scholarship,
and education by publishing worldwide in

Oxford New York

Auckland Cape Town Dar es Salaam Hong Kong Karachi Kuala Lumpur
Madrid Melbourne Mexico City Nairobi New Delhi Taipei Toronto
Shanghai

With offices in

Argentina Austria Brazil Chile Czech Republic France Greece
Guatemala Hungary Italy Japan South Korea Poland Portugal
Singapore Switzerland Thailand Turkey Ukraine Vietnam

Published in the United States
by Oxford University Press Inc., New York

British Library Cataloguing in Publication Data
Data available

Library of Congress Cataloging in Publication Data
Data available

ISBN 978-0-19-924427-0 (Hbk.) 978-0-19-289263-8 (Pbk.)

5 7 9 10 8 6

Typeset by Laserwords Private Limited, Chennai, India
Printed in Great Britain
on acid-free paper by
Ashford Colour Press, UK

FOR HAMISH

Acknowledgements

WRITING a book is a careful balance of individual endeavour and collective help. While taking full responsibility for the opinions and errors this one contains, I nevertheless have great pleasure in thanking all those who have enabled me to undertake and complete it. In the first place, I am grateful to Simon Mason at Oxford University Press for inviting me to write it, and, more recently, to Ruth Parr and all her team for their editorial encouragement and expertise. I could not have written without generous amounts of research leave, and for that I thank, in the first instance, the University of St Andrews, where I am grateful to my colleagues in the Department of Mediaeval History for accommodating my periods of withdrawal from teaching, and to the School of History Research Committee, for a subvention towards the cost of maps and diagrams. External funding has been essential to its completion, and I have been the privileged recipient of a Fellowship-in-Residence at the Netherlands Institute of Advanced Study (1999–2000), a fellowship at the Shelby Cullom Davis Center for Historical Studies, Princeton University (2001), and Arts and Humanities Research Board Research Leave (2003–4). I thank all those who elected me to these positions.

In the course of writing this book, I have drawn heavily on the assistance and friendship of many people. At St Andrews, special thanks are due to Duncan Stewart in Reprographics for preparing nine of the maps, and to Margaret Grundy and her staff in the Inter-Library Loans department of the University Library for cheerful efficiency in tracking down the material I needed. I am indebted to Alicia Correa for compiling the index with expert professionalism. Over the years, dozens of colleagues have responded generously to email, telephone, and conversational requests for bibliography and advice without necessarily realizing why I was consulting them: I truly appreciate this help. Julia Crick, John Hudson, Mayke de Jong, Tom Noble, and Alex Woolf all commented on one or more chapters in early draft, and I have benefited greatly from their suggestions. Four people read most or all of it and gave sustenance far beyond astute criticism and advice. Peter Brown and Chris Wickham scrutinized the entire manuscript towards the final stages of composition, and, in saving me from many errors and jejune remarks, showed me how to push the argument much further. Over the years, Jinty Nelson responded to most of it, and provided unstinting encouragement in good times and bad. Finally, Hamish Scott is not only the best of friends and, unofficially, the best of editorial critics, but has enabled the good times that have finally brought this book to completion. Its dedication is a small public token of a large private debt.

Contents

RESOURCES

IDEOLOGIES

List of Figures

Abbreviations

AASS	*Acta Sanctorum quotquot toto orbe coluntur*, ed. J. Bollandus et al. (Antwerp, Brussels, Paris, 1643–1940)
CCCM	Corpus Christianorum, Continuatio Medievalis
CCSL	Corpus Christianorum, Series Latina
CSEL	Corpus Scriptorum Ecclesiasticorum Latinorum
EHD	*English Historical Documents*, i: c.*500–1042*, ed. Dorothy Whitelock, 2nd edn. (London, 1979)
EME	*Early Medieval Europe*
MGH	Monumenta Germaniae Historica
AA	Auctores Antiquissimi
Epp.	Epistolae
Epp. Sel.	Epistolae Selectae
Poetae	Poetae latini medii aevi
SRG	Scriptores rerum Germanicarum in usum scholarum separatim editi
SRL	Scriptores rerum Langobardicarum et Italicarum
SRM	Scriptores rerum Merovingicarum
SS	Scriptores
PL	*Patrologiae Cursus Completus, Series Latina*, ed. J.-P. Migne, 221 vols. (Paris, 1844–65)
SC	Sources Chrétiennes
Settimane	Settimane di studio del Centro italiano di studi sull'alto medioevo

Note on Conventions

Persons

Where dates are given in parentheses after the names of rulers, counts, bishops, and popes, they refer to period of office. Dates of birth and death are indicated thus: b., d..

Personal names are given in common English forms, whenever possible.

Places

To aid location I have relied on Europe's major rivers and mountain ranges as prominent landmarks; they are marked on Figure 0.1. In addition, I have sometimes used modern nations (Scotland, France, Germany, etc.) as geographical descriptors: the reader is cautioned that these have absolutely no political validity for the period under discussion. Principal places mentioned in each chapter are marked on its first map.

Place names are given in standard English forms, where these exist, and otherwise in the dominant local language.

Sources

Notes are confined to identifying the editions of works from which I quote: all translations are my own unless otherwise indicated. Many early medieval texts, especially histories and saints' lives, are readily available in excellent translations, with or without the original language on the facing page, and I acknowledge whenever I have reproduced these. For those texts where the original is not available in the same volume as the translation I have cited, there follows in parentheses a reference to the best available edition. In those cases where I disagree with widely available English translations, I have provided my own translation but have usually noted the availability of an alternative English version.

Introduction

As concepts originating in the Italian Renaissance, 'Antiquity' and 'the Middle Ages' are deeply embedded in historical consciousness, and few would doubt that these catchwords stand for distinct phases of Europe's past. Scholars during the Renaissance, however, popularized the terms as antithetical poles of European culture, the former positive, the latter negative. When History emerged as a separate university discipline in the middle decades of the nineteenth century, the study of the past for its own sake became institutionalized. This occurred in a way that isolated Antiquity and the Middle Ages from each other in different museums and art galleries, libraries and academic departments. Certainly, serious scholars no longer treat the so-called medieval period as the bleak antithesis of the ancient world, even if the notion of a 'Dark Age' lingers in journalistic vogue. Nevertheless, debates about the relative contribution of 'Antiquity' and the 'Middle Ages' to the complex and problematic phenomenon of 'European Civilization' have persisted in juxtaposing the one against the other. In all this, the centuries in between have remained the poor relations, dismissively labelled as impoverished, barbarian, superstitious, or archaic. If the broad sweep of European history is conceived in linear or evolutionist terms, they are viewed as a period of national origins for narratives whose unfolding requires simple virtues, distinct identities, and suitable foundations for later progress. Alternatively, within a cyclical view of history, they become an interlude of lesser significance between two peaks of political and cultural achievement, the Roman Empire and the cosmopolitan Christian Europe of the twelfth and thirteenth centuries. Both frameworks impose value judgements rooted in the political needs and cultural preferences of post-Enlightenment Europe. This book rejects these hard-worn paradigms. It proposes that the dynamic transformation of Europe's cultures between Antiquity and the Middle Ages is of fundamental significance in its own right.

When did this transformation occur? Periodization can be the bane of historians. Scholarly arguments, each with their own premises, locate the end of the ancient world anywhere between the fifth century and the late tenth or early eleventh century. Where the caesura is placed depends on whether priority is given to political, institutional, social, economic, or cultural criteria as the basis of periodization: the neat half millennium of my subtitle is deliberately artificial. It serves as an approximate guide to the contents of this book, for this contested period forms its subject. At its opening, around the year 500, Roman imperial rule had already ceased to be operative in the West, but most other aspects of Roman culture and practice persisted, little affected by changing political structures: in 500, Europe was post-imperial, but not thereby post-Roman. By around 1000, quite different imperial polities dominated the political landscape, and the Roman cultural legacy had both been transformed and exercised a transforming effect over a vast area of Europe. Those changes are equally evident in the city of Rome itself, the former western imperial provinces, and the lands far beyond them. In order to establish their main contours, I pursue themes both before and after the rounded dates of AD 500 and AD 1000. This allows me to demonstrate that, within the overall matrix of social and cultural development across these centuries, change occurred at different times and speeds in different places.

Multiple terminologies accompany disputed periodization. The 'late Antiquity' of the ancient historian, the 'early Middle Ages' of the medievalist, the 'early historic period' or 'late Iron Age' of the archaeologist of non-Roman Europe reflect different disciplinary presumptions and analytical perspectives but can all refer to the same century. For simple convenience, I have generally preferred to use the phrase 'early Middle Ages' to cover the entirety of the matter discussed in this book, but that too is arbitrary.

The geographical scope is similarly less self-evident than my title might suggest. In mythological origin, Europa was a Phoenician princess. But the god Zeus, in the form of a bull, raped her and carried her off over the sea: her name came to refer to one of the three continents known in Antiquity. By the ninth century, the name 'Europe' was shedding its use as a geographical descriptor and acquiring instead strong overtones as a designator of the zone where Latin Christian traditions found allegiance. Indeed, for much of the Middle Ages, 'Europe' yielded to 'Christendom', the land of Rome-centred Christianity, as the preferred term of cultural identification. A legacy of confusion between geographical and cultural signification has persisted ever since. For most of the nineteenth and twentieth centuries, 'Europe' could be divided along political, religious, and social fault lines into 'western' and 'eastern' sections, with 'Mitteleuropa' assigned an ambivalent role and a contested location somewhere in between. Now, in the early twenty-first century, the meaning of 'Europe' is under renewed scrutiny, its geographical, cultural, religious, and political connotations more debated than ever before. Even at the most simplistic level of definition—the member states of the European Union—Europe has changed while this book has been in preparation.

My frame of reference certainly approximates to the expanded European Union that came into being on 1 May 2004, but with two significant qualifications. The first is the exclusion of Greece (together with its non-EU Balkan neighbours). Retaining a focus on the area that by the end of the first millennium was acquiring an identity as Latin Christendom has meant relegating the Byzantine world to an offstage role. The second is imposed by the evidence available. Some parts of 'Europe' were inhabited by preliterate peoples for part or most of these centuries, while others are poorly represented in surviving documentation. Scandinavia, the Slav regions, and the Danubian plain all fall into the former category; much of Scotland and Wales into the latter. Thus the contours of this book are inevitably those of the extant written word. I have avoided the temptation to fill the gaps by using texts from later centuries that purport to offer a window onto these earlier times, but instead have sometimes turned to material evidence to complement the textual record. Even so, the very uneven coverage of archaeological research and publication imposes its own constraints.

The story of the transition from Antiquity to the Middle Ages has conventionally been told in two parts. The first instalment tells of imperial decline, barbarian invasion, economic stagnation, and the decay of urban culture; its sequel hails the rise of national monarchies and an internationally organized Christian church accompanied by the gradual recovery of economic prosperity and civic life. Of the various forms of this grand narrative, the one most familiar today privileges France, Germany, and England and allocates occasional episodes to Italy. It defines its subject in terms of significance to the post-medieval history of nation building and high culture, thereby virtually ignoring everywhere that did not conform to the nineteenth-century paradigm of the nation state. While this overt teleology has certainly weakened since the 1960s, distinctive national historiographical traditions nevertheless still inform twenty-first-century approaches to the early Middle Ages. Additionally, much scholarly literature continues to take as its field of analysis either the modern polity or the early medieval ethnic or political grouping deemed to precede it, whatever specific topic is under investigation. The only place the reader of this book will find any trace of these approaches is at the back, in the Further Reading.

I have substituted three revisionist approaches, chosen for their combined analytical vigour. In the first place, I rebalance the usual historiographical emphasis on a 'core' region by attention to a much broader geographical field of vision stretching from Scandinavia to Spain and from Hungary to Ireland. As Figure o.1 suggests, this is a region of great natural differentiation between north and south, upland and lowland, coast and interior; this variation forms the backdrop to the chapters that follow. Secondly, I repeatedly move between polities, medieval or modern, cross-cutting national historiographical preoccupations and ignoring modern political boundaries. Finally, I reject any notion that Europe in the early Middle Ages can be characterized as a homogeneous culture-province. My premiss is diversity of experience, not analogy of historical outcome.

In place of teleological determinism, I substitute a comparative ethnography of the early Middle Ages. This method draws heavily, albeit indirectly, on the work of social and cultural anthropologists; its purpose is to enable questions of general applicability to receive locally specific answers. These cumulatively establish a cross-cultural analysis of early medieval societies and facilitate comparisons and contrasts between them. The organizing problem that I address in this fashion can be summarized thus: how did the men and women who lived between 500 and 1000 order their own worlds in social, cultural, and political terms? In answering it, I emphasize the variety of early medieval experience by highlighting both the omnipresence of localisms and micro-regions and the diversities inherent in gender and status distinctions.

Those around whom power congealed—strongmen, lords, kings, emperors—form the goal of my analysis, not my point of departure. Thus they tend to occur towards the end of each chapter, and especially the end of the book. I have chosen to get at them by addressing issues that pertain to the organization of almost all social groupings: language and communication; kinship and gender; the accumulation and symbolism of wealth; religious practice and ideology; personal and group identity; political legitimation and status. Rather than merely explaining what happened, these concerns analyse how and why things happened, how communities were organized, how people gave meaning to their lives and validated their own ways of doing things.

The book begins by establishing the 'ground rules' for subsequent chapters: not only the general limits of what we know about the early Middle Ages and how we can know it, but also the constraints of terrain, climate, and agricultural technology. The first two chapters thus introduce the many and varied environments within which men and women spoke, wrote, and thought, lived and died; together they establish diversity of experience and responsiveness to change as recurrent themes. The next pair

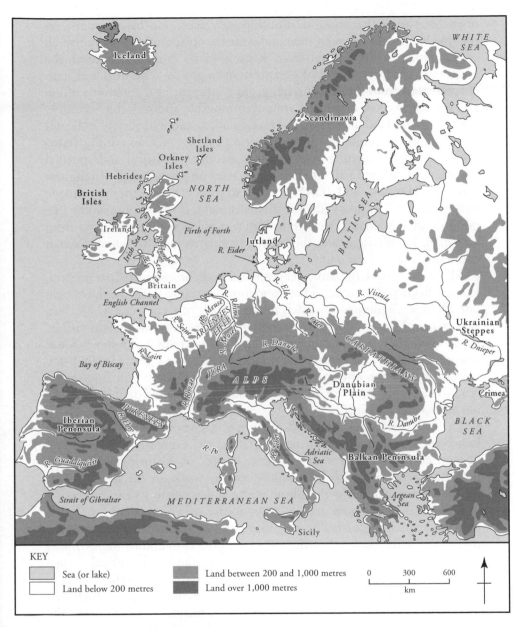

0.1. Europe: physical features.

of chapters argue that social relationships—between kin-based groups, on the one hand, and between men and women, on the other—organize all communities at every level from household to empire, whatever the locally specific forms of social organization might be. The fifth and sixth chapters turn from the power relationships inherent in distinctions of kin and gender to those organized around immovable and movable wealth—that is, around land and treasure. Once again, situational variety indicates a wide range of responses to the generic problem of maintaining status and hierarchy, of turning resources into enduring political and spiritual advantage. The final pair of chapters focuses on experiences of religious and political change and draws attention to ways in which they were made to seem 'natural' by heavy ideological investment. Both emphasize the importance of Christianity as a transmitter of cultural values derived from an earlier, Roman, age, and the many imaginative uses to which Roman cultural resources were put.

All chapters have the same geographical and chronological parameters, Europe from 500 to 1000. They function like transparent overlays: each one offers a diagrammatic sketch of one aspect of a complex whole, but, as they are placed one upon the other, the lower diagrams remain visible. Each is coherent; together the intersecting perspectives build up a full and nuanced picture. The reader who prefers to take these chapters in a different order to the one in which I have arranged them will find ample cross-referencing between chapters but no repetition of definitions, regnal dates, and so forth.

This is a new cultural history of Europe in several ways. Admittedly a loosely conceived genre of historical writing, the expression 'new cultural history' commonly refers to a diverse cluster of historiographical approaches, many of which have influenced my work. In the first place, it signals an engagement with 'culture' in its widest sense, as the expression of meanings, perceptions, and values by means of which people construct their understanding of reality, organize their experiences, and determine their actions. By implication, this approach prefers to endow the men and women of the past with agency, instead of understanding historical change as a series of forces, trends, or movements that reduce individuals to passive pawns in the grip of impersonal processes. Secondly, new cultural history is founded upon sensitivity towards language. It emphasizes the uncertain relationship between texts and the historical 'reality' they purport to represent—or that some historians aspire to find. While that sensitivity sometimes verges on denial of any relationship, I adopt a more moderate position but nevertheless draw readers' attention to some of the textual problems encountered by historians working on this epoch. There follows the proposition that culture is in the service of power, whether it occludes, displaces, or legitimizes its brute realities. Thus cultural history, so the argument goes, contributes to unmasking the realities of power, and revealing strategies of domination for what they are. Finally, it stems from each of these points, individually or in sum, that new cultural history evinces scepticism of grand narratives. In their place, it substitutes a belief in the value of micro-history and a healthy respect for the pluralism of historical experience.

For these reasons, this is a book not about European culture but about Europe's cultures. My approach allows repeated emphasis to be placed on three interpretative threads, all equally central. I have already indicated my insistence upon recognizing early medieval particularities from many different perspectives. The second is the attention I bring to the role of the Roman heritage in early medieval constructions of power. Whether in Rome's former provinces or in regions that were never within the imperial boundaries, I argue that the reception, reinterpretation, or abandonment of that inheritance made a formative contribution to all the cultures of early medieval Europe. The trace of the former political frontier, marked on Figure 0.2, influenced how that occurred: in cultural formation as well as historiographical periodization, the Middle Ages presuppose Antiquity. They cannot be sundered. The third is the dynamism of early medieval societies. The demonstration that the Europe of 1000 was very different from that of 500 is not an argument for any evolutionary grand narrative, but a recognition that, wherever and however one looks, change and fluidity are evident. Decline, stagnation, and rise have no place here; instead a kaleidoscope of multiple transformations, continuities, innovations, permutations.

One artefact sums up this book more eloquently than an extended introduction could do. At some point in the late eighth or early ninth century, a master sculptor fashioned a large box-shaped structure (177 cm wide, 90 cm deep, and 70 cm high) for the royal Pictish church of *Cennrígmonaid*, in eastern Scotland. Its carved panels of local sandstone slot together to form an object of disputed but indubitably Christian function—perhaps a tomb, an altar, or a shrine. Its richly carved front depicts the Old Testament scene of David wrestling with the lion, represented here in his Christian interpretation as king and saviour (see Frontispiece). He is flanked by an ancient eastern symbol of royalty, a lion-hunter on horseback, and an unmounted huntsman with his dogs, in pursuit of Scottish deer. Artistically, it offers a sophisticated amalgam of distinct stylistic traditions: Eastern Mediterranean, Roman, Irish, Anglo-Saxon, and Pictish.

BRITAIN
(until 410)

Rhine

GAUL

Danube

NORICUM

PANNONIA

Ravenna

Rome

Constantinople

1000 km

750

500

250

0

—— Boundary of Roman Empire, c.400

‑ ‑ ‑ Division between western and eastern
emperors' jurisdiction, from 395

○ Imperial capitals

Kingdom of the Suevi, from 409

Visigoths settled under a treaty with Rome, 418

Kingdom of the Vandals, from c.430

o.2. The Roman Empire in the early fifth century.

By the time of its manufacture, Roman rule in Britain had receded to a distant and shadowy memory in the minds of an educated few, and even when, in the middle of the second century, it had briefly reached into southern Scotland, the site of future *Cennrígmonaid* (modern St Andrews: see Figure 1.1) lay beyond the imperial frontier. Nevertheless, an urban religion originating on the eastern fringe of the Roman Mediterranean, Christianity, had become integral to the northern political, social, and imaginative world of the Picts. The so-called St Andrews sarcophagus thus represents my three themes of local identities, cultural dynamism, and the reception of the Roman heritage.

It stands as an icon for the issues addressed here in a second way. The Picts were typical of the many peoples of the Atlantic and North Sea regions of Europe north of the Roman frontier whose polities all had fundamentally different and rather simpler internal socio-political organizations than those of the Roman Empire. From a Roman perspective, the contrast was one of civilization and barbarism, of a divide between 'us' and 'them' based upon ancient Mediterranean beliefs that urban communities and the civic culture that they sustained were inherently superior to technologically and politically less complex, rural, warrior societies. From a twenty-first-century perspective, the artificiality of this categorization is painfully evident. 'Civilized' and 'barbarian' are subjective referents based upon perceptions and traditions designed to legitimize one group at the expense of others by affirming a hierarchy of cultural difference and moral worth. The sculptor of *Cennrígmonaid* associated a classically robed David with a traditionally armed Pictish warrior in a way that quite negates any antithesis between 'civilized' and 'barbarian'. European historiography too needs to transcend this ancient polarity: this book offers a contribution to that endeavour.

FUNDAMENTALS

I

Speaking and Writing

What we say passes, what we write remains.[1]

We hear God's books explained and read to us, the Gospel proclaimed, and His glories made known to men.[2]

CENTRAL to the historian's craft are the written relics of the past. Crudely scratched inscriptions, dry bureaucratic prose, inspired poetry, tax lists, abstract theological speculations, or beautifully illuminated manuscripts: these and many other forms of the written word are the materials on which historians base their constructions of past societies. In thinking about Europe's history in the centuries between 500 and 1000, we face at the outset the dilemma that much written material has not survived. Medieval writers sometimes mention or quote texts and documents to which they had access but which have since perished. In copying documents, scribes might struggle to read the handwriting, or might deliberately alter and update the text in front of them, only to throw the old version away when the new one was finished. The ravages of neglect, damp, fire, and warfare over many centuries have compounded deliberate disposal and accidental loss. For all these reasons, we can be sure that the surviving written record for the early Middle Ages is only a fraction of what must once have existed, even though we cannot measure quite how small it may be. The chapters in this book all take their cue from such written material as does remain.

The vagaries of survival are not the only constraint upon our enquiry. Had nothing been lost, we should still not be able to answer all the questions that we might wish to. For part or all of the period under discussion, people in some parts of Europe made no use of any form of writing. Even in those communities that were familiar with the techniques of writing and reading, these skills were practised by only a small proportion of the population: we can study the early Middle Ages through the words of only a few of the men—and even fewer of the women—who lived in those centuries.

Recognition of these limitations should encourage us to begin our enquiry into early medieval culture by exploring the place of writing within it. Let us remember at the outset that writing always happens in a specific language. It encodes speech in a widely shared repertoire of visual signs that represent the sounds that combine to form words. Thus it is never neatly separable from other verbal activities such as talking, reading, and thinking, and is only one of many different means of communication and expression available to any society. Historians of the modern world are often able to exploit a wide range of communicative media, but a more restricted range is available to scholars of the Middle Ages. Visual images were certainly important, as were numbers, gestures, and symbolic actions, but this chapter focuses on words, spoken as well as written—for we cannot consider the one without the other. Early medieval authors commonly composed by speaking out loud to a scribe who took down their dictation, and they generally did so in the expectation that their words would be communicated by being read out loud to an audience or voiced in a murmur by the individual, solitary reader. Knowledge central to a community's identity and functioning might be passed on orally for generations, whether or not its members were familiar with the techniques of writing and reading. Material from that oral storehouse of traditions and information from time to time found its way into written form, and written texts often acquired their social significance when voiced aloud to an audience of hearers. Thus meanings, thoughts, and ideas conveyed by words flowed back and forth between complementary spoken and written media. Although speaking and writing cannot be divorced from one another, historians must remember at all times that only the written words survive for us to analyse and appreciate: in the much-quoted dictum of Pope Gregory I 'the Great' (590–604): 'What we say passes, what we write remains.'[3] The quandary that faces the student of any pre-modern culture is the inaccessibility of the non-written word, despite its central importance in the lives of men and women.

This chapter thus approaches the question of writing from the perspective of spoken language. What languages did people speak in the early Middle Ages? And how readily could they understand one another? Why and how did the linguistic map of Europe change during these centuries? Of defining importance in their own right, these questions provide our starting point. They also introduce a major theme running throughout this book—the diversity of early medieval experience, so different from the universalizing tendencies of the ancient world.

The second section of the chapter analyses the interrelationship between Latin, the language of Roman imperialism and culture, and the local languages of early medieval Europe by asking what was committed to writing and in which language. A world of widely varying customs and local practices, of communities each with their own ways of going about life, acquires firm focus. Against the background of the political collapse of the western Roman Empire, the uses found for Latin in new contexts open up a world of shifting, dynamic cultural processes that contributed to novel forms of power and authority. The section concludes that, in their adoption, adaptation, or rejection of the language of the Roman Empire, early medieval Europeans were making choices about their own identity and about ways of organizing and expressing power in their own world. Here we meet the second overall theme of this book: that interaction with Roman traditions was of fundamental importance to all localities, including those far beyond the former Roman frontiers. The contribution of this legacy to the cultural formations of early medieval Europe cannot be ignored; this discussion demonstrates the point with respect to language and the uses of writing.

The third theme that runs through this chapter, as through all subsequent ones, is power. Building on the analysis of the relative prestige of different languages in the second section, the final part argues that literacy must be understood as a technology of power. There are two dimensions to this. The first concerns individuals and their access to the relevant technical skills that enabled the exercise of authority. The second has an institutional dimension, for ascetic Christian communities gradually emerged as the upholders of a normative, elite literary culture in a way that lacked precedent in the ancient world but nevertheless perpetuated its cultural prejudices. The overall purpose of this chapter is to make clear that the surviving written sources for early medieval history are never naive in conception or transparent in intent: their choice of language, form, and content betrays implicit cultural value judgements and power relationships. This argument is crucial for what follows: once we are aware of the extent to which the surviving written sources are themselves ways of constructing meaning and organizing power, we can proceed to exploit them to different purposes in subsequent chapters.

The Tower of Babel

Around 850, the wife of Count Hungerius of Langres gave birth to a daughter who was both deaf and mute. Treating her 'like a monster, a brutish animal, more wretched than the slave of one of their domestic

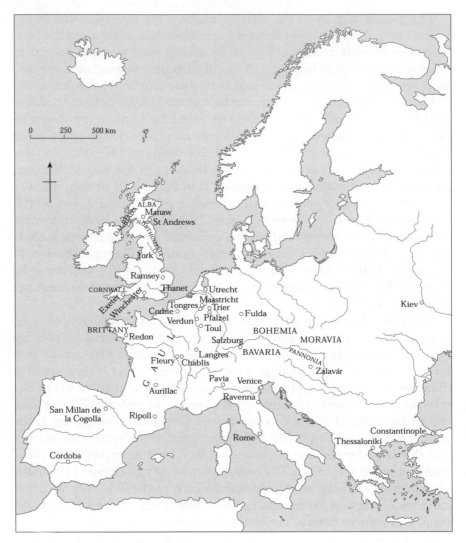

1.1. Principal places mentioned in Chapter 1.

serving girls', her parents rejected her. Somehow the girl survived and, as a grown adult, found her way to the shrine of St Martin at Chablis. Here the saint addressed her: 'Genovefa, my daughter, be not afraid.' As blood poured from her ears and mouth, she was healed. She had never heard speech before, and was Genovefa her name? Shortly thereafter, her brothers' serving-girl happened to visit the shrine and recognized the woman. The servant hailed her as 'my lady Genovefa' and acknowledged the miracle. Cured of her disabilities, Genovefa was restored to humanity.[4] For the monk who described this miracle, as for other writers in the early Middle Ages, the power of speech differentiated humans from animals. Language was a divine gift to humankind.

But in one part of the origin myth that Christians took over from the Jews, all the peoples of the earth had originally spoken the same language. This tale tells how, having constructed the marvellous Tower of Babel, its builders succumbed to pride in their achievement. To punish them, God 'established for earth-dwellers dissimilar tongues so that they had no success with [each others'] languages . . . nor did any people understand what another said.'[5] To this Anglo-Saxon translator of the biblical myth, it seemed evident that each people spoke its own language. Others were less certain, such as Isidore, bishop of Seville (599–636). He was sure that languages preceded peoples, but could not make up his mind quite how they correlated. 'In the beginning, there were as many languages as peoples, but later more peoples than languages, for many peoples arose out of one language.'[6] This constituted a tacit acknowledgement of the fluid, shifting interrelationship of language to people.

Isidore's intuition was certainly correct. We must dismiss the nineteenth-century misconception that there had ever existed a matching relationship of one people or polity to one language. Equally erroneous is the notion that there was linguistic uniformity within any medieval group that regarded itself as constituting a single people or nation. The relationship of languages to peoples in the early Middle Ages was far too complex to be reduced to simple formulae such as these. As we shall see, languages did not start and stop at political frontiers: they overlapped in various ways that took no account of political allegiances. Moreover, they were always characterized by marked internal dialectal variations and were continually evolving. Naturally, language change continued long after the end of our period, so we must bear in mind that the changes reviewed here form one segment of a much longer story—but it is an era of formative significance in European linguistic history, and one that has been central to arguments about the identities of the peoples of Europe since the eighteenth century.

With these points in mind, we can survey the languages of the region on which this book concentrates. Figure 1.2 shows four main language zones at the start of our period. The British archipelago was the main zone of Celtic speech, whose main forms were diverging in important ways in the later Roman period. By the eighth century, two mutually incomprehensible versions were spoken, Gaelic (or Q-Celtic) and Brittonic (or P-Celtic). Although modern philology has established their close affinity, no one in the Middle Ages was aware of this; to all intents and

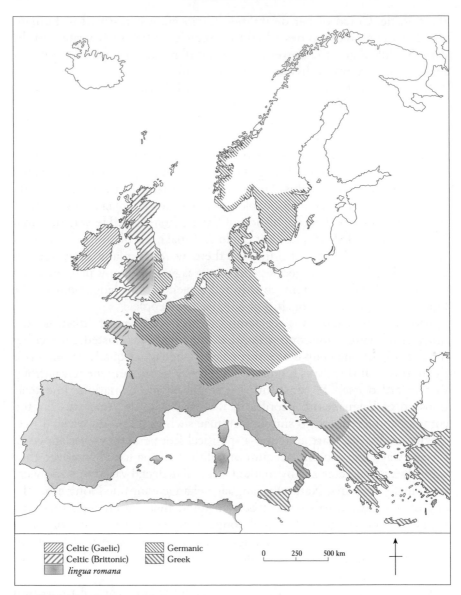

1.2. Main language zones, *c.*500.

purposes, they were two quite different languages. In *c.*500, Gaelic was spoken in Ireland, as well as by settlers across the Irish Sea. Its use along the western coasts of Cornwall and Wales in the fifth and sixth centuries was relatively short-lived, but not so further north, in what is now western Scotland. We shall return here shortly.

Brittonic, the indigenous language of Britain at the time of the Roman conquest, had remained in use alongside Latin during the centuries of Roman rule, but in the early Middle Ages developed distinctive regional forms, including Welsh, Cornish, Cumbric, and Pictish. Neither regional linguistic variation nor differing political fortunes destroyed a sense of shared identity among the British, and a tenth-century Welsh poet could prophesy that the time would come again when the Cymry, the speakers of Brittonic, would once again

> . . . possess all from Manaw [near Edinburgh] to Brittany,
> from Dyfed to Thanet . . .
> from the Wall to the Forth. . . .[7]

In the fifth and sixth centuries, British speakers were also to be found scattered along much of the Atlantic coast of continental Europe, with particular concentrations at the north-western tip of Spain and the westernmost peninsula of what is now France. Only in this latter region—Brittany—was their linguistic impact enduring: in the eleventh or twelfth century, a Welsh writer commented that the Welsh and the Bretons 'were of one language and one people, although geographically separate'.[8] This was the limit of medieval awareness of linguistic affinity in this region of Europe, for the designation 'Celtic' is a construct of eighteenth-century philological erudition infused with romantic-era political and cultural aspiration: it has no basis in medieval understanding.

As a comparison of Figures 1.2 and 1.3 reveals, the extent of Brittonic within Britain shrank greatly in the course of the early Middle Ages. It faced two challenges. Gaelic speakers applied the name Dalriada both to the north-eastern tip of Ireland and to their settlements in western Scotland. From its relatively modest origins in Dalriada around the year 500, Gaelic gradually diffused throughout almost the entire area north of the estuaries of the Solway and Forth. Its maximum extent, around 1100, corresponded to most of the medieval Scottish kingdom, known to its inhabitants as Alba. Within this area, Gaelic had competed with, and then gradually displaced, local Cumbric and Pictish versions of Brittonic. It remains far from clear exactly how this happened, and, while we know that the Irish monk Columba (b. *c.*521, d. 597) could preach Christianity to the Picts in northern and eastern Scotland only 'through an interpreter', it

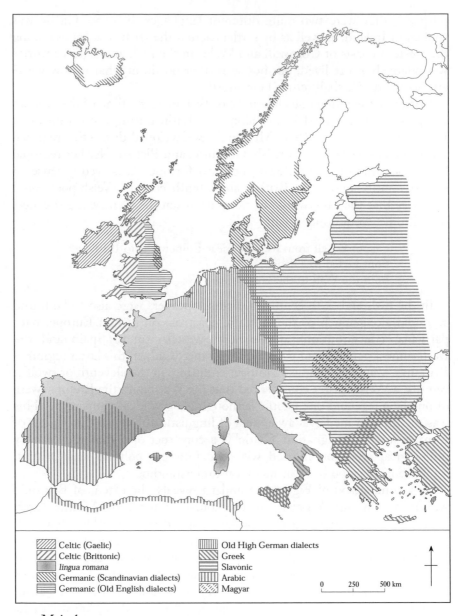

1.3. Main language zones, *c.*1000.

does seem that, in parts of central Scotland at least, a bilingual elite speaking both Gaelic and Pictish persisted until c.900.[9] Thereafter, the dominant language of the kingdom of Alba was Gaelic.

Germanic is the second language-group to consider, although this too is a post-medieval philological categorization. A version of this posed the second challenge to Brittonic, causing the latter's disappearance from southern and eastern Britain. Germanic-speaking elites, collectively—but anachronistically—designated 'Anglo-Saxons', had certainly established a presence on the eastern seaboard of the island during the fifth century. Thereafter, they gradually established political hegemony over all Britain south of the Firth of Forth and east of the Severn by c.750. How their political successes prompted a linguistic transformation so complete as to eradicate Brittonic throughout this area remains deeply contested, however.

The cluster of dialects spoken by the Anglo-Saxons are collectively known as Old English. They are best assessed within the broad Germanic language zone around the North Sea. It comprised the north-western quadrant of the European continent including southern Scandinavia, as marked on Figure 1.2. In the early centuries of the Christian era, Germanic was the speech of those peoples living along and north of the Roman imperial frontier that followed the Rhine and Danube, and its use had extended as far as the flood plain of the river Elbe in the north-east and the Ukrainian steppes in the south-east. The turbulence of the fourth, fifth, and sixth centuries carried its speakers far and wide throughout the western provinces of the empire, whether as isolated individuals, military detachments, entire armies, or even peoples. Among these were groups who styled themselves Goths, Franks, Saxons, Lombards, Frisians, Bavarians, to name only the most important. We shall meet them frequently in this book, as also the kingdoms they established within Roman imperial territories. One indication of the linguistic unity of the early medieval Germanic-speaking world is a remark of Paul the Deacon (b. c.720/30, d. c.799). He came from Italy to the court of the Frankish king Charlemagne (768–814), where his stay will have familiarized him with the sounds of the Germanic dialects north of the Alps. He recalled how the deeds of the Lombard king Alboin (c.560–72) were remembered 'not only among the Bavarians and the Saxons, but also among other men of the same tongue in their songs'.[10]

Except in eastern Britain, and in a broad swathe of territory in northern Gaul, Germanic speakers gradually became assimilated into the local communities, giving up their traditional language in the course of several generations. Social and political upheaval fostered rapid linguistic change within the Germanic zone, as it did within the Celtic zone: here too one sign of this was growing regional differentiation within the Germanic language continuum, with marked results by the end of the millennium. As divergent strands of Germanic emerged, it must have required increasing effort on the part of speakers of one version to comprehend those using another, particularly when the speakers each came from remoter parts of the dialect spectrum. We certainly should not assume that speakers would have held the same opinion about the degree of linguistic identity they shared, however. In the wake of Scandinavian settlement in England in the ninth–tenth century, some English writers differentiated the Scandinavian language from the English, yet, as late as the twelfth century, a descendant of the Scandinavian settlers in Iceland commented that the Icelanders and English 'are of one tongue'. He emphasized this, despite also acknowledging that 'one of the two tongues has changed greatly, or both somewhat'.[11] Speakers' perceptions of language identity or difference were as subjective in the Middle Ages as they remain today. Figure 1.3 acknowledges the growing differentiation between Scandinavian, Old English, and other Germanic dialect forms collectively known as Old High German.

The growing divergences affecting both the Celtic and Germanic languages had been given impetus by major changes in pronunciation, vocabulary, and word-forms, which were particularly rapid in the fourth, fifth, and sixth centuries. No single explanation of these linguistic changes suffices: complex social and political transformations must all be taken into consideration. Of all the contributory factors, population movement probably played only a minor part. More cogent explanations include conquest and Christianization, for these were both potent agents of linguistic change—and sometimes of language death. Additional stimuli came from the development of written forms of these languages and from the influence of Latin, the language of power, prestige, and Christianity, which influenced Celtic and Germanic languages alike.

With Latin, we reach the third important language zone of the early Middle Ages. In the post-imperial era, it continued to be spoken in those provinces less seriously affected by social or political disruption, and where Christian communities persisted undisturbed. In western Britain, Latin was certainly still spoken in the sixth century but died out thereafter. At about the same time, it ceased to be the dominant language in the Balkans, becoming concentrated in the western half of the Mediterranean and most of its Iberian, Gallic, and Italian hinterlands, as Figure 1.2 makes clear.

The fourth and final language marked on Figure 1.2 is Greek, which had been spoken and written throughout the eastern Mediterranean in

Antiquity. The central Balkans and the southernmost tip of Italy had long since stabilized as its western limits, and although knowledge of Greek had formerly been common among the educated elite of the western Roman provinces, this accomplishment had become rare by *c.*500. The declining use of Greek had an additional cause, however, in the appearance of Slavonic. Despite losing much ground to it during the early Middle Ages, Greek nevertheless remained the main language of the southern part of the Balkan peninsula, and in the course of the sixth century replaced Latin as the administrative language of Constantinople, capital of the Byzantine (eastern Roman) Empire. In Italy, where the southernmost provinces remained under Byzantine rule, Greek remained a language of elite literary culture alongside Latin for as long as the administrative bond with Constantinople persisted.

Slavs are first mentioned by Byzantine writers in the middle years of the sixth century, who located their kingdoms north of the lower reaches of the Danube. It is debatable whether the Slavs ever shared any sense of common identity, however. While it is clear that Slav conquests of the northern and central Balkans fostered the spread of their culture and language at the expense of Greek as far south as Thessaloniki at the head of the Aegean Sea, the causes of the cultural transformation remain contested, as elsewhere. By the eighth century, versions of Slavonic appear to have been spoken throughout much of central Europe east of the Elbe, including areas that had formerly been Germanic—some of which would become so again in later centuries. By *c.*1000, increasing amounts of evidence make the extent of Slavonic more certain, and this is shown on Figure 1.3.

There are two further languages marked on Figure 1.3, both spread by well-documented conquests: Arabic and Magyar. Muslim armies crossed the Straits of Gibraltar in 711 and conquered the southern and central provinces of the Iberian peninsula in the early eighth century; they introduced the Arabic language into Spain. Although Latin continued in use there, it lost its status and prestige as the local population gradually adopted Islam. By the early eleventh century, it remained the language of worship for such Christian communities as remained, but by then Arabic was firmly established as the language of government and elite literary culture. Finally, the Magyars (known to their opponents as Hungarians), in origin nomads from the Asiatic steppes, crossed the Carpathian mountains in the late ninth and tenth centuries on wide-ranging raids before establishing permanent settlements in the Danubian plain, where they introduced their own distinctive language.

Although Latin came under competition from other languages in many parts of the former western Roman Empire, it deserves detailed attention.

In and after late Antiquity, *lingua romana*, 'the Roman tongue', meant Latin, both spoken and written. When it was spoken in Antiquity, pronunciation varied considerably from one region to another and also between elite and non-elite speakers. As a written literary language, the Latin of Antiquity was much less susceptible to change, and retained an inbuilt tendency towards conservatism, standardization, and elitism. The term *lingua romana* referred to all these forms. By the twelfth century, however, *lingua romana* referred only to the spoken forms, 'the Romance tongue'—whether in its French, Walloon, Catalan, Spanish, or Italian versions—to distinguish it from the written Latin language. We can avoid the controversies about how, when, and why spoken Latin stopped and Romance began by referring to the form spoken in the early Middle Ages as simply the *lingua romana*.

It too evolved significantly in the course of the early Middle Ages. Regional divergences in the spoken *lingua romana* gradually become even stronger than in Antiquity, and pronunciation changed too, but not so much as to cause incomprehension between speakers from different regions. That started to happen only around 1200. This meant that, when Abd al-Rahman III, the Arabic-speaking caliph of Cordoba (912–61), exchanged envoys with the German king Otto I (936–73), in 953, they had no difficulty communicating. The caliphal representatives were members of the local Cordovan Christian community, men fluent in both Arabic and the local *lingua romana*. If they had been attentive as they travelled northwards, they might have noticed gradual local shifts of accent and vocabulary, until they finally arrived at Toul, a town still within the north-eastern reaches of the *lingua romana*, but also inside Otto's kingdom. Otto had chosen as his envoy John (b. *c.*900, d. 974), a monk of Gorze, who had been born in the area where the *lingua romana* intermingled with Germanic speech. In all probability bilingual in both these local languages, John travelled south with one of the Cordovan deputation: together they whiled away the long journey by 'talking about everything'.[12] Despite some regional differences, a single language was thus spoken all the way from the Guadalquivir to the Mosel, just as it had been in Roman times. By this date, the descendants of the Germanic speakers who created the fifth- and sixth-century kingdoms had long since abandoned their ancestral language. As a Spaniard who became bishop of an Italian city wrote in the early ninth century: 'Latin, though one language, has within its fold many peoples, like the famous and noble ones of our time: the Franks, the Gauls, the Italians (or Romans), the Lombards; and the Spanish, the Africans, the Asturians and the Basques.'[13] There is an element of linguistic imperialism at work here, for the Basques spoke—and still speak—an ancient language unrelated to Latin, but nevertheless, Claudius of Turin aptly expressed the truism that the *lingua romana* remained a single language spoken by many different peoples.

Latin followed a different trajectory as a written language, however. To track this, we must return from the Mediterranean basin to Ireland, where the spread of Christianity during the fifth century introduced the language of Christian worship used throughout the western Roman world. Irish scholars approached Latin as a language to be acquired by learning to read books in school, not from speaking to parents in the home. They soon developed methods for teaching it as a foreign language, which the new Christian communities in the Germanic parts of Britain also eagerly adopted. For Irish and Anglo-Saxon converts, then, Latin was a written, learned language, not a living, spoken one. They clung to traditional rules for spelling and grammar, in sharp contrast to the fluid usages of native speakers of the *lingua romana*. Only those monks and nuns who travelled to the Continent ever encountered the spoken forms of the language. When they did, they were startled at how different it was from the Latin they had learned to read, write, and pronounce in their schoolrooms. Boniface (b. *c*.675, d. 754) was a missionary from southern England who spent most of his life preaching among the Germanic peoples of the Continent, whose local versions of Germanic he evidently understood without difficulty. But when he visited Rome in 722, he was uncomfortable with the *lingua romana* spoken in the papal court and preferred to communicate important matters in writing. Boniface's written Latin posed no problem for his papal interlocutor, but his experience emphasizes the growing gulf between Latin as a mother tongue and Latin as a language learned in the classroom.

Half a century after Boniface, the Anglo-Saxon scholar Alcuin (b. *c*.740, d. 804) was invited to Charlemagne's court, where he became an influential teacher and counsellor. Among the achievements attributed to him are a reform of the spelling and grammar of the written form of Latin he encountered on the Continent. By bringing it back into line with late antique norms he had learned at school in York, Alcuin initiated reforms that stabilized the written language in a highly conservative way. Though these had no effect on the spoken language, they further exacerbated the growing gulf between the spoken and written language. It seems that preachers who used the learned, 'Alcuinian', Latin were liable to find that they were incomprehensible to audiences north of the Seine, who spoke the orally transmitted *lingua romana*.

This divergence between the spoken and written language, between the 'rustic' or 'vulgar' speech and the Latin of the clerically educated elite, developed only rather later in Mediterranean regions. Not until the very end of the millennium did such a distinction become evident in Rome. When Pope Gregory V died in 999, an inscription was placed above his tomb in St Peter's, commemorating the brief reign of this pope of German origin. Ignoring the turbulent politics of his pontificate, it praised the way he had 'instructed the populace with a threefold eloquence, using German, the vulgar tongue and the Latin language.'[14] Here in Rome, the original home of the *lingua romana*, 'Latin' was no longer the spoken language of the city's inhabitants by the end of our period.

Gregory was the papal name selected by Bruno, cousin and court chaplain to the German emperor Otto III (983–1002). As a career cleric in Germany, he would have acquired his knowledge of Latin entirely in the schoolroom. His elevation to the papal throne took him from the Germanic world into that of the *lingua romana*, which he evidently learned readily enough. Germanic, Celtic, and *lingua romana* were not mutually intelligible; except in the zones where two languages overlapped in frequent use, any bilingualism was an acquired effort, not the product of upbringing. But in the contact zones, the situation must have been rather different. Any place where two spoken languages were in simultaneous use was likely to have been socially complex. Commonly, one will have been the language of the ruling elite and thus enjoyed greater prestige, the other being relegated to the language of the peasantry. This limits the likelihood of widespread, full bilingualism. Active competence in one but general passive knowledge of the other is one possibility; equally probable is partial ability in the second language, for example in restricted spheres of life such as mercantile activity or estate management. Differentiations of social status will have further complicated the picture. Also, scattered communities where the minority language was locally dominant might occur, effectively speech islands.

Although complex linguistic nuances must have characterized areas where any two speech communities overlapped, they are most easily demonstrable where the *lingua romana* shaded off into Germanic. Intensive fifth-century Germanic settlement in areas south and west of the Rhine made Germanic the dominant language far further south than the present-day linguistic frontier between French and German and, for a while, a minority language over much of the northern half of the former Roman province of Gaul. Between the ninth and the thirteenth centuries, however, the border of dominant speech receded to approximately its current position, and any familiarity with Germanic further south faded away. Notwithstanding the dominance of Germanic around Gaul's northern and eastern peripheries, the *lingua romana* continued to be spoken in some cities, such as Tongres, Maastricht, and Trier, as well as in remote valleys in the Ardennes and Jura mountains. How the complex linguistic situation affected the peasantry is impossible to say, but there is good evidence that some members of the aristocracy from this area were bilingual until at least the ninth century. This doubtless facilitated their participation in the far-flung networks of imperial power established by Charlemagne, and, indeed, helped make those networks function. For as long as this empire held together, speakers of *lingua romana* might find themselves sent off to learn Germanic, or married to a husband with a different mother tongue. But the dissolution of the Carolingian Empire that began in the late ninth century lessened the political advantages of familiarity with both languages, except where the bilingual zone persisted along the southern bank of the Rhine. It is symptomatic of the change that, when the German emperor Otto II (973–83) met the leading West Frankish magnate, Duke Hugh (nicknamed Hugh Capet; French king 987–96) in 981, neither spoke the other's language. To communicate, Otto spoke in Latin, and one of the bishops in Hugh's retinue translated for the duke. Evidently Hugh's only language was the spoken *lingua romana* of northern France, and he had neither learned Latin nor understood Germanic.

In sum, we must appreciate the linguistic diversity of early medieval Europe. In this context, some people found it easier than others to strain their ears to make sense of dialectal variations of their own language, or to learn completely different ones. We may contrast the efforts of two Italian missionaries who travelled in 1001 to 'the land of the pagans of horrific-sounding speech'—the Poles. 'With excessive sweat' only one of them tackled the linguistic challenge, learning to understand Slavonic but only to speak it well enough to get by.[15] Although the German-speaking Otto I learned some words of both the *lingua romana* and Slavonic, he nevertheless lacked the confidence to speak them, at least in public. In Chapter 6 we shall meet slave-traders from Verdun who regularly journeyed to Cordoba and German merchants who crossed the Alps to trade in Pavia: certainly these men did not let language difficulties stand in the way of profit. Whatever its diversities and richnesses, language remained the index of humanity. Preaching to the people who dwelt around the southern shores of the Baltic, the ninth-century missionary Rimbert encountered strange dog-headed creatures with two legs. On seeking advice, he was reassured that a key diagnostic was the sound they made: 'humans speak but dogs bark.'[16] Humans shared the facility of language and thus of reason: this united them far more than any language difference divided them.

Languages of Authority

For centuries, Latin had been the language in which the citizens of Rome made love, scribbled graffiti, commemorated their conquest of an empire in monumental inscriptions, wrote laws, issued tax lists, formulated and preserved rich literary traditions. And, as Christianity spread westwards in the second and third centuries, among communities incapable of understanding the Greek in which the Christian holy texts were written, religious leaders naturally chose to debate, preach, worship, and write in the local language. In preparing Latin translations of the Judaeo-Christian scriptures—the Hebrew Old Testament and the Greek New Testament that comprised the Bible—and in using the same language for worship, fourth- and fifth-century churchmen in the western provinces of the Roman Empire were making their religion as widely accessible as possible. In *c.*500 Latin implied a whole system of learning, a social code, and a technology of power as well as a religion.

As imperial rule crumbled and political systems changed from ancient to early medieval ones, how was the privileged status of Latin as a medium of culture, control, and communication affected? In what language did new converts to Christianity, far beyond the former imperial frontiers, worship? In what ways did the social significance of Latin change, and what political or religious importance did other languages acquire? These are important issues in their own right; together, they help us understand why the surviving written sources for early medieval history take the form they do. This section begins by evaluating the fate of the late Roman bureaucratic apparatus in post-imperial times. It then explores the cultural prestige attached to different systems of writing, and concludes with an extended discussion of the relationship between language and authority. This pays particular attention to the choice of language for written use in contexts where ideology and identity were as important as communication of verbal meaning. By tracking regional variations in the use of Latin vis-à-vis the local languages of Europe, it emphasizes that sacred and secular authority both took many different written forms. The argument turns on the paradox that the use of Latin spread in geographical terms as the number of people able to understand it, let alone read and write it, diminished. By the end of the first millennium, Latin had become the mark of an elite, inseparably associated with the authority of kings and clergy alike throughout much—but not all—of the early medieval West.

At the outset, it is helpful to distinguish between the western Roman Empire as a political and territorial entity; its administrative and legal apparatus; and Latin as the language in which communication was maintained and authority imposed. Each had a differing fate in the post-imperial centuries: this uncoupling of polity, documentary procedure, and language helps explain some of the characteristic features of early medieval culture. The fate of the polity need not detain us here, for that will be the focus of Chapter 8. For the moment, it is enough to note that the deposition in 476 of the last western emperor, Romulus Augustulus, was of little political significance, and that the disintegration of the western empire into a cluster of kingdoms ruled by local warlords had already begun much earlier in the fifth century.

Understanding the shifting relationship between language and the exercise of power during the early Middle Ages requires attention to the fate of the highly complex Roman bureaucracy of the fourth and early fifth centuries, for this did not cease to function with the termination of imperial rule in the West. Its salient characteristics in western and eastern provinces alike included the linkage of governmental administration to an elite literary culture underpinned by a system of elementary and advanced Latin schooling. Scribal, stenographic, and notarial skills made the humble careers that sustained everything from military provisioning and the law courts to the book trade and estate management. Equally significantly, hard-won mastery of the canon of Latin classics was the access route to high office and the prestige it conferred. The conventional content of this education thus provided a homogeneous cultural code that obliterated heterogeneous geographical and social origins. Simultaneously, its high cost did much to reinforce the social exclusiveness of the ruling elite by making it beyond the reach of the less well-off.

While governing always relied upon direct personal contact and patronage, late Roman emperors also made extensive use of written administrative, fiscal, and legal procedures. Overall, inefficiency and internal contradiction vied with favouritism and corruption as the chief characteristics of the bureaucratic machinery that mediated between the emperors (one since 324 in Constantinople, the other, western, one since 408 in either Ravenna or Rome) and their subjects in the localities. In outlying western provinces, notably Britain and northern Gaul, much of this had probably collapsed rather earlier in the fifth century; further south, in Spain, central and southern Gaul, and Italy, Romulus Augustulus' removal did nothing to interrupt bureaucratic habits. All the kingdoms that emerged on the Continent during the fifth century relied directly on these inherited techniques of ruling. By appropriating traditional mechanisms of government for their own use, fifth- and sixth-century warrior kings asserted legitimacy, collected revenue, made law, and proclaimed their power.

If we take a long-term perspective, however, it is clear that inherited Roman bureaucracy did not endure. To assert that it decayed would be to adopt an inappropriate narrative of 'decline and fall'. Rather, its constituent elements—documentary forms, legal norms, tax accounting, judicial and archival procedures, and so on—disaggregated and thinned out. In places—but only in some places—fragments of the once-coherent bureaucratic regime then perished. Other fragments took on a new life. Men of property freed slaves, negotiated marriage contracts, endowed churches, and arranged their testamentary bequests in formal documents whose wording and appearance owed much to Roman precedent, but they did so in political circumstances that no Roman official would have recognized.

Establishing any precise chronology for these changes is extremely difficult, however, because of the patchy survival of evidence and the problems of dating what we do have. A few broad generalizations are nevertheless possible, if at the risk of oversimplification. Regarding the period between *c*.500 and *c*.750, the disaggregation tended to be slower in more southern areas than elsewhere, and was slowest of all in the papal bureaucracy in the city of Rome. Simultaneously, however, the nature of political elites was changing. Martial prowess gradually replaced a lengthy literary education as the quality that kings sought in their secular advisers—and that they rewarded with land and office. The bureaucratic expertise and the literary culture that had characterized the late Roman political elite became increasingly the preserve of Christian clergy, for the mastery of the written word remained as crucial for Christian worship as hitherto. Churchmen were thus becoming the new literate elite, experts in using the written word as a medium for negotiating power.

If we now extend our summary overview to the second half of our period, from *c*.750 to *c*.1000, then additional generalizations are possible. After the mid-eighth century, we encounter legal and administrative procedures of Roman origin being adopted, adapted, and transplanted across a wide area, parts of which had never formed part of the Roman Empire. Eighth-century Bavarian dukes promulgated law in self-consciously Roman style; tenth-century German kings made formal grants of land and legal privilege to churches founded amongst the Slavs by means of documents that stand in a recognizable relationship to late Roman exemplars, as do the coins minted by the early eleventh-century Přemyslid rulers of Bohemia. An idiom of power, clearly indebted to Roman precedent, helped bring new kingdoms into being, and clergy played the role of midwife, as Chapter 7 will make clear. In brief, Roman bureaucracy and legal procedure were gradually disarticulated from the fifth century onwards, but, instead of disappearing, they persisted in piecemeal fashion as a repertoire of ways of exercising authority from which Europe's early medieval power brokers could pick and choose.

Against this background, we may turn to the cultural significance of language, and, in particular, to written language. Throughout the ancient world, Latin implied cultural superiority. Like Greek, the *lingua romana* was regarded as the language of learning, law, and rationality—those hallmarks that, Romans opined, raised their own world to a higher level than those around them. To a Roman, the peoples who lived beyond the imperial frontiers were unkempt and ferocious, 'barbarians' whose way of life contrasted unfavourably with that of the inhabitants of the empire. The term 'barbarian' was laden with heavy cultural and linguistic prejudice: 'as much distinguishes a barbarian from a Roman as a four-legged creature from a two-legged one, or a dumb girl from a man with the power of speech', wrote the late-fourth-century poet Prudentius.[17] Above all, the gulf was educational, as we learn from Salvian. A Christian priest from the frontier city of Trier, he was among those displaced in the aftermath of the breach of the Rhine frontier in 406 by Germanic speakers and others, who then made their homes within Roman territory (see Figure 0.2). Writing in the middle years of the fifth century, he characterized the immigrants as 'lacking in Roman learning, indeed in any civilized human education' and 'ignorant of all literature and knowledge'.[18] Education—in the West the mastery of the Latin language in written and spoken form, and in the East, of Greek—entailed the whole cultural formation that underpinned Roman political hegemony. From an imperial perspective, Greek and Latin marked out a superior society that had no respect for the ignorant and uneducated.

Based on education, the distinction between Roman and 'barbarian' was cultural not racial, and thus never formed an impermeable barrier. Except as part of the mental furniture of the Roman elite, we should not take the prejudice too seriously. It is more fruitful to be alert to the ways in which political frontiers functioned as zones of intensive interaction and cultural osmosis, enabling those who originated beyond them to encounter Greek and Latin and either assimilate themselves into the late Roman world or, alternatively, appropriate techniques and uses of writing for their own purposes. Leaders of particular peoples might enter into diplomatic ties and treaties with the emperor that bound their subjects as a group. Assisted by secretaries and interpreters, some warlords, including the Hunnic leader Attila (d. 454), entered into written correspondence with imperial authorities, utilizing Roman norms of written, diplomatic communication to negotiate the standing of their entire following. Individuals often also found personal advancement through trading with the empire or through undertaking military service on its behalf. Priscus, a Greek envoy to Attila, noted that, in addition to the 'barbarous tongues' spoken by the various peoples under Attila's rule, 'those that have commercial dealings with the western Romans [speak] Latin'.[19] Certainly, a fair number of military men and merchants would also have acquired at least rudimentary practical writing skills in the course of their careers. Although it is impossible to evaluate how this might have contributed to individuals' professional success, the adoption of Latin words to do with warfare, writing, and trading into Celtic and Germanic languages is a clear sign of this acculturation.

In other contexts, those living outside the imperial borders appropriated aspects of the culture of writing to their own use rather differently—most notably the notion of symbolic representation of the sounds of which speech is constituted. Runes and ogam are both relevant here. The runic alphabet was a series of letter forms adapted during the first or second century AD from the Greek and Latin scripts to represent the sounds of Germanic speech. It was designed to be cut into wood, metal, or stone. The earliest surviving runes, on objects scattered sporadically throughout the Germanic-language zone, were employed for a range of practical and invocatory purposes, whether inscribing a woman's name on a precious brooch, announcing the name of a treasured sword blade or spearhead, invoking good luck, or even naming the gods. Although often hard to decipher, early runic inscriptions are an example of an important theme, writing as a form of cultural osmosis around the periphery of the Roman world.

Later runic inscriptions epitomize new forms of that interaction. Anglo-Saxon monks standardized the runic alphabet and utilized it for Christian memorial inscriptions in the monasteries and churches of late-seventh- and eighth-century Northumbria as a complement to Latin inscriptions in the Roman alphabet. In tenth- and eleventh-century Scandinavia, on the other hand, a new and vigorous tradition of commemorative inscribed rune stones seems to have been a local reaction to the pressures of foreign missionaries. In Norway runes coexisted with Christian, Latin literacy into the late Middle Ages, being turned to new administrative purposes, although always remaining primarily a script for carving not penning. Although they gradually lost out to the more prestigious Latin alphabet and authoritative texts introduced by Christian priests, runes were never condemned for their pre-Christian origins. Quite the opposite: the ways in which runes were co-opted to Christian uses, especially in Northumbria, reveal a spectrum of literate practices and a readiness to adapt to which we shall return shortly.

The history of ogam is not dissimilar, but takes us instead beyond the far western frontier of the Roman Empire. Around the Irish Sea, fourth-century speakers of Gaelic were in close contact with the Latin culture of late Roman Britain; probably on its eastern, British, shore individuals with a precise knowledge of the sound systems and spelling conventions of the Latin language developed an entirely new sequence of marks to represent the Gaelic language. Specifically designed for stone monuments to commemorate deceased persons of elite status in direct imitation of Roman epitaphs, ogam is testimony to the impulse to appropriate—on local terms—the evident association between writing and power. In the kingdom of Dyfed in south-west Wales, as elsewhere in western Britain, it was used until the seventh century for the Irish part of bilingual Old Irish–Latin epitaphs, in public assertions of the direct equivalence and high status of these two minority languages, and in Scotland, both Gaelic and Pictish ogam inscriptions occur. Across the Irish Sea, the many fifth- and sixth-century ogam stones of south-western Ireland are an idiom for emulating Roman memorial practices while shunning its language and script. They demonstrate the resonances of Roman hegemony beyond the empire long after its western half had ceased to exist as a political entity.

Like runes, ogam was adapted to Christian contexts, lingering longest in Scotland, into the tenth century. Its abandonment in eighth-century Ireland and replacement by Latin as the language for the display of secular status became possible only once Latin itself was no longer associated with powerful neighbours just across the Irish Sea. By then, Latin had acquired a completely different significance as a mark of Christianity. On any evaluation, the diffusion of this Roman religion beyond the boundaries of empire had a defining cultural significance in European history; crucial here is the stimulus to reading and writing presented by this book-based creed, for Christianity prompted the development of ways of writing local languages that had hitherto remained wholly or largely preliterate. It also introduced more ways of exploiting writing to enhance power and authority than either runes or ogam had ever expressed.

Over the course of the early medieval centuries, there emerged a richly textured and widely varying repertoire of languages of authority, of which Latin was only one. We can best survey this region by region, paying particular attention to the languages of Christian worship, of law, and of the expression of claims to landed property. To commence, we should remain in Ireland, where the impact of Christian book learning was startling, for two reasons. First, although the details of the conversion of the Irish during the fifth century in large part elude us, it is clear that the Irish had mastered 'Latin as a foreign language' by c.600. During the following century, they not only began composing their own texts in Latin but also adapted the Latin alphabet to writing in their own language. With the ability not merely to carve short inscriptions on stone but now to write lengthy Old Irish texts in fluent documentary hands, Irish *filid*—scholars, poets, and legal experts—appropriated the Roman alphabet to their own uses, creating a large corpus of Old Irish texts side by side with Christian Latin ones. This took many forms, including Old Irish poems, genealogies, mythical tales, but also a very large number of legal treatises, setting out the complexities of Irish social organization and detailing the norms that regulated everything from bee-keeping to the treatment of hostages or the qualifications for poets of different ranks. These law books were the work not of legislators making new law, but rather of judges and scholars systematizing past procedures and existing social practices into generalized normative statements whose impact on everyday living is unknown. How far the Irish ever supplemented these law tracts with practical administrative forms of writing cannot be said. It is impossible to determine whether the almost total absence of tribute lists, land documentation, and the like is the result of massive documentary losses or of a persistent preference for oral modes of remembering and regulating community affairs. We are left with only the vivid insights into how the elite of highly trained scholar-poets and jurists thought their communities ought to operate, but very little evidence about how they actually did. We shall encounter some of these ideal societies later.[20]

Secondly, the Irish preferred to keep their Bible and their worship in a foreign language. Hitherto, the seepage of Christianity beyond the frontiers of the Roman Empire had been accompanied by translation of the Bible into the local language, often also accompanied by development of a new script so as to keep each language in its own script. In the mid-fourth century, the priest Ulfilas (b. c.311, d. 383) had done exactly this for Christian Goths living north of the lower Danube and in the steppes north of the Black Sea.[21] But in Ireland, nothing comparable occurred. The Irish chose to keep their sacred books in Latin. They seized with enthusiasm upon the dictum of Isidore of Seville, that, among the variety of tongues after the Tower of Babel, there were three 'sacred languages', those of the sign posted over the dying Christ on the cross (John 19: 19–20) and of the Bible: Hebrew, Greek, and Latin.[22] For the Irish, the sacred books remained in the sacred language. To be sure, poetry, hymns, saints' lives, homilies, and a range of other religious texts composed in Old Irish mediated Christian stories and values to unlearned audiences, as tales of secular heroes composed by Christian authors also did indirectly. Moreover, Old Irish words were sometimes jotted above or beside difficult Latin words to aid comprehension (glosses), but the central texts of worship— the liturgy of the Mass, the Creed, the Lord's Prayer, and the Gospels— remained unintelligible to all except those who undertook the long rigours of learning Latin in the schoolroom.

By the later sixth century, Irish Christians were themselves active as preachers and missionaries outside Ireland, taking their sacred books in their sacred language to western Scotland, the Continent, and the Anglo-Saxons of eastern and central Britain. Among the Anglo-Saxons, their paths criss-crossed those of seventh-century missionaries sent out either from Rome, men whose native language was the *lingua romana*, or from Frankish Gaul, whose dialect of Germanic was fairly readily intelligible to the Anglo-Saxons but who also knew Latin. In the cultural melting pot of early Anglo-Saxon Christianity, the languages of authority underwent another reconfiguration.

Unlike western Britain, where Christianity, spoken Latin, and Roman techniques for documenting property rights continued uninterrupted throughout the sixth century, most or all of the Roman cultural apparatus of religion and bureaucracy had collapsed in eastern Britain during the fifth and sixth centuries. Aided as much by Irish as by continental missionaries, the Anglo-Saxons too developed a written version of their own Germanic dialects, supplementing the letters of the Latin alphabet with a few runic characters. England's early convert kings turned this towards law. Unlike those of the Irish jurists, however, their law books contained not only specifications of existing social conventions but also royal law, a promulgation of power that had Roman overtones but used the local language to spell out the king's command. In addition, from the late seventh century at the very latest, Anglo-Saxon kings began assenting to formal Latin documents that reorganized and recorded for posterity claims to landed property. Issued in the king's name but drafted by churchmen, these documents—known as charters—adapted the forms of Roman provincial bureaucratic documentation with which continental missionaries were familiar. That seventh-century Anglo-Saxon kings could neither have read nor understood these Latin documents mattered little: from a royal perspective this was symbolic writing and an assertion of a new form of power; from an ecclesiastical one a means of securing a landed endowment, establishing enduring institutional structures and enhancing the clergy's political influence.

Like the Irish, the first Anglo-Saxon Christians adopted the new religion as a Latin religion. But they approached the cultural and linguistic chasm differently. By the early eighth century, Christian texts began to acquire a new, Old English penumbra, sometimes in the form of an Old English interlinear gloss or 'crib' added in small letters between the lines of a magnificent Latin gospel book, at others in the form of explanations of the meaning of the Creed and the Lord's Prayer by educated priests to the people 'in their own language'.[23] Bede (b. *c.*673, d. 735), the most influential of early Anglo-Saxon scholars and teachers, even provided written Old English translations of these two central texts for priests and monks who knew no Latin 'in order that the faithful may learn how to be faithful'.[24]

Here we meet the central issue. Was Christianity a religion confined to a symbolic, prestigious language, incomprehensible to all except the few who, like Bede, had been intensively schooled in it since early childhood? Or was an effort to be made to make its sacred texts directly intelligible? Even in the tenth and eleventh century, by which time Old English had developed a sophisticated written form capable of being turned to a wide variety of legal, administrative, pastoral, historical, and poetic purposes, the words of the Mass itself always remained in Latin. As for the Bible, strategies included the reworking of biblical narratives into Old English, either in traditional poetic form or as homilies. By the late Anglo-Saxon period, Old English versions existed of the most frequently read parts of both the Old and the New Testaments, although these cannot have been widely available. Nor was translation uncontentious. Ælfric (b. c.950, d. c.1010) did translate the first part of Genesis for his noble patron Æthelweard, but warned him that this was an 'exceedingly dangerous' thing to do, for the polygamous habits of the Old Testament patriarchs ran counter to Christian teaching and needed to be made 'safe' by an experienced exegete.[25] Ælfric was one of a generation of scholars who shaped a distinctive Old English culture in late Anglo-Saxon England. The Anglo-Saxons never went as far as the Irish, who claimed that their own language was the best of all because their mythical ancestor Fénius Farsaid had invented it by combining the best features of all other languages. But they were far more willing to put their native tongue, the language of royal power and law, to the service of Christianity as a tool for teaching and preaching than seems ever to have occurred in Ireland.[26]

In brief, the imported Latin culture of early Anglo-Saxon England steadily mutated into a bilingual one in which Latin and Old English complemented each other as languages of power and authority. Tenth- and early eleventh-century kings and their counsellors legislated in Old English but heard Mass in Latin. They issued charters composed in Latin, with the property concerned specified in Old English. They sent out administrative letters (writs) in Old English and may perhaps have recited the Lord's Prayer in Old English as well as in Latin. One king, Alfred (871–99), took delight in books of Old English poetry—but that verse was as likely to be about biblical heroes as traditional Germanic ones. Another, Edgar (957–75), gave lavishly decorated Latin gospel books to favoured churches, whose clergy he also commissioned to translate key Latin texts into Old English. The powerful late Anglo-Saxon polity drew strength from finely calibrated linguistic strategies.

In the eighth century, Anglo-Saxon missionaries such as Boniface took to preaching and founding churches in the Germanic-speaking regions of continental Europe, north and east of the Rhine. Naturally, they took with them their appreciation of the advantages of using the local language to assist in training priests and explaining Christian doctrine, and, under Anglo-Saxon influence, the various dialects of Old High German began to be written in the Latin alphabet. As in England, vocabulary lists and glosses, to both religious and legal texts, preceded the composition of works entirely composed in the local language. When produced, these were mostly for classroom and pastoral use, helping to make sense of, but not replacing, the Latin of religious services. Thus alongside the Creed, the Lord's Prayer, and baptismal formulae, we find some sermons, prayers, and blessings. Slightly later, German poetic paraphrases of parts of the Bible, especially the Gospels, extended the repertoire of Christian German literature, although, as in England and Ireland, the Mass itself always remained in Latin.

Yet the churches and monasteries founded on the Continent by Boniface and his compatriots lay in the lands of rulers who legislated in Latin, unlike the Anglo-Saxon kings. It had been self-evident that fifth-, sixth , and seventh-century kings of the Goths, Burgundians, Franks, and Lombards should legislate and govern in Latin, not only because they often relied on the assistance of late Roman legal experts but also because they were deliberately insisting upon their role as successors of the Roman emperors. Moreover, their Germanic followers were all, more or less rapidly, abandoning their traditional language in favour of the *lingua romana*. To issue laws and charters in Latin was to do so in the language of most, if not all, of their subjects, and, if kings themselves did not fully understand, interpreters were always to hand. So the Carolingian dynasty of kings who seized the Frankish throne in 751, though themselves speakers of the Frankish dialect of Germanic, asserted their legitimacy by continuing to legislate in Latin. As their kingdom expanded through political manœuvring and outright conquest in the late eighth century, it became a huge, multi-ethnic and multilingual conglomerate, ultimately extending far beyond the area of Anglo-Saxon missionary activity. The subjects of the Carolingian kings and emperors spoke a wide variety of languages, from the Brittonic of Brittany through the full dialectal spectrum of the *lingua romana*, the Germanic of the Rhineland, Saxony, and Bavaria through to the Slavonic speakers of the eastern borderlands of the empire. Royal officials and preachers alike certainly used local dialects and languages to communicate with their audiences in the localities; on arrival at the royal court, they entered a multilingual environment. But Latin defined everyone's wider cultural identity, and, most especially, their religious identity. Latin law and Latin worship gave the Carolingian Empire a coherence that it otherwise lacked: the sacred language was also the language of imperial power.

From the middle years of the ninth century onwards, Carolingian preachers were active among the Slav principalities that lay along the empire's eastern flank. These lands were also sought out by Byzantine missionaries, most notably the brothers Constantine and Methodius, both bilingual in Greek and Slavonic and excellent linguists. It was they who first gave the Slavonic language written form, when the Byzantine emperor sent them to preach to the Slavs of Moravia in 863. Before departing, Constantine invented an entirely new alphabet, and began to produce Slavonic translations of the Greek Bible, the liturgy, and other service books all written in this, the Glagolitic alphabet. After his death in 869, his brother Methodius continued his missionary and literary endeavours, now working in Pannonia, until his own death in 885. Thereafter, German missionaries gradually succeeded in displacing the fledgling Slavonic liturgy in favour of the Latin liturgy and alphabet; the cultural project of Constantine and Methodius endured only among the Bulgars in the south-east Balkans and, from the eleventh century, far to the north-east among the Rus of Kiev. Amongst Bulgars and the Rus, another alphabet, this time directly adapted from Greek—Cyrillic—vied with the Glagolitic for writing in Slavonic, eventually winning more widespread acceptance. For the Slavs, the adoption of Christianity brought with it books for worship in their own language and distinctive scripts that were adaptable to a wide range of purposes, including laws, chronicles, spiritual and exegetical works, and inscriptions.

The achievements of Constantine and Methodius proved contentious in a way that casts a sharp light on the relationship between languages and power in the early Middle Ages. For the Byzantines, the use of a local language and writing system for Christian worship was normal; as Ulfilas's activities indicated, eastern Christianity was characterized by linguistic pluralism. Carolingian clergy, however, insisted that there were only three sacred languages. Moreover, they regarded Moravia and Pannonia as within their exclusive sphere of influence. En route to Rome from Zalavár, seat of Prince Kocel, Constantine and Methodius stopped in Venice in 867, where the bishop and clergy of the city met them with hostility, attacking Constantine 'like ravens against a falcon' for his translating enterprise.[27] When Methodius returned to Pannonia after his brother's death, he too came in for criticism, being disparaged by the clergy of Salzburg on the grounds that, 'behaving like a philosopher, he displaced the Latin language and Roman doctrine as well as the venerated Latin alphabet with a newly invented Slavic alphabet, and in that region he rubbished for everyone the Masses and Gospels and church services of those who conducted them in Latin'.[28]

What was at issue? Neither the clergy of Venice nor of Salzburg found it acceptable to use anything other than one of the sacred languages for worship. Resentment of the Greek brothers' intrusion into their own territory doubtless fuelled their antagonism, but their response betrayed deeper cultural anxieties about language and power. Like all Christians who spoke the *lingua romana*, the Venetians conducted religious worship in the language of their everyday speech, albeit in a register that may well have sounded old-fashioned. Similarly, everywhere in the zone of the *lingua romana* except that part of the Iberian peninsula governed by the Arabic-using bureaucracy of the caliphs of Cordoba, secular rulers and their officials issued laws, arbitrated disputes, administered property in Latin, simply the written form of local speech. In this respect, nothing really changed here during the early Middle Ages. The clergy of Salzburg, by contrast, were Germans. Their Latin had been learned from schoolmasters in monastic and cathedral schools. They read the Bible and conducted religious services in Latin but also used it to administer their estates, remember their dead, receive and respond to royal orders, record the outcomes of lawsuits, and fulfil a host of other purposes. Knowledge of Latin set them apart from their congregation, tenants, and servants, many of whom spoke the Bavarian dialect of Germanic while a number spoke Slavonic. Disparate in linguistic background, the clergy of Venice and Salzburg were united in feeling that Constantine and Methodius had impugned the sacredness of the Latin Bible and liturgy.

The two brothers must have been puzzled by the hostility they encountered. But their assumption that the sacred Christian texts could be translated into any local language highlights the peculiarity of western Christianity. From the conversion of the Irish onwards, western Christianity was essentially Latin Christianity, whatever the local language. First in Ireland, then in England, there was one language for religion and another for law. But in the Carolingian lands, the indispensability of Latin as the language of both sacred and secular authority was affirmed. Assisted by their clergy, tenth- and eleventh-century German kings and emperors enthusiastically followed suit and, through sponsoring missionary activity amongst the Poles, Hungarians, and Scandinavians, made sure that Latin was exported as the language and symbol of both German kingship and German Christianity. Everywhere north of the linguistic divide between Germanic and the *lingua romana*, the language of authority had to be learned from schoolmasters brandishing the cane. The rod thus instilled a technology of power, for Latin not only communicated information, ideas, commands: it conveyed status, prestige, identity, and allegiance. As for the British Isles, it took the onslaught of the Norman Conquest in 1066 to trigger the displacement of the local languages by Latin for the purposes of governing.

Despite its inherited cultural prestige and the mass of surviving manuscripts written in it, book-learned Latin was not the only language of power in the early Middle Ages. In using schoolroom Latin as the language of religion, law, and property, the clergy of Salzburg were out of step with large parts of the Europe of their own day. That this only much later became the normal experience must not be allowed to obliterate the fluid, multiform relationships between language and authority in early medieval Europe.

Local Literacies, Elite Literacy

In 721, Gregory, later bishop of Utrecht, visited his aunt Addula, the abbess of Pfalzel near Trier. As was common for noble youths, he spent his formative years in the retinue of the Frankish king—an education in courtliness, arms, and rudimentary literacy. Dinner at Pfalzel was accompanied by religious readings in accordance with monastic custom, and on this occasion Addula handed the Bible to her 14- or 15-year-old nephew. The dinner guests included the missionary Boniface, who, as Gregory's disciple Liudger later told the tale, addressed Addula's nephew. 'You read well, my son—if you understand what you're reading.' Gregory asserted that he did, so the holy man questioned him more closely. The youth began to read the passage again from the beginning, just as he had done before. 'I'm not asking you to speak out the passage like that, my boy. Explain your reading to me in your own language and in the everyday speech of your family.' Gregory confessed that he could not do this, and so Boniface began to expound the text, preaching to the whole family.[29] This encounter set young Gregory on the path to his own missionary career. It sets us in pursuit of the complexities of 'literacy' in the early Middle Ages.

The term is a capacious one, referring to individuals and social practices. It embraces many skills that were taught and learned separately in the early Middle Ages: the graphic art of wielding a pen, whether with unpractised effort or calligraphic fluency; the transformation of speech into text with or without the intermediary of a scribe between author and parchment; the cognitive skill of the reader, not always extending to comprehension of the text. The term also invites us to enquire into the contexts in which texts were read, written, and consulted, to consider the importance attached to these activities, and the mentalities associated with them. Gregory's encounter with Boniface exemplifies several of these strands. It reminds us that, wherever the *lingua romana* was not spoken locally, learning to read was accomplished in a foreign language. Furthermore, in its locales of palace and monastery, his early career draws our attention to the relationship between literacy and elite status, secular and ecclesastical. Finally, the tale cautions us to avoid creating a false antithesis between 'literacy' and 'orality'. For Gregory, reading was an oral performance in front of an audience of hearers, the usual way of experiencing a written text in the early Middle Ages. And the flow of words from speech to text always worked in both directions: in composing his life of Gregory, Liudger relied as much on stories narrated by the saint's family as on literary models of missionary sanctity. Literacy thus requires attention to both social situation and individuals.

It is immediately clear that not all communities regarded writing in the same way. A predisposition to utilize writing for a host of purposes from the most mundane to the most formal was certainly characteristic of many regions once within the Roman Empire. The spread of written language did little to encourage that predisposition elsewhere: some places remained more text-minded than others. Moreover, the relationship between literacy and power was liable to be reconfigured, as power relationships within and between polities themselves shifted over time. Aspirations towards intensive government commonly fostered the use of administrative writing more than geographically extensive assertions of power. Thus the two most powerful polities of the early Middle Ages—the Frankish empire of Charlemagne and his son Louis the Pious (814–40), and the late Anglo-Saxon kingdom of Edgar and his successors—were also those that relied most on written modes of government. In both these cases, subsequent political change brought with it different attitudes towards and uses of the written word. Comparable diversity is evident when we turn to the religious contexts of literacy. Though the sacrality of the Latin Bible was universal, its local cultural milieux varied both in the ways that churches received and adapted the literary heritage of late antique Christianity and in the ways in which they used administrative literacy in pursuit of their institutional goals. In short, early medieval Europe manifested a kaleido-

scope of cultures of literacy, combining and recombining in localized patterns that shifted over place and time but that steadfastly resist ordering
into a linear series from 'less' to 'more' literate.

It helps to distinguish between the reading and/or writing skills possessed by an individual and the access to those skills enjoyed by those who
lacked them themselves. Personal literacy is direct, the consequence of
education; participatory literacy is indirect, mediated through a scribe or
reader. The extent of the former is hard to assess even within a religious
context: not only is the patchy evidence susceptible to widely differing
interpretations, but also there can be no generally applicable criterion of
assessment. On balance, it is safe to conclude that significantly more
monks, nuns, and clergy than laity could write their name or vocalize the
letters on a page and that even in Italy, certainly the most 'literate' place
in the early Middle Ages, only a small minority of the population possessed either skill. Since personal literacy was uncommon, we shall focus
for the moment on participatory literacy. This was far more widespread,
as a sermon preached by Caesarius, bishop of Arles (502–42), suggests. He
told his congregation about merchants who, although unable to read and
write themselves, hired the services of those who could. With their em-
ployees to keep their accounts, they made a huge profit. By the same token,
Caesarius argued, illiteracy was no impediment to the spiritual profit of
reading the Bible. 'You who don't know your letters, whoever you are, why
don't you seek out for a fair price someone to read holy scripture to you
so that you can gain the rewards of heaven through them? Certainly,
brothers, he who goes about this diligently believes that he can benefit
from it in eternity; but he who neither wants to read the Bible nor to hear
it being read to him certainly does not believe that any good can come of
it.'[30] Here was a culture where personal literacy was never universal but
participatory literacy was extensive.

At other times, individuals might be caught up in a world of written
texts without it necessarily being to their own advantage. As a young
child, Fructuosus of Braga (d. 665) accompanied his father, a Goth of elite
birth and rank, on a trip to the family sheep pastures in the mountains
of north-western Spain. The boy wandered off while his father 'wrote
down [details of] the flocks and discussed the accounts with the shepherds'.[31] Even if the shepherds could not themselves maintain written
stock lists, they nevertheless had contact with, and contributed to, the
managerial documentation necessary to the smooth running of a large
landed estate.

Examples such as these could be multiplied throughout the early
medieval centuries, from many different secular and religious contexts. But

we should remain in the central-northern regions of the Iberian peninsula for further evidence of text-mindedness in the seventh and eighth centuries. Here, the discovery in archaeological contexts of over 150 slate slabs used as writing tablets reveals a distinctively local literacy. Although their badly chipped, poorly decipherable, condition prohibits conclusions about their scribes or readers, the slates nevertheless allow unmatched insight into the social contexts in which some people employed writing to conduct their affairs. They also exemplify the kind of particularities that gave early medieval practices of literacy such marked regional diversity.

Several of these slates are exactly the sort a landowner such as Fructuosus's father would have needed to run his estates—lists of livestock, slaves, and dues owed by tenants. Others relate to different aspects of property management, but had similarly short-term usefulness: a letter from an estate steward to his master, an inventory of stolen domestic objects and clothing complete with the monetary value of each item. Some slates have a religious rather than an administrative purpose: curses against named individuals, texts of prayers and psalms, invocations to archangels and saints; others again are classroom writing exercises—all lost or discarded when no longer needed but nevertheless revealing of local religious mentalities or individual efforts to acquire personal literacy. One group would have been of more lasting importance: formal documents of sales and exchanges of land between individuals, details of the guarantees that secured a deal, and precisions of the oaths sworn to complete them. Documents in this last category conform to late Roman legal provisions for validating property transactions and use standard local conventions for phrasing such documents. Indeed, legal procedural norms offer one of the most characteristic markers of regional particularity in the social uses of writing.

Elsewhere, the best surviving evidence for regional documentary practices mostly concerns landed property. And, since these records have survived only in ecclesiastical archives, they reveal most about local literacies in the spheres of influence of major churches. The insights such archives can offer into local social organization and landed economies are deferred until Chapter 5; here let us focus on the textual habits of one locality: eastern Brittany in the ninth century. This was a document-minded world of a few large landowners and many peasant proprietors who bought and sold land amongst themselves, bequeathed property to their heirs, raised loans, argued and settled disagreements, or stood surety for each other's behaviour. They took care to make their transactions in front of witnesses and announce them to their neighbours with public formality. They also ensured that local scribes recorded the deals in Latin formulae sanctioned by time-honoured local usage and included the names of those who had witnessed the transaction and affirmed its validity. When the monastery of Redon was founded in their midst in 832, the ensuing donations to the monks were equally precisely specified in writing. In turn, the monks exploited local documentary practices for their own interests, in so doing conserving hundreds of charters for their—and our—benefit.

A member of the region's elite of petty landowners, Riwalt functioned as local bigwig in villages close to Redon during the 830s and 840s. He and other members of his family epitomize the participatory literacy of this social group. Riwalt regularly witnessed the gifts, sales, and pledges of his neighbours. In 840, he had the donor, witnesses, and scribe assemble in his own house for the formalities and recording of Catworet's gift to Redon; when his own son Deurhoiarn killed Catworet a few years later, he made public recompense in a carefully documented pay-off. He took pains to have his own donation to the monks witnessed, including having Deurhoiarn attest and thus assent to his father's generosity. Whether Riwalt could read or hold a pen well enough to make his own mark of attestation is unimportant. The formal gesture of touching the parchment sheet with the hand commonly counted as the equivalent to a graphic mark of attestation or a signature, so Riwalt had no need to be able to write his name to keep his affairs in good order. Nor does it matter that he probably spoke Brittonic and so perhaps did not understand the Latin of his charter of donation, for he most certainly knew its gist. Riwalt shrewdly regarded written records of customary format as central to his activities, and knew how to turn the local documentary conventions to his own advantage.

In the 850–60s, Deurhoiarn, his wife Roiantken, and their son Iarnwocon all continued Riwalt's relationship with Redon, making sure valid records of their gifts were drafted in conformity with local conventions. The surviving documents include a charter recording a donation that Roiantken made with the agreement of her husband and son: it draws attention to women's participation in the documentary literacy of a rural community such as this. To the extent that married women had land under their own control or were central to wider family strategies for the disposition of property, they were in a position to issue and attest charters in conjunction with their husband or son, as Roiantken did. Only in widowhood or if vowed to a celibate life did they sometimes issue charters in their own name. The wider issues of management of the familial patrimony will be discussed in detail later, but, to anticipate briefly, women's opportunities to control land were universally limited.[32] As a result, their opportunities for active participatory literacy were commensurately few, a restriction reinforced by a widespread reluctance to call women to witness other people's transactions. With a few notable exceptions of rulers' wives, charter witness lists suggest that the meetings at which land transactions were completed, conflicts resolved, and community affairs regulated were essentially men's gatherings.

Here, then, was a culture that regarded both the verbal testimony of male eyewitnesses and the written record of charters as overlapping ways of proving ownership or settling a dispute. Across Europe, local communities might put more emphasis on the one rather than the other. Even in Ireland, where documentary forms of Roman origin (such as those in the Redon area) seem to have made little impact, 'godly old writing' was recognized along with valid witnesses, sureties, and ogam-inscribed boundary stones as a form of proof.[33] And in southern France, where Roman legal procedures with their heavy emphasis on written documentation persisted throughout the early Middle Ages, the sworn oral testimony of witnesses remained a vital complement to lost, falsified, destroyed, or disputed charters: judges ruled only after they had 'seen and heard' the evidence.[34] Whether in the reading-aloud of a disputed charter or the writing-down of witnesses' oaths, document-mindedness always presupposed an oral, spoken milieu. It never presumed the personal literacy of all participants.

Provided that a few individuals had the necessary skills to draw up records in the approved manner, widespread reliance on documentary practices was as possible for modest freeholders as for lay or ecclesiastical proprietors of vast landed estates. Such document-mindedness character-ized the small social elite, either lay persons of sufficient wealth and standing to own land and command the services of others, or the bishops, abbots, and abbesses who represented the institutional interests of cathedrals and monasteries. This general truth offsets the wide variation in local literacies. There is far more at issue here than simply a well-resourced lifestyle, however, for writing was integral to the functioning of political power in the localities and royal courts of Christian Europe alike. Whether as a medium for communicating, expressing an ideology, transmitting specialist legal knowledge, maintaining king-lists, proclaiming royal pedigrees, or keeping fiscal records, literacy was widely implicated in the articulation and maintenance of authority in the Christian regions of early medieval Europe. This is particularly true of those polities that actively sought to promote a degree of centralized control, but everywhere literacy had the potential to enhance legitimacy, build consensus, and convey intense symbolic meaning.[35] Those who were accustomed to dealing with documents and understood the social conventions surrounding their use could contribute what rulers sought. Like the landowner with a personal notary or village scribe at his elbow, the churchman skilled at drafting letters, charters, or estate memoranda contributed to the exercise of authority at local and central levels. Especially where Latin was one of the languages—or the only language—of power, but regional communities spoke Celtic or Germanic, only the elite had the necessary savoir-faire or technical assistance to participate in ruling and to mediate between courts and localities. Whether personal or participatory, document-mindedness was thus both a precondition for and a consequence of membership of the power-broking elite.

Early medieval literacy had a religious as well as a documentary aspect. By the fifth century, the conventions of Christian worship had crystallized into written form, reproduced in service books that encoded considerable regional variations in liturgical practice. Wherever adherence to Christianity was formalized into local congregations led by officially appointed, male priests, worship required the presence of such books and of a man capable of reading aloud from them. As a late-tenth-century Anglo-Saxon preacher put it, during worship 'we hear God's books explained and read to us, the Gospel proclaimed, and His glories made known to men'.[36] Christian liturgy was a verbal and visual drama, at the centre of which were God's books.

To complete the full annual cycle of services, a priest required several different books for fulfilling a community's sacramental needs, with additional books for any pastoral work he might undertake. How many minor rural churches, as distinct from cathedrals, monasteries, and other regional centres ever possessed the full set of texts in this period is open to question, but the uncertainty does not detract from the encounter with the written word that church attendance implied for everyone, of all social ranks. The form of that encounter doubtless depended, in part, on whether the language of worship was comprehensible in that locality, how effectively trained the officiating priest was, and whether he was separated from the congregation by a screen. Far more than the communication of verbal content was at stake, however. The centrality of books to the words and gestures of Christian ritual grounded religious authority and truth in writing. It thereby devalued unwritten opinion and oral tradition, and gave men but not women the opportunity to put their literate skills to work in public.

Emphasis on the Christian tradition of the written word found its fullest expression not in scattered local churches but in monastic communities. The roots of the early medieval monastic tradition lay in the distant past, in the early Christian impulse to reject land, wealth, sexuality, and family in favour of a life devoted to living out biblical precepts, sometimes accompanied by spectacular forms of self-denial and a reputation for miraculous achievements. This movement found expression wherever Christianity gained adherents, whatever the local social and political conditions. By the fifth century, those who withdrew into ascetic communities often found themselves balancing the self-discipline and social distancing that their commitment demanded with the popularity and flow of landed gifts that their reputation encouraged. Intense engagement with the culture of the Bible required that at least some members of the group could read and comprehend Latin—but this might also entail exposure to the vast non-Christian Latin literary tradition, as well as to the fourth- and fifth-century authoritative works of biblical interpretation. By the seventh century, and in some places rather earlier, monastic communities found themselves the main guardians of the educational traditions and literary heritage of Antiquity.

Ascetic existence turned on the Word of God—written in sumptuously decorated Bibles bound with gold and jewels, sung and spoken during worship, recited aloud and heard by all, read silently or in a low murmur for meditative reflection on its inner meaning. Monastic organization and ideology were sometimes codified in writing, but the monastic rule always functioned as a spoken text. 'Listen, my son, to the teachings of your master, and incline the ear of your heart,'[37] began what became the most popular and, by the ninth century, the most authoritative of such written rules, composed by Benedict of Nursia (b. c.480, d. 560). In monastic culture, words shifted endlessly back and forth between spoken and written form, but the fixed point of reference was always holy scripture, the oral teaching of Christ transmitted in words on the parchment page.

'The foundation, form and perfection of discretion is knowledge of the holy scriptures.'[38] Thus wrote Hrabanus Maurus (b. c.780, d. 856) in 819, the influential schoolmaster of the monastery that Boniface had founded at Fulda in the forests of central Germany. His parents and older brother were typical of the charter-using regional aristocracy of the central Rhineland, but, in contrast with their participatory literacy, Hrabanus became one of the most literate men of his age, a prolific author of works of biblical exegesis and monastic instruction as well as of complex Latin verse. Later, as abbot of Fulda (822–42), he presided over the largest monastic community north of the Alps (some 600 men). In this position, he developed its library into a major collection of both Christian and classical texts and oversaw the management of the monks' vast landed endowment of over 8,000 farmsteads, before ending his career as archbishop of Mainz, the counsellor of kings (847–56). Whether for poetic, pedagogical, spiritual, administrative, or political ends, Hrabanus always expressed himself in polished Latin. All this was possible because his parents had placed him in the monastery as a child of 7, young enough for extended years of schooling to foster his abilities and instil full mastery of the 'sacred language'.

Under Hrabanus's aegis, Fulda developed a distinctive literary culture. Although the common wellsprings of monastic learning encouraged monasteries to collect similar foundational texts of Latin grammar and biblical interpretation, even monastic literacy assumed characteristically local or regional forms. This only partly resulted from the sheer difficulties of obtaining books from far away; equally important was the continual reformulation, revision, and alteration of texts to suit local needs and preferences. Fulda, however, evinced additional particularities, for its abbots also fostered the formation of a written literature in Old High German, primarily but not entirely for pastoral uses. Their diligent searches also built up a unique collection of rare classical works, several of which have survived only thanks to the activities of the monastery's ninth-century copyists. Fully consonant with the common ideals of monastic life, Fulda nevertheless enjoyed a literary culture with its own, local quality.

Fulda was not alone in this. However widespread the Rule of Benedict had become by the ninth and tenth centuries, monasteries maintained locally traditional styles of liturgy. They also built their own intellectual life within the context of regional cultural norms, using whatever resources, opportunities, and contacts they could. In the Christian kingdoms of northern Spain monasteries such as the Catalonian houses of Ripoll and San Millan de la Cogolla benefited from their relative proximity to the brilliant intellectual culture of the tenth-century caliphal court at Cordoba, acquiring scientific and mathematical treatises unavailable elsewhere in the Latin West, including some translated from Arabic. Meanwhile, in tenth- and eleventh-century England, the monks and clergy of Exeter, Winchester, Ramsey, and elsewhere copied and collected books in Old English as enthusiastically as Latin works, pursuing eclectic tastes in Old English heroic poetry as well as biblical exegesis. When Gerbert, a young monk of Aurillac, travelled across the Pyrenees to Ripoll in 967 and Abbo, monastic schoolmaster of Fleury in central France, went to teach in England at Ramsey in 985–7, each encountered a familiar monastic lifestyle and liturgy offset by novel resources for study. Even the elite literacy of a monastic library displayed local particularities.

All this came at a price. Books required expert scribes and an abundant supply of high-quality animal skins for the parchment. Consider two of the most famous works from eighth-century Northumbria: Bede's

Ecclesiastical History, available today as a paperback of 290 pages, required the skins of about thirty animals for a single copy, while the magnificent, exceptionally large Lindisfarne Gospels was made from the skins of over 150 calves. Hildemar of Corbie (d. *c*.850) intimated that his monastery could sell a book made from thirty skins for 60 *denarii* (silver pennies), a sum approximately equivalent to the value of four fleecy sheep or fifteen piglets: Corbie's own library possessed over 300 titles, most of them recently copied. Stocking a library of this size was extremely expensive— and helps explain Hrabanus's care in organizing bound registers to preserve copies of the thousands of individual charters that witnessed Fulda's rights to land and income. Nor does this take into account the illustrated liturgical books that Fulda also produced in the ninth and tenth centuries, a single one of which might consume over sixty skins in addition to costly, imported pigments and gold leaf for the paint.

Despite the huge size of the Fulda community, its famous school, and the vast resources that sustained the monks and their library, few others of its ninth- and tenth-century monks authored works in Latin or Old High German, and none of them was nearly as prolific as Hrabanus. In any monastery, male or female, full participation in the monastic life demanded the ability to read. Community affairs would be aided if a few of the monks or nuns could copy books and draft charters. But compositional literacy remained a rarity throughout the early Middle Ages, an intellectual achievement that required exceptional resources as well as exceptional talent. Little wonder, then, that abilities of this sort were confined to an elite, or that Hrabanus and others like him graced rulers' courts. A privileged status and a privileged voice: theirs are the voices that have best survived the centuries.

> No work of men's hands but the weary years
> Besiege and take it, comes its evil day:
> The written word alone flouts destiny,
> Revives the past and gives the lie to Death.[39]

Hrabanus's words themselves flout destiny. But for the energy of a seventeenth-century printer, these verses would have been lost to us, long since destroyed along with the majority of the manuscripts in Fulda's medieval library. In these lines, Hrabanus expressed a perspective inherited from the Christian writers of late Antiquity and affirmed much that was central to the Christian, Latin culture of the Carolingian Empire: indebtedness to the past, respect for a culture of Latin book learning, profound conviction that no other medium, no other language, conveyed authority and truth. But we should not allow him to trap us into perpetuating that prejudice or replicating its presumption that Latin literacy necessarily represents a superior level of cultural attainment. Rather, we should view it as an agent of political transformation. As this chapter has argued, writing, and with it literacy, was deeply implicated in the exercise of power by strengthening, shaping, and justifying social hierarchies, ecclesiastical control, royal rule. Not for nothing did a freed slave receive a document confirming his or her manumission, for writing constructed power relationships of all sorts and ensured that they were remembered.

Nor should we allow Hrabanus to drown out other voices from other places. While Christianity certainly provided a powerful impulse to the written word, older, epigraphic runic and ogam habits persisted in Atlantic and northern Europe for some centuries after the arrival of Christian forms of literacy. We have also seen that, in practice, early medieval communities were extremely diverse in what they chose to commit to writing, in which script and in which language. Only a common attachment to the Latin Bible and liturgy helped create a degree of shared identity and enabled those who knew Latin to communicate wherever they travelled in Christian Europe.

Certainly, if we are looking for generalizations, we may conclude that it was in the early Middle Ages that Latin first emerged as an international mandarin language throughout most of Europe and, equally, that during these centuries education, book learning, and literacy became the overwhelming preserve of Christian churches. But this chapter has emphasized additional conclusions. It has drawn attention to the interplay between Latin and other languages. It has shown the facility with which lay landowners manipulated traditions of written documentation, whether in their own language or in Latin. In outlining some of the ways in which rulers relied on writing in legislating, governing, and evoking their authority, it has introduced themes to which the final two chapters of the book will return.

Finally, it has emphasized that a kaleidoscopic variety of local cultures of speaking and writing characterized early medieval Europe. Although our understanding of them is constrained by the erratic loss of books and documents sustained over the past millennium, it is beyond doubt that their characteristics were contingent upon individual preferences and needs as much as on local resources and precedents. Exceptionally, rulers intervened to encourage schools and book learning, in the hope of fostering correct Christian behaviour and tighter royal administration. But the written remains from the early Middle Ages introduce us to the localities as much as to the royal courts, and it is with these that we shall stay, as we turn in the next chapter to investigate matters as equally fundamental to human existence as speaking—birth and death.

2

Living and Dying

A storm-bowed maple,
I sorrow for my son,
My boy, who has bent
His body to earth:
Unhappy, he
Whose kin is hewn down
And must bear away the bones
From the bed.[1]

There came also a certain woman almost dead of starvation with a small child among the others seeking help. Before she could cross the threshold she collapsed from weakness and died. The child tried to pull the breast of his dead mother out from her clothes and suckle, which caused many of those who saw this to groan and weep.[2]

A FATHER mourning the drowning of his son, an infant suckling its famished mother's still-warm corpse: men and women in early medieval Europe lived intimately with deprivation and death. In the face of intermittent climatic disasters, periodic epidemics, and harsh everyday living conditions, the population of Europe laboured to produce a living from the land and to raise children to carry on their efforts. Most lived at or near subsistence level; others reflected on the meaning of human existence and its moral qualities amid the fearfulness of unexpected death and the likelihood of dearth. As in all cultures, the fundamental rhythms of living and dying framed human experience, not only shaping the age profile of any community, its members' life expectancy, and their search for security, but also affecting politics, informing understanding of the natural world, and situating humans in the cosmos.

This chapter enquires into the interaction of humans and their natural environment. It also reflects upon their understanding of it. It introduces questions that are not all amenable to textual enquiry but that can be addressed by the archaeological recovery and scientific analysis of material remains. Preliminary cautions are in order, however. The archaeological research necessary to answer environmental and demographic questions by tracking changes in climate, land use, and population levels is painstaking and expensive. It has been conducted only at a limited number of sites: to extrapolate beyond them is to risk overgeneralizing. Whereas the discovery of hitherto unknown textual evidence for the early Middle Ages is rare, new archaeological excavations and surveys are frequently undertaken and novel techniques of scientific analysis developed: conclusions based on data currently available remain liable to subsequent review.

With these provisos in mind, this chapter integrates archaeological evidence with the extant textual record in order to place the perceptions and social responses of early medieval men and women within the context of the landscapes in which they lived and the lifespans that they enjoyed. It thus approaches living and dying as both biological and cultural phenomena. The first section addresses the environment: climate, landscape, and settlement distribution. Against this background, the second turns to demographic questions, to estimate population levels and to suggest explanations for the fluctuating rates of fertility and mortality that seem to have been characteristic of the early Middle Ages. The final part asks how men and women coped with deprivation, disease, and death, and seeks answers in a range of cosmologies and curative strategies. In all these respects, a pattern of intense localism emerges.

Habitats

Early medieval men and women lived, worked, and died in environments affected not only by natural resources and climate but also by a long prehistory of settlement and exploitation. Over the millennia, human activities had created many landscapes out of Europe's complex physical geography. Always a dynamic process, that interaction continued throughout the early Middle Ages, shaping human habitats out of the natural world and lending a characteristically heterogeneous aspect to life in the early Middle Ages.

Let us take a brief glance at the richness and diversity of that natural world. Some aspects of its variegation are as obvious today as in the Middle Ages—for instance, the contrasts between the agricultural potential of the lowlands of the south-eastern corner of Britain and the upland economy of the mountainous zones to the north and west, or between the

2.1. Principal places mentioned in Chapter 2.

olives and vines of the Mediterranean littoral and the cereal cultivation of northern France. Differences such as these reflect a combination of geological structure and soil type interacting with the characteristic climatic patterns of the regions in question. Intensely local differences—between the soil in one field and the next or the amount of sunshine on one side of a valley rather than the other—are no longer so obvious in an age of urban sprawl and intensive mechanized farming. But in the early Middle Ages the distinctive nature of one small locality as compared with another was often as significant as the differences between entire regions, for each community was intimately attuned to the potentials and limitations of its own immediate environment. Farming, diet, textiles, clothing, pottery, building materials: all responded to locally available resources in this world of micro-regions. Interconnections came from the social, economic, and political bonds that later chapters will explore, as also from the rivers and coasts, roads and trackways that afforded contact between one settlement and the next.

Other aspects of the diversity of the early medieval landscape reflect the evolving impact of humankind upon the natural environment. One token of this was the push to bring new land under arable cultivation. Along the river Po, the northern Italian plain was still largely covered with oak forest at the end of Antiquity, and disafforestation made a major impact here only from the ninth century onwards. Likewise, the lands east of the Rhine and the Danube remained heavily wooded, and, although newly arrived settlers began making clearings in these wooded regions from the eighth century onwards, extensive felling did not reach east of the Elbe before the twelfth century. By the tenth century, drainage and the canalization of rivers were transforming landscapes dominated by rapidly shifting coastlines and low-lying salt marshes, such as the polderlands of Frisia, the East Anglian fens, and the Po delta. Although an anonymous ninth-century writer claimed that the Frisians 'almost live like fish in the water, by which they are surrounded on all sides',[3] archaeological evidence confirms that the coastal region of early medieval Frisia supported densely populated communities. Their inhabitants lived on artificially raised mounds (*terpen*), where they combined intensive agriculture with extensive exploitation of the surrounding salt marshes and waterways. From these settlements, they began to make inroads into the peat bogs that lay just above the tidal flood plain, digging drainage channels to carve small arable fields out of the bog from the ninth century onwards and founding new settlements on recently dried sites. The transformation of the Frisian landscape was well under way long before large-scale drainage efforts began in the late eleventh century. In regions such as this, a particular effort of imagination is required to envisage the changing aspect of the early medieval landscape.

In other circumstances, changes resulted from the spread of new crops and technologies. The Iberian peninsula is particularly notable in this respect, for the Arabs and Berbers who settled here in the wake of the Muslim conquest of 711 introduced new plants and techniques of irrigation. After the Umayyad dynasty had been ousted from power in Damascus in 750, leading members of the family fled to Cordoba and in 756 established the independent polity of al-Andalus in Spain. Encouraged by Umayyad amirs such as Abd al-Rahman I (756–88), who is said to have sent for pomegranate seeds and date palms familiar from his Syrian homeland, parts of southern Spain took on a new aspect, as a result not only of the introduction of new plants for cultivation but also of the establishment of the systems of intensive irrigation widely practised elsewhere in the Islamic world. Under Muslim rule, belts of irrigated fields around the cities of al-Andalus enabled the cultivation of such water-dependent crops as sugar cane, rice, and cotton, all of which were widely farmed in southern Spain by the late eleventh century. With the introduction during the tenth century of the orange, much appreciated for its ornamental qualities in formal gardens, Cordoba, Seville, and other cities in early medieval al-Andalus recalled to visitors' minds the landscapes of Syria.

Changing landscapes also need to be assessed in the context of climate and weather. Early medieval writers certainly had an intuitive notion of meteorological normality, and extreme aberrations in the weather drew comment. In 748, Ireland was afflicted by 'snow of unusual depth so that nearly all the cattle of the whole of Ireland perished, and the world afterwards was parched by unusual drought'. And in northern France in 874, a 'long, hard winter' produced 'such a tremendous amount of snow that no one could remember seeing anything like it'.[4] Commentators also noted the connection between climate and disease or harvest failure. Exceptional rains in 820 led, we are told, to widespread disease among humans and livestock, caused grain and vegetables to rot in the fields, and left that year's grape harvest small and bitter. Worst of all, perhaps—and certainly unusual for the precision with which it is recorded—was the 'great flood far beyond the usual coastal tides' that inundated Frisia on 26 December 838, breaching all the dunes, spilling sand everywhere, and washing away homes, cattle, and 2,437 people.[5]

However perceptive, early medieval observers could not have been aware that sudden crises such as these betokened a cycle of long-term climatic shifts that very gradually changed the world in which they lived. Only the combination of documentary witness and modern scientific techniques allows an outline of the climatic history of Europe in the first millennium AD to be reconstructed. Midway through the millennium (very approximately the years c.400–600), a significant drop in average temperatures of about 1.5°C throughout the northern hemisphere produced increased rainfall and flooding. Additional manifestations included rising sea levels along low-lying coasts of the North Sea, expansion of the peat bogs of south-western Ireland, the advance of Alpine glaciers, and the extension into the Mediterranean of the Atlantic climate pattern of wetter winters than had characterized the first part of the millennium. By *c.*700 a more continental climatic pattern, of hot, dry summers and severely cold winters, was leaving its mark. (The frequent heavy snows and frozen rivers of north-west European winters in the ninth century are among the indications of this.) Only in the last century of the millennium did temperatures again rise above their long-term average, building gradually to another climatic optimum in the twelfth century, nearly 2°C higher in northern Europe than in *c.*500.

Climatic change might affect the ability of marginal land to sustain cultivation and certainly contributed to some of the shifts in settlement sites noticeable in the early Middle Ages. The abandonment and rebuilding elsewhere of early medieval Frisian *terpen* corresponded with phases of marine transgression and regression. Likewise, as peat bogs expanded in upland areas of south-western Ireland and north-western Britain in the early Middle Ages, communities ceased to cultivate hillside fields, leaving them to revert to scrub and woodland. In Ireland, archaeological evidence for increased cereal production and pastoral farming activity on the fertile central and eastern lowlands suggests a redistribution of population in favour of these areas. A particularly well-studied example is the chalk hills of southern England. Here, a progressive lowering of the water table in the seventh to eighth centuries seems to have contributed to the abandonment of hilltop settlements to the south-east of Winchester. Combined with steady erosion of the soil on the hill slopes, this may have helped prompt communities to relocate to the heavier and more fertile soils of the coastal lowlands. By contrast, the climatic amelioration of the last third of the first millennium may help explain a notable increase in cereal cultivation in Scotland, and also its introduction to north Atlantic islands, notably the Shetlands and Outer Hebrides.

Changes in land use and rural settlement frequently also resulted from altered political and economic relationships between and within communities. Archaeological evidence suggests that in parts of southern Scandinavia, for example, intensification of agricultural production in the seventh century accompanied widespread political changes. A well-studied example concerns Borre in Vestfold, where larger fields and new crops signalled enhanced cultivation in association with the emergence of a new centre of elite occupation evidenced by massive, richly furnished burial mounds. Powerful chieftains were evidently forging larger kingdoms by imposing themselves upon the lesser farmers in the region, extracting produce or tribute by means we can only surmise, but leaving a changed landscape as evidence of their new-found power. Similar but less dramatic restructuring contributed to the well-known 'wandering-settlement' phenomenon that affected many rural habitation sites in much of north-western Europe. Until *c.*700 Anglo-Saxon settlements were liable either to shift gradually within their territorial boundaries or to relocate entirely; in Denmark settlements continued to wander around in this way until the eleventh or twelfth century. In all these cases, the emergence of less egalitarian, more exploitative social relationships, coupled with changing ecological conditions, manifested itself in spatial reorganization and agrarian change.

Towards the end of our period, the Italian peninsula provides a particularly well-studied variation on this theme. Textual and archaeological evidence agree that almost all rural Italy from Tuscany southwards underwent a redistribution of habitations in the tenth and eleventh centuries. In a process commonly known as *incastellamento*, dispersed rural households gathered together into a single fortified village. These were usually built on a previously unoccupied site located on higher ground than the former dwellings. Relocation to defended sites was only partly a response to the growing insecurity of the tenth-century Italian countryside, which was suffering persistent attacks by Saracens (Arab pirates from North Africa) and highly mobile Magyar raiding parties. Weakened princely authority also contributed, for it freed landowners to build and garrison their own fortifications, from which they could intimidate their neighbours. At least as important as threats of violence, however, transformations in the nature and organization of the agrarian economy stimulated *incastellamento*. Burdensome new rents and labour services enhanced landowners' domination of their rural workforce at a time of rising population, making it advantageous to rehouse tenants directly under the lordly gaze.

A different aspect of population movement is migration, whether voluntary or forced. Temporary or permanent population displacement probably accompanied much of the inter-ethnic violence of the early Middle Ages. We hear, for example, of the Daleminzi Slavs from around Meissen on the upper Elbe, who suffered repeated Magyar attacks in 906. This region was 'reduced to such miserable penury that the Daleminzi abandoned their own land and took service with other peoples in order to have something to eat'.[6] Largely unrecorded because lacking in political consequence, sufferings such as these must have been far more frequent than the evidence makes explicit. We occasionally also learn of deliberate ethnic cleansing, and it too must have had a temporary impact on settlement and land use. The fate of the Saxons living east of the Elbe is the best-known case: in 804 Charlemagne consolidated his conquest of Saxony by the mass deportation of many thousands of men, women, and children, whom he relocated in interior parts of his empire.

Displacements such as these are a sad but straightforward manifest-ation of settlement mobility. Much more controversial is the extent to which long-distance migration in northern Europe accompanied the col-lapse of the Roman frontier in the fifth century. The idea that entire peoples trekked south in search of new homes was first promulgated in the origin tales that the Franks, Goths, Lombards, and Anglo-Saxons told about themselves after they had successfully established their own king-doms within former imperial provinces. As we have seen, however, there are additional powerful explanations of the social and cultural changes of the fifth and sixth centuries.[7] While settlement archaeology does suggest that between the fifth and seventh centuries there was some reduction in the population around the base of the Jutland peninsula and along the North Sea coast of modern Germany, and, in places, an associated ex-pansion of forests, migration may not have been its sole, or even main, cause.

We are on safer ground if we turn our attention to what happened within frontier provinces of the empire, for organized evacuation formed a recognized instrument of imperial policy, and supplemented the flight of refugees away from zones of conflict to safer parts of the empire. The gradual collapse of the Danubian frontier was accompanied by deliberate evacuations of towns, starting along the southern bank of the river's upper course in the last two decades of the fifth century and then, a century or so later, along its lower, Balkan, reaches. In the 480s, townsfolk, clergy, and saints' relics from Noricum were resettled in Italy, and then, in the 580–90s, evacuees and refugees from Slavic attacks in the Balkans found safer homes in Greece, the Aegean islands, southern Italy, and Sicily. North-eastern Italy was not exempt from this disruption. Repeated in-vasions and raids across the eastern Alps from the Balkans and Danube basin created an atmosphere of insecurity, which lasted into the later seventh century. Vulnerable to attack, the cities and settlements on the dry lands above the head of the Adriatic Sea steadily declined in importance. Their inhabitants found safer refuges on the islands surrounding the Adriatic lagoons, where new communities developed, first temporary refuges and then permanent settlements. From c.800 onwards, the independent and increasingly powerful trading settlement of Venice grew rapidly on the island of Rialto: its rise marks the new predominance of island settlements over the depopulated *terra firma* in this region.

In situating the men, women, and children of the early Middle Ages in their habitats, two points emerge. First, we must envisage rural and urban settlements as dynamic and ever-changing, not static and timeless. Habitation sites were rarely stable or permanent: they occupied a landscape littered with the debris of former generations and ages, whether buildings, field walls, cemeteries, or monuments. As men and women shifted their dwellings and modified their farming practices, they left their mark on the continuously evolving European landscape. Climate, exploitation of natural resources, availability of cultivable land, choice of crops, habitation sites, forms of settlement, and modes of exploitation all gradually changed, each contributing to the European environment familiar today. Some of this evolution can be detected in the year-by-year events recorded by written documentation, but much of it occurred slowly, over decades and centuries, and is not readily identifiable except by intensive regional archaeology. That we now know as much as we do about the evolution of Europe's landscapes is the fruit of close collaboration between historians and environmental scientists, and a broadening in historical perspective beyond the events of political or ecclesiastical history towards a complementary focus on longer-term structural change in human societies.

Secondly, wherever we look, we encounter the regionalism, even localism, that is the dominant characteristic of the early Middle Ages. Landscape, natural resources, climate, farming systems, settlement distribution, and population density not only changed over time; they also differed from one part of Europe to another, from one locality to the next. The variation and diversity of habitats is of fundamental significance: although subsequent chapters will explore the human endeavour expended in overcoming the limitations of micro-regional living by forging networks of social association, economic contact, and political allegiance, the next section of this chapter will demonstrate ways in which human experience remained constrained by local conditions throughout the early Middle Ages. By thinking in local rather than generalized terms, we can make sense of the dynamics of living and dying in the early Middle Ages.

Birth and Death

After three years of marriage, Vilithuta, wife of Dagaulf, died in about 590. Aged 17, she passed away in childbirth, 'pregnant with her own doom'. 'Born in the jaws of death', her child died with her; her sorrowing husband 'in one death . . . grieved for burying two'. We know of Vilithuta's brief life and Dagaulf's grief only from the verses of consolation that her death occasioned, but this poem nevertheless reminds us that, however inextricably linked, birth and death are both the cultural experience of individuals and the biological fundamental of collective human existence over time.[8] The case of Vilithuta and Dagaulf invites us to consider a wide range of demographic questions about birth and death in the centuries between 500 and 1000. This section explores the nature of population change in the early Middle Ages. It then moves on to enquire into life expectancies and sex ratios in order to sketch the demographic profiles of the communities who form the subject of this book: Vilithuta's life story turns out to be not uncommon. Against the backdrop of regional and micro-regional landscapes outlined above, it also argues that birth and death are best comprehended in local contexts.

Inasmuch as they are both cultural and biological phenomena, birth and death are, in principle, amenable to study through both cultural and biological evidence—that is, through textual representation and human remains. In practice, however, neither separately nor even in conjunction do the two categories of evidence easily yield answers to the questions historians might wish to pose. We immediately find that things that seem important to us rarely mattered in the same way in the early Middle Ages. Take the question of age. One late Roman habit maintained by the literate urban elites of Italy, Gaul, Spain, and the Balkans until c.700 was the practice of erecting epitaphs to commemorate the dead. Many of these tombstones state the age of the deceased. The ages given are occasionally downright impossible, sometimes explicitly approximate—'Demetius lived more or less thirty-seven years'[9]—and often rounded off to a suspiciously neat number that was socially appropriate rather than factually accurate. It seems that few people knew exactly how old they were, and that age was more a matter of social role than a precise period of time. Analysis of skeletal remains offers an alternative approach, but, even so, can offer only approximations of the age at death of individuals whose remains have been excavated.

Nor was anyone concerned to count people, for the question about how many people lived in a place never arose in the early Middle Ages, and, even if it had, no one would have had the means to answer it exactly. Thus there is a fundamental absence of evidence for calculating Europe's early medieval population—not that this has prevented efforts at guessing. For what they are worth, estimates of the population from Scandinavia to the Balkans c.1000 fall either side of the 40 million mark. The nearest thing to a population census is a handful of estate surveys and descriptions of the workers on great ecclesiastical estates in the ninth-century Carolingian Empire. As will be seen, if used with care these can provide approximations of the density, sex ratios, and age profile of the specific settlements concerned. Even so, this evidence is exiguous and unreliable, for the compilers' aim was not a population census but a record of fiscal exactions and labour services in which individuals were generally recorded only in so far as they were burdened with taxes or labour services. This is the nub of the problem with the available evidence: statistical records of a population and its obligations are the product of cultures featuring both sophisticated document-mindedness and intensive government. As the previous chapter has indicated, extant documentation from such environments survives only from parts of the ninth-century Carolingian Empire and late-tenth-century England, and none at all remains from the highly bureaucratic regime of the amirs of al-Andalus. In Scandinavia, where any written documentation is absent before the eleventh century, there is nothing to fall back on except extrapolations from indirect evidence offered by burial archaeology, to the extent that such cemetery evidence has survived and been analysed. The same situation pertains in Ireland, for, if Irish uses of writing did extend to forms of record keeping, no traces of them have survived. As for the Slavs, who generally disposed of their dead by cremation rather than inhumation until at least the late tenth century, archaeological assessment of demographic questions necessarily excludes any skeletal analysis. It is best to accept that we cannot say what the population of early medieval Europe was.

Although we cannot measure numbers of people, we can deduce something about relative changes in population levels in the course of the early Middle Ages. Tracking these starts in the cities of the sixth-century Mediterranean, certainly crowded but many of them less so than they had been a couple of centuries earlier. Each town was not only the focal point for its rural hinterland but also a hub in inter-regional trade networks.[10] Thus the epidemic of bubonic plague that broke out at Pelusium on the Nile delta in 541 was able to spread rapidly from one seaport to another. Recurring frequently during the remainder of the sixth century, and thereafter at lengthening intervals, its demographic impact was especially severe in the eastern Mediterranean, where ongoing long-distance grain shipments facilitated its persistence. The disease reached the western Mediterranean basin in 542, repeatedly ravaging the cities of the Italian, French, and Spanish littoral as well as North Africa during the next two centuries, until a final outbreak in southern Italy in 767. But long-distance shipping declined somewhat earlier in the western Mediterranean than in the east, and this may have reduced the severity of the epidemic's impact here. On occasion, plague reached inland along major trade routes such as the Rhone, the Ebro, and the Po, but its virulence faded as it spread; only once did it reach north of the Loire valley.

Bubonic plague had unmistakable symptoms and killed fast. 'It was a sudden death. A wound like a serpent's bite swelled in the groin or armpit and those affected were so consumed by its poison that they died on the second or third day. The strength of the poison robbed sufferers of their senses.'[11] At its most noxious, the epidemic might have dramatic consequences: shortages of coffins, mass burials, flight, civic collapse. In the summer of 654, plague hit several Italian cities. Nearly 150 years later, the devastation seemed apocalyptic to Paul the Deacon. 'So great was the multitude of those dying that even parents with their children and brothers with their sisters were placed on biers two by two and conducted to their tombs in the city of Rome. And in like manner too this pestilence also depopulated Ticinum [i.e. Pavia] so that all citizens fled to the mountain ranges and to other places and grass and bushes grew in the market place and throughout the streets of the city.'[12] Whatever the actual death toll may have been, an outbreak such as this left traumatic memories and enduring perceptions of social dislocation.

In demographic terms, the impact of the plague undoubtedly varied from region to region and city to city. Locally severe on several occasions in Rome and Marseilles, a passing anguish in Trier and Toledo, non-existent in Nantes or Paris, these epidemics caused regional but not global decline in population. Indeed, bubonic plague rarely reached much beyond the busy trading ports of the Mediterranean and their immediate hinterlands, where the preconditions for its spread existed. Nevertheless, spasms of virulent disease certainly visited the more rural and sparsely populated areas of Atlantic Europe and the British Isles. Mentions of 'yellow pestilence', 'mortality of children', 'great mortality', and 'pox' occur in Irish and Anglo-Saxon sources for the sixth and seventh centuries, but these phrases cannot be reliably translated into modern medical terminology. Whatever their precise nature, these epidemics had serious consequences. Several kings succumbed to disease, their deaths inevitably plunging fragile kingdoms into turmoil. On occasion, it seems that whole localities were devastated too, as in 664, when one of these outbreaks ravaged first southern England, then northern regions, and finally spread to Ireland. According to Bede, in Northumbria, this 'most grievous pestilence . . . brought with it destruction so severe that in some large villages and estates once crowded with inhabitants, only a small and scattered remnant, and sometimes none at all, remained'.[13]

In assessing whether epidemics had a significant effect upon European population levels, we have no means of moving beyond literary impressions of disaster such as Bede's to any measure of how many people actually died or fled to uncontaminated places. Nor is it possible to determine whether the population level was reduced for more than a couple of generations. We should avoid any temptation to overgeneralize, and, rather than postulating any overall fall in population, it makes best sense to interpret the decline and dislocation induced by epidemics as short term and locally specific, varying from place to place.

The same holds true for the food shortages that are such a marked feature of the historical record from *c*.800 onwards. Famine recurred on average one year in four throughout the ninth century, dropped to only one year in ten in the tenth, but rose again in the eleventh century. Many of these were of regional impact: the Rhineland in 850, Saxony in 853, Bavaria in 882, 'here and there' in 889, for example.[14] In contrast, Ireland, a country especially dedicated to animal husbandry, endured recurrent bouts of murrain among cattle in the course of the early Middle Ages, with a profound impact on food supply and human resistance to disease. In 700, 'cattle mortality' broke out early in the year, with extreme consequences: 'famine and pestilence prevailed in Ireland for three years, so that man ate man.'[15] Only on one occasion is it clear that all Europe was affected simultaneously, however. In the famine of 1005, so great that 'no man ever remembered one so cruel',[16] cannibalism was again reported: this famine ravaged everywhere from the British Isles to Bavaria. The terrible hunger of 1005 was nevertheless exceptional. In general, dearth and disaster struck here one year, there another year. No long-distance trade in foodstuffs evened out the oscillations of scarcity and plenty; equally, no general cycle of misery afflicted all early medieval Europe.

The same emphasis on regionality also applies to the circumstances that might be conducive to population growth. A critical prerequisite for sustaining demographic advance is a regular and adequate food supply. Either extension of the area of cultivation or intensification of agricultural techniques might increase the availability of foodstuffs—to the extent permitted by climate and soil fertility, supply of labour and agricultural technology. Did agricultural change enable more intensive cultivation, and thereby population growth in the early Middle Ages? The most appropriate answer is again one that stresses regional distinctions. Consider a small part of France: watermills studded the area west of Paris from at least the late eighth century onwards, yet they remained rare until the eleventh century just 50 kilometres to the south, where different geology and patterns of landholding delayed their introduction. Whether the issue is the use of a heavy plough or the introduction of new crops, both of which are attested in many different places, the same picture emerges: change was localized, and dependent on many factors besides technical expertise. At the very least, as Chapter 5 will argue, the arrival of a new, energetic landlord could make a considerable difference. The one thing that seems not to have altered anywhere is extremely low grain yields, even on the most fertile soils. Although the quality of harvests was doubtless extremely erratic, to reap no more than two to three times the amount of grain as had been sown appears to have been common: and out of this harvest came next year's seed corn. If the population of rural areas grew in the early Middle Ages, more intensive food production was not the main cause.

By contrast, many different parts of Europe provide evidence to suggest that land clearance was common, certainly from the eighth century onwards, and in places perhaps from the seventh. Archaeological traces of new settlement sites, palaeobotanical analysis of pollen deposits, and documentary references to the extension of cultivation into areas of woodland all point in the same direction. Whether the evidence comes from Ireland, southern England, Scotland, central France, Catalonia, northern and central Italy, the Ardennes, Hesse, eastern Bavaria, or the western Polish heartland, it is consistent in suggesting the extension of cultivation and, in particular, of cereal-growing. Whether small-scale clearance on individual initiative, or larger projects pushed forward by the energy of lords, churches, and even kings, the felling of scrub or woodland constituted the main form of agricultural change in the early Middle Ages.

The extension of arable land should probably be associated with growth in the rural population of Europe inasmuch as it both presumes a supply of labour adequate to the task and results in an increased supply of foodstuffs. Certainly, those few ninth-century estate surveys that provide a snapshot of their workforce at a particular moment reinforce the view that there was considerable pressure on landed resources by this date. On the lands in southern Flanders belonging to the abbey of Saint Bertin in the middle years of the ninth century, the population probably reached an average density of twenty inhabitants per square kilometre. On the estates belonging to Saint-Germain-des-Prés in the Seine basin around Paris, the average was even higher, up to forty persons per square kilometre on certain estates.

To the suggestion that the cereal-growing lowlands of northern Europe were already supporting dense settlement in the ninth century can be added clues from the mountainous fringe of the Mediterranean. Indeed, in the upland valleys of Catalonia, the rural population may well have been as high as nineteenth-century levels. The only documentation that allows an estimate of demographic growth to be hazarded comes from the Provençal lands of Saint-Victor at Marseilles in 813–14. The evidence of this estate survey indicates that the population increased rather faster on some properties in the region than on others. Extrapolations suggest an overall growth rate on Saint-Victor's estates equivalent to a doubling of the population in the course of a century. If these calculations are at all reliable, they imply that, in at least some parts of ninth-century Europe, the population was capable of brief spurts of growth almost at the rate sustained in England towards the eve of the Industrial Revolution. In all, there are firm signs of considerable, if short-term, demographic growth in parts of Europe at various times from the ninth century onwards.

The summary picture for the eighth and ninth centuries is one of patchy, regional changes in agricultural methods and technology, widespread land clearance, and the capacity for substantial population growth. Yet these developments had only modest cumulative impact, for not until c.950–1050 is there clear evidence of widespread, prolonged population growth. Medieval Europe's sustained demographic upturn commenced, approximately, with the millennium. In the preceding two or three centuries, land clearance and population growth were tempered by outbreaks of disease, frequent famines, and the effects of climatic deterioration.

The most likely explanation for the lack of steady population growth in the early Middle Ages is that spasms of subsistence crisis, marked by food shortages and natural calamities, interrupted periods of growth and expansion. Since famine rarely struck universally, and since heavy rains, drought and other climatic disasters were similarly regional or local in impact, the oscillation between population growth and stagnation (or even short-term decline) is likely also to have been regional and inconsistent. All this suggests that, in the early Middle Ages, the resources were not widely available to sustain steady population growth over long periods of time. A population on the brink of subsistence crisis was not well equipped to withstand years when the crops failed or cattle murrain was rife. While there certainly were dense pockets of population, that density was neither uniform nor stable. In short, throughout the early Middle Ages, the rate of change in the population level fluctuated unpredictably from place to place. If the impact of dearth and disaster was erratic and uneven, so too was population growth.

For a population to grow, a sustained surplus of births over deaths is required. In the assessment of fertility and mortality, cemetery evidence is invaluable, for painstaking analysis can induce the bodies of the early medieval dead to yield up much valuable information on the sex ratios, life expectancies, patterns of disease, and forms of mortality prevalent within particular communities. With the caveat that skeletal analysis is not an exact science, and that a cemetery does not necessarily hold all (or even a representative sample) of a community's dead, burial evidence nevertheless throws into sharp relief the circumstances in which men and women lived, endeavoured to reproduce themselves, and died. Two cemeteries, widely separated in space and time, illustrate its potential.

The first is a site in south-eastern England, in use from the late fifth century until the middle of the eighth. At Buckland, at least 20 per cent of all the community died before they reached the age of 18, and only about 6 per cent lived to an age of 60 or more. Of the adult population, women outnumbered men by 3:2, but had a significantly shorter life expectancy, for the average age at death of adult women was 31, as compared with 38 for men. Approximate though these figures are, they indicate a population faced with very heavy child mortality, a high rate of female mortality in the child-bearing years, a surplus of women, which may imply that men frequently died away from home—at war or out hunting—and a community whose elderly members were far fewer and much younger than in recent centuries. Furthermore, since the people who lived in the vicinity of Buckland buried their infants under about age 5 somewhere separate from this communal cemetery, the real child mortality rate must have been very much higher. The sixth-century cemetery at Cannington in south-western Britain suggests a likelier figure: there 64 per cent of the entire population died before they reached 18 and, indeed, 15 per cent did not survive their first year.

The second example is the Münsterhof cemetery in the centre of Zurich. This served as the burying ground for the proto-urban settlement that formed around the Frauenmünster nunnery founded in 853, and it remained in use until the end of the twelfth century. Figure 2.2 indicates its overall population profile. Unlike Buckland, young children and some infants were buried here, but it seems that, before the eleventh century, stillborn babies and those dying in the first weeks of life continued to be laid to rest elsewhere. Of those who were buried in the Münsterhof, almost 50 per cent failed to reach age 18 and at least 30 per cent died in the first five years of life, two-thirds of whom died within their first year. In terms of perinatal, infant, and child mortality, the population of ninth- and tenth-century Zurich was depleted at a rate broadly comparable with that at Buckland or Cannington. By contrast, the adult population of Zurich was quite different. The ratio of women to men was much more nearly even, with six women for every five men, a ratio in line with many other cemeteries of the high Middle Ages. Also, the average age at death of the adult population suggests that the security of existence was measurably greater in Zurich than it had been in Buckland, for most adults died between 50 and 60 and a few lived on above 60. There was,

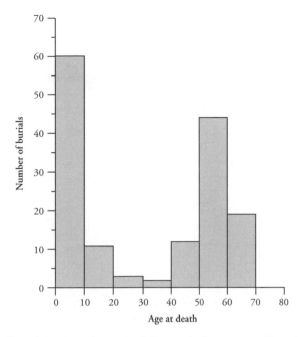

2.2. Age profile of the burials in the Münsterhof cemetery, Zurich. This graph emphasizes the very high rate of infant and child mortality and, for those who survived into adulthood, the likelihood of dying in their 50s. Based on J. Schneider, D. Gutscher, H. Etter, and J. Hanser, *Der Münsterhof in Zürich: Bericht über die vom städtischen Büro für Archäologie durchgeführten Stadtkernforschungen 1977/78* (Olten, 1982).

nevertheless, a clear difference between men and women, which Figure 2.3 reveals, for the average life expectancy of a 20-year-old male was 57, as compared with 49 for women of the same age. This was an environment in which childbirth remained an appreciable danger, for over one-third of adult women died during their fertile years.

Approximate though these figures are, they nevertheless suggest a few general observations. In the first place, regional and temporal variation is again noteworthy: the striking fluctuations in general population levels reflected locally varying fertility and mortality rates. Further, if on average one-half of the population died during infancy or childhood, this means that women underwent pregnancy and childbirth twice for every child that reached adulthood. For population levels to remain steady each couple had to produce four offspring, of whom two would survive; for the population to grow, even more. There is also the inescapable observation

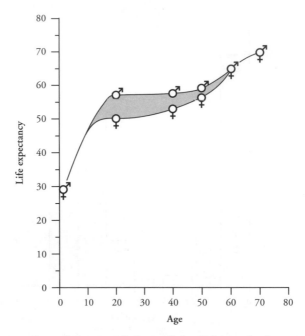

2.3. Life expectancy of the population of the Münsterhof cemetery, Zurich. Average life expectancy at birth was about twenty-eight years, but those who survived their first year of infancy might expect to live on to 36. By age 20 a clear gender differential is evident, which diminishes only in old age. Based on J. Schneider, D. Gutscher, H. Etter, and J. Hanser, *Der Münsterhof in Zürich: Bericht über die vom städtischen Büro für Archäologie durchgeführten Stadtkernforschungen 1977/78* (Olten, 1982).

that birth and death were intimately associated. The risk of death was always greatest within the very first year of human life—probably even the first weeks—and, for adult women, around the time of childbirth. In this respect, early medieval Europe was little different from those twenty-first-century communities that lack any access to modern hygiene and medicine. The population profile thus contrasts starkly with that of contemporary western Europe, as Figure 2.4 emphasizes.

Cemetery evidence from Buckland, Zurich, and elsewhere reveals something of the quality of life in the early Middle Ages. Among the symptoms betrayed by skeletal remains are: dental problems such as badly worn teeth and abscesses; broken limbs that had healed crooked or shortened; long-running inflammation and infections in joints whose sufferers had lived deformed from pain; uncomfortable and debilitating skeletal

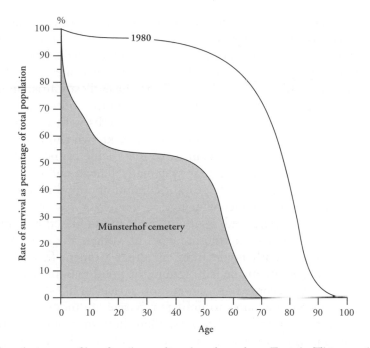

2.4. Population profile of early medieval and modern Zurich. This graph contrasts the demographic profile of the early medieval Münsterhof cemetery with the much lower rate of infant mortality and much longer life span of late-twentieth-century western Europe. Based on J. Schneider, D. Gutscher, H. Etter, and J. Hanser, *Der Münsterhof in Zürich: Bericht über die vom städtischen Büro für Archäologie durchgeführten Stadtkernforschungen 1977/78* (Olten, 1982).

conditions such as arthritis, osteoporosis, or spondylosis afflicting men and women in the middle and later years of life. Cemeteries sometimes also hint at communities in which diseases such as tuberculosis were endemic as well as at personal life stories otherwise unknown to us: an adult woman at Tuttlingen whose bow legs were the result of malnutrition in childhood; a man at Griesheim whose left leg had been amputated below the knee, but who had lived on into his 50s with a wooden leg fitted with a rust-proof bronze cap; a congenitally malformed child at Zurich who had been born with a severely twisted spine; a man in Kent who had been stabbed in the left eye and then sustained three decapitating blows on the back of his skull. Skeletal remains evoke a world pervaded by illness, pain, and deformity, exacerbated from time to time by the violence of personal hatred and warfare.

Cemetery evidence on its own does not, however, fully explain early medieval patterns of fertility and mortality, for both are also shaped by social conventions of a type not amenable to archaeological enquiry. For example, archaeology cannot elucidate whether fertility rates were affected by deliberate limitations of family size. From the earliest Christian times, churchmen had inveighed in vain against both contraception and abortion, and there is no doubt that common herbs with effective contraceptive and abortifacient properties were well known throughout early medieval Europe. Occasional instances of infanticide cannot entirely be dismissed, although arguments that systematic female child killing was practised in some ninth-century peasant communities and in Viking-age Scandinavia remain quite unconvincing.

There are two interrelated issues here. First, unlike the numerous cemeteries that suggest a sex ratio in favour of women, the ninth-century estate surveys consistently report more men than women. To explain this by invoking female infanticide is to ignore the good reasons why women tend to be under-recorded in surveys of agricultural estate workers. Secondly, deliberate measures to limit family size are more plausibly associated with the constraints of poverty than those of gender. To the extent that it is possible to estimate the number of surviving children born to each couple, only amongst the royal dynasties or the most rich and powerful continental aristocracies of the ninth and tenth centuries are families of more than three or four children at all common. A frequently repeated pronouncement against abortion offers vital evidence of the way in which the conscious limitation of family size might correlate with poverty: after imposing differential penalties for termination of a pregnancy within the first six weeks or after a foetus has quickened, the ruling continues: 'but it makes a great difference whether an impoverished woman does it on account of the difficulty of feeding the child or a prostitute for the sake of concealing her crime.'[17] Other texts too impose a much lighter penalty on the impoverished woman who slays a child. The recognition that poverty might drive a woman to abortion or even infanticide gradually became an established aspect of ecclesiastical law, but cemetery evidence can never reveal the extent to which this was practised.

If poverty constrained fertility at one end of the social spectrum, then lifestyle may have influenced mortality at the other. Analysis of animal bone remains from high-status sites suggests that early medieval elites enjoyed a diet rich in the meat of domesticated animals raised for early slaughter when the flesh was of optimum quality, supplemented with wildfowl and game such as boar and deer. Food remains from peasant sites, on the other hand, point to the consumption of the flesh of much older animals, livestock whose primary function may have been to provide wool, milk, or traction rather than meat. Better diet and access to such medical expertise as was available may have helped elite women survive the traumas of childbirth a little more readily than other women, but their menfolk were perhaps more susceptible to early death than the men of other social groups. The German aristocracy of the tenth century offers a well-studied and extreme example of this. Hunting, war, feuding, and judicial duels thinned out the ranks of the men of the Ottonian aristocracy, who were often long outlived by their female relatives, whether sisters dedicated to a life of Christian celibacy or widowed wives and mothers. In this context, mortality might have serious political repercussions. When the ruling dynasty itself was involved, a bitter succession dispute or the accession of a minor, usually under the tutelage of his mother, was the likely consequence.

In any society, demographic changes reflect a complex interaction between external factors such as climatic disaster and famine, on the one hand, and, on the other, such internal social conventions as constraints on family size, attitudes towards contraception and abortion, medical knowledge, and the prevalence of dangerous lifestyles among certain social groups. Fragmentary and impressionistic though the early medieval evidence is, it shows clearly enough the main patterns of fertility and mortality. The physical discomfort of chronic illness probably affected most people; endemic disorders were exacerbated from time to time by epidemics of infectious diseases, of which the plague was only one. Amid these difficulties, infants, women in labour, and aristocratic men all faced an enhanced risk of death, yet Europe's population nevertheless managed to increase in the course of the early Middle Ages. Although individual communities experienced fluctuating patterns of fertility and mortality, the overall upward curve is clear.

Moreover, as the millennium approached, erratic demographic change was giving way to a steadier rate of increase as the constraints on growth eased. Certainly, the climate was generally improving by the year 1000. Documentary evidence suggests that land clearance projects were taking place on an enhanced scale. Local and regional trade networks were intensifying, transporting foodstuffs to towns whose growth, especially in northern Italy and the Low Countries, must have relied upon surplus rural population.[18] By the opening years of the eleventh century the population and economy of Europe were entering an era of sustained growth that would last into the thirteenth century. The developments of the high Middle Ages did not suddenly develop out of nothing; but they did consolidate changes that had hitherto been faltering or spasmodic.

Responses to Calamity

For any early medieval community, everyday life involved facing death and disaster. Enduring this ever-present threat, men and women not only raised children and eked out a living; they also strove to make sense of the world in which they lived and to do whatever they could to ameliorate their lot. Their responses were informed by ideas and assumptions about the causes of good or bad fortune, about the place of humans within the cosmos, about what happened after death. But it remains virtually impossible to recover most of these mentalities, partly because of the difficulties in extrapolating from material culture to attitudes, beliefs, and rituals, partly because attempts to suppress older explanations for the fates of humankind accompanied the spread of Christianity. As will be seen, we can nevertheless pick up some traces of those other views, despite the dominance in the textual record of a Christian cosmology. What emerges from this survey are the variety and versatility of early medieval responses to the calamities that constrained existence.

Many different ways of dealing with ill health, disability, and disease are particularly well evidenced. It would be possible to categorize the range of curative techniques and resources thus: professional doctors, trained in book-learned medicine inherited from the ancient world; practitioners of local wisdom concerning herbal remedies; Christian faith healers, living and dead; clerical specialists expert in manipulating ecclesiastical rituals for curative purposes; traditional practices such as amulets, talismans, invocations, and charms. Yet, in practice, these were not clear-cut distinctions, for some holy men possessed medical knowledge, while clergy sometimes carefully copied out herbal recipes that were to be applied with a mixture of Christian prayers and charmlike incantations. What the evidence generally fails to offer is a sense of healing as practice rather than as textual strategy, not least because of the paucity of direct evidence for the application of most of these methods. It would seem, though, that the more specialist resources were thinly and unevenly distributed, and thus that the curative options available in any one locality were in all likelihood restricted. For all except the wealthy few, cost would anyway have prohibited virtually all forms of external help, for professional doctors charged fees for their services or for rare drugs; the nearest shrine might be far away and hard of access, its custodians likely to expect a significant gift. Most people were thrown back on whatever expertise was locally available—and free.

Far more is known about one form of healing than all the others, however: that offered by the shrines of Christian saints. Some were the tombs of men and women who had been martyred in the second and third centuries. Others were the graves of holy men or—less frequently—women, persons who had acquired a reputation in their lifetime for mitigating human affliction through their own religiosity and whose achievements had commonly included healing the sick through prayer and ritual, sometimes also identifying and expelling the demons whom Christians deemed to inhabit the bodies of the suffering. Whether martyred or not, all saints were understood to have the ability to intercede successfully with the God of Christian tradition to win beneficial intervention in human affairs: their importance reflected a clearly articulated cosmology that identified certain humans during and after their lifetimes as special conduits of supernatural assistance.

As Christianity spread, so clergy established new shrines, either by moving body parts of established saints to new locales, or by encouraging the veneration as saints of recently deceased religious leaders. In some places, these shrines perpetuated pre-Christian healing powers once vested in potent springs and trees or attributed to sites sacred to the local gods; in others, a quite new religious landscape emerged, competing with, and ultimately replacing, earlier ritual sites. Thanks to the clerical custom of keeping written records of the cures, exorcisms (expulsions of demons), and other intercessions attributed to the saints, the healing available at Christian shrines is far better documented than any other of the curative possibilities of the early Middle Ages.

We have already met one such saint, Martin, also one of the many cures achieved through his intercession. After a spectacular and controversial career as bishop of Tours (371–97), healer, and wonderworker, he had become the best-documented and most widely revered saint of the early Middle Ages, venerated from Scotland and Ireland to Spain and Germany. Although his tomb in the magnificently decorated fifth-century church just outside the city of Tours always remained the focal point of his cult, Martin's bodily remains had been removed to a church in Chablis for safekeeping between about 872 and 885, a time of threat from the Vikings, seaborne Scandinavian raiders.[19] It was there that Genovefa had been cured of her congenital deafness and lack of speech when she spent the night in silent prayer outside the doors of the church, along with other pilgrims congregated there. The clerical author who noted the details of her visit drew on commonplace religious motifs when he represented her cure in terms of a confrontation between a fire-spitting devil and the resplendent, white-haired saint, a conflict easily won by the latter. In so doing, the author relied upon the widespread

Christian understanding of the world as one in which the cosmic struggle of good and evil manifested itself in the symptoms displayed by the human body, a struggle in which Christian salvation was synonymous with physical healing. The fundamental tenet of Christian belief, that this redemption came through belief in Christ, easily accommodated saints as the channels through which divine beneficence or retribution flowed. 'I am Martin, through whom Lord Jesus Christ deigns to restore you to health' declared the saint as his healing touch cured Genovefa.[20]

Christian teaching relied on a cosmology that explained far more than the physical afflictions of individuals: it supplied reasons for death and disaster too. For one thing, the Bible provided a frame of reference and comparison. In 873, the 'ancient plague of the Egyptians' afflicted much of Europe—an infestation of locusts. When the swarm flew, it filled the air with the thrumming of wings: 'one could scarcely see the sky, as if looking through a sieve.' Clergy processed with crucifixes and the relics of saints through stricken areas, 'beseeching God to defend them from this plague'.[21] Above all, however, the Bible presented an exemplum of suffering and destruction as symptoms of a wrathful God angered by personal immorality or social disarray. No one contributed more to interpreting the afflictions of this world through the lens of Christian doctrine than Gregory I. Wracked by pain and illness for much of his life, he drew inspiration and comfort from the Old Testament story of Job, a man who exemplified persistence in faith undeterred by disease and suffering. What held good for Gregory in his private life held good also for the world around him. Elected pope in 590 as plague raged through Rome, claiming among its victims his predecessor Pelagius, Gregory explained the reason and remedy for this epidemic to his congregation:

Behold! The sword of heavenly anger strikes down the entire Christian community, as one after another they are laid low by sudden slaughter. No infirmity warns of the approach of death, but, as you see, death overtakes the onset of sickness. The smitten person is struck down without time for conversion to tears and penitence. Think, therefore, how the person who has had no time to repent of their actions will come into the presence of the stern Judge [at the Last Judgement]. Our townsfolk are not taken away piecemeal but they all collapse together: houses are left empty, parents attend the funerals of their children, their heirs precede them to the grave. So let each of us take refuge in repentance and lamentation of our sins whilst there is still time to weep before death strikes. Let us recall to the mind's eye how we have gone astray and what wrongdoings we have done and let us punish ourselves with tears. 'Let us come into God's presence in confession' and, as the prophet urges, 'Let us lift up our hearts with our hands to the Lord'.[22]

Whether the tribulation was induced by epidemic, famine, Viking attack, or any other calamity, the appropriate responses were fasting, prayer, and penance. From Rome to Ireland, wherever the Christian religion found adherents, Christians instinctively reacted by propitiating their God through penitential processions and prayers of intercession, as did the local clergy in the areas overrun by locusts in 873. Such measures could be universal as well as local. Faced with severe and widespread famine in the winter of 792–3, Charlemagne commanded all bishops, priests, monks, nuns, and clergy throughout the Frankish lands to say Masses and sing psalms, ordered everyone to fast, and required all lay and ecclesiastical landowners to give alms to support their tenants until the next harvest time. Similarly, with his kingdom under threat of imminent collapse from Viking invasions in 1009, the Anglo-Saxon king Æthelred II (978–1016) ordered identical action by 'all the nation' in order that 'we may obtain God's mercy and his compassion and that we may be able through his help to withstand our enemies'.[23] Prayer, penance, and almsgiving were the practical manifestations of a mentality that attributed human suffering to spiritual deficiency and found the remedy for physiological, environmental, and political dislocation in the rebalancing of relationships between humans and the divine.

Of the various crises facing early medieval communities, one in particular raised a host of moral and practical problems: famine. One issue was that of lawful foodstuffs. Christian teaching urged a concept of a community whose social boundaries had various markers. Among these were food laws, behavioural prescriptions whose transgression would pollute both the individual and the group. The flesh of several categories of animals was commonly proscribed as unclean: those who shared their living space with humans, such as cats, dogs, and rats; those contaminated by wrongful contact with blood or semen; those that had eaten carrion or human corpses; those found already dead. But, when food was scarce, few starving people can have thought in these terms. In the summer of 869, for example, famine hit central France especially severely. 'A huge number of people died a bitter death, to the extent that men are said to have eaten human corpses. And some are also said to have eaten the flesh of dogs.'[24] A rather different moral issue was the fair price for grain. In the spring of 585, as grain stores ran out long before the next harvest, merchants 'grievously despoiled people' by selling such wine and grain as remained at vastly inflated prices. Struggling households eked out what little flour they had by drying and grinding grape pips, hazel catkins, the roots of ferns, or the young shoots of corn in the field. We also know how those who could not afford any grain at all fared: 'many others, who had no flour

at all, gathered and ate various grasses, but they swelled up and died. . . .
The impoverished gave themselves into slavery in order to receive
a scrap of food.'[25] It was to alleviate situations like this that, in 792–3,
Charlemagne regulated grain prices in a move to prevent landlords from
pursuing profiteering rather than their almsgiving obligations. As
expressed in this legislation, prices and profits were more a matter for
religious concern than economic planning, but at least almsgiving had the
effect of redistributing food to those most in need.

However, Christianity monopolized neither explanations of disaster
nor available remedies. In places where it was of recent introduction,
the validity of the new religion might itself be at issue. The political elites
of southern England had accepted the new faith only a generation or so
before the epidemic of 664: in reaction to the spread of disease, the
East Saxons 'deserted the sacraments of the Christian faith and aposta-
sized. . . . They began to restore the derelict temples and to worship images, as if they could protect themselves by such means from the plague.'[26]
Centuries later, the German missionary bishop Bruno of Querfurt
(1002–9) preached to the Magyars, Poles, and Pechenegs of eastern
Europe. He also wrote an account of the missionary Adalbert of Prague,
using his own experiences to present insights into the difficulties Adalbert had faced immediately before his martyrdom near Gdansk in 997. In
describing the Prussians' hostility that culminated in Adalbert's death at
their hands, Bruno represented their opposition to Christianity as an
equation of the evangelizers' presence with the sterility of the land: '"On
account of these men," the Prussians said, "our land will not yield a
harvest, our trees will not bear fruit, new animals are not born and old
ones die".'[27] A sensitive missionary such as Bruno understood that, in the
struggle for prosperity, religion and disaster were as integrally associated
for non-Christians as for Christians.

Many men and women in early medieval Europe, however, neither enjoyed the learned outlook on the world of a man such as Gregory the
Great nor lived in non-Christian communities. Rather, their Christianity
was richly varied in its understanding of and responses to the world, for
the spread of the Christian religion was a slow process of extended cultural encounters that left its everyday content open to centuries-long negotiation. As Chapter 7 will argue, leading churchmen certainly had their
own firm views about appropriate Christian practice for addressing the
pressing concerns of a rural population struggling with subsistence—the
fertility of animals and fields, the health of children, good weather. They
met limited success in imposing them, however: local communities and
their rural priests persisted with a much wider range of solutions for deal-

ing with the difficulties of a harsh existence. This emerges clearly when
we consider the problem of weather, and especially the summer hailstorms
that could devastate a harvest. Two complementary beliefs are widely attested throughout the early Middle Ages: that the devil was responsible
for unwanted rain and hail; and that 'storm-makers' existed, men and,
occasionally, women who could be invoked to deflect bad weather—or to
rain hail down on a hated neighbour's lands. Techniques for achieving the
desired weather addressed saints, storm-makers, and others deemed able
to intervene through prayers and incantations; charms both spoken and
written, adjurations and invocations; the payment of protection money,
and much else.

Many of these are principally known from their repeated condemnation by clergy, but an exceptional text from north-western Spain does
allow us to see what one individual actually did to ward off hail. In the
late eighth or early ninth century, the 'servant of God' Auriolus wrote, or
had written out for him, a talisman to keep hail off his and his neighbours' fields. He folded then fastened its two slate leaves together, text
inside; after nine incantations to ensure its efficacy, he buried it in his
field near Carrio, where it remained until unearthed by farmers in 1926.
Auriolus adjured 'all you patriarchs Michael, Gabriel, Cecitiel, Oriel,
Raphael, Ananiel, Marmoniel, who hold the clouds in your hands' that
they 'go across the mountains and return neither when the cock crows nor
the hen clucks, neither when the ploughman [ploughs] nor the sower
sows'. He also adjured Satan not to harm the trees, harvest, vines, or fruit
bushes and added prayers to God attributed to St Christopher before ending 'in the name of the Father, the Son and the Holy Spirit, amen, amen,
ever amen, alleluia'.[28] Auriolus's slate not only indicates the persistence of
enduring regional textual habits;[29] it also suggests a broad-spectrum approach to eliminating hail, simultaneously invoking archangels, saints, and
Satan while mixing prayers, incantations, and adjurations in a powerful
cocktail of diverse traditional practices and local wisdom.

Auriolus's concerns were practical, but, to many in the early Middle
Ages, bad weather, pestilence, and other caprices of nature also had a
portentous place in human experience. The appearance of a comet, for
example, 'betokens famine or pestilence or war or the destruction of the
earth or fearful storms'.[30] Experts—in astronomy, in the sinfulness of the
kingdom—then pronounced upon its significance, while annalists and
commentators with a political point to make offered their own opinion
about the meaning of a comet, as they also did for locusts, disease, and
other such omens. Indeed, writers at ninth-century Carolingian courts
so frequently reported natural disasters as the immediate precedent of a

revolt, Viking attack, or the death of a king that some of these 'disasters' are as likely to have been rhetorical signals as actual sufferings. Disorder in the natural world had become a sign of decay in human society, a mirror image of perturbation and chaos. For some of the learned men who reflected upon the right ordering of human affairs, it was also a possible sign that the cosmic struggle of good and evil might be nearing conclusion in the manner of the prophetic vision of the biblical Apocalypse.

In the decades either side of AD 1000, reflection upon the end time (eschatology) and scrutiny of signs potentially suggestive of its approach both intensified. Archbishop Wulfstan of York (1002–23) was no stranger to these. Writing in the aftermath of the harsh famines of 1005 and in the midst of extreme political turmoil facing England in 1014, he circulated a sermon that summed up early medieval thinking about the relationship of natural calamity, the social order, and the end of the world.

Beloved men, realise what is true: this world is in haste and the end approaches; and therefore in the world things go from bad to worse, and so it must of necessity deteriorate greatly on account of the people's sins before the coming of Antichrist, and indeed it will then be dreadful and terrible far and wide throughout the world.
. . .
For it is clear and manifest in us all that we have previously transgressed more than we have amended, and therefore much is assailing this people. Things have not gone well now for a long time at home or abroad, but there has been devastation and famine, burning and bloodshed in every district again and again; and stealing and killing, sedition and pestilence, murrain and disease, malice and hate and spoliation by robbers have harmed us very grievously, and monstrous taxes have afflicted us greatly, and bad seasons have very often caused us failure of crops. For now for many years, as it may seem, there have been in this country many injustices and wavering loyalties among men everywhere.

Wulfstan concluded his address with the time-tested remedy: 'turn to the right and in some measure leave wrong-doing, and atone very zealously for what we have done amiss.'[31] However near the end of the world might seem, there was always time for repentance.

In the face of scholarly disagreement about when exactly it fell, the millennium came and went without the world coming to an end. That did not invalidate the point that calamity had meaning, whether as portent or punishment, for the association of human behaviour with the behaviour of the elements was far too fundamental to be so easily severed. Whether we address the theologically informed thinking of the learned elite, seek to comprehend the mentality of those for whom conversion to Christianity threatened to bring disaster, or survey the means by which hard-pressed peasants sought to control the hostile forces of nature, we find everywhere deeply rooted assumptions that human affairs were but one aspect of a much vaster cosmic order, an order that could be disturbed by wrong action or rebalanced by the appropriate mental effort and actions. In this light, the practical and intellectual responses to calamity surveyed here all make sense to us, even though many of them were dismissed or even ridiculed by high-minded bishops and legislators.

On 24 January 1002, Emperor Otto III died of a sudden fever at Paterno, just north of Rome, aged 21, unmarried and without an heir. Contemporaries ascribed his death to the 'Italian sickness', in all probability malaria.[32] Both his own early demise and that of his father Otto II eighteen years earlier at the age of 28 are sharp reminders that even the most powerful rulers of the early Middle Ages were as likely to succumb to disease and sudden death as anyone else. Otto II had at least secured the succession by having his infant son elected co-ruler six months earlier, but Otto III had made no provision for the succession: his untimely death threw into turmoil his empire, a sprawling conglomerate of lands from the Baltic to central Italy. Indeed, the political impact of death and disaster on this and countless other occasions during the early Middle Ages cannot be underestimated, for famine and disease could as easily halt a vital military expedition as sudden death could trigger a succession crisis. Perhaps because of his awareness of this fragility, perhaps the result of an outlook instilled by those who had tutored him as a boy, Otto III interpreted his rule as a renewal of the right political, religious, and social order needed to defer the beginning of the end time. To that purpose, his actions were decisive. He made Rome, the eternal city, the capital of his transalpine empire, the first ruler since the fourth century to pay anything more than a passing visit there.[33] In 1000, he travelled to Gniezno, where he inaugurated the cult of a new miracle-working saint, Adalbert of Prague. And as a reminder of what would happen when the world came to an end according to biblical prophecy, he surrounded himself with apocalyptic imagery. At his imperial coronation in Rome in 996, he had even clothed himself in a mantle 'on which the entire Apocalypse was embroidered in gold'.[34]

Otto's reign encapsulates many of the themes of this chapter. His sudden, fevered death was a characteristically Italian one in an age where disease, like famine, almost always hit locally rather than universally and where forms of morbidity varied from one region and habitat to another. From his birth near Nijmegen to his death at Paterno, he had travelled

vast distances both north and south of the Alps, and had a personal experience of the mosaic of landscapes and localities that constituted
Europe everywhere from the modern Nertherlands to Poland and Italy.
His preoccupation with eschatology was an effort to give his reign meaning in terms of Christian cosmology and to situate himself within the
grand narrative of human history, past, present, and future. His distribution of the relics of Adalbert of Prague expressed the universal Christian
view that healing and other forms of divine beneficence flowed from the
bones of sainted patrons. Yet, for all his acute sense of his own mission to
guide his empire towards Christian expansion and Roman renewal, Otto
cannot have been aware that he ruled a population now steadily growing
in number, as elsewhere in Europe, or that the climate of Europe was
improving. Nor, in his brief life, is he likely to have taken note of the
changing appearance of the landscape, as forests were cleared, new settlements founded, and old ones relocated. And, although Rome was central
to his politics and his world view, Otto cannot have realized the extent to
which this city had been transformed in the course of the centuries that
separated him from the last of the western Roman emperors. When we
visit Rome in Chapter 8, we shall find its population a fraction of what it
once had been, its cityscape ruralized and its topography transformed.
More than any other city, Rome epitomizes the highly localized changes
that made the world in which early medieval Europeans lived and died so
complex and, at the same time, so dynamic.

AFFINITIES

APPENDICES

3

Friends and Relations

In happy times a man's near relative will be fond of him; nevertheless each of them will have to turn from the other, since the Lord
means, by his sentence, to commit the wretched body to the earth.[1]

It befits as many things as nature has bound together to be in harmony—nature who joins to herself the friendship of kinsmen.[2]

THEY are indeed happy times in any community when a man's relatives
are fond of him, but, as an anonymous Anglo-Saxon poet recognized,
death severs and restructures familial relationships. Similarly, the affection
of kinsfolk, and in particular their friendship for each other, may be fitting, but reality rarely matches the myth of what is 'natural', for, though
the ties between parents and children, brothers and sisters, uncles and
nephews are some of the most cogent bonds in any human society, they
can also be amongst the most fraught. To explore the significance of
kinship in the early Middle Ages is thus to investigate one of the most
important ways in which men and women structured human relationships,
made choices about their social world, expressed emotions and ideals.
Reflection upon these ties also elucidates personal identities, forms of
affinity, and deeply ingrained habits of thinking.

Three themes run throughout this chapter: the locally varied social
forms and cultural expressions of kinship; their ubiquity as a matrix within
which to assert—or contest—power and authority; and the balancing of
affinities of blood with those of friendship. Different aspects are explored
in each section. In using patterns of name giving, modes of religious commemoration, and genealogical records to demonstrate that familial traditions helped construct individuals' sense of social identity, the first section
emphasizes the tendency for paternal traditions to take precedence over
maternal ones. The second turns to the situations in which men and

women might, in principle, expect support from their relatives, but argues that, in practice, ties of friendship were at least as important as those of family in the giving and getting of help. The final part explores the separate norms of honourable behaviour for men and women, arguing that the latter were far more grounded in familial relationships than the former. All three sections dismiss generalized assumptions about the functioning of kinship as a form of social process, stressing instead the importance of individual choices and contexts as well as wider power relationships.

We must be aware at the outset, however, that 'kinship' has two different, but not unrelated, connotations: first, the affiliation of an individual to a group defined in terms of consanguinity—that is, of shared blood—and, secondly, the alliances between groups of consanguineal kin effected by marriage or other strategies of association. In the early Middle Ages, both were important. In addition, we must note these affinities can be both objectively and subjectively defined—on the one hand, those people to whom an individual is deemed related in accordance with a clearly stated set of social rules, but, on the other, the persons whom an individual chooses to acknowledge as kin at any particular moment. As will become evident, early medieval men and women used both, often for different purposes. Much of the challenge of studying early medieval societies stems from the fact that the latter group was generally more important than the former.

Clearly, then, 'kinship' is a matter of socially constructed interrelationships, not simply of biologically determined ones. This is true at several levels beyond the answer to the question 'who are your kin?'. Adoption, common under Roman law but absent from other early medieval cultures except Ireland, is a particularly clear case in point where biological paternity and legally recognized fatherhood do not coincide. Fosterage, particularly important in early medieval Wales, Ireland, and Scandinavia, created another form of 'artificial' kinship, where the emotional bond between a boy and the adults who raised him did not coincide with his tie to the parents from whom he in due course inherited property, legal rights, and obligations. Christianity came to place great emphasis on the spiritual kinship created at baptism between godparents and godchild and between a child's natural and spiritual parents. It deemed the former bond as strong as that between a child and its natal parents; the latter—between 'co-parents'—it regarded as equivalent to that between full siblings. 'Nature', then, made a relatively modest contribution to early medieval 'kinship', which was in reality a far more complex and flexible notion than it may seem at first sight.

Full appreciation of all these nuances is hindered by the nature of the surviving sources. Jurists' and law-makers' preoccupation with property, violence, and the protection of the defenceless led them to take far more interest in the interactions between relatives than those between friends. Although there survives ample guidance on kinly affairs issued by kings or codified in lawyers' compilations, it is not distributed evenly either geographically or chronologically. Nevertheless, for some places and periods, such as sixth-century Gaul, seventh-century Ireland, or tenth-century Wessex, it allows us to construct a schematic model of how kinship relations (as also other forms of social relationship) were ideally supposed to work. Even so, to get beyond norms and expectations to social practices and conventions takes very different forms of textual record. Documentary forms of evidence are often anecdotal but provide only a narrow snapshot of a much wider picture. Other sources are either dramatized, poetic evocations of plausible but not historical situations, or clerical diatribes suffused with the authorial prejudices and narrow perspectives of a celibate elite trained to despise all aspects of family and sexuality. The historical reality of interactions among friends and relations is exceptionally hard to pinpoint, the more so because, when we can grasp that reality, it is usually only for upper social levels—local bigwigs, nobles, royalty—and virtually never for peasants.

We may take Lombard Italy of the seventh to eighth centuries as an example of some of these challenges. Ample royal legislation touching on familial interactions survives, most notably the Edict issued in 643 by King Rothari (636–52). In legislating on issues where the king had an active concern in the affairs of a free Lombard, such as the inheritance of property, the proper procedures for betrothal and marriage, or accusations of plotting the death of one's relatives, Rothari's laws are all framed in terms of relationship to the individual in question: father, mother, stepmother, brother, sister, uncle, cousin, nephew are all mentioned. The laws also refer frequently to other 'near relatives' without specifying exactly who these might be. As envisaged by legislators, therefore, Lombard kinship not only took the individual person as its point of reference but also acknowledged the needs of a particular situation. On occasion, however, much more distant relationships might matter, most particularly when the inheritance of property was at issue. Anyone claiming property, Rothari decreed, had to be able to proclaim the names of all ancestors for seven generations, and had to provide kin who would swear to the precise nature of their relationship in front of the judges of the royal law court. In the vital matter of ensuring that land was inherited only by those with a provable claim by blood, Lombard law, therefore, took as its definition of 'kin' a descent

group of seven generations. How many Lombards could name their ancestry for seven generations, trace those related to them by descent from
a common great-great-great-great-great-grandfather, and—crucially—
make their own story agree with that of their relatives? In claiming title
to land, then, legal theory fixed the limits of entitlement at seven generations, even though recorded court cases suggest that claims to kinship
may have worked very differently in practice.

Rothari's Edict shows clearly how multiple notions of kinship could
function simultaneously in one community, according to situation and
purpose. Lombard Italy was not unique: analogous conclusions can be
drawn for all early medieval cultures. But we may remain with Lombard
laws for the moment, for they exemplify a further general point. Rothari
assumed that free Lombards resided in households including domestic
slaves and semi-free men and women as well as their free members.
Although the king certainly envisaged that these households might be
focused on a husband, wife, and their children, his laws also take other
familial patterns for granted. A household might, for example, consist of
a brother, his widowed sister, and some unmarried sisters, in addition to
slaves and other dependants. It might be a group of brothers remaining
together in their father's house after his death, or it might be father and
grandsons, sons of a deceased son, perhaps also a still unmarried son. Another permutation mentioned by Rothari is father, children by a former
wife, and their stepmother. This last may have been a particularly common pattern: given what we know of early medieval mortality rates, many
children are likely to have grown up in households lacking one or both
natal parents.

Simply stated, Rothari's Edict makes clear that the main medieval
social unit was not the nuclear family. Rather, it was the household.
Modern thinking identifies the co-residential descent group as a discrete
social element consisting of parents and children, occasionally with the
addition of close relatives of a third generation (grandparents) or collat-
erals (a brother, his wife, and children, for example). But this way of
thinking has been habitual only since the eighteenth century. The
medieval word *familia* translates most effectively as household and there
is no term equivalent to the modern 'nuclear family'. Although in practice a *familia* commonly had a conjugal unit at its core, both the word
and the social grouping embraced servants, dependants, and sometimes
other close kin. Its precise membership will have been fluid, as older
members died, a widowed sister returned to her natal kin, foster sons
joined then left, or new slaves were purchased and dependants reallocated

to duties elsewhere. In practice, then, a *familia* comprised all those who were under the authority of the male head of the household at any one time and who resided, if not in his house itself, then elsewhere on his property.

That we must think in terms of households not nuclear families is clear wherever we inspect the residential patterns of the men, women, and children of the early Middle Ages. Even royal courts were but households writ large. Consider the exceptionally large empire of Charlemagne. At its domestic and political centre was his queen or concubine of the moment, his daughters but not his sons (for after infancy they were sent off to govern subkingdoms far from the parental palace), several grandsons in the emperor's latter years, and a staff of officials, domestics, stewards, clerics, scribes, huntsmen, cooks, and whoever else was needed for the maintenance of such a large household and the central governing of a huge empire. At the other end of the scale, the peasants of the early Middle Ages lived in households too, usually with their wife and perhaps offspring, and sometimes also with slaves or other semi-free dependants. If they were tenants on a large estate, their household may even have included spare or aged serfs allocated to it by the lord or his bailiff. Modern assumptions about the meaning of the word 'family' do not, therefore, map easily onto the Middle Ages; the following pages use the word 'family' exclusively as a diffuse and ill-defined shorthand term for all those with whom an individual acknowledges association by shared blood, ancestry, upbringing, or marriage.

Although 'family' in the sense of 'mum, dad, and the kids' was not a recognized social unit, this group nevertheless formed the core of most households in both affective and juridical terms at all social levels. Within this narrow group, children were raised in an environment shaped by maternal love and paternal authority, for the rights enjoyed by the male head of household over his dependants intersected with the complex emotional realities of family life. Early medieval sources reveal a world of strong affections between parents, children, and siblings—a world of joy at a safe and healthy birth, grief at the untimely death of a child, mutual conjugal love, maternal anxiety for the well-being of an adult son launched on his own career, fraternal help and friendship. By the same token, they also indicate the equally powerful disappointments, rivalries, and jealousies that could lead parents to reject a disabled infant, husband to abandon wife, brother to feud with brother, or son to kill father. Then, as now, parents, children, brothers, sisters, uncles, and aunts were relations, but not necessarily friends.

Identity

> . . . 'or of what ancestry are you?
> Name but one, the others I will know,
> Youth, in the kingdoms all the kindreds are known to me.'[3]

With these words the hero Hildebrand challenged his younger opponent according to a ninth-century poetic epic. He expressed a common sentiment, for in the early Middle Ages social identity remained firmly associated with kin throughout life for all except those who, like Bede or Hrabanus Maurus, had been given over to a monastic life as small children. Since the shaping of the social person commenced when the parents chose a name for their newborn child, enquiry into the significance of kinship should start with naming. The customs and preferences that influenced early medieval name giving varied over time and from region to region, but the broad outlines are reasonably clear. There certainly were no hard-and-fast rules to follow; rather, parental decisions often reflected deeply ingrained cultural habits. Except in the naming of some royal babies, where the name was of the utmost political importance, we cannot usually recover the precise reasons why parents chose a particular name. Nevertheless, it is clear that the naming of an infant gave the newborn an identity that situated him or her within a circle of relatives and might even single the child out for a future as a cleric or as the heir to ancestral lands. Another strategy, less common but certainly deployed, especially in Ireland and Scotland, named a child after a particular saint or religious patron.

The close association between kinship and name giving deserves particular attention. In the early imperial period (first–second centuries AD), formal Roman naming procedures used three names to identify each citizen as a member of a subset of a particular patrilineal clan—that is, a descent group in which fathers but not mothers transmitted membership and identity to their offspring. In response to social and political changes, more fluid usages had superseded these rigid conventions by the fourth century, enabling names to signal not only social rank but also, at least among the elite, maternal as well as paternal ancestry. In the late Roman West, aristocrats of the fourth, fifth, and sixth centuries typically bore two, three, or even more names, selected to transmit pride in illustrious ancestry and a strong sense of identity with close kin. The sixth-century historian Gregory, bishop of Tours (573–94), typifies these practices. His full name was Georgius Florentius Gregorius, and he was the descendant of rich, influential Gallic aristocrats on both paternal and maternal sides. His first

3.1. Principal places mentioned in Chapter 3.

name, Georgius, was the name of his paternal grandfather (d. 502/6), almost certainly a member of one of the wealthiest and most prestigious aristocratic lineages in fifth-century Gaul. The second name was his father's, but the third, the name by which he chose to be known, was the name of his mother's paternal grandfather. That Gregory of Tours went by the name of this maternal relative can have been no coincidence.

Gregorius Attalus had been count of Autun before becoming bishop of Langres in 506; he died in 539, within a year or at most eighteen months of the birth of his great-grandson, and was immediately hailed as a saint. By harking back three generations to a sainted ancestor on his mother's side, Gregory of Tours stressed in his own name his descent, his nearness to a saint, and his stronger identity with his maternal line than with his father's kin.

Gregory of Tours's multiple names indicate the way in which parents might choose names that would locate a child in relation to its family. But they also represent a weakening tradition, for, even where people continued to regard themselves as *Romani*, Romans, a single name was becoming customary by Gregory's time and, by the end of the seventh century, had become universal even in the Byzantine world. Changing onomastic habits among old Roman elite families are nevertheless only one of several important changes in the relationship between names and identities at the start of our period. During the fifth century, the dissolution of Roman governing structures and the coagulation of new kingdoms around Germanic-speaking elites gave prominence to the distinctive patterns of name formation shared by all the Germanic languages. The two pools of names did not remain separate for very long, however. In sixth-century Gaul, names reveal the adaptation of old elites to changing political circumstances, for some individuals of Roman origin abandoned their traditional naming habits in favour of those of their new Frankish masters; in Spain and Italy, by contrast, Goths and Lombards sometimes selected Roman names for their offspring. When parents with Roman names gave their children Germanic names, and vice versa, they made local decisions about cultural prestige and social identity that had everything to do with the desire for assimilation into the dominant group and nothing to do with spoken language.

It is worth pausing to note how names were formed in the Germanic languages, for, although the convention that a name associated a newborn with his or her ancestors and kinsfok was as strong among Germanic-speaking communities and their descendants as amongst the Romans, different linguistic and social principles were nevertheless at work. Germanic names (non-royal and royal) commonly consisted of two elements, a root and a suffix, which were transmitted and recombined in various ways, and through which ancestry, ethnicity, and social identity might all be signalled. Some of these elements were common to all Germanic languages, but others, characteristic of one language, became valued indicators of ethnic identity.

An example from the end of our period illustrates both the way in which

Germanic names were formed and the complex connotations that one name might have. In about 1008, a well-to-do Anglo-Saxon couple, the priest Æthelstan and his wife Wulfgifu, had a son, possibly their first. The child became a bishop and a saint, and his biographer records: 'He was given the name Wulfstan, made up of the first part of his mother's and the second of his father's. The child had fair hopes, and fair too the omen which gave him a name taken from both parents, considering that he was destined to pour into himself the sanctity of both, and perhaps to surpass it beyond all comparison.'[4] The omen of future sanctity emphasizes how parental name elements had been used to form the new name, but it seems also that the child was named after his maternal uncle, the famous archbishop of York. The name presumably marked the young Wulfstan out for an ecclesiastical career. When it came to naming the future bishop's two brothers, Æthelstan and Wulfgifu again signalled the boys' paternity, naming them Ælfstan and Byrcstan, but selected other elements to combine with the paternal suffix -stan. These decisions about the names of their children may be summed up as freely chosen variations around a common familial theme.

The young Wulfstan did indeed become a bishop (of Worcester, 1062–95). His name exemplifies the way in which elements were recombined to form a new name that nevertheless associated the child with his parents; it also emphasizes that name elements were handed down bilaterally—in other words, they might be as easily derived from the mother or maternal relatives as from the father or paternal relatives. Despite this, wherever a large enough sample of names has been preserved in ways that permit statistical analysis, it is clear that parents usually chose to associate a child with its paternal rather than the maternal kin. Certainly, among the aristocracy of the Carolingian Empire, almost all children were named after a close relative (parent, uncle or aunt, grandparent), yet fewer than one in five can be shown to have carried the name of a maternal relative. Not entirely shunning the use of other names, Frankish name-giving habits nevertheless preferred the names of close kin, and, within the circle of close kin, preferred to indicate paternal affiliations more frequently than maternal ones. Only when the maternal line was of more prestigious ancestry did parents tend to select names that associated a child with its mother's kin.

By the time Wulfstan, the future bishop of Worcester, was born, the custom of coining a name by varying the two elements had become archaic. In the sixth century, ruling dynasties in continental Europe had started to name their offspring by repeating the entire name of a deceased relative rather than varying the name elements. This custom spread gradually from kings to aristocracy, and, by the end of the tenth century, crossed the English Channel and began to influence Anglo-Saxon naming conventions too. By c.1000 it was universal for continental elites to use a restricted pool of names to identify members, and for the emphasis on patrilineal transmission of names to be even greater. When Hugh 'Capet' was crowned king in France in 987 after the demise of the old Carolingian ruling dynasty, he bore a name that clearly identified him as a member of one of the leading aristocratic families that had been prominent in France since at least the middle years of the ninth century. His male forebears all bore the names Hugh, Robert, or Odo; their sisters were commonly called either Emma or Adela. By the millennium, then, names remained a sign of identity, for parents continued to choose ones that associated their offspring with their close relatives and immediate ancestors. But, more than ever, names associated a child with its father's relatives rather than its mother's.

If naming a child at birth placed a newborn within a narrow familial circle, stretching to include cousins, grandparents, and occasionally great-grandparents, then death gave a new twist to the patterns of kinship and social identity. Within the Christian communities of the eighth century and later, concern for the welfare of the soul in the afterlife led many to enter on monastic registers the names of their relatives, living and dead, for whom they requested prayers of intercession. Such prayer bound the living and the dead together in a liturgical community that invoked the presence of the dead by naming them in the company of the living. Massive lists of names registered at several ninth- and tenth-century monasteries in France, Germany, and England survive, and they provide us with a complementary perspective on the ways in which individuals associated themselves with their kin. The German king Henry the Fowler (919–36) is typical: in 932 he requested prayers from the monastery of St Gall for himself, his wife, their three sons and two daughters, together with the husband of one of the daughters, his wife's parents, and her three sisters. Henry's concern for the spiritual welfare of his kin embraced three generations and extended beyond his own wife and offspring to include those associated with him by various marriages. In the context of religious commemoration, 'family' extended beyond an individual's natal family and the conjugal unit of which he or she formed one element, to include a wide, but still selective group of relatives. With the fate of the soul in the afterlife rather than the transmission of land or worldly office at issue, this form of kinship readily recognized women—mothers, wives, daughters—on the same terms as men.

In obtaining religious commemoration and in naming a child, differing ideas about the bonds of kinship thus came into play. Their most significant shared characteristics were, first, the recognition that kinship embraced two to three or, at the very most, four generations; and, secondly, an acceptance that women might sometimes make a significant contribution to the definition of familial identity. Neither of these points obtains in the third main way in which individuals used the associations of kinship to construct their social identity: genealogies. Genealogies are statements of descent modelled on biblical precedents. They usually take the form of 'X was the son of Y, son of Z', and, unlike most of the evidence discussed so far in this chapter, they cast a shaft of light on the cultures of the British Isles, particularly Wales and Ireland. Several royal genealogies survive from the Continent, but none traces the ancestry of non-royal personages before the end of the tenth century; in Ireland, by contrast, the many thousands of genealogies that survive from the eighth to tenth centuries pertain to Christian holy men and aristocrats as well as to kings. These genealogies present a form of kinship that is vertical (they may extend from a handful of generations to thirty or more), almost without exception totally male, and ruthlessly oblivious of siblings or collateral relatives.

Although many such genealogies have sections where the claimed relationships can be proven to be historically accurate, they are more important for the cultural and political assertions that they make. In all early medieval societies, claims to secular power, wealth, and status rested in large part upon descent: a genealogy legitimized those claims. The ties of kinship presented were those of immediate political significance and were thus liable to be remade and rearranged as political dictates demanded. Such manipulation could involve excision or augmentation of both the length of the pedigree and its collateral branches. The Carolingian dynasty (751–987) not only hitched itself onto the Merovingian dynasty (c.480–751), which it eventually replaced, but also appropriated the Roman past into its ancestry by a genealogy that claimed that its sainted (and historically attested) founder, Arnulf of Metz (d. c.643), was the grandson of the (mythical) Merovingian princess Blithild and her (equally mythical) husband Ansbert, hailed as a Roman senator. Two aspects of this are noteworthy. First, a fictional bride formed the key link in an otherwise male statement of descent. The deliberate omission of the historically attested women through whom the dynasty had, in reality, built up its position confirmed women's exclusion from formal authority, while the inclusion of a mythic ancestress nevertheless acknowledged women's essential contribution to dynastic reproduction and the transmission of family memories. Secondly, beyond the span of accurate human memory, seventh- and eighth-century historical fact shaded off into inventive ideological optimism, aided by access to textually transmitted knowledge of the distant Roman past. The political imperative to manipulate a genealogical statement by whatever means best suited the occasion is clear. As a way of using the past to assert contemporary political claims, this Carolingian genealogy was nevertheless relatively restrained. In Ireland, the need to stress the ancient length of a pedigree resulted in the common ancestor of the Érainn and the Dál Fiatach being named as 'Old son of Very Old son of Strong son of Very Strong'.[5] With this, we reach the apogee of biological fiction in the service of political legitimacy.

Genealogies make the point that kinship can be as much about socially constructed relationships, expressed in the fictions of biological descent and mythical ancestry, as it can be about genetic parentage. Further, they express more clearly than anything else the patrilineal inclinations of all early medieval cultures: pared down to bald statements of the descent of one powerful person after another, they emphasize that all that counted was the succession from 'father' to 'son'. But those masculine norms operated in a world that at no time had a single, stable understanding of kinship. Name-giving customs and the rituals of commemoration remind us that, in these situations, those who were acknowledged as kin were a close circle of relatives on both the male and the female side. Kinship, in effect, meant different things in different circumstances.

Friends by Blood

It is time to turn to the wider implications of kinship, for an extensive range of sources—legal, documentary, narrative, poetic, hagiographical— all confirm that interactions with relatives commonly had great social and political significance. They also insist that kinship cannot be disentangled from friendship. The practical expressions of these affinities were, however, immensely varied, and the reasons for this help explain the many roles that relatives—and friends—might play in each others' lives.

One manifestation of the cultural heterogeneity of early medieval Europe was the coexistence of diverse social norms. Much of our detailed knowledge of these derives from records of law, whose contents are as varied as their textual forms and sources of authority. Broadly speaking, three legal cultures can be identified, with widely differing expectations of social relationships, including those among relatives. In Mediterranean Europe, the legislative codifications of the late Roman Empire remained in force wherever continuity of population and administration enabled people to continue to think of themselves as *Romani*. To the north, Germanic-speaking settlers introduced their own social customs, which began to take normative, written form from the sixth century onwards. No hard-and-fast division separated these two legal cultures, for in one way or another all the law codes issued by post-imperial kings betray the influence of Roman law, and this is especially true of those originating from the more southerly areas of enduring Roman presence, notably the Burgundian, Lombard, and Iberian Gothic kingdoms. Much less amenable to Roman influence in either format or content was the third legal culture, that of the Celtic-speaking regions fringing Atlantic Europe, where direct Roman influence was limited or non-existent. Each of these three traditions proposes a different view of the social implications of kinship.

With the proviso that law only ever offers an oblique and highly schematic view of social reality, each of these legal cultures can be said to approximate roughly to a distinctive form of social organization. As codified in the fifth century AD, Roman law was intensely concerned to regulate marriage and to confirm the authority of the male head of the household over his wife and children; but it explicitly rejected any notion that an adult male's juridical identity was bound up with his relatives. Secular Irish legal treatises, by contrast, make clear that the kin group was the most fundamental form of social organization; they stipulate norms and procedures in such detail that elaborate reconstructions of the ideal interactions between relatives are possible.[6] Both late Roman and Irish juridical expectations of the roles relatives should play in each others' lives emerge clearly. Between these two extremes, however, lies much debate over the significance of kinship within Germanic-speaking communities.

Nineteenth-century historians constructed grand schemes of early Germanic society (first–seventh century) and organized it into large clans that functioned as political entities, peacekeeping and judicial organizations, units of military recruitment, and settlement groups. They endowed these kin groups (usually referred to by the German term *Sippe*) with constitutional importance and accorded them a prominent place in an evolutionist progression of European society from the clan to the nuclear family, and from the tribe to the state—in other words, from 'primitive' to 'civilized'. This paradigm of cultural advance has long since collapsed, but the underlying view of the social organization of early Germanic peoples has been slower to disintegrate: it too must be definitively discarded. In its place, we must substitute individuals, each of whom had a web of consanguineal relatives shared with no one except his or her full siblings, and a somewhat different range of interactions with the in-laws to whom he or she was related by marriage.

In practice, kin never endured as a group. Rather they every where existed as a category of persons, a web of latent affinities to be activated and mobilized as each separate situation required. Two aspects are deferred for discussion in the next chapter—namely, the conventions surrounding marriage and the strategies of inheritance. Here we shall draw on poetic, documentary, and legal evidence to emphasize the ambiguity and uncertainty inherent in kinship in a range of other situations.

Surviving in a single manuscript from around the year 1000 but probably of much earlier origin, the Old English epic poem *Beowulf* is set in a mythic Scandinavian past. Its ideals and values nevertheless resonated with its Anglo-Saxon audience, and also have close parallels in vernacular poetry from other parts of the early medieval west—Ireland, Wales, and Germany, for example. *Beowulf* derives much of its dramatic vigour from the tension between theoretical obligation and practical unreliability between kinsfolk. Although 'the bonds of kinship | nothing may remove for a man who thinks rightly', the poet also knew well enough that the time would come 'when the blood-feud should bring out again | sword-hatred in sworn kindred'.[7] For insight into how the tension between obligation and animosity between relatives might play out, we can turn to the Frankish *Pactus Legis Salicae*. Probably put together in the reign of Clovis (*c.*481–511), this is a compilation of customary procedure and royal pronouncement for Franks who now lived between the Rhine delta and the Loire but whose culture was not yet overly influenced by Roman norms and legal procedures. The *Pactus* makes it clear that kinsmen were expected to offer support to each other in a variety of ways. If a man needed to establish his status, or perhaps his insolvency, on oath, he had to find people to co-swear with him: these 'oath-helpers' were drawn from among his male relatives. Furthermore, if someone was killed, the slayer had to find a monetary compensation for the lost life or risk a blood-feud (to be discussed in the last section of this chapter), and the payment was to be divided between the dead person's children and relatives on both the paternal and maternal sides. If the slayer, on the other hand, could not raise the entire sum himself, then his relatives had to help out: first, his father and brothers, then, if the obligations still could not be met, his maternal and paternal kin.

Which kinsfolk were involved here? Certainly children and parents—

the close-knit conjugal group, central to identity, inheritance, and indeed survival. Beyond that, the laws did not specify, referring simply to 'relatives' both paternal and maternal. Any individual, then, was in a particularly close relationship with parents and offspring, but also had to negotiate to acquire whatever support was needed from a wider, bilateral circle of relatives. The composition of that circle was unlikely to be constant, as death removed parents and uncles, and as marriages introduced in-laws at different points in an individual's life. Furthermore, the *Pactus Legis Salicae* envisaged that an individual might formally sever the ties of kinship, and outlined how to achieve this:

He who wishes to remove himself from his kindred should go to court and in the presence of the thuningus or hundredman [a local judicial official] break four sticks of alderwood over his head and throw them in four bundles into the four corners of the court and say there that he removes himself from their oath-helping, from their inheritance, and from any relationship with them.[8]

Freed from obligation to provide cash (or its equivalent in land and live-stock), oaths, or any other support for kinsfolk, whoever went through this procedure would find that henceforth neither help nor inheritance would be forthcoming; such a person would face the world alone and unaided. On this evidence, Frankish kinship was not a cohesive bond among a specified range of people who functioned as a group in all circumstances. Rather, beyond the immediate parent–child tie, it was an undefined web of potential supporters, to be persuaded to action in time of need. At its bleakest, it was a network of unwelcome obligations and social embarrassments to be negotiated and, in the last resort, rejected.

Other potential supporters in time of need might be a man's neighbours, his lord, and his dependants within his *familia*. Since some of these people might well be related to him, kinship commonly overlapped with and reinforced other highly localized relationships. Those who could be relied upon to rally round in a crisis were thus all 'friends' of the hard-pressed individual, and it is striking how often sources refer to 'friends and relatives' without differentiation. Indeed, in Anglo-Saxon England the distinction at times collapses completely, for among the many Old English words meaning 'kin' one of the most commonly used, especially in law codes, is *freond*, the word from which the modern English 'friend' directly derives. The kinship that mattered was not the technicalities of precise genealogical relationship, but rather the kinship that made a difference in practice. As the late-eleventh-century biographer of Theoderic, bishop of Metz (963–84), affirmed, 'kinship without goodwill is an empty word, and friendship is inseparable from goodwill'.[9]

In Marc Bloch's memorable phrase, 'friends by blood' were the kin who could be relied on.[10]

In contrast to kinship, with its aura of being a 'natural' relationship, friendship is entirely socially constructed. As Chapter 5 will argue, social relationships in the early Middle Ages were predominantly ordered in hierarchical ways; friendship offered horizontal bonds of solidarity that softened the harsher contours of domination and subordination. The *Beowulf* poet knew this too; he makes Hrothgar, king of the Danes, describe his murdered friend Ashhere thus:

> 'He was my closest counsellor, he was keeper of my thoughts,
> he stood at my shoulder when we struck for our lives
> at the crashing together of companies of foot,
> when blows rained on boar-crests. Men of birth and merit
> all should be as Ashhere was!'[11]

So friends, in the early Middle Ages, were those men who provided each other with advice and support when needed, affirmed their loyalty, and backed it with appropriate action, even in battle. They might be neighbours, in-laws, members of a peer group, even kinsmen. Especially amongst the elite, friendship could be of great social advantage, its loss of gravest consequence. Heorot, Hrothgar's royal hall, had known happy times whose end *Beowulf* chronicles; as the poet also prophesied, friendship was no more reliable than kinship:

> Heorot's floor was
> filled with friends: falsity in those days
> had no place in the dealings of the Danish people.[12]

Kinly friendship might be of considerable political importance, and its consequences cannot be dissociated from forms of power and authority. There are two extremes to note here. On the one hand, fifth- to sixth-century Ireland contained hundreds of small lordships and kingdoms, whose rulers had only modest executive influence. Here, where the Old Irish word *fine* also means both 'kin' and 'friend', the loyalties of kinship tended to reinforce the loyalties of lordship, and the two together helped foster social cohesion and order. On the other hand, where royal authority was vigorous and largely effective, as it was in Carolingian Francia and in Anglo-Saxon England by the tenth century, the support that kin offered each other might be to the detriment of the kingly view of law and order. The English king Æthelstan was only one of several rulers vexed by criminals whose relatives protected them from the rigours of royal justice. He confronted the problem of thieves who were being sheltered by kindreds 'so strong and so large' that they were beyond the reach of royal officials. Clearly, local bosses and bigwigs were enforcing their grip on a locality by taking cattle-rustlers and the like into their retinue and *familia*; Æthelstan's solution was to authorize mounted posses of armed men to overawe and smash these local kin-based protection rackets.[13]

By the same token, the withdrawal of friendship between kinsfolk might have serious political repercussions, especially when the rifts occurred within the ruling family itself. The German emperor Henry II had died in 1024, leaving no son or other designated heir. Members of the German elite negotiated among themselves, and some weeks later agreed that there were two most suitable candidates to succeed to the throne, both called Conrad, who were cousins. During tense bargaining between the two, the elder Conrad—who prevailed and was duly crowned as Conrad II (1024–39)—is reported to have told his kinsman: 'it befits as many things as nature has bound together to be in harmony—nature who joins to herself the friendship of kinsmen'.[14] But the accord was fragile, and no one can have been surprised when Conrad the Younger was among those who rebelled less than a year later, and remained long thereafter a threat to his crowned cousin. On inspection, many of the most bitter political rivalries of the early Middle Ages turn out to be similar, for nothing bred competition more than kinship.

But what of individuals whose kinly rights and obligations had been severed, leaving them effectively kinless? These were most likely to be men, who had either exhausted their relatives' goodwill by habitually thieving, brawling, and stirring up feuds, or whose treachery and violence had been turned against their immediate family in acts of patricide, fratricide, or even incest with their own mother. In Anglo-Saxon England and on the Continent, those whose relatives were no longer prepared to support them by co-swearing or contributing to a hefty compensation payment were left to answer with the only thing left to them—their life—by penal servitude or hanging. In Ireland, the man guilty of betrayal, theft, or the slaying of kin was labelled a wolf and treated as such: he was left to wander in exile as a hated outcast, a feared outsider, devoid of status, identity, help—of humanity.

In the final analysis, kinlessness reduced the free man close to the abject social situation of a slave, lacking in rights or relatives. In a Christian society, it was a fate worse than death, for the man who had remained friends with his relatives could expect a decent burial and prayers for the sake of his soul. Social outcasts were flung out on the dung heap when they died; the kinless exile endured the living equivalent. Such utter degradation points up the central importance of kinship not for its genealogical affiliations but for its social importance, as the 'friendship' that helped keep communities together.

Nowhere did kin form a defined group with clear criteria of membership and invariable rules of behaviour; everywhere a person's relatives were a social resource to invoke, a source not only of identity but also of support as the situation demanded. Yet kinly relationships presupposed uncertainty, for the support had to be negotiated, coaxed into action. Such an interpretation of kinship takes little for granted, for it counterbalances reciprocity with unpredictability and affinity with rejection. It accepts that, in principle, a person's loyalties and obligations extended to both paternal and maternal relatives, and recognizes that kinship was established by marriage, godparenthood, or fosterage as well as by descent. And it helps explain how, notwithstanding the cultural and social heterogeneity of early medieval Europe, the bonds of kinship remained a fundamental source of social cohesion, whether in isolated villages or among wide-ranging imperial elites. By the same token, however, their rupture threatened the essence of the social fabric. No wonder that hell was a place 'where there is not any recognition of anyone closest to one . . . where a mother does not love her son or daughter, and a son does not respect his father'.[15]

Honour and Vengeance

As the *Pactus Legis Salicae* had elaborated, one of the ways in which relatives might help each other out was by paying the compensation owed by a slayer and his kin to the relatives of the person he had killed. Except where Roman legal principles remained vigorous, all early medieval communities put a monetary value on redeeming a person's life, termed wergeld in the Germanic languages. Its amount varied with rank, making explicit the much greater worth of a king or noble than of a peasant or slave; women and children generally enjoyed the wergeld of their father. Wergeld did not only apply in cases of homicide, however. Homicide certainly explains why wergeld is the price of a life, but either the wergeld itself or a proportion of it was due in less than fatal circumstances in which injury was suffered. That injury might be either physical or verbal: the Lombard laws of Rothari tabulate the compensation due for a huge range of injuries ranging from cutting off the little toe to gouging out the eyes, while the Frankish *Pactus Legis Salicae* stipulates a scale of penalties for verbal insults. These included accusing a woman of being a prostitute, and impugning a man's martial courage and loyalty by accusing him of being 'covered in shit', calling him a 'fox' or a 'hare'—accusations, in other words, of having soiled himself with fear, behaved treacherously, or fled the scene of battle.[16] We need, then, to assess how the value ascribed to a person's life encompassed social as well as physical selfhood, and to explore how different expectations of male and female conduct informed the behaviour of family and friends. As we shall see, these insults suggest a world of touchy pride that turned on women's sexual propriety and men's aggressive valour.

Since wounding words and injurious blows assailed social standing, wergeld was far more than a payment for physical damage. It expressed in monetary terms the slight done to familial pride, reputation, and integrity: the obligation to pay a wergeld imposed upon the offender and his relatives an equivalent degradation. In effect, wergeld recompensed a person's family for the damage done to their collective social esteem. Its dual nature both as reparation for loss and as a means of restoring respect is sharpened by comparison with the Irish procedure of making two discrete payments. The one compensated the dead, injured, or insulted person's paternal relatives for the loss or damage; the other, termed 'the value of a face' or the 'face-cleansing' payment, counterbalanced the affront done to both paternal and maternal relatives. That 'cleansing' a besmirched face removed the stain of loss, injury, and insult suggests a culture that intimately associated reputation with the human body: recovery of a person's social standing was 'saving face'. That both wergeld and the Irish value of a face were graduated according to rank indicates that those of high social standing risked a far greater loss of face than those lower down the social hierarchy. The following discussion focuses on these well-documented, high-value elites.

The mid-eighth-century Bavarian law code takes us a little further. It names five elite families ranked immediately below the ducal lineage who were entitled to 'double compensation' because they were granted 'double honor'.[17] 'Honour' is not susceptible to brief definition—except that, unlike compensation payments, it follows no tariff schedule. Anthropologists use the word as a short-hand term for a complex bundle of personal social attributes that together facilitate political influence and the accumulation of material wealth. Its essence combines the self-esteem of an individual with the respect accorded by others. Both self-regarding and other-regarding, it tends to dissipate unless constantly reasserted and reaffirmed through both general conduct and particular actions. By extension, therefore, it is never stable and cannot be hoarded. Further, the association with compensation payments hints that early medieval honour was as much familial as personal: it inhered in persons-in-groups and placed the individual firmly at the centre of a web of social relationships with relatives, friends, lords, and kings. And, since some forms of conduct were more liable to affirm or restore respect than others, the elite men and women of the early Middle Ages were acutely aware of the consequences of the wide range of words or actions that might tarnish or destroy it entirely. A rich vocabulary of shame, infamy, humiliation, and disgrace indicates ways in which dishonourable actions could lead to an infamous reputation in the eyes of others. At the negative end of the spectrum of social values, shame attached to actions detrimental to the pride and reputation of both individual and family. And, when the family in question was a royal one, the erosion of honour might be politically disastrous.

Early medieval writers rarely used a single word to sum up this abstraction. They preferred to think in terms of the action—to honour, show respect to someone. Honourable conduct emphasized generosity and the display of wealth, loyalty, sexuality, martial prowess, revenge. Running through these seemingly disparate aspects of behaviour are two interlocking themes, one concerning the correct disposition of the human body, whether in sexual or military affairs or through resplendent attire, the other concerning obligations towards others, whether of generosity, loyalty, or revenge. Leaving aside social display and generosity to Chapters 5 and 6 respectively, we can use other forms of honourable behaviour to pursue further our theme of interactions between friends and relations in the early Middle Ages.

Sexual conduct offers the most immediate indication of the way in which the activities of individuals affected the collective standing of their kinsfolk. At issue here were notions of sexual propriety, and the allocation of blame for the breach of deeply rooted conventions and taboos. The *Pactus Legis Salicae*, for example, regarded illegitimate children as 'marked with disgrace'.[18] In general, however, celibate Christian churchmen form our greatest source of information on early medieval sexuality. While it is certainly hard to disentangle lay social behaviour from the complaints of clerics quick to condemn whatever did not accord with their own ethical views, it is nevertheless clear that early medieval codes of strict sexual conduct commonly pertained to women much more than to men. 'In Old Saxony [i.e. in still-pagan northern Germany]', the Anglo-Saxon missionary Boniface reported in 746/7,

if a maiden stains with adultery her paternal home, or if a married woman breaks the bond of matrimony and commits adultery, they sometimes force her to end her life by her own hand, hanging herself by a noose; and when she has been burnt and cremated, they hang her violator over her pyre. Sometimes a crowd of women is gathered, and the matrons scourge her and lead her all over the district, striking her with rods and cutting off her garments to the girdle; and cutting and pricking all her body with wounds with their knives, they send her from village to village bloody and lacerated. And new scourgers are always joining them, prompted by their zeal for chastity, until they leave her dead, or barely alive; that others may be afraid of adultery and lasciviousness.[19]

Admittedly, Boniface had a point to make to his Christian audience, whose morals he considered far too loose, but his words nevertheless hint at a mentality that equated adultery with pollution of the integrity of a family.

Not only pre-Christian families responded to unsanctioned female sexual activity by putting the guilty woman to death or imposing an extreme form of censure. Le Mans had long been a Christian city when in 584 a woman of good birth dressed as a man to elope with her lover, a priest. When her relatives found out, they rushed 'to avenge the humiliation of their family' by burning the woman alive and imprisoning the priest.[20] Her behaviour had affected the reputation of all her kin, who took the only step open to them to redeem it. For the most part, early medieval societies left the punishment of errant women in the hands of their male kin, whether father and brothers or husband. Summary, familial retribution for a woman's flagrant breaches of her relatives' integrity counterbalanced the procedures for expelling a man from the kin group and condemning him to the life of an outcast.

'If a woman during her husband's lifetime commits adultery with another man, and it becomes known, let her afterwards become herself a public disgrace and her lawful husband is to have all that she owns, and she is to lose her nose and ears.'[21] Shame, loss of face (literal and metaphorical), family dishonour, and even death followed from female sexual activity outside recognized unions. They provided the largely unwritten sanctions that regulated women's conduct, and they mark out the intimate connection between the reputation of a family, on the one hand, and the control of women's sexuality, on the other. Women and sexual intercourse were so essential to the reproduction of any kin group that the honour of kinsmen was inextricably identified with the sexual purity and self-control of their sisters, wives, and daughters. Moreover, just as adultery brought dishonour through the way in which a woman used her body, so too retribution was visited upon her body, by stoning, disfiguration, or death.

A woman's sexual misdemeanours challenged the paternity of a man's heirs and thus threatened her entire family's social standing. But a woman could also make a positive contribution by controlling her own sexuality. 'A chaste and prudent wife, diligently attending to useful matters with a humble demeanor and cheerful speech,' one ninth-century writer opined, 'peacefully manages her children and family; and, on behalf of her husband's welfare, if necessary, she sets her life against death and defends his wealth with an honorable reputation'.[22] If a woman's honourable reputation contributed to the esteem in which her kin was regarded, it was also incumbent upon her male relatives to protect her from risk and to defend her good name. This point emerges from a lawsuit that came to the attention of Liutprand, king of the Lombards (712–44), in 733. A woman had been bathing alone in the river, having laid her clothes aside on the bank. 'A certain perverse man' took them, and she was forced to walk home naked, 'blushing with shame'. But the shame was not her fault, and Liutprand decreed that the thief had to pay his full wergeld in compensation for such a 'shameful' act on the grounds that, if the woman's father, husband, or other male relatives had been on hand, they would have jumped on the man and killed him. Having escaped unseen and unscathed, the thief therefore was required to provide the monetary equivalent of his life.[23] Implicit in the king's ruling was an acknowledgement that the woman's kinsmen had both the obligation and the right to defend her modesty and thereby her honourable reputation, if need be with violence.

A woman's conduct epitomized the way in which honour stood at the heart of relations between family members. Any sexual impropriety she committed brought disgrace to herself and her relatives; her chaste conduct upheld the social esteem of her husband, father, and brothers. In return for maintaining her—and their—honour, she could expect them to defend her from shameful treatment and false accusations. The maintenance of honour and the avoidance of shame suggested the conduct that would help maintain cordial relations among close relatives.

In defending their wives, sisters, and daughters from verbal or physical assault, early medieval men were quick to resort to violence. Indeed, masculine honour was as intimately associated with displays of aggression, courage, and martial skill as feminine honour was bound up with sexual propriety. By contrast, however, masculine honour was less exclusively attached to familial honour, at least among the elite. It was also a quality inhering in the right relationship between a warrior and the lord under whom he served, complementing rather than displacing the honour that associated a man with his family. As such, it was an avenue to social advancement and political influence.

In 843, an Aquitainian mother named Dhuoda wrote to her much-loved 15-year-old son, resident at the court of the West Frankish king, Charles the Bald (840–77), and learning the ways of courtly society. In pouring out moral and religious advice to William, Dhuoda touched upon the theme of honour, and its relation to family and lord. She opened her chapters of advice on how to be successful in the tense atmosphere of mid-ninth-century politics with the injunction that William 'should fear, love and be faithful to [his] lord and father, Bernard, in all things', and then, by linking honour towards his father with obedience to the Christian God, Dhuoda developed the point that honour and respect in the secular world might be achieved by this dual loyalty. She expected her son to be loyal to his lord, King Charles, but stressed that other loyalties would also bring William honour: 'I urge you to strive to act among your associates, peers, and faithful friends so that your life may hold to a good course, marked with no shame of disloyalty to your lords but with eagerness for good action, in a laudable fashion, worthy and proper.'[24] William's task was to earn respect by his loyalty and his actions towards not only his father but also the king and his courtiers. Separated now from his family, William had to uphold his own and his family's honour in the competitive environment of the royal court. Dhuoda's summary of her advice put the giving and garnering of honour at the centre of the precepts that, she believed, should govern upright behaviour in a world of turbulent politics. 'Therefore, my son William, cherish and show respect to whatever one or many persons you wish to respect you. Love, revere, stand by, and honour all, so that you may be found worthy to receive from everyone an appropriate return with the honour that pertains to it in the changeable situations of the world.'[25]

Dhuoda did not elaborate upon the acquisition of respect through martial prowess. To explore the connection between masculine honour and military skill, we can do no better than to turn to the epic poetry of the early Middle Ages. The problem of determining an honourable course of conduct in situations where loyalty to kin conflicted with loyalty to lord, and the demonstration of the hero's fearless courage in the face of his adversaries are twin themes that repeatedly preoccupied early medieval poets and their audiences across the entire spectrum of early medieval languages. In *Waltharius*, a Latin epic probably written in the late ninth or tenth century, the anxieties of honour versus shame and kinship versus lordship intertwine to offer a compelling glimpse of the imperatives of early medieval masculinity. The stuff of legend, not history, the events of the poem concern the deeds of a hero named Walter, who, like Dhuoda's son William, was an Aquitainian. Walter grows from youth to manhood as a hostage at a foreign court, that of Attila the Hun. Attila has also taken as hostages the Burgundian heiress and Walter's betrothed, Hildgund, and the Frankish nobleman Hagen, who has been surrendered in lieu of the still-infant Frankish prince Gunther. The three share Attila's hospitality and grow up to positions of eminence and importance in his court, Hildgund as companion to the Hunnish queen, Walter and Hagen as victorious commanders of Attila's army. But when Gunther becomes king of the Franks, Hagen flees back to serve him. Rather later, Walter and Hildgund also make their escape, taking as much of the Huns' treasure as they can manage. To reach Aquitaine, they must cross Gunther's kingdom, but the Frankish king learns of their presence in his lands and, with a squadron of twelve proven and courageous warriors, he marches out to seize the treasure Walter and Hildgund carry. Hagen is compelled to accompany Gunther. Walter makes his stand in a narrow gorge, and, when Gunther sends out his twelve warriors one by one, Walter slays each in turn. As Gunther's fury grows, there remains only Hagen, who has hitherto refused to fight against his friend. Anguished by the decision, he finally agrees to help Gunther tackle Walter, and, in the final combat of two against one, all three warriors are maimed but none dies.

As Walter works his way through the twelve single-handed combats, several themes preoccupy the poet. One, of course, is Walter's heroism, valour, and apparently limitless strength, for he is a man of 'accustomed bravery' who was 'utterly unmoved | by any fear'.[26] Another is the instinct to seek revenge as the warriors fall one after another, and most especially the impulse to avenge a relative's death. A third is the role of verbal boasts of prowess and courage, in combination with taunts and insults hurled at the opponent; a fourth, the imperatives of honour and manliness. All strands come together after the twelve warriors have been killed and when only Hagen and King Gunther remain alive to face Walter.

Before the combat had started, Gunther had tried to rouse Hagen to fight by insulting him, his family, and, by implication, his reputation as a man.

> 'As I observe, you are the image of your father;
> Hagathie also bore a timid heart inside
> A frigid chest, avoiding war with many words.'[27]

But Hagen had not risen to the taunts and instead remained at a distance, watching the fighting but not participating, even when his nephew fell to Walter's sword. But when only the two of them remain, Gunther intensified the taunting:

'Are you not shamed to disavow your manhood, with
So many friends and kinsmen killed?'[28]

The implications are clear. If Hagen will not fight, the price of failure
to avenge his nephew and his companions in arms will be the shame of
cowardice. Only women do not fight, so, in his shame, Hagen will be
reduced to womanliness. And yet,

> Still Hagen wavered and considered in his breast
> The faith so often pledged to Walter, and he pondered
> The outcome of the matter as it had transpired.
> But now the luckless king begged more insistently.
> Moved by the fervor of his pleading, he avoided
> His sovereign's gaze and thought about his reputation
> For valor, that it might be sullied if he should
> In any manner spare himself in this affair.[29]

Here, at the moral crux of the poem, all the conflicting values are laid bare.
Hagen's decision, reluctantly taken, is that manly honour demands that he
maintain his reputation as a valiant warrior prepared to risk his life in the
pursuit of glory. Only by agreeing to fight Walter can he avoid shame,
avenge his nephew, retain his king's goodwill, and remain a man. In the
last analysis, the unambiguous need to prevent the collapse of his reputation makes clear the course of action that Hagen must take.

In 991, a band of Anglo-Saxons were defeated by the Vikings in a well-
attested battle at Maldon on the Essex coast. Their leader slain, some of
the Anglo-Saxons had fled the battlefield. A contemporary Old English
poet recast the defeat in terms of traditional epic values, emphasizing not
the Anglo-Saxon reverse but the heroism of those who chose to stay and
fight on to the end:

> Proudly the thanes pressed forward,
> uncowed the warriors crowded eager
> for one of two things: each man wanted
> either to requite that death or to quit life.[30]

Stripped of their political ambiguities, the events at Maldon offered an
opportunity to restate a familiar theme—the inseparability of honour,
courage, vengeance, and loyalty to the point of death—and thereby to
remind a fast-changing world of age-old values. In real life, as distinct
from poetic representation, such conduct brought acclaim—and enhanced
dangers. In 801, Alcuin interceded with Charlemagne on behalf of
the Northumbrian nobleman Torhtmund, one of 'our friends'. In 796

Æthelred I, king of Northumbria, had been assassinated; Alcuin spoke up for Torhtmund as 'the faithful servant of King Ethelred, a man proved in loyalty, strenuous in arms, who has boldy avenged the blood of his lord'.[31] Torhtmund's act of vengeance can have left him no option but to flee abroad beyond reach of further reprisal. Alcuin was evidently confident that Charlemagne would not only take the imperilled man into his protection, but would regard his avenging valour as a mark of commendation.

An Irish prophecy of doom foretold social collapse into a world of 'women without modesty, men without valour'.[32] In pursuit of social order, early medieval men chose their course of action with reference to an ethic that was different from but complementary to the constraints of sexual modesty imposed upon women. Masculine honour was not only the avoidance of shame, for it also implied an aggressive pursuit of martial prowess and the constant reassertion of manliness in both speech and action. Those who failed, fleeing from the battlefield, behaved 'like women'.[33] Nor was it exclusively kin-centred, like feminine honour, for it demanded the approbation of a wider public, that of a man's friends as well as his relatives, his lord as well as his peers. Yet it too was concerned above all with reputation in the eyes of others, and was as closely bound up with speech, gesture, action, and body as was a woman's honour. Furthermore, masculinity often found expression in boastful vaunting and in the exchange of insult. Sometimes, especially in the intoxicated atmosphere of a feast, verbal aggression turned out to be the foreplay that preceded the exchange of physical blows and even killings. When honour demanded that shaming insult, injury, or homicide had to be requited, the threat of feud might loom on the horizon.

Except to the extent that the Roman juridical principle that an individual was solely and uniquely responsible for his own actions may have remained enforceable in some parts of the Mediterranean, early medieval Europe was a feuding culture, for feud is the manifestation of a notion of honour that associates virility with vengeance. It also encapsulates both the moral obligations amongst relatives and their fragility; for that reason it deserves consideration here. It should be said immediately that feud is neither a state of anarchy, whether temporary or persistent, nor one of constant bloodshed. Rather, it is an attitude of potential, latent, or actual hostility between groups, in which the very threat of vengeance killings may itself help to discourage violence and promote more orderly means of resolving conflict. Only when the spilling of blood seemed more honourable than the acceptance of honourably offered wergeld—or when sage advice could not temper young hotheads—did early medieval feud become bloody retributive justice. Much of the time, however, it seems that wergeld was paid in order to deflect the risk of vendetta. That land was sometimes sold off explicitly to raise the large sums needed to pay a wergeld suggests that a slayer's kin frequently saw the advantages of providing monetary compensation in the hope of placating the slain person's aggrieved relatives. Within small communities, where most neighbours were probably also relatives, the threat of violence may well have seemed far too terrible to contemplate.

Feud, then, is a form of managing conflict. It follows conventions that are more often embedded in social practice than articulated in explicit principles of action. A state of mind as much as a code of action, feud results in bloodshed only when other methods of repairing the insults done to injured honour have failed. Rarely do the written sources allow us to trace the beginning, course, and resolution of a vendetta or enable adequate assessment of the wider social context, but they do reveal clearly that feuding was about the reciprocal exchange of enmities, and that, once a blood-feud had developed, a desire for retribution contributed to its persistence and to the lack of any easy resolution. In seeking Charlemagne's protection, Torhtmund knew this well. For this reason, vendettas might be of brief duration, or might flare up spasmodically over years, sometimes over generations. Whereas decisions to sell off family land and settle financially are not the stuff of chronicles or heroic epics and achieve only fleeting mention in deeds of sale, conflicts that escalated into violence catch our attention—as they did that of early medieval chroniclers— because of their exceptional narrative allure.

Two incidents, approximately contemporary but from quite distinct cultural milieux, encapsulate the complexities of honour, compensation, and revenge. Both occurred around the year 590, one in western Ireland, the other in northern Gaul. Librán, a man from Connaught, tells his own story first:

While I still lived in my own district I killed a fellow. After this I was held in chains as a guilty man. But a relative of mine, in fact one of my immediate kindred, who was extremely rich, came to my rescue in the nick of time. He paid what was needed to get me off though I was bound in chains, and he saved me, though guilty, from death. After he had bought my release, I promised him with a binding oath that I should serve him all the days of my life.[34]

Librán had committed homicide and must have surrendered himself in admission of his guilt. That he was not at large minimized the risk of the dead man's kin setting out to undertake a vengeance killing, but equally Librán was evidently unable to raise the compensation and face-cleansing payments due in accordance with Irish law. His life was therefore at the mercy of the dead man's kin, who could slay him or sell him into slavery. That Librán had been rescued by a wealthy kinsman suggests the interest that kin had in each other's continued existence. Nevertheless, the price of that rescue was to be bondage to his own relative. In fact, he broke his oath and fled into exile a few days later, and it took the intervention of the holy man Columba to find a resolution that satisfied the honour of all of Librán's kin and also purged Librán's conscience of his guilt at the slaying and the broken oath.

In this instance, one slaying did not precipitate a chain reaction of counter-killings. Rather, all the pressures towards a peaceful settlement combined to restore honour without further dislocating the social order. But, in the other incident, the initial offence involved no bloodshed at all, yet it escalated into a protracted and vicious feud. Gregory of Tours's account is worth quoting in full:

A dispute arose among the well-born Franks of Tournai because the son of one was insistently rebuking the son of another, who had married his sister, angrily chiding him for having abandoned his wife for a prostitute. Since the accused man did not change his behaviour, the brother's anger [at the slight to his sister] became so intense that the lad fell upon his brother-in-law and killed him along with his own men. Then he himself and those who had come with him were cut down and no one from either group remained alive except only one man, who lacked a slayer. As a result, the relatives of both men feuded among themselves. They were repeatedly urged by Queen Fredegund to end their hostility and make peace, lest the continuation of their strife create even greater disturbance.[35]

Here, the heady cocktail of familial honour, sharp words, and hot blood triggered a sequence of vengeance killings that was finally ended only when Fredegund had the three ringleaders beheaded while drunk.

Its dramatic quality exposes some of the complexities of feuding to our attention. In the first place, although the immediate cause was the shaming of a woman by her husband, this vendetta, as all others, was conducted by men. Women's participation was at best indirect, either (as here) as the precipitating cause or in an instrumental role in rousing their menfolk to take action, as is especially well documented in Iceland and Ireland. Feuding was men's business, and was conducted by groups, not individuals. Those groups had to be assembled on an ad hoc basis if there was revenge killing to be done. As this Tournai example again shows, the ill feelings that manifested themselves in feud involved men in the same social network, neighbours who knew each other well. In Tournai, where brother feuded with brother-in-law, the dispute forced men to take sides within their own familial circle. Indeed, as many feuds occurred between men related to each other as between two distinct kin groups. Further, the circle of kinsmen who were liable to be sucked into a feud was not defined by social practice or explicit rules, whether in late-sixth-century Tournai or anywhere else. It depended on how successful the chief contestants were in persuading others to join them, and on how far the honour of those not directly involved might be impugned. And each time someone was killed, the circle of those affected would be recomposed. The shift from ill-feeling to violence in Tournai was the work of a hotheaded, unmarried young man, able to mobilize a group of supporters, not explicitly his kin. In the first bout of fighting, he and his brother-in-law with all their followers but one were killed. At that point, the circle of feuding men widened, as (other? older?) kinsmen of the antagonists became involved and the level of violence escalated. Entirely typical of other feuds whose details caught the attention of early medieval chroniclers, this one seems to have involved not only kinsmen, but also other associates of the two brothers-in-law. Ties of friendship, cameraderie, neighbourliness, or loyalty to a lord could as easily sweep men up into a feud as the obligations of kinship. But, just as feud could also range kinsmen against one another, so feud could also force apart sworn friends, much as Walter and Hagen were finally forced apart by Gunther. The outbreak of a feud, then, called into being a group in which the imperatives of kinship could either meld or conflict with other forms of association and obligation.

Finally, this conflict over a perceived slight to a woman's honour makes the point that feuding coexists with other forms of social regulation, in this case royal command. It would be mistaken to regard feuding as necessarily antithetical to royal authority, and, indeed, some of the best evidence for feuding procedures comes from the legislation of particularly powerful kings, such as the ordinance on feuding issued by the West Saxon king Edmund (939–46). All early medieval kings accepted the principle of feuding: their concerns were to prevent vendettas escalating to the point where they caused serious political disturbance and to reap the fiscal benefit for themselves by fining men for breaches of appropriate procedure. Rather than prohibiting feuding, they tried to co-opt the impulse towards vengeance and turn it to royal advantage. To that end, royal legislation made it advantageous and honourable to settle by accepting compensation. Rothari, for example, increased the level of compensation for a wide range of injuries 'in order that the faida, that is the blood feud, may be

averted after receipt of the . . . composition, and in order that more shall
not be demanded and a grudge shall not be held. So let the case be concluded and friendship remain between the parties.'[36] A strong king of firm
will could mobilize the full vigour of royal anger to force hostile parties
to make peace with each other to the general enhancement of their honour and royal power alike. Where royal authority was tenuous (as in tenth-
century southern France), or where kings were themselves implicated in
the feuding (as in tenth-century Germany), vendettas functioned as an
integral aspect of politics, as a way of asserting dominance and grasping
power in a highly competitive and unstable environment. If, for some, the
pursuit of resources, followers, status—of honour—encouraged feuding,
for others there remained the hope that feuding might undermine the
power of regional strongmen and remake the local realities of dominance
and subordination.

The last word goes to the Frankish king Guntram (561–92), mourning
the assassination of his brother, King Chilperic, in 584: 'I ought not to be
regarded as a man if I am unable to avenge his death this year.'[37] Early
medieval kings were driven by the need to defend their manliness, family, and reputation as much as other men, and vengeance could be as much
the mainspring of royal policy as it was of the quest for individual or
familial honour. In the early Middle Ages, men participated in a culture
that encouraged them to prove themselves in exchanges of boasts, insults,
blows, and killings. Through defence of his honour, the individual asserted
his place in the community of adult warriors: in so doing his reputation
redounded to the credit of his entire family. Alternatively, his actions
might drag his family into turbulent relations with other kinsmen, neighbours, even the ruler. With so much at stake, masculine honour was
volatile, virile, and vengeful. It had to be: the essence of 'friendship by
blood' was the willingness to lay down one's life in defence of family, or
perhaps of lord. Without kinsfolk, a man had no one to help defend his
honour; without honour, he lacked manliness; without manliness, he had
no social existence.

At its simplest level, kinship is about parents and children, husbands and
wives, and about the associated endearments, tensions, hatreds, and obligations that result from such fundamental human pairings. Yet it is also
much more than that. As this chapter has repeatedly demonstrated, discussions of kinship as a form of affinity are in effect discussions of politics at every level from the local to the imperial. The convergence enables
us to avoid simply pigeon-holing early medieval kinship as 'social history',
allowing us to recognize that it forms one of the fundamental ways in

which power was distributed and disputed, social control maintained or challenged, legitimacy asserted and achieved. Early medieval politics turned on the imperatives of kinship as much as on ideologies of authority, the benefits of office holding or sheer military force: to ignore that is fundamentally to misunderstand the nature of all early medieval societies. Prestigious ancestry offered a cogent rhetoric of legitimacy. Relationships between relatives provided identity, support, and legal standing. Among the elite, the urge to stop honour seeping away—and to enhance it— informed dealings with friends and relations, lords and neighbours. All these, at root, were issues of politics and power, whether or not kings were directly involved.

Yet at no stage has a simple definition of early medieval kinship been supplied, with good reason. In matters of name giving, 'friendship by blood', honour or feuding there were no hard and fast rules. Rather, kinship was a habitual amalgam of the conventions of a particular cultural group, the pressures of the moment and of individual strategies and choices. It was a resource to exploit, an identity to affirm, a custom to confirm, a norm to challenge. Its particular significance depended on the specific context.

Its social practices were neither uniform nor unchanging. In the Mediterranean areas where Roman law persisted, individuals had no formal right to seek support and help from their kinsfolk. Their only recognized recourse was to a judicial system that left the individual to face the force of the state alone and unassisted—but that did not stop people pursuing personal and familial interests by whatever means, peaceable or violent, they preferred. Elsewhere, customary law envisaged that kinship would fulfil some of the functions that the Roman state had once arrogated to itself, particularly in matters of regulating the behaviour of members of the group and in offering the means to resolve grievances and disputes. North of the Alps and in Anglo-Saxon England, the bonds of kinship sometimes competed with and sometimes complemented royal power and formal legal processes: here, aristocratic kinship and royal power coexisted in an unstable equilibrium that could as easily promote a ruler of exceptional power such as Charlemagne as it could throw formidable obstacles in the way of efforts to consolidate the authority of Æthelstan or Otto I. In the Celtic-speaking regions, where there was little or no direct Roman heritage, no contribution of Germanic settlement, and no stable, powerful, wide-ranging monarchies, the self-regulatory pressures of close ties of kinship—reinforced in all probability by close residency—provided much of the cohesion needed for ordered existence. It has sometimes been argued that royal authority grew in the course of the early Middle Ages by attacking and weakening the bonds of kinship. Such a sharp opposition is untenable, for ties of kinship were fundamental to all the different cultures of the early Middle Ages at all social levels: they were never the antithesis to strong royal government. Rather, the most successful rulers were generally those who could manage tensions amongst their own close family, co-opt the support of a wide circle of relatives, and turn all the strategies of kinship to their own advantage. An effective king was one who knew how to turn his own relatives into friends.

4

Men and Women

'Man' is the word for any strongminded and discerning person, but 'woman' refers to a mind that is weak and lacking discernment.[1]

Two people are mates. A man and a woman will bring a child into the world through birth.[2]

MINDS that are 'weak and lacking discernment' rarely figure in accounts of great deeds and political achievements. Conventionally told, the history of the early Middle Ages was one of men's politics, economics, and religion, where women were largely absent from the politics and economics and marginal to the religion. This presentation not only rested on the presumptions and prejudices of earlier generations of scholars, but also reflected the tenor of many early medieval chronicles, annals, and histories. But much has changed. Historians now realize that women are more likely to be mentioned in other types of medieval text, such as saints' lives, charters recording land transactions and law codes, than in narrative sources. Also, when the enquiry broadens to acknowledge the local and familial contexts in which people lived, then women take their place beside men as central subjects of historical and archaeological research. Undertaking this is not just a matter of drawing attention to the wives, mothers, and daughters of the kings, princes, bishops, and warriors who feature prominently in chronicles. This approach demands that we explore the disparities between men's and women's social roles and expose their underlying assumptions, values, and prejudices. In other words, it demands that we pay attention to gender as an integral aspect of both social organization and cultural expression during the early Middle Ages. As we do this, we find ourselves studying forms of domination and subordination in every aspect of daily existence in peasant huts as much as imperial palaces. That is the task of this chapter.

It has two premisses. The first has already been established: that literacy justified, promoted, and defended sacred and secular authority.[3] It follows that early medieval scribes and authors were never disinterested, neutral, or innocent reporters of the world around them. In serving the vested interests of those with most at stake, they were selective in their reporting, imbued with attitudes common to their place and time, and adroit at shifting attention away from those who were partly or entirely excluded from rights, resources, prestige, power. These rhetorical strategies easily reduced women to partial or complete invisibility alongside children, slaves, and peasants; this chapter draws attention to some of the gender games that early medieval writers played.

Its second premiss was implicit in the previous chapter but must now be made explicit: that, although most early medieval texts marginalize women, they are nevertheless crucial to the reproduction of any community. Their role is not only the biological reproduction of pregnancy and childbirth, but also the social reproduction of cultural assumptions, modes of behaviour, and mores from one generation to the next. Family names and advice from mother to son are aspects of this that we have already encountered.[4] Equally fundamentally, women contribute their labour to the task of sustaining a community, producing clothing, food, and much else. For the time being, it suffices to note that women's economic contribution complements their cultural and social role.

This chapter thus extends the exploration of the patterning of men's and women's behaviour begun in the previous chapter by taking gender disparities as its focus. It argues that, although early medieval gender relationships varied widely from place to place and changed greatly in the course of the centuries under discussion, there were nevertheless fundamental commonalities in mental attitudes and social practices throughout the early Middle Ages. Wherever we look, these turned on the inferiority of women to men. We shall begin with explicit statements and manifestations of the differing social worth of men and women, before moving on to two important subjects where the disparities between men and women were particularly marked, sexual partnerships and the negotiation of marriage, on the one hand, and access to landed property, on the other. In all three areas, the Roman legacy turns out to be vital.

Differences of Gender

Of all the forms that social distinction may take, gender is but one. Class or rank, age, ethnicity, and religion can also be prominent categories for

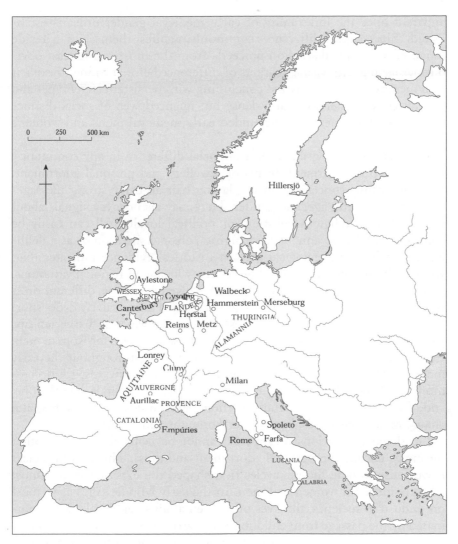

4.1. Principal places mentioned in Chapter 4.

regulating membership of a group, determining access to resources and
formulating identities. Alternatively put, these are all ways of privileging
some while restricting and demeaning others. In the early Middle Ages,
gender was arguably the most protean and the most pervasive of them,
the least amenable to alteration in the course of a lifetime. The fluidities
of social, religious, and ethnic identities will become more readily

apparent once the inflexibility of early medieval gender order is established.[5] Since gender differences commonly manifest themselves in a wide range of ways, this discussion proceeds from the most to the least obvious by starting with visible markers of difference before turning to explicit statements of social norms and concluding with persistent stereotypes and prejudices. We shall see that a dense but nuanced web of social distinction and cultural meaning surrounded early medieval men's and women's lives.

Perhaps the most visible aspect of social difference in any community is dress. Types of garment, forms of jewellery and personal adornment, ways of cutting, concealing, or displaying hair all carry strong messages about rank, wealth, age, and gender. They may also convey signals about ethnic identity, religious vocation, or political loyalty. All can easily be changed, whether to announce changing personal situation or as a deliberate disguise. Archaeological and art historical evidence indicates that, while early medieval costume showed many local and regional variations, and, especially for the wealthy elite, also evolved over time, different dress codes for men and women nevertheless remained universal. By c.500, short tunic and trousers had long since lost their opprobrium as 'barbarian' apparel and replaced the classical toga as the dress of choice for Roman men; they remained the universal basis of men's clothing throughout the early medieval West, except for clergy and, from c.800 onwards, royal ceremonial. Women, by contrast, always wore a calf- or ankle-length robe, and, for the few who could afford them, silks, fine woollen cloths, and changing fashions in display jewellery brought added variety.

Gendered distinctions of apparel cannot be isolated from the other meanings encoded in personal adornment and dress. This becomes clear if we pause to note the life cycles that shaped the experiences of almost all early medieval women and men. In the early Middle Ages as in most pre-industrial societies, the lives of women at all social levels were dominated by the passage from childhood to marriage at or soon after puberty and a move away from the parental home to reside with their husband, however near or far that might be. Then, if death in childbirth did not intervene, came another transition, from motherhood to old age. If widowed as young brides and mothers, they commonly entered a second or even third marriage, moving to wherever their new husband lived. Widowhood in later years commonly meant a different sort of move: an elderly peasant woman was liable to find herself shifted by her lord to a minor outlying dwelling on his estate, whereas elite widows often entered religious communities, which afforded protection and companionship. Only those girls whose parents committed them to the religious life in early childhood are likely to have resided in the same place for almost all their lives.

Men's lives followed a somewhat different rhythm, whatever their social status. Early years were shaped by the acquisition of the physical skills appropriate to their rank, whether the use of weapons or agricultural expertise, but, unlike their sisters, marriage did not intervene as soon as they reached physical maturity. By now sexually active, they commonly enjoyed a phase of full but unmarried adulthood. At the upper end of the social spectrum, they served as warriors in their lord's retinue and lived in his household, receiving training in courtliness and martial skills, as Gregory of Utrecht did at the royal court.[6] At its other end, young unmarried workers were vital members of a lord's agricultural workforce, often put to work on the main parts of an estate, but sometimes sent off to distant places to clear new land for cultivation. Marriage occurred at an older age than for their sisters, adding the roles of head of household and father. If his wife died young, a man was likely to remarry another woman significantly younger than himself: for him, old age brought physical senescence but far less commonly a lonely widower's existence. Even in old age, men still filled a valuable social role, for 'an old man knows most things, a man made wise by distant years, who has experienced a great deal before'.[7] They were the 'elders' whose knowledge and advice were frequently sought in the regulation of community affairs.

With these gendered life cyles in mind, we may return to dress and personal accoutrements. For the many preliterate communities of the early Middle Ages, funerary archaeology provides the crucially important evidence for these life cycles as well as for changing modes of apparel. When the men, women, and children of the fifth and sixth centuries died, they were sometimes buried in graves equipped with a rich variety of objects, commonly of great beauty, splendour, and wealth. Furnished burials are particularly characteristic of the social dislocation and fluidity that accompanied the arrival of peoples such as the Franks, Lombards, Goths, and Anglo-Saxons inside the Roman Empire. Later examples occur in places that, although distant from the former Roman lands, were nevertheless witnessing profound political and social reorganization, such as the western Slav lands in the ninth century and Denmark in the tenth century. They are not, it must be stressed, a product of a pagan, pre-Christian society whose beliefs presumed that the deceased would need the accoutrements of everyday life in the afterlife, for Christians carefully placed some of the most famous of these burials in churches. Rather, they are a symptom of unstable communities where economic, cultural, and military pressures were fostering stressful social change and competition for status and legitimacy. In such circumstances, the living frequently chose to affirm both their own and their dead relatives' social worth through this form of funerary provision. Especially where entire cemeteries of furnished graves have been excavated, they reveal ways in which the standing of individuals within their community fluctuated according not only to rank, but also to age and sex—in other words, according to the point in the gender-specific life cycle at which an individual died.

Sixth-century cemeteries from the region around Metz in north-eastern Gaul are a well-studied case in point. They reveal a world where families responded to the loss of a woman of adolescent or childbearing age with lavish burials containing specifically feminine objects—notably, necklaces, bracelets, earrings, and brooches, sometimes also spindlewhorls and bunches of household keys. Deposition of these objects both reflected the dead woman's social status and value to her family, and unequivocally identified her social value as one derived from her female, childbearing capacities. Both children and women over about 40 years of age, by contrast, were buried with either no grave goods at all, or only a few non-gender-specific items. Men, on the other hand, did not receive a furnished burial until aged about 20, by which time they would have reached the peak of their physical strength and be already fully established in adult male society. Their grave goods were, typically, sets of weapons such as throwing axes, swords, or spears; older men (above 40 or so) usually had far fewer objects buried with them, but nevertheless still ones of characteristically masculine nature. In effect, these graves suggest that women of marriageable or childbearing age, and male warrior heads of households, were in some senses more valuable to their families and communities than the very young and the very old. They also confirm the importance of dress and personal accoutrements in distinguishing men and women from each other and in signalling social role.

As we have seen, early medieval law codes are another valuable indicator of social norms and ideologies. They make explicit some of the disparities at which the material record hints, endowing them with durable, authoritative vigour. Many of these legal provisions pertain to rank, but, of those that deal with distinctions of age and sex, two are especially relevant here, wergeld and legal capacity. First, wergeld. In addition to putting an explicit value on a person's life according to social rank, it could also vary according to age and gender.[8] This is particularly clear in the *Pactus Legis Salicae*: roughly contemporary with these north-eastern Frankish burials, it offers a strikingly similar picture, using the heavy gold coin of late Roman imperial coinage (*solidus*; plural: *solidi*) as a unit of value. The standard wergeld for a free Frankish man or woman was 200 *solidi*, but a threefold increment to 600 *solidi* marked a woman who was pregnant or of childbearing age. After her fertile years had ended, a woman's wergeld dropped again to 200 *solidi*. A man's wergeld, by contrast, increased to 600 *solidi* when he was below 12 years of age or if, as an adult, he was in royal service. In juridical terms, the value of a life varied substantially across an individual's life cycle; in gender terms, the social worth of a sister was sometimes greater, sometimes less, than her twin brother's.

The second important distinction in this context is legal capacity. Early medieval law codes take the free, adult male as normative, and specify variations on the norm that apply to other groups, including women, children, semi-free, and unfree persons. In this context, several distinguish the legal capacity of adults from children and of men from women. Roman law had granted far fuller rights to bring a case or testify in a lawsuit to adult men than to minors or women, and of the post-Roman laws that impose similar restrictions, Rothari's Edict is firmest about restrictions on women's freedom of action, especially in property transactions. Rothari required a male protector or legal representative, normally father, brother, or son, to regulate a woman's interactions with the wider community, especially in any property transactions. In default of any male relative, the king would take on this responsibility—and doubtless benefit from the opportunity to intervene in family affairs. 'No free woman who lives according to the law of the Lombards within the jurisdiction of our realm', he declared, 'is permitted to live under her own legal control, . . . but she ought always to remain under the control of some man or the king. Nor may a woman have the right to give away or alienate any of her movable or immovable property without the consent of him who possesses her *mundium* [i.e. the right of legal authority over her].'[9] Although Rothari subjected the women of early Lombard Italy to greater legal disabilities than are found anywhere else, surviving early eighth-century charters indicate that his legislation did not reduce Lombard women to complete passivity. In practice, they retained greater freedom of manœuvre and somewhat more control over their own land-holdings than the letter of the law would suggest possible. Like other early medieval legislators, Rothari had seen women's position as an opportunity to extend his own sphere of action under the guise of protecting them: women's affairs provided a useful excuse for royal intervention. Taken on its own, Rothari's Edict might suggest that rigid gender distinctions infused all aspects of Lombard women's lives. In the context of the more nuanced picture provided by charter evidence, it provides another reminder of the importance of law as a statement of ideology not a description of social reality.

A similar slippage between prescription and practice emerges when we turn to peasant labour. Ecclesiastical efforts to impose Sundays as a day of rest began in the late sixth century; as the stipulations gradually became more specific, they incorporated explicit statements about the distinct but complementary roles for men and women. They culminated in Charlemagne's frequently copied declaration:

Manual labour is not to be carried out on the Lord's day—that is, men are not to engage in rural work by cultivating the vines, ploughing the fields, reaping, hay-cutting, hedging, assarting, tree-felling, stone-working, house building or gardening. . . . Women are not to engage in cloth-working or to cut out clothes or to sew or embroider; they are not to be allowed to card wool, to break flax, to launder in public or to shear sheep, that the *honor* [respect] and repose of the Lord's day may in all ways be preserved.[10]

Although the association of women with all aspects of cloth production, whether from wool or from linen, is confirmed throughout all parts of early medieval Europe, in practice the division of agricultural tasks varied according to local tradition—and changing technology. In some places the preparation of bread fell to men, in others to women, and, wherever village watermills were constructed for grinding grain, the allocation of domestic labour will have been affected by the abandonment of individual querns. Likewise, harvesting seems to have been men's work on some estates, but, on others, women went out into the fields too, and were sometimes explicitly charged with making sheaves and stooking them. In practice, then, rural labour was gendered, but neither inflexibly nor uniformly.

Not even powerful early medieval kings such as Rothari and Charlemagne could bring social reality fully into line with prescriptive norms. In practice, women characteristically lived their lives in the interstices of ideology and convention. As we shall see, that gap was often considerable, a cause of vulnerability for some but of opportunity for others.

To what extent did the spread of Christianity affect this? It is easy to point to institutional consequences—a valorization of celibate life that inverted the secular norms of masculine and feminine conduct; monastic alternatives to some or all stages of the male and female life cycles; an officialization of men's exclusive access to sacred power in the priesthood. The shifting nature of marriage, to be discussed shortly, fits here too. Equally importantly, however, Christian engagement with the Roman literary legacy reinvigorated deeply rooted stereotypes, while the fostering

of literacy provided a new means for articulating prejudice among formerly preliterate communities. Gregory I's comment that '"man" is the
word for any strongminded and discerning person, but "woman" refers to
a mind that is weak and lacking discernment' typifies this.[11] The massive
work in which he made this remark was much copied by medieval scribes.
Approximately 500 manuscripts of it survive, giving the aphorism a permanence and universality that belie its origins. In effect, the comment re-
cycles commonplaces of Roman tradition.

Isidore of Seville is our best guide to these. With a straightforward
play on Latin words that is lost in translation, he summarized conventional ancient wisdom on the qualities of men and women thus:

Man [*vir*] is named because there is greater force [*vis*] in him than in women,
whence also strength [*virtus*—the word means both physical strength and moral
uprightness] takes its name, or because he rules over women by force. Woman
[*mulier*], however, is named from softness [*mollities*], as if 'softer' [*mollier*] with a
letter changed and one taken away were 'woman' [*mulier*]. They differ from one
another in bodily strength and weakness, for the man's strength is greatest and
the woman's is less, so that she may be subject to the man.[12]

Isidore instructed his early medieval readers to regard the human body as
the key to moral disposition, much as it was in classical ethics. Since
women were softer or weaker than men, their moral strength was less than
men's—and so they were subject to men.

This position works by justifying moral differences between men and
women as the consequence of natural, physiological difference. And since,
from a Christian perspective, the entire natural world was a divine
creation, ancient thinking was easily transposed into a Christian framework. Social differentiation and the gender order originated with God and
'nature' alike. Weaving his thoughts around a string of biblical quotations,
Ambrose, bishop of Milan (374–97), had declared:

Thus it is written: 'A woman shall not be clothed with man's apparel, neither shall
a man use woman's apparel: for he that doeth these things is abominable before
God.' If you think about it hard, whatever nature herself abhors is incongruous.
Why would a man not want to be seen to be what he was born? Why assume an
alien appearance? Why pretend to be a woman, or you, woman, a man? Nature
clothes each sex in its own garments. Men and women have different habits, com-
plexion, movements, gait, strength and voice. Thus it is amongst other species of
animals: the lion and the lioness have different appearance, different strength, different voice. . . . Male peacocks are beautiful, but the females are not adorned
with the same varied plumage. . . . Surely they never change their appearance?
Why should we want to change ours?

. . .

But I think one would say it's not so much in clothing as in manners, or habits and behaviour, that one action is fitting for a man and another for a woman. Hence the apostle Paul says, as an interpreter of [divine] law, 'Let women keep silence in the churches: for it is not permitted them to speak, but to be subject, as also the law saith. But if they would learn anything, let them ask their husbands at home.' And also, 'Let the woman learn in silence with all subjection. But I suffer not a woman to teach, nor to use authority over the man: but to be in silence.' How disgusting it is for a man to perform woman's work![13]

Ambrose had neatly conflated divine command and the animal world to argue for inflexible gender distinctions of dress and behaviour. His and Isidore's words echoed through the early Middle Ages, copied or quoted by many who read them. From the Christian writers of late Antiquity, early medieval scholars inherited a ready-made view of normative gender relations whose subversion would threaten divine order, and they saw little need to develop it further.

But real life was not as straightforward as early medieval moralists might wish. One spring, the holy man Gerald of Aurillac (b. c.855, d. 909) encountered a woman ploughing. On being asked why she was doing this 'man's work', she explained that her husband had been ill for a long time and that, if she did not do the sowing, no one else would. Gerald's response was to give her enough money to hire a labourer to finish the work. His biographer Odo, abbot of Cluny (927–42), knew his Ambrose, however, and made a moral of the tale. 'Nature flees from everything artificial, as Ambrose says, and its author, God, abhors what is unnatural.'[14] A peasant woman's crisis had given a pious Christian the opportunity to give alms; a monastic moralist presented his readers with a tale of the restoration of the divinely ordained gender order.

Appeals to 'nature' constitute one of the common rhetorical gender games of clerical authors in the early Middle Ages—and for centuries thereafter. Another, as we shall see, was to withhold the name of a woman from the reader or audience of a text, for anonymity obliterates identity. Those who resorted to textual tricks such as these doubtless did so out of force of habit. But the habit itself is revealing—of ingrained assumptions about women's marginality, weakness, or inferiority. As a powerful cultural reflex, the notion of women's natural weakness served many purposes— political, legal, religious, literary. It could encourage exploitation as easily as protection; it could be turned to praise or slander at will. It made fame and good reputation hard to acquire and easy to lose. Above all, it re-inforced other social disparities, of age, rank, or resources, leaving women who did succeed in making their way in the world through whatever means available always vulnerable, caught within a web of meaning not of their own weaving.

Pairings of Conception

Sexual partnerships are essential to the reproduction of human society, not only as the means of procreation but also because the intimate group of parents and children is the forum in which cultural assumptions and values are most often transmitted from one generation to the next. Yet to speak without qualification of 'marriage' in the early Middle Ages is too simple. The word does not adequately describe the full range of accepted sexual partnerships that men and women made for themselves. By the end of the millennium, something recognizably similar to our modern notion of marriage as an enduring relationship between one man and one woman had developed in parts of Europe, but not without controversy. Examination of these issues will make clear the social organization of gender relations and take us to the heart of early medieval ideas about sexual mores. Building on the discussion of kinship in the previous chapter, it opens to scrutiny additional varieties of men's and women's experience.

Underlying early medieval cultural diversities, however, lay a persistent and universal imbalance. The less access to legal rights or economic resources a woman had, the more she was at the sexual disposal of men of higher status: everywhere elite men had sexual access to women of low social standing on their own terms. These informal liaisons were nothing to do with the partnerships through which property and cultural values were channelled or with the bonds of affection and familial identity that formalized partnerships enabled; they thus are rarely visible in the sources. Lacking in any political significance or ideological value, they seldom came to the attention of the lawyers and legislators whose models of social relationships expressed dominant values in terms of marriage and sexual conduct, as in much else.

Of the three legal cultures outlined in the previous chapter, the inherited Roman tradition provides our starting point, because it proved fundamental. It recognized two mutually exclusive forms of sexual partnership, concubinage and marriage. The former involved no property transactions and was simply an acknowledged, long-term, sexual partnership between a man of high status and a woman of vastly inferior rank; a concubine's offspring lacked any inheritance rights. Concubinage was an alternative rather than an adjunct to marriage, a sexual outlet for young, unmarried men or widowers who preferred not to remarry. As defined by Roman law, marriage expected husband and wife to be of equal rank, and it required a betrothal contract, the formal consent of both parties, and endowment of the new couple by the bride's parents. It thus defined a man's heirs as only those of his offspring whom his wife had born. Fourth- and fifth-century imperial legislation put an unprecedented emphasis on it as a permanent partnership, only dissoluble if one of the partners committed the sacrilege of grave robbing or resorted to witchcraft, or if the wife had intercourse with someone other than her husband. Idealized as a consensual partnership based on mutual affection and respect, these legal provisions remained in practice throughout the Mediterranean areas of the early medieval West. As we shall see, they also informed the views of a succession of bishops, and thereby came to influence ecclesiastical teaching throughout the Middle Ages.

Into this late Roman world, Germanic-speaking settlers introduced rather different values and conventions, in marriage as in kinship. Notably, both written law and social convention recognized several types of marriage, in contrast to the single definition of Roman law. Of these, only one involved property transfers and thereby rights of inheritance. The groom's family commonly paid a marriage price to the bride's father, which the groom supplemented with a 'morning gift' on the day after the consummation of the union. In addition, it became normal, by the ninth century at the latest, for the groom to specify a marital endowment out of his own property at the time of the engagement. Especially if she lacked brothers, the bride might also contribute property inherited from her own parents. Negotiated between the aspiring groom and the girl's father and kinsfolk and celebrated in a public ceremony with the participation of friends and relatives, this was a transaction between two groups of kin that not only endowed a new household but might also seal a political alliance to mutual advantage or even end a feud. As such, it could generally only be ended by the man, with serious economic implications for both partners. Well described as 'conjugal domination',[15] this first form of union had two further features. First, it also required the transfer of the father's *mundium* over his daughter to her husband, so that he acquired the rights to represent her legal interests and to exercise authority over her. Secondly, the bride went to reside on her husband's estate, however near to or far from her natal home that might be. By the very nature of its property transactions, this was a form of partnership characteristic of the wealthy elite.

Equally accepted, long term, and publicly celebrated was a form of marriage in which the woman's move to the man's home was unaccompanied by any transfer of *mundium*, even though she might have property of her own. Men had no need to choose between these two forms of union: the rich and powerful could easily afford to support more than one woman, and indeed multiple partnerships became an expression of status and a way of accumulating socially prestigious resources. One such man was the wealthy and influential Rhineland landowner Pippin of Herstal (b. *c*.650, d. 714), who is known to have fathered sons by three women. His two simultaneous wives Plectrude and Alpaida both came from powerful families of the Ardennes region, although possibly only the extremely wealthy Plectrude had been transferred to Pippin's *mundium*. In due course, their sons contested their father's inheritance. Much less is known about Pippin's third partner, but the lack of any record of her name and the exclusion of her son from any share in Pippin's inheritance both strongly suggest that this was a much more informal partnership.

This brief survey does not exhaust the ways in which men competed for status by attracting women, for early medieval law codes recognized a range of supplementary relationships. Women could be taken without their parents' consent either in enforced abduction or in a seduction in which they themselves were willing accomplices. Although the parents had to be compensated for the loss of their daughter, such unions were nevertheless recognized, and might also be made more formal by a subsequent property settlement. Finally, at the bottom of the social hierarchy, it was left to lords to authorize whatever marriages among their slaves and serfs best suited the exigencies of efficient estate management.

In sum, the descendants of Germanic speakers generally preferred to maintain their traditional spectrum of sexual unions long after they had assimilated into many other aspects of post-Roman provincial life. These unions were differentiated by their degree of permanence; by the ways in which the transfer of a woman from her natal kin to her husband was achieved; by the nature of the attendant property transactions, if any; and by the arrangements for legal authority over and protection of the woman. While it remains uncertain whether a girl had much opportunity to voice her opinion of a proposed union, high-status men certainly could foster their interests by strategic marriages and find ample scope for sexual satisfaction and the begetting of heirs. When, towards the end of the eleventh century, Adam of Bremen (d. *c*.1083) commented that among the Swedes 'a man according to his means has two or three or more wives at one time, rich men and princes an unlimited number. And they also consider the sons born of such unions legitimate', he was only reporting, with perhaps modest exaggeration, a centuries-old pattern of powerful men exploiting these opportunities to 'hoard' women and thereby confirm their superiority not only over the women but also over less successful men.[16]

In the third place, we should return to Ireland, where lawyers' treatises blended elements of Christian, late Roman marriage law with indigenous practices to delineate a range of types of sexual union. Seventh- and eighth-century Irish scholars categorized nine 'pairings of conception' and ranked them from the most to the least honourable.[17] In the most honourable form of union, the woman's kin gave her to the groom, and the new household was supported by substantial property endowments. Foremost among these was the union to which both sets of kin contributed property and livestock, establishing the bride as a 'wife of joint authority'.[18] Less conducive to enhanced status, the property could come solely from either the husband's or the wife's kin. The constitutive element of these three unions was a contract regulating the property provisions and the division of responsibility for administering it. Despite their complexity, such contracts could be terminated. In contrast with other early medieval cultures, Irish laws permitted a wide range of grounds for separation. In theory at least, a man could part from his wife if she betrayed him, damaged his honour, persisted in adultery, killed their children, or neglected household tasks. She could leave him if he were impotent, sterile, or homosexual, too fat to have intercourse, gossiped about her sexual performance, took a mistress, circulated a satire about her, or if, in exercising his right to rebuke her, he struck a blow that caused a blemish. Unfortunately, we lack the sort of evidence that would reveal whether Irish social reality corresponded at all closely with these idealized schemes.

Next in the Irish ranking of sexual unions came those that the woman's kin accepted but in whose negotiation they had not been actively involved. The 'pairing of conception' in which a man visited a woman in her parents' home with their consent was less formal and less honourable; even less honourable were unions in which the woman went away with a man with neither the participation nor the consent of her kin, or was secretly visited by him. At the very bottom of the scale came the 'pairing of conception' to which the woman herself had not consented (rape) or the union of two insane people. All these provisions potentially had important consequences for the distribution of property, for only if a woman's kinsfolk had not recognized the union did the sons of that alliance lose their right to inherit from their father, yet these sons could nevertheless inherit if their father chose to acknowledge them as his.

This spectrum of relationships allowed for multiple simultaneous relationships even more readily than in the successor kingdoms, for Irish law distinguished between the *cétmuinter*, the 'chief wife', and lesser-status wives.[19] The 'chief wife' had entered into a marriage contract in which her kin had fully participated, and which bound her more closely to her marital family than to her natal kin. Thus she was under the rule of her husband, and responsibility for two-thirds of her legal liabilities now lay with her sons and only one-third with her natal kin; her sons and her kin stood to inherit her property in equivalent proportions. Other wives, however, remained largely or fully within their natal kin in matters of legal liability, and enjoyed only half the status and entitlements of the chief wife. It was quite acceptable for a high-status man to have a chief wife, then acquire a second wife (on whom the *cétmuinter* was entitled to inflict non-fatal injuries during the first three days of this additional union), and also be visiting one or more women in their parental home. In the face of Christian clerical disapproval, Irish lawyers turned to the Old Testament for justification of traditional habits. 'There is dispute in Irish law as to which is more proper, whether many sexual unions or a single one: for the chosen people of God lived in plurality of unions, so that it is not easier to condemn it than to praise it.'[20] For those who could afford it, multiple sexual partnerships were normal.

Those who condemned a plurality of unions, in Ireland and elsewhere, were the clergy. The Christian doctrine of marriage was based firmly on the practice of the later Roman Empire, as encapsulated in a ruling of Pope Leo the Great (440–61) that a legitimate marriage was one between a free man and a free woman of equal rank, and that it involved the kin of the girl giving her in a formal betrothal into a marriage that was endowed with property and publicly celebrated. Leo's view, that 'not every woman joined to a man is a "wife" because not every son is heir to his father', asserted a distinction between the woman who was partner to the only form of sexual union recognized in Roman property law, marriage, and a woman in any other form of sexual liaison, such as a concubine or mistress.[21] To this legal definition of Roman origin, fourth- and fifth-century moralists had added a strong dose of a rigorous sexual ethic based largely on the New Testament. Paul of Tarsus (d. *c*.65) had declared that 'On account of fornication let every man have his own wife and every woman have her own husband' and 'Know ye not that the unrighteous shall not inherit the kingdom of God? Be not deceived: neither fornicators, nor idolaters, nor adulterers, nor effeminate nor abusers of themselves with men, nor thieves, nor covetous, nor drunkards, nor revilers, nor extortioners, shall inherit the kingdom of God,' and pronouncements such as these became the basis for a Christian morality of male and female sexual restraint that recognized heterosexual marriage as the sole legitimate relationship in which intercourse was permissible.[22] Promulgated by the clergy, this combination of Roman legal premises and uncompromising Christian morality cut across local conventions everywhere.

But to what extent did ecclesiastical opinions alter social practice? In Ireland, the Latin word for a woman having illegal intercourse, *adultrix*, supplied one of the Old Irish words for the secondary wife, *adaltrach*. Lexical borrowing by no means signalled the end of multiple sexual partnerships, however. The success of attempts to restrict the learned caste of poets, clerics, and judges to only one wife cannot be ascertained, and the view that 'lords, poets, commoners are impaired by illicit cohabitation' seems to have made little impact.[23] Genealogies certainly suggest that multiple partnerships remained common at least amongst kings, and, when the full force of high-minded continental clerical reform reached Ireland in the twelfth century, reformers were vigorous in their condemnation of the marital practices they found there.[24]

Outside Ireland, local habits and ecclesiastical expectations also diverged, as the experience of a seventh-century man named Barontus indicates. A nobleman from Lonrey in central France, he decided to end his days as a monk. Having entered his local monastery, he participated in its daily round of prayers and psalms. Then, in 678/9, he is reported to have had a near-death experience. On his return to full consciousness he recounted how devils had taken his soul on a tour of heaven and hell. At one of the gates of heaven, the apostle Peter asked the demons what charges they had against Barontus. 'They replied: "He had three wives, which was not permitted. He has also committed other adulteries and many other sins which we persuaded him to."'[25] Until he retired to the monastery, Barontus's behaviour was just like that of his contemporary, Pippin of Herstal. The difference is that we know about Barontus's multiple marriages from the perspective of a critical monastic author from whose high moral vantage point the normal behaviour of rich men seemed like the work of the devil.

Visionary literature was not the only means of censure, or elderly men its only targets, however. On the occasions when ecclesiastical disapproval turned against kings, the stakes were high, for dynastic succession could be at risk. 'Know that these boys will never bear the royal sceptre, for they were begotten in sin' prophesied the Irish ascetic Columbanus in 610, fulminating against the marital habits of the Merovingian Theuderic II (596–613).[26] Many Merovingian kings of Gaul, Theuderic included, had multiple sexual partners, most or all of whose sons they recognized as heirs. Those, like Columbanus, who dared to criticize, struck out at the practices that helped perpetuate the dynasty.

The stakes were raised even further during the eighth and ninth centuries, when councils of bishops in Italy and the Frankish lands launched a concerted effort to redefine marriage and to establish it as a religious, sacred undertaking. Starting at a synod in Rome in 721, ecclesiastical councils gradually added three further elements to Leo the Great's ideas: an emphasis on the permanence and indissolubility of marriage, a refusal to countenance more than one sexual relationship at a time, and a very much broader definition of incestuous, forbidden marriages. In this context, bishops were emphatic that both the spiritual kinship established through baptism and the relationships created through marriage were impediments to marriage. Godparents, god-siblings, co-parents, and all in-laws thus fell into the vast pool of prohibited marriage partners. In addition, some bishops tried to impose an additional disqualification—consanguinity extending all the way to a common ancestor within seven generations, way beyond the widely acceptable four-generation limit.

It remains contentious why some Carolingian clergy sought to extend the circle of incestuous relationships to such extremes, especially since there is no evidence that marriage to close relatives was common, let alone normal, prior to the middle of the eighth century. Whatever the underlying motives, the result was that, during the century and a half from 721, marriage, and sexual relationships of all sorts, became politicized in a new way. There are two main reasons for this. First, by the later eighth century, good kingship meant fostering Christian conduct.[27] Thus Charlemagne and his successors supported ecclesiastical efforts to enforce a revised marital morality, while finding their own sexual conduct and marital alliances open to new scrutiny. Indeed, as Lothar II (855–69) discovered to his great cost, bishops could turn these prohibitions against a king, leaving him heirless. Secondly, beyond the immediate context of the politics of kings' bedrooms, bishops' only real chance of changing marital practices came if they worked in alliance with rulers: they thus handed wily kings an effective weapon for asserting control over their powerful subjects.

A case that came to the attention of a council of Frankish bishops in 860 allows us a rare glimpse of the social complexities, emotions, and conflicting political interests involved in betrothal and marriage. It concerned Stephen, count of the Auvergne, and its setting was Aquitaine, where his royal lord Charles the Bald was having difficulty building a stable, loyal regime. The story was one of 'very great scandal to the church and detriment to the kingdom'. In Stephen's own words: 'In the weakness of youth, as was the custom, I had my way with a young woman.' Then, in about 857, acting 'with the consent of my family and friends', he negotiated with another leading Aquitanian count, Regimund, to be allowed to marry the latter's daughter. They reached agreement about the marital endowment Stephen would provide, and the couple were formally betrothed. But, before Regimund could publicly hand over his daughter or Stephen could effect the property transfers, Stephen had discovered that his fiancée was related to his previous sexual partner. He had then consulted his priest, who informed him that the proposed marriage would be incestuous, and therefore forbidden. Stephen's ensuing efforts to back out of the betrothal aroused the wrath of both the king and Regimund. Fearing exile and ruin, Stephen felt 'compelled by necessity' to take Regimund's daughter as his wife in a public ceremony, and to hand over the endowment intended for her. But he nevertheless declined to consummate the marriage, and his obduracy made the confrontation with Regimund increasingly violent. Angered and humiliated at his daughter's treatment, Regimund finally lodged a complaint with the bishops in 860.[28]

Faced with such complex issues of honour, property, contractual obligation, sex, and sedition, the council decided that the case should be heard simultaneously by a secular assembly presided over by the king and by an ecclesiastical assembly led by the archbishops of the provinces where both Stephen and Regimund had their lands, the former to deal with the issues of property and politics, the latter with the nature of the marriage. The council also had a report on the case prepared by Hincmar, archbishop of Reims (845–82), one of the most vigorous lawyer-bishops of the entire Middle Ages but in this, as much else, also Charles the Bald's agent. The archbishops' ruling has not survived, so we do not know the final outcome, but, if they did follow Hincmar's advice, their solution would have been a face-saving one for Stephen and Regimund, with scant regard for the well-being of the unwanted bride, whom the briefing never bothered to name. Hincmar's concern was not sex outside marriage, but sex within it. He advised the provincial ecclesiastics to interrogate the girl: if the marriage had indeed been consummated, it was incestuous and therefore invalid; but, since consummation was necessary to complete a marriage, it was not a proper marriage if the pair had not had intercourse. Either way, Stephen was released and the royal assembly must deal with the broken betrothal contract, the insult to Regimund, and the threats of political unrest.

Why had Stephen acted thus? He claimed that fear of losing face and encountering the king's wrath played their part, but there seems to have been more to it than this. He may have been an innocent victim of the recent rigorous prohibitions against marriage to anyone related to a previous sexual partner, or he may have been cleverly manipulating the law to wriggle out of a marriage alliance no longer politically convenient for him. Whatever the case, Charles the Bald's grip on Aquitaine was in question. However we choose to adjudge Stephen's behaviour, a conflict such as this would have been hardly conceivable a century earlier. Whether the tale of a hapless victim or an adroit schemer, the case is important for several reasons. In the first instance, it is a reminder of the importance of elite marriage as political negotiation. Secondly, in a society that more commonly consigned a girl of marriageable age to a role as pawn than as an active strategist, a woman's opinion and well-being mattered little. Indeed, to Hincmar, they meant as little as her name. Thirdly, it testifies to the reformulation of definitions of kinship in the service of a changing ethic of sexuality and marriage.

Finally, it is no coincidence that Stephen of the Auvergne was a man of high status, a member of the king's retinue. His prominence exposed his marital shenanigans to the critical gaze of courtier-bishops and a king quick to spot any potential way of exerting leverage over his followers. Far to the south, beyond the Pyrenees, his Catalonian contemporary Dela, Count of Empúries (862–94), had married his first cousin Quixilona, daughter of his father's brother. Cousin-marriage was the norm for the counts of late ninth- and early tenth-century Catalonia, for it reinforced the familial grip on power. Had they known, bishops at the Carolingian court might have been perturbed—but Catalonia had never enjoyed close contact with Carolingian centres of power and, by the late ninth century, was rapidly losing all contact with the northern lands. When, in the middle years of the tenth century, Catalonian counts did begin to look further afield for their brides, it was for reasons of political advantage rather than the result of any moral pressure. Similarly, in Wessex, King Edward the Elder (899–924) assured his claim to the throne by marrying Ælfflaed, daughter of his first cousin and rival Æthelhelm. Not for another fifty years or so did the Carolingian notion that close kinship was an insuperable impediment to marriage even begin to alter English practice. And it did so only because late-tenth-century Anglo-Saxon kings found a strategic political advantage in supporting moralizing bishops who had familiarized themselves with stringent continental ideals. In effect, the Carolingian redefinition of marriage—indissoluble, exclusive of any other simultaneous sexual partnership, prohibited to couples related to each other within at least four generations—began to affect people's behaviour only when the full resources of king and church were united in trying to enforce it.

Elsewhere, either beyond Carolingian purview, or where the will and the means to effect change were lacking, definitions of marriage long remained much more flexible. Scandinavia is a case in point, as Adam of Bremen reliably informs us.[29] The Dane Cnut conquered England and seized the throne in 1016, then shortly thereafter acceded to the Danish crown: in having two concurrent wives, Ælfgifu and Emma, he maintained the older, Scandinavian ways, while nevertheless bowing to ecclesiastical

pressure and legislating to fine those Anglo-Saxons who married close relatives or did not confine their sexual activity to marriage. Even further
away, quite beyond the sphere of Carolingian influence, Ireland remained
untouched by continental norms until the very end of the eleventh century. Indeed, an Irish woman who was her father's sole heir was likely to
be married off to her closest male relative precisely to prevent her property leaving the kindred, and, despite lip-service to the patristic ban on
marriage within four generations, Irish churchmen evidently acknowledged the need for cousin-marriage for heiresses.

To change marriage customs required both political persistence and
consistent norms on the part of aggressive kings and bishops acting in
tandem. But for long after the high tide of Carolingian moralizing, neither the alliance nor the will to action were much in evidence. Instead, at
least among the political elite, marriage long remained an uneasy balance
of political exigency and divergent norms, only sometimes tempered with
personal morality. A poignant early medieval love story from the close of
our period emphasizes these contradictions. Count Otto of Hammerstein
and his wife Irmengard were distantly related—Irmengard's great-
grandparents were Otto's great-great-grandparents. Their long-standing
marriage was interrupted when the vengeful German emperor Henry II
(1002–24) set out to destroy Otto, fearing he was becoming an over-mighty
subject. Henry attempted this by encouraging a renewed mood of moral
rigour among German bishops, some of whom were seeking to put new
force into the ninth-century proposals for a seven-generation definition
of incest. In 1018, Henry II presided over an ecclesiastical council that
excommunicated the couple and ordered them to separate. 'Blazing with
blind love', Otto nevertheless remained with Irmengard, and in 1020 he
assaulted his leading ecclesiastical opponent, the archbishop of Mainz.[30]
Henry II retaliated, besieging Otto in his castle at Hammerstein, razing
it, and then seizing all Otto's extensive lands. Still the couple clung together until, in 1023, another ecclesiastical assembly again ruled against
them. Fearful of the emperor, Otto finally submitted, but Irmengard remained defiant. In breach of the German bishops' refusal to let her
appeal to the pope, she journeyed to Rome in 1023 and successfully pleaded
her case. In affirming the validity of her marriage and denouncing the
German bishops who had annulled it, Benedict VIII (1012–24) provoked
a storm of protest for his interference. The following year, both king and
pope died, and with them, the controversy: Otto and Irmengard remained
married and enjoyed the favour of the new king, Conrad II, whose own
marriage elicited strong clerical criticism.

The travails of Otto and Irmengard reveal much about marriage at the turn of the millennium. In the first place, their own acceptance of it as permanent and monogamous indicates the long, slow reorientation of social assumptions that took place in large parts of early medieval Europe under Christian influence. They embodied the ideal that ecclesiastical teaching advocated, of marriage as an exclusive partnership of equals. Secondly, despite agreement on the principle that marriage should be between partners who were not related in any way, uncertainty persisted about where to set the limits of kinship. Thirdly, kings, bishops, and popes contested the right to arbitrate marriages. Originating in the era of vigorous Carolingian moral idealism, a distinctive notion of marriage had been formulated whose presuppositions had massive implications for local conventions about the nature and number of tolerated sexual partnerships, and for the social units in which women raised their children. Sometimes reinforced by royal promulgation, it spread wherever handbooks of Carolingian ecclesiastical legislation were copied, primarily on the Continent and, by the later tenth century, into England as well. But, as we have seen, formulation of that notion was one thing, its implementation quite another, and attempts to turn aspiration into reality remained fitful, controversial, and inconsistent long beyond 1050.

Women, Family, and Inheritance

If marriage long remained more a matter of politics than of Christian morality, it did so because it involved far more than regulation of sexual activity. At the very least, the arrival of a wife and daughter-in-law into a man's home increased the pool of labour available for women's work—the spinning, weaving, sewing, embroidering to which women of all social levels devoted their energies, and the food preparation and other tasks that slave and peasant women undertook. Among the elite, marriage also involved calculations about conserving, distributing, and augmenting family property so as to arrange its disposition across generations. With land came the wherewithal to survive and, for all property-owners above the meagre subsistence farmer, the possibility of a surplus. The next chapter will emphasize how rights over landed property opened the way to status, political power, and influence; here the focus is on inheritance of the patrimony as a means of negotiating gender disparities. This analysis argues that, while the distribution of resources among heirs reinforced men's and women's differential access to wealth, influence, and power, women's access to property was nevertheless crucial to early medieval familial interactions.

Open to the influence of political pressures, ecclesiastical opinion,

evolving local legal procedures, and changing ideas of family, early medieval inheritance customs varied widely from place to place. Yet, despite
widespread regional and temporal variation, some general points are clear.
The first is that sexual partnerships transmit property (movables and land)
from parents to children, and that the right to inherit is generally closely
related to the nature of the parents' partnership. The formal and publicly
acknowledged unions in early Ireland gave sons a greater right to their
father's property than those of less formal partnerships; elsewhere the
developing notions of Christian marriage strengthened the inheritance
rights of a man's child by his wife against claims by the children of less
formal unions. Secondly, the normal patterns for inheriting land diverged
from those for movable property such as cattle, slaves, or jewellery, and
procedures for inheriting political office might be different again. Thirdly,
parental property was in principle partible—in other words, was shared
between some or all children, albeit usually in unequal amounts. By the
eleventh century, however, some families were beginning to develop strategies for channelling most or all of their patrimony to a single son, as notions of family and identity continued to evolve. Fourthly, the transmission
of property from one generation to the next was rarely the concern of
parents and children alone. Kings were watchful, keen for an excuse to
intervene, and, except where Roman property law persisted, the wider kin
group was also involved. This discussion therefore locates men and women
among their relatives and also keeps an eye on the broader political contexts within which they lived. Finally and fundamentally, men's right to
inherit land was one of the commonalities of all early medieval cultures;
women's access to the family patrimony, on the other hand, varied greatly
from region to region, and from generation to generation. By tracing
women's differential access to land vis-à-vis their brothers, a gendered pattern of immense political significance emerges.

Identifying strategies of inheritance inevitably depends upon the
surviving documentation. In this context, it is germane to reiterate several points made earlier. On the one hand, the norms articulated in law
codes about the transmission of property are not an adequate guide to
how people behaved in practice: to get at that, we must juxtapose them
with the records of transfers of specific, named estates such as charters
of donation, wills, and bequests. Further, not only did the degree of
document-mindedness vary markedly from region to region, but the rate
of documentary survival has been much better in some places than others. A final point to recall is the gradual adoption across northern Europe
of testamentary practices of Roman origin, practices that affected methods of transmitting and recording title to property.[31] Overall, records

detailing land transfers generally survive in some numbers only from the late seventh century onwards in Italy and the Frankish lands, the late ninth century in northern Spain, the mid-tenth century in England, and even later elsewhere.

It is nevertheless possible to sketch some of the most obvious regional distinctions in inheritance custom. The two extremes are, as so often, Ireland, on the one hand, and the southern, enduringly Roman areas of continental Europe, on the other. In Ireland, the paternal land was divided equally between all recognized sons, but daughters were entitled to an equal share of movable property, most notably slaves and cattle. If a man died leaving a daughter but no sons, she might have a life interest in his estate, but on her death the property reverted to her male kinsmen on her father's side. These practices operated within a culture that emphasized that land was the property of a four-generation kin group, known as the *derbfine*, and in which alienation of land away from the *derbfine* was discouraged and difficult to achieve. Female inheritance would pose a threat to the kin group and its land, for recognized sons belonged to their father's *derbfine*, not their mother's: were a woman to inherit land and pass it to her sons, it would pass from one *derbfine* to another. This is why an heiress would find herself pressured to marry her father's nearest male relative.[32] By contrast, Roman property law of the fifth and sixth centuries operated on two quite different principles, which remained intact throughout the early Middle Ages, and long beyond. First, land was owned in full and outright ownership only by individuals: there was no notion of any collective interests or rights over land. Secondly, the law of the late Roman Empire was based upon the assumption that daughters had the right to inherit on equal terms alongside their brothers in the event of intestacy. Overall, it posed no legal obstacles to the full control and free disposal of property by women independent of any guardian. In areas such as Calabria and Lucania in southern Italy or Aquitaine and Provence in southern France, where Roman practices persisted throughout the early Middle Ages, women's access to property gave them in principle a degree of economic independence quite unthinkable in early Ireland.

But what of those regions between Ireland and southern Italy, in other words in the kingdoms where Germanic-speaking settlers and their descendants persisted in their own customs? Here, it is important to acknowledge a wide range of local differences, but with two significant common factors. First, rights to private, individual ownership of property were balanced alongside the interests of the kin, who might wish to claim it or to be consulted if its owner desired to sell or donate land to anyone

other than his offspring. Secondly, these traditions clearly preferred transmitting land to male heirs, and generally acknowledged inheritance rights
of daughters or sisters only when sons were lacking. More hostile to
women owning land than any other law code, the mid-eighth-century
compilation of Thuringian law specified that, in the absence of a son, the
property would go to the father's nearest male relative. The Thuringian
law is also useful for making more explicit than any other law code the
differential routes to be used in passing on movable goods as distinct from
land, for it stipulated that, although the latter went to the father's nearest
male relative, livestock and slaves went to his daughters, who would also
be the ones to inherit their mother's clothing, jewellery, and personal
ornaments.

And yet: prescribing written rules for inheritance and drawing up documents confirming individual land transactions were both devices adopted
from Roman tradition. The result of this is that, from the earliest moment
when the written record first allows us to glimpse inheritance strategies
in the post-imperial kingdoms, they are already touched by Roman norms.
This trend intensified only in the seventh, eighth, and ninth centuries.
The Lombard kingdom in northern Italy is a particularly clear instance
where the inheritance rights of Lombard women altered significantly
under the heavy pressure of the customs of their Roman neighbours, and,
by the end of the eighth century, Lombard daughters had a far greater
chance of inheriting a part of their father's property than did their predecessors who had lived under Rothari's rule. In effect, wherever the
documentation survives to reveal the specificities of property transactions,
women in the successor kingdoms could and did inherit land as well as
movables.

That is not to say, however, that women's access to property was ever
as great or as secure as men's. Rather, it remained limited, insecure, and
liable to be contested. Although statistical deductions are notoriously un-
reliable for the early Middle Ages, several rough calculations may help
focus this discussion. Late Roman women, it has been optimistically suggested, may have owned 30–45 per cent of all the landed property in the
empire. Admittedly, this is little more than guesswork, but it may be contrasted with figures for later centuries derived from differing types of
material. First, analysis of continental charters from the eighth century
onwards suggests sharp regional differences in women's access to land. In
areas where the influence of Roman legal traditions remained strong,
women may have controlled significant amounts of land—approximately
17 per cent in tenth-century northern Spain and 13 per cent in adjacent

regions of southern France. North of the Loire, in Germany and in Lombard Italy, women had less than 10 per cent, and probably less than 5 per cent of all land. For England, the evidence is rather different: Domesday Book, the national survey of landholding compiled for William the Conqueror (1066–87). In addition to reporting on landholding in 1086, Domesday records the pattern of landownership in Anglo-Saxon England on 'the day when King Edward was alive and dead', that is in 1066, and it offers a snapshot of property rights immediately before the Norman Conquest. Anglo-Saxon custom strongly preferred land to pass from man to man, and, in general, women's access was conditional and restricted. Domesday records only about 5 per cent of all the land in England as being owned by women in 1066: and there are good reasons for believing that somewhat more land was in female hands by 1066 than it had been in c.1000. These figures suggest—however tentatively—that, subject to the influence of legal cultures and local traditions, female property rights varied tremendously and that, even on the best possible estimate in the regions most favourable to women's property rights, the vast majority of all land remained under men's control.

Access to landed wealth was not only conditioned by the constraints of local social practice or legal restrictions. Specific familial circumstances were of equal significance, and might affect women just as much as men. First and foremost, the uncertainties of birth or the vagaries of sudden death might throw into confusion even the most carefully planned property distribution. Abba, the reeve—king's official—in Kent, had a childless marriage. Between 833 and 839 he drew up a will in which he made arrangements for several possible futures. 'It is my desire', he stated at the outset, 'that if God will give me a child, he shall have the land after me, and enjoy it with my wife; and similarly, and that after him my descendants shall continue to hold it as long as it is God's will that there be any of them able and qualified to hold land.' But Abba also envisaged a childless old age: 'If, however, it is my lot not to have a child, then I desire that my wife shall have it [my land] as long as she is willing to keep it without marrying again.'[33] Another possible future was that his widow Heregyth remarried. In that case, the land was to return to his own kinsmen, leaving her with only whatever property she had herself brought into the marriage. Finally, he made provisions in case Heregyth wished to enter a convent, provisions designed to ensure that she had adequate wealth to be accepted into the community but that the land remained with his own kin. Abba also gave some thought as to which of his kinsmen might expect to benefit if he did indeed die childless. His brothers were to pass the property to their heirs, if they had any; failing them, one Freothomund (cousin? uncle?) would inherit if he were still alive; if he had already died, then one of Abba's sisters' sons could claim the land. If his family died out completely, the land was to go to the local cathedral church, Christ Church in Canterbury. Abba had stared into an uncertain future, not knowing whether his wife would ever conceive, or which of his relatives might predecease him.

How did things turn out? We do know that, in her widowhood, Heregyth surrendered Abba's lands to his kin in a way that diverted some of the produce from them to Christ Church, Canterbury, to enable both their deaths to be properly commemorated there with regular intercessory prayer for the sake of their souls. She herself may have retired to a convent, or perhaps secluded herself back in the home of her natal family. Such a fate for a widow was far from unusual. Abba had left her a life interest in his lands, but had directed that ownership of those should be restricted to his male blood relatives. Abba's decisions exemplify a practice particularly common in, but not confined to, Anglo-Saxon England, a practice that channelled property from man to man through women. Heregyth and Abba's sisters could transmit the title but not hold it in their own right.

Occasionally, family circumstances might work out very much to a widow's advantage. The characteristic demographic profile of early medieval communities must have meant that it was not uncommon for adult children to die before their parents.[34] Whenever offspring who lacked children of their own predeceased their parents, their heirs were normally either siblings or parents. Reverse inheritance from children to parents is well attested, and may not have been all that unusual. An eleventh-century runic inscription from Hillersjö in Sweden reflects conventions widespread in northern Europe in the preceding two centuries. It runs as follows:

Read! Germund took Gerlög, a maiden, as wife. Then they had a son before he (Germund) was drowned and then the son died. Thereafter she had Gudrik as her husband. . . . Then they had children but only one girl survived, her name was Inga. Ragnfast of Snottsta had her as his wife. Thereafter he died and then the son. And the mother (Inga) inherited from her son. Then she had Erik as her husband. Then she died. Then Gerlög inherited from Inga her daughter. Torbjörn the skald carved the runes.[35]

Gerlög had outlived her first husband (Germund), her son by him, her second husband (Gudrik), her only surviving child by her second husband (her daughter Inga), her son-in-law (Ragnfast), and her unnamed grandson. Directly or indirectly, she was the heir to all of them. In the course of her long life, she accumulated by reverse inheritance from her own children the lands of her first husband, her second husband, and her son-in-law. Marriage normally transmits property from the older generation to the younger, and no one would plan for the grandmother to be the sole heir of all the wealth of the younger generations of her family. But, with all the uncertainties of mortality in the early Middle Ages, it could and, on this occasion, certainly did happen.

More commonly, widows found that their access to the property left to them by their husband either with a life interest or in outright ownership was contested by their dead husband's relatives. Abba had certainly foreseen that his brothers would prowl around his widow Heregyth, and had tried to co-opt their support for her. But, on occasions, the opposition might come not from the husband's kin, but from a woman's own son, eager to take immediate control of his paternal inheritance without having to wait for his mother to die. A famous dispute occurred at Aylestone in Herefordshire in the reign of Cnut (1016–35), when a man called Edwin brought a lawsuit against his unnamed mother. In consigning her to anonymity, the charter scribe nevertheless recorded that she successfully defended her right to bequeathe 'my land and my gold, and my clothing and my raiment, and everything I possess' to her kinswoman Leofflæd.[36] Such conflicts between a man's widow and his heir were hardly unusual, but, in all probability, widows won them infrequently. In this instance it may well have been the fact that Leofflæd was the wife of an important local landowner and power broker that enabled mother to fend off son.

Partible inheritance did not require a parent to divide land equally among heirs, whether sons and daughters, or just sons. The chances of squabbling were therefore high. Siblings might find themselves jockeying for more favoured treatment from one or both parents; cousins might also be eyeing lands formerly the possession of their common grandfather; the brother of a dead man might dispute with the adult sons of the deceased for control of his lands. Such tensions could spill over into hostility, even feuding, notoriously in Ottonian Germany. Although chronicles may narrate these familial animosities, charters normally only hint discreetly at them. An unusual example of frankness, and unusual too in revealing the strategies available to parents, comes from Spoleto, in central–southern Italy. Pando had given his wife Taneldis a life interest in his estate of *Cicilianus*, with directions to pass it on to their son Benedict if he behaved well towards his mother in her widowhood. But, Taneldis declared, Benedict 'insulted me and was hostile to me and inflicted many wrongs on me, as is known to many people', and so in 768 she gave his father's land in its entirety to the monastery of Farfa.[37] She doubtless acted not so much out of spite for her son but to secure her own income in her widowhood, for she nevertheless retained a life interest in the land that she had donated. Typical of many women who achieved relative security in their widowhood by associating themselves in one way or another with a monastery, Taneldis could live out her days assured of an adequate income and the assistance of an influential patron and protector in the person of the abbot of Farfa.

Although negotiating an elite marriage had always involved designating specific resources for a woman's maintenance, it was generally only in widowhood that she acquired direct control of its landed component. Like her marital endowment and her morning gift, any land she had inherited in her own right would have been administered conjointly with her husband's property for the duration of her marriage. Widowhood brought an end to 'conjugal domination' and inaugurated her direct access to landed resources, whether the widow enjoyed outright ownership of them or a life interest. For Taneldis, as for all the other identifiable early medieval women of property, access to land—and with that the potential for independent wealth and influence—came at a major turning point in the female life cycle. Indeed, wherever women did transfer property by written document in their own name, as Taneldis did, they only ever did so as nuns or widows, never as wives or daughters.[38] But widowhood might nevertheless entail social isolation, and it certainly left a woman vulnerable to challenge from the aggressive or the unscupulous. It is little surprise that Taneldis secured powerful and effective protection of her own interests.

The example of Taneldis makes the point that women's access to property in the early Middle Ages was conditioned by a complex cultural matrix, within which each woman had to negotiate as best she could. On the one hand, that matrix was influenced by local legal tradition, royal power, and ecclesiastical pressure. On the other, it was resolutely familial. Whereas men stood a chance of acquiring property from their lord or king as well as by inheritance, women generally had access to land only as a result of inheritance from their parents (and sometimes from their dead children) or under the terms of their marriage settlement. The effective result of this was to leave women as the conduit through which land was channelled from one generation to the next, or from a family to a church, with minimal opportunity for them to own it securely in their own name, unfettered by any other interests in it or claims to it. Women's access to property is therefore inherently an aspect of the wider question of men's strategies of heirship: once again, discussion of women cannot be separated from that of the families, natal and marital, to which they belonged.

However distinctive any particular family was—and no two families were ever the same in composition, ancestry, identity, or affections—all had roughly similar aims as they transmitted land from one generation to another. Two goals predominated. In the first place, families strove to maintain status from one generation to the next. Since status was in large part dependent upon access to wealth, the preservation of status called for the preservation of patrimony. For families who managed to raise more than one child to adulthood, however, the custom of partible inheritance and the familial frictions that it encouraged had to be carefully managed. Complementary to this goal, and of equal importance, once the Christian custom of prayer for the dead had become universal, was provision for commemoration of oneself and one's family in the afterlife. Liturgical commemoration made the dispersal of wealth an imperative, whether as charitable almsgiving or as endowments to monasteries. Strategies of heirship, then, had to be formulated to balance a range of competing priorities.

From at least the ninth century onwards, it is possible to glimpse some of those techniques and women's place in them. One obvious approach was to limit the number of heirs. Whether sexual self-restraint was practised in addition to the use of readily available herbal contraceptive or abortifacient agents cannot be said. What is clear, however, is that parents made decisions that directed their children either into a secular life of marriage, inheritance, and the perpetuation of the family or into a religious life of committed celibacy and asexuality. Born in 975, the historian Thietmar, bishop of Merseburg (1009–18), was the third of five sons of Siegfried, count of Walbeck, and his wife Kunigunde. The first two sons were raised for marriage and the life of an aristocratic warrior, the eldest succeeding to his father's countship in 991, the second achieving a more modest political career. Thietmar and his two younger brothers were all sent into the church and all eventually became bishops. The count of Walbeck thereby made a calculated gamble that, even if one of his secular sons died before producing an heir, the other would succeed and continue the family line. With three sons in the church, he was also attending to his family's spiritual needs.

Daughters too had an integral place in family plans. A century or so earlier, in 864, the ageing Eberhard, marquis of Friuli, and his much younger wife Gisela made a will, distributing their huge wealth in northern Italy, Alamannia, and Flanders amongst their children. The couple catches our attention for many reasons—and especially for the opportunity that their will affords for examining familial strategy in some detail. Of their five sons and four daughters, the eldest son, named after his father, had died in infancy. Of the surviving eight children, marriages were arranged for two sons, Unruoch and Berengar, and one daughter, Heilwig. A further two sons, Adalard and Rudolf, were sent into the religious life, becoming abbots of religious communities in Flanders. One daughter, named after her mother, was also dedicated to God and raised as a nun in northern Italy. The fate of the third and fourth daughters is unknown, but there are grounds for suspecting that they never married. In planning their children's futures, Eberhard and Gisela had shaped the family long before the time came for the children to inherit.

The testamentary disposition of their property evinces an equally firm parental strategy. Under the terms of their will, all eight surviving children stood to inherit precious objects and books from their parents; all except one daughter (of whom more in the next paragraph) received land as well. The lion's share of the patrimony, including all his father's land in Italy and Alamannia, went to Unruoch. As the eldest surviving son, he was intended to succeed to his father's political status and influence: as a token of this, he was allocated his father's sumptuous jewelled and gilded weaponry and gold-embroidered clothing, the symbols of high status and imperial office. The other three sons, two of them already in religious orders, all received much smaller portions of land in Flanders, as did Heilwig, the only married daughter. Her inheritance would have been indirectly intended for the grandchildren—and indeed, she was the only one of the three married offspring fortunate enough to succeed in raising another generation to adulthood.

The three children sent into the religious life also contributed to the family's future, for their share of the landed inheritance helped fulfil the family's need for religious commemoration. The gift of a child to a church established close links between parents and the religious house through the child; property conveyed via that child confirmed the link and made provision for intercessory prayer and Christian remembrance of all members of the family. Such arrangements rarely removed land entirely out of a family's sphere of influence: to the contrary, they established strongly reciprocal interests that often endured over generations. All this was at work in the planning undertaken by Eberhard and Gisela, and, since a daughter's monastic vow was customarily accompanied by a gift of land to the convent in question, provision for the religious daughter, Gisela, will have pre-dated her parents' will, whereas the property assigned in their will to Adalard and Rudolf simply took longer to enter ecclesiastical management. Of the three churches in question, one had strong associations with

Eberhard's family, another with Gisela's; the third they founded together at Cysoing, in Flanders. Eberhard and Gisela will have considered the land that followed Adalard, Rudolf, and young Gisela into their respective religious communities as effective an investment in their families' future as the estates distributed to their other children. Finally, we should note the place in these arrangements of the elder Gisela after her husband's death in 866. Widowed, she used her own inheritance to build up Cysoing as a place where the members of her family might be buried and remembered in prayer, and she appointed as its abbot first Adalard, then Rudolf. Some of her land was to be held by her sons before passing, on their death, to this family monastery, again meeting both the goals of immediate economic sustenance and long-term prayer.

In the generations after the deaths of Eberhard and Gisela, some aristocratic families began to develop another strategy for limiting the fragmentation of their property among an ever-expanding number of descendants. Tentatively and erratically, some experimented with appointing only a single heir and leaving the patrimony intact from one generation to the next. Precocious in this respect were the aristocratic families that rose to princely and even royal power as the Carolingian dynasty faltered after 888. Like their Merovingian predecessors, the Carolingian kings had tended to treat the kingdom as a partible familial inheritance. But the last few Carolingian kings, ruling western Francia from 898 until 987, had too little power or land to risk splitting it up. They, like the Ottonians who succeeded them as rulers of the East Franks, pioneered a tradition of appointing a single heir, leaving younger sons to find a career in the church or in service to their elder brother. A high-risk strategy, this laid the eldest son open to challenges and revolts by his siblings.

Where kings and princes led, aristocrats followed, especially in the heartlands of the former Carolingian Empire. Here, a gradual reconfiguration of the relationship between family and land began during the ninth century, encouraged by demographic and economic growth. By the twelfth century, elite families in north-western Europe commonly passed land undivided from father to one son, usually the eldest surviving one. The practice never became universal, however, for partible inheritance remained widespread in large parts of Europe up to the end of the Middle Ages and even beyond.

One thing never altered: access to land brought opportunities for status and influence. For men, that meant the possibility of participating in the political life of a kingdom, and seeking further reward in the service of a lord or king. For women, access to land as heiresses or widows certainly might bring influence, but it also reinforced vulnerability.

However wealthy, women could never combine their influence with formal office holding in royal government in the early Middle Ages. Institutional positions such as count, duke, sheriff, or reeve were bestowed on, or inherited by, men, as indeed were royal thrones, but women could only be the channel through which these offices passed from one man to another, their guarantor of status and legitimacy. Even when, from the late tenth century, counts' wives were increasingly referred to as 'countess', and when those of them whose widowhood involved governing on behalf of an infant heir began to use this as a formal public title, the shift in titulature did not signal any new ability to be appointed to office in their own right. Instead, it confirmed marriage and motherhood as the sources of their prestige and influence. Just as a queen might exercise huge political influence as the wife of a sickly or incompetent king or as mother of an under-aged monarch but could not inherit the throne or be elected to it in her own name, so, throughout the aristocracy, women's access to power came as wives, mothers, or widows. Landed wealth, then, might bring a woman wealth and influence; it could not bring her institutionalized power and authority.

Too much has been made in recent years of a shift in familial structures in the early eleventh century—from the amorphous, bilateral kin groups of the early Middle Ages to tightly focused patrilineal families in the high Middle Ages within which property passed from eldest son to eldest son to the increasing detriment of daughters and younger sons. To the extent that changes did occur, they happened neither abruptly nor universally, and were only ever one of a range of ways to accumulate land. Younger sons might maintain their status by finding an heiress to marry, receiving gifts from living relatives, benefiting from royal patronage, or finding other ways to acquire property—for example, by emigrating. Unexpected death might as easily upset a father's planned distribution of his lands in the twelfth century as it did in the eighth. From the perspective of women's place in familial strategies, they always remained the channel by which property flowed from one generation to another, and from one familial group to another. As daughters, they had just as good a chance of succeeding in default of brothers in the twelfth century as in the ninth. As wives, their marriage still required a carefully calculated property transaction agreed between their father and their husband. As widows, they remained in control of significant proportions of a family's land, vulnerable to others' interest in it but central to its transmission.

Family, sexual partnership, and, if wealthy, property inheritance: these formed the matrix within which early medieval men and women lived their lives. Despite changing notions of marriage, shifts in inheritance strategies, and wide regional variations in social practice, two themes have remained constant throughout this chapter. The first is the centrality of women to the affairs of their family. A girl dedicated to the religious life in childhood; a mother dead in her prime years and buried in a richly equipped grave; a magnate's daughter betrothed—then discarded—to suit her father's politics; a son's inheritance blocked by his mother; a wife's ride to Rome to save her marriage; a widow vacillating between the demands of her husband's relatives and shelter in a convent: all have emphasized the familial context of women's lives and the affinities that shaped them. The second theme is the disparities, sometimes negotiable, sometimes not, between women's experiences and men's opportunities. Despite the individuality of every family, the temperaments of individuals, the unpredictability of long life or early death, men were almost always at an advantage. Tacit social assumptions and explicit legal principles alike worked in their favour, whether in terms of sexual access to women and inherited access to land, or in terms of authority over their wives and daughters. Above all, when a boy was sent off into the household of an influential relative, his father's lord, or even the king, he left the immediate familial circle and started to find his way in a world where friends mattered as much as relations. For him, marriage and fatherhood supplemented other equally important affinities and political relationships.

As kings, magnates, and bishops, it was men who legislated, revised social norms, passed sentence. It was mostly they, or their subordinates, who copied charters, wrote histories and chronicles, composed moral treatises, delineated ideal social relationships. Legal, intellectual, and religious traditions inherited from the Roman world provided powerful justification for a world tilted in their favour. It is no wonder, then, that their voices are the loudest, or that many generations of historians found it easy to see the early Middle Ages as a man's world, or, at least, from men's perspectives. To some extent, this accurately reflected communities where men were indeed more likely to have far more wealth and power than women. But, as this chapter has stressed, there was often a considerable disjuncture between ideological expectations and social realities: we must not confuse or conflate them. If early medieval men and women occasionally found themselves hard up against stringent legal requirements or inflexible moral expectations, customary expectations and unvoiced assumptions shaped their interactions on a daily basis.

RESOURCES

5

Labour and Lordship

'What do you say, ploughman? How do you go about your work?'
  'Oh my lord, I work extremely hard. I go out at daybreak, driving
the oxen to the field, and I yoke them to the plough. There is no
winter so harsh that I dare linger at home, for fear of my lord. . . .
Yes, the work is hard because I am not free.'[1]

> Let each man cleave to his lord;
> let each man protect his territory.
> The top of each man is his lord;
> the root of each man is his territory.[2]

LAND, those who laboured on it, and those who lorded it over them are
themes that take us to the heart of social, economic, and political relationships. The overwhelming majority of Europe's inhabitants between
c.500 and c.1000 lived on the land and worked it directly: their lifestyle
was constrained by the physical toil needed to maintain the rhythms of
the agricultural year. Equally importantly, control of landed property and
the extraction of surplus produce were central to relationships between
individuals and groups. The previous chapter has shown how social distinctions between men and women in the early Middle Ages often turned
on differential rights over land; this one takes up the theme of social strati-
fication and the ways in which landholding underpinned untidy hierarchies of inequalities.

It contends that control over people and control over land cannot be
neatly separated. The combination was an essential aspect of political
organization in almost all early medieval communities, for lordship
embraced them both, separately or together. The owner of cattle, slaves,
or land was a lord by virtue of the power he exercised over them. So too
was the master of a household, by virtue of his authority over all members of his *familia*, from the most menial to the most distinguished.

Lordship was thus essentially a form of social power, rooted in relationships between persons and control of resources, especially land and livestock. As a term of address for a master, chieftain, king, emperor, or the Christian God, 'lord' acknowledged that power, implied deference, and showed respect for the one who was first and foremost. So a woman too could be a lord, when she controlled estates or ruled in her own name. In brief, early medieval inequalities were not simply those of material wealth and the lifestyle it brought, but of social influence and political power as well.

Our starting point is the straightforward observation that the groups into which people formed themselves in the early Middle Ages reveal differentials of resources, wealth, legal rights, and status, whether those groups were isolated village communities or large kingdoms and empires. These inequalities did not neatly correspond to each other, for legal rights were no guarantee of material wealth, any more than juridical rank reflected subjective perceptions of status. Although men and women lived in a world of domination and subordination, the gradient was never neatly ordered or systematized, except sometimes in the tidy-minded wording of law codes and schematic legal treatises. Rather, it resulted from the reality of power over others: those at the bottom were subordinated to those at the top by custom and tradition; legal constraints and sanctions; a wide range of forms of dependency and clientage; menacing behaviour and actual violence, or simply fear.

'The work is hard because I am not free': the ploughman's lament alerts us to the fact that the history of land, social hierarchy, and power also raises emotive issues of freedom and servitude. For this reason, it has often been contentious. History emerged as an academic discipline in an environment saturated with heated debates about the appropriate political order for modern times—absolutist or aristocratic, liberal or conservative, bourgeois or Marxist. Social theorists, polemicists, and historians alike found in the early medieval past harbingers of the freedoms they yearned for, causes of the oppressions they fought against, or justifications of the privileges they defended. In this atmosphere, they constructed schematic, generalized overviews of the early medieval centuries, and readily perceived them as either a golden age of peasant freedom or a crucible of exploitation and oppression—that is, a prelude to subsequent 'better' or 'worse' phases of human existence: the shadow of these older passions still lingers over debates about the early medieval peasantry.

The approach adopted here is different. It presumes that diversity of experience is characteristic of the early Middle Ages. Instead of seeking a unified story of the relationship of land, labour, and lords, it looks for varied localisms by following the fluid terminologies and multiple perspectives of the early medieval sources themselves. In referring to a wide range of political structures—large empires, small chiefdoms, compact, intensive polities, developing kingdoms—it argues that regional diversity and change over time were the hallmarks of all early medieval social hierarchies. The chapter starts at the bottom of the ladder by exploring slavery and serfdom and the implications of freedom. The first section argues that, although the distinction between free and unfree was of fundamental legal importance, social realities were far more complex than this neat antithesis suggests. The central section focuses on social inequalities organized around the control of land. In looking at the many different forms of lordship that touched peasants' lives, it argues for responsiveness to changing local situation and political context. The final section moves to the upper social echelons, to ask how high status was perceived, maintained, or contested, and how lordship also expressed political relationships.

Servitude and Freedom

'There is nothing other than the freeman or the slave': thus ran a Roman legal adage that Charlemagne found useful in adjudicating the status of children with one free and one unfree parent.[3] As in the ancient world, the distinction between freedom and servitude remained the fundamental legal cleavage in all early medieval communities. This was a pairing of opposites, a radical statement of juridical extremes. At its simplest, it distinguished the person inviolable in life and limb from the person whose physical well-being and existence remained at the mercy of others.

In practice, however, servitude and freedom did not constitute polar opposites. Rather, they formed the ends of a spectrum. Just as there were degrees of dependency, so there were degrees of freedom and the advantages it brought, for both servitude and liberty were relative notions. A sliding scale of domination and subordination ran the entire length of the spectrum: at the top, forms of dependency organized the elite's political relations with their ruler, and, at the bottom, structured the exploitation of the rural workforce. While the demeaning obligations imposed on the unfree lacked any honourable aspect, the service that a magnate rendered to a king enhanced status and honour. Both offered *servitium* to their superior. Service and lordship were two sides of the same coin at every point in the social gradient: only their form and social worth differed. In any case, dependency and freedom were not so much singular terms as bundles of restrictions and privileges that could be associated in many different combinations. Prominent among these were: freedom of movement;

5.1. Principal places mentioned in Chapter 5.

control over one's own body and its labour; the right to carry weapons; access to law courts; ownership of property; entitlement to marry or inherit; the recognition of one's own children; and the pursuit of honour. Each of these could be denied or recognized in more than one way, by judicial proceedings, custom, or social regard.

Crucially, however, one disability did not imply all of them. Wherever we look, we find a huge range of intermediate statuses that combine aspects of freedom with degrees of dependency. These defy classification; it is better to recognize the immense variety of local practice in this, as in so many other respects. It was possible to be servile yet of high status, as were the *adalschalks* (the 'noble unfree' of eighth-century Bavaria), and the *ministeriales* of late-tenth- and early eleventh-century Germany. Both groups lacked legal freedom but carried out honourable and skilled services for their lords. It was also possible to be free, yet dependent; we shall shortly meet examples of free men who made annual payments to a major church or monastery in recognition of its lordship.[4] A variant on this were the riding men (*radcnihts*, *geneats*) in western England in the tenth and eleventh century. These were propertied dependants, substantial enough to own horses, like those on the estates of Bath abbey at Tidenham, whose duties included the obligation to 'ride and furnish carrying service and supply transport and drive herds and do many other things'.[5] They were far from the condition of the slave girl whose lord was himself an unfree peasant and who exploited her sexually—and this suggests an even more abject female experience of subordination than men ever suffered.

Charlemagne's memorandum to his officials had used the traditional words for freeman and slave: *liber* and *servus*. The former is relatively straightforward: the *liber* enjoys liberties, in the sense of freedom to exercise certain rights, whatever his economic condition may be. The latter term is notoriously difficult. The ancient meaning of *servus* had been a chattel slave, an object possessed by a master, usually captured in war and imported from afar, who would be replaced by another human import when his working life ended. In the course of the early Middle Ages, it came to mean an unfree serf, recognized as a person though with minimal rights and, commonly, bound hereditarily to the land on which he laboured and on which, in due course, his offspring would work too. For much of this period, however, the word could mean either, or both. The new meaning did not displace the older one, and individual writers were not always consistent in exactly how they used the word. Nor is context always a reliable guide. There are two main reasons for the linguistic imprecision: first, its ancient meaning had specified a juridical condition but early medieval texts commonly used the word to describe a socioeconomic situation, not a legal one. Secondly, its shift in meaning was closely associated with changing ways in which lords used dependent labour to work their estates. For both these reasons, it has left a residue of controversy about whether the early medieval economy can be classified as a 'slave economy'.

The debate is unhelpful, for several reasons. Importantly, it risks reducing the social relations and agricultural economy of these centuries to a single, paradigmatic model and discourages appreciation of the immense variety of forms of dependency and unfreedom that coexisted even within a single locality. It also distracts attention away from a group of undoubted importance in many places, the free peasant proprietors, who are often hard to track in the sources except at the moment when they surrendered either their land or some of their freedom to a lord. Further, it tends to obliterate the wide range of other words in common use for dependent workers in Latin and in local languages, words that were used separately or in conjunction with *servus* and that had their own fluid meanings.

But the most important point is this: although the vocabulary of servitude hardly shifted, its social and political dimensions were quite different in the early Middle Ages from those of the ancient world. Some of the vast agricultural estates in Italy and other Mediterranean provinces of the Roman Empire had been worked by large gangs of imported slaves, who were housed in barrack-like conditions and denied any family life, but that method of exploitation and of human degradation had disappeared before the fourth century. Settled on individual plots of land, fourth- and fifth-century slaves came increasingly to resemble tied, dependent peasants in two ways: their recognition as persons, not objects, and their impoverished economic situation, social subjection, and heritable status. Yet there remained a fossilized juridical vocabulary, redolent of former times, that did not correspond with newer socio-economic realities.

By the time that early medieval records begin to show us the characteristic forms of lordship and subordination in any detail, agricultural slavery had become a thing of the past in the post-imperial provinces. In Christian regions of the Continent, the only slaves to be found were in aristocratic households and high-status urban residences, where they worked as either domestics or skilled craftsmen. By contrast, in England, agricultural slavery existed alongside other forms of servitude, as social practice and Old English vocabulary both make clear. Elsewhere in the British Isles and in Scandinavia, slavery formed the main source of unfree labour, its supply replenished by raiding and purchase. It persisted until northern French conquerors took their own traditions of agricultural exploitation and long-established moral strictures against the selling of humans to England after 1066, to Wales at the end of that century, and then finally to Ireland after 1169. The end of the slave trade points to a practical difference between early medieval serfs and slaves: although both could be put to work in the fields, the former generally remained tied to the particular estate on which they were born and were transferred with the land, whereas the latter could also be bought or sold in the marketplace, and made to work far from their place of birth.

Whether slaves or serfs, the unfree population entered lordly domination in various ways. As well as hinting at the harsh realities of subjection, these introduce us to some of the insecurities and uncertainties of life in the early Middle Ages. Many were subjected to a lord from birth, simply because their parents had been: from a lord's point of view, the distinction between freedom and servitude mattered most when, as commonly happened, sexual relationships or marriage across the legal gulf produced offspring whose status had to be decided. From a lord's perspective, the issue was to maintain control of the workforce. Some individuals lost their freedom as the penalty for a crime for which they were unable to scrape together the compensation owed; we have encountered others who gave themselves into servitude when desperate hardship and starvation made enslavement an acceptable price for a little grain and perhaps even some protection.[6] Being on the losing side in a war could result in capture and enslavement, and, indeed, around the periphery of Christian Europe, warfare and slave raiding were inseparable. 'I captured that slave beyond the border where the duke led the army': this declaration was adequate proof of ownership in eighth-century Bavaria.[7]

An individual could move back and forth between freedom and servitude, sometimes more than once in a lifetime. The altered status would touch future generations too, as this poignant text from northern England in the late tenth century bears testimony: 'Geatfleda has given freedom for the love of God and the sake of her soul [to] Ecceard the smith, Ælstan and his wife and all their children born and unborn, and to Arkil, Cole, Ecferth [and] Aldhun's daughter and all the people whose head she took for their food in those evil days.'[8] These starving men and women had stooped down, placing their heads between Geatfleda's hands to symbolize their subjection to her lordship: in return, she fed them. Later, she freed them in another, equally symbolic, ceremony at the altar of Durham cathedral.

Practised throughout Christian Europe and encouraged by the clergy as an act of piety, manumission was probably the most common way in which an individual's legal status was altered. Emancipation was nevertheless an act of lordship that, in religious terms, benefited the lord whose initiative it was. In legal terms, it removed several disabilities endured by the unfree person. On the Continent, Roman documentary forms were widely available, and the newly freed, clutching their charters, might be referred to as a 'charter-people'. In the British Isles, by contrast, records of manumission were commonly entered into Gospel books, and divine

sanctions invoked to uphold them. This is what the four sons of
Bleddri did in the early ninth century when they granted freedom 'in perpetuity' to Bleiddudd ap Sulien and his offspring. In the margins of an
old Gospel book kept in the church of St Teilo at Llandeilo Fawr in Wales,
they declared: 'Let he who keeps this grant of liberty to Bleiddudd and
his sons be blessed. But let he who does not keep it be cursed by God and
St Teilo, in whose Gospel this is written.'[9]

On other occasions, free status came not from lords but from servile
peasants' own actions. Reports of uprisings are rare in the extreme, but
references to the flight of individuals are much more common. Sometimes
a local church provided sanctuary—and, in these instances, flight was
probably a prelude to renegotiation with one's lord. On other occasions,
a nearby frontier provided an opportunity, and pacts regulating boundaries
between kingdoms sometimes made explicit provision for the return of
fugitives. In addition, anyone who aided and abetted the fleeing man or
woman was liable to harsh penalties. Since freedom of movement was
itself one of the marks of the free person, successful removal to a new
region might transform an individual's status. Less commonly, an enter-
prising lord in a sparsely inhabited region would offer freedom to all those
coming to settle there: thus, in 880, Wifred, count of Cerdanya, offered
freedom to all slaves or serfs who could escape their masters to settle south
of the Pyrenees in the frontier district of Cardona.

To win freedom was worth one's life savings or the perils of flight. To
defend it might be worth slaying an unfree relative who might disprove
one's status: Charlemagne prescribed the death penalty for anyone who
went to such lengths, and for good measure ordered that any free relatives
would fall into servitude too. But freedom could be defended by litig-
ation, especially since one of its privileges was access to royal law courts.
It also conferred the right to carry weapons. Freedom was not all advantages, however. It is as likely to have brought greater insecurity as any improvement in living conditions, for, in times of dearth, the independent,
free peasant had little chance of handouts from a lord's granary. So peasants who acquired their legal freedom often renegotiated another form of
subordination in return for their lord's continued protection. The legal
advantages and economic disadvantages of freedom were finely balanced,
since the distinction between freedom and servitude was slight by some
criteria but substantial by others, rendering the social barrier between the
two conditions permeable.

In principle, gaining freedom lessened the risk of being subjected to the
violence that accompanied subordination. While laws often stipulate
mutilations, floggings, and even capital sentences for serfs or slaves caught

stealing, damaging property, or breaching the peace, the equivalent pun-
ishments for freemen involved monetary compensation, although, in the
event that they were unable to meet it, they were liable to be reduced to
servitude. Beyond the remote world of legal prescription, however, lay a
more immediate culture of customary violence. Occasionally, law codes
themselves refer to it, such as this Bavarian provision: 'If a slavewoman is
maimed by any person in a way that causes her to lose the child she is
carrying, if it had not yet quickened, let him pay four *solidi* in compensation. If, however, it had already quickened, let him pay ten *solidi*.'[10] More
commonly, however, the fulminations of Christian moralists alert us to its
ubiquity. Only human society creates inequalities between persons, who
are all alike at the moment of birth, Jonas, bishop of Orleans (818–43), reminded Count Matfrid in about 820. 'Lords who are roused by their slaves'
mistakes to violent indignation and tremendous fury and who either beat
them with savage blows or mutilate them by cutting off their limbs' should
not be mistaken into thinking they could get away with it—but should
remember that there is only one God in heaven.[11] Such masters were unlikely to have cared much about the niceties of legal distinction between
an unfree serf and one whom he had freed but who remained in his
dependency. Precisions of legal status can have meant little when living in
extreme subjection meant living under the shadow of violence and, for
women, of sexual exploitation too.

In an effort to mitigate the more brutal realities of a hierarchical world,
late antique churchmen had preached the ethics of responsible power,
linking it to hopes of Christian salvation for the elite. One aspect of this
was emphasis on the redemptive effect of charitable giving. Bertechildis
was the wife of a notable at Bingen on the Rhine, who lived at an unknown point in the sixth or seventh century. She had absorbed this ethos,
and when she died aged 20, only one year into her marriage, an inscription was placed over her grave. It commemorated her pious generosity:
'loved by the people, she gave alms to the widows, orphans and the poor,
for the sake of her own sins.'[12] Such direct testimony to lay almsgiving is
rare, but it reveals what we know to have been common: a perspective that
attributed to the poor a role in assisting the salvation of the wealthy. By
accepting alms, the poor helped tilt the economy of salvation in favour of
the rich.

Early medieval bishops and moralists continued to take for granted the
existence of the *pauperes*, 'the poor', meaning not only widows, orphans,
and the impecunious, but all those who were vulnerable to exploitation
by the powerful and who lacked the resources of lordship with which to
defend their own interests. From the ninth century onwards, they broad-

ened the responsibilities towards the poor that they urged upon the
potentes, the powerful. The latter could not eliminate social inequalities,
but they could protect the poor; buy peasants' wine and grain at fair prices
and without rigging the measures; and give alms to the destitute—and, in
so doing, save their own souls.

The distinction between servitude and freedom, then, had social and
moral dimensions that were at least as important as any juridical difference or economic reality. Firm in legal theory, but highly permeable in
social practice, the one implied the possibility of the other. Lordship lay
at the heart of the relationship, for servitude presupposes domination, and
subjection was not restricted to those who were legally unfree. All early
medieval moralists accepted the gulf between the powerful and the poor.
They simply urged that each fulfil their allotted role and respect the rights
of each rank. In an ideal world, the unfree would labour to support the
free, and the lords would protect and defend everyone:

> For no free man can live without the unfree.
> When there's a job that they really want to see done,
> The king and bishops seem to serve their serfs.
> The lord is nourished by the serfs whom he should nourish.

In a Christian moral economy, lordship rested upon a careful use of power,
for it brought social responsibilities as well as rights, privileges, and wealth.
But Adalbero, the elderly bishop of Laon (977–*c*.1031), who penned these
lines in the early eleventh century, also knew better. He immediately
added:

> The groans and tears of the unfree have no end.[13]

The ploughman who dared not linger at home in the midwinter cold
would have agreed, and since, in an agricultural economy, lordship depended on the exploitation of land, we now turn to that.

Peasants and Lords

How then were social relationships organized around the need to produce
an agricultural surplus? In practical terms, how did peasant labour uphold
lords' position? What were the social and economic realities of lordship?
A remark of the fourth-century writer Palladius that 'there cannot be one
way of organizing the work when there are so many different types of
land'[14] offers a helpful starting point. Palladius explained this heterogeneity in terms of different soils and climates; we should add that practices varied from small to large estates, and that they changed over time

too. Late antique and early medieval landholding was characterized by a profusion of regional and local realities that we should keep in mind at all times.

One of those diversities was scale. Small-scale landowning was widespread but very unevenly distributed, mostly visible in the documentation only at the moment when ecclesiastical institutions took control of some or all of smallholders' property. Large-scale landowning was possible only within large polities, and the context of Palladius's observation was the huge size of late Roman elite landownership. Some members of the senatorial aristocracy of the western half of the empire had owned huge scatters of properties throughout the Mediterranean in the early fifth century, but the growing insecurity and the gradual collapse of unified Roman rule in the western empire in the course of that century eroded their landed fortunes: the establishment of the post-imperial kingdoms was accompanied by a shrinkage in the scale of property ownership.

The ending of Roman rule in the West had additional repercussions. In late Antiquity, the landed urban oligarchy of each region (the *curiales*) had been responsible for collecting taxes from proprietors of modest estates and independent smallholders, and passing their payments on to the state. Their intermediary role enabled them to extend their influence through extortion, threats, or false generosity. This is how Caesarius of Arles described what happened in early sixth-century Provence:

If [the rich man's] neighbor is a poor man who has been put in the position of having to sell or who can be pressured and forced into selling, his eye turns in that direction, and he hopes that he can take away either the estate or the tenant farm of his poor neighbor. He therefore inflicts troubles on him. For example, he secretly convinces those in power to have tax collectors entangle him or to appoint him to some ruinous public office. . . . Driven by necessity, [the poor man] goes to the rich man through whose wickedness he is being oppressed and afflicted, and ignorant of the fact that he is suffering because of his actions, says to him: 'I ask you lord to give me a few *solidi*, for I am in need; I am beset by creditors.'

Having tried to raise a loan, the poor man is finally forced to sell up. 'The rich man says that he will help his so-called friend', and buys the poor man out for far less than the true value of his land.[15]

As influential landowners interposed themselves between local men and the state, both peasant freeholders and small proprietors found their independence eroded. Their payments evolved into customary dues, and, on this basis, large landowners could gradually pull them into more tightly defined and subordinated positions of dependency. The transition from small freeholder to dependent peasant was rarely reversible; great estates expanded everywhere between the sixth and eleventh centuries, and small men lost out.

The process was hastened in another way. Insecurity in the fifth and sixth centuries blurred the difference between the parallel civilian and military professional cadres of the fourth century. Standing garrisons gave way to peasant militias, landowners began to offer armed protection to their tenants in times of invasion and insecurity—or to run protection rackets themselves. To ensure their own position, landlords became war-lords. And, following the precedent of the settlement of a Gothic war-band in Aquitaine in 418 (Figure 0.2), several armies originating north of the imperial frontiers were relocated under their own leaders in the coun-tryside of western Roman provinces, perhaps initially only drawing a por-tion of the tax revenue generated by rural estates, but sooner or later developing into a landowning military elite. This further enhanced the control of a lord over his dependants and neighbours. Thus the associ-ation between social elites and military leadership that characterized European society throughout the Middle Ages and beyond was cemented during the rapid changes that accompanied the disintegration of the Roman political order.

Relations between peasants and lords always implied a wider political environment. Military service, royal patronage, and, at times, additional financial levies had a direct effect on the leading men who had found their way into their rulers' entourage. Indirectly, peasants felt the impact, for the pressures of lordship trickled down to them in various ways. Shifting settlement patterns in north-western Europe in the seventh and eighth centuries are suggestive of tighter lordly control, probably coupled with demands for larger renders of produce and higher dues, and also enhanced artisanal production of specialist items. Peasants must have been adversely affected, although the details are elusive. By the late eighth century, lords were commonly demanding direct labour services as well, certainly in the Carolingian heartlands and possibly elsewhere. Although there was always pressure on peasants to produce more than sufficed for their own subsist-ence, so that the lord could profit from the surplus, trends in estate man-agement nevertheless varied, and, by the tenth and eleventh centuries, it seems that many lords preferred rents and payments in kind to direct labour services.

Beyond these generalities, we know frustratingly little about the details of secular landownership in the early Middle Ages, because no lay or royal collection of title deeds, charters, surveys, or estate memoranda has re-mained intact. Documents issued by the laity have generally survived only when they accompanied donations of property to churches. The archives that have endured are those of cathedrals and monasteries: as the following pages demonstrate, our fullest perspective on landownership and exploitation is thus an essentially ecclesiastical one. As we proceed, we can nevertheless keep an eye on relations between secular lords and their peasants.

Wherever the Christian religion was established, major churches had been acquiring land since the fourth century. Early phases are extremely hard to trace in any detail, in part because papyrus, the main late antique material for record keeping, is easily perishable. It is clear, however, that the rate of pious donation increased sharply from the early eighth century, as strategies for the disposition of familial resources shifted and the search for posthumous religious commemoration became more urgent. The spread of document-mindedness that accompanied this upsurge coincided with a switch to the highly durable medium of parchment in many parts of Christian Europe, and, as a result, both lay donation and ecclesiastical landholding become very much more easily visible from the eighth century onwards, especially on the Continent.

By the ninth century, approximately one-third of all cultivated land in the Carolingian Empire belonged to churches, although there was wide regional variation and not all these estates were retained in the long term. In England, on the eve of the Norman Conquest, the figure was similar—about one-quarter of all land. These imprecise, but nevertheless striking, figures have several implications that deserve attention.

First, as their landed wealth grew, churches became central to the economic organization of the landscape and its inhabitants. Regional specialization on ecclesiastical estates—in wine, salt, or wool, for example, and artisanal manufacture of cloth, pottery, and the like—gave a major impetus to regional and inter-regional trade. From the wealth that churches derived from their property, they also acquired ever-growing political clout. No study of lordship can afford to ignore this institutional dimension.

Secondly, whereas secular landed property was liable to be redivided, reallocated, and contested on the death of each owner, ecclesiastical estates commonly enjoyed enduring institutional ownership. To be sure, spasmodic and piecemeal rapacity by kings and local bigwigs caused losses, but, even so, a lord who was notorious for seizing the land of one church was often commemorated as a generous benefactor by a different one. A lesser form of attrition came through the tendency of tenancies to become hereditary; it took continual managerial vigilance and strong-mindedness to limit this form of quiet erosion. But nevertheless, ecclesiastical estates were on the whole islands of relative stability in a sea of tenurial fluidity. Supported by long institutional memory in the form of carefully stored archives of title deeds, church lands had a far greater permanency than early medieval secular estates.

Finally, because churches had developed into propertied institutions under imperial aegis, they functioned in accordance with late Roman property law. Wherever they went in the early Middle Ages, Christian missionaries took with them its presumptions of individual title in full ownership, forms of written documentation, and technical vocabulary. These often cut across traditional property relations, especially where rights over land were closely tied to membership of a kin group and were preserved in social memory by oral tradition. Everywhere from the mountainous hinterland of Rome itself to the rolling hills of Ireland, the Romanizing language of early medieval records frequently obscures tenurial practices considerably adapted to indigenous conventions.

For many reasons, then, relations between lords and dependent workers, whether slave, serf, or free, conform to no single pattern. Some customs were fairly widespread, but there was no norm, no paradigmatic system. Multiplicity, fluidity, and evolution were the hallmarks of early medieval landed estates, and we must recognize this. Since the spectrum of practices does not lend itself to summary presentation or representative examples, there follows a single case study chosen to illustrate this diversity.

The area in question is northern Flanders, and is shown in detail in Figure 5.2. Just within the former Roman border, it straddled the early medieval (and modern) linguistic frontier zone between Germanic speech and *lingua romana*. For the moment, our concern is with a religious community founded between 629 and 639, and dedicated to St Peter. Its site was the hill called *Blandinium*, overlooking the old Roman settlement of Ghent at the confluence of the rivers Scheldt and Leie, and close to the

5.2. Landowners in ninth-century Flanders. This map indicates the intermingling of the estates of Ghent's two abbeys, St Peter's and St Bavo's, along the rivers Leie and Scheldt. St Peter's, in particular, attracted many small donations here, consisting of tiny fields interspersed with meadows and, on the slightly higher ground, woodland. By contrast, the large estates of southern and western Flanders included extensive areas devoted to grain growing. Sheep pasturage in the coastal salt marshes was eagerly acquired by all monasteries, including more distant ones such as St Amand and Lobbes. In addition to Eberhard and Gisela, many other lay persons doubtless owned land in the region, but this is much harder to document.

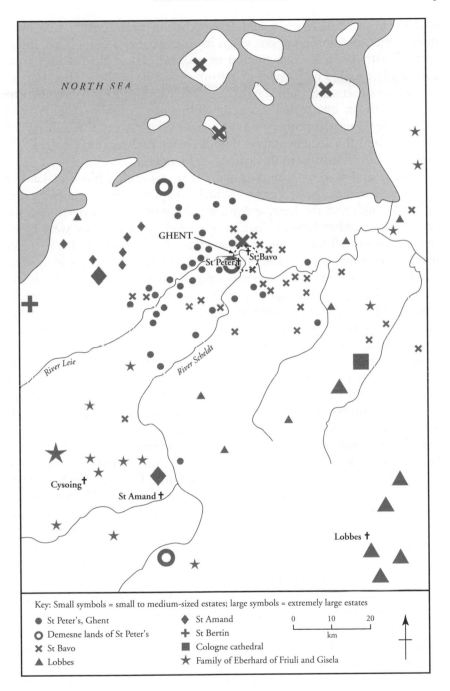

NORTH SEA

GHENT

St Peter's †St Bavo

River Leie

River Scheldt

Cysoing †

St Amand †

Lobbes †

Key: Small symbols = small to medium-sized estates; large symbols = extremely large estates

● St Peter's, Ghent
○ Demesne lands of St Peter's
✕ St Bavo
▲ Lobbes

◆ St Amand
✚ St Bertin
■ Cologne cathedral
★ Family of Eberhard of Friuli and Gisela

0 10 20
km

spot where a trading centre would develop by the ninth century. Like most monasteries, it enjoyed periods when its endowment accumulated, interspersed with periods of stagnation or erosion. These fluctuations were commonly coupled with cycles of 'reform'—that is, of the overhaul of ecclesiastical observances and standards of behaviour of its inhabitants conducted with an eye to widening the difference between religious and secular life. Over the centuries, St Peter's at Ghent went through several of these; from the documentation that has been left we can trace the shifting patterns of lordship in this corner of Flanders.

Initially endowed by King Dagobert (623–39) with a block of land in its immediate vicinity, St Peter's gradually acquired other estates further up the Scheldt and the Leie, and among the forests to the north and the coastal salt marshes beyond. As Figure 5.2 indicates, its lands were modest, and almost all lay within 30 kilometres of the abbey church—unlike many other monasteries, whose possessions were much more widely scattered. Later Merovingian kings seem not to have maintained interest in the new church. By the eighth century, as rival magnate power brokers contested for control over northern Gaul, St Peter's tried but failed to remain neutral. Inevitably, perhaps, it became sucked into the patronage of one of them, but seems to have lost lands in consequence.

Royal control was reasserted in the reign of Charlemagne. For St Peter's, Ghent, as for many other monasteries and cathedrals, Carolingian lordship brought immediate access to the royal court in any lawsuits. Further, within its own lands, the abbot substituted for local imperial administrative and judicial officials: in effect, he became the king's agent here. By the same token, Carolingian control meant vulnerability and obligation, as became evident when Louis the Pious appointed a new abbot in 815, whose task was to 'reform' the community. This was Einhard, loyal courtier, famous biographer of Charlemagne, and layman. He represented royal lordship within the very confines of the community, and was the channel through which the emperor tapped into the monastery's wealth. Administering some of its landed estates for personal or imperial advantage, Einhard nevertheless set aside specified lands for the upkeep of the twenty-four clerics who resided in St Peter's. He carefully registered their share, and associated documentation reveals how this particular ecclesiastical community organized and exploited its lands.

Although Einhard or one of his ninth-century successors as abbot assigned to the brothers a farm nearly 50 kilometres to the south, most of their land lay adjacent to the abbey itself, a modest unit comprising arable, hay meadows, a wood where pigs were kept, and part of a tiny vineyard. Associated with this were outlying sheep pastures in the coastal salt marshes. All this was called the *terra indominicata*, the demesne, meaning that it would be cultivated directly for the profit of its lord, in this case the community of St Peter's. The clerics also had assigned to them a larger block of land, adjacent to their demesne, which had formed part of the original seventh-century endowment. How it had been organized then remains unknown, but it is clear that by the early ninth century the tenurial arrangements had evolved considerably. By then, it was subdivided into units each cultivated by a dependent worker who had specified obligations to fulfil.

Let us look at one particular dependent, Folcric, who held one unit of land, one *mansus*. Each year he owed the abbey specified quantities of bread, beer, pigs, wood, roofing shingles, flax, eggs, and grain. In addition, every third year he paid two *solidi* (= 24 pennies) at harvest time instead of contributing his own labour to the demesne, on one of the intervening years he paid another two *solidi* towards meeting the abbey's military expenses, and in the other year he had no cash payments to make, only a shirt to stitch. Since we know neither the size of Folcric's *mansus*, nor whether he had a wife and children to help him, we cannot estimate the severity of these obligations, nor calculate how much produce would have been left to feed himself and any family. But we can be sure that bailiffs would have ensured that the brothers received a steady supply of bread, beer, and other produce; and that their managerial tactics would include graft, extortion, and flogging.

Folcric's daily routine must have been bounded by the fields he tilled, the woods he visited to chop and cart wood, and the flax he harvested for (presumably) his wife to make into linen cloth and then clothes, but he was nevertheless part of a much larger and more complex economy. His predecessors in the days of Charlemagne had possibly been subjected to labour services on the demesne, but, if so, these had been converted into a cash payment by Folcric's time. In the late eighth and ninth centuries, dependent peasants frequently owed labour services (of varying onerousness) on an estate's demesne, thus integrating the different parts of an estate, but this was far from universal. Landlords might substitute demands for cash in a move to exploit their lands more effectively and to provide a more flexible income. But they could do so only when peasants had access to a market where they might exchange small quantities of surplus produce for silver pennies. Living so close to the growing market centre of Ghent itself, St Peter's dependants evidently had no difficulty with this, especially after the establishment of a royal mint there after 840.

Beyond Folcric's fields, the local market, and the control over his life exercised by the abbey, royal power made itself felt. In paying two *solidi* every three years towards St Peter's military commitments, Folcric contributed to the cost of the Frankish army. Although details of the ways in which troops were levied in the ninth century remain controversial, great ecclesiastical landowners and secular aristocrats alike had to provide contingents. The core of each group was probably the landowner (or, in the case of a church, its lay representative), with his retinue of heavily armed, mounted followers. The impact of military obligation can be glimpsed at St Peter's. The fifty cartloads of hay produced each year by the demesne meadow would have sustained horses through the winter, as would the oats grown on part of the demesne. Some of the timber received from tenants may have been directed to the upkeep of the coastal defence fleet that had been built at Ghent in 810. And did the abbot pool the small sums the abbey's many dependants each paid and use the proceeds to buy in the equipment, pack animals, and warhorses needed to send heavily armed, mounted warriors off to the army? Or had he contracted to pay a regular lump sum into royal coffers in lieu of actually sending troops? From Folcric's point of view, it can have mattered little: he simply had to pay up. In this and other ways, the abbey's lordship mediated between himself and the ruler.

Some twenty-four other dependants each held a *mansus* on identical or similar terms to Folcric. During and after Einhard's abbacy, St Peter's acquired further plots of land for the clerics' own use that were organized on the same basis of demesne with dependent tenancies. The records of these gifts indicate that along with the land came its workforce, and that the peasants passed from the lordship of the donor to the beneficiary. These men and women can only be described as servile. Their children came with them, and inherited their status. By the end of the ninth century, the marks of their extreme subordination to the abbey were even clearer: in addition to their annual obligations, they had to make a payment when they married, and another upon their death. St Peter's domination thus had three chief qualities: it was patriarchal in that it touched all members of the monastic *familia*; patrimonial in that it was exercised over the entire monastic landed endowment; and obligatory in that it could not be avoided. Whether the lord was a church, a secular lord, or a king, these were the three main characteristics of all early medieval lordship.

Other men and women stood in quite different relationships to St Peter's. The demesne lands were farmed by twenty-nine unmarried people—young men and women and a few milkmaids to whom no individual plots of land had been assigned, and who must have been housed in the abbey's outbuildings. Whether we choose to call them serfs or slaves does not affect their position of total dependency. At the other end of the spectrum, some people enjoyed much looser and more honourable relationships with the abbey. Several 'free men' owed only substantial cash payments accompanied by limited dues in kind, usually of beer. They may have held tenancies on a basis whose details elude us. Or they may have been small freehold proprietors on land that had once been under loose subordination to the king but who now paid their customary dues to the abbey instead. Ecclesiastical lordship sat fairly lightly on these men, but St Peter's nevertheless asserted rights over their land and its profits.

Different again were the relationships between the clergy and some recent donors. Nordbert was one such: he had purchased an estate that he gave to St Peter's. But then in 830 he arranged with Einhard to continue to occupy and profit from the land, in return for the nominal annual sum of twopence in recognition of the abbey's lordship. Only on his death would the clergy acquire direct control: until that moment, Nordbert and the clergy had overlapping rights over the estate. Such an arrangement was made to the church's advantage, or benefit, and the land in question commonly designated a 'benefice'. Those advantages would have been social and political rather than economic. Did Nordbert act as Abbot Einhard's armed escort or fight in St Peter's detachment of troops? Did he use his influence in local affairs to protect and foster the abbey's interests? Might Einhard have used his position to help Nordbert? We shall see in the next chapter that he did that for others of his personal followers. These speculations simply reflect what we know of similar benefices elsewhere in the ninth century, but they also remind us that lordship could be about personal loyalty and political service as well as about managing land. It consisted of a spectrum running from economic exploitation through social links to political patronage.

Thus the relations between the community of St Peter's, Ghent, and its dependants fit no single, simple pattern. There were many ways of organizing the land and its workforce. A shrewd abbot such as Einhard was flexible, balancing local custom with a drive for efficiency. The natural resources available provided one set of opportunities and constraints, the accessibility—or remoteness—of markets another. It suited the abbey to impose heavy renders and obligations on some men and women, much lighter ones on others. The effective lord responded to changing circumstances, whether economic, demographic, or political; individually and collectively, lords' decisions helped shape a changing society.

How did the lands of St Peter's fit into the pattern of landowning in northern Flanders as a whole? There were other major landowners in the vicinity, notably the much richer abbey of St Bavo located at Ghent itself, whose lands up and down the Scheldt and Leie intermingled with those of St Peter's. For the most part, however, small-scale proprietors dominated the locality, each man or woman owning a few small fields that they worked with the assistance of a couple of dependants, or at most five or six. Fragmented landholdings were the rule: wealthier owners held their properties scattered in several locations. The overall effect was a patchwork of tiny fields and meadows cut out of the woodland, with water meadows along the rivers. And, as these peasant proprietors made their small donations to St Peter's, so the abbey's acquisition of a field here and a field there contributed another element to the changing landscape.

The valleys of the Leie and Scheldt were ideally suited for growing flax, and were notable for their very heavy concentration of linen production. Elsewhere in Flanders, the natural environment and its modes of exploitation differed, as Figure 5.2 makes clear. To the north, in the coastal salt marshes and peat bogs and on the islands in the Scheldt estuary, St Bavo's owned estates each large enough to support upwards of 1,000 sheep. Perhaps, like the monasteries with sheep-ranching interests further up the coast in Frisia, they made few demands on the peasants here, except for annual renders of finished cloth, for pastoral economies generally encouraged very different forms of lordship.

To the north-east, as well as to the south up the Scheldt around Tournai, lay some of the lands that Eberhard and Gisela would distribute in their will.[16] These were large, intensively farmed agricultural estates, which in all probability had been royal land for centuries until assigned to Gisela as her dowry by her father, Louis the Pious. They followed a mixed agricultural regime, producing several types of grain but also raising cattle, large numbers of pigs, and some sheep, in addition to poultry— and even peacocks.

Also to the south-west, the abbey of St Bertin was another major landowner. In the gently undulating countryside of southern Flanders, St Bertin had huge cereal-growing estates whose tenurial arrangements had been systematized in the first half of the ninth century. This monastery's peasants had a more onerous relationship with their lord than those of St Peter's, Ghent. In addition to specified payments and renders, each holder of a *mansus* was required to work three days a week on the abbey's demesne if he was servile, two days a week if he was free. This was the most efficient way of farming large cornfields. If there had ever been farms belonging to independent peasant proprietors here, they had disappeared by the mid-ninth century, swallowed up by their powerful ecclesiastical neighbour.

We can let this corner of Flanders stand as a microcosm of early medieval rural society as a whole. It demonstrates the interplay of arable and pastoral economies: although they complemented each other throughout Europe as a whole, few regions were as intensively devoted to sheep raising as the Flemish and Frisian coast—or to grain as the cereal-growing estates that stretched southwards from Flanders to the Paris basin. Inter-regional trade redistributed their surpluses; elsewhere other specialist regional products, such as wine or salt, were also transported to markets considerable distances away. Flanders also reminds us of the economic importance of woodland—here for both timber and fodder for pigs. And, above all, it demonstrates the ways in which tenurial regimes adapted to different environments. In this particular region, the forms of control over dependent labour varied according to the differing requirements of animal husbandry and tillage; in Mediterranean Europe, the cultivation of vines and olives was characterized by other, more suitable forms of tenure and, in the next chapter, we shall encounter quite different ones again in the cattle country of Ireland.

Throughout Europe, lords exploited their local natural environment as best they knew, controlling peasants and other dependants by balancing local possibilities with their own changing priorities. But we should also remember that they responded to the wider political environment as well. Einhard's administration of St Peter's, Ghent, was characteristic of the heyday of the Carolingian Empire, when royal patronage was the dynamo that temporarily converted fluid regional networks of lordship into an exceptionally large polity. By the end of the ninth century, however, the Frankish polity was in crisis, the result of competition for power within the royal dynasty rapidly followed by the failure to produce male heirs. In the mid-ninth century there were too many kings' sons, each hopeful for a kingdom, but by the end of the century not enough to maintain existing subkingdoms. As the dynamo faltered, regional elites turned to different power brokers and reconfigured themselves into multiple, smaller polities.

Flanders was one of these, its counts related by marriage and common political interests to the last Carolingians, the tenth-century West Frankish kings. By the end of the ninth century, Ghent emerged as the central stronghold from which the counts ruled a nascent polity, basing their power in a new wooden castle there. Within its confines, they behaved as power brokers in exactly the same ways as the Carolingians had done within their empire, and managed to maintain an effective grip on the ebb and flow of patronage—of land, office, and honour—within their region until the twelfth century.

With that in mind, we can return to the clergy of St Peter's, the secular landowners and peasantry of the vicinity, to see how the changing political context affected relations between peasants and lords. Another phase of 'reform' in the 940s has left a deposit of documentation that suggests not only losses of properties to be recovered, but also a rapidly changing world. St Peter's was now governed by Count Arnulf I (918–65) in his capacity as patron and lay abbot, and Ghent was a rapidly developing town. In 941, for example, Count Arnulf's benefactions to St Peter's included revenues from town houses and levies on cargo boats that passed through the port. Outside the town, the landscape was changing too, as lordship acquired a new, commercial, dimension. Mills were being built, and sheep raised in vast numbers throughout Flanders: St Peter's profited from both. As the tenth and eleventh centuries progressed, Arnulf's successors did much to encourage the clearance of woodland and the draining of the coastal floodplain.

We can deduce the implications for the Flemish peasantry. They found themselves participating in a growing cash economy, for lords now preferred money payments to labour services or renders in kind. Mills meant an end to the domestic grinding of corn and the release of peasant labour, usually female, for other tasks. But they also meant the obligation to pay for their use, an example of the spread of lordly 'customs' that created new forms of subordination. Land clearance implied a growing population, altered dealings with lords, and a degree of rural mobility. Other peasants must have been leaving the countryside altogether, for the rapid growth of Ghent and other Flemish towns can only have been the result of immigration from the countryside, with all its dislocating effects. Those that remained in the countryside will have been involved in producing enough food to feed the townsfolk as well as their families and lords. Finally, the emergence of an urban artisanal cloth industry introduced new forms of labour and lordship.

In these various ways, Flemish peasants were touched by wider economic currents and by the changing lordship of St Peter's abbey and the counts of Flanders. Though these developments were specific to the region around Ghent, peasants everywhere were caught up in and affected by the spread of lordly 'customs' and the ever-shifting networks of political power among the elite. We cannot ignore the great diversity of these customs by generalizing any more than this, for all lords, secular or ecclesiastical, instituted their own preferred techniques of extracting surplus from the land to sustain their lordly position. That different routes led to similar outcomes would not have surprised contemporaries. After all, an early eleventh-century Anglo-Saxon writer on estate management had echoed Palladius when, after summarizing the organization of a particular property, he continued: 'This estate-law exists on certain estates; at some places, as I have said, it is heavier, at some places also lighter; for all estate-customs are not alike. . . . He who looks after the administration is to take care that he always knows what is the ancient arrangement of the estate, and what the custom of the people.'[17] Local custom in a changing world: this was the matrix within which peasants answered to lordly domination.

In Search of Status

'Tell me, in what do your riches lie?' the tenth-century moralist Rather of Verona (d. 974) asked a fictional rich man in a literary dialogue. 'In my possession of estates, male serfs and female slaves, horses, oxen and other animals, in the obedience of my followers, in my delight in dogs and hawks, in my abundance of clothes, fine tableware, grain, wine and oil, of arms, silver, gold, jewels.'[18] Landed property, a servile workforce, a loyal retinue, costly possessions, and ostentatious display: the rich man's reply suggests the complexities of achieving high social status. He was asked about riches, and answered by combining power over people and material resources in just the way that was typical of lordship, as we have seen. He alluded to the lifestyle he so enjoyed, one of hunting, feasting, personal finery, and other forms of conspicuous consumption that set him apart from others. Naturally, his words presume a hierarchical view of human relationships, from the slave to the wealthiest, most powerful lord. This section explores some implications of this self-perception for those at the top of the early medieval social order.

Great diversity was also to be found at the upper end of the scale. Those who were designated by a wide variety of terms that simply mean leading men, bigwigs, the powerful, the best (*primores*, *potentes*, *optimates* in Latin; there is an equivalent range of terms in Old English and other languages) enjoyed the greatest possible cluster of liberties, but even so served a princely, royal, or imperial lord. Lesser notables, well-to-do free men who enjoyed privileges on a regional level, served them sometimes voluntarily, sometimes under duress. In some places, tight hierarchies bound each group tightly to those above and below, but, in others, the contacts, obligations, and forms of service were looser and lighter. Additionally, those who served a lord renowned for territorial expansion had quite different opportunities from those whose lord ruled a stable, or even shrinking polity, for royal or princely patronage depended, in part, upon available resources.

Take four men whom we have encountered earlier, all alive in the 830s: Abba, Eberhard, Riwalt, and Nordbert.[19] Riwalt and Nordbert were both locally substantial men who nevertheless chose to enter into dealings with an important local church, Riwalt with Redon and Nordbert with St Peter's, Ghent. In Brittany, any superior lordship sat very lightly on local landowners such as Riwalt, but, as we have just seen, tightening obligations of lordship were affecting Flanders in Nordbert's day. Abba and Eberhard both served their king directly, the former as reeve of Kent, the latter as marquis of Friuli, but the scale of their landholding, wealth, and political influence bears no comparison. Powerful and wealthy though he was in Kentish terms, Abba was puny in contrast with Eberhard of Friuli. The latter's family ranked among the Carolingian super-elite, and this had enabled his father and himself to benefit from the Franks' territorial expansion under Charlemagne, resulting in landed possessions stretching from Flanders to Italy.

Other than ownership of land, there is little in common between these four elite men and their families, except the fact that they all used land to establish an association with churches—and that, indeed, is why we know about them. The diversity suggests we should look carefully into what additional markers of status there may have been in the early Middle Ages. We shall see that the vastly disparate resources and variable terminology reflected the social fluidity of the upper echelons, and the lack of any firm criteria for membership of the elite. In the absence of any precise prescription for gaining or losing high status, we have to search for it in various ways. So, as we shall see, did early medieval men.

In the first place, it was visible to others. Leovigild, king of the Iberian Goths (568–86), gave an estate near Merida to an abbot called Nanctus, to support his monastic following. Its inhabitants went to visit their new master, and were appalled: 'When they went and had seen him in his wretched clothes and with his hair uncut, they despised him and said to one another, "it would be better for us to die than serve such a master"'— so a few days later they killed him.[20] For Nanctus, lack of personal grooming was a sign of asceticism, but his workers were not prepared to serve a master who looked like an abject slave, however holy he might be. A master had to look the part.

In addition to appearance, deportment and speech also conveyed high rank, as the seventh-century Northumbrian Imma found out. Taken prisoner in battle by the Mercians in 679, he pretended that he was not a king's retainer but only a poor peasant. His captors kept a close eye on him and, after a while, 'realized by his appearance, his bearing, and his speech that he was not of common stock as he had said, but of noble family'.[21] Evidently, attendance at the royal court promoted elegant manners and refined speech as well as the dress code that set the elite apart from peasants.

Courtliness fostered a distinct appearance in other ways too. By the time of Charlemagne at the latest, the royal entourage dressed with an eye to fashionable display, investing in costly silks and furs, together with jewelled, gilded weapons for the men and brooches, armbands, girdles, and necklaces for the women. Louis the Pious had to persuade his bishops and abbots—almost all of them men of high birth—not to dress like secular nobles. He urged them to give up 'the ornaments of secular glory'—namely, 'belts weighed down with golden sword-mountings and jewelled daggers, exquisite clothing and footwear decorated with spurs'.[22] These were exactly the prestigious items that Eberhard of Friuli bequeathed to his children and that, as we shall see in the next chapter, were used to cement bonds of patronage and favour. All signalled elite status, but sword belts had a special significance, for, jewelled or plain, they were badges of office as well. And this form of courtliness was catching: the trend that began at the Carolingian imperial court developed still further at the Ottonian court, and both set a fashion for luxurious high-status apparel that others emulated elsewhere. By the late tenth century at the latest, Anglo-Saxon kings and queens together with the nobles and their wives were following suit, dressing in patterned silks with ample gold embroidery overlaid with jewellery and heavy furs.

Attention to display extended to fine mounts and their harnesses, decked out with 'decorated medallions'.[23] Only the 'most renowned horses', plump, strong, and 'praiseworthy in every aspect', would do for Pope Hadrian I (772–95) to ride in processions.[24] And when (between 1036 and 1038) the 50-year-old Boniface of Canossa journeyed across the Alps to collect Beatrix, his bride of about 18, he shod his horses in silver. He deliberately attached the shoes so loosely that they were shed en route for the local populace to gather up: 'this way the people might find out who he was.'[25] No opportunity was lost to make status obvious.

Fine food was another aspect of elite lifestyle, as we saw earlier.[26] In addition to game and the succulent meats of domesticated animals reared especially for slaughter, a well-stocked table had fish from the sea, such as porpoise and herring, and dishes prepared with imported spices. It had all these in great abundance: to judge by preachers' complaints, bigwigs liked to eat and drink to excess. Despite this, food intake could, in principle, mark out graduations of status, for, when Louis the Pious specified the rations for his representatives going about imperial business, he stipulated precisely 'how much should be given to each according to his rank', whether bishop, abbot, count, or retainer.[27]

Membership of the elite also implied social distance. One expression of that was a personal retinue of armed men, domestic officials, and hangers-on. Another might be a defended residence, such as the tenth-to eleventh-century Anglo-Saxon hall at Goltho, where the main hall, outbuildings, and courtyard were enclosed by an earthwork rampart and ditch. It also demanded deference and the avoidance of threatening gestures. 'Servants are accustomed to hand knives to their masters [holding them] by the tip of the blade.'[28] Careful tactics might reinforce hierarchy: Tagino, archbishop of Magdeburg (1004–12), simply preferred 'nobility of lineage and manner' and declined to admit the low-born into his company.[29] Social climbers set out to erode that distance, however, for to emulate nobility was to court the deference due to it. Thus estate stewards of the monastery of St Gall 'learned to blow their horns in a way that made a different sound from the other peasants' and started carrying polished weapons and going hunting with dogs—at first just hares, but then even wolves, bears, and boars. '"The cellarers can look after the fields and meadows," they said. "We must look to our own advantages and indulge in hunting, as befits real men."'[30]

Elite status, then, implied a lifestyle and mores characterized by personal display and conspicuous expenditure. An eighth-century Irish treatise, surely over-systematizing but nevertheless true to its spirit, sums this up. The man who had twenty-seven clients in his retinue, a house 29-foot long with a 19-foot outhouse, lavish furnishing including eight beds and couches with cushions and rugs, a cauldron in his kitchen large enough to stew an entire ox, twelve gilded bridles and hunting dogs, and whose wife had a pet lap-dog, was a 'noble of the first rank'.[31]

In these terms, the fictional rich man with whom we opened had a good claim to be regarded as elite. He had the necessary wealth, lifestyle, and retinue. But were great riches and appropriate behaviour sufficient? Not necessarily. What defined the elite in early medieval perception was being 'noble'. An early eleventh-century Anglo-Saxon treatise on status acknowledged that, 'if a trader prospered, that he crossed thrice the open sea at his own expense, he was then afterwards entitled to the rights of a thegn [i.e. in Anglo-Saxon terms, a noble: see below]'.[32] Maybe some early medieval merchants did manage to ease themselves into the ranks of the thegns, but we have no evidence to prove it. What we do have, however, are many indications that more was involved in being noble than just luxuriating in wealth, as the rich man did.

'Noble' was yet another flexible term. It often described a person's high rank and position of power and privilege, but it could also refer to distinguished, upright conduct within the religious and social expectations of the day. One or both of these meanings might be intended in any particular context: they shared the implication of being notable and well known. While the rich man had a claim to be noble in the former sense, not all his peers would necessarily have regarded him in this light. There is a fundamental reason for that: despite its key place in medieval and early modern European social hierarchies, 'nobility' was not, in the early Middle Ages, a rank defined by objective, agreed criteria.

Rather, it was a quality. Conduct often mattered, as the word 'noble' itself suggested. But, in addition, ancestry counted, for two reasons. In the first place, there was a strong presumption of inherited status: knowledge of a person's parentage confirmed his or her nobility. A woman, in particular, inherited her father's rank, and was often the custodian of familial genealogical details. Secondly, except perhaps for the occasional merchant who made good, the main way of acquiring the resources necessary to support a noble lifestyle was inheritance. Since only nobles had the opportunity to assemble or inherit resources on anything more than a very modest scale, the possession of wealth did not automatically ennoble. Rather, it confirmed it. Conduct, ancestry, wealth: all contributed towards being hailed as noble.

Consider Gerald, count of Aurillac, whose celebrity as a holy man stemmed, in part, from his refusal to indulge in the ostentatious lifestyle of his noble peers. He was, nevertheless, of true blue blood: 'he was so illustrious by the nobility of his birth, that among the families of Gaul his lineage is outstanding both for its possessions and the excellence of its life. . . . And indeed the great quantity of estates endowed with serfs, lying in various places, which came to Gerald by right of succession, testifies to the extent of [his ancestors'] riches.' 'Excellence of life' in the form of 'modesty and religion' also ran in the family.[33] Gerald took nobility of living to new extremes, however. In general, nobles were expected to behave in the ways that brought honour to themselves, their family, and their lord: courage and martial prowess for lay men, sexual modesty and careful household management for women.[34] By shunning vengeance and the force of arms, and keeping himself quite chaste, the count of Aurillac simply stood traditional paradigms of gendered conduct on their head. Gerald, then, had all the tokens of nobility: ancestry, great landed estates, and that other, elusive, criterion—distinguished conduct, albeit of a rather odd sort. He was so noble, his biographer implied, that he did not need to confirm the fact by flaunting his wealth.

There remains one important additional avenue to nobility or its enhancement to consider: royal service. It is not by accident that many of the words that came to denote high rank originally meant a servant or domestic retainer: this is the root meaning of 'thegn', 'thane' (the main elite rank in Anglo-Saxon England and Scotland respectively), 'knight' (Old English *cniht*), and 'vassal' (Old French *vassallus*). At the very least, since that service was often military, the death in battle of one man might open the way for the rise of another at court; conversely, distinction in battle might bring reward, patronage, and higher social esteem. Service might also be more peaceable, in the secular and ecclesiastical administrative positions of great responsibility that supported the monarchies and empires of the early Middle Ages. And its rewards—prestige, influence, landed estates, even a royal bride—could be great indeed, as Eberhard of Friuli appreciated.

Access to these posts created a group of insiders, those who enjoyed and could exploit their closeness to the king for their personal and familial advantage. Further, while noble ancestry conveyed noble rank (or did so for so long as memory of that ancestry was cultivated and a noble lifestyle maintained), it need not be a prerequisite for access to high office. Liutward, bishop of Vercelli (880–900), exemplifies both these points. Of low birth, he rose through ability to hold the highest ecclesiastical positions in the court of Charles the Fat (876–87) and 'was honoured and feared by all more than the emperor'. He was also successful in promoting his family, and 'he carried off the daughters of the most noble men in Alemannia and Italy without opposition, and gave them to his relatives in marriage'.[35] Marriage to a woman of higher rank was an established means of social advancement, for women could transmit status as well as resources from one generation to another. We should remember, however, that privileges, wealth, and the power that arose from closeness to a ruler by no means always went together. Great noblemen often had obscure brothers, men of equally high birth and comparable wealth but of little political standing or influence.

Nor was royal confidence in a valued courtier necessarily matched by the trust of his peers. In the 570s, Leudast was count in Tours. He had acquired the position by winning the attention of King Charibert (561–7) and then his brother King Chilperic (561–84). The office brought responsibility for fiscal, military, and judicial administration on the king's behalf, and carried a presumption of nobility, but we only hear of Leudast through the eyes of his rival for influence in the town, Bishop Gregory. The latter asserted that Leudast was the son of a slave in a royal vineyard, who was put to work in the royal kitchens. As a scullion, Gregory alleged, Leudast had his ear mutilated for attempting to escape, but nevertheless managed to ingratiate himself at court, catching the eye of Charibert's queen, Marcofeva. Once appointed count, Leudast 'strutted around, bursting even more with prideful glory in his high office. He showed himself to be a rapacious plunderer, a brawling braggart, and a filthy adulterer. By sowing discord and fomenting malice, he amassed no small fortune.'[36] This may be a story of unusually successful upward social mobility; it was certainly Gregory of Tours's desperate attempt to vilify a dangerous political rival by denying him any nobility, despite his undoubted wealth, power, and royal favour. It was also the contest of a parvenu self-made through royal service with an aristocrat of ancient, inherited status often at odds with Leudast's royal patron.[37]

In the absence of any hard-and-fast criteria of nobility at any point in the early Middle Ages, tension between old and new blood probably characterized royal courts more often than not. After all, noble status was jealously guarded, to be defended against newcomers attempting to encroach upon it. 'The emperor made you a free man but not a noble, for that is impossible', was the accusation hurled by a ninth-century polemicist at a man whom he hated, an archbishop who coupled humble origins with loyal service towards his imperial patron, Louis the Pious.[38] The charge of humble origins could also be turned against those who were noble, but not of the right sort, as Hagano discovered in the early tenth century. He came from an important landed family in Lotharingia, a part of the East Frankish kingdom that the West Frankish king Charles the Simple (898–922) seized in 911, and rapidly won the trust of his new royal lord. In his native circles, Hagano would have undoubtedly been treated with all the respect due to someone known to be of distinguished nobility. But, at Charles the Simple's court, he encountered the rivalry of those with vested interests in the West Frankish networks of power, who resented the intrusion into their midst of an outsider—this 'man from the middling sort whom the king had made powerful'. The old elite complained to Charles about his habit of discussing royal affairs in private with Hagano, excluding his other—rightful—counsellors. They threatened to withdraw their own participation unless Charles dropped 'this man of obscure parentage [who] was doing immense damage to the king's dignity by giving him advice as if there were no nobles'.[39] Charles persisted in trusting Hagano—and, in 920, his critics finally rebelled and deposed the king shortly thereafter.

With these cases, we come to the crux of the matter. No distinguished conduct or pedigree, no amount of royal favour, wealth, social climbing, or power, could necessarily make a man noble in the eyes of his rivals. The essence of noble status was social acceptance by one's peers. No legal formula quantified the relative proportions of its constituent elements: in the absence of agreed, explicit status qualifications, nobility remained in the eye of the beholder. For that reason, it could be fragile, even evanescent. It encouraged the proclamation of pedigree through the reuse of ancestral names. It needed constant reaffirmation through conspicuous displays of wealth, influence, and appropriate conduct, and it needed defending against the risk of being upstaged by social climbers. Careful cultivation of friends and relations; a watchful eye for ways of enhancing honour; strategic marriage alliances for oneself and one's offspring; a reputation for generosity towards churches; careful disposition of the family patrimony; navigating the shifting sands of patronage and favour: all were means of advancing or, at least, of striving to contain the erosion of nobility.

That nobility was in large part a matter of social perception is crucial to one of the most important shifts to affect medieval elites: the emergence of knighthood. Although the roots of this gradual process are traceable in the ninth and tenth centuries, it was not complete until the twelfth, or in some places even the thirteenth century. There are three major strands to this, one ideological, one sociological, and one semantic. First, the warrior aristocracy of the Carolingian Empire embraced a specifically Christian ideology of martial values. Among the ninth-century nobility who fought on horseback, heavily armed, against the foes of Christendom, there developed a rhetoric that exalted and justified warfare. They delimited membership of this elite group by rituals of weapon giving, which were sometimes accompanied by religious ceremonies. Secondly, as tenth-century lords began to build castles and garrison them with armed followers, a group of free but non-noble men dedicated to warfare as a way of living became more prominent. These men were styled *milites*, meaning, in accordance with the word's classical usage, simply 'soldiers'. Thirdly, in a complex semantic shift that began in parts of France towards the end of the tenth century but can be traced elsewhere only rather later, the noble elite began to regard itself, and to be regarded by others, as *milites*. At the same time, the garrison *milites* began to claim noble status for themselves. From being a word of non-noble connotation, *miles* thus became a reputable status that nobles were keen to adopt. Only gradually did these three developments fuse to form the knightly cadre of the twelfth century and later. If knighthood was one of the most distinctive aspects of the high medieval nobility, then its roots lay in the functions, fluidities, and subjective perceptions of the early Middle Ages.

Thus, although the existence of elites of some sort was a social fact at all times, membership rested on no firmly defined criteria. Nor could it, for rulers did not distribute patronage and favour according to objective test, but rather followed the pressures of the moment—political need, loyalty, ability, and friendship. The most general statement that can be made is that nobility was relational, with respect to those both higher and lower in the social hierarchy. Those who claimed to be noble, and who were recognized by their peers as noble, ranged from individuals of comfortable but not extravagant means to those of vast landed fortunes. They comprised families whose nobility extended back for many generations, alongside those of a more recent vintage, for whom royal service provided the most common ladder of social mobility. Carefully chosen marriage partners and shrewd disposition of the family patrimony made women vital links in the transmission of ancestry, land, and claims to nobility from one generation to the next, within and between amorphous kinship networks. For many, though, the relationship that mattered most was with their ruler. Those not in a position to catch the king's eye directly might at least hope to find an opening in the retinue of one of his courtiers for themselves or their sons. And, as patronage and service pulled people towards the royal court, so fashions and tastes for luxurious living diffused outwards and downwards from it.

The search for status, then, required energy and effort as well as expenditure. It drew on inherited resources but also on the strengths of friendships, and it called for adroit political manœuvring, to protect reputation, enhance honour, win high office and landed reward. When Rather of Verona conjured up a rich man for his pastoral dialogue, he was not interested in his creation's political ambitions or successes, only in the fate that awaited the soul of one so greedy as he. Nothing, from Rather's point of view, was more precious. The search for earthly status, he implied, was fraught with spiritual risk.

Around the year 890, Alfred, king of Wessex, received a visitor, who brought him some fine walrus ivory. Ohthere lived in Norway, at the northernmost limit of settled agricultural activity. One summer, he extended his hunting expedition further even than the whale-hunters went, sailing right the way round the arctic coast of Scandinavia, as far as the White Sea, to find out whether anyone lived there. His gift of the very finest ivory came from those parts, uninhabited apart from the occasional camp of the *Finnas*, the Sami hunters and fishers of arctic Scandinavia.

Ohthere's detailed description of northern geography fascinated the West Saxons. They also questioned him about himself, and discovered that 'he was among the chief men of that country, but he had not more than twenty cattle, twenty sheep and twenty pigs, and the little that he ploughed he ploughed with horses'. Their surprise that such an important man had so little arable land and very modest flocks of domestic animals was tempered by the realization that Ohthere 'was a very rich man in those possessions which their riches consist of, that is in wild deer. . . . [which] they call reindeer'. The main source of the wealth of the men of that region, Ohthere reported, was the tribute of marten fur, reindeer hide, bearskin coats, sacks of feathers, whalebone, and rawhide ropes received from the Sami, each of whom paid 'according to his rank'.[40]

Neither herds of reindeer nor the personal dependencies of tribute-givers acknowledge precise territorial boundaries. That the wealth of rein-deer barons such as Ohthere came more from herding and tribute taking than from agriculture reflected the scarcity of arable land, its poor qual-ity, and the lack of tightly organized lordships so far north. Here was an economy that did not turn on the control of land, where the labour of the hunter rather than the ploughman upheld those of higher rank. There could not be a greater contrast to the agricultural economy of northern Flanders, with its highly regulated farming, demarcated plots of land, firm subordination to royal, comital, and ecclesiastical lordship, and its rapidly commercializing exchange. They form the extreme modes of labour and lordship in the early Middle Ages, but nevertheless share important fea-tures. Both were carefully organized to exploit the natural resources of the region, whether walrus tusk and bearskin or linen, oats, and wool. Both reveal local gradations of wealth and rank, which, although very different in absolute terms, manifested themselves in social and political inequal-ities on a regionally significant scale. Both contributed resources that kings and their retinues valued: rare furs; ivory for jewellery, delicate caskets, and precious book covers; oats for horses; timber for warships and castles. Both are suggestive of the varied ways in which powerful men and rulers obtained the resources that sustained their lordship, and what they did with those different resources once they had acquired them. The next chapter takes up these issues in more detail.

6

Getting and Giving

There is a fine fortress on the promontory,
Graciously each one there receives his share.
. . . . .

There is a fine fortress on a height,
Lavish its feasting, loud its revelry
Beautiful all round it, that fort of champions,
Is the flying spray: its wings are long![1]

Charlemagne liked foreigners, and took great care in welcoming
them, to the extent that their great number seemed, not unjustly, to
be burdensome not only to the palace but even to the kingdom.
But because of his magnanimous nature, Charlemagne was un-
troubled by burdens of this kind, since he was compensated for the
great inconvenience by praise for his generosity and the reward of a
good reputation.[2]

CHARLEMAGNE knew that a ruler needed a reputation for generosity.
His court, like that of Bleiddudd, lord of the Welsh 'fine fortress' of Tenby,
resounded with the sounds of feasting and revelry, part of the lavish
display and conspicuous consumption that successful rulership required.
According to one contemporary estimate, the daily consumption of Otto
I's court in 968 amounted to 'one thousand pigs and sheep, ten cartloads
of wine, another ten of beer, one thousand measures of grain, eight oxen,
in addition to vast quantities of chickens, piglets, fish, eggs, vegetables and
other foodstuffs'.[3] Even if an exaggerated report, it is suggestive of the
scale on which rulership needed to be resourced. Charlemagne's generosity (although not Bleiddudd's) must have been on a similar scale: that it
generated criticism is little surprise. The truly generous ruler could afford
to ignore complaints in the expectation of reaping political rewards from
his extravagant expenditure.

Displays of generous grandeur and maintenance of an elite lifestyle were but two of the uses to which lords and rulers might put their material resources. Endowing churches; rewarding followers; supporting the administration of a kingdom; conducting warfare; building residences, palaces, or castles; engaging in diplomacy; providing for relatives: all drained them. This chapter, then, explores ways of accumulating and distributing a wide range of forms of material assets. Taking its cue from Charlemagne's feasting of so many foreigners in order to enhance his reputation, its focus is the conversion of economic capital to symbolic capital—that is, of treasure, money, cattle, and agricultural produce into honour, political success, and divine approval.

The translation of the one into the other was fraught with difficulties. Land and its produce remained the predominant source of support for all early medieval elites, yet even kings remained constrained by the vagaries of bad weather and outbreaks of disease, for food shortages might make campaigning impossible or an outbreak of disease decimate an army. Income in the form of perishable foodstuffs could not be stored in treasure chests and required conversion into something more enduring. There were, of course, other sources of wealth, but they too were often unstable. Plunder could be won in battle, or lost. Indiscriminate generosity might exhaust both resources and reputation. Inheritance and marriage might bring enhanced wealth; providing for sons and daughters might drain it. Rulers might amass great treasure in the form of diplomatic gifts—but, by the same token, had to reciprocate generously in some way. Thus, although the attributes of a successful king included a well-filled treasure chest, and although his legitimacy rested, in part, on stewardship of precious ancestral heirlooms, we should not work with static images of gold hoards in mind. Rather, the translation of wealth into political power was a dynamic process of circulation and redistribution, of constant inflow and outflow. Kings hoarded in order to be able to disburse; they gave in order to get.

The conversion of material assets into social and political advantage tended to be concentrated at particular nodes. The first part of this chapter identifies the places where wealth and power tended to cluster, situates them within geographical networks, and comments on their relationship to the polities in which they lay. This section, then, explores ways of accumulating and distributing wealth within early medieval economies, and notes ways in which kings and others took advantage of them. It notes shifting patterns of commerce, and their relationship to other forms of exchange. The second part of the chapter shifts focus from places to people, from topographical to social networks. It addresses gift giving and

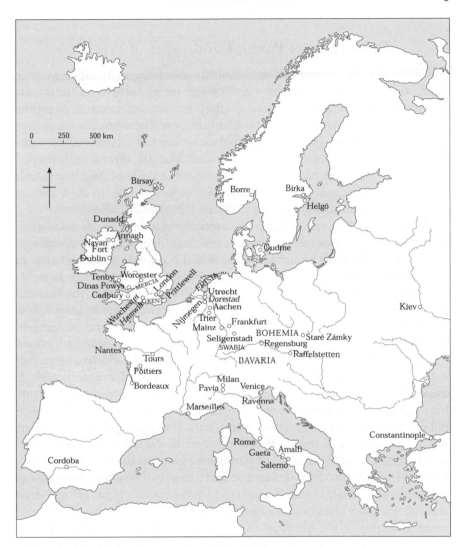

6.1. Principal places mentioned in Chapter 6.

patronage as strategies central to the ways in which early medieval lords and rulers used their resources to build and maintain their power. Finally, it argues that material wealth helped organize relationships between the human and the supernatural, and that its use offers insights into early medieval cosmologies.

Landscapes of Power, Landscapes of Wealth

In hierarchically organized agricultural societies, material resources, political leadership, and supernatural power are as liable to be unequally distributed in geographical terms as they are in social terms. Mapping textual and archaeological evidence would reveal a complex landscape, in which economic, religious, and political functions clustered in some places, but other locations had fewer roles. Making several such mental sketch maps for the early Middle Ages is the task of this section. It reveals great changes: charting these landscapes is an effective way to explore the dynamic human geography of the early Middle Ages.

We must start in the ancient Mediterranean, where the Roman Empire knitted together a mosaic of cities and their dependent territories into a vast and remarkably enduring political and economic system. Any map of this would emphasize the dominance of urban communities as political, religious, and economic focal points. Closer inspection would reveal their importance as places where local and imperial interests intersected, overlapped, or competed. Agriculture, wars, tribute, and state-organized production and supply had generated the vast resources needed to sustain this empire. Indeed, so great were the demands of the Roman state that it had sucked in resources from far beyond its political frontiers, seeking minerals such as gold and iron, prestige goods such as spices or furs and human resources, whether slaves or soldiers, wherever available. Its internal economy was a command economy, activated by imperial requisitioning, with transport systems directed to provisioning the army's many units and feeding the teeming cities of Rome and Constantinople. The massive fourth- to fifth-century bureaucracy and army had strained resources to the limit, yet lavish imperial and aristocratic spending on refined civic architecture and ceremonials continued to enhance the urban environment and project the ideology of empire against this backdrop. In late Antiquity, cities remained the central points for the consumption and display of wealth and for political activity, most visibly in the Mediterranean. Above all, Rome itself concentrated material wealth and political influence in one place, a supremacy it maintained long after the foundation of a second imperial capital on the Bosphorus at Constantinople in 324. Even the removal of the fourth-century western court first to Trier, then Milan, and finally Ravenna in 408 did little to dent Rome's predominance as the outstanding theatre of power. Nor, immediately, did the lapse of the western imperial title after 476. Although in many cases their population and inhabited areas were diminishing, the cities rimming the Mediterranean nevertheless still formed by far the wealthiest zone in Europe in *c.*500. State-driven exchange still regularly shipped large quantities of grain, wine, and oil as well as luxury items from one end of the Mediterranean to the other, replenishing imperial granaries and sustaining urban magnificence.

Crumbling imperial control in the West changed all this. The ending of imperial rule entailed the gradual unravelling—and sometimes deliberate dismembering—of its huge military and bureaucratic regime, and of the system of exactions, taxes, and coinage that had sustained it. It also left the tradition of civic munificence and imperial monument building to decay, quickly in some places, more gradually in others. In this changed climate, cities in peripheral provinces struggled to survive at all; nearer to the Mediterranean, most persisted, albeit on a reduced scale. As warrior elites carved new polities out of Roman territory, they established themselves as rural landowners, but maintained a generally respectful attitude towards cities as theatres of power, even if those urban centres were now dilapidated, partially abandoned, and economically impoverished.

The overall consequences for the fifth, sixth, and seventh centuries can be sketched. Secular elites became ever more rural and more militarized; everywhere civic display, urban lifestyle, and civilian ideologies were at best severely compromised, and in much of the West (unlike the East) collapsed altogether. Only bishops and clerics continued to build in cities; under their aegis, the multiplication of churches changed the appearance and character of the urban environment. Meanwhile, systems of exchange that had formerly moved goods over long distances disintegrated. By the mid-seventh century even the Mediterranean economy had dissolved into local zones of more-or-less autonomous activity within which a reduced volume of goods circulated, connected only by erratic sailings from one port to the next. The separate Mediterranean micro-regions did not continue to function at the same level, and in the western Mediterranean basin, in particular, economic activity slumped to far lower levels than at the eastern end. This affected Rome too: by the eighth century, the shrunken city was fed from its immediate hinterland only, and civic display had given way to ecclesiastical munificence.

The end of the Roman state-driven economy was a gradual, erratic process, which cannot be precisely dated, but whose results are clear. Although political imperatives and the need for resources had led the empire to seek raw materials and rare items far beyond its borders, the military frontier had nevertheless been the clear limit of the Roman fiscal system and its monetized economy. The end of the tax state and the cessation of regular minting of coinage effectively blurred the distinction between economic systems within and beyond the border. Furthermore, there emerged not a new, unified economy but a series of overlapping local and regional economies. Except in Italy, their characteristics and nodes were more rural than urban and their coinages switched from gold to silver.

Although these changes took place over approximately the same period as the formation of post-imperial kingdoms, the new political and economic topographies by no means coincided. This was particularly evident in Gaul, where the kings of the Franks looked south to exploit the trade in the Mediterranean and where eastern items continued to flow northwards through the trading city of Marseilles until the seventh century, but they also turned their attention north, to the mouth of the Rhine and beyond. Here, the rapidly expanding Frisian population enjoyed a gold-rich society by the late sixth century and shared in the culture common to all the North Sea littorals: by the early seventh century, Frisia was the magnet that pulled the Franks ever more into the northern European arena. The Frankish kingdom thus straddled both the Mediterranean and the North Sea economic zones.

Around the North Sea, new patterns of communication and exchange integrated regions formerly transected by the Roman political frontier. Their outlines are clear by the early seventh century. From the mouth of the Seine to the base of the Jutland peninsula on the Continent and from the Solent to the Humber Basin in England, new coastal or estuarine centres of production and exchange developed, known as emporia or *wics*. Only flourishing in the seventh, eighth, and ninth centuries, these were waterfront centres of artisanal production and trade that funnelled goods from regional hinterlands overseas to other territories and kingdoms. In this way, basalt quern stones quarried in the Eifel hills north of Trier reached the Rhine delta, travelled northwards through the Danish peninsula into the western Baltic, and crossed the Channel to the south coast of England in a traffic unbounded by political frontiers.

By c.800, emporia were also to be found throughout southern Scandinavia and the Baltic, whose exports of amber, furs, and ivory were exchanged for shipments of woollen cloth, wine, pottery, ceramics, and arms. Even where they did lie within the territory of the former Roman Empire, their sites were not old Roman cities but rather a new type of focal point for the distribution of goods. They were undefended, and often only seasonally occupied, mostly by men unaccompanied by women or children. Characteristically, emporia were not in themselves centres of royal or aristocratic lordship, but usually were located in close and probably direct relationship with them, as on the Solent, where *Hamwih* lay just south of the West Saxon royal centre of Winchester (itself an old Roman city), or in Frisia, where *Dorestad* was located near to the late Merovingian ecclesiastical centre in the Roman fort at Utrecht.

And, as small silver coins began to be minted in some North Sea emporia from the 670s, kings took an interest, finding ways to tap into their wealth by taxing transactions, exploiting the possibilities of acquiring prestige items for themselves and of generating income by selling the surplus produce of their own estates. Royal interest and encouragement were matched by ecclesiastical pursuit of wealth and luxury, and the emergence everywhere of cathedrals and monasteries as centres of wealth as well as of political influence is a characteristic feature of the seventh and eighth centuries. Thus, for example, the late eighth-century rulers of the landlocked Anglo-Saxon kingdom of Mercia imposed tolls on ships trading at *Lundenwic*, 'an emporium for many nations who come to it by land and sea' on the open riverside beach to the west of the old Roman city of London.[4] (London's *wic* is probably commemorated in the street name Aldwych.) Specifically exempted from these tolls were ships belonging to certain Kentish churches and to the bishops of London and Worcester. Although details of their trading activities are unknown, these churches, like the kings who privileged them with documents of exemption, found emporia central to the development of their own wealth and power. In this way, the interests of several different groups overlapped.

The intensification of long-distance exchange at points along the eastern coast of Britain coincided with its decline around the western coast. In late Antiquity, trade had linked the Mediterranean, via the Atlantic coast of Gaul, to Brittany and then to south-western Britain and the entire Irish Sea zone. Grain, wine, and oil travelled out, and ships returned with British tin, silver, and lead plus slaves and hunting dogs from Ireland. The link into the Mediterranean persisted into the middle of the sixth century, but thereafter, until *c.*700, only the northern sector of this route remained in use, conveying salt, wine, spices, and dyestuffs from Bordeaux and Nantes in south-western Gaul to the Irish Sea region in considerable quantities.

Whether merchants ever made the entire run from the Mediterranean to Ireland and even south-western Scotland, or whether goods passed through several intermediaries, remains disputed. Although this trade was of very modest proportions in Mediterranean terms, it was of significance to the kings who competed for influence and territory around the Irish Sea. These rulers based themselves in Iron Age fortifications on commanding hilltops, sites whose population must have been numbered in dozens or, at most, hundreds and whose modest economic role was far outstripped by their political and symbolic importance. These high-status sites included centres such as Cadbury, Dinas Powys, and Dunadd in Britain and the double complex at Navan Fort and Armagh in Ireland. Those who ruled from these sites—men like Bleiddudd of Tenby—commanded labour services and military obligations from their subjects. They also retained specialist craftsmen such as goldsmiths, jewellers, and enamellers, who worked within the safety of the hillfort residences to produce the luxury artefacts through which they flaunted their elite status. And, in regulating access to the goods from the Mediterranean and south-western Gaul, they enhanced their own position.

By the early eighth century, most of these fortified hilltops had been abandoned. In Ireland, artisanal production moved to monastic sites, but its distribution, such as there was, probably remained under royal control. In due course, the Irish Sea region gradually reoriented its economic and political connections away from the Gaul and the Bay of Biscay, instead turning northwards, via the Northern Isles to Scandinavia and the Baltic. Although the causes remain uncertain and the chronology approximate, they are in some way associated with an altogether larger shift that was affecting eighth-century Europe as a whole: the temporary abatement of economic activity around the western Mediterranean and its intensification in northern waters.

Access to the wealth of the North Sea and, beyond it, of the Baltic was just one of the reasons for relentless Frankish expansion northwards in the eighth century. Under the leadership of the Carolingian dynasty, the Franks succeeded by 800 in building a polity that controlled a land mass greater than any other post-Roman polity before the sixteenth century. With its political core in the regions between the Seine and the middle Rhine, their empire stretched from the Ebro to the Danube and from the Tiber to the Elbe (Figure 8.3). It embraced dozens of economically distinct regions, ranging from the relatively urbanized Po valley to the sparsely inhabited forests of northern Germany, and it certainly controlled far greater material resources than any other early medieval polity, even if nowhere near the level of those of the Roman state. Indeed, comparison ends at that point, for the Carolingians quite lacked the apparatus of a state-run command economy. Careful exploitation of the agricultural surplus of their own vast estates; adroit taxation of the growing volume of trade both in the localities and along the inter-regional routes that criss-crossed the empire and passed beyond its boundaries; and aggressive plundering of their neighbours all facilitated high levels of accumulation. Persistent efforts to co-opt the loyalty of local aristocrats and churches involved the redistribution of a proportion of that fortune, but won the kings indirect access to both secular and ecclesiastical landed wealth, as, for example, at Ghent.

Carolingian kings and emperors shunned the urban displays of power their Roman predecessors had cultivated. The Carolingians sought game in the forests of the Ardennes in the company of a select noble entourage, whereas Roman emperors had enjoyed the hunt in metropolitan amphitheatres, watched by many thousands of spectators. They preferred to endow huge rural monasteries, which functioned as additional centres of power and accumulation of treasure, rather than lavishing patronage on civic monuments in densely populated cities. Even when their palaces were located, as Aachen, Nijmegen, Frankfurt, and Regensburg all were, on Roman foundations, these were small, semi-rural establishments or old army camps on the northern Roman periphery, not cities at its heart.

Their empire was also polyfocal. Although in the second half of his reign Charlemagne developed a showpiece palace around the thermal springs at Aachen, it was never his sole abode, except in his final years. Nor was it ever the only administrative centre, for he and his successors generally set their sons to rule one or more provinces as junior or sub-kings, and provided each with his own retinue and governing centres. In the second half of the ninth century, intra-familial rivalries hardened these temporary administrative expedients into more enduring kingdoms, whose rulers were left either to found new palaces for themselves or to impose their entourage on monastic hospitality. Though Aachen remained the most prestigious, the most coveted, of ruling sites, multiple rulers meant multiple nodes in the geography of power. In the Carolingian era, as throughout the early Middle Ages, authority remained personal, not institutional, and so the king's presence, wherever he was, identified the nerve centre of political activity.

The Carolingian dynasty managed to meld many different webs of local political influence and economic resources, each of which had its own regional hub. Ghent was one of them, as we have seen, so let us visit a rather different one: Mainz. An old Roman frontier city, it lay on the middle Rhine, the great arterial waterway that led from the North Sea towards the Alpine passes to Italy and the Mediterranean. The dominant presence here was not royal, for there was no palace; instead it was ecclesiastical, for the origins of the archbishopric of Mainz lay in the late Roman era. In person or, more commonly, through their agents, rulers, magnates, and churches tapped into the lucrative trade that passed through the city. It presented a fragmented townscape, for, within its Roman walls, ecclesiastical and secular residential complexes each formed their own compound amid areas given over to agriculture or viticulture. Regional bigwigs and the abbots of major rural monasteries all had town houses here, which were used whenever they or their estate bailiffs came to town to conduct business or take agricultural produce to the market. With a royal mint to stimulate trade and also facilitate its taxation, the city also functioned as an important centre of production and exchange. Along the riverside, the 'Frisian quarter' comprised the warehouses and workshops of a sizeable colony of Frisian merchants, whose boats plied the Rhine, exporting the wine and grain of the regional hinterland, together with the fine metalwork produced in the city itself. By the early tenth century, Mainz was also a transit point for the shipment of goods brought across the Alps, including spices from the east, and was visited by Muslim and Jewish traders. But, by then, the Carolingian political experiment had foundered on the rock of regional differentiation and local interest. In the absence of means of rapid communication and reliable methods of compulsion, effective polities generally remained smaller in scale, even as local agricultural output rose and inter-regional trade intensified. In the localities of late- and post-Carolingian Europe, economic dynamism remained unaffected by political fragmentation.

The wealth and growing population of Frankish coastal emporia, rural monasteries, riverine ports, and local markets were among the best documented of the many targets to attract the attention of the Vikings. Particularly well recorded are the attacks that their highly mobile forces staged from the late eighth century onwards on the Carolingian heartlands and British Isles. Their raids became more frequent and more devastating in the course of the ninth century: by sacking church treasuries, targeting markets, and extorting tribute from rulers, they siphoned off quantities of coin and treasure, sometimes also cattle and humans. As their war bands grew larger, the Vikings also sought land to settle, whether by outright conquest or by concessions wrung from local rulers.

Confident seamen, able traders, canny raiders, the Vikings travelled far and wide from the late eighth until the early eleventh century. In the ninth and tenth centuries Scandinavian boats dominated the coasts of the British archipelago and the Northern Isles, ranging along the western seaboard of Europe, and occasionally passing through the Strait of Gibraltar into the Mediterranean. They crossed the Atlantic to settle Iceland and even sometimes sailed onward to Greenland and Newfoundland. They criss-crossed the Baltic and travelled the river routes of eastern Europe to reach the Black Sea. There the Vikings tapped into the vast wealth of the Muslim world, thereby sucking westwards massive quantities of Islamic silver coins. Stimulated by this traffic, powerful trading centres such as Kiev, on the river Dnieper, emerged by the 860s.

The finds from the Swedish settlement at Helgö are indicative of the breadth of Viking contacts, direct or indirect: they include glassware from the Rhineland; the intricately wrought head of an Irish crozier; a silver dish and a hoard of gold coins from Byzantium; a ladle made in Coptic Egypt, and a bronze statuette of the Buddha. Explanations for this dramatic (but sometimes overdramatized) phase of northern seafaring activity remain controversial. Southern Scandinavian society underwent profound transformations in the sixth to eighth centuries, developing into a more hierarchically ordered society in which resources became accumulated in centres controlled by local leaders, such as the one we have already encountered at Borre in Vestfold. The emergence of these powerful chiefdoms seems to have been closely associated with the ability to exploit and redistribute resources derived from trade as well as local agricultural and artisanal production. The wealth of the Baltic emporia— places such as Birka, which contained 'many rich merchants, and a large amount of goods and money'[5]—certainly helped fuel their growth, as the North Sea emporia did that of seventh- and eighth-century Anglo-Saxon and Frankish kings. Among these chiefdoms, the Danish one developed earliest into a dynastic kingdom and asserted a seaborne hegemony that extended beyond the Jutland peninsula to include the southern Scandinavian chiefdoms and the Slavic communities along the Baltic shore.

The growing concentration of power and resources in the hands of Denmark's kings was contested both within their kingdom and on its borders: political rivalries encouraged the formation of aggressive warrior bands and aristocratic elites. And Charlemagne's expansion into northern Saxony not only destroyed traditional alliances between the Danes and their Slavic neighbours east of the Elbe, for an imperial politics of patronizing client-kings also fostered the emergence of dominant local dynasties of new-found status and influence. Trading contacts over a wide area and a tradition of maritime travel coupled with political upheaval and the ever-pressing need to accumulate the resources that would reward a war band: these preconditions were sufficient to unleash the Viking raids on western Europe's accumulated treasure.

From a northern perspective, the 'Viking Age' was as much about the transformation of the power structures of Scandinavia as it was about exploiting the material resources of western Europe and the Muslim lands. From a British and continental perspective, it was also about the destabilization and transformation of established political landscapes. It was not merely that Viking raiders demanded tribute or presented a military challenge. In these terms, it is relatively simple to assess their impact, for their depredations demonstrated the ability of the Carolingian and Anglo-Saxon agrarian and artisanal economies to continue generating resources year after year. They also contributed to the development of efficient Frankish and English coinages run under tight control for royal profit. In this respect, although local damage was often severe and always traumatic, the overall effect of the Viking raids was transformative not destructive. Equally significantly, Franks, Bretons, Anglo-Saxons, Welsh, and Gaels had no qualms about making common cause with the Vikings when it suited their own political purposes. Roving Viking war bands were welcome participants in Carolingian familial feuding or inter-kingdom rivalries within the British Isles to an extent that contemporary chroniclers took pains to obscure. Their presence complicated or even destroyed local political conventions, in addition to subverting the regular rhythms of agricultural production, diverting tax revenues, and releasing the wealth of church treasuries into circulation.

The Viking impact was especially far-reaching in the British Isles, where a plethora of competing kings were only too ready to call on outside help to overcome a neighbouring rival. For example, the mid-ninth-century absorption of the formerly powerful Pictish kingdom into the Gaelic kingdom of Dalriada may well have been the work of tactical alliances between Gaels and Vikings. Perhaps, inadvertently, the Vikings prompted the emergence of the kingdom of Alba out of the Gaels' domination of the Picts. Certainly by the late ninth century, north-eastern Scotland and the Orkney Islands emerged as an aggressive and powerful lordship of Norse origin whose main place of power was the former Pictish settlement at Birsay. In Ireland, Norse raiders were notable for their rapid assimilation into Irish society. As keen participants in the violent rivalries between Irish kings, the founders of several coastal trading colonies, and settlers in the hinterland of these ports, they rapidly intermarried and left their mark on language, settlement, and politics.

For the Hiberno-Norse, as for other Scandinavian groups, raiding and conquest were part of a spectrum of activities that embraced colonizing as well as trading. Dense ninth- and tenth-century Hiberno-Norse settlement in the Hebrides largely obliterated all traces of earlier cultural groups and left a legacy that endures in the place names of these islands. In Iceland, Hiberno-Norse settlers joined migrants from western and northern Norway who had found an all-but-unoccupied land and settled there in some numbers between c.870 and c.930. There they replicated the political organization of their northern Scandinavian homelands—

a patchwork of small chiefdoms whose headmen presided over largely self-regulating farming communities—and remained distinctive for their lack of any kingship until Iceland passed under the control of the Norwegian crown in 1262.

From the early tenth century until the early eleventh century, Dublin, the richest and most influential of the Norse colonies in Ireland, was effectively another small kingdom, one whose political significance was enhanced by the accumulation of considerable commercial wealth. Its rulers built it up by extending their raiding, slaving, and military campaigning into northern England and south-western Scotland. Its denizens were doubtless sustained by a regionally generated agricultural surplus, but trade—especially in slaves—across the Irish Sea and beyond integrated this flourishing port into the Scandinavian web of trade routes that straddled the North Sea and Baltic and ultimately linked with Muslim traders in the Caucasus and Transoxania. Much of the trade and tribute that moved along these routes did so in the form of hacksilver (silver collars, arm rings, and the like cut into portions of roughly uniform weight) or silver coin, but, to assist their trading ventures, the Norse first imported foreign coins into Ireland, and then started to mint their own currency in Dublin. The Mediterranean and Near East had been familiar with metallic currency as a medium of exchange and assertion of a ruler's prestige and authority since the seventh century BC: that coins were not minted in Ireland until the 997 is a measure of the cultural difference between the Mediterranean and the non-Romanized parts of Europe.

Well before that date, the West Saxon kings had cleared the Viking warlords out of England, and had incorporated the heavily Scandinavianized eastern lowlands into a refashioned monarchy that aggressively asserted overlordship over the Welsh, British, Gaels, and Norse of western and northern Britain. In the south, in and beyond their West Saxon heartland, they built large defensive centres known as burhs, which not only served strategic military purposes in the fight against the Vikings but rapidly emerged as focuses for new forms of urban development. Although retaining close links to their agricultural hinterland, these late Anglo-Saxon towns were sophisticated and populous trading communities as well as centres of royal and ecclesiastical power. They provided regional markets for locally produced agricultural surpluses and artisan manufactures, and imported growing quantities of prestige goods such as silks and wine for the fashion-conscious elite. Above all, they housed royal mints and customs collectors, by means of which the late Anglo-Saxon kings sucked very large amounts of tax, in the form of silver pennies, out of the thriving English economy.

Was Anglo-Saxon England the richest kingdom in Europe by 1000? The case can be argued. Certainly by the late tenth century, when the supply of Islamic silver into Scandinavia dwindled and a resurgent Danish monarchy found expansion into the Baltic lands blocked by the Ottonian Empire, England was the most enticing source of profit, with large amounts of silver coins in circulation and flourishing local and regional urban markets. A new wave of attacks on England, organized by the Danish kings, culminated in the fall of the West Saxon ruling dynasty in 1016 and the accession of Cnut, who soon acquired the Danish throne as well. On this basis, he built a North Sea empire stretching from Dublin, via Scotland and Scandinavia, to the Baltic, but his personal hegemony did not outlast his death in 1035 (Figure 8.4).

Cnut's North Sea empire had relied upon the maritime connections and trading wealth built up by the Danes and Norwegians over the preceding 200 years. By the early eleventh century, such a territorially far-flung hegemony was characteristic of northern Europe rather than the lands south of the Loire and the Alps, where regionally intensive rather than imperially extensive polities were emerging. The fragmentation of France into regional or local lordships was a manifestation of this. The disjuncture between traditional political topographies and newer accumulations of material wealth was, however, most acute in northern Italy.

By the start of the new millennium, Italian towns were at the hub of a rapidly expanding urban and mercantile economy and were beginning to assert their own autonomy. While urban life never disappeared in Italy to anything like the extent that it did north of the Alps, the role of Italian cities as centres of production, exchange, and consumption in the period from c.600 to c.800 is hard to assess, although it seems clear that the pace of production and exchange began to intensify only rather later than in the North Sea area. As the evidence gradually becomes more plentiful, we can trace patterns unlike those of the late- and post-Roman Mediterranean, although it remains true that the changed nature of the evidence (documentary as well as archaeological) may exaggerate the impression of an economic transformation.

Northern Italy had been absorbed into the Frankish kingdom in 774. Carolingian control fell away after 888, but, in the middle of the tenth century, the Carolingians' German heirs, the Ottonians, reasserted a transalpine lordship from their main seats of power in distant, economically backward Saxony. North-east of the Rhine, the absence of long-established towns or markets and the lack of a well-developed coin-using economy left rulers reliant on other methods of resourcing their rule: itinerant kingship, vast landed estates, the tribute of dependent peoples, and the seemingly inexhaustible plunder of frontier warfare. Little wonder, then, that northern Italy attracted them, for here urban wealth was developing apace.

Of particular note is the growth during the ninth century of new Italian coastal towns well placed to develop long-distance trading contacts but in locations unfavourable to agriculture. At the head of the Adriatic, Venice exploited its location on the frontier between the Carolingian and Byzantine empires and, from at least 840, was effectively independent, with only its own interests to foster. Venetians put their energies into a trading economy that gave them a key role in the shipment of goods between western Europe, Byzantium, and the Islamic east, so much so that by the late tenth century the Adriatic Sea was, from a Muslim perspective, simply the 'gulf of Venice'.[6] The perception is important, for much of Venice's prominence probably derived from its role as an entrepôt in the slave trade. Here, slaves captured along Europe's eastern periphery were loaded for shipment to Egypt, and then transit onwards to major Islamic cities, where, unlike in the Christian world, slavery was a fundamental social and military resource. In return, Venetian merchants imported 'all the riches of the east from across the sea' and traded these prestige items on up the Po valley.[7]

On the rocky coast of the Tyrrhenian Sea in southern Italy, Amalfi too had originated as a stronghold against land-based invaders in the late sixth century. In the ninth and tenth centuries, Amalfitans used their fleet to support their Christian neighbours against Saracen pirates or to help Arabs against Christians as best suited their own ambitions, in the process establishing lucrative trading contacts with the ports of the Islamic Mediterranean. Through such political processes, shrewd merchants fostered the growth of a new, urban, and mercantile society that attracted attention for its 'richness and opulence'.[8]

What was the situation of older Italian towns at the end of the tenth century? The Roman city of Pavia had been the capital of the Lombard kingdom since the late sixth century and its palace remained the seat of royal government in Italy under the Carolingian then Ottonian rulers. Detailed regulations emanating from the royal treasury document the city's economic life at the end of the tenth century, a time when the city was frequently visited by the emperor and his retinue. Through his treasurer, the emperor collected tolls on the trade that passed through Pavia, regulating its mint and market activities both for his own financial profit and to maintain law and order. The ordinance also tells us of the urban community and its craftsmen—fishermen with their boats, tanners, shipowners, and sailors of large ships, gold-panners and soap-manufacturers—and of the traders who passed through the city. These included Anglo-Saxons and others—probably French and German—from beyond the Alps, who traded horses, slaves, wool, linen and canvas cloth, tin and swords. Italians came too: traders from Amalfi, Salerno, and Gaeta on the Calabrian coast, and especially rich Venetians trading up the Po valley, purchasing wine and grain but bringing with them goods from Byzantium and the Muslim world—spices, ivory combs, silver mirrors, and the like. So Pavia was an outlet for local agricultural produce, a place of production for artisanal products, and a marketplace for imported luxuries as well as a centre for administration and the display of imperial power. The Ottonians, as all rulers, found tolls on trade a lucrative source of income, and their treasury in Pavia was no exception.

But this was not to last. From the late tenth century, Pavia's citizens chafed against imperial control and rebelled on several occasions. When they heard the news of the death of the emperor Henry II in 1024, they destroyed the palace so completely that its location is now unknown. Their revolt signalled the end of an era. Centralized imperial administration in Italy was virtually at an end, and the pace of efforts to achieve urban autonomy throughout Italy quickened in the course of the eleventh century. The political landscapes that had emerged in the aftermath of the disintegration of the Roman Empire could no longer easily contain the new realities of Italian urban wealth.

Treasure, Gifts, and Patronage

The author of the Pavia toll regulations also noted a series of customary payments that were not part of the burgeoning commercial economy of Italy at the end of the tenth century. The wife of the king's treasurer could expect that merchants from other Italian cities would give her gifts of eastern manufactured goods and fine patterned silks. The treasurer himself was to make regular donations of lighting oil to Pavia's cathedral church and of clothing to its custodians. We meet here other forms of exchange, ones in which women were often expert, but in which commercial profit was not the aim. The giving of prestige gifts or of charitable donations to a religious institution signals very different forms of transactions, ones whose social, political, or religious dimension is to the fore. By shifting focus to social interactions that were characterized by patronage, gift giving, or forcible expropriation, we can understand better how material resources could be converted into symbolic capital—that is, into honour, prestige, and political influence.

The scene is set not in Rome but in imperial Ravenna. A glittering mosaic panel in the sixth-century church of San Vitale depicts Justinian (527–65), the last Latin-speaking emperor to rule in Constantinople, and the man who came near to realizing a dream of ousting the warrior kings of Italy, Spain, and North Africa and restoring these provinces to direct imperial control. Dressed in purple and gold, with a huge, heavily jewelled diadem on his head and a matching brooch on his shoulder, he is flanked by courtiers whose rank is indicated by their dress, from the lavish to the more modest. His consort Theodora faces towards him across the church, equally opulently adorned, her retinue also dressed to emphasize precise hierarchy. Both carry gifts of equal splendour: he bears a massive golden salver, she a golden cup studded with glittering gems. The representation of the imperial couple draws attention to the way in which ostentatious display and the giving of gifts were the outer trappings of power in the late Roman world. Expressed in dress, precious objects, art, and architecture, the late antique rhetoric of power and prestige included an idiom of visible wealth, expertly deployed by women and men in complementary ways.

Sumptuously embellished churches—gifts to the Christian God—still stand as a reminder to us of the massive disposable wealth of late Roman emperors and aristocrats. They also signal their donors' hopes that generosity might be rewarded by enhanced holy patronage and protection, for building and endowing churches projected into the realm of the supernatural customs and expectations that informed human relationships. Among the Romans, gift giving consolidated friendships between individuals and eased the exchange of political favours. In a culture where securing patronage was central to political and social advancement, gifts could cement the flow of support between patron and client. Their centrality reflected the basic truth that personal favours and direct contact were the real lubricants of power and influence in the late Roman world, not its cumbersome bureaucratic procedures.

On their accession, late antique emperors would shower coins into the crowds and distribute splendid silver dishes and tableware as largesse to favoured supporters. They also frequently made huge payments to neighbouring kings and warlords to win peace or compliance with other political goals. In this way, Roman prestige goods—gold coins and medallions, luxury silver tableware, the jewelled brooches that designated high rank—flooded across the imperial frontiers. Archaeologists have found their remnants everywhere from Scandinavia and the eastern Baltic to the Black Sea: the influx of fourth- and fifth-century Roman wealth into the treasure chests of the warrior chieftains of northern Europe and the Danube basin enhanced these leaders' prestige and power vis-à-vis their own followers. As they flowed through the political, social, and religious veins of the late antique empire, prestige items cloaked bureaucracy in the guise of direct personal relationships, helped win the support of the saints in heaven, conferred legitimacy, and structured the empire's relationships with its enemies and neighbours.

The post-imperial kingdoms of the early medieval West remained firmly within this political order. Kings took their cue—and much of their treasure—from the empire. Two sixth-century episodes reveal both the material richness and the political symbolism involved. The first concerns the victory of Clovis in 507 over the Goths of south-western Gaul and Spain under their king Alaric II, whom he killed. The battle enabled him to seize south-western Gaul for the Franks, thus confining the Goths to the Iberian peninsula, much to the annoyance of Alaric's father-in-law Theoderic the Great, king of Italy (493–526). Clovis's troops grabbed what they could of Alaric's treasure but, crucially, not the heirlooms that were central to his dynasty's identity. These included ancient political treasures, seized when the Goths under Alaric I had sacked Rome in 410: 'Among these were the treasures of Solomon, the king of the Hebrews, a most noteworthy sight. . . . Most of them were adorned with emeralds; and they had been taken from Jerusalem by the Romans in ancient times [i.e. the Roman sack of AD 70].'[9] These venerable markers of political identity— successively Jewish, Roman, then Gothic—signalled Alaric I's successors as legitimate players in Roman imperial politics. These treasures were far too precious to let fall into Frankish hands, so Theoderic took them into his own custody, returning them to his grandson Amalaric when he became of age to succeed to the throne. Whatever their worth as gold and gems, these heirlooms symbolized prestige, legitimacy, and dynastic continuity.

In the immediate aftermath of his victory, Clovis was rewarded with traditional imperial tokens of recognition and patronage by the Byzantine emperor Anastasius (491–548), whose political strategies his victory had also served. Clovis then signalled his increased status with a dramatic display of royal generosity directed towards his new subjects: in the course of a victory parade in Roman idiom, he made a great gift of the spoils of war to the church of St Martin at Tours and, clad in Roman dress, 'he mounted a horse and, by his own hand, and with the greatest goodwill, distributed gold and silver to the crowd along the road between the gateway of the courtyard [of St Martin's church] and the cathedral church in the city'.[10] By immediately redistributing the booty, Clovis established his credentials as a generous ruler, allied himself with one of the most important saints of the region, and put his new subjects under a moral obligation to reciprocate by giving him their support and loyalty. On this, as on many other occasions, Clovis was a shrewd manipulator of the symbolism of gifts and treaure: by giving, he gained.

Our second episode comes from near the end of the sixth century, and concerns Clovis's great-grandson, Childebert II (575–96). In 584, the Byzantine emperor Maurice (582–602) had presented him with 50,000 gold coins (*solidi*) as an inducement to invade Italy. The peninsula had been reconquered by Justinian at vast cost only a generation before, but then invaded by the Lombards under Alboin in 568, who extended their control throughout its northern half in the course of the next twenty years. Maurice's strategy was the time-honoured one of paying one warrior king to attack another; he hoped the Franks would drive the Lombards out of Italy.

To be effective, diplomatic gift giving presupposed that both giver and receiver recognized the implicit moral code, and that they had equal political interests in an exchange of treasure-for-peace. But, on this particular occasion, it failed. As Childebert marched into Italy, the Lombards avoided conflict by submitting, presenting him with gifts of their own to persuade him to leave. Maurice felt that Childebert had broken the terms of the payment and demanded its return: but the Frankish king was so confident of his power that he did not even deign to reply. In this game of political poker, Childebert was twice the winner. He had gained financially on two occasions, for Maurice's payment was approximately 227.5 kilograms of gold, and the 'many gifts' of the Lombards must also have been substantial.[11] But he had also twice enhanced his political standing: by rejecting the subordination to imperial wishes implied by Maurice's gift, and by receiving the Lombards' sub-mission that accompanied their gifts. He had thereby increased both his material and his symbolic capital.

As the events of 507 and 584 indicate, the amounts of treasure that facilitated post-imperial politics were enormous. They also show that access to and control of treasure were intimately associated with political legitimacy in the eyes of rival kings, one's own subjects, the Byzantine emperor. Yet Maurice's experience reminds us that the giving of political subsidies was unpredictable and fraught with difficulties: it might, or might not, achieve the donor's goals.

As a means for achieving political ends, gift giving did not have to be on the scale of cartloads of gold and jewels: it could involve nothing more costly than a bunch of flowers from a meadow or a thoughtfully composed letter. To observe this, let us remain in sixth-century Gaul a moment longer. In 566, an Italian poet arrived at the court of Sigibert (561–75), father of Childebert II. Venantius Fortunatus launched his career with great éclat by presenting the king with a skilfully composed nuptial ode on the occasion of his marriage to Brunhild. Fortunatus's charming Latin verses are commonly read as an indication of the continuing appreciation for classical literary culture in post-imperial Gaul. But, in addition to being an able poet, the Italian was also sufficiently adroit for the patronage he attracted eventually to bring him a bishopric. As we watch him winning friends and becoming more influential, we may also glimpse the ways in which gift giving was part of the patronage that articulated relationships between individuals.

Food was a subject often in Fortunatus's mind. He thrived—indeed survived—on invitations to banquets or gifts of food. His counter-gifts were poetic and laudatory:

> Nectar, wine, food, clothing, learning, opportunity:
> With your generous gifts, Gogo, you content me.[12]

Senior palace official in Sigibert's court, and man of wide-ranging contacts and influence, Gogo was a useful patron for the Italian poet. Through the relationship, Fortunatus enjoyed the 'fruits of friendship'.[13] A poem to Conda, a man who had risen from modest origins to become a key financial and administrative figure in Sigibert's retinue, hints at the political realities that informed the flow of benefits. Fortunatus comments that Sigibert has given Conda lavish gifts in reward for his able services: 'The king, more powerful than the rest, has provided rightly better rewards, and your case demonstrates what he values more highly.' Conda's own conduct is modelled on the king's: 'In generosity and kindness you bestow gifts in plenty on all, and bind men to you by your gifts.'[14] The king's example was one to be emulated throughout the social hierarchy, for at all levels generous giving created obligations. Power brokers such as Gogo and Conda were well placed to manipulate the flow of royal patronage if they chose: Fortunatus's eulogies were well aimed.

In the end, Fortunatus settled down with two particular patrons. One was Gregory, the hard-pressed bishop of Tours. The other was Radegund (d. 587), former queen of Chlothar I (511–61) but by this time cloistered at Poitiers. As a nun, she continued to practise her courtly skills, and, in pursuit of her own aims, exploited the traditionally feminine associations of fine dress and food. At Tours, Venantius commended himself to Gregory as a special 'humble servant'. The bishop's support for his versifying protégé ranged from presents of shoe leather to landed estates. In return, the Italian used his literary talent to support Gregory at moments of great political crisis. At Poitiers, Radegund and her abbess, Agnes, frequently sent Fortunatus gifts of food from their table—a jug of milk, dark plums, delicate titbits. Whether from the hands of a wealthy queen, a lord's wife, or a woman dedicated to monastic poverty, food was a gift that nurtured more than just a man's stomach. Fortunatus reciprocated with equally modest tokens—bunches of violets, a handmade basket of sweet chestnuts—and put his rhetorical skills to good use in furthering Radegund's plans for making peace between feuding kings and collecting earthly relics of the immortals in heaven. Behind the delicate poetic images, Fortunatus knew as well as Gregory or Radegund the unspoken rules of the courtly game of gift giving. All three were well aware that gifts, obligation, reward, and influence all went together, for they knew well how to convert material resources into social power, political influence, and saintly patronage. Shortly before 600, Fortunatus got his bishopric—in Poitiers.

The use of wealth to solidify political friendships or to maintain and refresh existing bonds of loyalty, dependence, and service was not confined to the late Roman world and its immediate heirs. Indeed, one reason why fifth- and sixth-century rulers so rapidly adapted to their own purposes the politics of redistribution and reciprocity was that analogous customs were integral to the culture of the war bands that had transformed the political map of the Roman West in the fifth century. The organization of the chiefdoms north of the Rhine–Danube frontier and in the non-Roman parts of the British Isles was undoubtedly much simpler than the bureaucratic culture of the imperial state, with its array of professional specialisms and massive military machine. Lacking administrative or coercive means of ruling, the kings of these polities could fall back on little more than bonds of personal influence and obligation.

They forged them from material wealth. The most famous expression of this occurs in *Beowulf*, but has close parallels in early medieval epics in many other languages. The good epic warlord or king is generous to his followers, rewarding valour in battle with lavish gifts, but thereby investing in the expectation of future service and support. An effective war leader will attract ambitious young warriors into his retinue, entertain them in his hall, feast them, and arm them: in the competition for power, rival lords use treasure, precious weaponry, and their own reputation to swell their own army and compete for victory. In *Beowulf*, Hrothgar son of Healfdene was a ruler of this sort:

> Then to Hrothgar was granted glory in battle,
> mastery of the field; so friends and kinsmen
> gladly obeyed him, and his band increased
> to a great company.[15]

Beowulf, a princely warrior from the land of the Geats, was among those who sought service in Hrothgar's retinue, and his exploits form an extended commentary on the social code of martial success, treasure, reward, honour, and rulership. When Beowulf returned from slaying the monsters who had attacked Heorot, the Danish king declared:

> You will lack nothing
> that lies in my gift of the goods of this world:
> lesser offices have elicited reward,
> we have honoured from our hoard less heroic men,
> far weaker in war. But you have well ensured
> by the deeds of your hands an undying honour
> for your name forever.

Then the hall was prepared for the banquet—'gold-embroidered tapestries | glowed from the walls'—and Hrothgar arrived to take his place:

> No people has gathered in greater retinue,
> borne themselves better about their ring-giver.
> Men known for their courage came to the benches,
> rejoiced in the feast; they refreshed themselves kindly
> with many a mead-cup.
>   .   .   .   .
> Then as a sign of victory the son of Healfdene
> bestowed on Beowulf a standard worked in gold,
> a figured battle-banner, breast and head-armour;
> and many admired the marvellous sword
> that was borne before the hero. Beowulf drank with
> the company in the hall. He had no cause to be ashamed of
> gifts so fine before fighting-men!

Hrothgar then added eight warhorses with gold and jewelled harness to the array of gifts, and, through the gift giving, the reputation of both men was enhanced:

> Thus did the glorious prince, guardian of the treasure,
> reward these deeds, with both war-horses and armour;
> of such open-handedness no honest man
> could ever speak in disparagement.[16]

Both Hrothgar and Beowulf had warded off the shame that was the dreaded undertow of a culture of honour and reward: Beowulf had fought his way to wealth and reputation while Hrothgar had demonstrated regal generosity. On the hero's return to the Geats, the circulation of these precious weapons continued, for he duly made his own spirit of generosity manifest by giving them to his kinsman, King Hygelac. Beowulf had proved that he was fit to succeed to the throne.

Beowulf is a great literary epic and its heroes legendary. That its social ethos is nevertheless a realistic indicator of the rituals and values surrounding gift giving in the highly martial culture of the early Middle Ages is amply confirmed by a wide range of historical sources from all parts of Europe. Their matter-of-fact narratives of plundering expeditions and lively descriptions of gifts exchanged at feasts and other ceremonial occasions give historical specificity to the values of epic poetry. Warfare, plundering, and feasting all had their place alongside other forms of exchange: these were the military and political complement to the concentration of agricultural, artisanal, or trading wealth on lordly or royal sites.

The treasures that figure so prominently in the pages of *Beowulf* were not confined to well-wrought weaponry and jewelled body armour. They included goblets and tableware, arm rings and collars, all made of gold. The items of personal adornment were worn and given away by women as well as by men, for women had an integral role in the interlocking traditions of expropriation, redistribution, and reciprocity that shaped all early medieval societies. They too were the givers of gifts, using whatever resources they had at their own command to exercise patronage for their chosen political and religious purposes, as we have seen Theodora and Radegund do. To them often fell the task of ensuring that courtly gifts and hospitality upheld the subtleties of rank and social precedence. A ninth-century guide to the complex organization of Charlemagne's royal household makes this explicit. 'The good management of the palace, and especially the royal dignity, as well as the gifts given annually to the officers (excepting, however, the food and water for the horses) pertained especially to the queen, and under her to the chamberlain.'[17] In overseeing the selection of gifts, the queen upheld the economy of honour upon which palace ritual depended.

In addition to being the agents of generosity, women might find themselves its objects. Hrothgar had betrothed his daughter Freawaru to the Danes' enemy Ingeld, hoping

> thus to end all the feud and their fatal wars
> by means of the lady.[18]

Although the *Beowulf* poet doubted the effectiveness of peacemaking marriage alliances, they are frequently attested in documentary sources of the early Middle Ages. One early example suffices: as a countermove to Clovis's defeat of the Iberian Goths in 507, Theoderic the Great gave his niece Amalberga in marriage to the Franks' enemy, the Thuringian

Hermanifrid. Sealing the marriage with the exchange of 'such gifts as the royal rank requires', Theoderic declared to Hermanifrid: 'May divine favour attend your marriage, that, as friendship has allied us, so may family love bind our posterity.'[19] Hrothgar would have recognized this sentiment—but would also have accepted that marriage alliances were no more predictable in their outcomes than gift giving.

Archaeological material from sites throughout Europe confirms the skill and technical abilities of early medieval goldsmiths and weapon-forgers. It also restores to us some modest fraction of the treasure that demarcated wealth, power, and prestige. But herein lies an irony, for much of the gold and jewellery recovered by archaeologists was deliberately buried, especially in the more northerly parts of Europe. Leaving aside the many caches whose owners buried them in times of insecurity with the intention of recovering them later, intentional deposits might mark sites and actions of ritual or religious significance. One of their social functions was to provide the spectacle of deposition—for whatever group of participants was privileged to watch. Another turned on the knowledge that thereafter the treasure was hidden from view, invisibly present. This is the context of the fifth-century bog sacrifices of war booty from Jutland and southern Sweden, which offer oblique comment on the way in which warring chiefdoms commemorated victory over an enemy. Cosmological significance also attaches to many of the deposits of gold at Gudme ('home of the gods'), a fifth- to sixth-century centre of political and religious power and trade on the Danish island of Fyn. Here we encounter a range of non-Roman and non-Christian associations between wealth and the supernatural, ones whose full religious or ideological implications cannot be fully recovered owing to the lack of written evidence to reveal the cosmology that informed them. Though mute, such deposits are suggestive.

Equally intentional was the funerary deposition of objects, mundane or prestigious. Archaeologists have uncovered—and continue to find—thousands of furnished inhumation burials from England and the non-Mediterranean continent in the period from c.400 to c.700, plus small numbers from Mediterranean regions. Such graves range from very modest through to immensely wealthy assemblages. Take the example of the East Saxon cemetery at Prittlewell in south-east England, where about 20 sixth- to seventh-century graves have been found. Some had no objects deposited in them at all; others no more than a knife, brooch, or a pot or two. One grave contained an exceptional chamber, whose discovery was announced in February 2004. Accompanied by his sword and shield, a warrior had been buried in the first half of the seventh century in a large, wood-lined cell. He had been laid to rest clothed in gold-braided fabric belted with a massive gold buckle, wearing gold-buckled shoes and with two small gold-foil crosses on his chest. His burial chamber was kitted out with a wide range of items that hint at far-flung contacts: a Byzantine flagon and inscribed silver spoon; a large Coptic bowl; two gold coins from Merovingian Gaul; hanging bowls from Ireland or northern England; and two pairs of Kentish glass jars. It also contained accoutrements suggestive of a ruler who liked to entertain his retinue in high style: a Roman-type folding seat perhaps from Italy; a tall stand for a torch (or perhaps a royal standard); decorated drinking horns; wooden drinking cups with gilded mounts; a lyre; gaming pieces and dice; plus hanging cauldrons, buckets, and a casket.

Like the handful of other richly furnished, probably royal, graves known from Anglo-Saxon England, the princely grave at Prittlewell undoubtedly had both a religious and a social context. On the one hand, it hints at the complexities and contradictions that often accompanied the spread of Christianity.[20] On the other, it suggests a good funeral, with a 'master of ceremonies' to orchestrate its grandeur, surviving relatives vying for the inheritance, and onlookers impressed by the spectacle. As we saw earlier, the burial rites employed as Roman rule collapsed and new kingdoms evolved were often an occasion for lavish displays of social status, not simply that of the deceased, but equally importantly of the heirs.[21] In view of the fluidity and uncertainty of early medieval inheritance practices, the death of a leading member of a kin group might well have been a moment of great crisis for his or her surviving relatives and their wider community, all the more so if the dead person were a ruler. Decisions about the weapons, jewels, and other objects to place in an early medieval grave were then deliberate choices about the uses of valuable items. The burial of these treasures was an assertion of prestige and influence at a crucial political moment, the funeral itself a suitable theatre for renegotiating power and reconfiguring social relationships.

Whether worked into items of personal adornment, elaborate tableware, or body armour and weaponry, gold, silver, and jewels were among the most durable forms of movable wealth in the early Middle Ages. Other forms perished, leaving only indirect trace. Prominent among them were the victims of plundering and warfare along the northern and eastern fringes of Europe, where slaving was habitual. Many human cargoes were shipped by Viking slavers from the British Isles to the Baltic, whence they were traded on into the Muslim east. Other convoys were marched westwards and southwards from the Slav lands of central Europe. Some were then embarked at Venice and other Mediterranean ports for transport to the Muslim east; others were taken via Verdun and then across the Pyrenees to supply the Umayyad court at Cordoba. The only material testimony to these unfortunates' existence is the neck irons, manacles, and chains with which they were bound, such as those from the stronghold of Staré Zámky, at the western end of the Carpathians. A convoy heading westwards from there would in all likelihood have made its way to the East Frankish border toll station at Raffelstetten in Bavaria. Here, Rus and Bohemian slave-dealers sold them on, quite probably to the Jews who were prominent in the early medieval European slave trade. The commercial value of these convoys must have been considerable, for the tolls taken at Raffelstetten in 906 indicate that a female slave was of equal value to a war stallion. She was an expensive item, prestigious in her own right, valuable in reproductive terms, and, in cash terms, worth four times as much as a male slave (or a mare).

The great worth of female slaves was also recognized in Ireland, where they formed a common unit of value. For example, the honour price of a provincial king was fourteen female slaves (*cumals*) in the estimation of an eighth-century treatise. By far the commonest form of currency for making payments in Ireland, however, was cattle. Central to the Irish economy, they were equally significant in political and social contexts. Irish law tracts reveal a world where lords bound clients to themselves by grants of cattle in ways that were simultaneously economic and political investments. This could happen in one of two ways, forming relationships of either 'free' or 'base' clientship. Common to both was a system that dispersed a lord's large herd widely, thus reducing the risk of malnourishment or disease, and where, over a period of years, a lord would receive back calves and heifers equal or greater in number to the size of the original grant of stock. Although cattle were only one element in a mixed arable–pastoral economy, they had a political significance and symbolic importance that other livestock lacked, as other aspects of the clientage arrangements reveal. In the case of a base tenant, his honour became subsumed within the lord's own, in a clear relationship of subjection. In addition, the base client paid annual food renders, provided manual labour on the lord's lands and fortifications, and demonstrated his subjection both by feasting the lord and his retinue for one night each winter and by fighting for him in his military retinue. A free client, on the other hand, enjoyed an honourable relationship with his lord. He might well be of noble status himself, and more than repaid the loan of stock on terms that imply that he had considerable herds of his own on which to draw should the lord's cattle fail to breed. There are other indications of his status too.

Unlike the base client, the free client suffered no loss of independence. All he had to do to mark the relationship was to rise to his feet when his lord stood up in the local political assembly, and probably provide fairly light labour services too. Through cattle clientage, a lord did not simply make arrangements for stockbreeding. He was fed and his own arable land was farmed. He acquired dependants commensurate with his wealth and rank, and a military following. With large herds of cattle he could acquire the attributes of a 'noble of the first rank' and enjoy all the prestige and power the status implied.[22]

All this makes sense for a population who used cattle as their equivalent of a unit of currency and lived in a natural environment that was particularly well suited to stock raising. But the methodical system suggested by the law codes must have been tempered by other, harsher realities: the episodes of cattle murrain that ripped through Ireland, intense competition among lords to acquire free clients, and the cattle raiding that formed the characteristic—and often deadly—form of Irish status rivalry among the numerous lords and petty kings. Paradoxically, cattle raiding was as integral to maintaining social equilibrium as it was dangerous to life and limb. But the paradox is only apparent, for, like feuding, cattle raiding had its own conventions. As with feuding too, contemporaries took its *raison d'être* for granted. A successful foray swelled a lord's stock of breeding cattle and might thus enable him to recruit more clients. It also provided an arena for displays of the masculine ethic of courage and military skill, and the likelihood that it would trigger a retaliatory raid raised the stakes. If a raid failed, a chief risked losing prestige, possibly also his life and the cohesion of his following. Cattle raids kept resources circulating and demanded frequent reassertions of military ability and solidarity. In so doing, they provided opportunities for negotiating codes of honour and binding a lord to his followers.

The surviving evidence makes it impossible to ascertain to what extent the Irish system of cattle-based patronage changed in the course of the early Middle Ages. Elsewhere, however, notable developments in the politics of generosity are more readily traceable. Above all, they concern the growing significance of landed estates as objects of patronage—and of competition. Many reasons for this have already been encountered: rising population; the precedent of inalienable ecclesiastical endowments; concern for the fate of the Christian soul after death; the gradually increasing ability to extract a significant cash profit from the land. From the seventh century on the Continent, and the eighth in England, grants of land became increasingly prominent forms of reward. While prestige items always remained the appropriate gift for another ruler, their role in relationships between a king and his entourage shifted to accommodate the pressure to acquire land.

Immovable property was the most potent, but also the most complex, form of gift or patronage. As such, it was central to the maintenance of honour, but liable to generate particular tensions. Unlike plunder or tribute, it was everywhere yet of finite quantity—unless, perhaps, there was an open frontier that invited aggression and land seizure. As a source of income, rights of lordship, and status, it had potentially enduring importance. But it usually came hedged around with qualifications, and was generally subject to multiple interests. If granted to the laity, it might be confiscated later for misbehaviour. If given to a church, it carried reciprocal obligations of prayer and military service. Then there might be the expectations of the heirs of a former owner to counter or accommodate, or sitting tenants to consider. And benefactors usually gave land to a church not in a single, limited moment of piety, but in the hope of forging enduring spiritual bonds with a religious community and its patron saint. Intertwined secular and religious favours together with ongoing commitments thus lay at the core of the politics of landed patronage.

We gain rare, vivid insights into the insecurities inherent in a land-based patronage system by once more taking Einhard as our guide. In the fifteen years after Charlemagne's death in 814, escalating tensions among the elite about inheritance, patronage, and reward exacerbated disputes about the imperial succession, and culminated in serious revolts in 830 and again in 833–4. In this atmosphere of political uncertainty, control of land became the key to political success more than ever before: competition for landed resources hereafter fuelled politics in an unprecedented way. These are the circumstances that Einhard's correspondence illustrates so effectively.

Through his letters, we see him negotiating with his own personal assistants and administrators in order to reap the financial benefits of his property. The reader is immediately struck by Einhard's attention to detail: he writes about such minutiae as arrangements for the distribution of the offal from slaughtered cattle, or the problem of securing a supply of wax after two years when the bees had failed to produce much honey. This attentiveness was in response to the sheer challenge of getting the right resources to the right place at the right time, whether food to maintain his retinue while he attended court at Aachen, or the difficulty of obtaining the building supplies he desired for the church he was constructing at Seligenstadt. Unlike the lordship of the clergy of St Peter's, Ghent, Einhard's personal lordship lacked a single administrative centre but shifted around his estates. Vigilance was also needed, for he also had to wrestle with negligent estate bailiffs and ensure that the income due to him was collected in full and in coins of good quality. Such administrative details inevitably had a political aspect. It was traditional—indeed obligatory—for Carolingian bishops, abbots, and lords to make annual 'gifts' to the ruler, and these generally took the form of prestige objects—horses, falcons and weaponry, silver, gold, and jewelled objects. This did not merely help to keep the royal treasure chests stocked: it defined the elite group who enjoyed access to the ruler. It also marked their deference to him. So Einhard duly wrote to his deputies instructing them to prepare and deliver his offerings to the palace. He can hardly have been unique in the exertions needed to make the most of landed property: his letters are simply more explicit about the difficulties than most other sources.

Einhard also hoped for something in return, usually in the form of political favours. He wrote on several occasions to Louis the Pious or members of his family to invoke their patronage and active help in building his church at Seligenstadt. He usually brought added pressure to bear by hinting at the spiritual support that Marcellinus and Peter, the Roman martyrs housed there, would bestow on those who patronized them, for Carolingian ideas of patronage embraced the saints as firmly as in late Antiquity. At other times, contacts—'friendships'—made at the earthly court could also be invoked to secure his goals, whether further resources for his building project, or favours for his political followers. Land also featured here, for, in the uncertain political climate of the 830s, Einhard's followers feared loss of their benefices—those estates to which they had only temporary rights—and, as their patron, he used his influence and the prestige of his name to do what he could for them. And, since the politics of patronage was a reciprocal process, many of his letters also reveal that he was himself importuned by others who sought to turn his influence to their own purposes. So he also wrote to palace officials, abbots, counts, and bishops to put in a good word or argue a case here and plead for an appointment there.

Against this backdrop of uncertainty and cronyism, Einhard emerges as a man whose influence was worth courting: as ever, personal contacts, patronage, and gifts together directed the flow of power and privilege and turned friendship into politics. In this respect, there is, however, a notable disparity between his great political capital and the relatively modest landed resources available to him. Perhaps, in making himself the earthly advocate of his beloved heavenly martyrs, Einhard had acquired spiritual resources to help bridge the gap. In addition, his long years at court, brilliant talents, and unfaltering loyalty first to Charlemagne and then to Louis the Pious had served him well, for they afforded him a central place in the web of social power that was spun around the imperial court. Proximity to martyred saints and emperors alike compensated for his limited material resources.

If Einhard's careful negotiation of the quicksands of court politics emphasizes the precariousness of lay careers built upon royal favour and grants of benefices, it also underscores the interconnectedness of secular and supernatural patronage. One of the main desires of kings and lesser laity alike was to win heavenly favour and intercession. Those who secured it on their behalf, put pious wishes into practice, and turned land into prayer were commonly their widows. This was why Heregyth, Abba's widow, had left land to Christ Church, Canterbury, and why Gisela devoted so much of her energies to the monastery that she and Eberhard had founded at Cysoing.[23]

Because of their potency as heavenly patrons, saints were not only the recipients of much land and treasure but could also themselves constitute the donated objects. Henry, duke of Saxony, had been chosen as king by the German nobility late in 918 and was formally installed on the throne the following spring. Lacking any ancestral claim to the throne, Henry built his rule on shrewd negotiating, military success, and the accumulation of holy relics through royal gift exchange. In 921, he reached an accord on equal terms with Charles the Simple, the last remaining Carolingian ruler, whose recognition enhanced his prestige and helped consolidate his position. In practice, though, Charles was the much weaker man, and the following year was defeated in battle and deposed by his own subjects. Desperate for support, Charles sent Henry a 'sign of faith and truth'—part of the body of the Carolingians' especial patron, the martyr Denis.[24] The gesture was one of defiance towards Charles's West Frankish opponents—but by the same token recognized Henry I as a rightful heir of the ancient Carolingian dynasty and the protector of its religious traditions. The arm of St Denis extended the aura of generations of Frankish kings to the new German ruler.

More prestigious even than remains of saints or martyrs were relics of Christ's crucifixion. In this Henry followed in Radegund's footsteps and made a notable acquisition. In 926, he ended his enmity with Rudolf II, king of Burgundy (912–37), persuaded him to recognize his overlordship, gave him rich gifts and transferred part of Swabia to him. The pact between the two kings was sealed when Rudolf gave Henry 'that thing whereby God had joined the things of earth to the things of heaven'— namely, the 'sacred spear' believed to have been used at the crucifixion and once owned by the first Christian Roman emperor, Constantine. This 'invincible weapon against all enemies, visible and invisible', had been a gift to Rudolf during his brief adventure as king of Italy (922–6).[25] Passing from him to Henry, who in turn bequeathed it to his son Otto I, the spear became an enduring symbol of legitimate rulership and German imperial authority, as the next chapter will demonstrate. Carried into battle, regarded as a holy relic and token of empire, it was kept at Aachen until the German empire ended in 1806, when, along with the rest of the imperial regalia, it was transferred to Vienna, where it remains on display.

The symbolism of ancient weapons, secular and sacred patronage all fuse in Henry I's relic collecting. Economic capital was transformed into symbolic capital; secular lordship expressed itself through spiritual patronage. The royal politics of gift giving and alliance building deployed many currencies: material wealth, sacred objects, territorial control, prestige, and legitimacy were inter-convertible. Although Otto I's empire bore minimal resemblance to that of Justinian 400 years earlier, kings and emperors continued to use similar strategies and strove for similar goals. Successful rulers adroitly manipulated all their convertible assets.

From the middle of the eleventh century, some of these attitudes began to change. First in northern Italy, where a mercantile economy was developing rapidly, and soon thereafter elsewhere, the acquisition of material resources no longer seemed such a straightforward sign of blessing. Although early medieval moralists had condemned the immoderate thirst for riches and regarded avarice as the worst of all vices, they had never called into question either the need to accumulate in a principled way or the reciprocity of giving and getting that defined and sustained political communities. But the surge in monetary transactions and commercial profit in cities such as Milan and Pavia short-circuited the ebb-and-flow of gifts and benefits. It also eroded the consensus that sustained it. Churchmen began to worry about the spiritual purity of those who accepted gifts in return for loyalty, and, especially, for ecclesiastical office and advantage. The involvement of bishops and abbots in the exchange of gifts and patronage became equated with moral corruption: the taint of heresy was detected. Then, as levels of material wealth rose still further, poverty began to seem to some the more godly option.

None of this would have made sense before the turn of the millennium. In the early Middle Ages, material wealth and political power had flowed along channels that were secular, sacred, or both simultaneously. Both were multiform, mutable, unstable, in need of constant reinforcement. In communities at risk of dearth, earthly riches betokened divine favour. Fitting offerings for the gods and the Christian saints, treasures, like land, conferred upon their owners and donors religious as well as political advantage. In this world where resources were hard-won but easily dissipated, their possession was one of the defining characteristics of the religious and lay elite. They used their wealth to display their status; uphold and reinforce their honour; establish and strengthen their ties to lords, rulers, and the saints in heaven.

Accumulating resources and distributing them generously were thus urgent imperatives. They demanded continuous attention, and no secular or ecclesiastical power broker could afford to let his or her attention slip. Full treasure chests little availed the lord who lacked the ability to manage their contents and manipulate their symbolism to political and religious advantage; a richly equipped altar did little for a church whose patron saint was a sluggish advocate of donors' interests. Yet conventions of gift giving and patronage followed no explicit rules. Their universally recognized moral and political expectations remained implicit, a consensus embedded in social practice and absorbed as part of childhood training in the courtly exercise of power. Intensely competitive, with both earthly honour and the fate of the soul at issue, the early Middle Ages remained a customary world of getting and giving. Having watched how kings turned their resources into political advantage, we must next ask how they justified that power and made it seem natural.

IDEOLOGIES

7

Kingship and Christianity

We pray that you bestow on King Louis unending prosperity.
We pray that you bestow on him life, health, and victory. Hear us!
. . .
We pray that you restrain the heathens steadfast in their savage
   religion. Hear us!
We pray that you humble the pagan heathens. Hear us![1]

First of all, my dearest son, I counsel, advise and persuade you thus:
if you desire to honour the royal crown, you should uphold the
catholic and apostolic faith with such diligence and good care that
you set an example to all the subjects committed to you by God, and
so that all sons of the church may deservedly call you a true man of
Christian profession. Know for sure that without this you will be
called neither a Christian nor a son of the church. And because faith
without works dies, those who believe falsely or who do not imple-
ment their faith in good works neither reign honorably nor share in
the eternal kingdom and its crown.[2]

WHEN the monks of the royal monastery of Lorsch prayed to the
Christian God for 'unending prosperity . . . life, health, and victory' for
their king, Louis the German (840–76), they invoked an ideology of kingship that had already been many centuries in the making. Prosperity for
ruler and subjects alike; the defence and propagation of Christianity; victory over enemies; upholding the rule of law: together, these formed the
core of early medieval thinking about the role of kings and the place of
Christianity in politics and society. By the early eleventh century, Europe
had evolved a culture distinctive for its integration of sacred and profane
power, characterized by kings who ruled in close association with the
personnel and institutions of the Christian religion, identified themselves
as 'Christ's own deputy',[3] and presided over efforts to promote their own

particular vision of a Christian society. The model of Christian kingship that had matured by the early years of the eleventh century is captured for us in the manual of advice quoted above, written by King Stephen of Hungary (997–1038) for his infant son. Stephen offered his heir a ten-point plan in which the king himself exemplified the Christian faith and its moral agenda, supported ecclesiastical institutions, and honoured its personnel. In his short, state-of-the-art treatise, royal power and Christian religion interlocked, supplying both a powerful ideology and practical code of conduct to mould the future king into the truly Christian ruler.

Such advice was timely: Pope Sylvester II had sent both his blessing and a diadem to Stephen in 1000/1, thereby making him the first crowned Christian king of the Hungarians. Otto III had given his approval, signified with a gift of a copy of the Holy Lance that his great-grandfather had received from Rudolf of Burgundy and had brandished as the insignia of Christian rulership. In that moment, Stephen took his place in an ordered hierarchy of Christian princes at whose apex Otto, as emperor, exercised pre-eminent authority.[4] Yet only a century and a half previously, the Hungarians (Magyars, in their own language) were the very 'heathens steadfast in their savage religion' whose attacks had so terrorized Louis the German and his subjects, and for whose defeat the monks of Lorsch had prayed. Their transformation from a cluster of semi-nomadic tribes in the western Asian steppe practising shamanism and spirit worship into a single people settled west of the Carpathian mountains and cohering into a Christian kingdom happened with remarkable rapidity. Notably, Stephen's coronation and anointing in 1000/1 accompanied the establishment of an archbishopric at Esztergom, and this joint institutionalization of church authority and Christian rulership is often regarded as the founding moment of the Christian kingdom of Hungary. Further, in the years immediately following, King Stephen not only wrote his manual of advice for his son; he also issued two law codes that took additional steps to strengthen royal power, establish a church hierarchy, promote Christian beliefs, and eradicate social and religious practices unacceptable to his Christian clergy. In this perspective, he was himself the model Christian ruler whom his son should aspire to emulate, a king whose vision of a truly Christian society achieved by legislation held out the possibility of realizing many a missionary bishop's dreams. When he was formally recognized as a saint by the Hungarian bishops in 1083, half a century after his death, Stephen's role as national founding father was formalized and commemorated.

In Stephen of Hungary we find a succinct illustration of the ways in

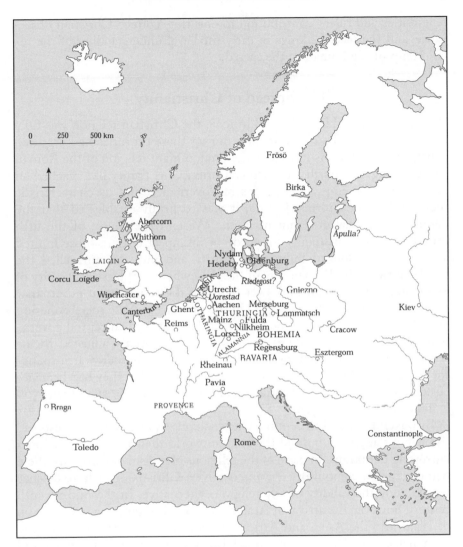

7.1. Principal places mentioned in Chapter 7.

which kings were central to the religious life of the early Middle Ages, fostering Christianity and benefiting from the ideology that this religion in turn promoted. This chapter will track three themes that associated rulers with religion: the royal role in fostering the spread of Christianity at the expense of other religious identities; the distinctions of both practice and perception between Christianity and other early medieval

religiosities and rulers' contribution to ensuring 'correct' Christian observance; and the place of kings in early medieval understanding of the relationship of the human to the sacred.

The Spread of Christianity

When Stephen of Hungary died in 1038, the Christian religion was fully
a millennium old. Its dissemination during these centuries had acquired
a distinctive profile. As it became the predominant religion of the Roman
world during the fourth and fifth centuries, Christianity had reached an
accord with the empire, its modes of governance, and its characteristic
social and cultural forms. Indeed, it was so firmly established that the
demise of imperial government in the West in the course of the fifth
century caused Christianity to recede or disappear only in those limited
areas where prolonged military insecurity and invasion unravelled the
whole fabric of the Roman way of life. Elsewhere, not least in the city of
Rome itself, churchmen took over many of the functions of governance
formerly fulfilled by the state. And in the provinces whose social cohesion
and identity had anyway come to depend less and less on central government, Christian communities and their leaders rapidly adjusted themselves to the establishment of new kingdoms, seeing in their warrior kings
the same possibilities for protection and patronage that they had been accustomed to enjoy under imperial aegis. The extent of Christianity in *c.*500
is indicated on Figure 7.2.

By the end of the fifth century, Christian observance was so widespread
throughout and even beyond the Roman world that its presence led to a
narrowing of options. In place of the religious pluralism of Antiquity, there
had emerged a compulsory—even coercive—Christianity, whose essence
was to deny the validity of any religious alternative. In the mid-seventh
century, however, the arrival of Arab conquerors bringing the new religion
of Islam into the Asian and African provinces of the Byzantine Empire
both helped harden the conceptual boundaries between religions and
greatly altered the geographical ones. In the face of the Arab advance, the
Byzantine Empire lost the majority of its non-European territories during the course of the seventh century, and the conquest of Spain in 711 left
only the mountainous north of the peninsula under Christian control. To
be sure, there remained thereafter extensive Christian communities under
Islamic rule, and Byzantium also managed to maintain control of ancient
Christian cities in Asia Minor, but, from the later seventh century, a religious frontier effectively threaded across the Mediterranean. That frontier came to be as much cultural and political as religious, and, with only

7.2. The extent of Christianity in the early Middle Ages. This map indicates the expansion of Christianity beyond its late Roman limits, as well as areas where it ceased to be a significant presence.

minor fluctuations, would remain unaltered until the eleventh century. Its presence defined identities in a new and sharper way.

North of the Mediterranean, another equally profound geographical transformation was occurring, as the old boundaries of empire along the Danube, the Rhine, and across northern Britain ceased to mark the limits of a Christian church organized to fit the Roman administrative template, with its division of the empire into dioceses and provinces. As Figure 7.2 shows, between the fourth and the seventh century, the Christian religion found its way to all corners of the British Isles; during the eighth and ninth centuries it extended from the Rhine to the Elbe, and then from the Danube to the Dnieper and the Baltic in the course of the tenth and early eleventh centuries. Indeed, Hungary was only one of several Christian kingdoms newly established around the turn of the millennium: the rulers of Poland, Bohemia, Denmark, Norway, and the Rus principality of Kiev all adopted Christianity within the decades 970–1030. Far out in the north Atlantic, even the communities of Vikings-turned-farmers who had settled on Iceland made a collective decision to adopt Christianity in 999/1000. In the course of the early Middle Ages, Christianity 'had gained many kingdoms and had triumphed over the mightiest kings and had crushed through its own power the necks of the proud and the sublime'. When Radbod, bishop of Utrecht (899–917), wrote those words in the early tenth century he cannot have known that they were as much prophetic as retrospective.[5]

How and why had this come about? Three salient characteristics of early medieval Christianity contribute to the explanation: its small-scale forms of organization, multiple social definitions, and doctrinal flexibility. As to the first, Christians had evolved a fairly standard form of organization by c.500, in which regional communities of worship (dioceses) were supervised by a bishop who had jurisdiction over professional ritual specialists (priests) who served local churches. The bishop of Rome—the pope—was widely acknowledged as the most senior leader of Christians in the West: if he was respected, it was out of deference, for, as the next chapter will explain, he commanded no jurisdictional obedience before c.1050. When groups of bishops acted in concert, they did so in a regional or sometimes a national level, but not a universal one. It became customary during the early Middle Ages for the pope to sanction the creation of new arch-bishoprics (such as Esztergom) as national or regional 'super-bishoprics', but new dioceses could be established, and new village churches built and staffed, wherever needed, without papal authorization. In addition, communities of celibate men or women living together established themselves wherever Christianity took hold. Although in the course of the early

Middle Ages these tended to become formalized to a common pattern, most monasteries nevertheless remained autonomous. In institutional terms, then, Christian modes of organization remained decentralized and could easily be replicated everywhere.

In social and doctrinal terms, early medieval Christianity evinced considerable fluidity. No consensus had emerged as to quite what being a 'Christian' meant except inasmuch as it designated a person who had made a public profession of this identity by undergoing the initiation ritual of baptism, or who had had that profession made on his or her behalf. Theologically speaking, that announcement implied that the individual was open to the possibility of eternal life after death. As Julian, bishop of Toledo (680–90), affirmed, 'everyone who is truly a Christian should in no way doubt that the flesh will be resurrected of all persons who have been born or will be born and who have died or will die'.[6] On this point, there was indeed agreement. The practical implications of the baptismal profession remained imprecise, however. More rigorous definitions of being a Christian emphasized ethical conduct, disengagement from the ties of secular society, and intellectual understanding of that belief. At its fullest, Christianity pulled all aspects of temporal, human existence into relationship with the divine in the course of a search for salvation in eternity. The precise doctrinal implications of that also remained negotiable. In the 500 years since its origins in Palestine, the religion's teachings had not been systematized into a single, coherent body of doctrine of undisputed meaning. Nor would that happen during the early Middle Ages: those who debated and wrote about its tenets had like-minded views on some but not all issues. Few indeed were equipped or inclined to participate in such learned discussions, not that these debates would have meant anything to the person baptized at birth into an isolated rural community visited occasionally by a barely literate priest. Being 'Christian' in the early Middle Ages was not susceptible to a standardized definition.

Thus, before c.1100, Christianity was organized in ways that were local but nevertheless replicable anywhere. Further, there was a spectrum of definitions of what it meant to be Christian and a range of interpretations of the core tenets of doctrine. In effect, early medieval Christianity was neither centralized nor systematized. Not a single, uniform cultural package to be adopted or rejected as an entity, it comprised a repertoire of beliefs, social practices, and organizational forms that could be adopted and adapted piecemeal. Thus Christianity jumped from one cultural and political context to another, repeatedly mutating and reconstituting itself in ways that preserved its core features. Differently put, a religion with an avowedly universal message managed to localize itself in a multitude of cultural contexts. Pluralisms and possibilities remained the hallmarks of early medieval Christianity—or, better, of early medieval Christianities— and enabled this universal religion to take endlessly varied local forms. Christianity thus reinforced the localisms so characteristic of the early Middle Ages.

Traditional narratives of the spread of Christianity do not take adequate account of these local variations. They offer a story of its diffusion from ancient Mediterranean centres of power through the work of famous men—emperors, kings, missionaries, and sometimes even popes. Inherent in this interpretation is a set of anachronistic assumptions about what constitutes normative Christianity. Those local particularities become much more evident when we start from a vantage point at the boundaries of Christendom, not at its centre. Kings and missionaries will concern us somewhat later.

As zones of cultural and economic interchange, early medieval frontiers were just as porous as Roman ones. Cross-border contacts made in the course of normal activities such as travelling and trading might be channels of encounter or dissemination through which Christianity seeped. The reception of passing merchants, missionaries, or political envoys offered moments of interaction, generating a modicum of familiarity with the Christian religion long before its adoption. Thus, when Franks and Danes met on the banks of the Eider to swear peace in 811, each group of envoys did so 'according to their own ritual and custom', the former taking an explicitly Christian oath, the latter doing something different.[7] The Magyars offer another example of a people whose contacts with Christianity preceded the arrival of Byzantine and German missionaries among them in the course of the tenth century, for in the early 880s the Greek missionary Methodius had travelled between Constantinople and the Slav lands through Hungarian territory along the Danube, where he was received with 'honor, solemnity, and joy' by their leader, who showered him with gifts.[8] Such encounters belong to the world of long-distance travel and took place at the level of elites and political leaders. But local cross-border encounters could also prompt the emergence of Christian communities in their hinterland. This is the likely explanation for the presence of organized churches in places such as Whithorn and Abercorn in the fifth and sixth centuries, north of the Roman frontier in Britain, or at Nilkheim in the early eighth century, beyond the eastern periphery of Merovingian Gaul.

Trade is a well-documented means of gaining knowledge of another religion. Doubtless the prayers and rituals of Christian merchants travelling beyond the limits of Christendom drew occasional comment. Better recorded, however, are the experiences of non-Christian merchants whose trade took them into Christian territories. Ninth-century merchants from the Scandinavian emporia encountered Christianity in the course of their travels. Some men from the Baltic emporium at Hedeby had been baptized at *Dorestad*, for example. Others recollected enough of what the Frankish missionary bishop Anskar (d. 865) had preached to suggest to the Swedes trying to sack the eastern Baltic settlement of *Apulia* that they appeal to the Christian god for help when their own deities were unwilling to assist.

Another notable form of encounter and dissemination of Christianity was cross-border raiding and slaving. Late Roman writers were well aware that Christian slaves sometimes spread Christianity to their captors: the most famous example is Patrick, the Romano-British Christian carried off into slavery by Irish raiders who escaped and later returned to Ireland to preach to his former masters at some point in the fifth century. In this respect, nothing changed with the political disintegration of the Roman Empire, for the slaving that marked the rim of all powerful polities in the early Middle Ages continued to function as a channel of religious interaction. Notably, on arrival at Birka, Anskar had found a considerable number of Christian captives. A tale from the 840s reveals how such people found themselves in transit around Europe's periphery. Fintan was a Christian, the son of a petty Irish ruler in Laigin, whose kin were busy feuding with a neighbouring warlord. To pre-empt further retaliation, his opponents resorted to guile: they invited Fintan to a feast on the beach and arranged for a group of Vikings in the neighbourhood to stage a raid and seize him. Fintan was rapidly and repeatedly sold on from one Viking to another, until he found himself the property of a man ready to return home, who shipped him off with his other captives. En route back to Scandinavia, the crew stopped overnight at an uninhabited island in the Orkneys, where Fintan managed to escape. Pledging himself never to return home, he swam to safety on a nearby island, and ended his days in 881 as a hermit in the foothills of the Alps at Rheinau.

The most notorious form of frontier violence is, of course, warfare, and this in its own way also contributed to the spread of Christianity. In the 250s, Goths living adjacent to the Roman frontier in the Crimea had frequently raided the southern, Roman shore of the Black Sea. On occasion, they returned with Christian prisoners, and from such inauspicious beginnings, the Goths acquired their first knowledge of Christianity. Some Goths converted; certainly the captive community preserved its religion for several generations until Ulfilas's imperially sponsored mission in the

340s–350s turned the Goths to the Arian interpretation of Christianity in vogue in imperial circles at that time.[9] Another perhaps more frequent scenario was the exposure to Christianity in imperial detention of prisoners and hostages taken from frontier peoples. Charlemagne's wars against the Saxons were notorious for their bloodshed and unremitting determination to crush Saxon society and religion, substituting Christianity at swordpoint.[10] A modest administrative memorandum from 805–6 records for us the names of thirty-seven Saxon hostages entrusted singly or in pairs to the safekeeping of the bishops, abbots, and counts of Alamannia. Their fates are unknown, but these were evidently men important enough to have had their lives spared—for refashioning as Christian subjects of the conquering emperor. Many other successful Carolingian and Ottonian campaigns against pagan enemies must have ended similarly.

From the late fourth century onwards, the periphery of the Christian Roman Empire was also a zone where not only individuals and small groups were in transit, but sometimes also armies and whole peoples. As warlords and their retinues crossed the frontier in search of new homes within the empire, so they found themselves settling among Christians. Some, such as the Goths and Vandals who settled within the empire in the early fifth century, were already Christians, albeit Arian Christians. For others, however, adoption of Christianity followed after migration into the empire. As the Franks expanded the area of their political control and settlement into the northern half of Gaul in the course of the fifth century, they must have had extensive contacts with the region's well-established urban Christian communities, and with such rural ones as existed. Here, religious change came not through travellers or missionaries, but through the sustained interactions of everyday life. Intermarriage was one aspect of that: whenever a Frankish warrior married a Christian woman, the household became a focus for religious change. In Gaul and elsewhere, the importance of Christian wives and mothers in spreading their religion cannot be overestimated. Only at royal level, however, does the surviving evidence enable us to track this in any detail. Clovis, the Frankish king whose acceptance of Christianity in (probably) 508 made him a trophy convert of great significance both to contemporaries and to posterity, had long been married to a Christian Burgundian princess. Chlothild's determination to have her children baptized and her personal influence over Clovis contributed to his decision to accept Christianity, earning herself a place in later legend as 'the mother of France'. From farmstead to palace, the domestic household was one of the most effective—if least well-documented—focuses for religious change and acculturation.

Except in the lower Rhineland, the gradual accommodation of the Franks to Christianity entailed no substantive disruption to Gallo-Roman Christianity. If anything, it enhanced the influence of leading churchmen. Elsewhere, however, the movement of armies and settlers often had a more deleterious effect. Christianity had spread throughout Britain by the late fourth century, but, when Anglo-Saxon settlers crossed the North Sea during the fifth and sixth centuries, its institutional organization crumbled throughout south-eastern Britain. Such Christianity as did survive here did so only as a few isolated pockets, bereft of clerical leadership. Perhaps the same happened in the Danube plain in the tenth century, for the western part of the region taken over by the Magyars included well-established Christian communities who seem to have passed their own vernacular religious terminology on to their conquerors.

In contrast to this slow, almost unchronicled cultural seepage, the political jolts that jump-started Christianity in new environments are highly visible in the sources. These form the second, quite different, means by which the religion spread: the decisive actions of powerful men and women whose impact was often rapid and wide-ranging. Whether as a narrative of rulers whose conversion harked back to that of the emperor Constantine (306–37), of queens who persuaded their consorts of a different understanding of their power, or of evangelizers obedient to Christ's injunction 'go ye and teach all nations, baptizing them in the name of the Father, the Son and the Holy Ghost' (Matt. 28: 19), the spread of Christianity is also a tale of high politics and of individuals whose fame Christian communities dutifully nurtured.

As a royal action, the acceptance—or rejection—of the new religion commonly took place against the background of a politics of hegemony. The assertion of influence by an overlord over a lesser ruler, the search by a petty king for support from a powerful neighbour, or simply the desire to emulate a proven recipe for succesful kingship all played their part. Whether on their own initiative or in response to royal instruction, preachers moved through the same channels of communication, only infrequently setting out for places unconnected even in any indirect way with their homeland. They brought with them political contacts, prestigious gifts, experience in magnificent ritual, and, not least, prior familiarity with the authoritative script for enacting successful conversion.

In these circumstances, acceptance of Christianity bore all the marks of political spectacle, carefully staged. When in 597/8 the Kentish king Æthelberht accepted Christianity from Augustine, a Roman monk working with the support of the Frankish overlords of Kent, 10,000 people, so it was claimed, were baptized as well. Demographically preposterous but rhetorically effective, the figure indicates an eye-catching occasion of immediate significance. The baptism of fourteen Bohemian princes with their retinues at the court of Louis the German at Regensburg in 845 must also have offered an impressive sight. Sometimes a superior king stood godfather to the convert ruler, sponsoring his change of identity and receiving him from the baptismal font, using baptism to assert a hierarchy of deference. Such were the circumstances in which Alfred of Wessex sponsored the baptism of his defeated enemy, the Viking leader Guthrum in 878. Royal baptism might also aim to tie future rulers into an alliance: during Otto III's visit to Gniezno in 1000, he became godfather to a newborn son of the Christian Polish prince, Boleslaw Chobry (992–1025), in a ceremony rich in symbolic importance. He also strengthened the bond by giving Boleslaw both a royal crown and another replica of the Holy Lance (still to be seen in Cracow).

To ask whether religious or political motivations underlay such baptisms is misplaced, for the distinction was meaningless in an age in which identities were as much social as personal and in which religious expression was more usually communal than individual. Petty or powerful, rulers needed to act out in visually dramatic form their political relationships with both superiors and underlings. Indeed, kings could function only with the support of their leading men. Anxieties about conversion, or conversion followed by apostasy, were thus the symptoms of conflict within a ruling group. In north-western Europe, the tensions between acceptance or rejection of the new religion could reflect choices about overlordship, perhaps also conflicts between older and younger members of a ruling elite. Æthelberht of Kent's death in 616 was followed by a reversion to pagan ways led by his son and successor, while a century later the Frisian ruler Radbod (d. 719) backed out of the baptismal font on being told that his pagan ancestors would not accompany him to the Christian heaven. Here, the issue of collective identity was expressed in terms of social cohesion between the living and the dead, but the hard reality was that Frankish aggression had fostered conflict within the Frisian elite.

Rulers in central Europe in the ninth, tenth, and eleventh centuries faced an additional dilemma in choosing between the Christianity sponsored by the Carolingian emperors and their Ottonian heirs, and that of the Byzantine emperors. As Chapter 1 emphasized, the former used Latin as its sacred language and looked to Rome for authenticity and sometimes even leadership, whereas the latter was prepared to adapt local vernacular languages for ritual use and had its jurisdictional centre at Constantinople. The choice was inevitably also one of political advantage, a dilemma particularly acute in the decades when the two empires, east and west, were actively competing for allies and influence. In the lower Danube basin, Khan Boris of the Bulgars (852–89) was a military threat and potential ally for Franks and Byzantines alike: both cultivated him and sought influence over him. This was the context of Boris's decision to adopt Christianity and of his baptism in 864/5. But political and cultural orientation remained an issue, and Boris negotiated at length with both Rome and Constantinople before opting for Greek Christianity in 870. A century or so later, the emerging Hungarian kingdom faced similar pressures. In the late tenth century, German and Byzantine missionaries worked simultaneously among the Magyars: the Greek clergy remained active long after King Stephen's coronation under papal and Ottonian auspices.

We should return briefly to Stephen's reign. He was a Christian king ruling subjects among whom local, unremarked, and unremarkable missionary work in spreading Christianity was gradually proceeding, and would long continue, interrupted by pagan revolts for some decades to come. Establishment of the archbishopric of Esztergom had to be followed by the gradual installation of the institutional infrastructure of a national Christianity—a network of bishops, the foundation and endowment of monasteries in which communities of men or women led a disciplined life of austerity and prayer, the training of local priests in ritual specialisms and the Latin language. Traditional procedures had to be renegotiated to meet the expectations of Christian clergy for legal protection and privileged status and for grants of land to be held in perpetuity. And the long, slow process of accommodation between traditional Magyar social conventions and the ethical demands of Christian doctrine had to be set in motion. In all this, Stephen of Hungary was exceptional only in the documentation that his zealous promotion of Christianity generated and in the alacrity with which he acted. His reign simply encapsulated a well-recorded, high-speed version of what many convert kings had faced in preceding centuries.

To achieve these goals took time and political determination. In areas where the spread of Christianity remained limited to informal contacts, institutionalization did not occur. In the absence of a priestly hierarchy or full literacy, we find improvisational forms of Christian living that flourished in ways that made sense to their practitioners but often met with suspicion or outright condemnation from the missionaries who finally caught up with these people. Such a one was Frideburg, a Christian woman living among the predominantly non-Christian Swedes in the middle of the ninth century. Knowing about a ritual involving wine sipped by the dying (the *viaticum*, in which consecrated wine is administered to the dying by a priest as part of rituals to ease the passage of the Christian soul to heaven), she purchased wine and set it aside with instructions to her daughter to give it to her to drink on her deathbed. Another such was Ørlygr Hrappson, a Norwegian who had been fostered in his youth by an Irish bishop in the Hebrides. In the early tenth century he journeyed to Iceland, equipped with the timbers to build a church, a liturgical book, and 'consecrated earth' to bury under its corner pillars. This last would have horrified anyone trained in the correct procedures for consecrating a new church. Ørlygr had named his church in honour of the Gaelic saint Columba, and there, three generations later, his descendants still 'believed in Columba although they were not baptized'.[11] Such 'do-it-yourself' Christianity was the concomitant of the slow seepage of religious change through informal channels of contact in the absence of an organized priesthood: although sparsely documented, it must have flourished all around the margins of institutionalized Christendom and in remote, internal pockets.

Whether we focus attention on the spread of Christianity by informal or by formal means, we are repeatedly reminded that religious change always occurred within social contexts, contexts that were frequently also political. It affected families and households, royal courts, armies, merchant communities, each in different and distinctive ways. Two general points can nevertheless be made. First, if early medieval men and women balanced views about the 'truth' of Christian doctrine against political or pragmatic motives in their acceptance of the new religion, we do not hear about it in their own terms. To be sure, deeply Christian writers believed this was what converts should do, and sometimes represented them as doing, but the actual reasoning that underlay religious change remains hidden from us. We may be sure, however, that the need to make a decision was much sharper for some than for others, sharper for rulers—or rebels—than loyal followers, for parents than children. Secondly, neither the baptism of a ruler and his retinue nor the domestic adoption of certain Christian practices necessarily resulted in a rapid and complete spiritual, moral, and social transformation. As previous chapters have made clear, shifts in burial rituals, sexual behaviour, responses to sickness, and much else besides, did occur but were slow, erratic, and extremely difficult to enforce. In neither geographical nor chronological terms can we detect an even momentum: the spread of Christianity followed many different routes and rhythms. Highly dependent on a shifting matrix of specific circumstances of place and time, it meant different things to different people. In sum, early medieval Christianity consisted of local knowledge not universal 'truth'.

Pagans and Christians

Despite their many local forms of organization, ritual, and social practice, the Christianities of early medieval Europe nevertheless had much in common. At the heart of the Christian world view lay the claim that this religion provided the only possible truth about the relationship of the supernatural (or divine), the natural (or earthly), and the human (or social). These universalizing notions appealed to rulers and their advisers because they reordered ideas of community, shaped new identities, identified new enemies, and supplied new justifications of royal power. As a mindset that opposed Christians and non-Christians solidified, it became the task of kings and clerics everywhere to extirpate 'error' wherever they might find it. In this way, Christianity transformed the imaginative landscapes of its adoptive societies. By providing a common stock of universal values, it offered them new ways of linking together. By promising warrior kings new ideologies and modes of communication, it encouraged them towards a shared ethic and even a common purpose.[12] Indeed, it succeeded so well in offering an overarching, umbrella identity that, by the early eleventh century, 'Christendom' and 'Europe' had become virtually synonymous. By the end of the first millennium, scattered communities of Jews formed the only significant non-Christian presence in Europe; treated with an ambivalent mix of disregard, tolerance, and hostility, they tested the limits of early medieval Europe's identity as a compulsory Christian community.

Compulsory Christianity rested on notions inherited from late Antiquity that deemed it not only a universal religion but also the only 'right' one. In this triumphalist perspective, the spread of Christianity was often represented as the eradication of 'wrong' religions. Hrabanus Maurus stated this pithily: 'Christianity destroys all errors.'[13] This rhetorical position denied any validity to other religions. Their gods were simply redefined as demons, their moral teachings and cult practices condemned as depraved.

Then the devil and his servant demons . . . began to appear to humankind in various forms and speak with them and demand of them that they offer sacrifices to them on high mountains and in leafy forests and they worship them as God. . . . One demon claimed to be Jupiter, who had been a magician and involved in so many adulteries that he had taken his own sister, Juno, as his wife and had corrupted his daughters, Minerva and Venus, and had even committed foul incest with his nieces and all his female relatives. Another demon called himself Mars, who had sown quarrels and discord. . . . Another demon imagined herself to be Venus; she had been a whore and not only participated in innumerable adulteries, but had even prostituted herself with her father, Jupiter, and her brother, Mars. . . . The demons even persuaded people to build temples to them and to place therein images or statues of wicked men and to set up altars to them, on which they should pour out for them blood both of animals and even of men.[14]

By thus inverting the religious valency of the traditional Roman deities, Martin, bishop of Braga (556–79), denatured them and ridiculed any attempt to assert their authenticity. His views circulated widely in the early Middle Ages, and were reiterated in various ways. For example, when baptism was administered in Germany in the vicinity of the missionary outpost of Fulda in the late eighth–ninth centuries, new Christians who accepted Christ promised to 'forsake all the works and words of the devils Thunor, Woden and Saxnot and all the fiends that are their companions'.[15]

Another way Christians dealt with indigenous gods was by denying their suprahuman status. By reducing gods to the status of mortals, Christians attempted to render rival deities innocuous. Daniel, bishop of Winchester (c.705–44), proffered this advice to Boniface on one of his preaching missions in Germany: 'You ought not to offer opposition to them concerning the genealogy of their gods, false though they are, but allow them to assert according to their belief that some were begotten of others through the intercourse of male and female, so that you may then at any rate show gods and goddesses born after the manner of humans to have been humans, not gods, and, since they did not exist before, to have had a beginning.'[16] Thus reduced to human status, gods might find themselves relegated to the distant past. Woden, one of the most widely venerated Germanic gods, suffered this fate, particularly among the various Anglo-Saxon peoples. Two and one half centuries after Christian missionaries had introduced their religion into southern England, Woden had been demoted from god to founding ancestor of royal dynasties, and from the primordial begetter of kings to descendant of Adam, the first human whom, according to scriptural tradition, the Judaeo-Christian God had created. Elsewhere—notably Ireland, Iceland, and Scandinavia—epics, sagas, and myths often kept these figures alive for many centuries more in a literary afterlife that filtered representations of the pagan past through long Christian experience.

From the fifth century onwards, Christian oppositional rhetoric also lumped together all non-Christians, except Jews, by dismissing them pejoratively as 'pagans'. Certainly no one would ever have used this as a term of self-identification. Its deployment hides from us the great variety of the indigenous religious traditions of early medieval Europe and deliberately obscures any understanding of their true nature. In attempting to assess this, we must proceed carefully. Whereas the thoughts and voices of upholders of the non-Christian religions of the Roman world have sometimes come down to us directly in writing, there is no comparable avenue into the religious attitudes or experiences of those men and women of the early Middle Ages who were not Christian, for, as Chapter 1 made clear, literacy in anything more than terse, incised inscriptions was a Christian introduction. We can rely only on material remains that may have had a religious significance, on linguistic traces (place names, for example), or on the accounts of non-Christian beliefs and practices offered by Christian writers.

With caution, we may nevertheless posit some broad outlines of the traditional religiosities that Christian preachers encountered as they moved outside the Roman world. Unlike Judaism, Christianity, or Islam, none of them depended upon a corpus of sacred texts, a prophetic tradition, or recognition of a single, universal deity. None had any doctrine and orthodoxy to defend, or a word expressing the complex abstraction 'religion'. They did not order the cosmos around a single, all-powerful figure, or even an opposed, dualist, pair, but found it to be inhabited by innumerable spirits who both influenced mortal affairs and were open to human manipulation. Everywhere, from the deepest earth to the most distant stars, the natural and the supernatural, the physical and the spirit, interlocked and interacted. Within this, the place of humankind was secured by means of myths, rituals, stores of sacred knowledge, or the activities of practitioners such as shamans, seers, or druids. Their rituals also offered ways of understanding and trying to control the elemental forces of life and death, fertility and sickness, war and prosperity. Propitiation of gods and spirits through sacrifice, binding, or invoking them with talismans and amulets; prediction of the future by means such as divination; and regulation of human conduct through taboos all appear to have been common. Thus sacral activities were so bound up with other aspects of human existence—familial, domestic, agricultural, political, military—as to make redundant any attempt to regard 'religion' as a discrete category of experience.

Despite these generalities, and despite apparently widespread cults of a few gods (such as the Germanic Woden), religious traditions were nevertheless very much about local identity, whether of group or of place. Many of the geographical specificities elude us, especially since we are much better informed about the religious traditions of some regions than of others. It is nevertheless clear that a god might be the primordial ancestor of a warrior elite; a natural feature such as an ancient tree might encapsulate the essence of a community; or a sacred site might be the ritual heart of a polity or a place of sacrifice. Thus, seventh-century Lombards believed they acquired their name when Woden promised the Langobards, the 'long-bearded men', victory in battle, whilst the southern tip of Ireland was ruled by the Corcu Loígde, the 'family of the Calf Goddess'. The German region of Lommatsch acquired its name from a sacred spring venerated by the local populace for its ability to predict the future by announcing peace and a good harvest with a scattering of wheat, oats, and acorns, but 'when the savage storms of war threaten, it gives a clear indication of the outcome with blood and ash'.[17] Perched upon their *terpen* above the tidal marshes along the North Sea coast, eighth-century Frisians identified in the forces of the flood tide a god to be placated by human sacrifice. By contrast, in the century following their overthrow of Ottonian rule in 983, the Liutizi Slavs organized their resistance to German rulers and their religion around their chief shrine, that of the god Swarozyc in the holy compound at *Riedegost*.

Archaeology helps elaborate this sketchy account. In Scandinavia and northern-central Europe in particular, traces of ritual sacrifices—animals, humans, weaponry—have been found, sometimes in special ritual enclosures, elsewhere as deposits in bogs, beside lakes, or around trees. Material remains and textual records alike confirm that sacred precincts could also contain pillar-shaped idols of wood or stone, but only in southern Scandinavia and the western Slav lands have statues of gods in figural form been found. Finds such as the Danish site at Nydam with its huge fourth- and fifth-century ritual deposits of weaponry and a boat; the figurines of gods and the remains of tenth-century horse sacrifices from Oldenburg, a Slavic stronghold on the Baltic coast of modern Germany; or the tenth- and eleventh-century remains of animals heaped around the trunk of a tree on Frösö, an island cult centre in northern Sweden, are all a graphic reminder of beliefs and practices that Christianity would in due course annihilate.

Inasmuch as modern scholars cannot study these indigenous religiosities through internal textual evidence, they are in a formal sense prehistoric. They should not thereby be assumed to be ahistoric. Ways in which they changed over time can indeed be detected, not least through interaction with neighbouring hegemonic cultures or with Christianity. The invention of the ogam alphabet by the pre-Christian Irish is one example already encountered. In the fifth and sixth centuries, Anglo-Saxon settlers in Britain may have begun to use special cult buildings either by taking over old Roman temples and churches or by building their own wooden shrines in deliberate imitation. In late-tenth- and early eleventh-century

Denmark, rune stones sometimes invoked the power of the god Thor in formulae whose wording betrays Christian influence. And the Liutizi, the Danes' neighbours, had not always worshipped in temples, nor had one sanctuary always taken precedence over others in their territory: as opposition to German rule hardened, so their indigenous religion acquired a structure and organization that mimicked their opponents' religion. When it came to the mutual reinforcement of political and sacral power, there was no better model than Christianity.

That indigenous religious traditions responded to the influence of a neighbouring Christianity should be no great surprise, for the porous nature of early medieval frontiers has already been stressed. In practice, religious beliefs and practices are never hermetically sealed systems, but develop through creative engagement, acculturation, or opposition with their wider social milieux. Thus, however stark the triumphalist antithesis of Christian truth and pagan error became, this conceptual dichotomy did not generally inform everyday religious experience, except for Christian armies urged into battle specifically to defeat pagans. For the most part, the reality of personal circumstance did not match up to a missionary ideology that presented conversion to Christianity as a total personal reorientation accompanied by complete rejection of the pre-Christian past.

Narratives about convert kings often make this clear: we may return to Hungary to make the point. King Stephen's father, Géza (c.970–97), had come to power at a moment when the Hungarians were poised between the two empires, Byzantine and German; under his rule, they swung their political allegiance decisively westwards. German missionaries from Bavaria supplemented the Greek ones already active amongst the Hungarians and baptized Géza himself in 972. Yet, battling other chieftains as he was to confirm his own paramount leadership over the Hungarians, he took whatever route he could to consolidate his position. A murderous man of quick temper, Géza, now Christian, 'turned his rage against his reluctant subjects, in order to strengthen this faith. Thus, glowing with zeal for God, he washed away his old crimes. He sacrificed both to the omnipotent God and to various false gods. When reproached by his priest for doing so, however, he maintained that the practice had brought him both wealth and great power.'[18] Like a considerable number of other rulers importuned by missionaries, Géza preferred religious pluralism to the rejection of old ways. Christian baptism complemented rather than replaced traditional worship. He seems to have recognized that the Hungarians' inherited religious beliefs and practices were too bound up with their identity and modes of living to be jettisoned without unravelling everything he sought to build. Géza, then, reminds us that baptism did not of itself eradicate traditional practices or rewrite the past. Conversion to Christianity should be seen as an extended encounter and interaction between different religious and cultural systems, not as the substitution of one for another that triumphalist historiography implies.

In late Antiquity, Christian leaders had come to realize that membership of the Christian community as marked by baptism was not enough to distinguish a Christian from a pagan. They began to move the goalposts, arguing that all forms of human behaviour must be distinctive. 'It is not enough for us to receive the name of Christians if we do not conduct ourselves as Christians', Caesarius of Arles warned his sixth-century audience.[19] Thus Christianity gradually became a religion of quotidian morality, which, as we have seen, concerned itself with the regular rhythms of daily life—times of work and worship, feasting and fasting, sex and abstinence—as well as with its unpredictable crises, such as fevered children, lame horses, or inclement weather. Thus Caesarius remonstrated that his Christian hearers should not respond to sickness by any means other than Christian ones. The peasant mother of Provence who drank a herbal drink to procure an abortion, who took a sick child to a diviner or a woman skilled in herbs, or who hung a written charm round the child's neck doubtless relied on practices that had been known for generations to be effective. A visit to a Christian priest or saint's shrine was only one of several therapeutic strategies available to her for coping with sickness and disaster. For Caesarius, however, these other strategies were all 'the persuasion of the devil'.[20] He demanded that his hearers abandon their traditional cosmology, in which the supernatural and the human came together and interacted in a wide range of persons and places, and instead seek out only those approved by their bishop: churches, saints, and priests. Even so, it was not enough to go to the right places, for he also told his congregation that to leap around dancing outside saints' shrines was 'to come to church Christian but leave pagan'.[21]

Caesarius threw a *cordon sanitaire* around Christianity, thereby staking out a clear distinction between 'right' Christianity and 'wrong' Christianity. In formulating the difference, he extended the condemnatory rhetoric formerly applied to non-Christian practices to cover anything his baptized congregation did that met with his disapproval. This language was the traditional polemic of 'superstition' and 'error'. 'Superstition' signalled any behaviour that the ecclesiastical elite deemed detrimental to the salvation of their Christian flock. As the persons, places, rituals, and words that mediated between humankind and the supernatural gradually all became subject to ecclesiastical claims to regulate them, 'superstition' was the term of abuse for anything that escaped that control and therefore lay on the wrong side of the conceptual boundary between right and wrong Christianity.

When Hrabanus Maurus declared that 'Christianity destroys errors', he defined these as 'idolatry, avarice and other vices', not bothering to distinguish non-Christian practices from inappropriate conduct by Christians.[22] Of wrong Christianity, Hrabanus doubtless had much direct experience. But of idolatry and other non-Christian practices he had at best a second- or third-hand knowledge, acquired from his reading or from his correspondence with missionary priests. His pagans were all in the mind, but that did not stop him pronouncing on how to deal with them. The method was clear: it was a royal one. As archbishop of Mainz, Hrabanus worked in close conjunction with his king, Louis the German. That it was a key task of kings to assist churchmen in the extirpation of error had been established by Louis's grandfather, Charlemagne. By a verbal association that the English language cannot reproduce, Isidore of Seville's popular encyclopaedic handbook, the *Etymologies*, had specified the correction of his subjects as an essential duty of a king. **Reges a regendo vocati.** . . . *Non autem regit qui non corrigit* ('kings take their title from the act of ruling. . . . However he who does not correct does not rule').[23] The point was more than wordplay: it sketched an entire moral agenda. Converted into a vigorous legislative programme first by the Iberian Gothic kings of Isidore's own day, adopted one and a half centuries later by Charlemagne, and subsequently disseminated wherever the ideals of his reign caught on, the royal responsibility for the correction of religious error gave a new twist to the distinction between Christian and pagan. An energetic Christian king such as Louis the German not only 'humbl[ed] the pagan heathens' on the battlefield; he worked closely with his leading bishops to inculcate correct Christianity amongst his subjects.

In such an environment, the do-it-yourself Christianity of remote areas might seem suspect, however authentic it was to its practitioners. 'Superstition' and 'error' were in the eye of the beholder not the perpetrator, for, during the early Middle Ages, the ecclesiastical elite arrogated to themselves the right to specify what constituted correct Christianity. One of Hrabanus Maurus's predecessors as archbishop of Mainz, Boniface had spent the second quarter of the eighth century travelling and preaching in the Frankish Rhineland, Thuringia, and Bavaria. Here he encountered no sharp frontier between Christianity and paganism but rather a spectrum of practices. One of its extremes was the disciplined monasticism in which he himself had been trained; its other the non-Christian practices of regions too remote to have had any previous interaction with

Christendom. Most people were somewhere in between, however—easy-going bishops whose values were more those of their aristocratic kinsfolk than of an ascetic; baptized peasants who made sacrifices to Christian saints or sought to predict the future from horse dung; do-it-yourself Christians who were unaware that their children were baptized with garbled ritual formulae. By the time Boniface died in 754, he had deployed Caesarius's notion of 'superstition' to reduce this blurred spectrum to a sharp conceptual polarity of right and wrong Christianity.

Boniface is important because of the key role he took in formulating norms of correct Christianity and in encouraging rulers to throw their weight behind them. As vast areas of Europe rapidly fell under Carolingian rule in the second half of the eighth century, so these norms were promulgated and further elaborated by bishops working in tandem with kings who had taken to heart the task of 'correction'. Charlemagne and his heirs strove hard to promote correct Christianity, and the enthusiastic reception given to this ideal in late Anglo-Saxon England and in Ottonian–Salian Germany ensured that it long remained influential. By the early eleventh century, we find the task of correction even at Europe's eastern periphery, for it informed the legislation of Stephen of Hungary. Correct Christianity—as defined from Boniface onwards—was well on its way to becoming the single permissible Christianity.

But what about Europe's western extremity? Ireland, Christianized in the fifth century, remained untouched by Carolingian or Ottonian political or cultural hegemony. Christianity in Ireland had long since accommodated its modes of organization to the small-scale kingdoms and the politics of cattle and kinship, and had adapted biblical precepts in ways that made local sense. It was simply one of the many early medieval Christianities, and it proved remarkably enduring. But, in the eyes of those for whom there was only one correct Christianity, the Irish version had come to seem distinctly odd by the later eleventh century. In 1070, William the Conqueror appointed a new archbishop to the see of Canterbury. Lanfranc had been born in Pavia, the old royal capital of Italy, in *c.*1010, and was familiar both with the traditional responsibility of kings for the welfare of Christianity, and with novel ideals of a centrally organized, uniform Christianity that were developing from the middle years of the eleventh century onwards. In *c.*1074, Lanfranc took it upon himself to point out to the high king of Ireland, Toirrdelbach ua Briain, king of Munster (1063–86), that his Christianity was the wrong sort. Baptism was not administered the way Lanfranc deemed proper, marriages did not conform to the requirements formulated by continental churchmen, bishops were not consecrated in the same way as elsewhere. Toirrdelbach must 'correct' these 'appalling . . . practices' and 'evil customs'.[24] The Irish did respond, but slowly, and certainly not fast enough to counteract the view that they persisted in error. In 1155, in the changed climate of the twelfth century—changed by the emergence of claims to universal papal monarchy and fusion of the many local Christian communities of earlier centuries into a single, much more homogeneous Christendom—Pope Adrian IV authorized the invasion of Ireland by the English king Henry II (1154–89) on the grounds that it would be to Henry's eternal credit 'to enlarge the boundaries of the church, to reveal the truth of the Christian faith to peoples still untaught and barbarous, and to root out the weeds of vice from the Lord's field'.[25] The Irish, then, were all but outright pagans, outside the church: their lack of correct Christianity justified invasion and conquest. When diverse local Christianities yielded to a single, standardized, normative Christianity at swordpoint, the early Middle Ages were truly over.

Good Kings, Bad Kings

In the spring of 961 Otto I prepared to undertake the dangerous march from Germany across the Alps to Rome. As part of his preparations, he had his 6-year-old son made king in order to secure the succession should he not return. The ceremony took place on 26 May in the chapel of the palace that Charlemagne had built at Aachen, the same spot where Otto had himself been consecrated at the beginning of his reign twenty-five years earlier. The young child, the future Otto II, found himself smeared with holy oil; then handed a symbolic sword, sceptre, and staff; crowned; and finally enthroned in a ceremony whose words, rituals, and gestures all had a long history, and which were as redolent of tradition as the location itself. At one level, the ceremony was a family affair, for, of the three archbishops who conducted the consecration, one was the new king's uncle, another his adult half-brother, and the third another relative. At another level, it bound both the junior and the senior Otto closely to the leading men of the realm, who were formally asked whether they were willing to submit to the rule of the new king, and to obey his commands. More complex still, it associated king, kingdom, and the Christian God in an intense bond, for Otto was asked, 'Do you wish to rule and defend the kingdom granted to you by God according to the justice of your ancestors?' and he replied with a formal promise that he would do so with God's help and the support of all those faithful to him.[26] As the consecration ceremony continued, it invoked all the complex ideas and ideologies of Christian kingship that had developed by the late tenth century. The king's role was to be the most strenuous of kings, the vanquisher of enemies, the guardian and defender of churches and the clergy. God was requested to crown him with 'the crown of justice and piety', to grant him victory over his enemies visible and invisible, and to bestow on him abundant harvests, health, peace, and heirs of his body. Divine help was invoked too to keep subject peoples loyal and magnates peaceable. In the course of the ceremony, Otto heard himself likened to the rulers of the ancient Israelites, leaders whom the Judaeo-Christian scriptures presented as anointed kings fighting in the name of God and ruling with justice and wisdom as mediators between God and people.

Much was going on here. Otto I had spent years crushing serious re-volts led by close members of his own family—his own brothers, son, and son-in-law—and so he sought to bind his relatives and subjects to his chosen successor. But the consecration resolved the tensions by trans-forming a political decision into something else: it incorporated young Otto's kingship into the God-given, and thus 'natural' order of the world. By setting the new king apart from other people as a person especially close to God, it made a human choice seem beyond challenge. In a vio-lent world, it gave one man the legitimate right to decree violence. Over-all, it made acceptable the very fact of kingship, the pre-eminent power of one man over everyone else that constituted the fundamental form of political organization throughout the early Middle Ages.

Indeed, it made kingship more than acceptable: it made it desirable. In the course of the ceremony, the new ruler was instructed in the tasks, moral responsibilities, and rewards that awaited him. Here was something for everybody. He was to be a vigorous warrior, protector of churches and churchmen, of widows and the poor, and the source of all justice in his kingdom. In this, he was to promote the Christian religion both by de-feating its enemies and by instructing and guiding his subjects. The pur-pose of warfare was to bring peace, not merely in the sense of the absence of warfare but in its much deeper meaning of a harmonious social order grounded in Christian principle and action. Here was the muscular Chris-tianity espoused by many generations of Frankish rulers, applauded by the monks of Lorsch in their prayers for Louis the German (see quotation at head of chapter), and supported by the *potentes*. Here too was a king pledged to 'correct' his subjects by promoting the welfare of God's churches and by extirpating 'superstition' and 'error' wherever they lurked. In all this, the keynote was 'justice', a word that extended beyond its judicial meaning of rendering judgement in lawsuits to embrace the moral equity necessary to achieving that rightful social ordering. Thus kingship should be a convergence of interests between the king and his leading subjects, clerical and lay, to the advantage of all persons in the realm, the powerful and the poor. Consecration, then, articulated that consensus in magnificent ritual splendour.

The prayers intoned over the new king also hinted that fulfilment of these responsibilities would bring the divine blessings of peace, prosperity, and progeny on ruler and realm. The king who fulfilled his responsibilities—the good king—was thus the linchpin of a world view that regarded the ordering of human society as an integral part of the wider ordering of the entire cosmos. And since, by the later tenth century, that cosmos had long since been understood within a Christian frame of reference, it also demanded that the good king function within that vision of a social order whose ultimate goal was eternal salvation for all. The ruler should act, then, in the hope of winning 'eternal joys in perpetual blessed-ness' for himself.[27] The king thus linked the present moment to eternity. Through the explicit biblical parallels, he also joined the Old Testament past to Ottonian present, taking his place as another in the line of monarchs protected by God and ruling in his name. So consecration enacted beliefs about the right ordering of the human and the divine, the sacred and the secular.

Supercharged with political, ritual, and cosmological significance, an early medieval royal inauguration was a highly specific event. A dramatic interlude of ritual clarity in the midst of the normal contention of court politics, it made explicit that ruling was as much an ideological as a prac-tical undertaking. As such, it both brought into sharp perspective ideas that were often much more fluid and set a standard for measuring a king's achievements. We may remain with Otto II for a moment longer, for the verdict passed on his reign by the historian Thietmar of Merseburg demonstrates this. Thietmar had lived through Otto II's reign, and as-sessed it by linking military failures to Christian morality and the conduct of his subjects to the condition of their king:

> Otto, the second bearer of this name . . .
> . . . was installed on the throne of his great father
> With worthy praise, he who helped all in need.
>
> .   .   .   .   .
>
> His youth was happy and fortunate, but sorrow arrived in his latter years
> Through the heavy burden of our sins.
> Then, this evil world did penance for rejecting the truth.[28]

In Thietmar's opinion, Otto II suffered because of the sins of his subjects: the king had lost good fortune, and the right ordering of society had slipped.

The high ideals of kingship that Otto strove to maintain had reached maturity in the reigns of Charlemagne and his immediate successors out of very much older traditions of both ritual and political thinking. They had congealed precisely because the unprecedented power that the Carolingians wielded required unprecedented justification. Charlemagne's power had taken many different forms—military success, attempts at regulation of many aspects of daily life, strenuous lordship manifested in vigorous economic exploitation of his lands and in successful manipulation of webs of aristocratic kinship—all of which imposed huge demands upon his subjects. The ideology and ceremonial of Christian kingship provided validation for this, deflecting attention away from the harsh realities of power. By stressing cosmic order not human oppression, divine legitimation made submission to such a strong ruler acceptable. And it offered kings access to a form of power that no quantity of treasure or fighting men could yield, for supernatural sanction was a form of legitimacy far more potent than mere political consensus, paternal designation, or success in battle. And when, from the mid-ninth century onwards, archbishops established a role—a prerogative, as they came to see it—in conveying the divine sanction to kings in the form of an ecclesiastical anointing, the synthesis of Christianity and kingship was complete. Thanks to clerical initiative, early medieval kings were the symbolic centre of a transcendent and explicitly Christian social order.

From the middle of the ninth century onwards, that Christian order also explicitly embraced a king's wife. In an innovation that lacked biblical precedent, a new ritual for consecrating a queen gave her a formal role in its maintenance. In addition to her well-attested courtly functions—domestic administration of a palace involved not only its provisioning but also regulating the flow of guests and gifts—the queen became a living icon of fertility, prosperity, and good conduct. It is no coincidence that queenship became both official and explicitly Christian in exactly the decades when Carolingian moralists were insisting on a new, tighter definition of marriage, and demanding that kings uphold it in their own lives. Through her new role as sole lifelong consort and chosen mother of the future heir, a queen's behaviour reflected directly upon her spouse. Her sexual modesty enhanced his reputation and epitomized the right ordering of society; her decorum betokened a king's wisdom in choosing her as his bride; her good counsel persuaded him to mercy; her fertility confirmed her husband's. Conversely, her barrenness might threaten political stability and seem a sign of divine disfavour; any hint of undue influence or allegation of sexual promiscuity undermined and unmanned a king's reputation for control of self, household, and society at large. Consecration, then, bestowed upon a queen heavy responsibilities for just rule and formalized her participation in upholding the transcendent order.

Once tapped in these ways, ideological power brought additional benefits. Protecting churches also meant endowing them generously. Among the Franks, the tomb of St Martin, among the Scots, the tomb of St Columba, among the Irish, the tomb of St Patrick—these and many others enjoyed landed wealth of royal origin. In return, kings and queens acquired the powerful spiritual patronage of the saints whose shrines they housed. At the same time, churches and monasteries made their huge landed wealth available to support royal power in various ways, as the clergy at St Peter's, Ghent, did for Louis the Pious. Royal nunneries had their place in these networks, as significant landowners in their own right, as homes for kings' daughters or widows, and as sources of intercessory prayer for their patroness and her family. Furthermore, churches put their considerable legal and administrative expertise at royal disposal, thereby transmitting at least some late Roman bureaucratic skills and judicial principles to early medieval rulers. The intense symbiosis of royal and ecclesiastical affairs was the practical expression of the early medieval ideologies of Christian rulership.

One corollary was the readiness of churchmen to lecture kings about their responsibilities. Whether by royal request or on their own initiative, clergy wrote letters, treatises, and admonitions to kings, encouraging, exhorting, or chastising. And there is enough evidence to suggest that at least some kings listened, and took the advice to heart. One king who certainly did was Charles the Bald, grandson of Charlemagne and ruler of the western third of his empire. And he needed to: his reign was a long struggle to deal with repeated conflicts with his brothers, nephews, and sons, worsening external threats posed by Viking raids, and diminishing internal resources. In addition, he faced assertive aristocrats and self-confident bishops. The most forceful and articulate of these was Hincmar of Reims, who had as clear views on the obligations of kings as he did on those of marriage.[29] Charles had read an earlier set of comments on kingship and questioned Hincmar about it, probably in 873. The archbishop replied with a treatise *On the Person of a King and the Royal Ministry*, whose words, he suspected, might leave the king feeling rather nettled. Its contents can be summarized thus: the Christian God appoints kings, permitting evil ones as well as enabling good ones. A good king rules in justice, punishing criminals, defending the church, and being equitable in judgement, and is thus a blessing to his subjects, bringing them peace, fruitful soil, and fertility. By contrast, a bad king brings only suffering, op-pression, invasion, and famine. In another treatise, Hincmar labelled such a king as tyrannical: nevertheless, he retains a place within the cosmologic-al whole, for God permits him to rule as a punishment for the sins of his people. Hincmar's good king is powerful and vigorous, in battle as in law. He exercises moral self-restraint, refusing to give in to flattery, partisan-ship, or pride. Humility is an essential precondition of good kingship, jus-tice its daily manifestation. The king thus becomes an exemplar of good conduct to his subjects. This can be quite compatible with shedding blood, if warfare will defend Christianity or if his subjects' terrible crimes justify the death penalty. In Hincmar's opinion, then, good kingship was vigor-ous morality in action for the sake of the welfare of the entire Christian social order. It was a *ministerium*, a ministry: a duty of responsible service to others. By means of the rule of good kings, human society embraced divinely inspired harmony, and the king ruled as Christ's deputy on earth.

On the Person of a King and the Royal Ministry marks a late and sophis-ticated stage in the development of early medieval thinking about royal power. Within that tradition, ideas of diverse origin had gradually fused, but this tract nevertheless allows us to identify exactly what the constituent elements were, for Hincmar worked by naming his sources and quoting from them extensively. In so doing he laid bare the intellectual antecedents of his—and much other early medieval—thinking about the nature and disposition of power. In the first place was the Bible, both the Old Testament books, which expounded the relations between God, kings, and people in ancient Israel, and the New Testament exposition of the teach-ings of Christ and his followers on social and political obligation within the Roman Empire. In the second place were the great theologians and moralists of late Antiquity and the very early Middle Ages. Ambrose and Augustine had been writing when the Roman Empire was still a power-ful political reality; Gregory the Great experienced both the enduring vigour of the eastern, Byzantine Empire and the dissolution of stability in Italy. Each in his own distinctive way, these writers combined scriptural ideas with strong Roman views on the ethics of power and the nature of law. The fourth writer from whom Hincmar drew heavily he believed, er-roneously, to be Cyprian of Carthage (d. 258). He was, in fact, an anony-mous seventh-century Irishman whose ideas were a fascinating *mélange* of biblical, patristic, and indigenous Irish wisdom literature.

At risk of oversimplifying, we may, therefore, locate the origins of early medieval ideas about good and bad kings in three different cultural tradi-tions: Roman, biblical, and Irish. Three admonitions to kings, all dating from the late sixth to seventh centuries, help us to disentangle their respective contributions. The author of the first was Martin of Braga; its recipient Miro, king of the Suevi (570–83), a people who had settled in north-western Iberia in 409 and maintained an independent kingdom there until absorbed by their powerful Gothic neighbours in 585 (see Figures 0.2 and 8.2). Martin's *Formula for an Honest Life* was intended as simple advice for the king and 'those who assisted in his royal ministry', and was explicitly independent of Christian teaching. He outlined the four cardinal virtues that should inform all the king's actions: prudence, magnanimity of spirit, self-restraint, and justice. In so doing, Martin stressed the need for self-discipline, ethical conduct, service to others, and equitable behaviour in all things. Avoiding vice, the king should be the 'corrector without reproach' of others and an exemplar of good conduct. All these ideas derived directly from the writings of the Roman philosopher Seneca (*c*.4 BC–AD 65); in one way or another, all resurface in Hincmar's advice to Charles the Bald. Martin's straightforward treatise was hugely popular throughout the entire Middle Ages, a reminder of the enduring legacy of the Roman belief that self-restrained moral conduct was the necessary precondition for the exercise of authority over others.[30]

The second strand, the scriptural, was rich, complex, and subject to endless reinterpretation. Nevertheless, the letter that Gregory the Great wrote to Æthelberht of Kent in 601 shows one way in which it could be presented in straightforward terms appropriate, as here, for a warleader who had just accepted Christianity. Gregory's succinct premiss condenses the whole tenor of biblical history into a single truism: 'Almighty God raises up certain good men to be rulers over nations in order that he may by their means bestow the gifts of his righteousness upon all those over whom they are set.' Behind this sentence lies awareness of ancient Israelite cosmology, which identified the king as a sacred person, protected by God and consecrated by being anointed with oil by the priests. As Gregory implied, he was the conduit between the divine and the human; his good governance brought God's gifts of fertility, prosperity, and peace. In Gregory's thinking, certain consequences followed from this ancient premiss. First, Æthelberht has responsibilities towards God—to further the spread of Christianity, to set an example of Christian conduct, and to change his people's conduct by 'exhorting, terrifying, enticing and correcting' them.[31] Secondly, if he does this, God will reward him with honour, a glorious reputation, and eternal life promised to Christians. Here, the king is the fulcrum of the Christian polity with simultaneous obligations towards both the Christian God and his own subjects. This was central to much of Gregory's thought, and he expressed his views on the responsibilities of

rulers in many other works besides this one letter. Their wide dissemination ensured that his ideas too became part of the common currency
of early medieval political thinking; Hincmar was only one of many to
acknowledge indebtedness to Gregory's contribution.

The third strand is perhaps the most unexpected. We encounter it in a
seventh-century treatise, *The Testament of Morann*, a work of instruction
from an Irish sage, the *fili* Morann, to King Feradach Find Fechtnach.
Both are legendary characters, but this is one sample of an Old Irish
wisdom literature addressed to kings. Morann's purpose is to bring to the
king 'the virtue of rectitude, | which each ruler must have'.[32] Through his
messenger, he tells Fechtnach about the *fír flathemon*, the 'king's justice',
a rich term meaning equity combined with truth and integrity.

> Tell him, it is through the justice of the ruler that plagues and great
>   lightnings are kept from the people.
> It is through the justice of the ruler that he judges great tribes and
>   great riches.
> It is through the justice of the ruler that he secures peace,
>   tranquillity, joy, ease, and comfort.
> It is through the justice of the ruler that he dispatches great
>   battalions to the borders of hostile neighbours.
> It is through the justice of the ruler that every heir plants his
>   house-post in his fair inheritance.
> It is through the justice of the ruler that abundances of great tree-
>   fruit of the great wood are tasted.
> It is through the justice of the ruler that milk-yields of great cattle
>   are maintained.
> It is through the justice of the ruler there is an abundance of every
>   high, tall corn.[33]

Morann goes on to spell out in detail how the true ruler must behave to
uphold the rightful order of society and win these abundances for his
people. He also refers to the antithesis, the 'un-ruler' or usurper whose
reign is spent in violence and warfare, against whom 'there is always
bellowing with horns'.[34]

Once again, we find that royal conduct is integrally associated with the
welfare of the people, the fecundity of the soil, and the maintenance of
peace through external warfare and internal good governance. Good rulership presupposed that the king's 'justice' would regulate social relations
effectively and fairly. These ideas were part of a wider complex of traditions current in Ireland before the introduction of Christianity, traditions
that placed a high symbolic value on the king as the embodiment of both
social and supernatural order. As in ancient Israel, kings were perceived

to be central to a way of thinking that regarded social well-being as but one aspect of the well-being of the wider world—its soil, its weather, and its rulers—and that drew a tight analogy between political malaise and a discordant cosmos.

Not surprisingly, *The Testament of Morann* remained unknown beyond Ireland, for it was written in Old Irish. But its ideas about the true ruler as opposed to the un-ruler and about the importance of the king's 'justice' informed a Latin tract also written in seventh-century Ireland and widely read in England and on the Continent from the eighth through the twelfth century, commonly entitled *On the Twelve Abuses of the World*. This was the work that Hincmar thought had been written by Cyprian, and whose definitions of good and evil kings he quoted in full.

Now ancient Israel, pre-Christian Ireland, and the ninth-century Carolingian Empire were all very different societies. They all had kings in abundance, however, and accepted kingship as the only possible political order. All assumed the interpenetration of the supernatural, the earthly, and the social in various ways, an assumption that manifested itself differently in each culture. But they shared the presupposition that the king was one of the key nodes of this interaction and that his conduct was a conduit through which the divine, the natural, and the human affected each other. For this reason, beliefs about the nature of kingship derived both from the Old Testament and from Irish learning were readily appropriated in the warrior kingdoms that emerged out of the Roman Empire. If early Germanic-speaking peoples had ever regarded their kings within a cosmological context, the huge upheavals and transformations of the fourth and fifth centuries had been far too disruptive to sustain such beliefs. Instead, the inheritance of Roman Christianity and classical standards of ethical conduct for the exercise of power provided a cultural context receptive to the assimilation of other texts and ideas about good kings and bad kings.

That melding had commenced in the immediate aftermath of the adoption of Christianity by the Roman emperor Constantine, and the patristic theologians on whom Hincmar drew had played no small part in it. But thinking about the tasks of kingship never remained static, and the political transformation of the western Roman Empire in the fifth century provided another impetus. As empire yielded to kingdoms and as Christianity spread among them, the urge to formulate norms of Christian kingship became irresistible. Hincmar's several treatises on kingship represent the culmination of that long, slow process.

Not only his sophisticated political thought and his copious writings make Hincmar important. He also specialized in inventing royal rituals to enact in dramatic form the political theology he espoused. It was his shrewd political judgement that had introduced the king's formal promise to his people into the consecration ceremony, and, more than any single other person, he regularized the tradition of anointing kings and queens. Otto II, and the many subsequent generations of medieval rulers whose reigns were inaugurated with the same words and religious rituals, participated in a sacred drama that was in large part the product of Hincmar's fertile mind. While consecration at the hands of archbishops could not of itself make a good king, it did make a king and it did instruct him how to be a good one. And, for the ruler who was already married, unlike the young Otto II, the consecration of his queen implicated her in the maintenance of good rule.

What difference did these ideals make to the practice of rulership? They were no substitute for hard-won experience, let alone a remedy against defeat in battle. Rather, their importance lay in establishing an agreed yardstick by which to measure a king's performance, and in providing the criteria for criticism, whether by disaffected lay subjects, clerical critics, or those anxious to oust a rival. Early medieval kings were not bad simply for being sly, promiscuous, incompetent, or unsuccessful in war: they were bad when they lost the respect and cooperation of their leading subjects, lay and ecclesiastical. In short, bad kingship was the wilful destruction of the consensual partnership that made governance work. In a cosmological perspective, it was the perversion of divine order.

It could take several forms. One was sexual and gendered. A ruler's self-restraint had to start with the control of his own body lest, 'governed by lust, [he stain] the fame of [his] glory before God and men by the sin of lasciviousness and adultery'. Such conduct, Boniface warned King Æthelbald of Mercia (716–57) in 746–7, was both 'a disgrace in the sight of God and the ruin of your reputation among men'. Far more serious, though, was the accusation that Æthelbald had vented his lust on those whom he ought to protect, nuns dedicated to God in the convents of his kingdom: this conduct was 'the snare of death and the pit of hell and the whirlpool of perdition'.[35] Whereas a good ruler 'should first rule himself with reasonable and meritorious discipline; second his wife, his children, and his household; and third, the people entrusted to him', the bad king combined lack of self-control with a wanton wife. 'A foolish wife is the ruin of a household, the exhaustion of wealth, the fullness of crimes, and the abode of all evils and vices.'[36] Accusations of queenly adultery became a weapon for attacking kings, as Louis the Pious and his empress, the beautiful Judith, discovered to their joint cost in the 830s. The truth of the matter

was irrelevant, for queenly modesty had become so integral to good kingship that insinuation and allegation against the queen sufficed to identify
the bad king.

Another form of bad kingship was taking bad counsel, or no counsel at
all. The best advice came from God, as set out in the Bible. Two further
precepts followed: 'a prudent man summons other prudent men into
counsel and does nothing without their advice; but a foolish man
deliberates by himself and does whatever he hastily desires without the
counsel of others. . . . The third rule in counsels to be observed is that a
just ruler should not have deceitful and pernicious counselors. Who,
indeed, should trust the counsels of the wicked? . . . As good counselors
raise the state upwards, so evil ones press it downwards in ruinous
calamity.'[37] Counsellors might be condemned as evil if they blocked
others' access to the king, as Hagano did in the reign of Charles the
Simple, or came, as Charles the Fat's adviser Liutward of Vercelli did,
from the wrong social background. The political consequences could be
serious: Zwentibold of Lotharingia (895–900) was deposed not only
because he plundered church property but because, 'settling the affairs of
the kingdom with women and men of lower rank, he disparaged his
more honourable and noble followers and stripped them of their offices
and dignities'.[38]

Most dangerous of all, however, was the form of bad kingship identified as early as the seventh century by pseudo-Cyprian: disregard for
justice. One of the 'twelve abuses', the 'unjust king' dishonoured his
subjects, disregarding their rights and interests. This was the tyranny of
oppression about which Hincmar would in due course warn Charles the
Bald. But Charles learned this lesson the hard way, for in his early years
he had ruled so vigorously that in 858 his subjects rebelled, amid complaints that his rule had become 'tyranny' when, they alleged, he destroyed
their property with 'evil savagery' and broke the oaths and pledges he had
made to his people. In short, 'all despaired of his good faith'.[39] Charles,
his opponents asserted, ruled without regard for the common welfare and
ignored the even-handed identity of interests and purpose between ruler
and ruled that lay at the heart of good kingship and successful governance
alike.

Accusations of bad kingship made for vigorous political opposition;
from the pen of a historian, they damned in posterity. Thietmar of Merseburg—or his informant—had no time at all for the Danish king Swein
Forkbeard (c.987–1014), a Christian. He condemned the Dane not only for
his attacks on England, but for wasting his own kingdom: he was 'not a
ruler but a destroyer. . . . he traded security for constant wandering, peace

for war, a kingdom for exile, the God of heaven and earth for the Devil.'[40]
In effect, Thietmar turned Swein into an icon of bad kingship, who dis-
played the opposite of the good ruler's qualities in a perversion of the
Christian cosmological scheme.

Bad kingship reminds us that good kingship was a highly sophisticated
political and ideological construct. As a moral undertaking, based upon
obligation, justice, and self-restraint, it was greatly indebted to ecclesiastical visions of the right ordering of the social world, but it was not
confected out of purely clerical ingredients, for kingship was far too
fundamental to be left entirely to churchmen to define. It remained
grounded in the harsh practicalities of leadership in war, and presupposed
the consent and cooperation of the secular elite. Without that, a king could
not function: he would be reduced to uselessness, an un-ruler. So we
should be careful not to think in dualistic terms, of one prescription of
kingship for clergy, and another for laity. Churches relied on strong
warrior kings to defend their lands as well as to spread Christianity,
nobles were happy to let some of the sacred aura of kingship brush off
onto themselves. Principles of justice and self-restraint were as much a
shrewd political strategy for aristocrats keen to enhance their own position as they were a code of conduct for kings.

After all, as Jonas of Orleans, Adalbero of Laon, and others emphasized, Christian ethics of the responsibilities of power had come to apply
not only to kings but also to the *potentes* who constituted the ruling elite.[41]
At its most ideologically effective, royal authority presumed a complementary balance between the just exercise of power by kings and their
leading subjects: good kingship was the ideological and cosmological abstraction of a social order grounded in good lordship more generally. No
one knew that better than Adalbero's contemporary, Wulfstan of York,
whose association between the collapse of civil society and the moral
transgressions of the Anglo-Saxons has already been quoted.[42] At about
the same time as his castigation of the Anglo-Saxon elite spelled out the
connection between natural disaster and social disarray, he articulated
trenchantly the king's side of this same relationship:

> For the Christian king
> it is very fitting
> that he be in the position of a father
> to the Christian people.
> And in watching and warding over them
> be Christ's deputy,
> as he is called.[43]

These lines, written in about 1010, summed up centuries of reflection on the task and nature of kingship in a Christian society. A few years later, Wulfstan elaborated the underlying logic:

> Through the unwise king
> the people will be made wretched
> not once, but very often
> because of his misrule.
> Through the king's wisdom
> the people will be blessed
> and prosperous and victorious.
> And therefore the wise king
> must expand and exalt
> christendom and kingdom,
> and heathendom shall he always
> hinder and abhor.[44]

The early medieval convergence of interests that represented the king as 'Christ's deputy' reached its high point in the 1020s in England and in Germany, but was not to remain uncontested much longer. In the 1070s, fierce ideological warfare broke out, first in the German empire, then elsewhere, about the appropriate relationship of king to God and clergy. Institutional changes followed, transforming the exercise of priestly authority and the means of implementing royal justice by the end of the twelfth century. Wulfstan of York would have found it strange indeed that the role of 'Christ's deputy' had been claimed exclusively for the pope, yet the exercise of justice remained the cornerstone of Christian kingship. Hincmar of Reims, on the other hand, would have felt quite at home at the inauguration of any new ruler, for the consecration formula used for Otto II looked directly back to his inspiration but remained a living tradition for many centuries to come.

During Antiquity, 'Europe' signalled one of the three continents of the known world. But in the centuries from c.500 to c.1000, much of the continent came to adopt a new identity, as Christendom, the community of all baptized believers in Christ and the Christian God. Men and women from the Mediterranean to the Arctic Circle now had something in common. And, as is the nature of any group identity, Christendom defined itself as much vis-à-vis those outside as those within. Propagated by powerful words and sharp swords alike, Christendom did its best to silence alternative visions of the world. As a dominant core of beliefs and values, it influenced the history of Europe and the wider world for centuries to come.

This much is self-evident. But the significance of the alliance between kings and the Christian religion that emerged in the early Middle Ages is deeper than this. Early medieval Christianity was even more a religion of the powerful, the *potentes*, than of the poor, the *pauperes*. In Antiquity, Europe beyond the Roman imperial frontier had been occupied by numerous petty peoples and their fragile, shifting confederations. By the end of the millennium, however, powerful and enduring kingdoms had emerged there. Previous chapters have sketched some of the reasons for this: the impact of Christianity supplements them, for it offered resources, infrastructures, ideology, and, importantly, identity. Differently put, Christianity brought with it the late Roman legacy of institutionalized power, well resourced, ideologically justified, and of cosmological significance.

In those Mediterranean parts of Europe that had passed from imperial officials to warrior kings in the fifth century with little structural disruption, the association of Christianity and rulership was already firmly entrenched. Continuity of administration and bureaucracy in both secular and ecclesiastical life assisted this. But, even here, Christianity brought kings new justifications for ruling, new tasks and obligations, new powers to exercise. And, when effective royal government broke down in southern France and Italy in the later tenth and early eleventh centuries, the ideals and obligations of ethical power were maintained and asserted by churches. At the same time, muscular Christianity offered the small kingdoms of northern Spain a ready-made justification for beginning steady aggression against the Muslim warlords of the central and southern parts of the Iberian peninsula. However dislocating the ideological disputes and juridical reorganization of Christendom in the late eleventh and twelfth centuries were, the early medieval alliance of warrior kings and Christianity remained unassailed.

8

Rome and the Peoples of Europe

The ... mighty sea has also in its arctic region ... a great island named Scandza, from which my tale (by God's grace) shall take its beginning. . . . Now from this island of Scandza, as from a factory of peoples or a womb of nations, the Goths are said to have come forth long ago under their king.[1]

To the king who had been intent on war came a longing for travel, bearing a pilgrim's staff. The lord, dear to the emperor, friend of Peter, reaped a portion of Rome's glory.

Few generous princes will thus have measured the southward path with their feet.[2]

AT the centre of the Roman Empire lay the Great Sea around whose sun-drenched shores the imperial provinces sprawled. Roman geographers organized their knowledge of the world from this Mediterranean vantage point: *mare nostrum*, our sea, divided the land mass into three continents, Europe, Asia, and Africa. Around the whole of the world flowed Ocean, the tidal girdle that 'surrounds its coasts like a wreath'.[3] At the furthest edge of Europe, Ocean contained islands, with only some of which the Romans were familiar: Britain they ruled, Ireland they visited occasionally, the Orkneys they acknowledged by repute. Beyond these and 'separated from the others by an indefinite space and ... known to barely a few' lay Thule, the island of summer midnight sun and the winter night that lasted for a full six months, where the sea was dark and frozen.[4] Also in its arctic region Ocean was believed to contain the 'great island named Scandza', also called 'Scadinavia'. Here was the outermost edge of the world.

From Rome to Scandinavia was a long stretch of the imagination. In Antiquity, Roman ethnographers filled the space beyond the imperial frontiers with 'imagined communities', whose names, numbers, physical and moral characteristics they described in detail on the basis of limited knowledge and much stereotyping. Those who lived beyond the frontiers have left ample archaeological evidence of their existence, including their characteristic forms of settlement, furnished burials, and deposits of elite riches and weapons, yet we cannot use material remains such as these to deduce with any confidence what their political organization, far less their self-perceptions, may have been.[5] In the absence of any documentary records from these communities, who employed only occasional runic or ogam literacy, the historian thus encounters them through the interpretations of Roman commentators: the mentalities and social identities that informed life beyond the frontier remain effectively unknown.

These were the peoples whom, whatever their irrecoverable individualities, Romans categorized as 'barbarians', distinguishing only the sedentary and uncultured from the nomadic and utterly alien. As has been emphasized, 'barbarians' fulfilled an important cultural role by epitomizing the absence of the beneficial effects of the Roman way of life and its more 'civilized' values.[6] Yet these groups were far more than the essential 'other' of ingrained prejudices, for they also held a crucial, if ambivalent, place in imperial politics. While their restiveness provided the ongoing *raison d'être* for the military machine of the western provinces, their manpower was nevertheless crucial to the replenishment of Roman armies. And when, in the fifth century, some of these troops crossed the frontier and eventually founded new kingdoms, the infinitely distant Scandza, where—according to Mediterranean imagination—people had nothing to do except procreate during the long winter months, took on the aspect of the 'womb of nations'. Here, then, sixth-century writers located the first cause of the movements of peoples, battles, and political upheavals that in the course of the fifth century had turned the western Roman imperial provinces into separate kingdoms under their own rulers.

Rome and Scandinavia form the geographical frame of reference of this final chapter. Its conceptual dimension is indicated by two transformations. The first concerns Scandinavia, the 'womb of nations' of late Roman ethnographical imagination, where Christian kingdoms were rapidly developing from the late tenth century. It is emblematic of the early eleventh-century state of affairs that the road from Scandinavia to Rome was a real journey for King Cnut, grandson of the first Christian king of the Danes, for it was he whom the poet Sighvatr described as the prince who 'measured the southward path with [his] feet' in 1027. By the time of his pilgrimage, the geopolitical map of Europe's cultures and polities had achieved a form that would not fundamentally alter for some centuries to come. Together with the spread of Latin Christianity, the development of kingdoms based on ethnic groupings and of new imperial hegemonies had so reorganized the political topography of Europe that the old imaginative framework was quite redundant. Once the unknown periphery, Scandinavia was now incorporated within the political community of Latin Christendom on much the same terms as other regions.

Rome had been transformed too. Although vastly diminished since its imperial maximum of approximately 0.5 million inhabitants, the population of the city that Cnut visited was nevertheless far larger than that of any other in Latin Christendom. Cnut, as so many other visitors and pilgrims, would have encountered pockets of dense settlement among gardens and vineyards on the sites of the tenements that in antiquity had housed the city's teeming population. On his way to the shrines and churches, many already venerable with age, he would also have passed the crumbling, debris-filled monuments of the city's imperial past. For Rome had undergone profound changes in the early Middle Ages. In c.500, although no longer the administrative capital of the empire, it retained its ancient prestige and remained the seat of the senate, the body that had participated in governing Rome as city, kingdom, republic, and empire since the earliest times. The city remained a forum of political life for aristocrats of ancient families, who hailed it as 'that fertile mother of eloquence, that vast temple of every virtue, that city which cannot be called an alien place',[7] and at the same time was home to the pope and Latin Christendom's holiest shrines. Ecclesiastical presence asserted steadily growing influence on the politics and material fabric of fifth- and sixth-century Rome, so that, by the later eighth century, it had become a city of the papal church. By the time of Cnut's visit, however, it was in political terms a peripheral city, a southern outpost of northern polities wedged on the volatile frontier with the Byzantines of southern Italy, and only occasionally visited by emperors whose power base lay far north of the Alps. Splendid traditions of senatorial governance had long since given way to a ruling elite who exercised control through the papal bureaucracy. In the late tenth and early eleventh centuries, interest groups that fused ecclesiastical and secular interests played for high stakes in an urban politics characterized by aristocratic factionalism, popular unrest, and occasional imperial intervention.

Even so, Rome's hold over the imagination of all the inhabitants of Christian Europe was long since assured. Northern writers dreamed on, without mundane reality interrupting their idealized visions of the 'queen of cities'.[8] 'Famed throughout the triple world by Franks, | faithful

Christians and emperors', it was secure in its reputation as 'mother of kings and glory of Italians',[9] 'the mother of martyrs, the domicile of the apostles',[10] 'the capital of the world . . . mother of all churches'.[11] By the early years of the second Christian millennium, Rome was Europe's 'imagined community' par excellence, geographically marginal but symbolically central, a powerful idea but a shabby urban experience. Rome's twin roles as historic seat of political power and contemporary Christian holy place expressed different aspects of the same past.

Between these two poles—Scandinavia and Rome—this chapter establishes how political, religious, and cultural identities were formed and reformed throughout the early Middle Ages. Rejecting any view of the period from c.500 to c.1000 as significant primarily for the foundations of the events of later epochs, it dismisses narratives of 'the origin of nations' and 'the rise of the papacy'. It also refuses to cast the history of the early Middle Ages in terms of such Rome-centred normative evaluations as 'barbarian invasion' or 'ideals of empire'. Instead, the heart of this chapter is an exploration of Rome's role as an urban reality with such a rich political, cultural, and religious past that it exerted a powerful grip on the imagination of all who encountered it directly or indirectly. Each section presents a different aspect of this central theme; each is introduced by a journey to or from Rome. The first argues that there is nothing primordial about the ethnically based kingdoms that developed in the course of the early Middle Ages, but rather that these political identities were as much the product of specific cultural configurations and historical moments as kin-based, gendered, or religious ones. It pays particular attention to the contribution of Roman and Christian literature to the origin myths that explained and propagated early medieval ethnic identities. The second section turns from kingdoms to empires, as both concepts and polities. By asking how empires were established and legitimated, it assesses the extent to which Romanness was a political ideology that informed the early medieval political order. In this context, it also considers the transformation in Rome's role as the capital of empire. Visitors to the city form the thread through the final section. Their experience puts imperial ceremonial in context and also brings Christian Rome into focus. The chapter ends by juxtaposing the Rome experienced by the city's visitors with the evocations of Rome recreated in many parts of Christian Europe, arguing that the city's Christian identity formed a recurrent leitmotiv of early medieval cultural expression. It emerges that, in multiple ways, the political and cultural legacy of the Roman Empire formed a counterpoise to the particularisms and local identities so characteristic of Europe after Rome.

8.1. Principal places mentioned in Chapter 8.

Rome, AD 500

In AD 500, a Gothic warrior king visited Rome. The unchallenged ruler of Italy since 493, Theoderic the Great had established his military court at Ravenna, headquarters of the former imperial army and, since 408, a supplemental capital to Rome. Fifth-century Rome had remained a civilian city and its guardians were still members of the senatorial aristocracy.

By the end of the fifth century, however, their traditional domination of the city's politics and patronage faced increasing challenge from papal officials and the growing wealth of the city's many Christian churches, the foremost among which housed the tomb of St Peter, leader of the apostles. So in 500 Theoderic expressed his deference by going first to St Peter's, on the opposite bank of the Tiber from the ancient city: there 'Pope Symmachus and all the senate and people of Rome came joyfully to meet him outside the city'. Only then did he enter the city itself, where he addressed the senate and 'promised that, with God's help, he would uphold inviolably everything that previous Roman emperors had decreed'. Next, in traditional imperial fashion, he paraded in triumph through the city to the palace, staged circus games for the populace, distributed food, and allocated expenses for repairing the city walls.[12]

Adept at manipulating Roman conventions of rulership, Theoderic was in origin a frontier warlord who had spent his formative adolescent years as a hostage in the imperial court at Constantinople. Probably born in 451, the son of a mother who may conceivably have been Roman and a Gothic father who at that date led part of a Gothic army settled on imperial soil in Pannonia, Theoderic died in 526, western emperor in all but name (see Figure 8.2). In 489, he had led from the Balkans into Italy his following, a heterogeneous group drawn from various ethnic war bands but which, under his strong leadership, was rapidly acquiring a coherent group identity as 'Goths'. At the request of the Byzantine emperor Zeno (474–91), he seized control of Italy from Odoacer, the warlord who had dominated the peninsula since the deposition of the western child-emperor Romulus Augustulus in 476. In due course Zeno's successor Anastasius acknowledged Theoderic as the legitimate ruler of Italy; the Goth always took care to defer to Anastasius as emperor. Governing the mixed population of Romans and 'Goths'—indigenous inhabitants and in-comers of various origins—Theoderic won a reputation as a vigorous ruler, managing for most of his reign to maintain a careful balance between the touchy pride of the old senatorial elite and his own retinue of military par-venus. During his reign, Ravenna hosted a far more stable, magnificent, and respected court than under the last emperors, while in Rome the sen-ate enjoyed an Indian summer of influence and erudition. The pope also benefited from the rapport between Goths and senators, notwithstanding Theoderic's allegiance to Arian Christianity. The contemporary verdict was firm:

A most warlike and strong man . . . outstanding and of good will in all things, he reigned thirty-three years. During his time, Italy enjoyed thirty years of good

Kingdom of Theoderic the Great, at its maximum extent after 510
Kingdom of the Franks to 507
Visigothic to 507, thereafter Frankish
Kingdom of the Burgundians to 534, thereafter Frankish
Kingdom of the Suevi
Kingdom of the Vandals
Kingdom of the Visigoths

Theoderic's marriage alliances

1 Audefleda, sister of Clovis king of the Franks, married to Theoderic
2 Ostrogotho, daughter of Theoderic, married to Sigismund, king of the Burgundians
3 Thiudigotho, daughter of Theoderic, married to Alaric II, king of the Visigoths
4 Amalfrida, sister of Theoderic, married to Thrasamund, king of the Vandals
5 Amalberga, niece of Theoderic, married to Hermanifrid, king of the Thuringians

8.2. The World of Theoderic the Great.

fortune and prosperity, so that there was peace to those who were going about their business, and he did nothing improperly. Thus he ruled two peoples in one, the Romans and the Goths, and although he himself was of the Arian sect, he nevertheless attempted nothing against the Catholics, so that by the Romans he was hailed as another Trajan or Valentinian and by the Goths . . . was adjudged their most powerful king in all things.[13]

All around the western Mediterranean, other warlords had also leveraged their military ability for institutional authority as kings in the middle and later decades of the fifth century, profiting as much from the enduring vitality of Roman administrative and legal traditions as from the effectiveness of their armed followings. In such circumstances, the distinction between Roman and non-Roman inevitably blurred in practice, if not always in ideology or rhetoric. Although arguably not the most successful from a longer perspective, Theoderic's reign is certainly the best documented of these sixth-century kingdoms. In the unremitting competition for land, influence, and reputation among their rulers, he affirmed his pre-eminence through a canny combination of military skill, ruthless politics, and dynastic marriage alliances, including those with Hermanifrid and Alaric II.

In both domestic and external affairs, therefore, Theoderic replicated traditional discourses of power and successfully inserted himself into imperial networks of influence. But from the perspective of the eastern empire's court in mid-sixth-century Constantinople, the rapidly shifting western politics half a century or so earlier came to be seen as something very different: the demise of the old order. With the benefit of hindsight, the coup against Romulus Augustulus became a turning point, as a Constantinopolitan court official emphasized towards the end of Theoderic's reign. 'With this Augustulus perished the western empire of the Roman people, which the first Augustus, Octavian, began to rule in the seven hundred and ninth year from the foundation of the city. This occurred in the five hundred and twenty-second year of the kingdom of the departed emperors, with Gothic kings thereafter holding Rome.'[14] In sum, Theoderic's life spanned three-quarters of a century of immense and irreversible political change: his visit to the city in 500 is a convenient vantage point from which to take stock of the changing interactions between Rome and the peoples of Europe.

To do this is to investigate both the relationship of political formations to collective ethnic identities and, equally importantly, early medieval perceptions of it. Viewed from the perspective of the politics and passions of nineteenth- and twentieth-century Europe, this relationship became a highly charged issue, but it is important to be clear that the conceptual distinction between polity and ethnicity had no place in early medieval thinking. Nor did the modern dichotomy between culturally constructed ethnicity and biologically determined race. Instead, it is best to begin with political vocabulary. In the first place, both Roman and Judaeo-Christian conceptions of political organization viewed the entire world as divided into many peoples. From a Roman perspective, some of these had been subsumed into their empire with its pretensions to world rule; in biblical tradition all of them shared a common descent from the sons of the mythical founding ancestor, Noah—although only those acknowledging the Judaeo-Christian God could claim to be the 'people of God'. Secondly, central to Latin and the various local languages of the early Middle Ages were words that denoted in undifferentiated fashion a group whose members shared one or more of the following: putative descent from a common ancestor; common cultural attributes; organization into a single polity. Capable of being translated as 'people', these include the Latin terms *gens, genus, natio, plebs*; in the Germanic languages *folk* (Old High German), *þiuda* (Gothic), *þeod* (Old English); in the Celtic languages *tuath, cenél* (Old Irish), *tud* (Old Welsh). Writing between 906 and 913, Regino of Prüm echoed a millennium-long tradition and encapsulated the assumptions inherent in this vocabulary when he declared: 'the various nations of peoples are distinguished from each other by descent, customs, language and laws.'[15] This conventional reformulation of a commonplace notion underlines the absence of any distinction in ancient and early medieval thinking between groups whose membership was determined by biological descent (real or fictive) and groups defined by such socially constituted features as shared behavioural traits, names, political identity, or beliefs. Nor did any of these words specify the size, internal organization, or cultural characteristics of the peoples of early medieval Europe. It must be emphatically stated that the nuances of modern political and cultural terminology would have been meaningless in early medieval perspective.

That said, earlier chapters have already hinted at some of the issues involved in assessing what constituted a people in the early Middle Ages. Of Regino's diagnostics of ethnic identity, Chapter 1 examined language and Chapters 3 and 4 dealt with law and 'customs': although sometimes linguistic and/or legal communities approximately correlated with ethnic groups, for the most part they did not. Also important is the demonstration in Chapter 3 that genealogies organized gendered claims to power, above all for kings, claims that, as Chapter 7 indicated, often had cosmological overtones. However fictional, descent thus functioned as a persuasive metaphor for the legitimate transmission of power and status among a male ruling elite; by the same token, it provided mythical cogency in explaining the identity of an entire people. As for women, their role as agents of familial and cultural reproduction usually remained implicit, but, as we shall see, myths of descent did occasionally make this explicit.

Early medieval sources recount origin myths for many—indeed most—of the peoples of Europe. Such tales link an aboriginal homeland, final place of settlement, and genealogy of the ruling dynasty of a people; they may also explain key social and moral attributes, such as hairstyle, weaponry, nobility, or bravery. Some reach us via the pens of members of the ethnic group whose history they purport to narrate: in answering the question 'who are we?' they offer a vehicle for acknowledging collective identity and legitimating leadership. Others offer the perspective of outsiders and either emphasize separateness or seek schematic explanations of the multi-ethnic reality of the early Middle Ages. Whether their perspective is internal or external, these myths assert identity through difference and manipulate the past in service of the present. By explaining the present with reference to a past generally more imagined than real, they justify the restriction of authority to certain families and conceal the flux of political life in a cloak of natural, primordial metaphor.

Inevitably, we know of these myths only when they took written form. Although they may contain elements of preliterate tradition, whether the stories were told by warriors around the camp fire, by mothers to their children, or by court poets as lordly entertainment, the genre as it has come down to us is a product of the extended encounter between Christianity and the peoples of Europe outlined in the previous chapter. Because Christianity was the main vector for the transmission of the literary culture of the Roman world and churches the main agents of its preservation, the form and content of these myths were liable to be influenced by both biblical and classical origin tales.[16] Thus, for example, writers of the seventh, eighth, and ninth centuries commonly presented the Franks as descended from the Trojans. According to Rome's own myth of origins, as retold in the first century BC by the epic poet Virgil, the Trojan hero Aeneas had come to the land of the Latins, where his heirs founded Rome. By subsuming Roman history into that of ancient Troy, Virgil's ever popular myth invited his Frankish readers to claim parity with the Romans through shared Trojan origins. By contrast, Irish mythographers emphasized that Fénius Farsaid, inventor of the Gaelic language and eponymous ancestor of the *Féni*, the Irish, enjoyed a biblical descent from Magog, son of Japhet, son of Noah.[17]

This broad cultural template—of familiar biblical and classical paradigms, sometimes with an unquantifiable admixture of oral tradition—
applied in a wide range of settings. We can best survey the origin legends
of the peoples of Europe by starting far beyond the former imperial
boundaries, and gradually moving ever nearer to Rome itself. In the world
of Gaelic language along north-western Europe's Atlantic edge, the Irish
were well aware that their linguistic, legal, and cultural uniformity complemented their division into competing kingdoms, of which there were
probably over 100 in the fifth and sixth centuries, although no more than
a dozen of any political consequence by the tenth. They saw no tension
between identifying each kingdom in genealogical terms as a descent-
based group, such as the Corcu Loígde, and simultaneously expressing the
common characteristics of the Irish as an ethnic group. Irish scholars
achieved this by accumulating an impressive body of myth that slotted the
many hundreds of Irish ruling dynasties, real and legendary, into a historical framework derived from the Bible. In the process they provided
the Irish with a secure place in universal history and a known origin comparable with that of all other peoples of the world.

What began in the seventh century as scholarly manipulation of Latin
texts imported into Ireland's ecclesiastical libraries culminated in a widespread origin myth by the eleventh century. This was a story of the suc-
cessive migrations of heroic ancestors and their wanderings through
Africa, Asia, and Europe, culminating in the settlement of the originally
uninhabited island of Ireland. The method employed was threefold: narrative, chronology, and genealogical etymology. Narrative archetypes taken
from the Old Testament provided the literary scaffolding; computational
facility adjusted this to chime with the outlines of world history as constructed by fourth-century Christian chroniclers; plausible etymologies
provided the names for founding ancestors, of whom Fénius Farsaid is one
example.

By the early ninth century, all the main elements of the Irish origin
myth had been formulated, and were circulating widely in various genres
and with varying details, in Ireland and elsewhere. Here is the form in
which part of it reached a British audience:

When the children of Israel crossed through the Red Sea, the Egyptians came
and pursued them and were drowned, as may be read in the Law [i.e. the Old
Testament: see Exod. 14: 21–31]. Among the Egyptians was a nobleman of Scythia,
with a great following, who had been expelled from his kingdom, and was there
when the Egyptians were drowned, but did not join in the pursuit of the children of God. The survivors took counsel to expel him, lest he should attack their

kingdom and occupy it, for their strength had been drowned in the Red Sea. He was expelled and he wandered for 42 years through Africa, and they came to the Altars of the Philistines . . . [and many other named places] and their people multiplied exceedingly. After they had come to Spain, and 1002 years after the Egyptians had been drowned in the Red Sea, they came to the country of Dal Riada, at the time when Brutus was ruling among the Romans.[18]

Inasmuch as the Scythians of the Eurasian steppe were the archetypal noble savages (real and imagined) of Graeco-Roman ethnography and Brutus was the legendary first consul and founder of the Roman Republic, this tale deftly inserted the Irish into Roman and biblical history simultaneously. The linkage was strengthened, when ingenious etymologizing provided the anonymous Scythian nobleman with a wife: 'Scota, the daughter of Pharoah king of Egypt', herself explicitly the eponym of the *Scotti* and thus primordial mother of all the Irish.[19] Elaborated to include Scota's marriage to the Scythian, the origin myth achieved its definitive form throughout the Gaelic culture province common to Ireland and northern Britain. And in northern Britain, as the Gaelic kingdom of Alba evolved into the high medieval kingdom of the Scots, old myths served the rulers of this multi-ethnic, multilingual kingdom well, providing impeccable genealogical legitimation. Indeed, when the child-king Alexander III was consecrated king of Scots at Scone in 1249, his ancestry was proclaimed in full—all the way back to Scota, daughter of Pharoah.

Like the Irish, the British combined a strong sense of their own historical and ethnic identity with the reality of fragmentation into discrete, often competing, kingdoms. Unlike the Irish, however, they had no need to invent an attachment to the Roman past. In the legendary Brutus they identified an obvious eponym; via Brutus (or Britto, as he was sometimes called) their descent from the Trojans was easily asserted. Additionally, historical figures from Britain's era of Roman rule morphed into legendary ancestors of early Welsh dynasties, most prominently the late-fourth-century general and aspirant ursurper Magnus Maximus (d. 388). Migration, invasion, and settlement provided the political context for the development of British myths of ethnic origin, but a context in which the British were victims not victors. Faced with loss of hegemony over southern and eastern Britain to the sixth-century kingdoms coalescing around Germanic-speaking elites, the Britons' claim to be the aboriginal, rightful inhabitants of the island provided them with both an ethnic origin and the basis on which to prophesy the eventual expulsion of the hated invaders.

A remarkable Welsh monument at Llantysilio-y-Ial indicates the inseparability of British origin myth, descent-based kingship, and legitimation of territorial claims. Cyngen, king of Powys (d. 854), erected an inscribed column 2.4 metres high to the memory of his great-grandfather Eliseg, who had reconquered the inheritance of the kings of Powys from the English. Commencing by naming four generations of his own genealogy, Cyngen lauded Eliseg's achievements and spelled out his distinguished, if legendary, pedigree. This transforms the names of historical persons into ruling ancestors, legitimating Eliseg's position (and, by implication, Cyngen's) by descent not only from Britu but also from 'Maximus the king who slew the king of the Romans'.[20] Here we see clearly the appropriation of a common British legend for specific dynastic purposes in Powys, in much the same way as individual Irish kingdoms associated themselves with a common ethnic origin story.

This discussion of the Irish and British origin legends that emerged in the early Middle Ages has emphasized the significance of Roman history and Christian Latin texts as the cultural rubble out of which fundamentally different edifices could be built, even in places at or beyond the outermost margins of former imperial rule. It has also drawn attention to the theme of migration and settlement as context or content—or both—of origin myths. We find variants on both these points when we turn from the Celtic-language areas of Atlantic Europe to the Germanic-speaking peoples who had emerged amid the military imperatives and cultural porousness of the fourth- and fifth-century Rhine–Danube frontier.

This was an environment where prolonged encounter with the armies and institutions of the Roman Empire promoted the formulation of such stories—and not least because the need to assert a collective identity was enhanced by the destabilizing effect of the constant formation and re-formation of ethnic groups in the course of warfare, migration, settlement, and intermarriage. Such instability characterized the fifth and early sixth centuries in particular. Thereafter—from the seventh century—origin myths developed in altered circumstances. In some instances, they provided ideological glue for successful kingdoms whose populations were in practice always a mixture of Roman and heterogeneous non-Roman elements, but that gradually came to take their political identities from the ethnic self-perception of their ruling dynasty. Notable instances of this include not only the Frankish kingdom; the kingdoms of Angles, Saxons, and Jutes in south-eastern Britain; the kingdom of the Lombards, who had established dominance over the central and northern Italian peninsula in 568; and the Iberian kingdom that emerged in the fifth and sixth centuries under the leadership of Alaric's dynasty and subsequently acquired the designation 'Visigothic' to distinguish it from the Goths under Theoderic's rule in Italy. In other instances, the formulation or elaboration of persuasive Germanic origin legends was the product of political defeat not of success, and offered a retrospective on peoples whose cultural identity had outlasted their existence as a separate polity: this was notably the case for the Burgundians, whose Rhone valley kingdom was conquered by the Franks in 534. In similar fashion, the Lombard origin myth found its literary apogee shortly after the Franks had eliminated the Lombard kingdom in 774. Both these instances also indicate that, directly or indirectly, the Franks' political hegemony involved manipulating the ethnic identities of peoples absorbed into their aggressively successful polity.

The single kingdom that fits neither model was Theoderic's. Alone of fifth-, sixth-, and seventh-century kings, he actively encouraged the formation of ethnic mythology that asserted his right to the Gothic kingship by descent from founding ancestors of the Goths. Genealogy as ideology found expression in the names he gave his offspring, which were those of putative ancestral heroes. From Cassiodorus, the learned Roman senator who held the senior court offices of Quaestor and Praetorian Prefect, he even commissioned a twelve-volume history of the Gothic people, now unfortunately lost, but which is known to have given this new people an old history and to have flaunted Theoderic's supposedly ancient pedigree. We can only speculate about why the king was so determined to articulate a flawless Gothic identity for himself and his dynasty: perhaps the insecurity of a parvenu; perhaps the political priority of melding his fissiparous war band of disparate followers into a more ordered whole; perhaps the challenge to a newcomer of ruling the Roman imperial heartland, where 'Romanness' must have seemed a far more self-evident and monolithic identity than it actually was in practice.

It remains impossible to assess how much acceptance this Gothic identity commanded beyond its proponents within Theoderic's court circle. But it is certain that its mythological development did not cease when his dynasty failed in 536 and sixteen years later his kingdom collapsed, fatally undermined by a lengthy and destructive Byzantine campaign to reconquer the Italian peninsula. Having read Cassiodorus's Gothic History, a bureaucrat in Constantinople, himself of Gothic extraction, marked the resumption of Byzantine rule in Italy by writing his own account of the 'origin and deeds of the Goths'. Jordanes opened his work with Ocean's girdle around the three known continents, for 'the same mighty sea has also in its arctic region, that is, in the north, a great island named

Scandza, from which,' he declared, 'by God's grace my tale shall take its beginning'. From Scandza, 'as from a factory of peoples or a womb of nations, the Goths are said to have come forth long ago under their king, Berig by name. . . . And even to this day it is said to be called Gothiscandza.'[21] Claiming to prefer the rich, though inconsistent, traditions of ancient ethnography and the history of Rome that commenced with the city's mythic Trojan origins to the Goths' 'old wives' tales' that he had heard,[22] Jordanes equated the Goths with the Scythians and mentioned theories of their descent from Magog, thus fitting them into the geography and chronology of both Roman and biblical history. He endowed them with a magnificent past, one that commenced with migration from primeval beginnings in Scandza, and led, through wanderings and sufferings in the vast space between the mouth of the Danube and the boundaries of Asia, to encounter and conflict with Huns and Romans and then eventuated in Theoderic's triumphal march from the Balkans to conquer Italy. It was a past replete with the names of legendary kings— names that Theoderic's own children bore—and ancestors—'such heroes as admiring antiquity scarce proclaims its own to be'—of whose deeds 'in earliest times they [the Goths] sang . . . in strains of song'.[23]

Like Theoderic's kingdom, Jordanes's account was a product of its own time and place. Inasmuch as Theoderic and his immediate heirs were all dead and his kingdom restored to direct imperial rule, it was a product of the failure to establish a viable Gothic kingdom in Italy. For all its relentless narrative and anecdotal detail, Jordanes's vision of the past functioned as all origin tales do, by projecting the present political order into the distant past, and it achieved this so effectively that many generations of readers have been seduced by its attractive explanation of Gothic origins. Moreover, it rapidly gained such popularity that it acted as the template for subsequent origin tales for several other peoples such as the Lombards, who also came to acquire a mythic homeland in Scandza. Despite the dissimilar political context of composition, Jordanes had much in common with the anonymous Irish mythographers in purpose, narrative emplotment, balancing of oral tradition with literary sources, even some of the names out of which he spun his story. Like theirs, his work was exploited for quite different purposes in later centuries. Nevertheless, his—and their—great achievement was to show that ethnic and Roman histories cannot be disentangled and that the one presumes the other. Without Rome, its literature, legends, and Christian religion, the peoples of sixth-century Europe had no past, no present—and no future.

Paderborn, AD 799

In the summer of 799, Pope Leo III (795–816) journeyed north, to visit Charlemagne in Saxony at Paderborn. Not long thereafter, a skilled poet envisioned their meeting. Writing in Latin, he began by introducing Charlemagne, 'the beacon of Europe':

> Charles, powerful warrior, merciful victor and triumphant king,
> surpasses in goodness all the kings in the world,
> stands out as more just and more powerful than them all.
>
> .   .   .   .   .   .
>
> King Charles, head of the world, love and adornment of his people,
> venerable summit of Europe, very best father, hero,
> august lord in a city where a second Rome newly flowers,
> rising to great heights with its massive walls,
> touching the stars with its high domes.[24]

Then, after a vivid narration of the circumstances of Leo's journey, the poet returned his audience's attention to Charlemagne as he awaited the travel-weary Leo. Clad in a golden helmet, the Frankish king towered above everyone else as he sat astride his warhorse, surrounded by the units of his army drawn up in a circle for a full dress parade. Adjacent choirs of priests in their long vestments held aloft banners with that most Christian of symbols, the cross. As Leo approached, 'he is astounded how varied in their customs, languages, clothing, and armour are the various peoples from different parts of the world'. The ruler, now dismounted, and the pope met: 'the king, the father of Europe, and Leo, the chief pastor of the world' embraced.[25]

The so-called Paderborn epic used deliberately classicizing expressions and a rich vocabulary of ancient imperial imagery in order to present Charlemagne as the Christian world ruler, king over so many peoples that his rule was tantamount to rule over Europe. So powerful was this monarch that Aachen, Charlemagne's newly built prestige palace complex, has become 'a second Rome'. Only by such imperial analogies could his position be accurately represented. The poetic evocation of the Paderborn 'summit meeting' between Frankish king and Roman pope thus alerts us to the appropriation of Rome's imperial past as an element of early medieval political ideas and attitudes. It opens up for inspection two themes: the early medieval language of 'empire' in the representation of power, and the city of Rome as the capital of empire.

To put these broad themes in context, we should take time to explore the situations in which king and pope found themselves in 799, in order to establish why Leo's visit to Paderborn constitutes such a useful avenue of approach. We start with the city of Rome at the close of the eighth century and the circumstances of the pope's long journey. Leo left behind him a city whose population had shrunk far below the levels of Theoderic's day, perhaps as low as 25,000, but which was nevertheless notably cosmopolitan. Its permanent population comprised families of Greek, Syrian, and Sicilian origin in addition to those of local, Roman descent. Numbers were swelled by a transient population of pilgrims—Anglo-Saxons, Irish, Frisians, Franks, Greeks—and of merchants, including Arabs, Venetians, and southern Italians.

By this time, Rome was developing into a substantial artisanal and mercantile centre, where pottery and metalwork were produced in some quantity and where eastern goods—textiles, spices, precious metals—seem to have been exchanged for slaves. Certainly, by the late eighth century there were adequate funds available for extensive renovation of the crumbling urban fabric. Following the example set by his predecessor Hadrian I, Leo III was energetically restoring the city's monuments, repairing its ancient churches and overseeing the construction of new ones. His lavish endowment of churches, old and new, marks him out as one of Rome's great builders, as does his commissioning of palatial papal accommodation on a scale of unprecedented grandeur. But Leo had nevertheless fled a city in turmoil, for earlier that year he had been physically attacked in the course of a major religious procession through the city streets. The attack, which seems to have been accompanied by a move formally to depose him and by allegations of severe misconduct, nevertheless failed to inflict the horrific and irreversible mutilation that would have disqualified him from office. The position of pope was fast becoming the target of aristocratic factional ambition in a characteristically Roman form of politics. For Leo to leave the city for the four- to five-month round trip to Paderborn was to risk his position still further.

Paderborn was also a building site, albeit of a very different nature. Since 772 Charlemagne had been conducting frequent military campaigns against the Franks' northern neighbours, the Saxons; the forced conversion to Christianity that accompanied their ruthless subjugation has already been mentioned.[26] Founded in 776 at a strategically convenient location as a base for military and missionary endeavours in Saxony, this new *urbs Karoli*, 'Charles's city', had already been twice burned by the Saxons: in 799 a new church 'of amazing size' was erected and the royal palace rebuilt, larger than before.[27] With its sturdy fortifications, stone buildings, stained glass, frescoed walls, elevated balconies, and luxury imported tableware, the church and palace complex made an

8.3. The World of Charlemagne.

unequivocal statement about the power of the Saxons' new ruler and new religion.

And powerful indeed he was (see Figure 8.3). By 799, Charlemagne had surmounted all internal Frankish opposition to his rule, successfully co-opting the loyalty and resources of secular and ecclesiastical elites. He had appropriated the rapidly crystallizing ideals of Christian kingship as his own and, as Chapter 7 noted, fashioned from them a manifesto for 'correct Christianity' that he urged on all his subjects. He patronized scholars such as the Anglo-Saxon Alcuin, the Visigoth Theodulf, the Lombard Paul the Deacon, and the anonymous author of the 'Paderborn epic' as much for his own greater renown as for their contribution towards building a Christian kingdom. Envoys and exiles from far and wide sought him out, extending yet further the range of his influence and reputation. His vast project of military and cultural imperialism is notable for its geographical scope, economic investment, and human cost—and for the prestige he thereby accrued. But at the time of Leo's visit, protracted Saxon resistance was still posing a formidable challenge to Charlemagne's ambitions, and, as Charlemagne's biographer Einhard later said, 'No war taken up by the Frankish people was ever longer, harder, or more dreadful'.[28] The reconstruction of Paderborn in 799 symbolized the king's 'greatness of spirit and steadfast determination' in the face of the 'faithlessness of the Saxons'.[29]

The conquest of Saxony was not completed until 804, and was exceptional only for its bitterness and duration. The enforcement of Frankish rule marked a new phase in the development of the political organization and ethnic identity of the Saxons, making the situation in Saxony comparable to that elsewhere in Charlemagne's vast realm. Everywhere that Charlemagne and his aristocracy extended their rule, either older ethnic identities were reformulated or new ones emerged. Frankish domination certainly did not eradicate other ethnic groupings—far from it. If anything, it strengthened them, albeit in ways that increasingly associated a particular people with a specific region and a specific legal tradition. Carolingian rule thus fostered the creation of territorially bounded ethnic groups each with their own conventions encoded in law. As for the Franks themselves, their own ethnic identity was so fluid in its expression but so politically compelling that it functioned as a 'super-ethnicity', complementary not antagonistic to the peoples pulled into its orbit. When the poet of the 'Paderborn epic' put words (lifted from Virgil) into Leo's mouth expressing amazement at the many different peoples constituting Charlemagne's army, he was merely articulating the multi-ethnic quality that made the Frankish polity so distinctive.

Leo's visit was not Charlemagne's first encounter with a pope—that had taken place in 754 when Charlemagne was only 5 years old. In that year, Stephen II (752–7) had crossed the Alps both to confer legitimacy on the coup that had brought Charlemagne's father Pippin III to the Frankish throne in 751 and to enlist Frankish political and military help for himself. In 754, the papal predicament derived from the very real threat of Lombard aggression, exacerbated by the recent collapse of the Byzantine administration of central Italy, an administration that had endured here since Justinian's reconquest of the peninsula. In seeking out the assistance of the upstart Carolingian dynasty, Stephen acknowledged that Rome's ecclesiastical bureaucrats were in no position to take adequate military measures to protect their city. In 799, however, Charlemagne was himself the king of the Lombards and in 781 and 787 had confirmed that an extensive territory in Rome's hinterland was to be under direct papal rule. Leo III was thus left to continue Hadrian I's work of puzzling out how the popes, who until around 750 had been subjects of Byzantine imperial administration, could turn themselves into autonomous territorial rulers. That the rapidly shifting and poorly defined position of the pope had led to factionalism and street fighting within Rome hints at how high the political stakes must have been.

The meeting at Paderborn brought together a hugely powerful king, well disposed by family tradition to be respectful towards the bishop of Rome, and a weakened, supplicant pope. In no sense can it have been a meeting of equals. How to characterize it more precisely is impossible, however. That we do not know what was discussed has not prevented historians' attempts at guessing. Nor do we know what relationship, if any, there was between this meeting and Charlemagne's coronation as emperor in Rome during a papal Mass on 25 December 800, when the Frankish king had travelled south to take definitive action to restore Leo's position. If the Paderborn meeting raises more questions than answers, even more so does Charlemagne's imperial coronation. The conflicting viewpoints and aspirations of the two key players themselves were promptly obfuscated by factitious and partisan reportage put around by papal and Frankish spin doctors alike. The politics of contested interpretation inherent in the very events of 799–800 was thus coupled with a calculus of retrospective significance that began immediately afterwards.

In acquiring the title of emperor, Charlemagne set a precedent that future generations were keen to emulate. It took until 850 to establish the convention that the only route to the imperial title was papal coronation in Rome, a tradition that endured, off and on, until 1452; detached from any Roman association thereafter, the imperial title persisted north of the Alps until the Napoleonic era.

Inasmuch as popes, emperors, and historians of later ages repeatedly turned to Leo's impasse and Charlemagne's coronation to justify actions or legitimate claims in quite different circumstances, the events at Paderborn in 799 and at Rome the following year have suffered from extreme teleological over-interpretation. We can avoid that, however, by maintaining the figurative perspective with which this section began, and focusing on the use of 'Rome' and 'empire' as powerful imaginative devices that shaped the cultural parameters of early medieval thinking. Another poem (quite possibly by the same poet) underscores the point that both were transferable notions, equally potent as metaphors as they were as institutions:

My Palaemon [Charlemagne] looks out from the lofty citadel of the new Rome and sees all the kingdoms forged into an empire through his victories.
Our times are transformed into the civilisation of Antiquity.
Golden Rome is reborn and restored anew to the world![30]

The transformation at work here was not, of course a transformation of the world of *c*.800 'into the civilisation of Antiquity' but rather the transformation of phrases, ideas, and values drawn from the ancient world into the grandiose rhetoric of the powerful Frankish hegemonic kingship. That Constantinople had been officially designated 'new Rome' since 381 in no way detracted from the suitability of the epithet for Aachen: 'Rome' was a cipher that stood for the capital of empire in all its architectural grandeur and political importance.

In using an imperial, Roman *mise-en-scène* to add glamour and legitimacy to the political realities of their own day, Carolingian writers tapped into long-standing habits of thought, for empire (*imperium*) was a term central to the Latin political vocabulary of Antiquity. Since early medieval authors frequently relied on Isidore of Seville's *Etymologies* as a concise guide to classical culture, we should do the same. It included a synopsis of world history that drew readers' attention to two points. In the course of identifying two polities that were 'more glorious' than all others, the Assyrian and the Roman, Isidore explained that 'other kingdoms and other kings' were held in a relationship to them 'like appendices'.[31] Overlordship or other forms of hegemony over dependent kingdoms was thus one key descriptor. The other was more specific to the history of Rome itself, the title of 'emperor'. Isidore noted, correctly, that the word *imperator* had originally referred to a general in command of an army, but that the senate had bestowed it as a title on Augustus (d. AD 14) 'in order that he would be distinguished from the kings of other peoples', and that his successors had retained the title.[32]

If 'emperor' became a distinctively Roman title for a ruler whose position was based on military conquest and rule over dependent kingdoms, then an empire was, more generally, any such polity. A reader of the Latin Bible encountered references to many ancient empires, of which the Roman was simply the most recent. Together, the Latin Bible and Isidore ensured that the idea of 'empire' was integral to Christian Latin learning.

The Old Testament, in particular, demonstrated its value as a term for any militarily powerful, multi-ethnic kingdom, especially one that had managed to subordinate other kings to its own ruler. The New Testament provided the basis on which fourth- and fifth-century thinkers had developed theological justifications for the existence of empires as integral to the Christian scheme of divinely ordained redemption of humankind.

'Empire', *imperium*, was thus a useful word for a wide range of early medieval political situations, Christian and non-Christian. It could function neutrally, to describe an exceptionally powerful ruler, as, for example, in Bede's ascription of *imperium* to a sequence of sixth- and seventh-century Anglo-Saxon kings who managed to 'rule over all the southern kingdoms [of Britain], which are divided from the north by the river Humber and the surrounding territory'.[33] Similarly, writing of events much nearer his own day but on the Continent, Bede described Pippin of Herstal, 'duke of the Franks', as exercising 'imperial authority' in southern Frisia after having expelled its ruler and annexed his territory in 690.[34] Alternatively, a king's admirers and propagandists could use the word as a 'puff', to talk up the influence and prestige of kings such as Theoderic the Great.

The word *imperator*, 'emperor', could also be used for laudatory purposes, especially in military situations. The Northumbrian king Oswald (634–42) certainly exercised hegemony over much of the northern half of Britain, and his reign had commenced with a great victory over 'the most powerful king of the Britons', Cadwallon of Gwynedd, in 634. After Oswald's death, emphatic significance was placed on his success: 'Oswald returned as victor after battle and was afterwards ordained by God as emperor of all Britain.'[35] In tenth-century Germany, Otto I's defeat of the Magyars at the river Lech in 955 was afterwards deemed to have been similarly decisive: 'Seizing his shield and the Holy Lance, he turned his horse to face the enemy fulfilling the role of the strongest soldier and the best commander (*imperator*).'[36]

The benefit of hindsight was not an essential prerequisite for such flattery, however. Brian Boru, king of the Dál Cais in Munster (976–1014), broke the traditional mould of Irish politics by defeating not only the minor kings of southern parts of the island and the Hiberno-Norse colony of Dublin but also the traditional overkings of the northern half of Ireland, the Uí Néill. Taking tribute, hostages, and plunder wherever he went, Brian asserted a vigorous overlordship throughout Ireland. In 1005, he put a generous gift of gold on the altar of St Patrick at Armagh, a shrine normally under the patronage of the Uí Néill. A priest recorded the donation in the church's ancient gospel book 'in the sight of Brian, emperor of the

Irish'.[37] Brian certainly did not hold any formally bestowed office or title of emperor, but clerical bombast accurately captured the essence of his position as the king who dominated all other Irish kings of his day.

In sum, empire and emperors were often in the eye of the beholder. Oswald, Otto I as he rode into battle against the Magyars, and Brian Boru were emperors in the opinion of the learned men of their times, in much the same way as Theoderic, Pippin of Herstal, and others enjoyed *imperium*. Those who knew their Bible and their Isidore had at their disposal a vocabulary well suited to describe a characteristic early medieval political formation, one built upon dependent peoples. Their subordination might be established through battle, maintained by taking tribute, hostages, and troops from sub-kings, or consolidated by direct annexation and the removal of local kings: all were normal early medieval forms of *imperium*. When Charlemagne dismounted to meet Leo III at Paderborn, his kingship was exactly analogous. Only Charlemagne's ceremonial installation as emperor in Rome the next year was novel. It supplemented the traditional, descriptive vocabulary of empire and emperorship with an appointed office that was redolent of Roman Antiquity, and it gave the pope a vital role in bestowing that title.

Centuries earlier, the warlords who established kingdoms within the provinces of the crumbling western Roman Empire had legitimized their position by eagerly appropriating symbols of Roman rule—portraits on coins, seals, dress, insignia of office, flattering epithets. As Theoderic had said to Anastasius: 'Our kingship is an imitation of yours, modelled on your good design, a copy of the only Empire. By as much as we follow you, so much we precede all other peoples.'[38] If direct imperial imitation was the sincerest form of flattery in Italy in *c*.500, the aggressively competitive kings of later generations and more distant places also did their best to cash in on the act. Wrenched from its original context, imperial symbolism was thus transmitted across the centuries as a repertoire of royal procedures and attributes.

Charlemagne's installation as emperor in 800 gave renewed impetus to this much older practice, for papal officials were experts in Byzantine imperial ceremonial. Increasing diplomatic contact between the Frankish and Byzantine courts also enabled direct observation and emulation, for the prestige of the *Romaioi*, the Romans, as the Byzantines understood themselves to be, elicited a mixture of grudging admiration and keen imitation throughout the early Middle Ages—and for long thereafter. Whether at the Carolingian or, later, the Ottonian imperial court, appropriation of aspects of Byzantine court culture and ceremonial took place in an atmosphere of mutual edginess, a rivalry sharpened by the competition for political and religious influence all the way from the Balkans to the Baltic.

Just as the cultural prestige of the Byzantine court was a reflex of its political influence, so we find the same at the courts of the western—Carolingian and Ottonian—emperors. Alongside Charlemagne's lavish entertainment of visitors at Aachen, Paderborn, and elsewhere can be placed the appropriation of Carolingian styles of government in other kingdoms. In the ninth century, Alfonso II of Asturias (791–842) and Alfred of Wessex both found useful precedent in Carolingian ideologies of royal authority; at the end of the tenth century, the influence of Ottonian hegemony on the newly Christian kingdoms of central Europe—Poland, Hungary, and Bohemia—was also marked.

Thus we should not think of 'empire' only with reference to the two specific early medieval polities, Byzantine and (after 800) western, whose rulers were formally vested with the title of emperor. Far more than that, 'empire' was a widely used term for a particular kind of successful kingdom. It implied domination and hegemony—military, political, cultural. Furthermore, imperial practices provided a repertoire of inherited ways of presenting and enacting royal power for showy display and enhanced legitimacy: almost everywhere, kings avidly drew upon this stock of motifs, adding an imperial lustre to less grandiose realities.

Although rulers commonly took contemporary empires as their point of reference, on occasion they turned to the past, above all to the Roman Empire. When Charlemagne placed the motto 'the renewal of the Roman Empire' on his seal in the spring of 801, he had already left Rome, never to return—and was certainly not outlining a practical political programme. Rather, he was investing his new-found title with the rhetorical mantle of historical authentication. Subsequent emperors generally followed his example and spent minimal time in Rome itself, except for Otto III. Having revived Charlemagne's slogan, in the slightly but significantly altered form of 'the renewal of the empire of the Romans', Otto attempted to take it literally rather than metaphorically. In 998, he rebuilt the old imperial palace in Rome and set about governing from there, the first emperor to do so since the early fourth century. But no amount of 'renewal' could save him from the rough-and-tumble of Rome's urban politics, and the city's traditional rulers soon put paid to his ambition, expelling him early in 1001.

Otto died before he could learn the lesson that, for a transalpine emperor, Rome was more useful as an idea than as a centre of government. As an idea, it drew on the antique past to confer a potent form of legitimacy; as a place of power, it was best left well alone, distant but powerfully evocative. Though the rhetoric of Romanness added a patina of ancient respectability to the new forms of hegemonic kingship that emerged in northern Europe from the end of the eighth century onwards, most early medieval ideologues knew very well how to distinguish 'Rome' from 'empire'. In their separate ways, both were powerful master ideas: but we can never know precisely what part Leo III's visit to Paderborn may have played in the decision to conflate them into a novel institutional form.

Rome, AD 1027

We come, finally, to Cnut's journey from Scandinavia to Rome. King of Denmark by inheritance, of England by conquest, and aspirant ruler of Norway, he strove to protect and extend his North Sea empire. This gave him occasion to assert overlordship or take military action everywhere from the Irish Sea to the southern eastern Baltic (Figure 8.4). In 1025, he had come to an agreement with the newly elected German king Conrad II about their joint strategic interests in Poland and the Baltic Slav peoples; Cnut then spent the summer of 1026 in southern Sweden confronting a joint Norwegian and Swedish attack. Thereafter, he 'measured the southward path with [his] feet',[39] all the way to Rome. 'Generous prince' that he certainly was, Cnut showered gifts on the churches he visited en route, and arrived in Rome in time for the celebration of Easter in 1027. Together with King Rudolf III of Burgundy (993–1032), the German and Italian nobility and around seventy archbishops, bishops, and abbots, Cnut was in the audience in St Peter's on Easter Sunday when Pope John XIX (1024–33) crowned Conrad and his wife Gisela. The festivities were more magnificent than any previous early medieval imperial coronation, perhaps because of the persistent challenges to Conrad's rule. To impress the rebellious German and Italian aristocracy, he needed all the external political support he could muster: in an imposing display of imperial dignity, his two royal neighbours Cnut and Rudolf escorted the new emperor as he processed out of the basilica to his lodgings and the banquet that doubtless awaited them there.

If Conrad was an emperor who needed to be seen with a retinue of kings, Cnut too had much to gain from his place of honour at Conrad's side. Heading back to Denmark, he wrote to his English subjects, announcing that he had just been to Rome.

I would have you know that there was a great gathering of nobles there at the Easter solemnity with our lord Pope John and the Emperor Conrad, to wit, all the princes of the peoples from Monte Gargano [southern Italy] to this nearest sea [the North Sea], who all gave me a respectful welcome and honoured me with

8.4. The World of Cnut.

magnificent gifts. In particular I was honoured by the emperor with sundry gifts and precious presents: vessels of gold and silver and very precious fabrics and robes.[40]

Imperial gifts and papal honour enhanced the regality of a king whose rule over the English was based on conquest: those who were not in Cnut's retinue in Rome should nevertheless be aware of the prestige that accrued to their king. 'Dear to the emperor', Cnut had indeed 'reaped a portion of Rome's glory'.

For many of those in Rome that Easter, Conrad's coronation was an opportunity to conduct business. Whether at local, national, or imperial level, early medieval governance was not a constant process but rather the subject of intense bursts of activity on specific occasions of limited duration: the Easter gathering of 1027 was one such. For the three weeks of Conrad's visit, Rome functioned as Europe's political centre. Indeed, the flurry of activity on this occasion was all the greater because of the exceptionally large number of secular and ecclesiastical notables in attendance. When tenth- and early eleventh-century rulers summoned their subjects to debate major decisions or issued formal written documents, it was most usually done in the context of important religious festivities, and Conrad's coronation gathering was no exception. In the first place, pope and emperor presided together in a large ecclesiastical assembly in the Lateran basilica in an attempt to resolve two disputes about status and precedence between proud Italian prelates. The archbishops of Milan and Ravenna had suddenly erupted into unseemly rows as to which of them should lead Conrad into St Peter's, while the acrimony between the archbishops of Aquileia and Grado had been rumbling on for centuries already. A formal record detailed the names of the council's many participants, their deliberations and decisions. Such procedural and documentary grandeur was itself a form of political action, an expression of consensus far more important than the subsequent—contested—outcome.

In addition, bishops and abbots from far and wide petitioned the pope and the emperor on behalf of their own churches, requesting confirmation of their landholdings, the renewal or extension of their legal rights and privileges. In the course of Conrad's stay in Rome, both he and John XIX issued many such charters. Large in format, florid in the conventions of their bureaucratic prose, and formal in appearance, both the imperial and papal documents ultimately derived from standard late Roman bureaucratic procedures, as has been indicated.[41] For pope and emperor alike, the act of issuing such a charter was a mark of political goodwill and a means of ordering networks of alliance; for the recipients, the value of these documents as trophies of momentary closeness to the centres of power usually outstripped their ability to turn papal or imperial gracious-ness into any meaningful political advantage. Very often, it took the prox-imity of pope or emperor to enforce the contents of such privileges. Such opportunities were rare: while Conrad II's court was ceaselessly peri-patetic, John XIX's entourage restricted its movements to Rome and its immediate hinterland, and few of those who left Rome clutching grants and confirmations can have had any idea whether they would ever see the issuer again.

Cnut was amongst those who pursued political ends amidst the festiv-ities—and the street brawling—that accompanied the imperial coron-ation. He negotiated with both Conrad and Rudolf to secure a reduction in the tolls paid by Anglo-Saxon and Danish merchants and pilgrims trav-elling across the Alps to Italy, and with John XIX about the huge sums extorted from Anglo-Saxon archbishops whenever one of them collected his *pallium* (the item of dress bestowed by the pope on each incoming archbishop as a symbol of office). 'All the requests which I made of my lord the pope and of the emperor and of King Rudolf and the other princes through whose territory we have to pass on the way to Rome, for the bene-fit of my own people, were readily granted, and the concessions confirmed on oath, on the testimony of four archbishops and twenty bishops and an immense multitude of dukes and nobles who were present', he proudly reported to the English.[42] Public formalities and many witnesses offered the only real hope that the deals that Cnut had struck would be honoured in the future.

As well as alerting us to the integration into Europe's politics of emerg-ing Scandinavian and Slav polities, Cnut's visit to Rome reminds us of the centrality of honour and gift giving to early medieval politics. It also of-fers an excellent example of dramatically staged Christian rulership in action. It concerns us here for an additional reason, however—its religious dimension. In writing to his English subjects, Cnut opened by announ-cing his spiritual concerns: 'I give you notice that I have lately gone to Rome to pray for the redemption of my sins and the salvation of my king-doms and of the peoples who are subject to my rule.' Made in fulfilment of a long-standing vow, his journey was a pilgrimage that took him not only to the churches of Rome's two apostolic patrons, Peter and Paul, but also to 'every sanctuary that I could learn of within the city of Rome or outside it'.[43] For Cnut, as for many others in the early Middle Ages, Rome's importance was above all religious.

The Christian city had two contrasting dimensions, that of popes and that of pilgrims, which we will consider in this order. Whatever the broader political context, each pope was, first and foremost, Rome's bishop, whose time and energies were split between two main challenges. One task was to direct the elaborate ceremonies of worship around which the city's ritual life turned and to oversee its many churches, numbering approximately 200. The other was to administer the bishopric's extensive lands, direct their revenues to the upkeep of the urban fabric and the sustenance of the inhabitants and, in so doing, cope with the tendency of ecclesiastical lands to fall under the control of local bigwigs. Additional responsibilities accumulated when direct rule of the region around Rome passed to the pope in the 780s. Not only were there the intricacies of aristocratic politics to negotiate, as Leo III had found to his cost, but since, from the late eighth century, popes anyway came from local aristocratic families, there were also their relatives' affairs to foster. Defence of the papal lands formed another priority. From the early ninth until the early eleventh centuries, the main threat came in the form of Saracen plundering and slaving raids launched from Muslim north Africa and Sicily: the sack of St Peter's basilica in 846 jolted popes into action up and down the Italian coast. From the late tenth century onwards, resurgent Byzantine rule in southern Italy posed somewhat different problems. In this context, building urban defences, mustering troops, equipping ships, and negotiating military alliances all became urgent papal activities.

Faced with these local and regional priorities, it was of no direct relevance to tenth- and early eleventh-century popes that in the distant past, between c.400 and c.700, their predecessors had also been preoccupied with claiming pre-eminent status within an empire no longer directly governed from Rome, or that they had taken a leading part in the heated late antique debates about the correct definition of Christian doctrine. Certainly, no one doubted that the pope ranked first among the clergy, but in the early Middle Ages this high dignity neither conferred general authority nor commanded obedience. If early medieval bishops, abbots, lay persons, and kings chose to seek papal advice or support on specific matters, popes responded. But it was not their role to intervene in the wider world unless asked, far less to initiate. Nor, indeed, had they any means of enforcing their decisions, except perhaps in the vicinity of Rome: when a papal privilege for one church upset another's interests, or advice on a point of Christian conduct conflicted with established local norms, papal pronouncements frequently remained a dead letter.

In all this, John XIX was entirely typical. Son of the count of Tusculum near Rome, he abandoned a secular career as senator to succeed his brother as pope in 1024, and turned his considerable political skills to papal ends. Like other early medieval popes, he had no contact with large parts of western Christendom, for it was only in Anglo-Saxon England, the lands that had once comprised the Carolingian Empire, and those now ruled by the German emperor where there was any tradition of even occasional liaison with Rome. Most of the churchmen who obtained an audience with him simply sought confirmation of existing ecclesiastical lands and privileges; the most favoured returned home with their rights forcefully restated and their ceremonial splendour enhanced. A few others brought with them charters issued locally, in the hope that a papal countersignature would strengthen their legitimacy. Figure 8.4 indicates the extent of these contacts. Only in and around the city of Rome did the pope have anything more than fine words to give, when the senior clergy of his own entourage were the beneficiaries. Conrad II's coronation was the only occasion known to have brought any of Europe's rulers into direct personal contact with John XIX; the remainder of the time his channels of contact beyond the duchy of Rome were much the same as those of his predecessors. In addition to ecclesiastical delegations, his visitors from north of the Alps included a few powerful laymen who had broken ecclesiastical norms of conduct regarding marriage or the use of violence. Some had been excommunicated by their local bishop but came to Rome in search of papal absolution; others sought a penitential sentence directly from the pope rather than risking justice at the hands of local courts and clergy. But, for the most part, John XIX conducted the church services required of him, reorganized the bureaucratic hierarchy of the churches around Rome, and, in conjunction with his family, administered the papal lands to his and their mutual benefit.

Of the early medieval visitors to Rome, only a proportion sought out the pope. Most came not as petitioners to the pontiff but as pilgrims, to pray in its many shrines. We have met a few of them in other contexts, including Gerald of Aurillac, Fintan of Rheinau, and Cyngen, king of Powys. One of many centres of pilgrimage in the early Middle Ages, the city was sometimes in active competition with other shrines, such as St Martin's at Tours, but the great number of martyr saints venerated in churches in and around Rome exerted a cumulative attraction greater than anywhere else. From the time of Damasus I (366–84) onwards, popes had encouraged worship at the scores of early Christian graves in the extramural cemeteries and associated churches. Its martyrs were the city's spiritual adornment, its link with the early Christian era and an earthly anticipation of a heaven populated with saints. At their head were the apostles Peter and Paul: 'O lucky Rome, stained purple with the precious blood of such great princes, you excel all the beauty of the world, not in your praise but in the merits of your saints, whom you slew with bloody swords.'[44]

By the sixth century, Rome was no longer just the centre of local or regional pilgrimage (Figure 8.5). Worshippers were travelling increasing distances, and, by the first half of the seventh century, the Roman clergy were organized for their reception, providing accommodation and guidebooks. Arriving in Rome in 631, Irish monks found themselves 'in one lodging in the church of St Peter with a Greek, a Hebrew, a Scythian and an Egyptian';[45] by the end of the eighth century, Anglo-Saxons, Franks, Frisians, Greeks, and Lombards each had their own permanent establishment catering to their needs. From their hostels, pilgrims set out to tour the holy sites, equipped with precise itineraries. 'You go east until you reach the holy martyr Emerentiana, who is buried in the upper church, with two martyrs in the catacomb below, Victor and Alexander. Then follow the street *via Numentana* to the church of St Agnes, which is beautiful, in which she rests alone. Pope Honorius restored this with wonderful craftsmanship.'[46] This is typical of the careful detail with which a guidebook from the pontificate of Honorius I (625–38) steered pilgrims round the city. To visit all the catacombs and churches would have required a protracted stay, which not all chose to make, and concentrations of pilgrim graffiti suggest that some sites were indeed more popular than others. In the seventh and eighth centuries, women such as the Anglo-Saxon Fagihild and the Greek Anastasia joined men such as the Lombard Anwald, the Frank Lotharius, and many others in scratching their names onto the walls of the catacomb of Marcellinus and Peter on the *via Labicana*, an enduring testimony to the popularity of this particular site.

'. . . and thus you enter the street *via Vaticana* until you come to the basilica of St Peter, which Constantine, emperor of the whole world, built and which stands out above all other churches. At the western end of this beautiful church his holy body lies.' Any visit to Rome culminated at the tomb of St Peter, where the visitor would 'pour our tears of penitence'.[47] 'Friend of Peter', as Sighvatr described him, Cnut was blunt about the advantages of praying here: 'I have learnt from wise men of the great power which the holy Apostle Peter had received from our Lord of binding and loosing, and that it is he who bears the keys of the kingdom of Heaven; and for this I thought it very profitable to seek his advocacy in particular with God.'[48] Cnut's words echo those of Christian scripture, which claimed that Christ had said to his follower Peter: 'I will give to thee the keys of the kingdom of heaven. And whatsoever thou shalt bind upon earth, it shall be bound also in heaven: and whatsoever thou shalt loose on earth, it shall be loosed also in heaven' (Matt. 16: 19). A Bavarian song of *c*.900 expressed in simple but strong terms the underlying beliefs that made St Peter's 'advocacy' so desirable:

8.5. The ecclesiastical topography of early medieval Rome. Of the approximately 200 churches in early medieval Rome, this map shows four of the five papal basilicas and those churches and shrines mentioned in Chapter 8. Based on R. Valentini and G. Zucchetti, *Codice topografico della città di Roma*, 2, Fonti per la Storia d'Italia, 88 (Rome, 1942).

> Our Lord has transmitted authority to St Peter,
> that he may save the man who places hope in him.
> Lord have mercy, Christ have mercy.
>
> He keeps guard by his words over the gates of heaven
> and can place therein him whom he would save.
> Lord have mercy, Christ have mercy.
>
> Let us beseech God's beloved, all together, in full voice,
> that he may deign to have mercy on us sinners.
> Lord have mercy, Christ have mercy.[49]

In short, within the Christian cosmology of a world permeated by sin, St Peter's was the help most likely to aid the sinner achieve salvation. For this reason more than any other, men and women made the arduous journey to Rome, risking Alpine brigands; Saracen pirates; profiteers and prostitutes out to turn a quick penny from gullible foreigners.

City of St Peter, Rome was intensely familiar even to those who never visited it. To worship 'in the Roman manner' was to adopt the most authentic possible form of liturgy.[50] Narratives of the sufferings of Rome's martyrs and of the lives of the early popes circulated widely in the early Middle Ages: to read them was to enter the city in the mind's eye. One monk whose experience was entirely in the mind was an unnamed Irishman in the monastery of Kilbarry. He had vowed to go on pilgrimage to Rome, but had failed to obtain his superior's permission. The concerned abbot called the monk into his cell, so that they could pray and fast together for three days and nights. But, while his master prayed, the disciple fell asleep. When he awoke, he recounted what he had seen as he slept:

'I saw myself undertaking the pilgrim's journey, on which a very beautiful young man accompanied me. Having crossed the ocean, I reached Rome, with the same companion leading me along the right way. With the young man, I completed in due order the pilgrimage that I had vowed to undertake, in accordance with my intention. The same young man led me back here by the same road. Departing from me with great cheerfulness, he declared that he was the angel of God and he also stated that I had completely fulfilled the pilgrimage that I had vowed to undertake.'[51]

At Europe's outer margins, Rome was impossibly distant for all save the wealthiest few. But, as a place of holiness where the pious Christian dead lay buried in their multitudes, it could nevertheless be replicated and rendered accessible. The Irish did this by using the word 'Rome' to refer to a monastic cemetery. On Devenish island on Loch Erne, Molaisse (d. 564/71) had established 'a common cemetery [*ruaim*] for the Gaels':

here was 'God the Father's own domain'.[52] The same was done in west-ernmost Britain. Bardsey Island lies off the north-west coast of Wales, and is difficult of access. A twelfth-century Welsh writer explained why this was 'the Rome of Britain':

In ancient British custom, it is proverbially called 'the Rome of Britain' on account of the length and difficulty of the sea crossing, for it is situated on the very edge of the country, and also on account of the holiness and attractiveness of the place; holiness because the bodies of twenty thousand saints—confessors and martyrs—lie buried there; attractiveness because it is surrounded on all sides by the sea, with a high cliff on the eastern side and flat, fertile land with a spring of sweetly flowing water on the western side. The coast abounds with dolphins and the island is completely lacking in snakes and frogs.[53]

This Rome was paradise on an Atlantic island. Other recreations emphasized different aspects of the earthly city, most notably its buildings, church dedications, or topography. Remaining in the British Isles for a little longer, we shall switch attention to the Anglo-Saxon communities along the eastern seaboard, where papal missionaries were active for most of the seventh century. Canterbury, itself a former Roman city of regional importance, was the centre from which the earliest missionaries worked. Here, Augustine and his fellow Roman monks made for themselves a home from home. As Figure 8.6 indicates, they did so by dedicating the churches they founded to the principal patrons of Rome's own churches, old and new, and by copying their topographical relationship to the walled urban area. Rome's cathedral, the Lateran, lay within the city walls and was dedicated to Christ the Saviour, and its adjacent baptistery church was dedicated to St John: thus Augustine built his cathedral, Christ Church, within Canterbury's Roman defences, next to which his successor Cuthbert (740–60) added the church of St John the Baptist. At Rome, the papal basilicas of St Peter and St Paul both lay outside the city walls: at Canterbury, Augustine founded an extramural burial church, dedicated to Sts Peter and Paul together. And, since the popes who sent the missions to Canterbury, Gregory I and Honorius I, were especial patrons of Rome's extramural church of St Pancras and the city-centre church of the Four Crowned Martyrs, so too seventh-century Canterbury soon acquired an external church to St Pancras and an intramural one honouring the Four Crowned Martyrs. In all these churches, Augustine and his immediate successors placed relics of Rome's martyrs and followed the distinctively Roman way of singing the liturgy: the ruins of Roman-era Canterbury had been transformed into a replica of Christian Rome.

The presence of a ruined Roman city was nevertheless not essential for

1 Cathedral of St Saviour (Christ Church)
2 St John the Baptist
3 ? Four Crowned Martyrs
4 St Peter and St Paul
5 St Pancras
6 St Martin

River Stour

Roman City Walls

✠ Cathedral ✝ Church

⌐ ⌐ Main ecclesiastical precincts

0 100 200
metres

8.6. The ecclesiastical topography of seventh-century Canterbury. Based on N. P. Brooks, 'Canterbury, Rome and the Construction of English Identity', in Julia M. H. Smith (ed.), *Early Medieval Rome and the Christian West: Essays in Honour of Donald Bullough* (Leiden, 2000), with permission of Brill Academic Publishers and the author.

this sort of imitation of Rome. Much further north, where in former times the Roman Empire had shaded off into a militarized frontier zone, a Northumbrian monk founded twin monasteries near the mouth of the river Tyne, at Wearmouth in 674 and Jarrow in 681. Benedict Biscop had already travelled repeatedly to Rome and was determined to replicate the visual splendour and modes of worship he had observed there. To achieve this, he imported stonemasons and glaziers to build his churches 'in the Roman style he had always loved so much' and stocked them with the books, liturgical vestments, and pictures he had brought back with him.[54] He fetched a Roman singing master to teach his Northumbrian novices to sing Roman chant and dedicated his churches to Rome's two most important patrons, Wearmouth to St Peter and Jarrow to St Paul.

From this Northumbrian Rome, another followed. In *c.*713/14 Nechtan, king of the Picts, wrote to the abbot of Wearmouth–Jarrow requesting details of Roman liturgical procedure and builders 'to build a church of stone for his people after the Roman fashion, promising that it should be dedicated in honour of the blessed chief of the apostles'. A passing twelfth-century reference to a place called *Egglespethir* (Peter's church) near Restenneth is all that remains of this Scottish Rome. 'Remote though they were from the Roman people and their language', Nechtan promised that the Picts would replicate the practices of the Roman church. [55] In the far north, where no Roman missionary ever ventured and where local building techniques relied on wattle and timber, a stone church dedicated to St Peter in which Roman ecclesiastical customs prevailed would indeed have been a powerful evocation of Rome itself.

Such local renditions of Rome were not confined to the British archipelago. But they were characteristic of regions where Christian communities lacked their own direct link to the Roman era, whether that association was expressed through the veneration of their own local martyrs in ancient churches or an unbroken sequence of bishops stretching back to the third or fourth century. The replication of Rome through name transference, building forms, liturgy, dedications, and imported martyrial relics signalled a strong desire for attachment to authoritative narratives of Christian origins and apostolic authenticity in the absence of locally available proofs.

The main other region where Christian communities found imaginative ways to import Rome to their own locality was Germany. In the ninth century, abbots and bishops sometimes went to great lengths to acquire corporeal relics of Roman martyrs as one expression of this. Some also directly copied the most distinctive feature of Rome's ecclesiastical architecture: the ground plan of St Peter's, with its unusual western orientation and circular crypt around the apostle's tomb. To build such a crypt was to build in a deliberately Roman style. By the tenth century, German bishops were finding even more elaborate ways of transporting Rome to their own locality. A good example of this is Konstanz, a city on the banks of the upper Rhine, illustrated in Figure 8.7. Here, Bishop Conrad (934–75) rebuilt his see, in much the same way as Augustine had established Canterbury, reflecting the spiritual topography of Rome but also revealing his close links with Otto I. Next to the cathedral of St Mary a new church in honour of St John the Evangelist and St John the Baptist evoked the Lateran, whose dedication to Christ the Saviour had been superseded by the cult of both Johns by the late eighth century. Beyond the built-up area, foundations to St Lawrence and St Paul recalled Rome's extramural papal basilicas dedicated to these saints. Together with St Maurice, St

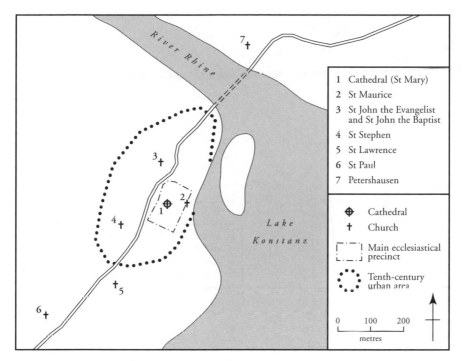

8.7. The ecclesiastical topography of late-tenth-century Konstanz. Based on H. Maurer, *Konstanz als ottonischer Bischofssitz,* Veröffentlichungen des Max-Planck-Instituts für Geschichte, 39 (Göttingen, 1973), with permission of the Max-Planck-Institut für Geschichte.

Lawrence had brought victory over the Magyars to Otto I in 955, so a rotunda in honour of Otto's especial patron, St Maurice, completed Conrad's building activities. His successor but one, Gebhard (979–95), went even further. Since St Peter's lay on the opposite bank of the Tiber from the city of Rome, Gebhard went to great effort to acquire a site on the opposite bank of the Rhine from his cathedral city. Here he founded a monastery 'constructed in accordance with the layout of the church of the prince of the apostles at Rome'—with a western orientation and a relic crypt—'and for this reason he called the place Petershausen [Peterhouse]'. Gebhard affirmed the Roman connection by enshrining part of the head of Pope Gregory I in it.[56]

We end back in Paderborn, where a fire had razed the town in 1000. Bishop Meinwerk (1009–36) set about rebuilding it on a far grander scale then ever before and in a way that reflected his own earlier career as one

8.8. The ecclesiastical topography of early eleventh-century Paderborn. This map shows the city as Meinwerk left it on his death in 1036; he did not live to complete his plan for two further churches, one to the north and one to the south of the town. Based on E. Herzog, *Die ottonische Stadt: Die Anfänge der mittelalterlichen Stadtbaukunst in Deutschland* (Berlin, 1964).

of Otto III's most trusted clerical courtiers. Figure 8.8 shows the town as he left it on his death. He planned to build five churches 'in the manner of a cross', with the rebuilt cathedral at its centre and four religious communities to mark the arms: thus through prayer 'the city might be marked by the crucifix and defended against all the darts of the Enemy'.[57] Of the new churches, the eastern one was a replica of the Church of the Holy Sepulchre in Jerusalem: dedicated to the Virgin Mary and Sts Peter and Andrew and housing relics fetched back from the Holy Land, it encapsulated Christ's life story and offered an earthly reflection of the heavenly Jerusalem. Opposite it, to the west, was a miniature of early Christian Rome, a Benedictine monastery dedicated to Sts Peter and Paul, with a western apse and a circular relic crypt. In it, Meinwerk placed an altar that

Leo III had dedicated on his visit in 799. With its strong papal associations, he used this as the episcopal funerary church where he reinterred his predecessors' remains, and where in due course he was himself buried. To the north and south of Paderborn were to be a further two churches. In laying out his cathedral city, Meinwerk also made precise reference to contemporary Rome, that of Otto III, by dedicating two other new chapels to saints whose cults Otto had himself launched in Rome, St Alexius and St Bartholomew. Meinwerk's death before he could complete his ambitious Christian theme park in no way detracts from the point that Rome, and indeed Jerusalem, could be relocated at will. Through architectural analogy, saints' relics, and episcopal liturgy, the holiest places in Christendom could be rebuilt and the events associated with them reenacted elsewhere. In the early Middle Ages, Rome was the ideal type of a Christian holy place.

Rome was the city that, so legend held, the heirs of the Trojan hero Aeneas had founded and that had gone on to conquer an empire spanning most of the known world. It was the city that had made martyrs of its earliest Christian inhabitants and then become the capital of a Christian empire. The history, myth, and legend of its long past, bloody and glorious, weighed heavily on the men and women of the early Middle Ages. First the foundation of a new imperial capital at Constantinople, then the formation of new kingdoms and ethnic identities in and around the western provinces, had rendered obsolete Rome's role as the capital of that ancient empire—but yet its central significance lived on.

From his Scandinavian perspective, Sighvatr unerringly identified the 'glory' that Cnut reaped in Rome. It came from being 'dear to the emperor, friend of Peter'. However much the political map of Europe had been transformed between c.500 and c.1000, Rome could not shake off its association with empire. Rather, its imperial dimension was reconfigured, formed anew to suit the needs of the powerful warrior kings of early medieval northern Europe. Glory, legitimacy, a secure past, and a cultural heritage—Rome provided aspiring emperors and their subjects with all these and more in abundance. Above all, the very notion of empire offered a way of organizing political life that might stand some chance of overcoming the local roots of all early medieval political power.

And, if empire was the city's enduring political attribute, Peter remained at the heart of its religious identity. From his tomb on the Vatican hill on the opposite bank of the Tiber, the prince of the apostles influenced the beliefs and devotions of early medieval Christians in their local churches and in their long journeys in search of Christian salvation. Manifested in liturgy and ritual, place names and architecture, affection for St Peter transcended the localisms and particularities that so characterized early medieval society.

Those identities and attachments found resonances far and wide. Not only in their travels but also in their stories and libraries, buildings and ceremonies, early medieval men and women transposed Rome, gave its history new meanings, imagined it in new ways, constructed it afresh. Whether encountered in books and documents or in bricks and mortar, it formed a storehouse of every conceivable kind of cultural resource, a repository of ideas and artefacts to be transvalued and transported wherever and however people wished. By stocking the imagination, the city—unique and particular as it was—was suggestive of a shared culture. In Rome, the peoples of Europe found a common fascination.

Epilogue

In 1049 another pope named Leo crossed the Alps. With Leo IX's journey to Reims, a different story begins. It tells of the formation of a papal monarchy, exercising authority throughout Latin Christendom by means of a centralized judicial and administrative machinery of government. This story reaches its apogee in the thirteenth century, when the city of Rome functioned as the jurisdictional headquarters of an international ecclesiastical institution, regulating theological doctrines, social norms, political procedures, and rituals of worship throughout the Latin west. It interprets conflict between popes and rulers as the opportunity to shed supposedly archaic notions of monarchy, as the first step towards specifically western—and thus more modern—modes of power. Additional strands in the narrative emphasize a striving towards a particular vision of conformity—expansion at the expense of Islam and Byzantium, elimination of Europe's last pagans, intolerance of internal dissent, and persecution of Jews. Its traditional corollaries are the celebration of cosmopolitan high culture and professional national governments, developments made possible by rapid urbanization and the formation of a self-sustaining, international mandarin class. In an echo of the vigorous rhetoric of novelty and new beginnings employed by eleventh- and twelfth-century writers, this version of the history of Europe is often presented in triumphalist terms, as a phase of enduring significance whose religious, institutional, and cultural parameters long outlived the Middle Ages. It identifies the period from approximately the turn of the first millennium as the decisive era of fresh starts in virtually every field of human endeavour—agricultural, economic, religious, institutional, military, literary, artistic. In this paradigm, the location of power shifted, forever, in the course of the long twelfth century.

Change the perspective, however, and this becomes a story of loss—of diversity, local identities, customary habits, plural solutions to common problems. Turned around, the traditional narrative recounts the erosion of the varied complexities of early medieval Europe's cultures. Its inversion tracks the ways in which presumptions of local knowledge faded as aspirations towards uniformity grew. It suggests that local values and regional issues lost out to lay and ecclesiastical hierarchs whose centralizing ambitions became the main agents of change. It marks the waning of diversity and the waxing of deviance.

This reorientation is not simply an intellectual exercise. The thematic tension in European historiography between diversity and uniformity derives its creative vigour from the strong, if oblique, relationship that has always existed between the content of historical writing and its immediate political context. Certainly, the familiar story of the high Middle Ages served the nation states of nineteenth- and twentieth-century Europe well, for they found in the medieval past resonances of more modern preoccupations. But, at the start of the third millennium, when the very notion of the nation state is being eroded from all directions, that well-worn narrative can no longer be sustained. A Europe in which regional identities of early medieval origin are being rediscovered—Mercia, Burgundy, Fife, Lombardy, Carinthia, and many others—needs a different story. So too does a Europe urgently striving for new forms of pluralism and coexistence in cultural, religious, social, and economic affairs.

This book has sought to offer that with respect to the centuries from 500 to 1000. It has balanced exploration of the ways in which common themes were manifested in diversity of experience with arguments for the cultural dynamism of these centuries. In 500, the many differences that distinguished one region of Europe from another all mapped onto a single spectrum. At one end, around the western Mediterranean, lay profoundly Roman but nevertheless post-imperial polities—Christian, relatively urbanized and populous, wealthy, literate, internally divided by steep gradients of status, wealth, and gender. Beyond them, around or straddling the former frontiers, new polities of rather weaker Roman character, which marched with those beyond the border, where Roman influence was always indirect. At its furthest reach, far away from the Mediterranean in an arc from the northern Atlantic to the Baltic and on to the Black Sea, were thinly populated polities characterized by shallow social hierarchies, some of whom made occasional use of inscriptional literacy (in runic or ogam) but which otherwise exercised power in non-literate, non-bureaucratic, non-urban modes. Their contacts with the Roman world were spasmodic, but so prestigious that power congealed around those very few with access to Roman contacts, Roman goods, Roman religion.

By 1000, that simple spectrum had dissolved. While varying population densities doubtless still existed, plague and de-urbanization around the Mediterranean had reduced the differential with more northern areas; in any case, the population was rising rapidly everywhere long before the millennium. Across the western Mediterranean there had come to be a shifting zone where Christianity shaded off into the dominance of Islam. To its north, the cultural hegemony of the Roman way of life had yielded to a matrix shaped by Christianity, a religion into which many separate Roman cultural elements had been gradually subsumed. Its dominance demanded vast landed resources, treasures, ideological reinforcements. It called for a reordering of daily life, sexual relationships, and family bonds. Its language, technologies of power, cosmology, and far-flung web of contacts together sharpened distinctions of status and gender and fostered new, steeply graduated, hierarchies of power, at whose apex were rulers whose wealth, power, and prestige lacked precedent in those localities. It prompted the emergence of new imperial polities whose centres lay in that northern arc; while to its south, around the western Mediterranean, the large kingdoms of post-imperial times had mostly disintegrated into numerous tiny polities. Lacking any injection of new ideologies or techniques of ruling, the latter competed bitterly among themselves for access to limited resources and prestige, for only some of them were in a position to profit from trading with Byzantium and the Islamic world, and even fewer had any scope for territorial aggrandizement at the expense of a non-Christian neighbour.

In short, from a world of Roman culture within which Christianity was one element in 500, by 1000 Europe had become a Christian world of which Roman cultural attributes formed one aspect. From a world of large polities in the south and small, simpler ones to the north and west, Europe had turned into a world of territorially extensive northern but modest southern ones.

In arguing this, I have adopted a perspective that has neither the city of Rome as its focal point nor the imperial frontiers as its frame. To do that would have simply reinstated the greatest Roman conceit of all, that of the dissemination from Rome of the benefits of a 'superior' civilization. In chronological terms, my emphasis on Europe after the collapse of imperial rule in the West has also been a concentration on Europe before the emergence of Rome as the seat of a European papal monarchy. Nor—except in my title—have I allowed the word 'Rome' to stand for anything other than the city of that name, in contrast to its frequent shorthand usage to designate the Roman Empire, bundled with its cultural attributes. This mode of presentation makes visible many different reinterpretations and imaginative appropriations of the Roman legacy—multiple strands and shifting patterns of coloured threads interwoven through a rich tapestry of cultural diversity.

This tapestry does not have neatly hemmed edges: in both geographical and chronological terms they are ragged, and deliberately so. I have defined the early Middle Ages by a cluster of phenomena whose common characteristics are, on the one hand, regional diversity and localism and, on the other, the omnipresence of aspects of the Roman cultural, religious, and political inheritance. In so doing, I have also demonstrated that, in the dynamic cultures of early medieval Europe, the location, pace, and direction of flux were far from uniform. And I have emphasized not generalized change, but multiple changes—abrupt or gradual, deliberate or contingent—in order to bring into focus both the social constraints that framed men's and women's lives and the many active choices each person made about his or her own affairs.

Viewed in this way, the early Middle Ages cannot be said to have begun, or ended, at particular dates on a time line, or to have been confined to this or that place or region. This approach avoids any necessity to privilege political, or economic, or religious, or any other theme as the determinant of periodization. By the same token, it blurs any attempt sharply to differentiate one historical period from another. Arguments that suggest that the eleventh century was the decisive period that ushered in a 'take-off' or 'first European revolution' in many—or all—aspects of European life misrepresent the dynamism of preceding centuries and cannot be allowed to stand. As I have presented them here, the early Middle Ages can in no way be seen as static, primitive, or underdeveloped, as simply the launch pad for take-off. Of the various novelties claimed for the eleventh and twelfth centuries, only a shift in the modalities of change remains, a shift in which centralizing institutions, lay and ecclesiastical, emerged as new, vigorous agents of change.

Instead, I have posited an early medieval 'syndrome' whose symptoms appeared early in some places, acquired a particular intensity in others, lingered longer elsewhere. The list is long, and could easily be lengthened: generally low population levels despite spasmodic growth; distinct but overlapping local economies combining low-output peasant agriculture and variable levels of urban activity with lavish conspicuous consumption by the elite; strongly gendered hierarchies of domination that commonly conflated the familial and official; the heavy presence of the past as a source of authenticity, legitimization, and meaning; polities incapable of harnessing sufficient economic, political, and cultural resources to overcome their innate tendency to collapse under the weight of their own success; the role of Christianity as a transmitter of many other aspects of Roman culture besides its normative creed. All of these are subsidiary, however, to its critical diagnostic: a cluster of dominant ideologies in which Rome held a central, inspirational place but no ascendant political role as it once had in Antiquity and would again, differently conceived, under papal guidance. To that extent, Europe *after* Rome is also Europe *before* Rome—after the crumbling of the political hegemony of the western Roman Empire but before the ecclesiastical hegemony of the international Roman Church. As I have presented the half millennium from 500 to 1000, we are freed from the historiographical tyranny of institutional frameworks and their teleologies, freed to focus on the ways in which men and women, peasants and lords, rulers and clergy experienced their world, endowed it with meaning and shaped it by their actions—freed to fashion a new cultural history for a new Europe.

Notes

CHAPTER I. SPEAKING AND WRITING

1. Gregory the Great, *Moralia in Iob*, XI.xlv.61 and XXXIII.iii.7, ed. M. Adriaen, 3 vols. with continuous pagination, CCSL 143, 143A, 143B (Turnhout, 1979–85), 620; also at 1675.
2. *The Blickling Homilies*, 10 (Rogation Wednesday), ed. and trans. Richard J. Kelly (London, 2003), 78–9.
3. Above, n. 1.
4. M. Coens, 'Un miracle posthume de S. Martin', *Analecta Bollandiana*, 50 (1932), 284–94, quotations at 291, 293, 294. For the religious context, see p. 73.
5. 'Genesis A', lines 1684–90, ed. A. N. Doane, *Genesis A: A New Edition* (Madison, WI, 1978), 161; cf. Gen. 11: 7.
6. Isidore, *Etymologiae*, IX.i.1, cf. IX.i.14, ed. W. M. Lindsay, 2 vols. (Oxford, 1911), i. 343, 345.
7. *Armes Prydein*, lines 172–4, ed. Ifor Williams and trans. Rachel Bromwich (Dublin, 1982), 12–13.
8. *The Text of the Book of Llan Dâv*, ed. J. G. Evans and J. Rhys (Oxford, 1893), 181.
9. Adomnan of Iona, *Life of St Columba*, II.32, trans. Richard Sharpe (Harmondsworth, 1995), 179 (*Adomnan's Life of Columba*, ed. A. O. Anderson and M. O. Anderson (Edinburgh, 1961), 396).
10. Paul the Deacon, *History of the Lombards*, I.27, trans. William Dudley Foulke (Philadelphia, 1974), 52 (*Historia Langobardorum*, ed. G. Waitz, MGH SRL (Hanover, 1878), 70).
11. *The First Grammatical Treatise*, ed. and trans. Hreinn Benediktsson (Reykjavik, 1972), 208–9.
12. *La Vie de Jean, abbé de Gorze*, 119, ed. Michel Parisse (Paris, 1999), 146.
13. Claudius of Turin, *Chronicle*, cited by Michael Idomir Allen, 'The Chronicle of Claudius of Turin', in Alexander Callander Murray (ed.), *After Rome's Fall: Narrators and Sources of Early Medieval History* (Toronto, 1998), 288–319 at 305. I have slightly adapted Allen's translation.
14. MGH Poetae V, pt. 2, p. 337, lines 11–12.
15. Bruno of Querfurt, *Vita quinque fratrum*, 9, 10, 13, MGH SS XV, pt. 2, pp. 725, 727, 729.
16. Ratramnus of Corbie, Letter to Rimbert, MGH Epp. VI, pp. 155–7.
17. Prudentius, *Contra Symmachum*, II.816–17, ed. Maurice P. Cunningham, *Aurelii Prudentii Carmina*, CCSL 126 (Turnhout, 1966), 239.

18. Salvian, *De gubernatione Dei*, V.ii.8, ed. G. Larrigue, *Salvien de Marseille: Œuvres*, 2 vols., SC 176, 220 (Paris, 1971–5), ii. 316. Cf. the English translation by Eva M. Sanford, *On the Government of God* (New York, 1930).

19. Priscus of Panium, fragment 11, ed. R. C. Blockley, *The Fragmentary Classicising Historians of the Later Roman Empire*, ii (Liverpool, 1983), 266, slightly adapted from translation in Alexander Callander Murray, *From Roman to Merovingian Gaul: A Reader* (Peterborough, ONT, 2000), 145.

20. See pp. 95, 127–30.

21. See pp. 225–6.

22. *Etymologiae*, IX.i.3, ed. Lindsay, i. 343.

23. Council of Clovesho of 747, clause 10. *Councils and Ecclesiastical Documents Relating to Great Britain and Ireland*, ed. A. W. Haddan and W. Stubbs, 3 vols. (Oxford, 1869–71), iii. 366.

24. Bede, Letter to Egbert, *EHD*, 799–810, at 801 (*Councils and Ecclesiastical Documents*, ed. Haddan and Stubbs, iii. 314–25).

25. Ælfric, *Praefatio Genesis anglice*, ed. Jonathan Wilcox, *Ælfric's Prefaces* (Durham, 1994), 116.

26. On Fénius Farsaid see also p. 262.

27. *Life of Constantine*, 16, trans. Marvin Kantor, *Medieval Slavic Lives of Saints and Princes* (Ann Arbor, 1983), 71.

28. *Conversio Bagoariorum et Carantanorum*, 12, ed. Fritz Lošek, *Die Conversio Bagoariorum et Carantanorum und der Brief des Erzbischofs Theotmar von Salzburg*, MGH Studien und Texte, 15 (Hanover, 1997), 130.

29. Liudger, *Vita Gregorii abbatis Traiacensis*, 2, ed. O. Holder-Egger, MGH SS XV, pt. 1, pp. 67–8.

30. Caesarius of Arles, *Sermones*, 6, ed. G. Morin, 2 vols., CCSL 103–4 (Turnhout, 1953), i. 31. Cf. the translation by Mary Madeleine Mueller, *Saint Caesarius of Arles: Sermons*, 3 vols. Fathers of the Church, 31, 47, 66 (Washington, 1956–73).

31. *Vita Fructuosi*, 2, *AASS Apr.* II, col. 431. Cf. the translation by A. T. Fear, *Lives of the Visigothic Fathers* (Liverpool, 1997).

32. See pp. 135–46.

33. 'Berrad Airechta: An Old Irish Tract on Suretyship', trans. Robin Stacey, in T. M. Charles-Edwards, M. E. Owen, and D. Walters (eds.), *Lawyers and Laymen: Studies in the History of Law Presented to Professor Dafydd Jenkins* (Cardiff, 1986), 210–33, at 221.

34. Narbonne judgement of 955, cited by Patrick Geary, 'Oblivion between Orality and Textuality in the Tenth Century', in Gerd Althoff, Johannes Fried, and Patrick J. Geary (eds.), *Medieval Concepts of the Past: Ritual, Memory, Historiography* (Cambridge, 2002), 111–22, at 120.

35. The point is developed on pp. 239–47.

36. See p. 13.

37. *La Règle de S. Benoît*, ed. Jean Neufville and trans. Adalbert de Vogüé, SC 181–186a (Paris, 1971–7), i. 412. Many English translations are available.

38. Hrabanus Maurus, *De institutione clericorum*, III.2, ed. Detlev Zimpel (Frankfurt am Main, 1996), 438.

39. Hrabanus Maurus, 'To Eigilus on the book he had written', in Helen Waddell (ed. and trans.), *Medieval Latin Lyrics* (Harmondsworth, 1952), 119 (*Carmina* 21, MGH Poetae II, p. 186).

CHAPTER 2. LIVING AND DYING

1. Lament attributed to Egil Skalla-Grimsson (d. *c.*990), from *Egil's Saga*, trans. Hermann Pálsson and Paul Edwards (Harmondsworth, 1976), 205 (*Egils Saga Skalla-Grímssonar*, ed. S. Nordal, Íslenzk Fornrit, 2 (Reykjavik, 1933), 247).

2. *The Annals of Fulda*, trans. Timothy Reuter (Manchester, 1992), 31 (*Annales Fuldenses*, a. 850, ed. F. Kurze, MGH SRG (Hanover, 1891), 40).

3. *Vita altera Bonifatii*, 9, ed. W. Levison, *Vitae Sancti Bonifatii archiepiscopi Moguntini*, MGH SRG (Hanover, 1905), 68.

4. *Annals of Ulster (to AD 1131)*, ed. S. Mac Airt and G. Mac Niocaill (Dublin, 1983), 203; *The Annals of Saint-Bertin*, trans. Janet L. Nelson (Manchester, 1991), 185 (*Annales de Saint-Bertin*, ed. F. Grat, J. Vielliard, and S. Clémencet (Paris, 1964), 195).

5. *Annals of Saint-Bertin*, trans. Nelson, 42 (*Annales de Saint-Bertin*, ed. Grat, Vielliard, and Clémencet, 28).

6. Widukind, *Res gestae Saxonicae*, I.20, ed. P. Hirsch and H.-E. Lohmann, MGH SRG 60 (Hanover, 1935), 29–30.

7. Cf. pp. 22, 31–2 on alternative explanations, and pp. 262–7 on origin myths.

8. *Venantius Fortunatus: Personal and Political Poems*, trans. Judith George (Liverpool, 1995), 9–15 (*Carmina*, IV. 26 in *Opera poetica*, ed. F. Leo, MGH AA IV, pt. 1, pp. 95–9), quotation from lines 46, 56, and 64.

9. Sixth-century inscription from Narbonne, cited by Mark A. Handley, *Death, Society and Culture: Inscriptions and Epitaphs in Gaul and Spain, AD 300–750* (Oxford, 2003), 92.

10. See further pp. 186–8.

11. Gregory of Tours, *Libri historiarum decem*, IV.31, ed. B. Krusch and W. Levison, MGH SRM I, pt. 1 (Hanover, 1937–51), 165–6. Cf. the inaccurate translation by L. Thorpe as *The History of the Franks* (Harmondsworth, 1974).

12. Paul the Deacon, *History of the Lombards*, VI.5, trans. William Dudley Foulke (Philadelphia, 1974), 255 (*Historia Langobardorum*, ed. G. Waitz, MGH SRL (Hanover, 1878), 166).

13. Bede, *Life of St Cuthbert*, 33, in *Two Lives of Saint Cuthbert*, ed. and trans. Bertram Colgrave (Cambridge, 1940), 258–61.

14. *Annals of Fulda*, trans. Reuter, 118 (*Annales Fuldenses*, a. 889, ed. Kurze, 117).

15. *Annals of Ulster*, ed. Mac Airt and Mac Niocaill, 159.

16. *Anglo-Saxon Chronicle* for 1005, *EHD*, 240 (*Two of the Saxon Chronicles Parallel*, ed. C. Plummer, 2 vols. (Oxford, 1892–9), i. 136).

17. *Poenitentiale Baedae*, IV.12, ed. A. W. Haddan and W. Stubbs, *Councils and Ecclesiastical Documents Relating to Great Britain and Ireland*, 3 vols. (Oxford, 1869–71), iii. 330 (cf. the translation of another version of this same text under the less misleading title of 'Penitential of Ps-Bede', II.11, in *Medieval Handbooks of Penance*, trans. John T. McNeill and Helena M. Gamer (New York, 1938, repr. 1990), 225).

18. For a specific example see p. 172.

19. See pp. 192–4 on the Vikings.

20. See pp. 16–17.

21. *Annales Xantenses*, a. 873, ed. B. von Simson, MGH SRG (Hanover, 1909), 33. The 'ancient plague of the Egyptians' refers to the plague of locusts in Exod. 10: 14–15.

22. As quoted by Gregory of Tours, *Libri historiarum decem*, X.1, ed. Krusch and Levison, 479. The biblical citations are Ps. 95: 2 and Lam. 3: 41.

23. 'Edict when the "Great Army" came to England', *EHD*, 447–8 (F. Liebermann, (ed.), *Die Gesetze der Angelsachsen*, 3 vols. (Halle, 1898–1916), i. 262).

24. *Annales Xantenses*, a. 869, ed. von Simson, 26.

25. Gregory of Tours, *Libri historiarum decem*, VII.45, ed. Krusch and Levison, 365.

26. Bede, *Ecclesiastical History of the English People*, III.30, ed. and trans. Bertram Colgrave and R. A. B. Mynors (Oxford, 1969), 322–3.

27. Bruno of Querfurt, *Vita Adalberti*, 25, ed. G. H. Pertz, MGH SS IV, p. 608.

28. *Documentos de época visigoda escritos en pizarra (siglos VI–VIII)*, ed. Isabel Velázquez Soriano, Monumenta Palaeographica Medii Aevi, series hispanica, 2 vols. (Turnhout, 2000), no. 104, i. 113–15, ii. 124–6.

29. See pp. 42–3.

30. *Byrhtferth's Manual*, ed. and trans. S. J. Crawford, Early English Text Society, 177 (London, 1929), 132–3.

31. Wulfstan of York, *Sermo Lupi ad Anglos*, in *EHD*, 929–34, quotations from pp. 929–30 and 934 (*The Homilies of Wulfstan*, ed. Dorothy Bethurum (Oxford, 1957), no. xx (version in mss E, I), 266–75).

32. *Annales Hildesheimenses*, ed. G. Waitz, MGH SRG (Hanover, 1878), 28.

33. For the political significance of this see p. 276.

34. *Miracula Alexii*, 9, *AASS Jul.* IV, col. 259.

CHAPTER 3. FRIENDS AND RELATIONS

1. 'The Rune Poem', lines 59–63, ed. and trans. T. A. Shippey, *Poems of Wisdom and Learning in Old English* (Cambridge, 1976), 82–3.

2. Wipo, *The Deeds of Conrad II*, trans. Theodor E. Mommsen and Karl F. Morrison, *Imperial Lives and Letters of the Eleventh Century*, 2nd edn. (New

York, 2000), 63 (*Wiponis opera*, ed. H. Bresslau, MGH SRG (Hanover, 1915), 17).

3. 'Hildebrandlied', trans. Patrick J. Geary, *Readings in Medieval History*, 3rd edn. (Peterborough, ONT, 2003), 118 (ed. Wilhelm Braune, *Althochdeutsches Lesebuch*, 16th edn. (Tübingen, 1979), 84–5).

4. William of Malmesbury, *Vita Wulfstani*, I.1, ed. and trans. M. Winterbottom and R. M. Thomson, *William of Malmesbury: Saints' Lives. Lives of SS. Wulfstan, Dunstan, Patrick, Benignus and Indract* (Oxford, 2002), 14–15.

5. Quoted by John V. Kelleher, 'The Pre-Norman Irish Genealogies', *Irish Historical Studies*, 16 (1968–9), 138–53 at 145.

6. See p. 34 on the nature of Irish legal treatises.

7. *Beowulf: A Verse Translation*, trans. Michael Alexander, 2nd edn. (Harmondsworth, 2001), lines 2597–8 and 83–4, pp. 93 and 6, with line numbering specific to this edition (*Beowulf: A Student Edition*, ed. George Jack (Oxford, 1994, rev. 1997), lines 2600–1 and 84–5, pp. 178 and 33, with line numbering following the manuscript).

8. *The Laws of the Salian Franks*, trans. Katherine Fischer Drew (Philadelphia, 1991), 123, slightly adapted (*Pactus Legis Salicae*, title LX.1, ed. K. A. Eckhardt, MGH Leges Nationum Germanicarum IV, pt. 1, p. 225).

9. Sigebert of Gembloux, *Vita Deodorici episcopi Mettensis*, MGH SS IV, p. 465, quoted by Régine Le Jan, *Famille et pouvoir dans le monde franc (VIIe–Xe siècle): Essai d'anthropologie sociale* (Paris, 1995), 84 n. 184.

10. Marc Bloch, *Feudal Society*, trans. L. A. Manyon, 2nd edn., 2 vols. (London, 1965), i. 123–4.

11. *Beowulf*, lines 1324–8, trans. Alexander, p. 49 (ed. Jack, lines 1325–29, p. 107).

12. *Beowulf*, lines 1016–18, trans. Alexander, p. 38 (ed. Jack, lines 1017–19, p. 86).

13. VI Æthelstan 8.2–3, *EHD*, 425 (F. Liebermann (ed.), *Die Gesetze der Angelsachsen*, 3 vols. (Halle, 1898–1916), i. 178–9).

14. Above, n. 1.

15. Paulinus of Aquileia, *Liber exhortationis*, 49, *PL* 99, col. 253.

16. *Pactus Legis Salicae*, title XXX.1–5, ed. Eckhardt, 118–19, following translation suggested by Guy Halsall, *Warfare and Society in the Barbarian West, 450–900* (London, 2003), 11.

17. *Laws of the Alamans and Bavarians*, trans. Theodore John Rivers (Philadelphia, 1977), 129 (*Lex Baiwariorum* III.1, ed. E. von Schwind, MGH Leges Nationum Germanicarum V, pt. 2, p. 313).

18. Drew, *Laws of the Salian Franks*, 78 (*Pactus Legis Salicae*, title XIII.11, ed. Eckhardt, 62–3).

19. *EHD*, 819 (ed. M. Tangl, *Die Briefen des hl. Bonifatius und Lullus*, no. 73, MGH Epp. Sel. I (Berlin, 1916), 146–55).

20. Gregory of Tours, *Libri historiarum decem*, VI.36, ed. B. Krusch and W. Levison, MGH SRM I, pt. 1 (Hanover, 1937–51), 307.

21. II Cnut 53, *EHD*, 463 (Liebermann (ed.), *Gesetze*, i. 348).

22. *Sedulius Scottus: On Christian Rulers and the Poems*, trans. Edward Gerard Doyle (Binghamton, 1983), 60 (*De rectoribus christianis*, 5, ed. S. Hellmann,

Sedulius Scottus, Quellen und Untersuchungen zur lateinischen Philologie 1, pt. 1 (Munich, 1906), 35).

23. Laws of Liutprand, clause 135, trans. Katherine Fischer Drew, *The Lombard Laws* (Philadelphia, 1973), 204–5 (*Leges Langobardorum*, ed. F. Bluhme and A. Boretius, MGH Legum IV, p. 466).

24. *Handbook for William: A Carolingian Woman's Counsel for her Son*, trans. Carol Neel (Lincoln, NE, 1991), 21, 33 (Dhuoda, *Manuel pour mon fils* III.1, 9, ed. Pierre Riché, SC 225 bis, 2nd edn. (Paris, 1997), 134, 170–2).

25. *Handbook for William*, 35–6, slightly adapted (*Manuel pour mon fils*, III.10, ed. Riché, 178).

26. *Waltharius*, lines 177, 696–7, ed. and trans. Dennis M. Kratz, in Waltharius *and* Ruodlieb (New York, 1984), 11, 35.

27. Ibid., lines 629–31, trans. Kratz, 33.

28. Ibid., lines 1079–80, trans. Kratz, 53.

29. Ibid., lines 1089–96, trans. Kratz, 53–5.

30. *The Battle of Maldon*, lines 205–8, trans. Michael Alexander, *The Earliest English Poems*, 3rd edn. (Harmondsworth, 1991), 107–8 (*The Battle of Maldon*, ed. D. G. Scragg (Manchester, 1981), 63).

31. *EHD*, 863–4 (Alcuin, *Epistolae* 231, 232, ed. E. Dümmler, MGH Epp. IV, pp. 376–7).

32. *Cath Maige Tuired*, quoted by Philip O'Leary, 'The Honour of Women in Early Irish Literature', *Ériu*, 38 (1987), 24–44 at 37.

33. Asser, *Life of Alfred*, trans. Simon Keynes and Michael Lapidge, *Alfred the Great: Asser's* Life of Alfred *and other Contemporary Sources* (Harmondsworth, 1983), 74 (*Asser's Life of King Alfred, Together with the Annals of St Neots Erroneously Ascribed to Asser*, ch. 18, ed. William Henry Stephenson with introduction by Dorothy Whitelock (Oxford, 1959), 17–18).

34. Adomnan, *Life of St Columba*, II. 39, trans. Richard Sharpe (Harmondsworth, 1995), 189 (*Adomnan's Life of Columba*, ed. A. O. Anderson and M. O. Anderson (Edinburgh, 1961), 422).

35. Gregory of Tours, *Libri historiarum decem*, X.27, ed. Krusch and Levison, 519–20.

36. Edict of Rothari, clause 74, trans. Drew, *Lombard Laws*, 65 (*Leges Langobardorum*, ed. Bluhme and Boretius, 23–4).

37. Gregory of Tours, *Libri historiarum decem*, VIII.5, ed. Krusch and Levison, 374.

CHAPTER 4. MEN AND WOMEN

1. Gregory the Great, *Moralia in Job*, XI.xlix.65, ed. M. Adriaen, 3 vols. with continuous pagination, CCSL 143, 143A, 143B (Turnhout, 1979–85), 623.

2. 'Maxims I', lines 24–6, ed. and trans. T. Shippey, *Poems of Wisdom and Learning in Old English* (Cambridge, 1976), 64–5.

3. See Ch. 1.

4. See pp. 89–92, 105.
5. See Chs. 5, 7, and 8.
6. See p. 40.
7. 'Maxims II', lines 11–12, ed. and trans. Shippey, *Poems of Widsom and Learning*, 76–7.
8. For wergeld as an expression of rank see pp. 100–1.
9. Edict of Rothari, clause 204, trans. Katherine Fischer Drew, *The Lombard Laws* (Philadelphia, 1973), 92 (*Leges Langobardorum*, ed. F. Bluhme and A. Boretius, MGH Legum IV, p. 466).
10. P. D. King, *Charlemagne: Translated Sources* (Kendal, 1987), 218–19 (*Admonitio generalis*, clause 81, MGH Capitularia I, ed. A. Boretius (Hanover, 1883), 61).
11. Above, n. 1.
12. Isidore, *Etymologiae*, XI.ii.17–19, ed. W. M. Lindsay (Oxford, 1911), ii. 23.
13. Ambrose of Milan, Letter IV.15. *Sancti Ambrosii opera*, x: *Epistularum libri I–VI*, ed. Otto Faller, CSEL 82 (Vienna, 1968), 112–13. The biblical quotations are Deut. 22: 5, 1 Cor. 14: 34–5, and 1 Tim. 2: 11–12.
14. Odo of Cluny, *The Life of St Gerald of Aurillac*, trans. Thomas F. X. Noble and Thomas Head, *Soldiers of Christ: Saints and Saints' Lives from Late Antiquity and the Early Middle Ages* (University Park, PA, 1995), 313 (*Vita Geraldi*, I.21, PL 133, col. 656).
15. *Capitula* of Arichis of Benevento, 12 (*Leges Langobardorum*, ed. Bluhme and Boretius, 209).
16. Adam of Bremen, *History of the Archbishops of Hamburg-Bremen*, trans. Francis J. Tschan (New York, 1959), 203 (*Gesta Hammaburgensis ecclesiae pontificum*, IV.21, ed. B. Schmeidler, MGH SRG (Hanover, 1917), 251).
17. Quoted by T. M. Charles-Edwards, *Early Irish and Welsh Kinship* (Oxford, 1993), 462.
18. Quoted by Fergus Kelly, *A Guide to Early Irish Law* (Dublin, 1988), 70.
19. Ibid. 70–1.
20. Ibid. 71.
21. Letter 167 to Rusticus, bishop of Narbonne, in 459, PL 54, col. 1204.
22. 1 Cor. 7: 2 and 6: 9–10.
23. Quoted from a law tract on privileged ranks by Donnchadh Ó Corráin, 'Marriage in Early Ireland', in Art Cosgrove (ed.), *Marriage in Ireland* (Dublin, 1985), 5–24 at 19.
24. See pp. 238–9.
25. 'Visio Baronti', 12, trans. J. N. Hillgarth, *Christianity and Paganism, 350–750: The Conversion of Western Europe* (Philadelphia, 1969), 199 (ed. W. Levison, MGH SRM V, p. 386).
26. Jonas, *Life of St Columbanus*, 32, trans. Edward Peters, *Monks, Bishops and Pagans: Christian Culture in Gaul and Italy, 500–700* (Philadelphia, 1975), 94 (*Vita Columbani*, I.19, ed. B. Krusch, MGH SRM IV, p. 87).

27. For a full discussion see Ch. 7.
28. All quotations from Hincmar, *Epistolae*, 136, ed. E. Perels, MGH Epp. VIII, pt. 1, pp. 87–107 at 88–9.
29. See p. 127.
30. *Annales Quedlinburgenses*, a. 1020, MGH SS III, p. 85.
31. See pp. 29–30, 41–2, 85–6.
32. See p. 134.
33. F. E. Harmer (ed.), *Select English Historical Documents of the Ninth and Tenth Centuries* (Cambridge, 1914), no. 2, pp. 3–5 with translation pp. 40–2.
34. See pp. 65–8.
35. Quoted in translation by Birgit Sawyer, *Property and Inheritance in Viking Scandinavia: The Runic Evidence* (Alingsås, 1988), 17.
36. *EHD*, 602–3 (ed. A. J. Robertson, *Anglo-Saxon Charters*, 2nd edn. (Cambridge, 1956), 150–3).
37. *Codice Diplomatico Longobardo*, v, ed. H. Zielinski, Fonti per la Storia d'Italia, 66 (Rome, 1986), no. 50, pp. 177–80.
38. See also p. 44.

CHAPTER 5. LABOUR AND LORDSHIP

1. *Aelfric's Colloquy*, ed. G. N. Garmonsway, 2nd edn. (Exeter, 1978), 20–1. Cf. the translation by Michael Swanton, *Anglo-Saxon Prose* (London, 1975), 108–9.
2. Old Irish verse, cited by Jane Stevenson, 'The Beginnings of Literacy in Ireland', *Proceedings of the Royal Irish Academy of Ireland*, 89C (1989), 127–65 at 159.
3. *Responsa misso cuidam data*, clause 1, MGH Capitularia I, no. 158, ed. A. Boretius (Hanover, 1883), 145.
4. See p. 169.
5. Survey of the manor of Tidenham (between 956 and 1061), *Anglo-Saxon Charters*, 109, ed. and trans. A. J. Robertson, 2nd edn. (Cambridge, 1956), 204–7.
6. See p. 76.
7. *Laws of the Alamans and Bavarians*, trans. Theodore John Rivers (Philadelphia, 1977), 162, slighted adapted (*Lex Baiwariorum*, XVI.11, ed. E. von Schwind, MGH Leges Nationum Germanicarum V, pt. 2, p. 439).
8. W. de Gray Birch, *Cartularium Saxonicum*, 3 vols. (London, 1885–93), iii. 358–9.
9. Lichfield memoranda, no. 5, in *The Text of the Book of Llan Dâv*, ed. J. G. Evans and J. Rhys (Oxford, 1893), p. xlvi.
10. *Lex Baiwariorum*, VIII.22–3, ed. von Schwind, 365. Cf. the translation by Rivers, *Laws of the Alamans and Bavarians*, 142.

11. Jonas of Orleans, *De institutione laicali*, II.xxii, *PL* 106, col. 215.
12. Walburg Boppert, *Die frühchristlichen Inschriften des Mittelrheingebietes* (Mainz, 1971), 108–18, at 109.
13. Adalbero of Laon, *Poème au Roi Robert*, ed. C. Carozzi (Paris, 1979), lines 290–4, p. 22.
14. Palladius, *Opus agriculturae*, I.6.3, quoted by C. R. Whittaker and P. Garnsey, 'Rural Life in the Later Roman Empire', *The Cambridge Ancient History*, xiii, ed. Averil Cameron and Peter Garnsey (Cambridge, 1998), 296.
15. Caesarius of Arles, Sermon 154, quoted with minor adaptations from William E. Klingshirn, *Caesarius of Arles: The Making of a Christian Community in Late Antique Gaul* (Cambridge, 1994), 205–6 (*Sermones*, ed. G. Morin, 2 vols., CCSL 103–4 (Turnhout, 1953), ii. 629).
16. See pp. 143–5.
17. From the so-called *Rectitudines Singularum Personarum*, trans. Swanton, *Anglo-Saxon Prose*, 22–3, under the title 'Duties and Perquisites' (F. Liebermann (ed.), *Die Gesetze der Angelsachsen*, 3 vols. (Halle, 1898–1916), i. 447–8).
18. *The Complete Works of Rather of Verona*, trans. Peter L. D. Reid (Binghamton, NY, 1991), 52, with adaptations (*Praeloquia*, I.33, *Ratherii Veronensis opera*, ed. Peter L. D. Reid, 2 vols., CCCM 46 (Turnhout, 1976–84), ii. 34).
19. See pp. 44, 139–40, 143–5 and 169.
20. Lives of the Fathers of Merida, 3: Nanctus, trans. A. T. Fear, *Lives of the Visigothic Fathers* (Liverpool, 1997), 57 (*Vitas sanctorum patrum Emeretensium*, ed. A. Maya Sánchez, CCSL 116 (Turnhout, 1992), 23).
21. Bede, *Ecclesiastical History of the English People*, IV.22, ed. and trans. Bertram Colgrave and R. A. B. Mynors (Oxford, 1969), 402–3.
22. 'Astronomer', *Vita Hludowici*, 28, ed. E. Tremp, *Thegan, Die Taten Ludwigs des Frommen (Gesta Hludowici imperatoris). Astronomus, Das Leben Kaiser Ludwigs (Vita Hludowici imperatoris)*, MGH SRG 64 (Hanover, 1995), 378.
23. Odo of Cluny, *The Life of St Gerald of Aurillac*, trans. Thomas F. X. Noble and Thomas Head, *Soldiers of Christ: Saints and Saints' Lives from Late Antiquity and the Early Middle Ages* (University Park, PA, 1995), 310 (*Vita Geraldi*, I.16, *PL* 133, col. 653).
24. *Codex Carolinus*, 81, MGH Epp. III, ed. W. Gundlach, 614.
25. Donizo of Canossa, *Vita Mathildis*, I.10, line 806, MGH SS XII, p. 368.
26. See pp. 70–1.
27. *Capitulare missorum* of 819, clause 29, MGH Capitularia I, p. 291.
28. Notker, *Gesta Karoli*, II.18, ed. H. F. Haefele, MGH SRG, NS 12 (Berlin, 1959), 88.
29. *Ottonian Germany: The Chronicle of Thietmar of Merseburg*, trans. David A. Warner (Manchester, 2001), 282 (*Thietmari Merseburgensis episcopi chronicon* VI.65, ed. R. Holtzmann, MGH SRG, NS 9 (Berlin, 1935), 354).
30. Ekkehard of St Gall, *Casus Sancti Galli*, 48, ed. H. F. Haefele (Darmstadt, 1980), 108–10.

31. *Crith Gablach*, clause 112, trans. Eoin MacNeill, 'Ancient Irish Law: Law of Status or Franchise', *Proceedings of the Royal Irish Academy*, 36C (1923), 281–311.
32. *Geþyncðo*, *EHD*, 469 (ed. Liebermann, *Gesetze*, i. 456).
33. Odo of Cluny, *The Life of St Gerald of Aurillac*, trans. Noble and Head, *Soldiers of Christ*, 298 (*Vita Geraldi*, I.1, PL 133, cols. 642–3).
34. See pp. 100–8.
35. *The Annals of Fulda*, trans. Timothy Reuter (Manchester, 1992), 101 (*Annales Fuldenses*, a. 887, ed. F. Kurze, MGH SRG (Hanover, 1891), 105).
36. Gregory of Tours, *Libri historiarum decem*, V.48, ed. B. Krusch and W. Levison, MGH SRM I, pt. 1 (Hanover, 1937–51), 258.
37. See pp. 88–9 on Gregory's ancestry.
38. *Thegan, Die Taten Ludwigs des Frommen*, 44, ed. Tremp, 23. Cf. the translation by Paul Edward Dutton, *Carolingian Civilization: A Reader* (Peterborough, ONT, 1993), 151.
39. Richer, *Histoire de France*, I.15, ed. Robert Latouche, 2nd edn., 2 vols. (Paris, 1964–7), i. 38.
40. *Two Voyagers at the Court of King Alfred: The Ventures of Ohthere and Wulfstan together with the Description of Northern Europe from the Old English Orosius*, ed. Niels Lund and trans. Christine E. Fell (York, 1984), 20.

CHAPTER 6. GETTING AND GIVING

1. 'Etmic Dinbych', lines 33–4, 84–51, trans. Ifor Williams, in *The Beginnings of Welsh Poetry: Studies by Sir Ifor Williams*, ed. Rachel Bromwich, 2nd edn. (Cardiff, 1972), 163–6.
2. Einhard, *Vita Karoli*, 21, ed. O. Holder-Egger, MGH SRG (Hanover, 1911), 26. Many English translations are available.
3. Annalista Saxo, a. 968, MGH SS VI, p. 622.
4. Bede, *Ecclesiastical History of the English People*, II.3, ed. and trans. Bertram Colgrave and R. A. B. Mynors (Oxford, 1969), 142–3.
5. C. H. Robinson, *Anskar, Apostle of the North, 801–865: Translated from the Vita Anskarii by Bishop Rimbert his Fellow Missionary and Successor* (London, 1921), 65 (*Vita Anskarii auctore Rimberto*, 19, ed. G. Waitz, MGH SRG (Hanover, 1884), 41).
6. Ibn Hauqal, *Configuration de la terre (Kitab surat al-Ard)*, ed. and trans J. H. Kramers and G. Wiet, 2 vols. (Beirut, 1946), i. 196.
7. Notker, *Gesta Karoli*, II.17, ed. H. F. Haefele, MGH SRG, NS 12 (Berlin, 1959), 86.
8. Ibn Hauqal, *Configuration de la terre*, 197.
9. Procopius, *History of the Wars*, V.xii.42, ed. and trans. H. B. Dewing, *Procopius*, 7 vols. (Cambridge, MA, 1914–40), iii. 128–9.
10. Gregory of Tours, *Libri historiarum decem*, II.38, ed. B. Krusch and W. Levison, MGH SRM I, pt. 1 (Hanover, 1937–51), 88–9.

11. Gregory of Tours, *Libri historiarum decem*, VI.42, ed. Krusch and Levison, 314.

12. Venantius Fortunatus, *Carmina*, VII.2, lines 1–2, ed. F. Leo, MGH AA IV, pt. 1, p. 154.

13. Ibid., VII.3, line 6, ed. Leo, 155.

14. *Venantius Fortunatus: Personal and Political Poems*, trans. Judith George (Liverpool, 1995), 66–7 (Venantius Fortunatus, *Carmina*, VII.16, lines 43–4, 55–7, ed. Leo, 170–2).

15. *Beowulf: A Verse Translation*, trans. Michael Alexander, 2nd edn. (Harmondsworth, 2001), lines 63–6, p. 5 (*Beowulf: A Student Edition*, ed. George Jack (Oxford, 1994, rev. 1997), lines 64–7, p. 32).

16. *Beowulf*, trans. Alexander, lines 948–54, 993–4, 1010–14, 1019–25, 1045–8, pp. 35–6, 37, 37–8, 38, 39 (ed. Jack, lines 949–55, 994–5, 1011–15, 1020–6, 1046–9, pp. 83, 85, 86, 86–7, 88–9).

17. Hincmar of Reims, *On the Governance of the Palace*, trans. Paul Edward Dutton, *Carolingian Civilization: A Reader* (Peterborough, ONT, 1993), 493 (*De ordine palatii*, 22, ed. R. Schieffer, MGH Fontes iuris Germanici antiqui in usum scholarum separatim editi (Hanover, 1980), 72).

18. *Beowulf*, trans. Alexander, lines 1027–8, p. 73 (ed. Jack, lines 2028–9, p. 146).

19. *The Variae of Magnus Aurelius Cassiodorus Senator*, IV.1, trans. S. J. B. Barnish (Liverpool, 1992), 74 (*Variae*, ed. T. Mommsen, MGH AA XII, p. 114).

20. See pp. 235–6.

21. See pp. 119–20.

22. See p. 176.

23. See pp. 140 and 145.

24. Widukind, *Res gestae Saxonicae*, I.33, eds. P. Hirsch and H.-E. Lohmann, MGH SRG (Hanover, 1935), 45–6.

25. *Liudprand of Cremona: The Embassy to Constantinople and Other Writings*, trans. F. A. Wright, ed. John Julius Norwich (London, 1993), 114–15 (*Antapodosis*, IV.25, in *Liudprandi opera*, ed. J. Becker, MGH SRG (Hanover, 1915), 119).

CHAPTER 7. KINGSHIP AND CHRISTIANITY

1. Prayer to be said over Louis the German, quoted from the MS by Eric J. Goldberg, "'More devoted to the equipment of battle than the splendor of banquets": Frontier Kingship, Martial Ritual and Early Knighthood at the Court of Louis the German', *Viator*, 30 (1999), 41–78 at 71.

2. Stephen of Hungary, *Libellus de institutione morum*, 1, ed. J. Balogh, in *Scriptores rerum Hungaricarum tempore ducum regumque stirpis Arpadianae gestarum*, gen. ed. E. Szentpétery, 2 vols. (Budapest, 1937–8), ii. 621.

3. Ælfric of Eynsham, Homily IX, line 48, ed. J. C. Pope, *Homilies of Ælfric: A Supplementary Collection*, 2 vols., Early English Text Society, 259–60 (Oxford, 1967–8), i. 380.

4. For the notion of emperor, see pp. 274–5.

5. Radbod of Utrecht, *Libellus de miraculo sancti Martini*, MGH SS XV, pt. 2, p. 1240, trans. Wolfert van Egmond, 'Converting Monks: Missionary Activity in Early Medieval Frisia and Saxony', in Guyda Armstrong and Ian Wood (eds.), *Christianizing Peoples and Converting Individuals* (Turnhout, 2000), 40.

6. Julian of Toledo, *Prognosticon futuri saeculi*, III.14 (quoting Augustine of Hippo, *Enchiridion*, 84). *Sancti Iuliani Toletanae sedis episcopi opera, pars I*, ed. J. N. Hillgarth, CCSL 115 (Turnhout, 1976), 90–1.

7. *Annales regni Francorum*, ed. F. Kurze, MGH SRG (Hanover, 1895), 134. Cf. English translation by Bernhard Scholz, *Carolingian Chronicles* (Ann Arbor, 1972).

8. *Life of Methodius*, 16, trans. Marvin Kantor, *Medieval Slavic Lives of Saints and Princes* (Ann Arbor, 1983), 125. (Kantor's identification of the 'king' in this passage with the Frankish Charles the Fat is erroneous.)

9. See p. 34.

10. See pp. 57–8, 269–71.

11. *Landnámabók*, 15, ed. Jakob Benediktsson, 2 vols. (Reykjavik, 1968), i. 52–5. Cf. English translation by Hermann Pálsson and Paul Edwards, *The Book of Settlements: Landnámabók* (Manitoba, 1972), 23–4.

12. See Ch. 1 on new, literate modes of communication, and pp. 239–51 on ideologies.

13. Hrabanus Maurus, *Expositio in Epistolam I ad Corinthios*, 2, PL 112, col. 23.

14. Martin of Braga, *Reforming the Rustics*, trans. Claude W. Barlow, *Iberian Fathers*, i: *Martin of Braga, Paschasius of Dumium, Leander of Seville* (Washington, 1969), 74–5, slightly adapted (*De correctione rusticorum*, 7–8, ed. Claude W. Barlow, *Martini episcopi Bracarensis opera omnia* (New Haven, 1950), 186–8).

15. *Niederdeutsche Taufgelöbnis*, ii, in *Althochdeutsches Lesebuch*, ed. Wilhem Braune, 16th edn. (Tübingen, 1979), 39.

16. *EHD*, 795, translation slightly altered (ed. M. Tangl, *Die Briefen des hl. Bonifatius und Lullus* 23, MGH Epp. Sel. I (Berlin, 1916), 38–41).

17. *Ottonian Germany: The Chronicle of Thietmar of Merseburg*, trans. David A. Warner (Manchester, 2001), 69 (*Thietmari Merseburgensis episcopi chronicon*, I.3, ed. R. Holtzmann, MGH SRG, NS 9 (Berlin, 1935), 7).

18. *Chronicle of Thietmar of Merseburg*, trans. Warner, 364 (*Chronicon*, VIII.4, ed. Holtzmann, 496).

19. Caesarius of Arles, *Sermones*, 16, ed. G. Morin, 2 vols., CCSL 103–4 (Turnhout, 1953), i. 77.

20. Ibid. 52, ed. Morin, i. 230–3, quotation at p. 232.

21. Ibid. 13, ed. Morin, i. 67.

22. Above, n. 13.

23. *Etymologiae*, IX.iii.4, ed. W. M. Lindsay, 2 vols. (Oxford, 1911), i. 362.

24. Lanfranc, letter 10, *The Letters of Lanfranc, Archbishop of Canterbury*, ed. and trans. Helen Clover and Margaret Gibson (Oxford, 1979), 70–3.

25. Privilege of Adrian IV, preserved in Gerald of Wales, *Expugnatio Hibernica*, ed. and trans. A. B. Scott and F. X. Martin (Dublin, 1978), 144–5.

26. *Ordo ad regem benedicendum* (= Ordo LXXII), *Le Pontifical romano-germanique du dixième siècle*, ed. Cyrille Vogel and Reinhard Elze, 3 vols., Studi e Testi 226, 227, 269 (Rome, 1963–72), i. 246–61, quotation at p. 249.

27. Ibid. 253.

28. *Chronicle of Thietmar of Merseburg*, trans. Warner, 126 (*Chronicon*, III, prol., ed. Holtzmann, 94).

29. See p. 132.

30. *Formula honestae vitae*, in *Martini episcopi Braracensis opera omnia*, ed. Barlow, 236–50; quotations from pp. 237, 244. Cf. translation by Barlow, *Iberian Fathers*, i. 87–97.

31. Bede, *Ecclesiastical History of the English People*, I.32, ed. and trans. Bertram Colgrave and R. A. B. Mynors (Oxford, 1969), 111–13.

32. *Audacht Morainn*, ed. and trans. Fergus Kelly (Dublin, 1976), 2–3.

33. Ibid. 6–7.

34. Ibid. 18–19.

35. *EHD*, 817–18 (ed. Tangl, *Die Briefen des hl. Bonifatius* 73, pp. 146–55).

36. *Sedulius Scottus: On Christian Rulers and the Poems*, trans. Edward Gerard Doyle (Binghamton, NY, 1983), 59–60 (*De rectoribus christianis*, 5, ed. S. Hellmann, *Sedulius Scottus*, Quellen und Untersuchungen zur lateinischen Philologie 1, pt. 1 (Munich, 1906), 35).

37. *Sedulius Scottus: On Christian Rulers*, trans. Doyle, 61–2 (*De rectoribus christianis*, 6, ed. Hellmann, 38).

38. *Reginonis abbatis Prumiensis chronicon*, a. 900, ed. F. Kurze, MGH SRG (Hanover, 1890), 148.

39. *The Annals of Fulda*, trans. Timothy Reuter (Manchester, 1992), 42 (*Annales Fuldenses*, ed. F. Kurze, MGH SRG (Hanover, 1891), 49–50).

40. *Chronicle of Thietmar of Merseburg*, trans. Warner, 333 (*Chronicon*, VII.36, ed. Holtzmann, p. 442).

41. See pp. 159–60.

42. See p. 78.

43. Wulfstan of York, *Institutes of Polity*, version I, §1–2, ed. Karl Jost, *Die 'Institutes of Polity Civil and Ecclesiastical'*, Schweizer anglistische Arbeiten, 47 (Bern, 1959), 40, quoting MS D.

44. Ibid., version II, §§13–15, p. 47, quoting MS X.

CHAPTER 8. ROME AND THE PEOPLES OF EUROPE

1. *The Gothic History of Jordanes*, trans. C. C. Mierow (Princeton, 1915), 53, 57, with minor adaptation (*Getica*, I.9, IV.25, ed. T. Mommsen, MGH AA V, pp. 55–6, 60).

2. Sighvatr, 'Knútsdrápa (Tøgdrápa)', verses 10–11, *EHD*, 338 (ed. Finnur Jónsson, *Den Norsk-Islandske Skjaldedigtning*, 4 vols. (Copenhagen, 1912–15), vol. B–1, p. 234.

3. *Gothic History of Jordanes*, trans. Mierow, 52 (*Getica*, I.6, ed. Mommsen, 55).

4. Orosius, *Seven Books of History against the Pagans*, trans. Roy J. Deferrari (Washington, 1964), 16 (*Histoire (contre les païens)*, I.2.79, ed. Marie-Pierre Arnaud-Lindet, 3 vols. (Paris, 1990–1), i. 32).

5. See pp. 56–7, 119–20, 206–7 for the material evidence.

6. See p. 31.

7. *The Variae of Magnus Aurelius Cassiodorus Senator*, trans. S. J. B. Barnish (Liverpool, 1992), 76 (Cassiodorus, *Variae*, IV.6, ed. T. Mommsen, MGH AA XII, p. 117).

8. *Liudprand of Cremona: The Embassy to Constantinople and Other Writings*, trans. F. A. Wright, with introduction by J. J. Norwich (London, 1993), 22 (*Antapodosis*, I.25, in *Liudprandi opera*, ed. J. Becker, MGH SRG (Hanover, 1915), 21).

9. *Sedulius Scottus: On Christian Rulers and the Poems*, trans. Edward Gerard Doyle (Binghamton, NY, 1983), 107 (*Carmina*, II.7, lines 62–4, ed. L. Traube, MGH Poetae III, p. 174).

10. Bruno of Querfurt, *Vita Adalberti*, 12, MGH SS IV, p. 600.

11. *Ottonis III. Diplomata* no. 389, ed. T. Sickel, MGH Diplomata regum et imperatorum Germaniae II, pt. 2, pp. 819–20.

12. 'Anonymous Valesianus', 65–7, ed. Ingemar König, *Aus der Zeit Theoderichs des Grossen: Einleitung, Text, Übersetzung und Kommentar einer anonymen Quelle* (Darmstadt, 1997), 82–4.

13. 'Anonymous Valesianus', 58–60, ed. König, 78–80.

14. *The Chronicle of Marcellinus*, ed. and trans. Brian Croke (Sydney, 1995), 27.

15. *Epistola ad Hathonem archiepiscopum missa*, in *Reginonis abbatis Prumiensis chronicon*, ed. F. Kurze, MGH SRG (Hanover, 1890), p. xx.

16. See pp. 30, 47–9.

17. See p. 36 and cf. Gen. 10: 1–2.

18. *Historia Brittonum*, 15, ed. and trans. John Morris, *Nennius: British History and the Welsh Annals* (London, 1980), 21, with Latin p. 62.

19. *Sanas Cormaic (Cormac's Glossary)*, line 1162, ed. Kuno Meyer, Anecdota from Irish Manuscripts, 4 (Halle 1912), 102.

20. http://www.ucl.ac.uk/archaeology/cisp/database/site/ltysl.html. See also 'The Pillar of Eliseg', *Early Welsh Genealogical Tracts*, ed. and trans. P. C. Bartrum (Cardiff, 1966), 1–3.

21. Above, n. 1.

22. *Gothic History of Jordanes*, trans. Mierow, 60 (*Getica*, V.38, ed. Mommsen, 64).

23. *Gothic History of Jordanes*, trans. Mierow, 62 (*Getica*, V.43, ed. Mommsen, 65).

24. *De Karolo rege et Leone papa*, lines 12, 27–9, 92–6, ed. Franz Brunhölzl, Studien und Quellen zur westfälischen Geschichte, 36, Beiheft (Paderborn, 1999), 10, 16. Cf. the translation of the first third of this poem in Peter

Godman, *Poetry of the Carolingian Renaissance* (London, 1985), no. 25, pp. 196–207.

25. *De Karolo rege et Leone papa*, lines 495–6, 504, p. 44.

26. See p. 226.

27. *Annales Petaviani*, a. 776, *Annales Laureshamenses*, a. 799, ed. G. H. Pertz, MGH SS I, pp. 16, 38.

28. *Vita Karoli*, 7, ed. O. Holder-Egger, MGH SRG (Hanover, 1911), 9.

29. Ibid. 9–10.

30. Modoin, *Ecloga*, lines 24–7, ed. and trans. Godman, *Poetry of the Carolingian Renaissance*, 192–3.

31. *Etymologiae*, IX.iii.2–3, ed. W. M. Lindsay, 2 vols. (Oxford, 1911), i. 362.

32. Ibid., IX.iii.14, ed. Lindsay, i. 364.

33. Bede, *Ecclesiastical History of the English People*, II.5, ed. and trans. Bertram Colgrave and R. A. B. Mynors (Oxford, 1969), 148–9.

34. Ibid., V.10, ed. and trans. Colgrave and Mynors, 480–1. Translation adapted.

35. Adomnan of Iona, *Life of St Columba*, I.1, trans. Richard Sharpe (Harmondsworth, 1995), 110–11 (*Adomnan's Life of Columba*, ed. A. O. Anderson and M. O. Anderson (Edinburgh, 1961), 198–200).

36. Widukind, *Res gestae Saxonicae* III.46, ed. P. Hirsch and H.-E. Lohmann, MGH SRG (Hanover, 1935), 127–8.

37. *Liber Ardmachanus: The Book of Armagh edited with Introduction and Appendices* by John Gwynn (Dublin 1913), 32.

38. Cassiodorus, *Variae* I.1, ed. Mommsen, 10.

39. Above, n. 2.

40. Letter of Cnut to the English, as quoted by William of Malmesbury, *Gesta regum Anglorum*, II.183, ed. and trans. R. A. B. Mynors, R. M. Thomson, and M. Winterbottom, 2 vols. (Oxford, 1998–9), ii. 326–7.

41. See pp. 29–30.

42. Letter of Cnut to the English, ed. and trans. Mynors, Thomson, and Winterbottom, 326–7.

43. Ibid. 324–5.

44. Paulinus of Aquileia, *Carmina*, V.7, ed. E. Dümmler, MGH Poetae I, p. 137.

45. *Cummian's Letter 'De controversia paschali' together with a Related Irish Computistical Tract*, ed. Maura Walsh and Dáibhí Ó Cróinín (Toronto, 1988), 93–5.

46. *Notitia ecclesiarum urbis Romae*, ed. Roberto Valentini and Giuseppe Zucchetti, *Codice topografico della città di Roma*, 4 vols., Fonti per la Storia d'Italia, 80, 88, 90, 91 (Rome, 1940–53), ii. 78–9.

47. Ibid. ii. 94, 97.

48. Letter of Cnut to the English, ed. and trans. Mynors, Thomson, and Winterbottom, 324–7.

49. 'Petruslied', trans. Cyril Edwards, in 'German Vernacular Literature', in Rosamond McKitterick (ed.), *Carolingian Culture: Emulation and Innovation*

(Cambridge, 1994), 162 (ed. Wilhelm Braune, *Althochdeutsches Lesebuch*, 16th edn. (Tübingen, 1979), 131).

50. Ps-Alcuin, *De divinis officiis*, 17, *PL* 101, col. 1209.
51. 'Vita Berachi', 25, ed. C. Plummer, *Vitae Sanctorum Hiberniae*, 2 vols. (Oxford, 1910; repr. Dublin, 1997), i. 85–6.
52. *Félire Óengusso Céli Dé: The Martyrology of Oengus the Culdee*, ed. Whitley Stokes (London, 1905), 206–7.
53. *The Text of the Book of Llan Dâv*, ed. J. G. Evans and J. Rhys (Oxford, 1893), 83–4.
54. Bede, *Lives of the Abbots of Wearmouth and Jarrow*, trans. J. F. Webb, *The Age of Bede* (rev. edn., Harmondsworth, 1988), 191 (*Historia abbatum*, 5, ed. C. Plummer, *Venerabilis Bedae opera historica*, 2 vols. (Oxford, 1896), i. 368).
55. Bede, *Ecclesiastical History*, V.21, ed. and trans. Colgrave and Mynors, 532–3, slightly adapted.
56. *Vita Gebhardi*, 13, ed. W. Wattenbach, MGH SS X, p. 587.
57. *Vita Meinwerci episcopi Patherbrunensis*, 218, ed. F. Tenckhoff, MGH SRG (Hanover, 1921), 131.

Further Reading

ORIENTATION FOR ENGLISH-LANGUAGE READERS

General

Anglophone readers are now well served by volumes addressing part or all of the period covered in this book. Overviews include Peter Garnsey and Caroline Humfress, *The Evolution of the Late Antique World* (Cambridge, 2001); Rosamond McKitterick (ed.), *The Early Middle Ages: Europe 400–1000* (Oxford, 2001), and Heinrich Fichtenau, *Living in the Tenth Century: Mentalities and Social Orders*, trans. Patrick J. Geary (Chicago, 1991). *The Cambridge Ancient History* and *The New Cambridge Medieval History* are authoritative and large-scale statements by leading experts, containing both political narrative and detailed analytical approaches to a comprehensive range of subjects plus detailed bibliographical guidance. The period *c.*500–1000 is covered by the following: *The Cambridge Ancient History*, xiv: *Late Antiquity. Empire and Successors, AD 425–600*, ed. Averil Cameron, Bryan Ward-Perkins, and Michael Whitby (Cambridge, 2000); *The New Cambridge Medieval History*, i: c.500–c.700, ed. Paul Fouracre (forthcoming); ii: c.700–c.900, ed. Rosamond McKitterick (Cambridge, 1995); iii: c.900–1024, ed. Timothy Reuter (Cambridge, 1999).

In the absence of any firm chronological distinction between 'late Antiquity' and the 'early Middle Ages' there is considerable debate about the place of the early Middle Ages in wider conceptions of pre-modern European history. See Peter Heather, 'Late Antiquity and the Early Medieval West', in Michael Bentley (ed.), *Companion to Historiography* (London, 1997), 69–87; Lester K. Little and Barbara H. Rosenwein (eds.), *Debating the Middle Ages: Issues and Readings* (Maldon, MA, 1998); R. I. Moore, *The First European Revolution, c.970–1215* (Oxford, 2000).

Sources

Editions of sources are listed in the above-mentioned volumes of *The Cambridge Ancient History* and *The New Cambridge Medieval History*. A convenient listing of available English-language translations can be found in McKitterick (ed.), *The Early Middle Ages*.

Electronic Resources

Much useful material is now available on the Internet. Images of early medieval objects in museums and libraries can be found on the websites of several major institutions including The British Library, The British Museum, The Dumbarton Oaks Museum, and The Cloisters branch of the Metropolitan Museum of Art.

There are also many university-based websites dedicated to medieval resources, especially translations of texts, subject-specific bibliographies, and some maps. The following websites are well maintained and reliable access points:

http://www.fordham.edu/halsall/sbook.html
A public-access website based at Fordham University, the Internet Medieval Sourcebook has a large number of online English translations of late antique and early medieval texts. It also provides links to many other useful sites.

http://labyrinth.georgetown.edu
Based at Georgetown University, this is the oldest, and most sophisticated, portal for accessing online medieval resources.

http://www.netserf.org
An index of links to thousands of other sites with medieval resources.

http://www.wmich.edu/medieval/research/rawl/index.html
The Rawlinson Center of Western Michigan University hosts a wide range of useful research tools (bibliographies, texts, etc.) for Anglo-Saxon England and Old English studies.

http://www.medievalsources.co.uk
Subscriber-only access to electronic versions of translations published by Manchester University Press, plus public-access portal with links to a range of other medieval sites.

http://www.itergateway.org
A University of Toronto-based bibliographical database for the Middle Ages and Renaissance, part of which is public access.

Regional Approaches

Regional and national historiographies have a strong presence in writing on the early Middle Ages, with many books being devoted to the medieval antecedents of modern polities. The following is a short English-language selection. Where relevant, they all provide bibliographic guidance to foreign-language titles.

British Isles, including Ireland
After Rome, ed. Thomas Charles-Edwards (Oxford, 2003) and *From the Vikings to the Normans*, ed. Wendy Davies (Oxford, 2003), both volumes of 'The Short Oxford History of the British Isles'; *The Oxford Companion to Scottish History*,

ed. Michael Lynch (Oxford, 2001); *The Oxford Companion to Irish History*, ed. S. J. Connelly, 2nd edn. (Oxford, 2002); *The Blackwell Encyclopaedia of Anglo-Saxon England*, ed. Michael Lapidge, John Blair, Simon Keynes, and Donald Scragg (Oxford, 1999); David Hill, *An Atlas of Anglo-Saxon England* (Oxford, 1981).

France

Edward James, *The Origins of France: From Clovis to the Capetians, 500–1000* (London, 1982); Ian Wood, *The Merovingian Kingdoms 450–751* (Harlow, 1994); Pierre Riché, *The Carolingians: A Family who Forged Europe*, trans. M. I. Allen (Philadelphia, 1993); Jean Dunbabin, *France in the Making, 843–1180*, 2nd edn. (Oxford, 2000).

Spain

Roger Collins, *Early Medieval Spain: Unity in Diversity, 400–1000*, 2nd edn. (Basingstoke, 1995); Thomas F. Glick, *Islamic and Christian Spain in the Early Middle Ages* (Princeton, 1979).

Italy

Chris Wickham, *Early Medieval Italy: Central Power and Local Society, 400–1000* (London, 1981); Cristina La Rocca (ed.), *Italy in the Early Middle Ages, 476–1000* (Oxford, 2002); *Medieval Italy: An Encyclopedia*, ed. Christopher Kleinhenz, 2 vols. (New York, 2004).

Germany

Timothy Reuter, *Germany in the Early Middle Ages, 800–1056* (London, 1991); Benjamin Arnold, *Medieval Germany 500–1300: A Political Interpretation* (Basingstoke, 1997); *Medieval Germany: An Encyclopedia*, ed. John M. Jeep (New York, 2001).

Scandinavia

Birgit Sawyer and Peter Sawyer, *Medieval Scandinavia: From Conversion to Reformation, circa 800–1500* (Minneapolis, 1993); *The Cambridge History of Scandinavia*, i: *Prehistory to 1520*, ed. Knut Helle (Cambridge, 2003); *Cultural Atlas of the Viking World*, ed. James Graham-Campbell (New York, 1994); *Vikings: The North Atlantic Saga*, ed. William Fitzhugh and Elisabeth Ward (Washington, 2000).

Central Europe

John V. A. Fine, Jr., *The Early Medieval Balkans: A Critical Survey from the Sixth to the Late Twelfth Century* (Ann Arbor, 1983); P. M. Barford, *The Early Slavs* (London, 2001); Pál Engel, *The Realm of St Stephen: A History of Medieval Hungary, 895–1526*, trans. Tamás Pálosfalvi (London, 2001); Paul R. Magosci,

Historical Atlas of East Central Europe from the Early Fifth Century to the Present, 2nd edn. (Seattle, 2002).

CHAPTER 1. SPEAKING AND WRITING

Marco Mostert (ed.), *New Approaches to Medieval Communication* (Turnhout, 1999), offers useful methodological reflections and an extremely full bibliography of themes covered in this chapter.

The history of the languages and non-Latin literatures of the early Middle Ages have naturally attracted much attention; an accessible overview is Philippe Wolff, *Western Languages, AD 100–1500,* trans. Frances Partridge (London, 1971). Vivien Law, *The History of Linguistics in Europe from Plato to 1600* (Cambridge, 2003), takes an accessible and stimulating look at how language was conceptualized and studied.

Recommended introductions to Old English are Albert C. Baugh and Thomas Cable, *A History of the English Language,* 4th edn. (London, 1993), and *The Cambridge Companion to Old English Literature,* ed. Malcolm Godden and Michael Lapidge (Cambridge, 1991). Catherine Hills, *Origins of the English* (London, 2003), outlines the controversies surrounding the historical circumstances in which Latin and British gave way to Old English.

J. Knight Bostock, *A Handbook of Old High German Literature,* 2nd edn. (Oxford, 1976), remains the only English-language discussion of this corpus and is usefully supplemented by Wolfgang Haubrichs, *Geschichte der deutschen Literatur,* vol. 1 pt. 1, *Die Anfänge: Versuche volkssprachiger Schriftlichkeit im frühen Mittelalter (ca. 700–1050/60)* (Frankfurt, 1988). D. H. Green, *Language and History in the Early Germanic World* (Cambridge, 1998), offers a comparative approach. For Slavonic, see Alexander M. Schenker, *The Dawn of Slavic* (New Haven, 1995).

The Celtic regions are surveyed by Thomas Charles-Edwards, 'Language and Society among the Insular Celts, 400–1000', in Miranda J. Green (ed.), *The Celtic World* (London, 1995), 703–36. For ogam, see Damian McManus, *A Guide to Ogam* (Maynooth, 1991); for runes, Ralph W. V. Elliott, *Runes: An Introduction,* 2nd edn. (Manchester, 1989), and David N. Parsons, *Recasting the Runes: The Reform of the Anglo-Saxon futhorc* (Uppsala, 1999).

On Latin, two historically sensitive interpretations are Michel Banniard, *Viva voce: Communication écrite et communication orale du IVe au IXe siècle en Occident latin* (Paris, 1992), and Roger Wright, *A Sociophilological Study of Late Latin* (Turnhout, 2002), both of which offer technical guidance on the philological issues underlying the transition from Latin to Romance.

Much scholarly attention has recently focused on a range of issues clustered around the 'orality'—'literacy' antithesis, with 'memory' bridging them. The poles of the debate are marked by Michael Richter, *The Formation of the Medieval West: Studies in the Oral Culture of the Barbarians* (Dublin, 1994), Rosamond

McKitterick, *The Carolingians and the Written Word* (Cambridge, 1989), and Patrick J. Geary, *Phantoms of Remembrance: Memory and Oblivion at the End of the First Millennium* (Princeton, 1994). Several volumes of essays from the 1990s are of central methodological importance, commencing with Rosamond McKitterick (ed.), *The Uses of Literacy in Early Medieval Europe* (Cambridge, 1990). Alan K. Bowman and Greg Woolf (eds.), *Literacy and Power in the Ancient World* (Cambridge, 1994), includes late Antiquity and the successor kingdoms, while Huw Pryce (ed.), *Literacy in Medieval Celtic Societies* (Cambridge, 1998), has much to say on regions too readily ignored in the debates.

Other useful collections of essays are A. N. Doane and Carol Braun Pasternak (eds.), *Vox Intertexta: Orality and Textuality in the Middle Ages* (Madison, 1992), Ursula Schaefer (ed.), *Schriftlichkeit im frühen Mittelalter* (Tübingen, 1993), Rudolf Schieffer (ed.), *Schriftkultur und Reichsverwaltung unter den Karolingern* (Opladen, 1996), and Walter Pohl and Paul Herold (eds.), *Vom Nutzen des Schreibens: Soziales Gedächtnis, Herrschaft und Besitz im Mittelalter* (Vienna, 2002). Monographic approaches include Seth Lerer, *Literacy and Power in Anglo-Saxon Literature* (Lincoln, NE, 1991); Nicholas Everett, *Literacy in Lombard Italy, c.568–774* (Cambridge, 2003); Michel Zimmermann, *Écrire et lire en Catalogne du IXe au XIIe siècle* (Madrid, 2003). For women's literacy, see Rosamond McKitterick, 'Women and literacy in the early Middle Ages' in ead., *Books, Scribes and Learning in the Frankish Kingdoms, 6th–9th Centuries* (Aldershot, 1994), ch. XIII.

The challenge of Christian, Latin literacy in the insular world was put on a new footing by Bernhard Bischoff, 'Wendepunkte in der Geschichte der lateinischen Exegese im Frühmittelalter', in id., *Mittelalterliche Studien: Ausgewählte Aufsätze zur Schriftkunde und Literaturgeschichte*, i (Stuttgart, 1966), 205–73, and has been approached rather differently by G. Hardin Brown, 'The Dynamics of Literacy in Anglo-Saxon England', *Bulletin of the John Rylands Library*, 77 (1995), 109–42, and Roy Liuzza, 'Who Read the Gospels in Old English?', in Peter S. Baker and Nicholas Howe (eds.), *Words and Works: Studies in Medieval English Language and Literature in Honour of Fred C. Robinson* (Toronto, 1998), 3–24.

On reading, there are insightful contributions in Jonathan Boyarin (ed.), *The Ethnography of Reading* (Berkeley, 1993), and Guglielmo Cavallo and Roger Chartier (eds.), *A History of Reading in the West*, trans. Lydia Cochrane (Cambridge, 1999). D. H. Green, *Listening and Reading: The Primary Reception of German Literature, 800–1300* (Cambridge, 1994), Armando Petrucci, *Writers and Readers in Medieval Italy: Studies in the History of Written Culture*, trans. Charles Radding (New Haven, 1995), and Simon Franklin, *Writing, Society and Culture in Early Rus, c.950–1300* (Cambridge, 2002), are all of wider significance than their titles suggest.

On monastic reading, Jean Leclercq, *The Love of Learning and the Desire for God*, trans. Catherine Misrahi (New York, 1961), retains its classic status. Pierre Riché, *Education and Culture in the Barbarian West, 6th–8th Centuries*, trans. John J. Contreni (Columbia, SC, 1975), and *Écoles et enseignement dans le haut moyen âge, fin du Ve siècle–milieu du XIe siècle*, 3rd edn. (Paris 1999), survey schools and curricula. Bernhard Bischoff, *Manuscripts and Libraries in the Age of Charlemagne*, trans. Michael Gorman (Cambridge, 1994), is important on the transmission of classical texts and much else.

While law and administration have traditionally been seen as aspects of constitutional and institutional history, newer approaches place them at the centre of subjects addressed in this chapter. In particular, see Patrick Wormald, '*Lex scriptum* and *verbum regis*: Legislation and Germanic Kingship from Euric to Cnut', in P. H. Sawyer and Ian N. Wood (eds.), *Early Medieval Kingship* (Leeds, 1977), 105–38; Robin Chapman Stacey, 'Law and Order in the Very Old West: England and Ireland in the Early Middle Ages', in B. T. Hudson and V. Ziegler (eds.), *Crossed Paths: Methodological Approaches to the Celtic Aspect of the European Middle Ages* (Lanham, MD, 1991), 39–60, and T. M. Charles-Edwards, 'Law in the Western Kingdoms between the Fifth and the Seventh Century', in *The Cambridge Ancient History*, xiv. 260–87. The accommodation of Roman law and associated documentary forms to the social practices of the successor kingdoms is a complex subject, but two accessible articles, both germane to the subject matter of Chapters 3 and 4, are: Patrick Wormald, 'The *Leges barbarorum*: Law and Ethnicity in the Post-Roman West', in H.-W. Goetz, J. Jarnut, and W. Pohl (eds.), *Regna and Gentes: The Relationship between Late Antique and Early Medieval Peoples and Kingdoms in the Transformation of the Roman World* (Leiden, 2003), 21–53, and Antti Arjava, 'The Survival of Roman Family Law after the Barbarian Settlements', in Ralph W. Mathisen (ed.), *Law, Society, and Authority in Late Antiquity* (Oxford, 2001), 33–51. Patrick Wormald, *The Making of English Law: King Alfred to the Twelfth Century* (Oxford, 1999), has much to say on continental as well as Anglo-Saxon law.

The study of charters in their socio-political context was opened up by the ground-breaking essays edited by Wendy Davies and Paul Fouracre, *The Settlement of Disputes in Early Medieval Europe* (Cambridge, 1986); Karl Heidecker (ed.), *Charters and the Use of the Written Word in Medieval Society* (Turnhout, 2000), contains several valuable contributions on the earlier Middle Ages. Useful studies of document-mindedness are Kathryn A. Lowe, 'Lay Literacy in Anglo-Saxon England and the Development of the Chirograph', in Phillip Pulsiano and Elaine M. Treharne (eds.), *Anglo-Saxon Manuscripts and their Heritage* (Aldershot, 1998), 161–204; and Cristina La Rocca, 'La legge e la pratica: Potere e rapporti sociali nell'Italia dell' VIII secolo', in Carlo Bertelli and Gian Pietro Brogiolo (eds.), *Il futuro dei Longobardi: L'Italia e la costruzione dell'Europa di Carlo Magno: Saggi* (Milan, 2000), 45–69. See also Warren Brown, 'When Documents are Destroyed or Lost: Lay People and Archives in the Early Middle Ages', *EME* 11 (2002), 337–66. Patrick J. Geary, 'Land, Language and Memory in Europe, 700–1100', *Transactions of the Royal Historical Society*, 6th ser., 9 (1999), 168–84, and Robin Chapman Stacey, 'Texts and Society', in *After Rome*, ed. Charles-Edwards, 221–57 (p. 315 above), put due emphasis on the oral, performative nature of texts.

The slate documents discussed on pp. 42–3 are published by Isabel Velázquez

Soriano, *Documentos de época visigoda escritos en pizarra (siglos VI–VIII)*, Monumenta Palaeographica Medii Aevi, series hispanica, 2 vols. (Turnhout, 2000). The Redon charters discussed on pp. 43–4 were edited by Aurélien de Courson, *Cartulaire de l'Abbaye de Redon en Bretagne* (Paris, 1863). For Hrabanus and Fulda, see Raymund Kottje and Harald Zimmermann (eds.), *Hrabanus Maurus: Lehrer, Abt und Bischof* (Mainz, 1982), and Gangolf Schrimpf (ed.), *Kloster Fulda in der Welt der Karolinger und Ottonen* (Frankfurt, 1996).

CHAPTER 2. LIVING AND DYING

A judicious introduction that puts many of the issues discussed here into a broad perspective is E. L. Jones, *The European Economic Miracle: Environments, Economies and Geopolitics in the History of Europe and Asia* (Cambridge, 1981). Packed with graphs, maps, and plans, and provocative but not always accurate, is Klaus Randsborg, *The First Millennium AD in Europe and the Mediterranean: An Archaeological Essay* (Cambridge, 1991). For an emphatic word-sketch of the human dimension, see Karl Leyser, 'The Tenth-Century Condition', in his *Medieval Germany and its Neighbours, 900–1250* (London, 1982), 1–9. A wide-ranging survey incorporating the fruits of recent scholarship on themes covered in Chapters 2–6 is Philippe Depreux, *Les Sociétés occidentales du milieu du VIe à la fin du IXe siècle* (Rennes, 2002).

The environmental history of the early Middle Ages is in its infancy, although settlement studies and landscape history often address many of the same issues. For an accessible introduction to scientific approaches, see Petra Dark, *The Environment of Britain in the First Millennium AD* (London, 2000). Matthew Stout, 'Early Christian Ireland: Settlement and Environment', in Terry Barry (ed.), *A History of Settlement in Ireland* (London, 2000), 80–109, reviews issues and evidence for Ireland. A contrasting approach is Paolo Squatriti, *Water and Society in Early Medieval Italy, AD 400–1000* (Cambridge, 1998). See also Squatriti (ed.), *Working with Water in Medieval Europe: Technology and Resource-Use* (Leiden, 2000). On Europe's climate, consult Hubert H. Lamb, *Climate, History and the Modern World* (London, 1982), esp. ch. 9, and also 'Climate from 1000 BC to 1000 AD', in Martin Jones and Geoffrey Dimbleby (eds.), *The Environment of Man: The Iron Age to the Anglo-Saxon Period*, British Archaeological Reports British Series, 87 (Oxford, 1981), 53–65.

There are various approaches to settlement history. Helena Hamerow, *Early Medieval Settlements: The Archaeology of Rural Communities in North-West Europe, 400–900* (Oxford, 2002), surveys continental and Anglo-Saxon settlement sites. For a well-illustrated study of a single site, see *Un Village au temps de Charlemagne: Moines et paysans de l'abbaye de Saint-Denis du VIIe siècle à l'an Mil* (Paris, 1988). Chris Wickham, 'European Forests in the Early Middle Ages: Landscape and Land Clearance', *L'ambiente vegetale nell' alto medioevo*, 2 vols. Settimane, 37 (1990), ii. 479–545, is important (repr. in id., *Land and Power: Studies in Italian and European Social History, 400–1200* (London, 1994), 155–200); for al-Andalus, see Thomas F. Glick, *Islamic and Christian Spain in the Early Middle Ages* (Princeton, 1979), esp. ch. 2, and Andrew M. Watson, *Agricultural Innovation in the Early Islamic World: The Diffusion of Crops and Farming Techniques, 700–1100* (Cambridge, 1983). Though dated, Jean Chapelot and Robert Fossier, *The Village and House in the Middle Ages*, trans. H. Cleere (London, 1985), remains useful.

There is no satisfactory overview of early medieval demographic issues. Instead, readers should consult a range of key articles. On the plague, J.-N. Biraben and J. Le Goff, 'The Plague in the Early Middle Ages', in Robert Forster and Orest Ranum (eds.), *The Biology of Man in History: Selections from Annales* (Baltimore, 1975), 48–80, is of central importance. Controversy surrounding the geographical range and demographic significance of the plague is clear from Dick Harrison, 'Plague, Settlement and Structural Change at the Dawn of the Middle Ages', *Scandia*, 59 (1993), 15–48, and J. R. Maddicott, 'Plague in Seventh-Century England', *Past and Present*, 156 (1997), 7–54. Peter Sarris, 'The Justinianic Plague: Origins and Effects', *Continuity and Change*, 17 (2002), 169–82, argues for its catastrophic impact.

Epigraphical evidence from the post-Roman West is presented by Mark A. Handley, *Death, Society and Culture: Inscriptions and Epitaphs in Gaul and Spain, AD 300–750*, British Archaeological Reports International Series, 1135 (Oxford, 2003), with comments on its demographic implications; post-750 demography is best approached through the incisive survey of Pierre Toubert, 'The Carolingian Moment', in André Burguière, Christiane Klapisch-Zuber, Martine Segalen, and Françoise Zonabend (eds.), *A History of the Family*, i: *Distant Worlds, Ancient Worlds*, trans. Sarah Hanbury Tenison, Rosemary Morris, and Andrew Wilson (Cambridge, 1996), 379–406, and Jean-Pierre Devroey, *Économie rurale et société dans l'Europe franque (VI–IXe siècles)* (Paris, 2003), both with further bibliographic guidance. G. M. Schwartz, 'Village Populations According to the Polyptyque of the Abbey of St Bertin', *Journal of Medieval History*, 11 (1985), 31–41, is one of the few English-language contributions to debates about how to handle the ninth-century estate survey evidence. In the absence of any documentary base from which to proceed prior to the Domesday Book of 1086, there has been no demographic study of any part of the British Isles in the early Middle Ages.

The debate over female infanticide was sparked by Emily Coleman, 'Infanticide in the Early Middle Ages', in Susan Mosher Stuard (ed.), *Women in Medieval Society* (Philadelphia, 1976), 47–70, and supported by Carol Clover, 'The Politics of Scarcity: Notes on the Sex Ratio in Early Scandinavia', *Scandinavian Studies*, 60 (1988), 147–88. The detailed counter-arguments have mostly been in French: Monique Zerner, 'La Population de Villeneuve-Saint-Georges et de Nogent-sur-Marne au IXe siècle d'après le polyptyque de Saint-Germain-des-Prés', *Annales de la Faculté des Lettres et Sciences Humaines de Nice*, 37 (1979), 17–24, and Jean-Pierre Devroey, 'Les Méthodes d'analyse des polyptyques du haut moyen âge', *Acta Historica Bruxellensia*, 4 (1981), 71–88. There are sane comments on infanticide together with a fundamentally important discussion of the practice of contraception and abortion in John M. Riddle, *Contraception and Abortion from the Ancient World to the Renaissance* (Cambridge, MA, 1992). Ecclesiastical teaching is set out by J. T. Noonan, *Contraception: A History of its Treatment by the Catholic Theologians and Canonists* (Cambridge, MA, 1986). Intentional or accidental infanticide in the ninth century is the subject of Gerhard Schmitz, 'Schuld und Strafe: Eine unbekannte Stellungnahme des Rathramnus von Corbie zur Kindestötung', *Deutsches Archiv für die Erforschung des Mittelalters*, 38 (1982), 363–87.

Discussions of early medieval agriculture and productivity have often been too preoccupied with controversies about the dating of technological change; for a clear and concise appraisal, see Adriaan Verhulst, 'The "Agricultural Revolution" of the Middle Ages reconsidered', in B. S. Bachrach and D. Nicholas (eds.), *Law, Custom and the Social Fabric in the Middle Ages: Essays in Honour of Bryce Lyon* (Kalamazoo, 1990), 17–28. This can usefully be supplemented by *La Croissance agricole du haut moyen âge: Chronologie, modalités, géographie*, published by the Centre culturel de l'abbaye de Flaran (Auch, 1990). The implications of early medieval agriculture for nutrition and health are explored by M. Montanari, *L'alimentazione contadina nell'alto medioevo* (Naples, 1979), for Italy, and Kathy L. Pearson, 'Nutrition and the Early Medieval Diet', *Speculum*, 72 (1997), 1–32, for north-western Europe.

The essential work on famine remains F. Curschmann, *Hungersnöte im Mittelalter: Ein Beitrag zur deutschen Wirtschaftsgeschichte des 8. bis 13. Jahrhunderts* (Leipzig, 1900), though there is a detailed discussion of Charlemagne's response to the famines of his reign by Adriaan Verhulst, 'Karolingische Agrarpolitik: Das Capitulare de Villis und die Hungersnöte von 792/3 und 805/6', *Zeitschrift für Agrargeschichte und Agrarsoziologie*, 13 (1965), 175–89. Food taboos are examined by Pierre Bonnassie, 'Consommation d'aliments immondes et cannibalisme de survie dans l'occident du haut moyen âge', *Annales: Economies, Sociétés, Civilisations*, 44 (1989), 1035–56.

For archaeological evidence of sickness and disease, see K. Manchester, 'Resurrecting the Dead: The Potential of Palaeopathology', in E. Southworth (ed.), *Anglo-Saxon Cemeteries: A Reappraisal* (Stroud, 1990), 87–96, and, for more detail, A. Czarnetzki, C. Uhlig, and R. Wolf, *Menschen des frühen Mittelalters im Spiegel der Anthropologie und Medizin*, 2nd edn. (Stuttgart, 1983). On the social and cultural history of disease, Peregrine Horden, 'Disease, Dragons and Saints: The Management of Epidemics in the Dark Ages', in Terence Ranger and Paul Slack (eds.), *Epidemics and Ideas: Essays on the Historical Perception of Pestilence* (Cambridge, 1992), 45–76, is stimulating. See also the papers on a wide range of aspects of early medieval medical history in 'The Year 1000' issue of *Social History of Medicine*, 13/2 (2000), 197–321, ed. Peregrine Horden and Emilie Savage-Smith. M. L. Cameron, *Anglo-Saxon Medicine* (Cambridge, 1993), is also valuable.

Of the huge literature on early medieval saints' cults, Peter Brown, *The Cult of the Saints: Its Rise and Function in Latin Christianity* (Chicago, 1981), has become a classic; two collections of studies indicate more recent approaches: James

Howard-Johnston and Paul Anthony Hayward (eds.), *The Cult of Saints in Late Antiquity and the Early Middle Ages* (Oxford, 1999), and Alan Thacker and Richard Sharpe (eds.), *Local Saints and Local Churches in the Early Medieval West* (Oxford, 2002).

Early medieval cosmologies have also attracted attention. Monica Blöcker, 'Wetterzauber: Zu einem Glaubenskomplex des frühen Mittelalters', *Francia*, 9 (1981), 117–31, is essential. Valerie Flint, *The Rise of Magic in Early Medieval Europe* (Princeton, 1991), is a vigorous and controversial attempt to explore a wide range of strategies for handling illness, bad weather, and much else. On apocalyptic thinking, see the essays edited by Richard Landes, Andrew Gow, and David C. Van Meter, *The Apocalyptic Year 1000: Religious Expectation and Social Change, 950–1050* (New York, 2003).

The demographic details on pp. 66–8 are derived from Don Brothwell, 'Palaeodemography and Earlier British Populations', *World Archaeology*, 4 (1972), 75–87; Vera I. Evison, *Dover: The Buckland Anglo-Saxon Cemetery* (London, 1987), and Jürg Schneider, Daniel Gutscher, Hansueli Etter, and Jürg Hanser, *Der Münsterhof in Zürich*, 2 vols. (Olten, 1982).

CHAPTER 3. FRIENDS AND RELATIONS

The best introduction to the subjects of Chapters 3 and 4 is Burguière et al. (eds.), *A History of the Family*, (p. 321 above), esp. chs. 8–9, 'Barbarian Europe' and 'The Carolingian Moment'. Geoffrey S. Nathan, *The Family in Late Antiquity: The Rise of Christianity and the Endurance of Tradition* (London, 2000), guides the reader through the late Roman heritage. David Herlihy, *Medieval Households* (Cambridge, MA, 1985), and Jack Goody, *The Development of the Family and Marriage in Europe* (Cambridge, 1983), are both important and contentious. Newer approaches, more alert to intra-familial interactions, are Katrien Heene, *The Legacy of Paradise: Marriage, Motherhood and Women in Carolingian Edifying Literature* (Frankfurt, 1997), Sally Crawford, *Childhood in Anglo-Saxon England* (Stroud, 1999), and Pauline Stafford, 'Parents and Children in the Early Middle Ages', *EME* 10 (2001), 257–71.

Naming practices in the ancient world are outlined by B. Salway, 'What's in a Name? A Survey of Roman Onomastic Practices from c.700 BC to AD 700', *Journal of Roman Studies*, 84 (1994), 124–45; late Roman conventions are explored in detail by Martin Heinzelmann, 'Les Changements de la dénomination latine à la fin de l'antiquité', in G. Duby and J. Le Goff (eds.), *Famille et parenté dans l'occident médiéval*, Collection de l'École Française de Rome, 30 (Rome, 1977), 19–24.

The most accessible introduction to Germanic names remains H. B. Woolf, *The Old Germanic Principles of Name-Giving* (Baltimore, 1939), now supplemented by Régine Le Jan, 'Personal Names and the Transformation of Kinship in Early Medieval Society (6th–10th centuries)', in G. T. Beech, M. Bourin, and P. Chareille (eds.), *Personal Names Studies of Medieval Europe: Social Identity and*

Familial Structures (Kalamazoo, MI, 2002), 31–50. Dieter Geuenich, Wofgang Haubrichs, and Jörg Jarnut (eds.), *Nomen et gens: Zur historischen Aussagekraft frühmittelalterlicher Personennamen* (Berlin, 1997), presents a range of new approaches to personal onomastics. Women's names are exhaustively analysed by Hans-Werner Goetz, '*Nomen Feminile*: Namen und Namengebung der Frauen im frühen Mittelalter', *Francia*, 23/1 (1966), 99–134; peasants' names by Carl I. Hammer, 'Servile Names and Seigneurial Organisation in Early Medieval Bavaria', *Studi Medievali*, 3rd ser., 36 (1995), 917–28, and J. Bessmerny, 'Les Structures de la famille paysanne dans les villages de la Francia au IXe siècle', *Le Moyen Âge*, 90 (1984), 165–93.

For Irish names (which lack any clear connection with patterns of kinship), see Brian Ó. Cuív, *Aspects of Irish Personal Names* (Dublin, 1986).

Introductions to burial archaeology are Guy Halsall, *Early Medieval Cemeteries: An Introduction to Burial Archaeology in the Post-Roman World* (Glasgow, 1995), and Edward James, 'Burials and Status in the Early Medieval West', *Transactions of the Royal Historical Society*, 5th ser., 39 (1989), 23–40. Megan McLaughlin, *Consorting with Saints: Prayer for the Dead in the Early Middle Ages* (Ithaca, NY, 1994), ch. 2, outlines Christian rituals for commemorating the dead. For kinship in this context, see C. Bouchard, 'Family Structure and Family Consciousness among the Aristocracy in the Ninth to Eleventh Centuries', *Francia*, 14 (1986), 639–58.

L. Génicot, *Les Généalogies*, Typologie des sources du moyen âge occidental, 15 (Turnhout, 1975), offers a general introduction to genealogies; for more detailed discussion, see Kenneth Sisam, 'Anglo-Saxon Royal Genealogies', *Proceedings of the British Academy*, 39 (1953), 287–348; D. N. Dumville, 'Kingship, Genealogies and Regnal Lists', in P. H. Sawyer and I. N. Wood (eds.), *Early Medieval Kingship* (Leeds, 1977), 72–104, and David Thornton, 'Orality, Literacy and Genealogy in Early Medieval Wales and Ireland', in Pryce (ed.), *Literacy in Medieval Celtic Societies*, 83–98 (p. 318 above). Gender issues of commemoration, memory, and identity are discussed by Matthew Innes, 'Keeping it in the Family: Women and Aristocratic Memory, 700–1200', in Elisabeth van Houts (ed.), *Medieval Memories: Men, Women and the Past, 700–1300* (Harlow, 2001), 17–35, and Ian Wood, 'Genealogy Defined by Women: The Case of the Pippinids', in Leslie Brubaker and Julia M. H. Smith (eds.), *Gender in the Early Medieval World: East and West, 300–900* (Cambridge, 2004), 234–56.

Much has been written on early medieval kinship, often informed by outdated or inappropriate legal and anthropological models: the sane comments on method and conceptualization of Anita Guerreau-Jalabert should be heeded in 'Sur les structures de parenté dans l'Europe médiévale', *Annales: Economies, Sociétés, Civilisations*, 36 (1981), 1028–49, and 'La Désignation des relations et des groupes de parenté en latin médiéval', *Archivum Latinitatis Medii Aevi*, 66–7 (1988), 65–108. Outdated notions of early medieval 'clans' are attacked by Pierre Guichard, 'De l'antiquité au moyen âge: Famille large et famille étroite', *Cahiers d'Histoire*, 24 (1979), 45–60, and definitively demolished by Alexander C. Murray, *Germanic*

Kinship Structure: Studies in Law and Society in Antiquity and the Early Middle Ages (Toronto, 1983).

Fundamental to the approaches and issues of this book are Isabelle Réal, *Vies de saints, vie de famille: Représentation et système de la parenté dans le royaume mérovingien (481–751) d'après les sources hagiographiques* (Turnout, 2001), Régine Le Jan, *Famille et pouvoir dans le monde franc (VIIe–Xe siècle): Essai d'anthropologie sociale* (Paris, 1995), and Karl Leyser, 'The German Aristocracy from the Ninth to the Early Twelfth Century: A Historical and Cultural Sketch', *Past and Present*, 41 (1968), 25–53. For a good example of a heavily Romanized culture, see P. D. King, *Law and Society in the Visigothic Kingdom* (Cambridge, 1972), ch. 8, 'The Family'.

On Anglo-Saxon England, Lorraine Lancaster, 'Kinship in Anglo-Saxon Society', *British Journal of Sociology*, 9 (1958), 230–50, 359–77, is central; H. R. Loyn, 'Kinship in Anglo-Saxon England', *Anglo-Saxon England*, 3 (1974), 197–209, remains useful. T. M. Charles-Edwards, *Early Irish and Welsh Kinship* (Oxford, 1993), repays careful attention.

On peasant households and kinship, see T. M. Charles-Edwards, 'Kinship, Status and the Origins of the Hide', *Past and Present*, 56 (1972), 3–33, supplemented by Carl I. Hammer, 'Family and *familia* in Early Medieval Bavaria', in R. Wall, J. Robin, and P. Laslett (eds.), *Family Forms in Historic Europe* (Cambridge, 1983), 217–48.

Important studies of the forms of artificial kinship promoted by Christianization are Joseph H. Lynch, *Godparents and Kinship in Early Medieval Europe* (Princeton, 1986), and id., *Christianizing Kinship: Ritual Sponsorship in Anglo-Saxon England* (Ithaca, NY, 1998). On kinlessness, T. M. Charles-Edwards, 'The Social Background to Irish *peregrinatio*', *Celtica*, 11 (1976), 43–59, is important.

For friendship, Verena Epp, *Amicitia: Zur Geschichte personaler, sozialer, politischer und geistlicher Beziehungen im frühen Mittelalter* (Stuttgart, 1999). Gerd Althoff, *Family, Friends and Followers: Political and Social Bonds in Early Medieval Europe*, trans. Christopher Carroll (Cambridge, 2004), and id., *Amicitiae und Pacta: Bündnis, Einung, Politik und Gebetsdenken im beginnenden 10. Jahrhundert*, MGH Schriften, 37 (Hanover, 1992), are valuable.

Except for Celticists, early medieval historians have been reluctant to tackle issues of honour and shame, which otherwise generally remain the preserve of literary analysis; see T. M. Charles-Edwards, 'Honour and Status in Some Irish and Welsh Prose Tales', *Eriu*, 29 (1978), 123–41, and M. E. Owen, 'Shame and Reparation: Women's Place in the Kin', in D. Jenkins and M. E. Owen (eds.), *The Welsh Law of Women* (Cardiff, 1980), 40–68. Judicious cautions against oversimplistic use of poetic sources are to be found in Katherine O'Brien O'Keeffe, 'Heroic Values and Christian Ethics', in *Cambridge Companion to Old English Literature*, ed. Godden and Lapidge, 107–125 (p. 317 above). Nira Pancer, *Sans peur et sans vergogne: De l'honneur et des femmes aux premiers temps mérovingiens* (Paris, 2001), provides the only detailed attempt to extend the analysis to the Continent and is restricted to the sixth century.

The seminal work that first addressed early medieval feuding remains essential: J. M. Wallace-Hadrill, 'The Blood-Feud of the Franks', in his *The Long-Haired Kings* (London, 1962), 121–47. To this should now be added W. I. Miller, 'Choosing the Avenger: Some Aspects of the Bloodfeud in Medieval Iceland and England', *Law and History Review*, 1 (1983), 159–204, and *Bloodtaking and Peacemaking: Feud, Law and Society in Saga Iceland* (Chicago, 1990), which, although primarily concerned with 12th–13th-century Iceland, nevertheless has much of general value to the early medievalist. Guy Halsall, 'Violence and Society in the Early Medieval West: An Introductory Survey', in Halsall (ed.), *Violence and Society in the Early Medieval West* (Woodbridge, 1998), 1–45, offers an unduly restricted understanding of 'feud'. Richard Fletcher, *Bloodfeud: Murder and Revenge in Anglo-Saxon England* (London, 2002), is an accessible, colourful piece of eleventh-century micro-history.

CHAPTER 4. MEN AND WOMEN

Gendered analysis of early medieval society is largely the work of anglophone scholars. For the issues involved, see Janet L. Nelson, 'Family, Gender and Sexuality in the Middle Ages', in Bentley (ed.), *Companion to Historiography*, 153–76 (p. 314 above); Pauline Stafford and Anneke Mulder-Bakker (eds.), *Gendering the Middle Ages* (Oxford, 2001), and Brubaker and Smith (eds.), *Gender in the Early Medieval World: East and West, 300–900* (p. 324 above), all with full references to additional bibliography. Contrasting approaches are sketched by Julia M. H. Smith, 'Did Women have a Transformation of the Roman World?', in Stafford and Mulder-Bakker (eds.), *Gendering the Middle Ages*, 22–41, and Guy Halsall, 'Gender and the End of Empire', *Journal of Medieval and Early Modern Studies*, 34 (2004), 17–39.

There are several books specifically on early medieval women, none of which is entirely reliable; these include Suzanne F. Wemple, *Women in Frankish Society: Marriage and the Cloister 500–900* (Philadelphia, 1981); Christine Fell, *Women in Anglo-Saxon England* (London, 1984); Lisa M. Bitel, *Land of Women: Tales of Sex and Gender from Early Ireland* (Ithaca, NY, 1996); ead., *Women in Early Medieval Europe, 400–1100* (Cambridge, 2002), and Patricia Skinner, *Women in Medieval Italian Society, 500–1200* (Harlow, 2001). There is much of value in Hans-Werner Goetz, *Frauen im frühen Mittelalter* (Cologne, 1995).

For men, see J. J. Cohen and B. Wheeler (eds.), *Becoming Male in the Middle Ages* (New York, 1997), D. M. Hadley (ed.), *Masculinity in Medieval Europe* (London, 1999), and Mathew Kuefler, *The Manly Eunuch: Masculinity, Gender Ambiguity and Christian Ideology in Late Antiquity* (Chicago, 2001). Carol Clover, 'Regardless of Sex: Men, Women and Power in Early Northern Europe', *Speculum*, 68 (1993), 363–87 (repr. in Nancy Partner (ed.), *Studying Medieval Women: Sex, Gender, Feminism* (Cambridge, MA, 1993)), offers a thoughtful comparative perspective based on early Icelandic evidence.

The key studies of burial, gender, and life cycle are Guy Halsall, 'Female Status and Power in Early Merovingian Austrasia: The Burial Evidence', *EME* 5 (1996), 1–24; id., *Settlement and Social Organization: The Merovingian Region of Metz* (Cambridge, 1995), and N. Stoodley, *The Spindle and the Spear: A Critical Enquiry into the Construction and Meaning of Gender in the Early Anglo-Saxon Burial Rite*, British Archaeological Reports British Series, 288 (Oxford, 1999).

The gendered aspects of domestic and agricultural work are analysed by Ludolf Kuchenbuch, '*Opus feminile*: Das Geschlechtsverhältnis im Spiegel von Frauenarbeit im früheren Mittelalter', in H.-W. Goetz (ed.), *Weibliche Lebensgestaltung im frühen Mittelalter* (Cologne, 1991), 139–75, and Jean-Pierre Devroey, 'Femmes au miroir des polyptyques: Une approche des rapports du couple dans l'exploitation rurale dépandante entre Seine et Rhin au IXe siècle', in Stéphane Lebecq, Alain Dierkens, Régine Le Jan, and Jean-Marie Sansterre (eds.), *Femmes et pouvoirs des femmes à Byzance et en Occident (VIe–XIe siècles)* (Villeneuve-d'Ascq, 1999), 227–49.

Marriage and sexual relationships are surveyed from the perspective of legal sources in James A. Brundage, *Law, Sex and Society in Medieval Europe* (Chicago, 1987). Key discussions of forms of marriage are Raymund Kottje, 'Eherechtliche Bestimmungen der germanischen Volksrechte (5.-8. Jh.)', in Werner Affeldt (ed.), *Frauen in Spätantike und Frühmittelalter: Lebensbedingungen, Lebensnormen, Lebensformen* (Sigmaringen, 1990), 211–20, and the papers in *Il Matrimonio nella società altomedioevale*, Settimane, 24, 2 vols. (1977). The late Roman background is evaluated by Judith Evans Grubb, *Law and Family in Late Antiquity: The Emperor Constantine's Marriage Legislation* (Oxford, 1995). For Anglo-Saxon England, Margaret Clunies Ross, 'Concubinage in Anglo-Saxon England', *Past and Present*, 108 (1985), 1–34, is crucial, while, for Ireland, Donnchadh Ó Corráin's articles, 'Marriage in Early Ireland', in Art Cosgrove (ed.), *Marriage in Ireland* (Dublin, 1985), 5–24, and 'Women and the Law in Early Ireland', in Mary O'Dowd and Sabine Wichert (eds.), *Chattel, Servant or Citizen: Women's Status in Church, State and Society* (Belfast, 1995), 45–57, are accessible complements to Charles-Edwards, *Early Irish and Welsh Kinship* (p. 325 above). See also Ruth Mazo Karras, 'Concubinage and Slavery in the Viking Age', *Scandinavian Studies*, 62 (1990), 141–62.

Mayke de Jong, 'To the Limits of Kinship: Anti-Incest Legislation in the Early Medieval West', in Jan Bremmer (ed.), *From Sappho to de Sade: Moments in the History of Sexuality* (London, 1989), 36–59, introduces the attempts to restrict choice of marriage partner, a subject surveyed in more detail by Patrick Corbet, *Autour de Burchard de Worms: L'Église allemande et les interdits de parenté (IXe–XIIe siècle)* (Frankfurt, 2001). Comparative analyses include: Bart Jaski, 'Marriage Laws in Ireland and on the Continent in the Early Middle Ages', in Christine Meek and Katharine Simms (eds.), *'The Fragility of her Sex'? Medieval Irishwomen in their European Context* (Dublin, 1996), 16–42, and Daffyd Walters, *The Comparative Legal Method: Marriage and Divorce and the Spouses' Property Rights in Early Medieval European Law and in Cyfraith Howel* (Aberystwyth, 1982).

Two studies by Carl I. Hammer address the issue of sexual relationships and marriage involving slaves, and of marriages among slaves: 'The Handmaid's Tale: Morganatic Relationships in Early-Mediaeval Bavaria', *Continuity and Change*, 19 (1995), 345–68, and 'A Slave Marriage Ceremony from Early Medieval Germany: A Note and a Document in Translation', *Slavery and Abolition*, 16 (1995), 243–9. Catalan comital marriage practices are surveyed in Martin Aurell, *Les Noces du comte: Mariage et pouvoir en Catalogne (785–1213)* (Paris, 1995).

Women, property, and inheritance are no longer the preserve of legal historians. For the late Roman background and the legislation of the successor kingdoms through to the seventh century, Antti Arjava, *Women and Law in Late Antiquity* (Oxford, 1996), is thorough, and can be supplemented by Karl Kroeschell, 'Söhne und Töchter im germanischen Erbrecht', in Götz Landwehr (ed.), *Studien zu den germanischen Volksrechte: Gedächtnisschrift für W. Ebel* (Frankfurt, 1982), 87–116.

There is now important work available on marital property transfers, women's access to property, and their role in familial inheritance strategies. Two recent conference volumes take thematic approaches to many different regions: 'Les Transferts patrimoniaux en Europe occidentale, VIIIe–Xe siècle: Actes de la table ronde de Rome, Mai 1999', published as *Mélanges de l'École Française de Rome—Moyen Age*, 111 (1999), pt. 2, and François Bougard, Laurent Feller, and Régine Le Jan (eds.), *Dots et douaires dans le haut moyen âge*, Collection de l'École Française de Rome, 295 (Rome, 2002).

Additional studies include Cristina La Rocca, 'Pouvoirs des femmes, pouvoirs de la loi dans l'Italie lombarde', in Lebecq et al. (eds.), *Femmes et pouvoirs des femmes*, 37–50 (p. 327 above); Brigitte Pohl-Resl, '"Quod me legibus contanget auere": Rechtsfähigkeit und Landbesitz langobardischer Frauen', *Mitteilungen des Instituts für Österreichische Geschichtsforschung*, 101 (1993), 201–27; Ingrid Heidrich, 'Besitz und Besitzverfügung verheirateter und verwitweter freier Frauen im Merowingischen Frankenreich', in Goetz (ed.), *Weibliche Lebensgestaltung*, 119–38 (p. 327 above). Inscriptional evidence from tenth- to eleventh-century Scandinavia is analysed by Birgit Sawyer, *Property and Inheritance in Viking Scandinavia: The Runic Evidence* (Alingsås, 1988). For late Anglo-Saxon England, the work of Pauline Stafford is crucial: see *Queen Emma and Queen Edith: Queenship and Women's Power in Eleventh-Century England* (Oxford, 1997), and references there to her earlier work on a wide range of issues.

The key study of the connections between family, commemoration, and inheritance strategy is Barbara Rosenwein, *To be the Neighbor of Saint Peter: The Social Meaning of Cluny's Property, 909–1049* (Ithaca, NY, 1989). The central role of women in commemoration and inheritance in Anglo-Saxon England is emphasized in two papers by Julia Crick: 'Women, Posthumous Benefaction, and Family Strategy in Pre-Conquest England', *Journal of British Studies*, 38 (1999), 399–422, and 'Posthumous Obligation and Family Identity', in William O. Frazer and Andrew Tyrrell (eds.), *Social Identity in Early Medieval Britain* (Leicester, 2000), 194–208. Brigitte Pohl-Resl, 'Vorsorge, Memoria und soziales Ereignis:

Frauen als Schenkerinnen in den bayerischen und alemannischen Urkunden des 8. und 9. Jahrhunderts', *Mitteilungen des Instituts für Österreichische Geschichtsforschung*, 103 (1995), 265–87, argues along similar lines.

Recent work suggests that widows hold the key to understanding many of these issues: see Janet L. Nelson, 'The Wary Widow', in Wendy Davies and Paul Fouracre (eds.), *Property and Power in the Early Middle Ages* (Cambridge, 1995), 82–113; Rolf H. Bremmer, 'Widows in Anglo-Saxon England', in Jan Bremmer and Lourens van den Bosch (eds.), *Between Poverty and the Pyre: Moments in the History of Widowhood* (London, 1995), 58–88, and Emmanuelle Santinelli, *Des Femmes éplorées? Les Veuves dans la société aristocratique du haut moyen âge* (Villeneuve-d'Ascq, 2003).

The argument that strategies of heirship changed in the eleventh century to permit the transfer of a family's entire inheritance from eldest son to eldest son was propounded by Georges Duby in a famous series of articles during the 1960s and 1970s; see chs. 3 and 6 of his *The Chivalrous Society*, trans. Cynthia Postan (London, 1977) for English versions. Criticisms of this outdated orthodoxy are Theodore Evergates, 'Nobles and Knights in Twelfth-Century France', in T. N. Bisson (ed.), *Cultures of Power: Lordship, Status and Process in Twelfth-Century Europe* (Philadelphia, 1995), 11–35, and Pauline Stafford, 'La Mutation familiale: A Suitable Case for Caution', in Joyce Hill and Mary Swan (eds.), *The Community, the Family and the Saint: Patterns of Power in Early Medieval Europe* (Turnhout, 1998), 103–25.

The figures on pp. 138–9 for the percentage of property owned by women are derived from the following studies: Arjava, *Women and Law in Late Antiquity* (p. 328 above); David Herlihy, 'Land, Family and Women in Continental Europe, 701–1200', *Traditio*, 18 (1962), 89–120, and Marc A. Meyer, 'Women's Estates in Later Anglo-Saxon England: The Politics of Possession', *Haskins Society Journal*, 3 (1991), 111–29.

The will of Eberhard and Gisela and associated charters used on pp. 143–5 are edited by Ignace de Coussemaker, *Cartulaire de l'abbaye de Cysoing et ses dependences*, 2 vols. (Lille, 1880), i. 1–11; see also the detailed analysis of Cristina La Rocca and Luigi Provero, 'The Dead and their Gifts: The Will of Eberhard, Count of Friuli and his Wife Gisela, Daughter of Louis the Pious (863–864)', in Frans Theuws and Janet L. Nelson (eds.), *Rituals of Power from Late Antiquity to the Early Middle Ages* (Leiden, 2000), 225–80.

CHAPTER 5. LABOUR AND LORDSHIP

The literature on early medieval social hierarchies is piecemeal and remains constrained by national historiographies. Almost the sole exception is Werner Rösener, *The Peasantry of Europe* (Oxford, 1994). For Anglo-Saxon England, see Pauline Stafford, *Unification and Conquest: A Political and Social History of England in the Tenth and Eleventh Centuries* (London, 1989); W. G. Runciman,

'Accelerating Social Mobility: The Case for Anglo-Saxon England', *Past and Present*, 104 (1984), 3–30; and Rosamond Faith, *The English Peasantry and the Growth of Lordship* (Leicester, 1997). David Pelteret, *Slavery in Early Medieval England from the Reign of Alfred to the Twelfth Century* (Woodbridge, 1995), is important. On Ireland, N. B. Aitchison, 'Kingship, Society and Sacralisation: Rank, Power and Ideology in Early Medieval Ireland', *Traditio*, 49 (1994), 45–75, and Paul Holm, 'The Slave Trade of Dublin, 9th–12th Centuries', *Peritia*, 5 (1986), 317–45, are both fresh and stimulating.

For the Continent, the standard but now outdated work on slavery is Charles Verlinden, *L'Esclavage dans l'Europe médiévale*, 2 vols. (Bruges, 1955; Ghent, 1977). The debate about the transition from slavery to serfdom has at times been intense, but still generally takes its cue from Marc Bloch, 'How and Why Ancient Slavery Came to an End', in *Slavery and Serfdom in the Middle Ages: Selected Essays by Marc Bloch*, trans. William R. Beer (Berkeley, 1975), 1–31. An important polemical contribution originally published in French in 1985 is Pierre Bonnassie, 'The Survivival and Extinction of the Slave System in the Early Medieval West (Fourth to Eleventh Centuries)', in id., *From Slavery to Serfdom in South-Western Europe*, trans. Jean Birrell (Cambridge, 1991), 1–59. Carl I. Hammer, *A Large-Scale Slave Society of the Early Middle Ages: Slaves and their Families in Early Medieval Bavaria* (Woodbridge, 2002), continues the debate. Wendy Davies, 'On Servile Status in the Early Middle Ages', in M. L. Bush (ed.), *Serfdom and Slavery: Studies in Legal Bondage* (London, 1996), 225–46, is both a sane analysis and a unique attempt to discuss continental and insular societies in tandem.

Nobility has inspired no such comparative treatment. Continental issues are well served by wide-ranging survey discussions in English that will guide the reader to all the relevant foreign-language literature. See Timothy Reuter, 'The Medieval Nobility in Twentieth-Century Historiography', in Bentley (ed.), *Companion to Historiography*, 177–202 (p. 314 above), J. B. Freed, 'Reflections on the Medieval German Nobility', *American Historical Review*, 91 (1986), 553–75, and Jane Martindale, 'The French Aristocracy in the Early Middle Ages: A Reappraisal', *Past and Present*, 75 (1977), 5–45 (repr. in ead., *Status, Authority and Regional Power: Aquitaine and France, 9th to 12th Centuries* (Aldershot, 1997), ch. IV). Paul Fouracre, 'The Origins of the Nobility in Francia', in Anne J. Duggan (ed.), *Nobles and Nobility in Medieval Europe: Concepts, Origins, Transformations* (Woodbridge, 2000), 17–24, is a concise update.

Le Jan, *Famille et pouvoir dans le monde franc* (p. 325 above), is important for all aspects of the continental nobility. Karl Ferdinand Werner, *Naissance de la noblesse* (Paris, 1998), is stimulating on cultural aspects and controversial on institutional ones. See also Hans-Werner Goetz, '"Nobilis": Der Adel im Selbstverständnis der Karolingerzeit', *Vierteljahrschrift für Sozial- und Wirtschaftsgeschichte*, 70 (1983), 153–91; Karl Bosl, '*Potens* und *pauper*: Begriffsgeschichtliche Studien zur gesellschaftlichen Differenzierung im frühen Mittelalter und zum "Pauperismus" des Hochmittelalters', in id., *Frühformen der Gesellschaft im mittelalterlichen Europa* (Munich, 1964), 106–34; Karl Leyser, 'Early Medieval Canon Law and the Beginnings of Knighthood', in Lutz Fenske, Werner Rösener, and Thomas Zotz (eds.), *Institutionen, Kultur und Gesellschaft im Mittelalter: Festschrift für Josef Fleckenstein zu seinem 65. Geburtstag* (Sigmaringen, 1984), 549–66 (repr. in id., *Communications and Power in Medieval Europe*, i: *The Carolingian and Ottonian Centuries*, ed. Timothy Reuter (London, 1994), 189–213).

Important essays on elite lifestyle are Timothy Reuter, 'Nobles and Others: The Social and Cultural Expression of Power Relations in the Middle Ages', in Duggan (ed.), *Nobles and Nobility*, 85–98 (p. 330 above), and Robin Fleming, 'The New Wealth, the New Rich and the New Political Style in Late Anglo-Saxon England', *Anglo-Norman Studies*, 23 (2000), 1–22.

Landlordship has generated a vast literature for the early medieval continent. See, in general, the sensitive if now somewhat old analysis of Georges Duby, *Rural Economy and Country Life in the Medieval West* (London, 1968). It is updated well by Philippe Contamine, Marc Bompaire, Stéphane Lebecq, and Jean-Luc Sarrazin, *L'Économie médiévale* (Paris, 1993), and Devroey, *Économie rurale et société* (p. 321 above). David Herlihy, 'Church Property on the European Continent, 701–1200', *Speculum*, 36 (1961), 81–105, attempts to assess how much land was in ecclesiastical hands, region by region, while Davies and Fouracre (eds.), *Property and Power in the Early Middle Ages* (p. 329 above), explores how land sustained political authority.

Most of the literature on estate organization deals only with the Frankish empire; an excellent introduction is Jean-Pierre Devroey, 'The Large Estate in the Frankish Kingdoms: A Tentative Dynamic Definition', in id., *Études sur le grand domaine carolingien* (Aldershot, 1993), ch. I. Adriaan Verhulst, *The Carolingian Economy* (Cambridge, 2002), is a useful overview, with detailed bibliography of the extensive technical literature. The following are particularly stimulating discussions: Ludolf Kuchenbuch, 'Die Klostergrundherrschaft im Frühmittelalter: Eine Zwischenbilanz', in Friedrich Prinz (ed.), *Herrschaft und Kirche: Beiträge zur Entstehung und Wirkungsweise episkopaler und monastischer Organisationsformen* (Stuttgart, 1988), 297–343; Fred Schwind, 'Zu karolingerzeitlichen Klöstern als Wirtschaftsorganismen und Stätten handwerklicher Tätigkeit', in Fenske et al. (eds.), *Institutionen, Kultur und Gesellschaft im Mittelalter*, 101–23 (above); Pierre Toubert, 'Il sistema curtense: La produzione e lo scambio interno in Italia nel secoli VIII, IX e X', in *Storia d'Italia: Annali, 6: Economia naturale, economia monetaria* (Turin, 1983), 5–63 (and reprinted in id., *Histoire du haut moyen âge et de l'Italie médiévale* (London, 1987), ch. VIII); Wickham, 'European Forests in the Early Middle Ages' (p. 320 above).

For the military aspects of lordship, Dick Whittaker, 'Landlords and Warlords', in John Rich and Graham Shipley (eds.), *Warfare and Society in the Roman World* (London, 1993), 277–302, is useful on the militarization of late Roman society throughout the empire. For a succint summary of debates about early medieval military recruitment, see Timothy Reuter, 'The Recruitment of Armies in the Early Middle Ages: What Can We Know?', in Anne Nørgård Jørgensen and Birthe L. Clausen (eds.), *Military Aspects of Scandinavian Society in a European*

Perspective, AD 1–1300 (Copenhagen, 1997), 32–7. See also Edward James, 'The Militarisation of Roman Society, 400–700', in ibid. 19–24; Bernard S. Bachrach, *Merovingian Military Organisation, 481–751* (Minneapolis, 1972); id., *Early Carolingian Warfare: Prelude to Empire* (Philadelphia, 2000); Richard Abels, *Lordship and Military Obligation in Anglo-Saxon England* (Berkeley, 1988); F. Prinz, *Klerus und Krieg im früheren Mittelalter: Untersuchungen zur Rolle der Kirche beim Aufbau der Königsherrschaft* (Stuttgart, 1971); Guy Halsall, *Warfare and Society in the Barbarian West, 450–900* (London, 2003).

The various networks of lordship that linked localities and regions, and then came together in the Carolingian polity, have received much attention recently in anglophone scholarship. Contrasting configurations, all with ample reference to foreign-language bibliography, are presented by Wendy Davies, *Small Worlds: The Village Community in Early Medieval Brittany* (London, 1988), Paul Fouracre, *The Age of Charles Martel* (Harlow, 2000), Matthew Innes, *State and Society in the Early Middle Ages: The Middle Rhine Valley, 400–1000* (Cambridge, 2000), and Simon MacLean, *Kingship and Politics in the Late Ninth Century: Charles the Fat and the End of the Carolingian Empire* (Cambridge, 2003). Susan Reynolds, *Fiefs and Vassals: The Medieval Evidence Reinterpreted* (Oxford, 1994), is refreshingly controversial on early medieval benefices.

Intense controversy currently swirls around the late tenth and early eleventh centuries. The emergence of knighthood, castles, and local lordships are specific themes within much larger debates about the relationship of social and political order, above all in France. Their flavour can be gauged from *Debating the Middle Ages*, eds. Little and Rosenwein, 105–210 (p. 314 above). The essays in Pierre Bonnassie and Pierre Toubert (eds.), *Hommes et sociétés dans l'Europe de l'an mil* (Toulouse, 2004), are thoughtful evaluations.

Details of the lands of St Peter's, Ghent, at the time of Einhard and Arnulf I, discussed on pp. 164–72, are derived from *Diplomata belgica ante annum millesimum centesimum scripta*, ed. M. Gysseling and A. C. F. Koch, i (Brussels, 1950), documents 49–56, pp. 123–49. See also Adriaan Verhulst, 'Over de stichting en vroegste geschiedenis van de Sint-Pieters en de Sint-Baafsabdijen te Gent', *Maatschappij voor Geschiedenis en Oudheidkunde te Gent*, niewe reeks, 7 (1953), 3–53, and Georges Declercq, 'Einhard und das karolingische Gent', in Hermann Schefers (ed.), *Einhard: Studien zum Leben und Werk* (Darmstadt, 1997), 223–46. For the town of Ghent, see Adriaan Verhulst and Georges Declercq, 'Early Medieval Ghent between Two Abbeys and the Count's Castle', in G. Decavele (ed.), *Ghent: In Defence of a Rebellious City* (Antwerp, 1989), 1–52 (repr. in Verhulst, *Rural and Urban Aspects of Early Medieval Northwest Europe* (Aldershot, 1992), ch. XII), and, for the broader context, David Nicholas, *Medieval Flanders* (London, 1992).

All this is but the tip of a bibliographical iceberg with vast dimensions and a deeply embedded historiographical problematic. Those interested in the latter can get a flavour of the issues from Otto Brunner, 'Feudalism: The History of a

Concept', in Frederic L. Cheyette (ed.), *Lordship and Community in Medieval Europe: Selected Readings* (New York, 1968), 32–61; J. W. Burrow, '"The Village Community" and the Uses of History in Nineteenth-Century England', in Neil McKendrick (ed.), *Historical Perspectives: Studies in English Thought and Society in Honour of J. H. Plumb* (London, 1974), 255–84, and Walter Pohl, 'Herrschaft', *Reallexikon der germanischen Altertumskunde*, 14 (1999), 445–57.

CHAPTER 6. GETTING AND GIVING

The literature on early medieval trade and exchange remains divided into many subspecialities, archaeological or historical, urban or rural, late antique or medieval. As an exercise in formulating an overview, Richard Hodges and David Whitehouse, *Mohammed, Charlemagne and the Origins of Europe: Archaeology and the Pirenne Thesis* (London, 1983), is stimulating and always controversial. For important new approaches, see Richard Hodges and William Bowden (eds.), *The Sixth Century: Production, Distribution and Demand* (Leiden, 1998), in conjunction with Inge Lyse Hansen and Chris Wickham (eds.), *The Long Eighth Century: Production, Distribution and Demand* (Leiden, 2000).

On the socio-economic aspects of the end of the western Roman Empire, I have taken my cue from Chris Wickham, 'The Other Transition: From the Ancient World to Feudalism', *Past and Present*, 113 (1984), 3–36, and 'Italy and the Early Middle Ages', in Klaus Randsborg (ed.), *The Birth of Europe: Archaeology and Social Development in the First Millennium AD* (Rome, 1989), 140–51 (both repr. in Wickham, *Land and Power* (p. 320 above). See also Michael Hendy, 'From Public to Private: The Western Barbarian Coinages as a Mirror of the Disintegration of Late Roman State Structures', *Viator*, 19 (1988), 29–78. For the contrary position, see Jean Durliat, *Les Finances publiques de Dioclétien aux carolingiens (284–889)* (Sigmaringen, 1990).

Michael McCormick, *The Origins of the European Economy: Communications and Commerce, AD 300–900* (Cambridge, 2001), combines important work on the Mediterranean region with a controversial argument about the centrality of the slave trade to economic change. For some of the issues it raises, see Edward James et al., '"Origins of the European Ecomony": A Debate with Michael McCormick', *EME* 12 (2003), 259–323. Peregrine Horden and Nicholas Purcell, *The Corrupting Sea: A Study of Mediterranean History* (Oxford, 2000), emphasizes Mediterranean micro-economies and webs of local 'connectivities'. The older study of Dietrich Claude remains crucial: *Untersuchungen zu Handel und Verkehr der vor- und frühgeschichtlichen Zeit in Mittel- und Nordeuropa, ii: Der Handel im westlichen Mittelmeer während des Frühmittelalters* (Göttingen, 1985).

Northern trading networks are the focus of *Untersuchungen zu Handel und Verkehr der vor- und frühgeschichtlichen Zeit in Mittel- und Nordeuropa, iii: Der Handel des frühen Mittelalters*, and iv: *Der Handel der Karolinger- und*

Wikingerzeit, both edited by Klaus Düwel, Herbert Jankuhn, Harald Siems, and Dieter Timpe (Göttingen, 1985 and 1987). The important contribution of Frisian traders is documented by Stéphane Lebecq, *Marchands et navigateurs frisons du haut moyen âge*, 2 vols. (Lille, 1983). Olivier Bruand, *Voyageurs et marchands aux temps carolingiens: Les Réseaux de communication entre Loire et Meuse aux VIIIe et IXe siècles* (Brussels, 2002), emphasizes the interplay of local, regional, and long-distance trade.

For the Irish Sea zone, see the contrasting interpretations of Jonathan M. Wooding, *Communication and Commerce along the Western Sea Lanes, AD 400–800*, British Archaeological Reports International Series, 654 (Oxford, 1996), and Ewan Campbell, 'The Archaeological Evidence for External Contacts: Imports, Trade and Economy in Celtic Britain, AD 400–800', in Kenneth R. Dark (ed.), *External Contacts and the Economy of Late Roman and Post-Roman Britain* (Woodbridge, 1996), 83–96. Mary A. Valante, 'Reassessing the Irish "Monastic Town"', *Irish Historical Studies*, 31 (1998), 1–18, offers a cautious assessment of exchange in pre-Viking Ireland. Sally Foster, Allan Macinnes, and Ranald MacInnes (eds.), *Scottish Power Centres from the Early Middle Ages to the Twentieth Century* (Glasgow, 1998), and Stephen T. Driscoll and Margaret R. Nieke (eds.), *Power and Politics in Early Medieval Britain and Ireland* (Edinburgh, 1988), pay proper attention to hillforts and other high-status sites.

Towns—attempts to define them, the fate of Roman cities, urban origins in non-Roman Europe—are the subject of intense debate. J. H. W. G. Liebeschuetz, *The Decline and Fall of the Roman City* (Oxford, 2001), draws a huge specialist literature together; a contrasting, succinct overview is S. J. B. Barnish, 'The Transformation of Classical Cities and the Pirenne Debate', *Journal of Roman Archaeology*, 2 (1989), 385–400. Richard Hodges, *Towns and Trade in the Age of Charlemagne* (London, 2000), argues enthusiastically for a new Carolingian economic order. Italian cities have their own special debates: Bryan Ward-Perkins, 'Continuists, Catastrophists and the Towns of Post-Roman Northern Italy', *Papers of the British School at Rome*, 65 (1997), 157–76, and Ross Balzaretti, 'Cities and Markets in the Early Middle Ages', in G. Ausenda (ed.), *After Empire: Towards an Ethnology of Europe's Barbarians* (Woodbridge, 1995), 113–42.

The Cambridge Urban History of Britain, i: *600–1540* (Cambridge, 2000), ed. David Palliser, includes judicious overviews of the large literature on Anglo-Saxon towns; on relationships between towns and regional economies, see Christopher Scull, 'Urban Centres in pre-Viking England?', in John Hines (ed.), *The Anglo-Saxons from the Migration Period to the Eighth Century: An Ethnographic Perspective* (Woodbridge, 1998), 269–310, and Robin Fleming, 'Rural Elites and Urban Communities in Late Saxon England', *Past and Present*, 141 (1993), 3–37. Trading privileges in London are discussed by Susan Kelly, 'Trading Privileges from Eighth-Century England', *EME* 1 (1992), 3–28.

Adriaan Verhulst, *The Rise of Cities in North-West Europe* (Cambridge, 1999), reviews recent work on towns and emporia throughout the Low Countries. Details of Scandinavian emporia are accessible in either Helen Clarke and Björn

Ambrosiani, *Towns in the Viking Age* (Leicester, 1991), or Johan Callmer, 'Urbanization in Scandinavia and the Baltic Region, 700–1100: Trading Places, Centres and Early Urban Sites', in Helen Clarke and Björn Ambrosiani (eds.), *The Twelfth Viking Congress: Developments around the Baltic and the North Sea in the Viking Age*, Birka Studies, 3 (Stockholm, 1994), 50–90. On non-Roman Europe, see H. B. Clarke and Anngret Simms (eds.), *The Comparative History of Urban Origins in Non-Roman Europe: Ireland, Wales, Denmark, Germany, Poland and Russia from the Ninth to the Thirteenth Century*, British Archaeological Reports International Series, 255, 2 vols. (Oxford, 1985).

The extensive, specialized literature on coinage is best approached through Peter Spufford, *Money and its Uses in Medieval Europe* (Cambridge, 1988), and Philip Grierson and Mark Blackburn, *Medieval European Coinage with a Catalogue of the Coins of the Fitzwilliam Museum, Cambridge*, i: *the Early Middle Ages (5th–10th centuries)* (Cambridge, 1986).

All discussions of giving and getting go back, in various ways, to Philip Grierson, 'Commerce in the Dark Ages: A Critique of the Evidence', *Transactions of the Royal Historical Society*, 5th ser., 9 (1959), 123–40 (repr. in Grierson, *Dark Age Numismatics* (London, 1979)). On gift exchange, see also Jürgen Hannig, '*Ars donandi*: Zur Ökonomie des Schenkens im früheren Mittelalter', in Richard van Dülmen (ed.), *Armut, Liebe, Ehre* (Frankfurt, 1988), 11–37, and Arnoud-Jan Bijsterveld, 'The Medieval Gift as Agent of Social Bonding and Political Power: A Comparative Approach', in Esther Cohen and Mayke de Jong (eds.), *Medieval Transformations: Texts, Power and Gifts in Context* (Leiden, 2001), 123–56.

Critical approaches to treasure are set out in Sauro Gelichi and Cristina La Rocca (eds.), *Tesori: Forme di accumulazione della ricchezza nell'alto medioevo (secoli V–XI)* (Rome, 2004). Some of the papers in E. M. Tyler (ed.), *Treasure in the Medieval West* (York, 2000), are also relevant. A wide range of textual and material evidence is assessed by Matthias Hardt, 'Royal Treasures and Representation in the Early Middle Ages', in Walter Pohl and Helmut Reimitz (eds.), *Strategies of Distinction: The Construction of Ethnic Communities, 300–800* (Leiden, 1998), 255–80. On changing forms and uses of material wealth, see Cristina La Rocca, 'Segni di distinzione: Dai corredi funerari alle donazioni "post obitum" nel regno longobardo', in L. Paroli (ed.), *L'Italia centro-settentrionale in età longobarda* (Florence, 1997), 31–54. Timothy Reuter, 'Plunder and Tribute in the Carolingian Empire', *Transactions of the Royal Historical Society*, 5th ser., 35 (1985), 75–94, is now classic.

For women's participation in gift giving, see Michael J. Enright, 'Lady with a Mead Cup', *Frühmittelalterliche Studien*, 22 (1988), 170–203; also Bonnie Effros, *Creating Community with Food and Drink in Merovingian Gaul* (New York, 2002), and the Further Reading for Chapter 7 on queens. Additional aspects of the social context are suggested by Donald A. Bullough, *Friends, Neighbours and Fellow-Drinkers: Aspects of Community and Conflict in the Early Medieval West*, H. M. Chadwick Memorial Lecture (Cambridge, 1990).

The social and symbolic values of weapons are discussed by Régine Le Jan,

'Frankish Giving of Arms and Rituals of Power: Continuity and Change in the Carolingian Period', and Heinrich Härke, 'The Circulation of Weapons in Anglo-Saxon Society', both in Theuws and Nelson (eds.), *Rituals of Power*, 281–309, 377–99 (p. 329 above). See also Charlotte Fabech, 'Booty Sacrifices in Southern Scandinavia: A Reassessment', in P. Garwood, D. Jennings, R. Skenates and J. Toms (eds.), *Sacred and Profane: Proceedings of a Conference on Archaeology, Ritual and Religion, Oxford 1989* (Oxford, 1991), 88–99.

Irish cattle-clientage is analysed in Nerys Patterson's stimulating and controversial *Cattle Lords and Clansmen: The Social Structure of Early Ireland*, 2nd edn. (Notre Dame, IN, 1994). A. T. Lucas, *Cattle in Ancient Ireland* (Kilkenny, 1989), and Fergus Kelly, *Early Irish Farming* (Dublin, 1998), are both thorough, technical assessments.

Details on pp. 197–8 of the royal treasury in late-tenth-century Pavia are recorded in the *Instituta Regalia*, incorporated into the *Honorantiae Civitatis Papiae*, ed. Carlrichard Brühl and Cinzio Violante, *Die 'Honorantie Civitatis Papie'* (Cologne, 1983).

For the 'Prince of Prittlewell' described on pp. 206–7, see the feature on 'Prittlewell: Treasures of a King of Essex', *Current Archaeology*, 16/10 (February 2004), 430–6, and, for updates as post-excavation work continues, the regularly maintained website of the Museum of London Archaeology Service, http://www.molas.org.uk .

The sketch of Einhard on pp. 210–12 is derived from his letters, trans. in Paul Edward Dutton, *Charlemagne's Courtier: The Complete Einhard* (Peterborough, ONT, 1998), 131–64, and ed. K. Hampe, MGH Epp. V, pp. 105–42; see also Julia M. H. Smith, 'Einhard: The Sinner and the Saints', *Transactions of the Royal Historical Society*, 6th ser., 13 (2003), 55–77.

The Holy Lance discussed on pp. 212–13 is studied by Percy Ernst Schramm, 'Die "Heilige Lanze", Reliquie und Herrschaftszeichen und ihre Replik in Krakau', in his *Herrschaftszeichen und Staatssymbolik*, MGH Schriften 13, 3 vols. (Stuttgart, 1954–6), ii. 492–537.

CHAPTER 7. KINGSHIP AND CHRISTIANITY

In view of the fact that Christianity and Christian monarchy were hugely influential in shaping medieval and modern national identities, the bibliography on this subject is vast. Valuable surveys are Richard Fletcher, *The Conversion of Europe: From Paganism to Christianity, 371–1386 AD* (London, 1997), and Arnold Angenendt, *Das Frühmittelalter: Die abendländische Christenheit vom 400 bis 900* (Stuttgart, 1990). Peter Brown, *The Rise of Western Christendom: Triumph and Diversity, AD 200–1000*, 2nd edn. (Oxford, 2003), is a magisterial summation from a cultural history perspective.

Pre-Christian religious traditions are hard to grasp, and should not be con-fused with the retrospective mythologies presented by literary sources of the twelfth century and later. Beliefs and practices in Ireland and other Celtic-speaking regions are especially elusive, owing to a lack of archaeological evidence for cult practices from the immediately pre-Christian period. For Slavic regions of central-northern Europe, see Lleszek Paweł Słupecki, 'Au déclin des dieux slaves', in Michel Rouche (ed.), *Clovis: histoire et mémoire. Le Baptême de Clovis, son écho à travers l'histoire*, Actes du colloque internationale d'histoire de Reims, 2 vols. (Paris, 1997), ii. 289–314, and id., *Slavonic Pagan Sanctuaries* (Warsaw, 1994). Michael Müller-Willer, *Opferkulte der Germanen und Slawen* (Stuttgart, 1999), is an excellent photographic record and brief discussion of cult places and sacrifices.

Germanic religious traditions have been intensively studied since the early nineteenth century. Among recent work, see Green, *Language and History*, chs. 1, 15 (p. 317 above), Ian Wood, 'Pagan Religions and Superstitions East of the Rhine from the Fifth to the Ninth Century', in Ausenda (ed.), *After Empire*, 253–79 (p. 334 above), and Heinrich Beck, Detlev Elmers, and Kurt Schier (eds.), *German-ische Religionsgeschichte: Quellen und Quellenprobleme* (Berlin, 1992). A judicious survey of the Anglo-Saxon textual material is J. D. Niles, 'Pagan Survival and Popular Belief', in Godden and Lapidge (eds.), *Cambridge Companion to Old Eng-lish Literature*, 124–41 (p. 317 above).

Ian Wood, *The Missionary Life: Saints and the Evangelisation of Europe, 400–1050* (Harlow, 2001), explores early medieval literary representations of missionary achievements. See also Richard E. Sullivan, *Christian Missionary Activity in the Early Middle Ages* (Aldershot, 1994), and Knut Schäferdiek (ed.), *Kirchengeschichte als Missionsgeschichte*, ii: *Die Kirche des früheren Mittelalters* (Munich, 1978). Conversion within the household and women's contribution more generally is the subject of Cordula Nolte, *Conversio und Christianitas: Frauen in der Christianisierung von 5. bis 8. Jahrhundert* (Stuttgart, 1995). Parts of this book's arguments can be sampled in ead., 'Gender and Conversion in the Merovingian Era', in James Muldoon (ed.), *Varieties of Religious Conversion in the Middle Ages* (Gainesville, FL, 1997), 81–99.

Regional and national approaches to the spread of Christianity are as follows:

British Isles: Charles Thomas, *Christianity in Roman Britain to AD 500* (London, 1981); T. M. Charles-Edwards, *Early Christian Ireland* (Cambridge, 2000); Richard Gameson (ed.), *St Augustine and the Conversion of England* (Stroud, 1999); John Blair, *The Church in Anglo-Saxon Society* (Oxford, 2005); Barbara E. Crawford (ed.), *Conversion and Christianity in the North Sea World* (St Andrews, 1998).

Frankish lands: of the vast literature on the baptism of Clovis, Danuta Shanzer, 'Dating the Baptism of Clovis: The Bishop of Vienne vs the Bishop of Tours', *EME*, 7 (1998), 29–57, is crucial and has extensive references to earlier bib-liography. J. M. Wallace-Hadrill, *The Frankish Church* (Oxford, 1983), surveys

Merovingian and Carolingian Christianity. An alternative approach is Lutz E. von Padberg, *Mission und Christianisierung: Formen und Folgen bei Angelsachsen und Franken im 7. und 8. Jahrhundert* (Stuttgart, 1995). On Frisia and Saxony, see, respectively, Stéphane Lebecq, 'Les Frisons entre paganisme et Christianisme', in *Christianisation et déchristianisation*, Publication du Centre de Recherches d'Histoire Religieuse et d'Histoire d'Idées, 9 (Angers, 1986), 19–45, and Ruth Mazo Karras, 'Pagan Survivals and Syncretism in the Conversion of Saxony', *Catholic Historical Review*, 72 (1986), 553–72.

Norse world: Birgit Sawyer, Peter Sawyer, and Ian Wood (eds.), *The Christianisation of Scandinavia* (Alingsås, 1987), can now be accompanied by Birgit Sawyer, *The Viking-Age Rune Stones: Custom and Commemoration in Early Medieval Scandinavia* (Oxford, 2000), ch. 6 ('Conversion'). For Iceland, Jenny Jochens, 'Late and Peaceful: Iceland's Conversion through Arbitration in 1000', *Speculum*, 74 (1999), 621–55, is illuminating.

Central Europe: the best survey is in J.-M. Mayeur, C. Pietri, L. Pietri, A. Vauchez, and M. Venard (eds.), *Histoire du Christianisme*, iv: *Évêques, moines et empereurs, 610–1054* (Paris, 1993), pt. IV, chs. 1–2. See also Premysław Urbańczyk, *Early Christianity in Central and East Europe* (Warsaw, 1997), and Michael Müller-Wille (ed.), *Rom und Byzanz im Norden: Mission und Glaubenswechsel im Ostseeraum während des 8.–14. Jahrhunderts*, 2 vols. (Mainz, 1997–8).

The evolution of norms of correct Christianity from their late antique origins can be tracked through William Klingshirn, *Caesarius of Arles: The Making of a Christian Community in Late Antique Gaul* (Cambridge, 1994), and Robert Markus, 'From Caesarius to Boniface: Christianity and Paganism in Gaul', in Jacques Fontaine and J. N. Hillgarth (eds.), *Le Septième Siècle: Changements et continuités* (London, 1992), 154–72. On their Carolingian implementation from Boniface onwards, see Rosamond McKitterick, *The Frankish Church and the Carolingian Reforms, 789–895* (London, 1977). Dieter Harmening, *Superstitio: Überlieferungs- und theoriegeschichtliche Untersuchungen zur kirchlich-theologischen Aberglaubensliteratur des Mittelalters* (Berlin, 1979), is crucial on the concept of 'superstition'.

The best introduction to early medieval political thinking is *The Cambridge History of Medieval Political Thought c.350–c.1450*, ed. J. H. Burns (Cambridge, 1988). For an emphasis on kingship, see J. M. Wallace-Hadrill, *Early Germanic Kingship in England and on the Continent* (Oxford, 1971), Marc Reydellet, *La Royauté dans la littérature latine de Sidoine Apollinaire à Isidore de Séville* (Rome, 1981), and Hans Hubert Anton, *Fürstenspiegel und Herrscherethos in der Karolingerzeit* (Bonn, 1986). There has been much discussion of whether early medieval kingship was in some sense 'sacral'. Wallace-Hadrill, *Early Germanic Kingship*, ch. 1, cautiously restates the traditional view, but see now Green, *Language and History*, ch. 7 (p. 317 above), and Eve Picard, *Germanisches Sakralkönigtum? Quellenkritisches Studien zur Germania des Tacitus und zur altnordischen Überlieferung* (Heidelberg, 1991). The highly technical literature on royal consecration rituals is best approached through the articles of Janet L. Nelson, assembled in her *Politics and Ritual in Early Medieval Europe* (London, 1996), esp. ch. 12, 'Inauguration Rituals'.

On queens and queenship, see Pauline Stafford, 'The King's Wife in Wessex, 800–1066', *Past and Present*, 91 (1981), 3–27; ead., 'Queens, Nunneries and Re-forming Churchmen: Gender, Religious Status and Reform in Tenth- and Eleventh-Century England', ibid. 163 (1999), 3–35; Janet L. Nelson, 'Early Me-dieval Rites of Queen-Making and the Shaping of Medieval Queenship', in Anne Duggan (ed.), *Queens and Queenship in Medieval Europe* (Woodbridge, 1997), 301–15; Geneviève Bührer-Thierry, 'Les Reines adultères', *Cahiers de Civilisation Médiévale*, 35 (1992), 299–312.

The connections between ideology and politics are underlined by Pauline Stafford, 'The Laws of Cnut and the History of Anglo-Saxon Royal Promises', *Anglo-Saxon England*, 10 (1981), 173–90, and Janet L. Nelson, 'Bad Kingship in the Earlier Middle Ages', *Haskins Society Journal*, 8 (1996), 1–26. On Hincmar of Reims, see Nelson, *Politics and Ritual*, ch. 7, 'Kingship, Law and Liturgy in the Political Thought of Hincmar of Rheims', and Jean Devisse, *Hincmar, archevêque de Reims, 845–882*, 3 vols. (Geneva, 1975–6). For the influence of the Bible on political ideas, see Raymund Kottje, *Studien zum Einfluss des Alten Testamentes auf Recht und Liturgie des frühen Mittelalters* (Bonn, 1970), and, more recently, 'The Power of the Word: The Influence of the Bible on Early Medieval Politics', a collection of articles in *EME* 7 (1998).

An overview of kingship in the Celtic-language zone is Wendy Davies, 'Celtic Kingships in the Early Middle Ages', in Anne Duggan (ed.), *Kings and Kingship in Medieval Europe* (London, 1993), 101–24. A succinct assessment of Irish conceptions is Philip O'Leary, 'A Foreseeing Driver of an Old Chariot: Regal Moderation in Early Irish Literature', *Cambridge Medieval Celtic Studies*, 11 (1986), 1–16; for a fuller discussion, see Bart Jaksi, *Early Irish Kingship and Succession* (Dublin, 2000). On similarities and differences between Irish and Germanic kings, Patrick Wormald, 'Celtic and Anglo-Saxon Kingship: Some Further Thoughts', in Paul E. Szarmach (ed.), *Sources of Anglo-Saxon Culture* (Kalamazoo, MI, 1986), 151–83, is fundamental.

Hincmar's treatise *De regis persona et regio ministerio* discussed on pp. 243–4 is edited in *PL* 125, cols. 833–56. One of Hincmar's other treatises on kingship is available in English translation: 'On the Governance of the Palace', in either David Herlihy, *A History of Feudalism* (New York, 1970), 209–27, or Paul Edward Dutton, *Carolingian Civilization: A Reader* (Peterborough, ONT, 1993), 485–99.

Pseudo-Cyprian, mentioned on pp. 247 and 249, is edited by Sigmund Hell-mann, *De duodecim abusivis saeculi*, Texte und Untersuchungen zur altchristlichen Literatur, 3rd ser, 4 (Leipzig, 1909), and is ably assessed by Rob Meens, 'Politics, Mirrors of Princes and the Bible: Kings and the Well-Being of the Realm', *EME* 7 (1998), 345–57.

The law codes of Stephen of Hungary referred to on p. 218 are translated in *The Laws of the Medieval Kingdom of Hungary*, ed. and trans. G. Bónis, J. M. Bak, and J. R. Sweeney, 2 vols. (Bakersfield, CA, 1985–90); Hartvic's Life of St Stephen is available in *Medieval Hagiography: An Anthology*, ed. Thomas Head (New York, 2000).

CHAPTER 8. ROME AND THE PEOPLES OF EUROPE

The study of the formation of early medieval kingdoms has been transformed in recent years by attention to ethnicity as a complex, shifting, social phenomenon involving the cultural and political projections of notions of self and others. In the absence of any full new synthesis, the best introduction in English is the short, suggestive essay of Walter Pohl, 'The Barbarian Successor States', in Leslie Webster and Michelle Brown (eds.), *The Transformation of the Roman World*, AD 400–900 (London, 1997), 33–47. On images of 'barbarians', see Peter Heather, 'The Barbarian in Late Antiquity: Image, Reality and Transformation', in Richard Miles (ed.), *Constructing Identities in Late Antiquity* (London, 1999), 234–58, and Yves-Albert Dauge, *Le Barbare: Recherches sur la conception romaine de la barbarie et de la civilisation* (Brussels, 1981).

On the emergence of early medieval ethnicities, recent debates owe much to the stimulus of German and Austrian conceptualizations, and generally take the continental 'Germanic' peoples as their frame of reference. The starting point for all recent work is Reinhard Wenskus, *Stammesbildung und Verfassung: Das Werden der frühmittelalterlichen Gentes* (Cologne, 1961). Wenskus's approach has now been developed into a theory of ethnogenesis; see Patrick Geary, 'Ethnic Identity as Situational Construct in the Early Middle Ages', *Mitteilungen der anthropologischen Gesellschaft in Wien*, 113 (1983), 15–26, and, with more sophistication, Walter Pohl, 'Tradition, Ethnogenese und literarische Gestaltung: Eine Zwischenbilanz', in Karl Brunner and Brigitte Merta (eds.), *Ethnogenese und Überlieferung: Angewandte Methoden der Frühmittelalterforschung*, Veröffentlichungen des Institut für Österreichische Geschichtsforschung, 31 (Vienna, 1994), 9–26. Herwig Wolfram, '*Origo et religio*: Ethnic Traditions and Literature in Early Medieval Texts', *EME* 3 (1994), 19–38, is a succinct English-language expression of the views of one of the leading exponents of ethnogenesis theory. Wolfram's approach also informs the recent general, though controversial, overview of Patrick Geary, *The Myth of Nations: The Medieval Origins of Europe* (Princeton, 2001). For ethnicity in the Carolingian period, see Walter Pohl, 'Zur Bedeutung ethnischer Unterscheidungen in der frühen Karolingerzeit', *Studien zur Sachsenforschung*, 12 (1999), 193–208.

To sample the debates and criticisms surrounding the 'ethnogenesis' approach, the following volumes of essays are useful: Pohl and Reimitz (eds.), *Strategies of Distinction* (p. 335 above); Andrew Gillett (ed.), *On Barbarian Identity: Critical Approaches to Ethnicity in the Early Middle Ages* (Turnhout, 2002), and Hans-Werner Goetz, Jörg Jarnut, and Walter Pohl (eds.), *Regna and Gentes: The*

Relationship between Late Antique and Early Medieval Peoples and Kingdoms in the Transformation of the Roman World (Leiden, 2003).

A traditionally important line of approach is philological—and it is only modern linguistic classification that imposes a unified view on Europe's invaders as 'Germanic': see Green, *Language and History* (p. 317 above), and Walter Pohl, *Die Germanen* (Munich, 2000). On literary representations of identity and origin legends, see Walter Goffart, *The Narrators of Barbarian History (AD 550–800)* (Princeton, 1988); specifically on Jordanes, see Peter Heather, *Goths and Romans, 332–489* (Oxford, 1991), 3–67, which supersedes previous discussions.

Archaeologists contribute complementary approaches, which are crucial for northern Europe. Lotte Hedeager, *Iron Age Societies: From Tribe to State in Northern Europe, 500 BC to AD 700* (Oxford, 1992), led the way; in addition see Howard B. Clarke, Máire Ní Mhaonaigh, and Ragnall Ó Floinn (eds.), *Ireland and Scandinavia in the Early Viking Age* (Dublin, 1998), and Tania Dickinson and David Griffiths (eds.), *The Making of Kingdoms* (Oxford, 1999).

The insular world is well represented in the archaeological literature but largely absent from the 'ethnogenesis' debates. Exceptions from an Anglo-Saxon perspective are John Moreland, 'Ethnicity, Power and the English', in William O. Frazer and Andrew Tyrrell (eds.), *Social Identity in Early Medieval Britain* (London, 2000), 23–51, Nicholas Brooks, 'The English Origin Myth', in his *Anglo-Saxon Myths: State and Church, 400–1066* (London, 2000), 79–89, and Patrick Wormald, '*Engla Lond*: The Making of an Allegiance', *Journal of Historical Sociology*, 7 (1994), 1–24. Approaches to Scottish, Welsh, and Irish material remain predominantly text-historical, conceptualized with reference to shifting historiographies of the British Isles and the heavy weight of English hegemony within them. On Ireland, see Donnchadh Ó Corráin, 'Nationality and Kingship in Pre-Norman Ireland', in T. W. Moody (ed.), *Nationality and the Pursuit of Independence* (Belfast, 1978), 1–35, and John Carey, *The Irish National Origin-Legend: Synthetic Pseudohistory*, Quiggin Pamphlets on the Sources of Medieval Gaelic History, 1 (Cambridge, 1994). On Wales, there are valuable comments in P. P. Sims-Williams, 'Some Functions of Origin Stories in Early Medieval Wales', in Tore Nyberg, Iørn Piø, Preben Meulengracht Sørensen, and Aage Trommer (eds.), *History and Heroic Tale: A Symposium* (Odense, 1985), 97–131; and for Scotland, a recent important contribution is Dauvit Broun, 'The Origin of Scottish Identity', in Claus Bjørn, Alexander Grant, and Keith Stringer (eds.), *Nations, Nationalism and Patriotism in the European Past* (Copenhagen, 1994), 34–55.

In addition to the Further Reading on political ideas cited for Chapter 7, for the concept of 'empire', see Karl Ferdinand Werner, 'L'Empire carolingien et le Saint Empire', in Maurice Duverger (ed.), *Le Concept d'empire* (Paris, 1980), 151–202. Three articles by Steven Fanning take a helpful look at the use of the word *imperium*: 'Jerome's Concept of Empire', in Loveday Alexander (ed.), *Images of Empire* (Sheffield, 1991), 239–50, 'Bede, *imperium* and the Bretwaldas', *Speculum*, 66 (1991), 1–26, and 'Clovis Augustus and Merovingian *imitatio imperii*', in Kathleen Mitchell and Ian Wood (eds.), *The World of Gregory of Tours*

(Leiden, 2002), 321–35. For the appropriation of imperial vocabulary and rituals of rulership in the successor kingdoms, see Michael McCormick, *Eternal Victory: Triumphal Rulership in Late Antiquity, Byzantium and the Early Medieval West* (Cambridge, 1986).

Of the vast literature on Charlemagne and his imperial coronation, the best overview remains Donald Bullough, *The Age of Charlemagne* (London, 1965). The sumptuous catalogue from the 1999 exhibition at Paderborn is accompanied by many valuable essays on a wide range of subjects: Christoph Stiegemann and Matthias Wemhoff (eds.), *799: Kunst und Kultur der Karolingerzeit. Karl der Grosse und Papst Leo III. in Paderborn*, 3 vols. (Mainz, 1999). For the empire and cultural world of Otto I, see the equally lavish catalogue and essay volume from the 2001 exhibition at Magdeburg: Matthias Puhle (ed.), *Otto der Grosse: Magdeburg und Europa*, 2 vols. (Mainz, 2001). On Otto III, Gerd Althoff, *Otto III.* (Darmstadt, 1996), is now available in English translation (University Park, PA, 2003). Otto III's empire building in central Europe is put into broad cultural context by the third major international exhibition catalogue of recent years, Alfried Wieczorek and Hans-Martin Hinz (eds.), *Europas Mitte um 1000*, 3 vols. (Darmstadt, 2000); *Europe's Centre around 1000*, 2 vols. (Stuttgart, 2000), is an English translation of the essays but lacks the illustrations. Stefan Weinfurter, *The Salian Century: Main Currents in an Age of Transition*, trans. Barbara M. Bowlus (Philadelphia, 1999), takes Germany into the eleventh century. Detailed accounts are available of both Cnut and Conrad II: M. K. Lawson, *Cnut: the Danes in England in the Early Eleventh Century* (Harlow, 1993), and Herwig Wolfram, *Konrad II. 990–1039: Kaiser dreier Reiche* (Munich, 2000).

The place of Rome in medieval imagination is the subject of Andrea Giardina and André Vauchez, *Rome: L'Idée et le mythe du moyen âge à nos jours* (Paris, 2000), and, for the insular world, should be supplemented by Éamon Ó Carragáin's important essay, *The City of Rome and the World of Bede* (Jarrow, 1994). Richard Krautheimer's classic presentation of the city itself, *Rome: Portrait of a City, 312–1308* (Princeton, 1980), is now significantly modified by recent archaeological and architectural work. Several volumes of essays make this, and much more, accessible: Julia M. H. Smith (ed.), *Early Medieval Rome and the Christian West* (Leiden, 2000); *Roma nell'alto medioevo*, Settimane, 48, 2 vols. (Spoleto, 2001), and *Roma fra oriente e occidente*, Settimane, 49, 2 vols. (Spoleto, 2002). All these have useful material on pilgrimage to Rome; see also Clare Stancliffe, 'Kings who Opted out', in Patrick Wormald, Donald Bullough, and Roger Collins (eds.), *Ideal and Reality in Frankish and Anglo-Saxon Society: Studies Presented to J. M. Wallace-Hadrill* (Oxford, 1983), 154–76, and Kathleen Hughes, 'The Celtic Church and the Papacy', in C. H. Lawrence (ed.), *The English Church and the Papacy in the Middle Ages* (London, 1965), 3–28 (repr. in Hughes, *Church and Society in Ireland, AD 400–1200*, ed. David Dumville (London, 1987), ch. XV).

No subject has suffered from the search for the linear antecedents of later developments more than the papacy, a problem that not even the best recent survey, Bernhard Schimmelpfennig, *The Papacy*, trans. James Sievert (New York,

1992), has avoided. An alternative approach is sketched by Thomas F. X. Noble, 'Morbidity and Vitality in the History of the Early Medieval Papacy', *Catholic Historical Review*, 81 (1995), 505–40, while the papers in Michele Maccarrone (ed.), *Il primato del vescovo di Roma nel primo millennio: Ricerche e testimonianze* (Vatican City, 1991), offer context-sensitive evaluations of papal ideology and practice. Peter Llewellyn, *Rome in the Dark Ages* (London, 1971), remains useful. Important recent studies of specific issues include: Federico Marazzi, *I 'Patrimonia sanctae Romanae ecclesiae' nel Lazio (secoli IV–X): Stuttura amministrativa e prassi gestionali* (Rome, 1998); Thomas F. X. Noble, *The Republic of St Peter: The Birth of the Papal State, 680–825* (Philadelphia, 1984); Arnold Angenendt and Rudolf Schieffer, *Roma—caput et fons: Zwei Vorträge über das päpstliche Rom zwischen Altertum und Mittelalter* (Opladen, 1989); Gerd Tellenbach, 'Zur Geschichte der Päpste im 10. und früheren 11. Jahrhundert', in Fenske et al. (eds.), *Institutionen, Kultur und Gesellschaft im Mittelalter*, 165–77 (p. 331 above).

Details of the recipients of John XIX's letters and charters as plotted on Fig. 8.4 can be found in Harald Zimmermann (ed.), *Papsturkunden 896–1046*, 2 vols., Österreichische Akademie der Wissenschaften, philosophisch-historische Klasse, 174, 177 (Vienna, 1984–5), ii. 1043–126.

Chronology

324	Foundation of Constantinople
337	Death of Constantine, the first Christian emperor
340s	Ulfilas converts the Goths to Arian Christianity
388	Capture and execution of Magnus Maximus, general of the Roman army in Britain who had usurped imperial power in the western provinces in 383
397	Death of Martin, bishop of Tours since 371
406	Vandals, Suevi, and others cross the Rhine
408	Ravenna begins to be used as western imperial capital
409	Vandals and Suevi enter Iberia, where Suevi settle in the north-west and Vandals conquer southern provinces in 422
410	Sack of Rome by Goths under Alaric I (known as Visigoths)
418	Visigoths settle in south-western Gaul under treaty with the Romans
429	Vandals cross to North Africa, make treaty with Rome in 435, and seize Carthage in 439
c.450	Patrick's mission in Ireland, probably at some point during the middle or late 5th century
451	Huns under Attila invade western empire but defeated in eastern Gaul by a coalition of Romans, Franks, Visigoths, and others
454	Death of Attila
476	Odoacer deposes western emperor Romulus Augustulus and is proclaimed king by army in Italy
c.481	Accession of Clovis, king of the Franks, in northern Gaul establishes Merovingian dynastic kingship
489	Zeno, Byzantine emperor (474–91), sends the Ostrogoth Theoderic the Great to invade Italy
493	Theoderic the Great captures Ravenna, kills Odoacer, and establishes Ostrogothic kingdom in Italy
c.500	*Pactus Legis Salicae* probably compiled during the reign of Clovis
500	Theoderic the Great visits Rome
507	Clovis defeats Visigoths under Alaric II and seizes south-western Gaul; Visigoths retreat to Spain

508	Probable date of Clovis's acceptance of Christianity
511	Death of Clovis; division of his kingdom among his four sons
526	Death of Theoderic the Great
534	Frankish takeover of Burgundian kingdom in Rhone valley
536	Justinian, Byzantine emperor since 527, invades Italy, having reconquered North Africa from the Vandals
c.540	Benedict of Nursia (d. 560) composes his monastic *Rule*, which becomes the normative guide to monastic observance from c.800
541	Bubonic plague erupts in Egypt
542	Death of Caesarius, bishop of Arles since 502, author of many sermons and other works
542–3	Bubonic plague reaches western Mediterranean; subsequent serious outbreaks in 570–1, 580, 590, and 654
552	Completion of Byzantine conquest of Italy and final collapse of Ostrogothic kingdom
561	Death of Chlothar I, last remaining son of Clovis; division of the Frankish kingdom among four of his sons, Charibert, Sigibert I, Chilperic, and Guntram
563	Irish monk Columba (c.521–97) founds island monastery of Iona in Scottish Dalriada and from there preaches to Picts
565	Death of Justinian, having returned North Africa, south-eastern Spain and Italy to imperial (Byzantine) rule
566	Italian poet Venantius Fortunatus arrives at court of the Frankish king Sigibert I (561–75) in Reims
568	Lombards invade northern Italy under King Alboin (d. 572); by 574 in control of Po valley cities and by 580 of Tuscany. Spoleto and Benevento established as independent Lombard duchies
584	Maurice, Byzantine emperor (582–602), pays subsidies to Childebert II, king of the Franks (575–96), who invades Po valley at Maurice's request but promptly settles with the Lombards and retreats, to imperial annoyance
585	Leovigild, king of the Visigoths (568–86), takes over the Suevic kingdom
589	Under Reccared (586–601), Visigoths renounce Arian Christianity and accept Catholicism
591–615	Irish monk Columbanus active on the Continent, founding monasteries and warning kings
594	Death of Gregory, bishop of Tours since 573, author of *Ten Books of Histories* and many hagiographical works

597	Augustine arrives in Kent to preach Christianity to the Anglo-Saxons, having been sent by Pope Gregory I in 595/6; establishes his see at Canterbury
597/8	Æthelbert, king of Kent, accepts Christianity and is baptized by Augustine; subsequently issues law code in Old English
c.600–	Fitful spread of Christianity to other Anglo-Saxon kingdoms; conversion of last pagan region, the Isle of Wight, in 686–7
604	Death of Gregory I (the Great), pope since 590, author of widely read pastoral and exegetical works
616	Death of Æthelbert of Kent; successor Eadbald at first rejects Christianity but then converts
634	Oswald, king of Northumbria, defeats Cadwallon, king of Gwynedd, and establishes domination over the northern half of Britain
636	Death of Isidore, bishop of Seville since 599, author of the *Etymologies* and numerous other works
639	Death of Dagobert I, king of the Franks since 623
642	Death of Oswald, king of Northumbria
643	Rothari, king of the Lombards (636–52), issues his Edict
664	Serious epidemics in Britain and Irelandn peninsula
674	Benedict Biscop founds monastery of Wearmouth (Northumbria)
678/9	The vision of Barontus
681	Benedict Biscop founds monastery of Jarrow (Northumbria)
711	Muslim invasion of Iberian peninsula
713/14	Envoys of Nechtan, king of the Picts, come to Wearmouth–Jarrow for advice about Roman liturgical practices and building techniques
716	Boniface, Anglo-Saxon monk, begins missionary activity on the Continent, preaching to the Frisians and reforming the Christian communities in Germany
721	Ecclesiastical council in Rome begins changes to marriage legislation
735	Death of Bede, monk of Wearmouth–Jarrow, author of the *Ecclesiastical History of the English People* and biblical commentaries, translator of St John's Gospel
744	Boniface founds monastery of Fulda in central Germany
744	Death of Liutprand, king of the Lombards since 712
751	Deposition of last Merovingian king of the Franks; accession of Pippin III marks start of Carolingian dynasty
754	Pope Stephen II (752–7) crosses the Alps to consecrate Pippin III
754	Boniface martyred by the Frisians at Dokkum

756	Establishment of Umayyad dynasty in Cordoba
757	Death of Æthelbald, king of Mercia since 716; accession later that same year of Offa (d. 796)
767	Last recorded outbreak of bubonic plague, in southern Italy
768	Death of Pippin III; division of his kingdom between his two sons Charlemagne and Carloman; on the latter's death in 771, entire Frankish kingdom passes to Charlemagne
772	Charlemagne commences campaigning against the Saxons
774	Charlemagne conquers and annexes the Lombard kingdom and duchy of Spoleto; duchy of Benevento remains independent into the eleventh century
776	Paderborn founded
781, 787	Charlemagne agrees limits of territory under direct papal rule; subsequently confirmed by Louis the Pious and Otto I
786–94	Alcuin of Northumbria (d. 804) among the scholars resident at Charlemagne's court
788	Charlemagne annexes Bavaria
789	Charlemagne begins to develop Aachen into a showpiece palace complex; from 802 in semi-permanent residence there. After Charlemagne's death, Aachen retains a highly symbolic role as the centre of legitimate kingship until 1804
789	Charlemagne promulgates the 'General Admonition', a full statement of 'correct Christianity'
792–3	Severe famine in the Frankish kingdom; Charlemagne legislates to alleviate it
793	Vikings raid the Northumbrian island monastery of Lindisfarne, the first securely dated Viking raid on western Europe. Increasingly frequent raids on Ireland, Scotland, and the isles thereafter
795	Death of Hadrian I, pope since 772, close friend of Charlemagne and energetic rebuilder of Rome
796	Assassination of Æthelred I, king of Northumbria
799	After an attempt to depose him, Pope Leo III (795–816) visits Charlemagne at Paderborn
800	In Rome, Leo III crowns Charlemagne emperor (25 December)
c.800–	Vikings trade with Byzantium and Islam via the river routes between the Baltic and the Black and Caspian Seas
804	Deportation of Saxons from Elbe valley marks conclusion of Charlemagne's Saxon wars
810	Viking raids on Frisia and Flanders begin; Charlemagne orders construction of a fleet at Boulogne and Ghent
811	Franks and Danes make peace on banks of river Eider

814	Death of Charlemagne and burial at Aachen; accession of his son Louis the Pious
815	Einhard becomes abbot of St Peter's monastery, Ghent
819	Death of Louis the Pious's first wife, Irmingard, and his remarriage to Judith; birth of her son Charles the Bald in 823 threatens his adult half-brothers' succession rights and contributes to political unrest
829	Frankish monk Anskar begins missionary work in Scandinavia; becomes bishop of Hamburg in 831
830	Revolt against Louis the Pious
830s	Viking raids extend to southern England, interior of Ireland, and Atlantic coast of Gaul
832	Foundation of monastery of Redon (Brittany)
833	Revolt against Louis the Pious; deposed by his sons but restored to full power in 834
833–9	Abba, reeve of Kent, makes his will
840	Death of Einhard, counsellor of Charlemagne and Louis the Pious, author of *Life of Charlemagne*, lay abbot of St Peter's, Ghent and founder of Seligenstadt
840	Death of Louis the Pious; contention between his sons is temporarily resolved by the partition of 843, which confirms Lothar I (840–55) as emperor and king of the middle kingdom, Louis the German (840–76) as king of the East Frankish kingdom, and Charles the Bald (840–77) as king of the West Frankish kingdom
841	Vikings establish base at Dublin; despite their temporary expulsion 902–17, Dublin develops into important urban centre and seat of a Hiberno-Norse kingdom, stretching until 954 across both sides of the Irish Sea
841–3	Dhuoda writes her *Handbook* for her son William
842	Death of Alfonso II, king of Asturias since 791, who established Asturias as a powerful Christian kingdom following Visigothic and Carolingian precedents and successfully defended it from Muslim attack
843	Kenneth mac Alpin ousts last Pictish king as Viking attacks on Scotland intensify
845	Vikings destroy Hamburg; Anskar becomes bishop of Bremen and resumes missionary work in Scandinavia
846	Saracens sack St Peter's, Rome
856	Death of Hrabanus Maurus, abbot of Fulda (822–42) and archbishop of Mainz since 847, author of numerous biblical commentaries

860	Frankish bishops adjudicate the marriage of Stephen, count of the Auvergne
860s	Kiev emerges as major Rus settlement and from *c*.880 extends rule over east Slavic peoples
862	First recorded Magyar raid, on the East Frankish kingdom
863	Constantine and Methodius commence preaching to the Slavs; Constantine dies in 869; Methodius dies in 885
864	Eberhard of Friuli and Gisela make their will
864	Baptism of Khan Boris of the Bulgars (852–89); turns to Pope Nicholas I for advice about Latin Christianity
865	Death of Anskar
866	Viking conquest of East Anglia soon followed by takeover of Northumbria in 876 and eastern Mercia in 877
870	Khan Boris decides in favour of Greek Christianity
c.870–930	Vikings settle in Iceland
871	Accession of Alfred, king of Wessex and exponent of Carolingian style kingship
873	Plague of locusts devastates much of Europe
878	Alfred, king of Wessex, wins victory over Vikings and stems their advance; Danish leader Guthrum submits to baptism, with Alfred as his godfather
881	Death of Fintan, an Irishman captured by Vikings in the 840s, who escaped in the Orkneys and later became a monk at Rheinau
882	Death of Hincmar, archbishop of Reims since 845, counsellor of kings, liturgical impressario, and author of treatises on kingship, marriage, and much else
884–7	Carolingian Empire reunited by Emperor Charles the Fat (d. 888)
888	Carolingian dynastic crisis; election of non-Carolingian kings in Italy, Provence, and, temporarily, west Francia
c.894	Magyars move west of the Carpathian mountains and begin to settle in the Danubian plain, taking over eastern Bavaria in 900 and Moravia in 902; Magyar raids on East Frankish kingdom become frequent
899	Death of Alfred of Wessex; accession of his son Edward the Elder, who commences conquest of East Anglia and eastern Mercia from the Vikings
909	Death of Gerald, count of Aurillac and holy man; his life and miracles subsequently described by Odo, abbot of Cluny (927–42)
911	Accession of Conrad I, first non-Carolingian king of the East Franks (Germans)

911	West Frankish king Charles the Simple (898–922) cedes Rouen and adjacent region to the Viking leader Rollo, thus establishing the duchy of Normandy
918	Death of Conrad I
919	Accession of Henry I, duke of Saxony, as king of the Germans
921	Charles the Simple sends Henry I the arm of St Denis
922	Defeat and deposition of Charles the Simple
924	Death of Edward the Elder, having extended West Saxon rule as far north as the river Humber; accession of Æthelstan
926	Henry I gives Swabia to Rudolf II, king of Burgundy (912–37), and acquires the Holy Lance in exchange
927	Æthelstan asserts his overlordship over the northern half of Britain and in 934 campaigns into Alba; hereafter West Saxon kings commonly referred to as kings of the English
936	Death of Henry I; accession of his son Otto I as king of Germany
939	Death of Æthelstan; accession of Edmund as king of England
941	Arnulf I, count of Flanders (918–65), begins reform of St Peter's, Ghent, and makes rich donations to the clergy
946	Death of Edmund; accession of Eadred as king of England
951	Otto invades Italy and is installed as king in Pavia
953	Embassy of John of Gorze to the court of Abd al-Rahman III (912–61) at Cordoba
954	King Eadred's capture of York ends Viking rule within England
955	Death of Eadred; accession of Edgar as king in Mercia and Northumbria; then, in 957, in Wessex
955	Otto I defeats Magyars at the battle of the river Lech; thereafter Magyar attacks diminish
961	Otto I has his 6-year-old son Otto II crowned king of Germany at Aachen, and then crosses Alps into Italy
962	Otto I crowned emperor in Rome
967	Gerbert of Aurillac visits Ripoll
967	Otto II crowned emperor
972	Baptism of Géza, king of Hungary (c.970–97)
973	Death of Otto I; sole rule of Otto II
975	Death of Edgar, king of England since 957, having fostered Carolingian-style 'correct Christianity' within England; accession of Edward 'the Martyr'
978	Assassination of Edward 'the Martyr'; accession of Æthelred II 'the Unready' to the English throne
980	Viking raids on England resume

980	Otto II meets Hugh Capet
983	Death of Otto II; accession of 3-year-old Otto III
983	Liutizi Slavs revolt against German dominance and reject Christianity
985–7	Abbo of Fleury teaches at Ramsey
987	Death of last Carolingian king of West Francia; coronation of Hugh Capet as king of the West Franks (French)
c.988	Prince Vladimir of Kiev and the Rus accept Christianity
991	Anglo-Saxon defeat by the Vikings at Maldon on coast of Essex; subsequently commemorated in the epic poem *The Battle of Maldon*
996	Having come of age in 994, Otto III crowned emperor in Rome
997	Adalbert of Prague martyred by the Prussians at Gdansk
997	Accession of Stephen of Hungary
997–1016	Date of the sole manuscript of the Old English epic poem *Beowulf*
998	Otto III rebuilds former imperial palace in Rome in an attempt to make Rome his permanent capital
999	Death of Gregory V, the first German pope
999/1000	Icelanders adopt Christianity
1000	Otto III visits Gniezno to inaugurate the cult of Adalbert of Prague, bestow a crown and a replica of the Holy Lance on Boleslaw Chobry (992–1025), and stand godfather to his son; establishment of Polish archbishopric at Gniezno
1000/1	Pope Sylvester II sends a crown to Stephen of Hungary and Otto III sends a replica of the Holy Lance; establishment of Hungarian archbishopric at Esztergom
1001	Otto III expelled from Rome
1002	Death of Otto III; succession crisis ends when Henry II elected king in Germany
1004	Henry II elected king in Italy
1005	Great famine throughout Europe
1005	Brian Boru (976–1014) visits Armagh and makes gifts to shrine of St Patrick
1009	Bruno of Querfurt martyred by the Prussians
1013	Swein Forkbeard, king of Denmark, conquers all England north of the river Thames; Æthelred II exiled
1014	Death of Swein Forkbeard; Danish army in England recognizes his son Cnut as king but Anglo-Saxons recall Æthelred II from exile

1014	Defeat at the battle of Clontarf ends Brian Boru's dominance of Ireland
1014	Henry II crowned emperor
1016	Cnut, son of Swein Forkbeard, conquers England; death of Æthelred II
1018	Death of Thietmar, bishop of Merseburg since 1009, chronicler
1018–23	Hammerstein marriage dispute
1023	Death of Wulfstan, archbishop of York since 1002, homilist and counsellor of kings
1024	Death of Henry II without heir; election of Conrad II
1024	Death of Benedict VIII, pope since 1012; accession of his brother John XIX
1026	Cnut fights the Norwegians and Swedes at the battle of Holy River in southern Sweden
1027	Conrad II crowned emperor in Rome, with Cnut and Rudolf III of Burgundy in attendance
1032	Death of Rudolf III, king of Burgundy since 993
1033	Death of John XIX
1035	Death of Cnut, king of England, Denmark, and Norway
1036	Death of Meinwerk, bishop of Paderborn since 1009, leaving his rebuilding of Paderborn unfinished
1038	Death of Stephen of Hungary; canonized in 1083
1039	Death of Conrad II

Index

Page numbers in italic refer to maps and diagrams in the text.

Elementary Circuit Properties of Transistors

Semiconductor Electronics Education Committee, Volume 3

Campbell L. Searle
Massachusetts Institute of Technology

A. R. Boothroyd
The Queen's University of Belfast

E. J. Angelo, Jr.
Polytechnic Institute of Brooklyn

Paul E. Gray
Massachusetts Institute of Technology

Donald O. Pederson
University of California, Berkeley

John Wiley & Sons, Inc., New York · London · Sydney

\# 568745

1-89

Foreword

The importance of transistors and other semiconductor devices is now well established. The subsequent development of microminiaturized electronic circuits has blurred the dividing line between the "device" and the "circuit," and thus has made it increasingly important for us to understand deeply the relationship between the internal physics and structure of a device, and its potentialities for circuit performance. Furthermore, the small size and efficient operation of semiconductor devices make possible for the first time a much closer integration between the theoretical and laboratory aspects of the educational process.

To prepare new educational material which would reflect these developments, there was formed in the Fall of 1960 a group known as the Semiconductor Electronics Education Committee (SEEC). This committee is comprised of university and industrial members, brought together by several of the faculty of the Electrical Engineering Department at the Massachusetts Institute of Technology, with Professor C. L. Searle acting as Chairman and Professor R. B. Adler acting as Technical Director. The committee undertook the production of a multipurpose course in semiconductor electronics, designed primarily for use in universities at the third or fourth year undergraduate level.

The success of the high-school physics course developed by the Physical Science Study Committee (PSSC) lead the SEEC to believe that the same kind of combination used there—text, laboratory experiments, and films, in a complementary format— would be the most practical way of providing uniformly high-quality instruction over the wide range of material involved. It was hoped that this arrangement would lead to broad applicability of the course in the academic world, and also in some professional training activities of industry and government. This book is one in the SEEC series, all volumes of which are listed here:*

These books have all gone through at least one "preliminary edition," many through two or more. The preliminary editions were used in teaching trials at some of the participating colleges and industrial training activities, and the results have been used as a basis for revision.

*Minor changes in title or authorship may take place in some of the volumes, which are still in preparation at the time of this writing.

It is almost impossible to enumerate all those people who have contributed some of their effort to the SEEC. Certain ones, however, have either been active with the Committee steadily since its inception, or have made very major contributions since then. These may be thought of as "charter members," deserving special mention.

From Universities

California, Berkeley: D. O. Pederson
Imperial College, London: A. R. Boothroyd△
Iowa State: H. L. Ablin*
M.I.T.: R. B. Adler, P. E. Gray, A. L. McWhorter, C. L. Searle, A. C. Smith, R. D. Thornton, J. R. Zacharias, H. J. Zimmermann (Research Laboratory of Electronics), J. N. Harris (Lincoln Laboratory)
Minnesota: E. R. Chenette
New Mexico: W. W. Grannemann
Polytechnic Institute of Brooklyn: E. J. Angelo, Jr.
Stanford: J. F. Gibbons, J. G. Linvill
U.C.L.A.: J. Willis

From Industries

Bell Telephone Laboratories: J. M. Early, A. N. Holden, V. R. Saari
Fairchild Semiconductor: V. R. Grinich
IBM: D. DeWitt
RCA: J. Hilibrand, E. O. Johnson, J. I. Pankove
Transitron: B. Dale,† H. G. Rudenberg‡
Westinghouse Research Laboratories: A. I. Bennett, H. C. Lin, R. L. Longini§

General management of the SEEC operations is in the hands of Educational Services, Inc. (abbreviated ESI), Watertown, Mass.,

△ Now at Queen's University, Belfast.
* Now at the University of Nebraska, Department of Electrical Engineering.
† Now at Sylvania Corp.
‡ Now at A. D. Little, Inc.
§ Now at Carnegie Institute of Technology, Department of Electrical Engineering.

a nonprofit corporation that grew out of the PSSC activities and is presently engaged in a number of educational projects at various levels. In addition to providing general management, ESI has supplied all the facilities necessary for preparing the SEEC films. These are 16-mm sound films, 20 to 40 minutes in length, designed to supplement the subject matter and laboratory experiments presented in the various text books. Two of the films are already available:

> "Gap Energy and Recombination Light in Germanium"— J. I. Pankove and R. B. Adler
> "Minority Carriers in Semiconductors"—J. R. Haynes and W. Shockley

At this writing two more films are still in the early stages of preparation: one deals with the *pn* junction, and the other with the relationship between physical structure, fabrication processes, and circuit performance of transistors. Pending arrangements for commercial distribution, completed films are available (purchase or rental) directly from Educational Services, Inc., 47 Galen Street, Watertown, Mass.

The committee has also endeavored to develop laboratory materials for use with the books and films. This material is referred to in the books and further information about it can be obtained from ESI.

The preparation of the entire SEEC program, including all the books, was supported at first under a general grant made to the Massachusetts Institute of Technology by the Ford Foundation, for the purpose of aiding in the improvement of engineering education, and subsequently by specific grants made to ESI by the National Science Foundation. This support is gratefully acknowledged.

Campbell L. Searle
Chairman, SEEC
Richard B. Adler
Technical Director, SEEC

Preface

The purpose of this book is to impart a thorough familiarity with the elementary circuit properties of single-stage transistor circuits. The issues of what measurements to make to determine numerical element values in transistor models, how the values of the various parameters change as a function of temperature, operating point, etc., how to perform both large-signal and small-signal circuit analysis by using these transistor models, and how to bias single-stage transistor circuits are treated in considerable detail.

This book is the third of seven volumes being prepared by the Semiconductor Electronics Education Committee. The entire series is designed to be taught at the junior or senior level, and, therefore, assumes some previous contact with introductory passive circuit theory and introductory electronic circuits. In particular, the authors of this book have assumed that the reader has already learned such things as simple circuit models for active devices (incorporating dependent sources), graphical characteristics, and elementary biasing calculations.

The authors envision two possible orders in which the SEEC books may be taught (and undoubtedly other orders will evolve). The first order involves starting with *Introduction to Semicon-*

ductor Physics (ISP) then passing to *Physical Electronics and Circuit Models of Transistors* (PEM), where the hybrid-π small-signal circuit model and the Ebers-Moll nonlinear circuit model are developed from detailed considerations of semiconductor physics. These books would then be followed by the present volume, *Elementary Circuit Properties of Transistors* (ECP). An alternate sequence, for those who prefer not to begin the course with a detailed treatment of semiconductor physics, is to start with the transistor circuit material in this book and follow this with the semiconductor physics material in ISP and PEM. A considerable effort has been made in the writing of this book (ECP) to make it possible to teach the material in either of these two orders. However, some compromise is always involved under these conditions. For those who follow the first sequence, the semiconductor physics material in Chapter 1 will appear as a somewhat unnecessary review of the material in ISP and PEM. Those who follow the second order of presentation can expect to find the introductory chapter altogether too brief, and be left with a definite feeling that they are somehow missing some of the physical background necessary for both the understanding and cataloging of the information. This problem should be particularly acute in Chapter 4.

We are indebted to all the members of the SEEC who, over the past three years, have by comments and criticisms contributed either directly or indirectly to the preparation of this book. In particular, however, the authors wish to acknowledge the help of Professors R. B. Adler and R. D. Thornton, who made major technical contributions to the writing in the course of innumerable heated discussions.

The SEEC texts have been extensively rewritten as a result of teaching trials conducted during the past three years. Thus many students have contributed to this book via their instructors at various SEEC "feedback meetings." Most of these students are unknown to us; we hope that they will accept this somewhat formal expression of our thanks. In addition, several M.I.T. students have contributed directly to the book, by working with us at the SEEC summer workshops. Specifically, much of the measurement work in Chapters 3 and 4 was done by Alton Tripp, and the experimental work in Chapter 9 was done by Huber Graham. The remaining curve plotting and all of the 'scope photography was done by John Kassakian. Willis North and Jim Maskasky served as student reviewers and proof readers. We gratefully acknowledge this help.

We also wish to acknowledge the continuing cooperation of the staff and directors of the Research Laboratory of Electronics, M.I.T.

CAMPBELL L. SEARLE

A. R. BOOTHROYD

E. J. ANGELO, JR.

P. E. GRAY

D. O. PEDERSON

Cambridge, Mass.
October, 1964

Contents

xlii

List of Symbols

A	gain, or junction area
A_0	mid-frequency gain
b	radius of admittance circle
C	capacitance
C_b	base charging capacitance
C_d	collector diffusion capacitance
$\left.\begin{array}{l} C_{be} \\ C_{bc} \\ C_{ce} \end{array}\right\}$	extrinsic capacitances in the hybrid-π model
$\left.\begin{array}{l} C_{ie} \\ C_{oe} \\ C_{fe} \\ C_{re} \end{array}\right\}$	capacitive parts of y-parameters. When primed, indicates *slope* of imaginary part of y-parameter.
C_j	incremental junction space-charge-layer capacitance
C_{jc}, C_{sc}	incremental collector space-charge-layer capacitance components
C_{je}	incremental emitter space-charge-layer capacitance
C_{ob}	output capacitance of transistor in the common-base connection
C_t	Thevenin equivalent capacitance which includes the effects of C_π and C_μ *for resistive loads*
C_μ	feedback capacitance in the hybrid-π model ($C_{jc} + C_d$)
C_π	capacitance in the hybrid-π model ($C_b + C_{je}$)
D	charge-carrier diffusion coefficient—see Note 1
E, e	source voltage—see Note 2
e_{trig}	triggering voltage in multivibrator

$\mathcal{E}$	electric field
$\mathcal{E}_0$	electric field at the metallurgical boundary of a pn junction
f_T	the frequency where $|\beta| = 1$
f_β	frequency where $|\beta| = 0.707\ \beta_0$
G,g	conductance
g_{ie} g_{oe} g_{fe} g_{re}	conductive parts of y-parameters
g_m	incremental transconductance of a junction transistor
g_o	output conductance in the hybrid-π model
g_μ	feedback conductance in the hybrid-π model
g_π	conductance in the hybrid-π model
h_i h_o h_f h_r	h-parameters. A second subscript indicates the transistor connection: b, common base; c, common collector; e, common emitter
I,i	electric current—see Note 2
I_{ci}	coordinate of common-emitter output curves where all curves cross
I_{CO}	collector-junction saturation current with the emitter open
I_{CS}	collector-junction saturation current with the emitter shorted to the base
I_{EO}	emitter-junction saturation current with the collector open
I_{ES}	emitter-junction saturation current with the collector shorted to the base
I_{BF}, i_{BF}	forward component of base current
I_{BR}, i_{BR}	reverse component of base current
I_{CF}, i_{CF}	forward component of collector current
I_{CR}, i_{CR}	reverse component of collector current
I_s	saturation current of an idealized junction diode
J	electric current density. Subscripts h and e denote hole and electron current densities
k	Boltzmann's constant, or, after a resistor value, 1000 ohms
L	inductance
m	turn-off overdrive factor in switching circuit, or mismatch factor in tuned amplifier
n	electron concentration, (see Note 3) or turn-on overdrive factor in switching circuit
n'	excess electron concentration—see Note 3
P	power
pf	picofarads
p	hole concentration—see Note 3
p'	excess hole concentration—see Note 3
q	magnitude of the electronic charge
q_b, q_B	total excess minority-carrier charge stored in the base

q_{BO}	charge stored in the base at the point of entry of the saturation region
q_e	total excess stored electron charge
q_F	forward component of excess minority-carrier charge stored in the base
q_h	total excess stored hole charge
q_i	charge in either half of the dipole layer of the space-charge region at a junction
q_R	reverse component of excess minority-carrier charge stored in the base
q_S	excess saturation charge stored in the base
q_{VE}	emitter junction space-charge-layer charge measured with respect to the charge for $V_{EB} = 0$
q_{VC}	collector-junction space-charge-layer charge measured with respect to the charge for $V_{CB} = 0$
R,r	resistance
r_e	emitter resistance in the common-base T model
r_o	output resistance in the hybrid-π model
r_x	base resistance in the hybrid-π model
r_μ	feedback resistance in the hybrid-π model
r_π	resistance in the hybrid-π model
s	complex frequency variable
T	absolute temperature
t_d	turn-on delay time
t_f	10%–90% fall time
t_r	10%–90% rise time
t_s	storage delay time
T'_{BF} T_{BR} T_F T_R T_S	total charge control parameters. Similar to corresponding charge control parameters τ, except that they include linearized space-charge-layer effects
V,v	terminal-pair voltage—see Note 2
V_{CEi}	voltage coordinate where all common-emitter output characteristics cross
$V_{BE}(T)$, $V_{BC}(T)$	temperature-dependent voltage sources
W	width of the neutral base region in a transistor or thin-region diode
x	longitudinal position coordinate in the one-dimensional model
Y,y	admittance
y_i y_o y_f y_r	short-circuit y-parameters. Second subscript indicates transistor connection: b, common base; c, common collector; e, common emitter
Z,z	impedance
α	incremental common-base short-circuit current gain

α_F	large-signal forward-injection common-base short-circuit current gain
α_R	large-signal reverse-injection common-base short-circuit current gain
α_0	low-frequency value of α
β	incremental common-emitter short-circuit current gain
β_F	large-signal forward-injection common-emitter short-circuit current gain
β_R	large-signal reverse-injection common-emitter short-circuit current gain
β_0	low-frequency value of β
ρ	space-charge concentration
τ	lifetime of excess charge carriers—see Note 1
τ_{BF}	effective base-region lifetime with forward injection
τ_{BR}	effective base-region lifetime with reverse injection
τ_F	forward injection charge-control parameter
τ_R	reverse injection charge-control parameter
τ_S	saturation region charge-control parameter
φ	electrostatic potential
φ_0	thermal equilibrium electrostatic potential barrier at a pn junction (contact potential)
ω_0	center frequency of tuned circuit
ω'	frequency deviation away from ω_0 ($\omega' = \omega - \omega_0$)
ω_α	frequency where $|\alpha| = 0.707\,\alpha_0$
ω_β	frequency where $|\beta| = 0.707\,\beta_0$
ω_T	frequency where $|\beta| = 1$

Note 1

In designating diffusion coefficients, mobilities, lifetimes, diffusion lengths, the subscripts e and h are used *with reference to diodes* to indicate that the parameters describe the dynamical properties of minority carrier electrons or holes, respectively. *With reference to transistors*, the subscripts e, b, and c are used to indicate that the parameter applies to the minority carriers in the emitter, base, and collector regions. In those few cases where majority carrier diffusion coefficients or mobilities are used, double subscripts are employed if there is possibility of confusion.

Note 2

Currents and voltages at the terminals of diodes and transistors are designated by subscripts which indicate the terminal at which the current flows or the terminal pair at which a voltage appears.

dc or operating point variables—upper case symbols with
upper case subscripts
total instantaneous variables—lower case symbols with upper
case subscripts

incremental instantaneous variables—lower case symbols with
lower case subscripts
complex amplitudes of incremental components—upper case symbols
with lower case subscripts

Note 3

In designating carrier concentrations, the semiconductor region is indicated by a subscript n or p for a diode or e, b, and c for a transistor. The use of a second subscript o denotes the thermal equilibrium value of the corresponding concentration.

1

Transistor Physical
Electronics and Circuit Models

1.0 SEMICONDUCTOR DEVICES AND MODELS

The purpose of this book is to help the reader become thoroughly familiar with basic single-stage transistor circuits, from the point of view of design as well as analysis. We shall consider at the elementary level both amplifier circuits and switching circuits. The common thread which runs through the entire book is the problem of choosing the most appropriate way to represent and analyze the important electrical properties of the transistor for the particular circuit application at hand. That is, each application requires the use of an electrical circuit model which represents to some sufficient degree of accuracy those electrical properties of the transistor that are of major importance in that application.

Inasmuch as we consider several distinctly different modes of transistor operation, several different circuit models are required. While this proliferation of models may at first seem unfortunate, we must remember that any single model of sufficient generality and completeness to suffice for all circuit applications would necessarily be too complex to be useful to the circuit designer.

Because a variety of different circuit models is essential to our purpose, it is desirable to have some understanding of the common ground from which they emanate, and to appreciate the relationships among models as well as the principal limitations of each. Such knowledge can be obtained only by studying the internal physical mechanisms of the device and how these mechanisms determine its electrical behavior at the terminals. Consequently, our investigation of circuit models includes some consideration of physical electronics, not only to guide us in model development, but also to provide a framework to which all the models can be tied.

1.1 THE MODELING PROCESS

The principal steps employed in obtaining a circuit model for any electronic device, and in particular for a transistor, are:

1. *Defining the Area of Applicability of the Model.* For example, is the application one in which the nonlinear nature of the device is an important factor, or are the expected variations in currents and voltages small enough so the relationship between these small signals may be regarded as approximately linear? Are the currents and voltages at the terminals changing very slowly, or are rapid changes of major importance? How precisely must the predictions of the model agree with the behavior of the real device?

2. *Deciding upon a Model Configuration.* That is, what network comprised of idealized electrical-circuit elements, such as resistors, capacitors, and dependent generators, should be used to represent the electrical behavior of the device under the conditions of interest? We must recognize that there is no unique answer to this question. Several different models can be used to yield similar answers, differing principally in simplicity of representation and in degree of accuracy.

3. *Determining Numerical Values for the Circuit Elements in the Model.* That is, what are the values of the parameters of the model for a particular transistor, and how do they depend on its electrical and physical environment?

Before we consider specific circuit models, let us indicate briefly the structure of this chapter in terms of the three steps in the modeling process described above. First, all the circuit models used in this book can be placed in one of two categories:

Small-Signal or Incremental Models. These are used whenever the changes in the terminal currents and voltages are small enough so that the relationships between these changes are approximately *linear.* Such models are therefore useful in the analysis and design of circuits in which the transistor is used as a linear signal-processing device.

Nonlinear Models. These are used when the ranges of values of the terminal variables are large enough to place the nonlinear nature of the transistor in evidence. Nonlinear models are used principally in those applications where the transistor functions as a switch, as in pulse circuits for the processing of digital information.

Second, in each case we use our knowledge of the internal physical behavior of the device as a guide in the choice of a model configuration, but we also strive for a configuration in which maximum advantage is taken of the simplification that is obtained only by limiting considerably the range of conditions over which the model is expected to apply.

Finally, we have adopted the philosophy in this book that the numerical values for the elements which appear in each model must be determined from electrical measurements made at the terminals of the device. Although analysis of the internal physical behavior shows how the values of the elements depend on the properties of the semiconductor, the physical structure of the device, and the electrical and environmental operating conditions, this analysis cannot in general be used as a basis for assigning numerical values to the parameters. The uncertainties introduced by changes in the material parameters during the manufacturing process, or by insufficient control over some of these processes, prohibit such reliance on internal physical parameters. We therefore cannot escape the need for electrical measurements made at the terminals of the device. The issue of *which* terminal properties to measure is decided primarily on the basis of a combination of measurement convenience and the ease of relating the measurements to the model parameters.

The discussion of circuit models presented in the following sections is, of necessity, brief and qualitative. However, it should serve to make plausible the various models which we require and should indicate the region of applicability and the limitations of each model.*

1.2 CHARGE CARRIERS IN SEMICONDUCTORS

1.2.1 *Holes and Conduction Electrons*

Semiconductors, of which germanium and silicon are examples, differ from metallic conductors in that they can support an electric current by the motion of either of two distinct and independent charge carriers. These two types of mobile charge carriers are *conduction electrons*, which transport negative charge, and *holes*, which transport positive charge. Although any semiconductor contains both holes and electrons,† these two types of carriers usually are not present in comparable numbers. The more populous carrier is called the *majority carrier*, and the less populous is referred to as the *minority carrier*. The difference between the population of majority carriers and the population of minority carriers is determined by the concentration of certain chemical impurities which are present in the semiconductor in extraordinarily minute quantities. For example, a sample of germanium in which the principal impurity is indium in an amount of one part per million (one indium atom for every million germanium atoms) has, at room temperature, a majority carrier hole population of about 4×10^{16} per cm^3 and a minority carrier electron population of about 1.5×10^{10} per cm^3. This material is designated as *p-type* because the holes, which are charged positively, are the majority carriers. Materials containing different impurities, in consequence of which electrons are the majority carrier, are known as *n-type* semiconductors. Both types of material are electrically neutral in spite of the concentration imbalance of *mobile* carriers. This neutrality is maintained because in *p*-type material the dominant impurity

---

* Because this short discussion cannot establish the analytical basis of these models, the reader is strongly urged to study at greater depth the physical background of semiconductors and transistors. Two other books in this series deal with appropriate material. These are: R. B. Adler, A. C. Smith, and R. L. Longini, *Introduction to Semiconductor Physics;* and P. E. Gray, D. DeWitt, A. R. Boothroyd, and J. F. Gibbons, *Physical Electronics and Circuit Models of Transistors,* hereafter referred to as ISP and PEM, respectively.

† Henceforth we refer to *conduction electrons* simply as *electrons*.

atoms (called *acceptors*) provide just enough *immobile negative charge* to balance the mobile positive charge resulting from the excess of holes over electrons, whereas in n-type material the dominant impurities (called *donors*) carry *immobile positive charge* which balances the excess of electron charge over hole charge.

Analytical treatment of the hole and electron populations in a semiconductor shows that over broad ranges of temperature the majority-carrier concentration depends primarily on the impurity concentration and is therefore relatively constant. On the other hand, the minority-carrier concentration is extremely temperature-dependent. For example, the minority-carrier electron population in p-type germanium doubles (approximately) for every temperature increase of 10°C.

1.2.2 Drift and Diffusion

In semiconductors, electrical currents are the result of the motion of *either* holes or electrons, and are associated with either of two distinct mechanisms.

The first is *drift* in an electric field, which occurs because the holes and electrons are charged particles, and therefore experience forces when acted on by an electric field. Although the carriers are accelerated by the field, the additional energy thus received is usually small compared to the energy of their random thermal motion. The motion of a single charge carrier is complicated and tortuous because of its random thermal motion and the collisions which it makes at random in the solid, and this motion is only slightly altered by the field. However, the average current resulting from small perturbations in motion produced by the field acting on each of a very large number of charge carriers is significant because the random thermal motion by itself gives *no* average current. It turns out that over and above their thermal motions, the charge carriers move in response to an applied field as though they were immersed in a viscous fluid, and the *drift velocity* added to the thermal motion by moderate applied fields is linearly dependent upon the force, and therefore on the field. Thus the current, like the drift velocity, is proportional to the field and the drift current obeys Ohm's law. Holes drift in the direction of the applied field whereas electrons drift in the opposite direction, because of their negative charge. In both cases the electric current associated with the average drift of charge carriers is in the direction of the field, and proportional to it.

The second mechanism by which holes and electrons move, thereby creating a current, is *diffusion* in the presence of a concentration gradient. Because of their random thermal velocities, each species of charge carrier tends to equalize its concentration over the entire volume in which it can move. Therefore, holes and electrons tend to *diffuse* from regions of high concentration to regions of low concentration. This diffusive motion is analogous to the spread of color which occurs when a drop of ink falls in a glass of water. Although the diffusion mechanism does *not* depend on the charge associated with the holes and electrons, diffusing charge carriers, of course, produce electric current. Analysis of the diffusion mechanism shows that for moderate gradients the average current density is proportional to the concentration gradient. If the concentration of holes, for example, varies in the x-direction, the x component of the hole current density caused by diffusion is

$$J_{hx} = -qD_h \frac{dp}{dx} \tag{1.1}$$

where D_h is the *diffusion coefficient* for holes. Inasmuch as the charge carriers diffuse from regions of high concentration to regions of lower concentration, the current density associated with diffusion of the positively charged holes is opposite in direction to the concentration gradient, whereas the current density associated with diffusion of the negatively charged electrons is in the same direction as the concentration gradient.

If a moderate electric field and a moderate concentration gradient are simultaneously present in a semiconductor, both drift and diffusion occur independently. The net current density of either the holes or the electrons is then simply the sum of the corresponding drift and diffusion component currents.

1.2.3 *Injection and Recombination of Excess Carriers*

Because semiconductors contain two groups of independent charge carriers, which have charges of opposite sign, it is possible by adding electrical, optical, or thermal energy to the material to increase almost equally the concentrations of *both* holes and electrons without causing significant deviations from electrical neutrality. The carrier concentrations increase as a consequence of the breaking of valence bonds in the semiconductor. Thus the mobile charge-carrier concentration can be increased without creating the enormous internal electric fields and currents normally associated with the deviations from neutrality that would accompany such increases in single-carrier conductors (e.g., metals). This fundamental difference between metals and semiconductors, which is a consequence of the two-carrier nature of semiconductors, is directly responsible for the operation of most semiconductor junction devices. Processes which cause the carrier concentrations to increase above their equilibrium values are referred to as *carrier injection* mechanisms, and the added carriers are called *excess carriers*.

Inasmuch as excess carriers in a semiconductor constitute a disturbance from the equilibrium situation, their presence is opposed by a *recombination* process in which holes and electrons are effectively removed from circulation as charge carriers by mutual annihilation. This recombination process may be visualized as the completion of a previously broken valence bond. Analysis of the detailed processes by which excess carriers recombine shows that the average time-space rate of recombination is in many practical cases approximately proportional to the excess minority carrier concentration. That is, in n-type material, for example, the net rate of recombination of excess holes with excess electrons can be approximated by

$$\text{Recombination rate} = \frac{p - p_o}{\tau_h} \tag{1.2}$$

where τ_h is the *lifetime* of the excess carriers, and $p - p_o$ denotes the *excess* hole concentration, i.e., the amount by which the actual minority-carrier hole concentration p exceeds the equilibrium hole concentration p_o. Similarly, in p-type material, the recombination rate would be described in terms of the excess minority-carrier electron concentration $n - n_o$, and a lifetime τ_e. In either case, the excess concentrations of both types of carriers are approximately equal because the semiconductor is nearly electrically neutral.

In summary, semiconductors have both holes and electrons as charge carriers. The equilibrium concentrations of the two-carrier types can be adjusted by controlling the type and quantity of chemical impurity added to the semiconductor crystal. The motion of holes and electrons, either by drift in an electric field or by diffusion in a concentration gradient, gives rise to currents. Excess carriers can be introduced without significant deviations from electrical neutrality by electrical, optical, or thermal injection mechanisms, and excess carriers tend to disappear by mutual recombination at a rate which is determined by the excess concentration.

1.3 pn-JUNCTION DIODES

The simplest semiconductor junction device is a *pn*-junction diode. It consists of a semiconductor in which the distribution of impurities produces a region of *p*-type material and a region of *n*-type material separated by a relatively thin region of transition from one type to the other. A representative diode structure is shown in Fig. 1.1*a*. We shall use the simple physical model shown in Fig. 1.1*b* in our descriptions of diode behavior because it preserves the principal physical feature of nearly all junction diodes, i.e., a rather abrupt transition from one conductivity type to the other in a single piece of semiconductor. The standard symbol for a junction diode is shown in Fig. 1.1*c*. The "arrowhead" in this symbol always points from the *p*-type region to the *n*-type region.

1.3.1 *The Diode in Equilibrium*

The dominant charge carriers in the *p*-type material are holes, whereas the dominant charge carriers in the *n*-type material are electrons. Clearly, the hole concentration is much greater on the *p*-type side than on the *n*-type side. Similarly, the electron concentration is much greater on the *n*-type side than on the *p*-type side. Normally, each carrier concentration differs by at least four or five orders of magnitude on the two sides of the junction, as illustrated in Fig. 1.2*a*. The diffusion effect of the large concentration gradients which exist for both carriers near the junction must be "balanced" by the drift effect of an electric field at the junction, so that no net current of either holes or electrons exists.

The equilibrium electric field at the junction, shown in Fig. 1.2*b*, is produced by a *dipole layer* of space charge that straddles the

Fig. 1.1. A *pn*-junction diode. (*a*) Physical structure of a diffused *pn*-junction diode. The diode is manufactured by diffusing a *p*-type impurity into the *n*-type starting material. Consequently, a portion of the semiconductor is converted to *p*-type. Electrical connections are made through metals which are soldered, vapor deposited or compression-bonded to the semiconductor. (*b*) Physical model. (*c*) Diode symbol.

junction as shown in Fig. 1.2c. The portion of this *space-charge region* that lies on the *p*-type side of the junction contains negative charge because holes have vacated this region, leaving behind immobile, negatively charged acceptor impurity ions. Similarly, the charge on the *n*-type side is positive.

The electrostatic potential, Fig. 1.2d, is different at the two edges of the space-charge region because of the electric field in the dipole layer. The electrostatic potential is higher in the *n*-type

Fig. 1.2. Electrical behavior near a germanium *pn* junction in equilibrium. (*a*) Hole concentration *p*, and electron concentration *n*. (*b*) Equilibrium electric field in the regions where the mobile carrier concentrations are changing. (*c*) Space-charge concentration showing the dipole layer which straddles the junction. *q* denotes the charge on an electron, 1.6×10^{-19} coulombs. (*d*) Electrostatic potential barrier at the junction.

region outside the space-charge layer than in the p-type region on the other side of the layer. Consequently, holes, which carry positive charge, are inhibited in moving from the p-type region to the n-type region by the change in potential. That is, the diffusion effect of the large concentration gradient of the holes is balanced by the electrostatic potential difference that appears across the space-charge layer. A similar balance occurs for the electrons, which find it difficult to move to regions of lower electrostatic potential because they are negatively charged. This potential difference across the space-charge layer which prohibits the diffusive flows of carriers is frequently referred to as the *internal potential barrier*. Because it is a consequence of a junction or contact between two electrically dissimilar materials, it is sometimes called the *contact potential*. Of course, it does not appear as a voltage difference at the terminals of the diode in equilibrium, because it is cancelled by the contact potentials which exist at the metal-semiconductor junctions.

1.3.2 The Effect of a Voltage

Diodes are interesting and useful electrical devices because of a nonlinear relationship between the terminal current and the terminal voltage. Because of the enormous asymmetry of the hole and electron distributions near the junction, the current depends very much on the polarity of the applied voltage.

Most junction diodes are constructed so that current-caused voltage drops at the contacts and in the semiconductor *outside* the space-charge layer are negligible for modest currents. Therefore, almost all of the voltage applied to the terminals of the diode appears across the space-charge layer as a change in the height of the potential barrier. If the polarity of the applied voltage is such that the p-type region is positive with respect to the n-type region, as shown in Fig. 1.3a, the height of the electrostatic potential barrier at the junction is reduced, thereby permitting a flow of holes from the p-type region, where they are plentiful, to the n-type region, where they are scarce. Electrons can also readily flow the other way because of the decreased barrier height. These hole and electron flows produce a current at the terminals in the same direction as the applied voltage, and this current increases rapidly as the voltage increases. This situation of relatively large current is called *forward bias*.

On the other hand, if the applied voltage is reversed so that the *p*-type region is negative with respect to the *n*-type region, as

(a) Forward bias

(b) Reverse bias

Fig. 1.3. The effects of a bias voltage on a *pn*-junction. (*a*) Forward bias produces large terminal current; i.e., *I* is large and positive. (*b*) Reverse bias produces small terminal current; i.e., *I* is small and negative.

shown in Fig. 1.3*b*, the height of the potential barrier increases, and very little current appears at the terminals. That current which does occur is the result of minority holes in the *n*-type side falling down the barrier to the *p*-type side, and of minority electrons in the *p*-type side "falling" up the barrier in the opposite direction. The resulting current is very small because the populations of the minority carriers are small. The bias polarity which produces relatively small current is called *reverse bias*.

1.3.3 *Internal Excess Carrier Distributions*

The current that appears at the terminals when a voltage is applied to a *pn* junction diode is intimately related to an internal redistribution of the holes and electrons. The change in the height of the potential barrier produced by an applied voltage causes the concentrations of charge carriers at the edges of the space-charge region to change. A closer study of the dependence of these carrier concentrations on the applied voltage shows that the total minority-carrier concentrations *at the edges* of the space-charge layer change by a Boltzmann factor $e^{qV/kT}$, where q is the electronic charge, V is the applied voltage, k is Boltzmann's constant, and T is the absolute temperature.* That is,

$$p_n|_{edge} = p_{no} e^{qV/kT}$$

$$n_p|_{edge} = n_{po} e^{qV/kT}$$

where p_n is the total minority-carrier (hole) concentration in the *n*-type material, p_{no} is the equilibrium concentration of holes in the *n*-type material, and similar definitions apply to n_p and n_{po} in the *p*-type material. Accordingly, the *excess* minority-carrier concentrations are given by:

$$p_n'|_{edge} = p_n|_{edge} - p_{no} = p_{no}(e^{qV/kT} - 1)$$
$$n_p'|_{edge} = n_p|_{edge} - n_{po} = n_{po}(e^{qV/kT} - 1)$$

$$(1.3a,b)$$

Equations 1.3 show that with forward bias ($V > 0$), for example, the excess minority-carrier concentrations at the edges of the space-charge layer increase strongly as V increases. These excess holes, which are *injected* across the junction into the neutral *n*-type

---

* The factor kT/q, which is frequently called the *thermal voltage*, has the value of approximately 25 mv near room temperature (290°K).

region, are transported into the n-type region by diffusion, as shown in Fig. 1.4a. The n-type region remains approximately neutral in spite of the injection of excess holes because a neutralizing charge of excess majority-carrier electrons is drawn from the right-hand contact to the region near the junction. In a similar manner, excess electrons are injected into the nearly neutral p-type region, where they diffuse away from the junction. These distributions of excess carriers decay toward zero (that is, the total carrier concentrations decay toward their equilibrium values) at positions far away from the junction because the recombination mechanism tends to reduce the injected concentrations of excess carriers. In fact, all of the excess minority carriers injected across the junction eventually disappear in the neutral regions near the junction by recombination with excess majority carriers which are supplied from the contacts. Inasmuch as the rate of recombination is approximately proportional to the excess carrier concentration, the total static diode current must be proportional to the total number of excess carriers. That is,

$$I = q_h/\tau_h + q_e/\tau_e \tag{1.4}$$

where I designates the total diode current, and q_h and q_e denote the total numbers of excess minority holes in the n-type region and of excess minority electrons in the p-type region, respectively. The constants τ_h and τ_e designate the lifetimes which characterize the recombination processes in the two regions of the diode, as introduced in Eq. 1.2ff. This linear relationship between the static or dc steady-state current and q_h and q_e, usually called the excess carrier *stores*, is of major importance in the behavior of junction devices.

Quantitative analysis of the distribution and flow of injected carriers shows that the stores of excess minority carriers are linearly related to the concentrations of excess carriers at the edges of the space-charge layer, because both the diffusion and the recombination mechanisms are linear. That is, for the hole store q_h,

$$q_h \sim p_n'|_{\text{edge}} \tag{1.5a}$$

whereas for the electron store q_e,

$$q_e \sim n_p'|_{\text{edge}} \tag{1.5b}$$

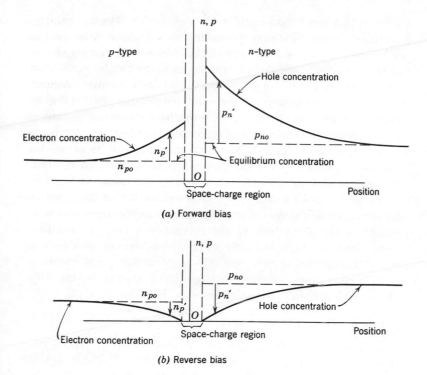

(a) Forward bias

(b) Reverse bias

Fig. 1.4. The effects of a bias voltage on the minority-carrier concentrations near the junction. Inasmuch as linear coordinates are used, the majority-carrier concentrations cannot conveniently be shown on these sketches. Because the regions outside the space-charge layer are neutral, the excess majority-carrier concentration equals the excess minority-carrier concentration.

Equations 1.4 and 1.5 show that, under static conditions, the excess carrier store and thus the total diode current are linearly dependent on the excess minority-carrier concentrations at the edges of the space-charge region. Inasmuch as these edge concentrations are proportional to $(e^{qV/kT} - 1)$,

$$I \sim (e^{qV/kT} - 1) \tag{1.6}$$

It is important to recognize that while the diode current-voltage relationship is highly nonlinear, the nonlinearity is entirely the consequence of the imbalance produced in the space-charge region by disturbing the height of the potential barrier. The mechanisms governing carrier flow and recombination in the neutral regions are *entirely linear*. We shall find this idea of internal linearity extremely useful in our description of transistor behavior.

Although the preceding discussion is phrased in terms of forward bias, the general features are the same for reverse bias. When the diode is reverse-biased, the *excess* minority-carrier concentrations at the edges of the space charge region become negative, as shown by Eqs. 1.3a and b. That is, the total minority-carrier concentrations are depressed below their equilibrium values, and minority carriers are extracted from the neutral regions as shown in Fig. 1.4b. Equations 1.4 and 1.5 still apply, although q_h and q_e are negative. The corresponding reverse current is small and substantially independent of the magnitude of the reverse-bias voltage because a reverse bias of about 0.1 volt $(4kT/q)$ suffices to produce the carrier distribution shown in Fig. 1.4b, and further increases in reverse-bias voltage produce no significant change in the edge concentrations, or in the distributions, as shown by Eqs. 1.3.

1.3.4 Static Diode Characteristics

The volt-ampere characteristics of a germanium pn-junction diode are shown in Fig. 1.5. Figure 1.5a, with a voltage scale of 0.5 volt per division, shows the highly nonlinear nature of the static diode characteristic. The rated forward current of most diodes is usually at least four orders of magnitude greater than the reverse

Fig. 1.5. Volt-ampere characteristics of a germanium pn-junction diode. (a) Characteristic at 25°C. (b) Expanded-scale characteristics, 25°C. (c) Expanded-scale characteristics, 75°C.

current. Figure 1.5b, with a voltage scale of 50 millivolts per division, shows the behavior of the diode near the origin. The diode volt-ampere characteristic is extremely sensitive to temperature, as shown by Fig. 1.5c, which illustrates the consequences of a 50°C increase in temperature. For any nonzero voltage, the magnitude of the diode current increases strongly as the temperature increases.

The static volt-ampere characteristic of an idealized pn-junction diode is, in accordance with Eq. 1.6, of the form:

$$I = I_s(e^{qV/kT} - 1) \qquad (1.7)$$

where I_s is called the *saturation current*. Since kT/q is approximately 25 millivolts at room temperature, changes in the forward-bias voltage of fractions of a volt produce large changes in current. This equation shows that for V large and negative, $I = -I_s$, so that I_s is identified as the asymptote of the diode reverse current. Inasmuch as this reverse current results from the extraction of minority carriers across the junction, I_s shows the same strong temperature dependence as the equilibrium minority-carrier concentrations. This temperature dependence of the saturation current, which is responsible for the diode temperature dependence shown in Fig. 1.5c, is shown explicitly in Fig. 1.6.

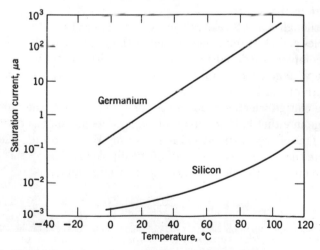

Fig. 1.6. Temperature dependence of the reverse current of two representative junction diodes.

1.3.5 *Dynamic Diode Behavior*

The transient electrical behavior of a diode differs from the static or quasi-steady-state behavior of the same device, solely because the *changing* internal charge-carrier distributions require components of the terminal current in addition to those required to feed recombination. That is, Eq. 1.4 must be replaced by:

$$i = \frac{q_h}{\tau_h} + \frac{dq_h}{dt} + \frac{q_e}{\tau_e} + \frac{dq_e}{dt} \tag{1.8}$$

where we have used lower-case rather than upper-case symbols to emphasize that the variables i and q are now functions of time. If the internal excess carrier stores, denoted by q_h and q_e, change very rapidly, as in applications involving fast transients or high-frequency signals, nearly all of the terminal current i may be devoted to changing the charge stores. In other words, dq_h/dt and dq_e/dt may be much larger than q_h/τ_h and q_e/τ_e. In terms of carrier injection across the junction, this means that some of the injected carriers are being added to the store of excess carriers rather than simply recombining, as in the static case. Although the situation is in some respects similar to the charging of a capacitor, the dynamic behavior of the diode is complicated by the distributed nature of the device.

Although Eq. 1.8 relates the excess carrier stores to the current of holes and electrons injected across the junction, it does not yield the complete diode current in dynamic situations. Whenever the diode voltage changes rapidly with time, an additional component of current is required to charge and discharge the dipole layer of space charge which straddles the junction, because the amount of charge in either half of the dipole layer depends on the diode voltage. This charge distribution is shown for $V = 0$ in Fig. 1.2c. If we denote the charge in either half of the dipole layer as q_j, the current which changes the charge in the space-charge region is

$$i_j = -\frac{dq_j}{dt} = -\frac{dq_j}{dv} \cdot \frac{dv}{dt} \tag{1.9}$$

Clearly $(-dq_j/dv)$ represents a capacitance, and is often called the space-charge capacitance C_j. It is dependent on the bias voltage V and is usually most important for reverse bias or small forward bias, where the current i_j is the dominant term in the total diode current.

The space-charge capacitance depends on the details of the impurity distribution near the junction. For bias conditions in which the displacement current dominates at moderate frequencies, the voltage dependence of the capacitance can be approximated by:

$$C_j = K(\psi_0 - V)^{-n} \qquad (1.10)$$

where K is a constant, ψ_0 is the contact potential, V is the bias voltage, and n lies between $\frac{1}{2}$ (which applies for an abrupt junction) and zero.

1.3.6 *Summary of Diode Behavior*

A junction diode has nonlinear $V - I$ characteristics because of the asymmetry of hole and electron concentrations which exists on the two sides of a region of abrupt transition from p-type to n-type material. Because there are many carriers available to produce current in the forward direction, but very few carriers available to support junction current in the opposite or reverse direction, the diode conducts readily in the forward direction but poorly in the reverse direction. The current of a diode is closely related to the stores of excess carriers which exist in the neutral regions near the junction. Consequently its time dependence is in many ways similar to the behavior of a capacitor, with the principal complications caused by nonlinearities and the distributed nature of the diode.

1.4 JUNCTION TRANSISTORS

The physical configuration of a junction transistor is that of two pn-junction diodes back-to-back, with a common n-type or p-type region between them. Figure 1.7 shows the general physical structure of two important classes of junction transistors. The most important feature of these structures is the *thin* n-type region, separating the two p-type regions, which is referred to as the *base*. The p-type regions are referred to as the *emitter* and *collector*. A device in which the conductivity types of the emitter, base, and collector are ordered in this manner is called a *pnp* transistor. Similar structures having an *npn* arrangement are equally useful.

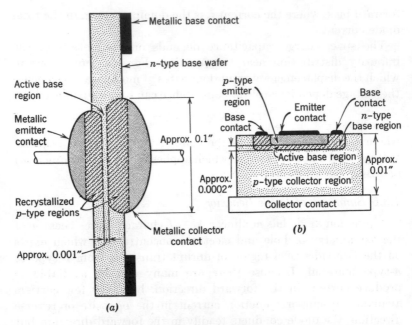

Fig. 1.7. Physical structures of junction transistors. The alloy unit is made by alloying a metal containing large amounts of p-type impurity into the n-type semiconductor wafer. When the wafer cools, the semiconductor recrystallizes with a preponderance of p-type impurities in the recrystallized regions. The diffused unit is made by diffusing n-type and p-type impurities into the p-type collector region.

Just as in the simple junction diode, excess carriers may be injected into or extracted from the base at either pn junction by applying a voltage to that junction. The base region in all transistors is so thin (usually in the range from 0.05 to 1.5 mils) that carriers can be transported across it with very little chance of recombination along the way. The probability that a carrier will recombine in the base is proportional to the average time that carriers spend in the base, and this time is very short if the base region is narrow. If the emitter-base junction is forward-biased, nearly all of the holes injected into the base at the emitter move across the base without recombining with majority-carrier electrons and are swept into the collector region by the electric field in the collector-junction space-charge layer. This field, which opposes the diffusion of majority carriers across the junction, is directed from the n-type to the p-type side for *both* polarities of collector junction voltage. Similarly, most of the holes injected into the base by a forward bias at the collector junction move across the base without recombination and are swept into the emitter region. In either case, base current comprises a flow of *majority-carrier* electrons which move into the base region to feed the recombination of hole-electron pairs in the base and to supply those electrons which are injected into or extracted from the emitter and collector. The base current is small compared with the corresponding emitter or collector current.

1.4.1 *A Static Transistor Model*

The preceding discussion suggests that the emitter and collector currents of the transistor can each be resolved into two independent components. Such a resolution is justified because the mechanisms governing the distribution and flow of carriers in the neutral regions are linear. As with the diode, the only nonlinearities are introduced by the Boltzmann factors discussed in connection with Eq. 1.3, relating to the concentrations of carriers at the space-charge layer edges.

In this resolution, both the emitter current and the collector current are expressed as the sum of two component currents. One component of the emitter current corresponds to minority-carrier injection or extraction at the emitter junction and is controlled by the emitter-base voltage. The associated component of the collector current is the result of minority-carrier transport across the base region and is similarly controlled by the emitter- base voltage. These components of the emitter and collector current are independent of the collector-base voltage. Analysis of the structure shows that these current components, which are associated with *forward operation** of the transistor, are given by

$$I_{EF} = I_{ES}(e^{qV_{EB}/kT} - 1)$$

$$I_{CF} = -\alpha_F I_{EF}$$

$$(1.11a,b)$$

---

* As used here, the adjective *forward* refers not to the polarity of the junction voltage but only to the fact that the forward components of the currents are under control of the emitter-base junction voltage.

The other component of the collector current corresponds to minority-carrier injection or extraction at the collector junction and is controlled by the collector-base voltage. The associated component of emitter current, which results from transport across the base, is similarly controlled by the collector-base voltage. These component currents, associated with *reverse operation*† of the transistor, are given by:

$$I_{CR} = I_{CS}(e^{qV_{CB}/kT} - 1)$$

$$I_{ER} = -\alpha_R I_{CR}$$

$$(1.12a,b)$$

The polarities of voltage and current used in these equations are defined in Fig. 1.8a.

Equations 1.11 show first that the forward component of emitter current is related to the emitter-to-base voltage exactly as in a simple isolated *pn*-junction diode, and second that a fraction α_F of the emitter current is transported to the collector junction. The coefficient α_F, which is known as the *forward short-circuit current gain*, usually lies in the range 0.9 to 0.995. Although its numerical value can be controlled by the designer, it is always slightly less than unity for two reasons:

(1) A small fraction of the holes injected into the base at the emitter recombine in the base or on its surface before reaching the collector.
(2) Not all of the emitter current is the result of hole injection into the base. Even in a well-designed transistor, some of the emitter current is the result of electrons which are injected *into* the emitter by the base (see Fig. 1.4.). These carriers clearly do not contribute to the collector current.

The equivalent diode saturation current I_{ES} is usually in the range of a few nanoamperes for silicon transistors to a few microamperes for most germanium units. It displays the same temperature dependence as the saturation current of a simple junction diode, which is shown in Fig. 1.6.

The interpretation of the second pair of equations describing the *reverse* components of current is entirely analogous to the

† As used here, *reverse* describes those current components which are controlled by the collector-base voltage, and does not refer to the polarity of a junction voltage.

Fig. 1.8. (*a*) Definition of transistor terminal variables. (*b*) The Ebers-Moll model.

previous discussion. The reverse short-circuit current gain α_R may vary from near unity to much less than unity, depending on the parameters and structure of the transistor.

Equations 1.11 and 1.12 can be combined to give the total emitter and collector currents, with the following results:

$$I_E = I_{EF} + I_{ER} = \quad I_{ES}(e^{qV_{EB}/kT} - 1) - \alpha_R I_{CS}(e^{qV_{CB}/kT} - 1)$$

$$I_C = I_{CF} + I_{CR} = -\alpha_F I_{ES}(e^{qV_{EB}/kT} - 1) + \quad I_{CS}(e^{qV_{CB}/kT} - 1)$$

$$(1.13a,b)$$

These equations represent the static current-voltage characteristics of a somewhat idealized transistor. They have a simple interpretation in terms of a circuit model commonly called the Ebers-Moll model, involving only dependent generators and idealized junction diodes, as shown in Fig. 1.8*b*. In this model the processes of injection or extraction at either junction are accounted for by the idealized diodes having saturation currents I_{ES} and I_{CS}, and the processes of minority-carrier transport across the base are accounted for by the two current-actuated dependent current generators. This transistor model has broad utility because it applies for arbitrary polarities of the voltages applied to the junctions.

1.4.2 *Dynamic Transistor Models*

The superposition of independent currents which produces the Ebers-Moll model can also be used as the basis for a dynamic model which is useful in estimating the transient behavior of the transistor in switching applications. This dynamic model is based upon a one-to-one correspondence between the forward or reverse components of the emitter and collector currents and the corresponding components of the excess minority-carrier store in the base. That is, we envision the total *excess* hole charge q_B in the base as resolved into two components q_{BF} and q_{BR}, as indicated schematically in Fig. 1.9*a*, and recognize that under static conditions, and even under relatively slowly changing dynamic conditions, there is a simple proportionality between the forward component of base charge and the corresponding component of collector current. More precisely, as shown in Fig. 1.9*b*, the slope of the triangular static charge distribution is proportional to the area under the distribution.

If the cross-sectional area of the base region (normal to the direction of flow of minority carriers) is A, the forward component of the base hole store is:

$$q_{BF} = q[\tfrac{1}{2}p_b{}'(0)WA] \qquad (1.14a)$$

where $p_b{}'(0)$ denotes the excess hole concentration at the emitter edge and W is the width of the neutral base region. Furthermore, the forward component of the collector current, which flows across

Fig. 1.9. Excess carrier distributions in the base region of a transistor. (a) Resolution of total excess charge into forward and reverse components. (b) Current and charge are proportional.

the base by diffusion as a consequence of the nearly constant concentration gradient $-p_b'(0)/W$, is given by

$$I_{CF} = -qAD_b \frac{p_b'(0)}{W} \qquad (1.14b)$$

where D_b designates the diffusion coefficient for minority carriers in the base. Consequently, the ratio of the forward component of the base charge to the corresponding component of the collector current is

$$\frac{q_{BF}}{I_{CF}} = -\frac{W^2}{2D_b} \equiv -\tau_F \qquad (1.15a)$$

This proportionality, which is based on the triangular *static* charge distribution, is valid under dynamic conditions as well if the rate of change of q_{BF} is low enough so that the instantaneous charge distribution changes as a succession of triangular steady-state distributions. This limitation is satisfied for most dynamic switching applications of transistors.

A corresponding proportionality applies for the reverse components. It is:

$$I_{ER} = -\frac{q_{BR}}{\tau_R} \qquad (1.15b)$$

Furthermore, each component of base charge is uniquely related to the corresponding component of the *base* current by a differential equation which is completely analogous to Eq. 1.8. Because the base region is approximately electrically neutral, the excess majority-carrier charge must be equal in magnitude to the excess minority-carrier charge. Furthermore, majority carriers can enter the base region only at the base terminal because there is very little flow of electrons across either junction in a well-designed transistor. Under dynamic conditions some of the electrons fed into the base region are used to increase the store of excess carriers in the base, while the rest feed the small amount of recombination which occurs in the base. Consequently, the forward component of base current may be written

$$-i_{BF} = \frac{dq_{BF}}{dt} + \frac{q_{BF}}{\tau_{BF}} \qquad (1.16a)$$

where τ_{BF} is a parameter determined by the recombination process in the base for forward operation. The analogous result for the reverse component is

$$-i_{BR} = \frac{dq_{BR}}{dt} + \frac{q_{BR}}{\tau_{BR}} \qquad (1.16b)$$

The two pairs of equations (Eqs. 1.15 and 1.16) are usually referred to as the *charge control* relationships of the transistor, because they emphasize that the forward component of the collector current (for example) is controlled by the forward component of the base charge which is in turn controlled by the forward component of the base current.*

* This characterization in terms of charge stores in the base must be modified if there is appreciable charge storage elsewhere in the transistor, e.g., in the collector region.

Equations 1.15 must, of course, reduce to the corresponding parts of the Ebers-Moll equations under static conditions. This reduction requires:

$$q_{BF} = \alpha_F I_{ESTF}(e^{qV_{BB}/kT} - 1)$$
$$q_{BR} = \alpha_R I_{CSTR}(e^{qV_{CB}/kT} - 1)$$

(1.17a,b)

It is entirely reasonable that each component of the base hole store should depend on the corresponding junction voltage as $(e^{qV/kT} - 1)$ because each component of the hole store is linearly dependent on the corresponding edge concentration (as in Eq. 1.14), and the edge concentration is exponentially dependent on the junction voltage because of the Boltzmann factor at that junction. Equations 1.17 show that a junction voltage can change sign only when the corresponding component of excess hole store in the base passes through zero. We shall have frequent recourse to this fact in our use of the charge-control equations.

The charge-control equations cannot readily be interpreted in terms of a circuit model unless we are willing to study the internal behavior of the transistor in considerably more detail. The large-signal dynamic behavior of the transistor is one example of an aspect of transistor electronics in which a complete understanding of the circuit performance of the device is inseparable from a thorough knowledge of the internal physical behavior of the device.

1.4.3 The Transistor as an Amplifier

In most applications where the transistor is used as an amplifier, it is operated with the emitter forward-biased and the collector reverse-biased, as shown in Fig. 1.10a. These conditions define the *normal mode* of operation. In the normal mode, the reverse components of current and charge are usually completely negligible in comparison with the forward components, so that the hole store in the base is as shown in Fig. 1.10b and the Ebers-Moll model may be approximated by the simple model of Fig. 1.10c.

The model of Fig. 1.10c shows that because of the exponential dependence of current on voltage, small changes in the emitter-to-base voltage produce relatively large changes in collector current. For example, a 10-mv change in V_{EB} produces approximately 50% change in I_C. Furthermore, the corresponding change in base

Fig. 1.10. The transistor as an amplifier. (*a*) The basic amplifier configuration. (*b*) Hole store in the base. (*c*) The amplifier circuit with an approximate form of the Ebers-Moll model.

current is much smaller than the change in collector current. As shown in Fig. 1.10c, the ratio of the base current to the collector current is $(1 - \alpha_F)/\alpha_F$. Since α_F is nearly unity, the base current is very small compared with the collector current. Inasmuch as all the currents as well as the voltages in the emitter-base circuit are essentially independent of the exact value of the reverse voltage on the collector junction, as long as this reverse voltage exceeds a few tenths of a volt, the change in load voltage which results from the change in V_{EB} can be permitted to become quite large. In other words, a large load resistance may be used in the collector circuit without altering the collector current swing produced by a given emitter voltage swing. Therefore, a transistor biased in the normal mode can exhibit large ratios of load power to input power because large swings in collector current and load voltage can be produced by relatively small changes in emitter-to-base voltage and base current. The power gain of a single-stage transistor amplifier can easily be as large as 10^4.

In the operation of a transistor as an amplifier, the changes in emitter-to-base voltage are often small enough so that the changes in the current and voltage thereby produced are *linearly* related to the change in V_{EB}. Consequently, a linear model of the device is desirable for use in circuit analysis. Such a linear model is particularly useful because it can describe small-signal dynamic operation as well as static operation.

1.4.4 A Small-Signal Transistor Model

With the emitter junction forward-biased and the collector junction reverse-biased, excess holes are injected from the emitter into the base, transported across to the collector junction, and swept into the collector body by the electric field in the collector-junction space-charge layer. We shall now consider the effects of a small positive increment in emitter-to-base voltage v_{eb}* (an increase in the forward voltage at the emitter junction) on the excess charge distributions in the base, and on the terminal currents. The excess hole distribution in the base before and after this change in volt-

---

* Lower-case variables with lower-case subscripts are used to designate instantaneous incremental components. The polarities are identical to those defined in Fig. 1.8a.

age is shown in Fig. 1.11. If the voltage does not change too rapidly, the distribution maintains its triangular shape during the change. It is clear from this sketch that application of v_{eb} has three consequences:

(1) The hole store in the base increases because the hole concentration at the emitter edge of the base increases. Because electrical neutrality is preserved, a transient component of base current must occur to supply the extra stored majority carrier electrons to the base region.

(2) Because of the increase in the base excess carrier store, more recombination occurs in the base. Consequently, the base current must increase to feed the increased recombination.

(3) The increase in base hole store causes an increase in the hole concentration gradient, thereby producing an increase in the collector current.

For small changes in v_{eb}, the corresponding changes in collector current and base current are directly proportional to v_{eb}. Therefore,

$$-i_c = g_m v_{eb} \qquad (1.18)$$

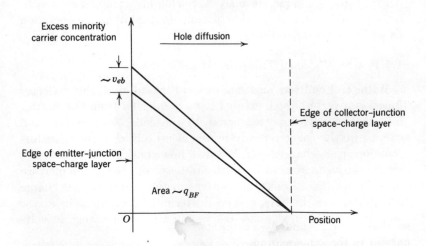

Fig. 1.11. The minority-carrier distribution in the base depends on the incremental emitter-base voltage.

The constant of proportionality, g_m, is known as the *transconductance* of the transistor. The transconductance can be evaluated directly from the change in slope depicted in Fig. 1.11. It can also be obtained by direct differentiation of the forward component of the equations describing the Ebers-Moll model, in particular Eq. 1.11b, (assuming $e^{qV_{EB}/kT} \gg 1$):

$$g_m = -\frac{dI_{CF}}{dV_{EB}} = -\frac{q}{kT}I_{CF} \qquad (1.19a)$$

Therefore, because $|I_{CF}| \gg |I_{CR}|$ in the normal mode, the transconductance may be written

$$g_m = \frac{q}{kT}|I_C| \qquad (1.19b)$$

where $|I_C|$ denotes the magnitude of the quiescent collector current.

As described above, the base current may be resolved into two components. One component is the result of the incremental increase in base region recombination which accompanies the incremental increase in excess charge stored in the base. This component is designated as $g_\pi v_{eb}$. The second component consists of the flow of carriers which provide the increase in excess carrier store in the base, and is designated as $C_b dv_{eb}/dt$. The total base current is:

$$-i_b = g_\pi v_{eb} + C_b \frac{dv_{eb}}{dt} \qquad (1.20)$$

The increase in recombination in the base is $-dI_{BF} = dq_{BF}/\tau_{BF}$ according to Eq. 1.16a, and $dq_{BF} = -\tau_F dI_{CF}$ in view of Eq. 1.15a. Therefore,

$$g_\pi = -\frac{dI_{BF}}{dV_{EB}} = -\frac{\tau_F}{\tau_{BF}}\frac{dI_{CF}}{dV_{EB}} = g_m\left(\frac{\tau_F}{\tau_{BF}}\right) \qquad (1.21a)$$

and

$$C_b = \frac{dq_{BF}}{dV_{EB}} = -\tau_F \frac{dI_{CF}}{dV_{EB}} = \tau_F g_m \qquad (1.21b)$$

so that both C_b and g_π are proportional to quiescent collector current in the same manner as is g_m.

Inasmuch as the charges and current in the transistor are, at least to first order, sensibly independent of the incremental component of the reverse bias on the collector junction, we can use Eqs. 1.20 and 1.21 to construct the simple incremental model shown in Fig. 1.12. This model describes the basic gain mechanism of the transistor for small-signal dynamic as well as static situations. It is useful for all frequencies at which the device has appreciable current gain.

Fig. 1.12. First-order small-signal model.

When the load impedance of the amplifier is such that the incremental voltage gain of the transistor is large (in the neighborhood of 10^3), a second-order mechanism requires a modification of the small-signal circuit model. This mechanism, which is referred to as *base-width modulation,* results from voltage dependence of the width of the collector junction space-charge region, which causes the effective base width to be voltage dependent. Figure 1.13 shows the consequences of the base-width modulation produced by an increment in collector junction bias. The change in collector junction voltage clearly has three consequences:

(1) The collector current changes because the slope of the minority-carrier distribution in the base changes.
(2) The change in stored base charge must be accompanied by a transient component of base current which supplies the additional stored majority carriers.
(3) The component of base current which feeds recombination must change to accommodate the change in stored base charge.

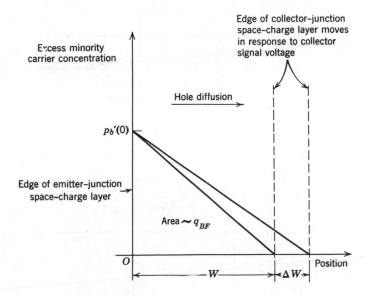

Fig. 1.13. The consequences of base-width modulation.

These changes are accounted for in the circuit model by adding two conductances, g_o and g_μ and the capacitor C_d shown in Fig. 1.14a. Because $\Delta W/\Delta V_{CE}$ is very small, both g_o and g_μ are very small compared with g_m, and C_d is much less than C_b; consequently, these elements influence the circuit performance appreciably only when the voltage gain is large. Because the stored excess base charge and the change in slope are proportional to $p_b(0)$ (see Fig. 1.13), the parameters g_o, g_μ, and C_d are proportional to I_C in the same manner as g_m (see Eqs. 1.14 and 1.19).

To complete the small-signal circuit model for the transistor, we must recognize that the emitter and collector junctions have space-charge-layer capacitances, which must be added as shown in Fig. 1.14b.

Finally, we should account for voltage drops in the base region which are caused by the transverse flow of majority carriers in the base *along* the thin dimension of the base region. In many cases these voltage drops can be modeled with sufficient accuracy simply by adding a series resistance to the base lead, although for some

Fig. 1.14. Evolution of a small-signal model for the transistor. (*a*) Model which includes base-width modulation effects. (*b*) Model with space-charge layer capacitances added. (*c*) Model which includes base resistance and space-charge layer capacitances.

applications a π network of series resistance and shunt resistance and capacitance is required. Because of transverse voltage drops in the base, it is frequently necessary to split the collector junction space-charge capacitance into two components: one which is charged through the base resistance or impedance and one (the so-called "overlap diode" capacitance) which is not. The relative values assigned to these capacitors depends vitally upon the geometrical arrangement of the transistor, as can be visualized by reference to Fig. 1.7.

Figure 1.14c shows the model which results when the base resistance r_x, the emitter junction space-charge capacitance C_{je}, and the two components of the collector junction space-charge capacitance C_{jc} and C_{sc} are added. Note that now the voltage which controls the dependent current generator at the collector is no longer equal to the incremental emitter-base voltage. To conform with usual circuit practice, we have reversed the polarity of both the dependent generator and the voltage which actuates it and have used V rather than v to designate that voltage; this notation refers to the complex amplitude of the incremental voltage. Finally, we have repeated the model in Fig. 1.15 with parallel capacitors combined and with the notation we use subsequently. Representa tive element values for a small-signal silicon transistor at an operating point of $I_C = 2$ ma, $V_{CE} = 5$ volts are also shown.

This small-signal model, which is usually called the hybrid-π* model, faithfully describes the incremental behavior of a transistor for all frequencies at which the device has reasonable gain. Although it appears complicated, we shall see in Chapter 3 that it is relatively simple to use for most applications, because it is seldom necessary to consider the effect of all of the circuit elements in any single calculation.

---

* The standard notation for the hybrid-π parameters, $r_{b'e}$, etc., is convenient for general discussion because the notation indicates the location of the element in the model. However, for circuit analysis the double subscripts with primes become cumbersome. We therefore use a single-subscript notation as follows:

$$r_x = r_{bb'} \qquad r_\mu = r_{b'c}$$
$$r_\pi = r_{b'e} \qquad C_\mu = C_{b'c}$$
$$C_\pi = C_{b'e} \qquad r_o = r_{ce}$$

$r_x = 50$ ohms

$r_\pi = 1/g_\pi = 1200$ ohms

$C_\pi = 200$ pf

$C_\mu = 5$ pf

$r_\mu = 1/g_\mu = 1$ megohm

$g_m = 0.08$ mho

$r_o = 1/g_o = 12$ kilohms

$C_{sc} = 3$ pf

Fig. 1.15. The small-signal transistor model with representative element values for an operating point of $I_C = 2$ ma, $V_{CE} = 5$ volts.

$$2$$

Circuit Models for Transistor
Volt-Ampere Characteristics

2.0 INTRODUCTION

In this chapter we study the characteristics of the Ebers-Moll nonlinear transistor model introduced in Sec. 1.4.1. We shall then compare these characteristics with those measured on some real transistors, and show how the four parameters in the Ebers-Moll equations, α_F, α_R, I_{ES}, and I_{CS}, can be determined from the measured curves or from information supplied in manufacturers' data sheets. In addition, we shall develop another nonlinear model called the *ideal-diode model*, which is somewhat simpler than the Ebers-Moll model, and consequently gives a correspondingly cruder approximation to transistor behavior. It should be emphasized at the outset that both of these nonlinear models can be used only over a restricted frequency range: namely, frequencies low enough that dynamic effects in the transistor can be ignored.

2.1 THE EBERS-MOLL MODEL

2.1.1 *Model Controlled by Terminal Voltages* (*or Diode Currents*)

The equations for the Ebers-Moll model of a *pnp* transistor, as postulated from a brief study of transistor physics in Chapter 1 (and developed analytically in more detail in PEM), are

$$I_E = \quad I_{ES}(e^{qV_{EB}/kT} - 1) - \alpha_R I_{CS}(e^{qV_{CB}/kT} - 1) \quad (2.1)$$

$$I_C = -\alpha_F I_{ES}(e^{qV_{EB}/kT} - 1) + \quad I_{CS}(e^{qV_{CB}/kT} - 1) \quad (2.2)$$

The four parameters α_F, α_R, I_{ES}, and I_{CS} are by definition positive numbers. The corresponding relations for an *npn* transistor are

$$I_E = -I_{ES}(e^{-qV_{EB}/kT} - 1) + \alpha_R I_{CS}(e^{-qV_{CB}/kT} - 1) \quad (2.1a)$$

$$I_C = \alpha_F I_{ES}(e^{-qV_{EB}/kT} - 1) - I_{CS}(e^{-qV_{CB}/kT} - 1) \quad (2.2a)$$

In the remainder of this section we will use the *pnp* transistor as the basis for discussion. The development, of course, applies to either, but suitable changes in sign must be made in the equations for application to *npn* transistors. Equations 2.1, 2.1a, 2.2. and 2.2a provide the needed information for these sign changes.

The model which corresponds to Eqs. 2.1 and 2.2 is shown in Fig. 2.1a (repeated from Fig. 1.8). Although the equations are written with the terminal voltages V_{EB} and V_{CB} as independent variables, to preserve linearity in the model we control the dependent sources by the *diode* currents. The diode currents are related to the terminal voltages by Eqs. 1.11 and 1.12. It is clear from the model or Eqs. 2.1 and 2.2, that I_{ES} is the reverse saturation current of the emitter diode when the collector terminal is *shorted* to the base ($V_{CB} = 0$), whereas I_{CS} is the collector saturation current when the emitter is shorted to the base.

The four parameters α_F, α_R, I_{ES}, and I_{CS} in the foregoing equations are not independent. This can be shown by considering the consequence of applying very small dc voltages to the transistor. Under these conditions, Eqs. 2.1 and 2.2 reduce (by series expansion) to

$$I_E = I_{ES}\left(\frac{q}{kT}\right) V_{EB} - \alpha_R I_{CS}\left(\frac{q}{kT}\right) V_{CB} \quad (2.3)$$

$$I_C = -\alpha_F I_{ES}\left(\frac{q}{kT}\right) V_{EB} + I_{CS}\left(\frac{q}{kT}\right) V_{CB} \quad (2.4)$$

On physical grounds, it is plausible that the transistor must now be indistinguishable from a simple block of resistive material with three leads. Thus it must possess under these conditions all the properties of such an element, including the property of *reciprocity*. It follows that

$$\alpha_R I_{CS} = \alpha_F I_{ES} \quad (2.5)$$

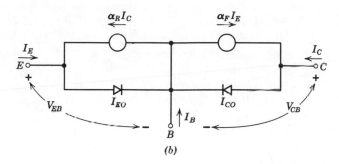

Fig. 2.1. Ebers-Moll model. (*a*) Model with dependent generators controlled by diode currents. (*b*) Model controlled by terminal currents.

2.1.2 *Model Controlled by Terminal Currents*

Many times it is desirable to transform the Ebers-Moll model to a form where the dependent sources are controlled by *terminal* currents, rather than *diode* currents. To find the desired model, we must recast Eqs. 2.1 and 2.2 to make them parametric in the terminal currents. Specifically, we first change the parameter in Eq. 2.1 from terminal voltage V_{CB} to terminal current I_C, by substituting for $I_{CS}(e^{qV_{CB}/kT} - 1)$ from Eq. 2.2 and defining new saturation-currents (also positive numbers):

$$I_{EO} = I_{ES}(1 - \alpha_F \alpha_R) \tag{2.6}$$

$$I_{CO} = I_{CS}(1 - \alpha_F \alpha_R) \tag{2.7}$$

The resulting equation for I_E is

$$I_E = -\alpha_R I_C + I_{EO}(e^{qV_{EB}/kT} - 1) \qquad (2.8)$$

A similar change of parameter in Eq. 2.2 from V_{EB} to I_E is accomplished by substituting from Eqs. 2.1 and 2.7:

$$I_C = -\alpha_F I_E + I_{CO}(e^{qV_{CB}/kT} - 1) \qquad (2.9)$$

The model which corresponds to Eqs. 2.8 and 2.9 is shown in Fig. 2.1b. It can be seen from the figure or from Eqs. 2.8 and 2.9 that I_{EO} is the reverse saturation current of the emitter diode when the collector is open-circuited ($I_C = 0$), whereas I_{CO} is the reverse saturation current of the collector diode when the emitter is open-circuited ($I_E = 0$).

The two models shown in Fig. 2.1 are, of course, completely interchangeable. The most important difference between them is that the dependent sources in Fig. 2.1b are *terminal current controlled*, whereas in Fig. 2.1a they are controlled by the *terminal voltages* or, equivalently, by the *diode currents*. We will have occasion to use both of these models in circuit analysis. The key factor in determining which model to use is whether the external circuit tends to constrain terminal *voltage* or terminal *current*.

2.1.3 *Regions of Operation*

The Ebers-Moll model describes the behavior of a transistor at its electrical terminals for arbitrary bias voltages. That is, either or both junctions can be forward- or reverse-biased. Often we can simplify circuit calculations by dividing transistor operation into four broadly defined states and developing simplified models appropriate for each. The states or regions of operation of a transistor are defined by the bias voltages on the two junctions. Because each junction may be either forward- or reverse-biased, four combinations are possible.

(1) *The Cutoff Region.* The condition of operation occurring when both junctions are reverse-biased is referred to as the cut-off region. We see from Eqs. 2.1 and 2.2 that the terminal currents are constant and essentially independent of the magnitudes of the reverse bias voltages, if these voltages are in excess of a few kT/q. The model for this case is shown in Fig. 2.2a. In constructing this model we have used the reciprocity relationship, Eq. 2.5.

(a) Cut-off region

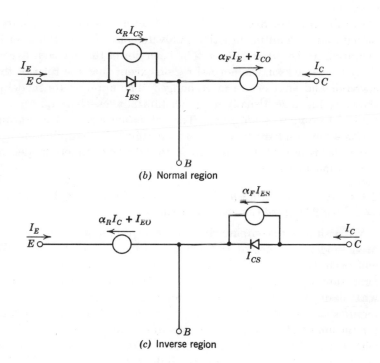

(b) Normal region

(c) Inverse region

Fig. 2.2. Simplified Ebers-Moll models.

(2) *The Normal Region.* The transistor is operating in the *normal region* when the emitter junction is forward-biased and the collector junction is reverse-biased. We have already encountered this condition of operation in Chapter 1, where we developed incremental models which describe *small* excursions in this region. If

the collector-junction reverse bias exceeds a few kT/q, the large-signal volt-ampere equation for the output circuit, Eq. 2.9, can be written as

$$I_C = -\alpha_F I_E - I_{CO} \tag{2.10}$$

This equation, together with Eq. 2.1, can be represented by the normal-region model of Fig. 2.2b. In many cases the current source in parallel with the idealized diode in the model may be neglected because it is small in comparison with typical normal-region emitter currents.

(3) *The Inverse Region.* If the collector junction is forward-biased and the emitter junction is reverse-biased, the transistor is operating in the *inverse region*. The behavior of the device is essentially the same as in the normal region except that the roles of the collector and emitter are interchanged. The appropriate model is shown in Fig. 2.2c. Usually α_R is substantially less than α_F.

(4) *The Saturation Region.* The *saturation region* of operation is defined by forward bias on both junctions. No simplification of the model is possible in this state; either of the complete models of Fig. 2.1 must be used.

2.1.4 *Comparison between Characteristics of the Ebers-Moll Model and Measured Common-Base Curves*

We wish now to compare the curves corresponding to the Ebers-Moll model with actual measured transistor characteristics. We will make the comparison first in terms of the common-base configuration, because the Ebers-Moll equations and model are somewhat easier to understand in this form. The common-base characteristics are usually plotted in current-controlled form. That is, for the input characteristics for instance, we plot I_E versus V_{EB} with I_C as the parameter. Therefore, Eqs. 2.8 and 2.9 are the appropriate form of the Ebers-Moll equations to use for the comparison.

The common-base curves corresponding to Eqs. 2.8 and 2.9 have been plotted in Fig. 2.3a and c, respectively. The corresponding set of transistor volt-ampere characteristics photographed from a curve tracer are shown for comparison in Fig. 2.3b and d. The general shape of the Ebers-Moll curves is seen to compare very favorably with the measured characteristics.

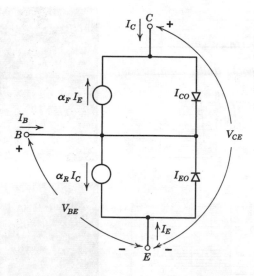

Fig. 2.4. Ebers-Moll model with common-emitter variables.

related to V_{BE} by the idealized semiconductor diode equation, Eq. 1.7, except that the voltage in the exponent is offset by an amount V_{CE}. For $(V_{CE} - V_{BE})$ more negative than -0.1 volt, the second term in Eq. 2.11 reduces to a constant, and again the relation reduces to a simple diode equation. This explains the shape of the so-called input curves shown in Fig. 2.5a.

For the output curves, operation of the transistor in the normal region is directly explained by Eq. 2.12. For the *pnp* transistor, if $(V_{CE} - V_{BE}) < -0.1$ volt, the exponential term in Eq. 2.12 is approximately zero, and the equation simplifies to

$$I_C = \left(\frac{\alpha_F}{1 - \alpha_F}\right) I_B - \frac{I_{CO}}{1 - \alpha_F} \tag{2.13}$$

The shape of the curves in most of the third quadrant of Fig. 2.5c is now obvious from the equation.

Note the important fact that for V_{BE} negative and $(V_{CE} - V_{BE}) < -0.1$ volt, which corresponds to third-quadrant (normal-region) operation for this *pnp* transistor, the input characteristics are virtually independent of the output voltage and current. In

Fig. 2.5. Common-emitter characteristics. (*a*) Ebers-Moll input curves. (*b*) Measured input curves. (*c*) Ebers-Moll output curves. (*d*) Measured output curves.

terms of Fig. 2.5, for V_{BE} one-tenth or two-tenths of a volt negative (forward bias on emitter diode) V_{CE} must be more than two- or three-tenths of a volt negative to satisfy the above condition. We conclude from Fig. 2.5*c* that the *input characteristics are virtually independent of the output voltage and current for normal-region operation.* This fact makes normal-region bias calculations very simple, because it is not necessary under these conditions to transfer load lines from input to output characteristics in order to find the operating point.

Manufacturers rarely show the set of curves appearing in the first quadrant of Fig. 2.5*c*, but this operating region (the inverse region) can be extremely useful for switch applications, as we shall see in Sec. 2.3. We can again use Eq. 2.12 to describe these first-quadrant curves, but it is simpler to start from Eq. 2.8, and eliminate I_E by Kirchhoff's law. Solution for I_C then yields

$$I_C = -\frac{I_B}{1 - \alpha_R} - \frac{I_{EO}}{1 - \alpha_R} (e^{-qV_{BE}/kT} - 1) \qquad (2.14)$$

We are looking for a set of curves which result when V_{CE} is positive and I_B is negative. From the model, Fig. 2.4, we see that if the collector voltage V_{CE} is more than half a volt positive, the collector diode is forward-biased, and the emitter diode reverse-biased, assuming a current-source base drive to make I_B negative. Thus V_{BE} is positive; in fact, it is almost as large as V_{CE}. Under these conditions the exponential factor in Eq. 2.14 goes to zero, and the equation can be rewritten as

$$I_C = \frac{-I_B}{1 - \alpha_R} + \frac{I_{EO}}{1 - \alpha_R} \qquad (2.15)$$

The shape of the curves in the first quadrant can now be deduced easily from this equation. The entire first-quadrant behavior can also be explained by considering the transistor to be in *common-collector* configuration with the role of the emitter and collector interchanged. Thus this region is the *inverse region* defined above.

We see from Fig. 2.2a that when both the emitter and collector diodes become reverse-biased, there are no further degrees of freedom in the model, and all currents are determined. That is, all three currents assume fixed limiting values of the order of I_{CO}, *regardless of the value of* V_{CE}. The exact limiting value for I_B can be found from Fig. 2.2 or Eq. 2.11:

$$I_B = I_{CS}(1 - \alpha_R) + I_{ES}(1 - \alpha_F)$$
$$= I_{CS}[1 - \alpha_R + (\alpha_R/\alpha_F)(1 - \alpha_F)] \qquad (2.16)$$

Substitution of typical values for α_F and α_R will show that this limiting value for I_B is close to I_{CO}. The limiting value for I_C is

$$I_C = -I_{CS}(1 - \alpha_R) \qquad (2.17)$$

which is between $-I_{CO}$ and $-I_{CO}/2$ for typical values of α_F and α_R.

The overall shape of the actual curves is reproduced well by the model curves, as shown by the comparison between the common-emitter curves of the Ebers-Moll model, Fig. 2.5a and c, and measured common emitter curves for a germanium transistor, Fig. 2.5b and d. But in detail the agreement is obviously not as favorable as the common-base comparison. There are two reasons why the model curves do not match the measured curves more closely. First, the effect upon α_F, α_R, I_{CS}, and I_{ES} of changes in base width caused by space-charge-layer widening has been ignored in the model. Second, α_F and α_R have been considered to be independent of current in the model, whereas actually they both depend on minority-carrier injection level. Both the voltage and the current dependence of the parameters are accentuated in the common-emitter connection because of the $(1 - \alpha)$ terms in the equations.

2.1.6 *Determination of Parameter Values*

One way of finding the Ebers-Moll parameters α_F and α_R is to match the Ebers-Moll curves to the measured curves. Working first from the common-base curves, Fig. 2.3, we see from Eq. 2.9 that the parameter α_F is the common-base short-circuit current gain in the normal-gain region. Therefore, α_F can be found readily from the measured common-base curves by noting the "average" vertical spacing between the curves in the output family. Similarly, the parameter α_R can be found from the common-base input curves.

Alternatively, the parameters can be determined by matching the common-emitter curves, Fig. 2.5. Here it is clearly impossible to achieve an exact fit between the Ebers-Moll curves and the measured ones, because the actual curves change in both slope and spacing as a function of collector current and voltage. The best that can be achieved is some kind of "average fit" over the region of interest. The spacing between the Ebers-Moll common-emitter output curves in the normal-gain region (third quadrant for *pnp* transistors) is, from Eq. 2.13,

$$\left. \frac{\Delta I_C}{\Delta I_B} \right|_{\substack{(V_{CE} \,=\, \text{constant} \,<\, 0, \\ \text{normal-gain region})}} = \frac{\alpha_F}{1 - \alpha_F} \equiv \beta_F \qquad (2.18)$$

Thus β_F can be found by noting the "average" spacing of the common-emitter output curves in the normal region. Then α_F can be calculated from Eq. 2.18.

The spacing of the output curves in the inverse region (first quadrant for *pnp* transistors) is from Eq. 2.15:

$$\left. \frac{\Delta I_C}{-\Delta I_B} \right|_{\substack{(V_{CE} \,=\, \text{constant} \,>\, 0, \\ \text{inverse-gain region})}} = \frac{1}{1 - \alpha_R} \qquad (2.19)$$

Thus α_R can be determined from Eq. 2.19 by finding the average spacing of the actual output curves in the inverse region. [If the measurement is made on a curve tracer, greater accuracy can often be obtained by interchanging emitter and collector leads and making the determination in the normal region of the *inverted* connection. Then from Eq. 2.18, the spacing between the curves gives $\beta_R = \alpha_R/(1 - \alpha_R)$, and from this we can calculate α_R.]

Sometimes manufacturers supply enough information in transistor data sheets to determine β_F (or α_F). If the output characteristics in the normal region are given, Eq. 2.18 can be used to make the determination. Even if characteristics are not given, data sheets usually do contain information on the low-frequency current gain measured with the output short-circuited (called h_{fe}, see Sec. 3.2.2). This current gain h_{fe} is actually a small-signal parameter, but does give some indication of an appropriate value for the large-signal parameter β_F.

The values of the saturation current parameters can be determined most accurately by direct measurement on the transistor, as indicated in Fig. 2.6. The experiment shown in Fig. 2.6a sets V_{CB} to zero. In this case, Eq. 2.1 reduces to:

$$I_E = I_{ES}(e^{qV_{EB}/kT} - 1) \qquad (2.20)$$

We determine I_{ES} by plotting $\log I_E$ versus V_{EB} for $V_{EB} > 0.1$ volt, and extrapolating *back* to zero V_{EB}.

The experiment indicated in Fig. 2.6b, determines the corresponding reverse parameter I_{CS}. The appropriate equation which applies for $V_{EB} = 0$ is

$$I_C = I_{CS}(e^{qV_{CB}/kT} - 1) \qquad (2.21)$$

(a)   (b)

Fig. 2.6. Determination of the parameters of the Ebers-Moll model. (a) Determination of I_{ES} by measuring I_E and V_{EB}. (b) Determination of I_{CS} by measuring I_C and V_{CB}.

The values of I_{CO} and I_{EO} can now be calculated from I_{CS} and I_{ES} by using Eqs. 2.6 and 2.7. Note that these two equations, together with Eq. 2.5, yield the reciprocity relation in terms of I_{CO} and I_{EO}:

$$I_{EO}\alpha_F = I_{CO}\alpha_R \qquad (2.22)$$

a relation which is often helpful for parameter determination.

It is clear from Eq. 2.13 that the amount of collector current flowing when $I_B = 0$, for common-emitter operation in the normal-gain region is equal to $I_{CO}/(1 - \alpha_F)$. Thus another method of determining I_{CO} is to find from actual output characteristics the value of I_C when $I_B = 0$, and then multiply this value by $(1 - \alpha_F)$. The problem with this measurement is that it is made at small collector currents, and, as we shall see in Chapter 4, α_F will be much smaller at these low currents than it is at normal operating currents. The model does not take these variations of current gain into account, and thus the value of I_{CO} will only be approximate when determined in this manner. The problem is particularly acute in silicon because $I_{CO}/(1 - \alpha_F)$ will be at most a few microamperes so that the calculated value of I_{CO} is liable to be in error by at least an order of magnitude.

The choice of current level for all of the above measurements is complicated by the following considerations:

(a) If the coefficients are measured at current levels that correspond to high injection levels in the base, the model does not apply and the fit between the measured and calculated curves will be poor.

(b) If the coefficients are measured at very low current levels but high voltages, by applying a large reverse bias to the junction, the measured currents will contain large components caused by surface leakage. In spite of this problem, manufacturers often specify in data sheets an "I_{CO}" measured in this way. Thus the data-sheet value for I_{CO} does not correspond directly with the I_{CO} in the Ebers-Moll model, particularly for silicon.

(c) If the coefficients are measured at very low forward currents and voltages, surface leakage effects will be small but in the space-charge region substantial recombination of carriers will take place. Therefore, the values of α and β measured in this region will be substantially smaller than those measured at higher voltages and currents.

2.2 IDEAL-DIODE MODEL

For many applications, particularly those involving large swings of I and V, it is appropriate to use a model which is simpler and less accurate than the Ebers-Moll model. This simpler model is derived by replacing each of the exponential diodes in the Ebers-Moll model with an *ideal piecewise-linear diode*. The square-box circuit symbol for the *ideal diode*, and its volt-ampere characteristic are shown in Fig. 2.7. This diode has, by definition, zero forward resistance and infinite back resistance; therefore, the characteristic is made up of two straight-line segments intersecting at the break-point $V = 0$, $I = 0$. The ideal-diode transistor model is shown in Fig. 2.8a. The corresponding set of curves shown in Fig. 2.8b can be derived from the model by the method of assumed-states, or breakpoint analysis. The reasonably close correspondence between these curves and actual common-base curves (Fig. 2.3) support the use of this simple model for large signal-swing applications. Remember, however, that the ideal diodes are invariant with temperature. Thus this model will not predict performance as a function of temperature.

The common-emitter curves corresponding to the ideal-diode model are shown in Fig. 2.9. Again the derivation can be made by either the assumed-states or breakpoint method, but the analysis problem is not as simple as it might appear. All breakpoints occur

(a)   (b)

Fig. 2.7. Ideal piecewise-linear diode. (a) Symbol. (b) Characteristic.

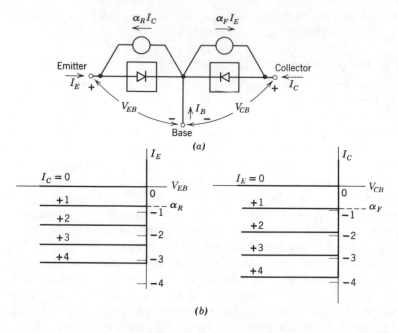

Fig. 2.8. (a) Ideal piecewise-linear-diode transistor model. (b) Common-base curves of ideal diode model.

on the I_C axis ($V_{CE} = 0$), so care must be exercised in keeping the various states sorted out.

Comparison of the idealized curves shown in Fig. 2.9b with actual common-emitter curves, Fig. 2.5, shows reasonable similarity, but the correspondence is not as close as it was in the common-base connection (as was the case with the Ebers-Moll model, and for the same reason).

An alternate common-emitter model, in which the collector current source depends explicitly on the input current I_B, is shown in Fig. 2.9c. The relation between β_F and α_F is given by Eq. 2.18.

Because we have used ideal diodes in this model, the saturation currents I_{CO} and I_{EO} are by definition zero. Thus there are only two parameters in the model, α_F and α_R, which can be found by the same methods given for the Ebers-Moll parameter determination. Of course, saturation currents can always be added to the ideal-

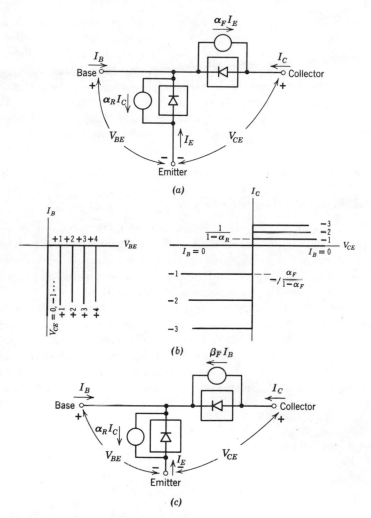

Fig. 2.9. (*a*) Ideal-diode model; common-emitter. (*b*) Corresponding curves. (*c*) Ideal-diode model with collector current-source modified.

diode model, if desired, by adding two current generators of values I_{EO} and I_{CO} in parallel with the emitter and collector diodes, respectively. As usual, the price paid for this increased accuracy of representation is increased complexity.

The ideal-diode model is extremely useful for first-order analysis and design of nonlinear circuits. For example, a glance at the ideal-diode model will quickly tell the designer which bias polarities to use for a given configuration in order to keep the emitter diode on and the collector diode off. In addition, the model can be used for order-of-magnitude small-signal calculations. Approximate current gains can readily be calculated, and the designer can get some idea of whether impedance levels in a circuit are high or low.

2.3 EXAMPLES OF NONLINEAR OPERATION

2.3.1 *Elementary Transistor Switch*

To illustrate the use of the Ebers-Moll model and the ideal-diode model, let us first analyze a simple transistor switch. The transistor is well suited for this application because, as we shall see, it can control the flow of large amounts of power while losing only small amounts of this power in internal dissipation.

Let us first discuss the properties of the *ideal switch* shown in Fig. 2.10*a*. When the switch is OFF, the resistance measured between the switch terminals is infinite, and when the switch is ON, the resistance is zero. In terms of a volt-ampere plot, the "output characteristics" of the ideal switch consist of straight lines representing the ON and OFF states, as shown in Fig. 2.10*b*. Note that

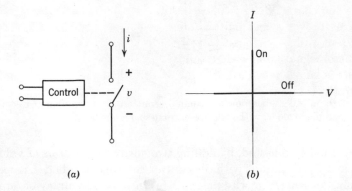

(a)   (b)

Fig. 2.10. Characteristics of an ideal switch.

these characteristics imply that the output part of the switch is lossless, because the product VI is always zero.

The control circuit shown in Fig. 2.10a causes the device to switch between its ON and OFF states. Ideally, the control circuit should consume no power. Also, there should be zero *feed-through* between the control circuit and the switch, where feed-through is that portion of the control signal which appears in the output circuit.

A simple *npn* transistor switch is shown in Fig. 2.11a. The transistor is switched between saturation and cutoff by the square wave e_M, and thus the current in R_L is switched from V_{CC}/R_L to zero. Both examples in this section will be worked with *npn* transistors, to complement the development in terms of *pnp* transistors in preceding sections.

The operation of the switch can best be explained in terms of the ideal-diode model, Fig. 2.11b. Note that we have changed here to lower-case letters with capital subscripts, indicating that the variables are total instantaneous quantities. However, the analysis is restricted to the *low-speed* aspects of the problem. The transients that occur during rapid switching intervals will be analysed in Chapter 9.

If we drive the base circuit with a square wave of peak amplitude E, then the base current will be either zero or E/R. Under these conditions the output characteristics are as shown in Fig. 2.11c. According to this analysis, it is clear that the circuit has the characteristics of the ideal switch postulated in Fig. 2.10, at least over some limited range of collector current. The load current will be changed from zero to V_{CC}/R_L in response to the control signal applied at the base, if the base current for the ON state is large enough to drive the transistor into saturation, that is, into the (1, 1) state.* For our circuit, this requires that

$$\frac{\beta_F E}{R} > \frac{V_{CC}}{R_L} \tag{2.23a}$$

---

* The notation (1, 1) is a convenient shorthand way of describing the diode states in problems involving ideal diodes. A "1" indicates the diode is ON, a "0" indicates OFF. The two numbers in parentheses indicate, respectively, the state of the *emitter* diode and the state of the *collector* diode.

Fig. 2.11. (*a*) Simple *npn* transistor switch. (*b*) Ideal-diode circuit model. (*c*) Ideal-diode output characteristics for $I_B = 0$ and $I_B = E/R$. Diode states indicated as follows: (D_e, D_c).

for V_{CC} positive, and

$$\frac{1}{1 - \alpha_R} \frac{E}{R} > \frac{|V_{CC}|}{R_L} \tag{2.23b}$$

for V_{CC} negative, where E is the peak amplitude of the driving square wave.

If we now move a step closer to reality and analyze the circuit in terms of the Ebers-Moll characteristics, Fig. 2.12, we find that the performance, while still excellent, is no longer ideal because three specific defects show up: (1) Current still flows when the transistor switch is OFF. (2) A small voltage drop remains across the transistor when it is ON. (3) The input circuit will dissipate a small amount of power (see Fig. 2.5a).

The collector current which remains flowing through the transistor in the OFF state would be $I'_{CO}/(1 - \alpha_F)$, if the base current were set to zero in this state. However, I_C is substantially reduced (by more than an order of magnitude) when the base-to-emitter voltage V_{BE} is driven negative. Under these conditions both the emitter and collector diodes become reverse biased, and the base

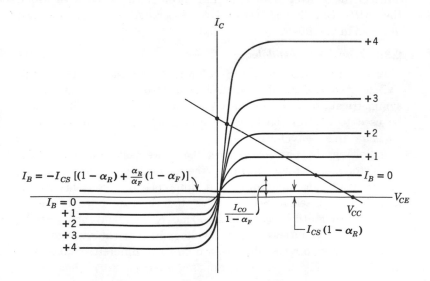

Fig. 2.12. Ebers-Moll output characteristics, *npn*.

and collector currents reduce to limiting values whose *magnitudes* are given by Eqs. 2.16 and 2.17, respectively. Because we are using *npn* transistors here, the limiting value of I_B will be negative, and I_C positive. These limiting values are both approximately equal in magnitude to I_{CO} for typical values of α_F and α_R.

The voltage across the transistor in the ON condition is the difference between the voltage drops across the two forward-biased diodes. Typical voltage drops across a germanium transistor in the ON state might thus be a few tenths of a volt for collector currents of several hundred milliamps. A typical value of I_{CO} for the same transistor might be 1 μa. Thus it is relatively easy to achieve ratios of ON current to OFF currents of 10^5 or 10^6, with an efficiency of greater than 95%; that is, a switch which can control more than twenty times as much power as it dissipates.

The maximum current limit on the switch is set either by the permissible dissipation of the transistor or by the available base drive, Eqs. 2.23. The maximum positive limit on V_{CC} is set by the reverse breakdown voltage of the collector diode (see Section 4.5). The maximum negative limit is dependent on the reverse breakdown of the emitter diode. The limitation on the speed with which the switch can change from ON to OFF or OFF to ON is discussed in detail in Chapter 9.

2.3.2 *Transistor Modulator*

In the circuit discussed in Sec. 2.3.1, the transistor was used to switch or control the flow of dc current. However, because of the symmetrical properties of the transistor, the same circuit can also be used to control the flow of *ac* current; that is, to switch or *modulate* an ac waveform.

Following the pattern of Sec. 2.3.1, we will first discuss the transistor modulator in terms of the ideal-diode model, as shown in Fig. 2.13. The first important difference between this circuit and that discussed in Sec. 2.3.1, is that the load line, instead of passing through the fixed point V_{CC}, moves back and forth parallel to itself, always intersecting the voltage axis at the voltage $e_I(t)$. The load lines corresponding to a number of different values of e_I are shown in Fig. 2.13c. It is apparent that $e_O = e_I$ whenever i_B is zero, and $e_O = 0$ whenever i_B is positive enough to saturate the transistor.

Fig. 2.13. Transistor modulator. (*a*) Circuit. (*b*) Ideal-diode circuit model. (*c*) Output characteristics. Diode states indicated as follows: (D_e, D_c).

The operation of the modulator in the normal region (the first quadrant for this *npn* transistor) is as follows. Assume a fixed positive value of e_I. Then for e_M negative, both the emitter and collector diodes are OFF $(0, 0)$, and all currents are zero. When e_M is made positive, the emitter diode closes $(1, 0)$ and base current starts to flow. If the base current is made sufficiently positive by increasing e_M, the collector diode also closes and the transistor saturates $(1, 1)$.

Operation of the modulator in the third quadrant (e_I negative) requires some further explanation. For e_M negative, and also more negative than e_I, both diodes must be OFF $(0, 0)$ and all currents must be zero. Under these conditions $e_O = e_I$. To turn the modulator ON, we make e_M positive. However, the sequence of diode closing is different from the first-quadrant case discussed above. If we assume e_I fixed at some negative value, when e_M becomes less negative than e_I the *collector* diode turns ON $(0, 1)$. The emitter diode is still OFF, because the base voltage V_{BE} is still negative. When e_M becomes positive, the emitter diode is turned ON $(1, 1)$ and the transistor is saturated. Another way of looking at the operation of the modulator with e_I negative is that the transistor is operating common-collector in the inverted mode; that is, with the roles of emitter and collector interchanged.

The waveforms of the modulator for a sinusoidal input waveform and a square-wave modulating signal e_M are shown in Fig. 2.14. The driving square wave appears to chop or modulate the input sine wave. Every time the square wave is negative, the transistor

Fig. 2.14. Waveforms for ideal-diode transistor modulator.

is OFF, so the input signal appears unattenuated at the output. When the driving square wave is positive, the transistor is switched ON, and the output is reduced to zero. Those familiar with balanced modulators will recognize that if the output waveform $e_O(t)$ were filtered to remove the low-frequency component at the frequency of e_I, the resulting waveform would represent the balanced modulation of e_I by e_M. Remember, however, that the voltage e_M must have a negative excursion larger than the peak negative value of e_I to keep the collector diode OFF when e_M is negative. If this condition is not met, the output waveform $e_O(t)$ will flatten out or saturate.

Now that the basic properties of the modulator are understood, let us use a more realistic model, the Ebers-Moll model, in order to study more carefully some of the fundamental limitations of the circuit. In Fig. 2.15a, c, and e the Ebers-Moll common-emitter output characteristics are drawn to different scales to emphasize different parts of the characteristics. In a, the overall shape of the curves is illustrated. The current scale has been greatly expanded in c to show the cutoff region more clearly. In e, both the voltage and current scales have been again expanded to show in detail the characteristics in the vicinity of the origin. One important feature shown by these curves is the fact that, according to the Ebers-Moll equations, all characteristics pass through a common intersection point. To find this point, we rewrite the Ebers-Moll output relation, Eq. 2.2a, in terms of V_{BE} and V_{CE} by substituting $V_{CB} = V_{CE} - V_{BE}$:

$$I_C = I_{CS} - \alpha_F I_{ES} + e^{qV_{BE}/kT}[\alpha_F I_{ES} - I_{CS} e^{-qV_{CE}/kT}] \quad (2.24)$$

If there is a point (I_{Ci}, V_{CEi}) which is independent of I_B, then it also must be independent of V_{BE} (see Eq. 2.12). Thus it follows from Eq. 2.24 that

$$\alpha_F I_{ES} - I_{CS} e^{-qV_{CEi}/kT} = 0$$

or

$$V_{CEi} = \frac{kT}{q} \ln \frac{1}{\alpha_R} \quad (2.25)$$

and

$$I_{Ci} = I_{CS} - \alpha_F I_{ES}$$
$$= I_{CS}(1 - \alpha_R) \quad (2.26)$$

Fig. 2.15. (*a*), (*c*), and (*e*) Ebers-Moll *npn* common-emitter output curves, drawn to three different scales. The size of the base current steps has been appropriately adjusted in each plot. (*b*), (*d*), and (*f*) Measured common-emitter output curves plotted to the same scale.

For the characteristics shown in Fig. 2.15, these coordinates have values $V_{CEi} = 2.5$ mv, $I_{Ci} = 1\mu a$.

Actual output curves for a germanium transistor, Fig. 2.15b, d, and f, show good correlation with the Ebers-Moll plots. The "intersection point" given by the Ebers-Moll model has become an intersection area, but it still can be treated with reasonable accuracy as a point. For silicon, the agreement would not be as good, particularly in regard to I_{Ci}, which might well be an order of magnitude larger than predicted by Eq. 2.26 because of the falloff in β at low currents.

A study of these curves will show three defects of the transistor modulator:

1. From Fig. 2.15a, when the modulator is ON, the output voltage will not be zero.

2. From Fig. 2.15c, when the modulator is OFF, the output voltage e_O will not be exactly equal to e_I, but will be smaller than e_I by a small amount if e_I is positive, and larger than e_I by the same small amount if e_I is negative.

3. Illustrated in Fig. 2.15e is the fact that there will still be an output e_O when $e_I = 0$, that is, when the load line passes through the origin. This voltage, the feed-through voltage, will be a replica of the square-wave driving signal.

Defect 1 will be a symmetrical effect, influencing the positive and negative portions of the output waveform by the same proportion. However, defects 2 and 3, both resulting from the nonzero crossover point of the characteristics, influence the output voltage in an unsymmetrical manner, and therefore represent an undesired imbalance in the modulator. For a typical modulator, these defects might give rise to undesired output voltages of the order of 10 to 20 millivolts, which might well be smaller than the desired output voltage by a factor of 100 or 1000.

The maximum current limit for this modulator circuit is exactly the same as for the switch, Sec. 2.3.1. The maximum voltage limits are somewhat more complicated. As discussed above, to hold the collector diode OFF for e_I negative, e_M must be more negative than e_I. Thus the maximum negative value of e_I is set by the maximum negative value of e_M or by the reverse breakdown voltage of the collector diode. The maximum positive value of e_I is set by the reverse breakdown voltage of the collector diode. Specifically, e_I must be less than the reverse breakdown voltage minus $|e_M|$.

2.3.3 *The Inverted Connection*

The performance of the modulator discussed above would under many circumstances be entirely satisfactory. However, in many instances it is important that the modulator imbalance be reduced to as small a value as possible. The imbalance can always be reduced by using the transistor in the "inverted" connection; that is, by interchanging the emitter and collector leads in the circuit. A quick glance at the Ebers-Moll model or the ideal-diode model, Figs. 2.4 or 2.8, shows that when this interchange is made, the basic operation of the circuit will remain virtually unchanged. All the previous discussions are valid if we merely interchange the terms α_F and α_R, and also I_{CO} and I_{EO}. Thus from Eqs. 2.25 and 2.26 we obtain a new set of equations for V_{CEi} and I_{Ci} as follows:

$$V_{CEi} = \frac{kT}{q} \ln \frac{1}{\alpha_F} \tag{2.27}$$

$$I_{Ci} = I_{ES}(1 - \alpha_F) \tag{2.28}$$

If we now compare Eq. 2.27 with 2.25 and Eq. 2.28 with 2.26, we can readily see the value of the inverted connection. The values of V_{CEi} and I_{Ci} for the inverted connection will always be smaller than the corresponding values for the normal connection. (It should be clear that α_F is by definition larger than α_R, otherwise we could assume that the transistor manufacturer had labeled the leads incorrectly in the first place. It follows from Eq. 2.5 that I_{CS} is always larger than I_{ES}). Substantial improvement in performance results when a germanium transistor with α_F close to unity is used in the inverted connection. For I_{Ci}, an order of magnitude improvement is realized. Because $\beta_R < \beta_F$, and the emitter breakdown voltage is usually smaller than the collector breakdown voltage, the inverted connection is used primarily in low-level modulator applications.

Some variations of the basic modulator circuit are included in the problems. (See Problems P2.8 to P2.11.)

2.3.4 *Simple Pulse Inverter*

Another example of the nonlinear operation of a transistor is the simple *npn* transistor pulse inverter shown in Fig. 2.16. The corresponding ideal-diode circuit model is also shown in this figure. Suppose we wish to find the voltage-transfer function v_O versus v_I for this circuit. Because we have chosen to use the ideal-diode model, all characteristics will be made up of straight-line segments, so the analysis is simple. We start by drawing the circuit models for the saturation (1, 1) state and the cutoff (0, 0) state, Fig. 2.17a and b. In the (0, 0) state, $v_O = V_C$. From Fig. 2.16, any value of v_I less than zero will maintain the circuit in this state.

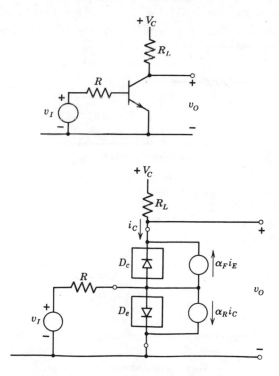

Fig. 2.16. Simple transistor pulse inverter (*npn*).

(a) Saturation (1, 1) state

(b) Cut-off (0, 0) state

(c) Transfer function

Fig. 2.17. Transistor pulse inverter.

For the $(1, 1)$ state, $v_O = 0$, and $i_C = V_C/R_L$. To maintain this state, there must be at least enough base current to produce this value of i_C. That is,

$$i_B \geq \frac{i_C}{\beta_F} = \frac{V_C}{\beta_F R_L} \tag{2.29}$$

The corresponding condition on v_I is

$$v_I \geq \frac{V_C R}{\beta_F R_L} \tag{2.30}$$

If the end-points of the $(0, 0)$ and $(1, 1)$ state lines are joined by a straight line corresponding to the $(1, 0)$ state, the transfer function shown in Fig. 2.17c results. The gain of the circuit in the $(1, 0)$ state is clearly $\beta_F R_L/R$. The circuit is called a pulse inverter because if a pulse is applied at the input and the gain is large, a pulse of fixed amplitude V_C but opposite polarity appears at the output. To insure an inverter gain greater than unity, it follows from Eq. 2.30 that we must meet the condition $\beta_F R_L/R > 1$.

2.3.5 *Bistable Multivibrator*

If we cascade two pulse inverters, and connect the output back to the input, the resulting circuit is a *bistable multivibrator*. To show this, we first find the transfer function of two identical inverters connected as in Fig. 2.18a. The three transfer functions shown in the figure are drawn on the basis that the second stage does not load the first, that is, $R \gg R_L$, in which case Fig. 2.18b and c are identical to Fig. 2.17c. Note that because β_F is usually large (that is, of the order of 100) the assumption that $R \gg R_L$ is nonetheless consistent with the assumption that the inverter gain is greater than unity, i.e., $\beta_F R_{Lo}/R > 1$, an assumption we need later on to insure multivibrator action.

Let us trace through the over-all transfer curve v_3 versus v_1, Fig. 2.18d, a step at a time. First, assume that v_1 is negative. From Fig. 2.18b, $v_2 = V_C$ and the first transistor T_1 is cut off. We find from Fig. 2.18c that under these conditions $v_3 = 0$, and the second transistor T_2 is saturated. If we now increase v_1, then for $v_1 = 0$, T_1 enters the normal region. If the inverter gain $\beta R_L/R$ is greater

(a)

(b)   (c)

(d)

Fig. 2.18. Two cascaded pulse inverters.

than one, then $v_{2a} < V_C$ so T_2 will remain in saturation. For $v_1 > v_{1a}$, where v_{1a} is defined in Fig. 2.18b and c, T_2 will come out of saturation and v_3 will start to rise. For $v_1 = v_{1b}$, T_1 saturates and T_2 reaches cutoff simultaneously, so for $v_1 > v_{1b}$, the output v_3 is at the cutoff value of V_C.

The circuit as drawn in Fig. 2.18 is not particularly useful. But because the circuit now has *positive* gain, which can be greater than one, the possibility arises of using the circuit to supply its own input. That is, we can use the voltage v_3 in place of the voltage source v_1, as shown in Fig. 2.19a. (The circuit is redrawn in a more conventional form in b.) Essentially we have added to Fig. 2.18a a linear constraint $v_1 = v_3 + e_{trig}$, where e_{trig} is a triggering voltage required to cause the multivibrator to change state. In Fig. 2.19c this constraint has been superimposed on the transfer function, yielding an operating point A, with transistor T_2 cut off, and T_1 saturated. If e_{trig} is now reduced to zero, point A will move to the left, but T_2 will remain cut off and T_1 will remain saturated. However, if e_{trig} is made negative enough, the constraint line $v_1 = v_3 + e_{trig}$ no longer intersects the transfer curve at $v_3 = V_C$, but intersects at $v_3 = 0$. This condition is indicated by the dashed constraint line in Fig. 2.19c. Thus the circuit abruptly changes to a new operating point B with T_2 saturated and T_1 cut off. In other words, in response to the change in trigger voltage, the circuit has changed state. If e_{trig} is returned to its original value, the circuit will return to its original state. Successively applied positive and negative trigger pulses will therefore cause the circuit to switch alternately from one state to the other.

We have assumed in drawing the figure that the transistors are identical, and $\beta R_L/R > 1$, thereby assuring that the slope in the normal region is greater than 1. These conditions are sufficient to insure the existence of only two stable states. Other methods of showing this are presented in Digital Transistor Circuits.*

We conclude that the circuit in Fig. 2.19b has two stable states and that it can be made to "flip" from one stable state to the other by applying a suitable trigger pulse, hence the name *bistable multivibrator* or *flip-flop*. The circuit has wide application in pulse and digital circuit designs.

---

* J. N. Harris, *Digital Transistor Circuits* (hereinafter referred to as DTC).

(a)

(b)

(c)

Fig. 2.19. Bistable multivibrator.

2.4 TEMPERATURE DEPENDENCE

We conclude this chapter by discussing the variation of transistor volt-ampere characteristics as a function of temperature. The common-emitter input and output characteristics of a *pnp* germanium-alloy transistor measured at three different temperatures are shown in Fig. 2.20. For simplicity we have plotted only the normal operating region, that is, emitter diode forward-biased and collector diode reverse-biased. Also, we have followed the convention of plotting the normal region in the first quadrant, even though this means plotting negative current versus negative voltage for the *pnp* transistor.

For the choice of coordinates in the figure, the dominant motion of the input characteristics is downward and to the left with increasing temperature. The output characteristics on the other hand suffer a pronounced shift upward with increasing temperature. The latter displacement amounts to nearly 5 ma for this particular transistor at 75°C. It is important to observe, however, that the lower boundary of the normal region does *not* move substantially, in spite of the large displacement. The figure shows clearly that a new set of curves for *positive* base current begins to appear on the characteristics below the $I_B = 0$ line.

The variation of transistor characteristics as a function of temperature can be explained readily in terms of the Ebers-Moll model. We saw from Eq. 2.11 and the ensuing discussion that the common-emitter input curves amount essentially to diode curves. Thus we would expect that the dominant temperature effect would be a change in the "saturation current," which for these characteristics is given by Eq. 2.16. This current, because it depends directly on I_{CS}, is extremely temperature-dependent, as shown by Figs. 1.5 and 1.6.

The $V_{CE} = 0$ curve of the input characteristics must always pass through the origin, because for $V_{CE} = V_{BE} = 0$, all currents must be zero. This fact, coupled with the known temperature dependence of the current defined in Eq. 2.16, allows us to predict the shift of the input curves with temperature.

Often in biasing calculations it is helpful to express the temperature dependence of the input characteristics in terms of the change in V_{BE} for constant I_E. The required relationship can be found

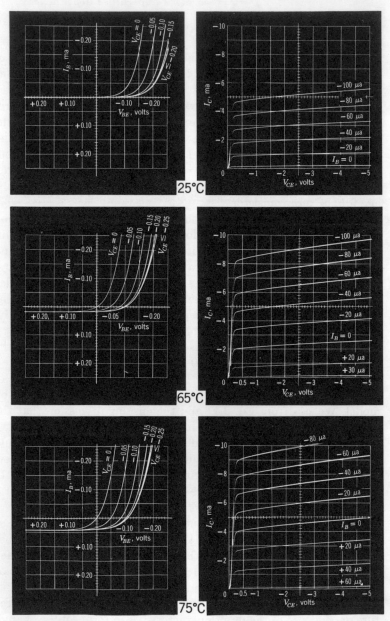

Fig. 2.20. Common-emitter characteristics of a *pnp* germanium-alloy transistor, measured at 25°C, 65°C, and 75°C.

Fig. 2.21. Common-emitter characteristics of an *npn* silicon transistor measured at 25°C, 75°C, and 105°C.

73

from the Ebers-Moll relations and the expression for the temperature-dependence of the saturation current*

$$\frac{\partial |V_{BE}|}{\partial T}\bigg|_{I_E = \text{constant}} \cong 2 \text{ mv/degree C} \qquad (2.31)$$

This value turns out to be nearly the same (within about $\pm 50\%$) for all types of transistors, and all normal values of I_E.

Turning now to the output characteristics, we see that the entire set of curves moves up with increasing temperature by an amount proportional to the change in I_{CO}. Specifically, from Eq. 2.12 the $I_B = 0$ curve in the normal region is always displaced above the $I_C = 0$ axis by an amount equal to $I_{CO}/(1 - \alpha_F)$. From Chapter 1, we know that I_{CO} is an exponential function of temperature. For germanium transistors, I_{CO} is of the order of a few microamps at room temperature, and doubles for every $10°C$ increase in temperature (see Fig. 1.6). Thus the displacement of the $I_B = 0$ curve can well amount to several milliamps at 60 or 70°C, as is borne out by the curves shown in Fig. 2.20.

The appearance of new curves for positive base current in the normal region can be explained by noting that the boundary between the normal and cutoff regions is defined by the emitter-to-base voltage and not by the base current. That is, the change of state occurs at $V_{BE} \cong 4kT/q$. From Eq. 2.17 the normal region thus extends down to $I_C = -(1 - \alpha_R)I_{CS}$.

A set of input and output characteristics for an *npn* silicon planar transistor measured at three different temperatures is shown in Fig. 2.21. For the choice of coordinates shown in the figure, the input characteristics again shift downward and to the left with increasing temperature, but I_{CS} is so small that it is difficult to see any appreciable downward shift on the scale plotted here. Equation 2.31 is probably the most useful form of analytic expression for the temperature dependence of these characteristics.

In silicon transistors, the displacement of the output characteristics is hardly noticeable, because I_{CO} is so small. This is true in spite of the fact that I_{CO} actually increases faster with temperature in silicon than in germanium, doubling every seven degrees at high temperatures in silicon. The principal change in the output charac-

* PEM, Sec. 3.3.4.

teristics that we observe in Fig. 2.21 is a substantial increase in β_F with increasing temperature, brought about by the increased carrier thermal motion.

PROBLEMS

P2.1 A *pnp* transistor has $\alpha_F = 0.95$, $\alpha_R = 0.70$, $I_{CS} = 50\ \mu a$. What are the terminal currents when the transistor is biased in the cutoff mode as shown in Fig. 2.22? Compare with I_{CO}.

Fig. 2.22.

P2.2 Two sets of measurements made on a *pnp* transistor are shown in Fig. 2.23*a* and *b*. Assuming that the transistor can be represented by the Ebers-Moll model, estimate I_C and V_{CE} for the circuit in Fig. 2.23*c*. Make reasonable assumptions.

$I_E = 2\ \text{ma}$, $I_B = -0.05\ \text{ma}$

$I_C = -10\ \mu a$

(a)   *(b)*

(c)

Fig. 2.23.

P2.3   Find either by breakpoint analysis or by assumed-state analysis the common base and common emitter input and output curves for the ideal-diode model. Check your answers with Figs. 2.8 and 2.9.

P2.4   Plot and dimension the output waveform for the circuit of Fig. 2.24. Assume that the transistor may be represented by the ideal diode model.

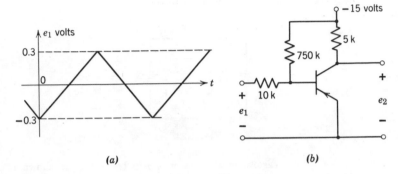

<table>
<tr><td>(a)</td><td>(b)</td></tr>
</table>

Fig. 2.24.

P2.5   The circuit of Fig. 2.25 is a simple transistor regulator for a d.c. power supply. Assuming that the transistor can be represented by the ideal-diode model with $I_{CO} = I_{EO} = 0$, determine and plot
    (a) e_2 versus e_1;
    (b) i_1 versus e_1.

Fig. 2.25.

P2.6   The transistor whose characteristics are shown in Fig. 2.15b is used as a switch in the circuit shown in Fig. 2.26.
    (a) When $v_d(t) = +5$ volts, the transistor should present a low impedance at the terminals a and a'. What range of values of the closed-switch current i can be tolerated under these conditions?

(b) When $v_d(t) = -5$ volts, the transistor should present a high impedance at the terminals a and a'. What range of values of the open-switch voltage v can be tolerated under these conditions?

Fig. 2.26.

P2.7 (a) Which of the circuits shown in Fig. 2.27a and b can be used to perform the function of the single-pole double throw switch shown in Fig. 2.27c?

(b) During which interval of time (A or B) is the transistor switch in Position 1? Assume $V = 10$ v, $R = 1$ k, $\beta_F = 40$, $\beta_R = 20$. Also

Fig. 2.27.

assume that no junction has a reverse breakdown voltage less than 80 volts.

The transistor is used to switch a *sinusoidal* signal.

(c) What is the maximum peak amplitude of sinusoidal current that can be applied to the ''closed'' circuit of the switch?

(d) What is the maximum peak amplitude of sinusoidal voltage that can be applied to the "open" circuit of the switch?

P2.8   In Fig. 2.28, two transistor modulators are connected in cascade. In what way is this circuit better than the single-transistor modulator, Fig. 2.13a.

Fig. 2.28.

P2.9   In Fig. 2.29, a *pnp* and an *npn* transistor are combined to produce a single pole, double-throw switch. Describe the operation of this circuit, using an ideal-diode model for the transistors.

Fig. 2.29.

P2.10 Several two-transistor modulator circuits have been devised which overcome some of the modulator imbalance problems discussed in Secs. 2.3.2 and 2.3.3. Two such circuits are shown in Fig. 2.30. Discuss the operation of these circuits in terms of the Ebers-Moll model, paying particular attention to modulator imbalance problems.

(a)

(b)

Fig. 2.30.

P2.11 The transistor modulator circuit can be used in any of the generic line of applications which develop from any basic balanced modulator circuit; for example, phase detectors, synchronous detectors, pulse stretchers, phase modulators, etc. An example of this, a transistor phase detector, is shown in Fig. 2.31. In this application the incoming signal $e_I(t)$ and the driving signal $e_M(t)$ are at the same frequency, and it is desired to derive a dc output voltage which is approximately proportional to the phase angle between the two signals. For the case of square-wave drive shown in the figure, show that the dc output voltage e_C at the output of the RC filter is proportional to the time delay τ between the two signals.

Fig. 2.31.

P2.12 Use the data of Fig. 2.20 to *estimate* I_{CO}, I_{EO}, α_F, and α_R at 25°C, 65°C, and 75°C. What conclusions can you draw about the temperature dependence of α_F and β_F? Plot log I_{CO} versus T. Why is this relationship approximately linear?

Parameter Determination and Circuit Properties of Hybrid-π Model

3.0 INTRODUCTION

In Chapter 1 we developed the configuration of the hybrid-π model by considering the physical processes that go on inside a transistor. In this chapter we first show how this model can be simplified to permit more rapid circuit calculations. Then we show how the element values of the hybrid-π model can be determined from electrical measurements at the transistor terminals.

3.1 SIMPLIFIED HYBRID-π CIRCUITS

At first glance it may appear that the hybrid-π model is somewhat complicated for circuit analysis. We shall show, however, that some elements in the model play dominant roles over certain frequency ranges or load impedance values, while over the same ranges other elements can be neglected completely. Only rarely is it necessary to use the complete model. Thus in this section various simplified models are studied in detail, because they represent the key to the understanding and application of the hybrid-π model.

It is important to recall from our physical considerations that the small-signal response of the transistor changes not only as a function of frequency, but also as a function of both operating point and temperature. For simplicity, however, we restrict the discussion in this chapter to the behavior of the transistor circuit as a function of frequency only, reserving until Chapter 4 the discussion of the effects of operating point and temperature.

3.1.1 *The Three Frequency Ranges*

Our first and most important step is to see how, at a given operating point and temperature, the hybrid-π model can be broken down into a series of simpler models, each one applicable over a limited frequency range. This discussion requires the introduction of numerical values as a basis of assessing the relative importance of the various elements in the model at various frequencies. Numerical values are therefore given in Fig. 3.1 for the hybrid-π elements of a silicon planar transistor at $V_{CE} = 10$ volts, $I_C = 10$ ma, and $T = 290°K$. Remember, however, that the numbers given in this figure, while representative for the given operating point, are by no means universal. As we shall see, both $r_π$ and g_m, for example, change by approximately an order of magnitude if the current I_C is changed by that amount. Also, the values of $C_π$ and $C_μ$ are markedly different for different transistor types, even at the same operating point. But although the numbers involved in this and the succeeding discussion change with temperature, operating point, and transistor-type, the principle of devising simplified models of course remains valid.

Fig. 3.1. Hybrid-π model with representative numerical values for a silicon planar transistor at $V_{CE} = 10$ volts, $I_C = 10$ ma.

As a first step, let us make a rough calculation to find out the relative importance of the two elements r_μ and C_μ in the feedback path of the model. At a frequency

$$\frac{1}{2\pi C_\mu r_\mu} = \frac{1}{(2\pi)(6)(10^{-12})(10^6)} \cong 27 \text{ kc} \qquad (3.1)$$

the resistance of r_μ is equal to the reactance of C_μ. Therefore, at frequencies much above this, the capacitor C_μ becomes dominant compared with r_μ, and r_μ can be neglected. Conversely, at frequencies much lower than this, the resistor r_μ becomes dominant compared with C_μ, and C_μ can be neglected.

In a similar way, we can make a rough calculation of the relative importance of r_π and C_π. At a frequency much above

$$\frac{1}{2\pi C_\pi r_\pi} = \frac{1}{(2\pi)(200)(10^{-12})(150)} \cong 5.2 \text{ mc} \qquad (3.2)$$

the capacitor C_π will be dominant over r_π, and at frequencies much below this frequency, r_π will be dominant over C_π.

These calculations are intended to give "ball-park" figures only; but even at that, it is clear that the two frequencies calculated in Eqs. 3.1 and 3.2 are more than two orders of magnitude apart. Thus these two frequencies serve in a very rough way to divide the electrical behavior of the hybrid-π model into three separate frequency ranges: a "low-frequency" range where both capacitors C_π and C_μ can be neglected; a "middle-frequency" range where r_μ and C_π can be neglected; and a "high-frequency" range where both the resistors r_μ and r_π can be neglected.

The models corresponding to the low- and high-frequency ranges as defined above are shown in Fig. 3.2a and b. The middle-frequency-range model mentioned above (but not shown in Fig. 3.2) has only limited usefulness. It is much more common to work with the model shown in Fig. 3.2c, in which both capacitors C_μ and C_π are left in, and only the resistor r_μ is neglected. This model is therefore applicable over both the middle- and high-frequency ranges. Let us discuss these simplified models one at a time.

3.1.2 *Low-Frequency Models*

Over the low-frequency region, in this case below 15 or 20 kc, the completely resistive model shown in Fig. 3.2a applies. But even

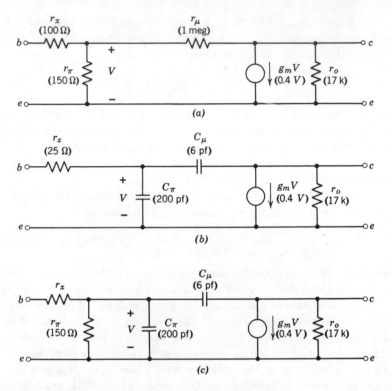

Fig. 3.2. Simplified hybrid-π models. (a) Model suitable for low-frequency use. (b) Model for use at high frequencies, where $f_\beta < f < \omega_b/2\pi$. ($c$) Model for use in middle- and high-frequency range, up to $\omega_b/2\pi$. (The frequency ω_b is defined by Eq. 3.46.)

this fairly simple model can be further simplified for many circuit applications. To show this, let us calculate the low-frequency voltage gain of the oversimplified transistor circuit shown in Fig. 3.3a. The appropriate circuit model using the low-frequency hybrid-π model is shown in Fig. 3.3b. We assume that both the biasing resistor R_b and the coupling capacitor C are large enough in value so that they have negligible effect on circuit performance over the frequency range of interest here.

The circuit can best be analyzed on the node basis, so for convenience the elements in the model are shown as conductances

(a)

(b)

Fig. 3.3. (a) Simple transistor amplifier. (b) Circuit model using low-frequency hybrid-π model. Element values are in units of millimhos.

($g_\pi = 1/r_\pi$, $g_x = 1/r_x$, etc.). The element values are given in units of millimhos. We choose as the two unknown variables the output voltage V_o and the voltage V which controls the dependent source. The resulting node equations are

$$(G_s' + g_\pi + g_\mu)V - g_\mu V_o = G_s'V_i \qquad (3.3a)$$

$$(g_m - g_\mu)V + (g_\mu + g_o + G_L)V_o = 0 \qquad (3.3b)$$

where we have set $G_s' = 1/(R_s + r_x)$.

To see which, if any, of these terms can be neglected, we should solve Eqs. 3.3 for the desired ratio of V_o/V_i, and then compare the relative sizes of the multiplied-out terms. However, in this case we can see by inspection that the only negative term in the denominator of V_o/V_i is going to be $(-g_\mu{}^2)$, a very small term. Thus *no cancellation* of the large terms in Eqs. 3.3 is going to occur, and we are justified in making approximations directly in these equations before we solve for V_o/V_i.

The conductance g_μ appears four times. In the first term of Eq. 3.3a, it represents loading on the input node. Here its effect is almost always negligible compared with g_π. The $g_\mu V_o$ term in Eq. 3.3a represents current fed *back* from the output node to the input node. This is an important term if the voltage gain of the transistor is high, as we shall see. In the first term of Eq. 3.3b, the g_μ term represents signal fed *forward* from input to output. This signal is always completely swamped by the signal fed forward by the dependent source $g_m V$. In the second term of Eq. 3.3b, the g_μ term represents loading on the output, and is usually negligible compared with g_o. Substitution of the numerical values given in Fig. 3.3 into Eqs. 3.3a and b confirms that the above approximations introduce errors of less than 1% for this example. Thus the only place that the g_μ term must be retained for further consideration is in the second term (the feedback term) of Eq. 3.3a.

Substitution of numerical values also shows that the g_o term is usually negligible compared with G_L, unless the load resistance is large (of the order of 10 k). On this basis, Eqs. 3.3a and b simplify to

$$(G_s{}' + g_\pi)V - g_\mu V_o = G_s{}'V_i$$

$$g_m V + G_L V_o = 0 \qquad (3.4)$$

These equations may be solved for the voltage gain V_o/V_i by simple elimination of V, with the result:

$$\frac{V_o}{V_i} = \frac{-g_m G_s{}'}{(G_s{}' + g_\pi)G_L + g_m g_\mu} \qquad (3.5)$$

The importance of the one remaining g_μ term in this equation depends on the relative size of the two terms in the denominator. Specifically, if

$$g_m g_\mu \ll (G_s{}' + g_\pi)G_L \qquad (3.6)$$

then the g_μ term in Eq. 3.5 can be neglected. Note that this is a distinctly different kind of approximation from those involving g_μ in the previous paragraphs. There we were comparing relative sizes of the various transistor model conductances appearing *in the same term* of the node equations. In Eq. 3.5 we are comparing the relative sizes of multiplied-out terms in one specific expression, in this case the voltage gain V_o/V_i. However, Inequality 3.6 involves only the denominator of V_o/V_i, which is the determinant of the network. Thus the first set of approximations and those based on Inequality 3.6 apply for all calculations involving this circuit.

Inequality 3.6 implicitly contains the source resistance R_s. It is desirable, however, to establish a criterion for neglecting g_μ which will apply for all values of R_s. Such a condition is

$$g_m g_\mu \ll g_\pi G_L \qquad (3.7)$$

which is clearly more stringent than Inequality 3.6 (assuming R_s positive). Inequality 3.7 can be expressed in terms of the voltage gain from the internal node V to the output V_o as follows:

$$g_\mu \ll \frac{g_\pi}{V_o/V} \qquad (3.8a)$$

or

$$r_\mu \gg r_\pi \frac{V_o}{V} \qquad (3.8b)$$

Because r_μ is typically more than three orders of magnitude larger than r_π, we see from Inequality 3.8b that unless the internal voltage gain V_o/V approaches several hundred, the feedback resistor r_μ can be ignored completely in calculating the voltage gain. If such is the case, the voltage gain expression, Eq. 3.5, reduces to

$$\frac{V_o}{V_i} = -g_m R_L \frac{G_s'}{G_s' + g_\pi} = -g_m R_L \frac{r_\pi}{R_s + r_x + r_\pi} \qquad (3.9)$$

Similar derivations show that Inequality 3.8 is also the correct condition for neglecting r_μ when calculating the current gain and the input impedance. Thus, for all these calculations, the much simpler *unilateral* low-frequency hybrid-π model shown in Fig. 3.4a can be used. The model is sufficiently simple so that expressions like Eq. 3.9 can be obtained by inspection. This model and the model in Fig. 3.4b, further simplified by neglecting r_x, are useful for first-cut calculations at low frequencies.

(a)   (b)

Fig. 3.4. Elementary (unilateral) low-frequency models, useful for first-order calculations. Both neglect feedback from output node to input node, and output resistor r_o.

3.1.3 *Middle- and High-Frequency Models*

The model shown in Fig. 3.2c is probably the most widely used form of the hybrid-π model, because it is applicable over the entire middle-frequency and high-frequency ranges, which for this example means from 30 or 40 kc to about 50 megacycles. If g_μ can be neglected at low frequencies as discussed above, the model in Fig. 3.2c is *good all the way from dc to 50 megacycles!* To illustrate its use, let us calculate the ratio of output voltage to input current for the simple amplifier shown in Fig. 3.5a.

We have chosen to drive the transistor with a current source in this example principally because it simplifies the subsequent discussions. Nonetheless, it raises the question: Which transfer function calculation should we make to describe the amplifier performance? There are basically two ways of calculating amplifier performance for prescribed source and load impedances:

1. We can find the Thevenin (or Norton) equivalent at the output terminals of the amplifier when it is driven by the prescribed source. This involves calculating the open-circuit voltage (or short-circuit current) and the output impedance of the *transistor-source combination*. After either of these equivalent circuits has been formed, it is a simple matter to calculate the amplifier transfer function for the prescribed load impedances.

2. Alternatively, we can calculate the input impedance and a forward transfer gain of the *transistor-load combination*. That is, these calculations are made with the given (or arbitrary) load impedance connected to the transistor output terminals. Then it is a simple matter to calculate the amplifier performance for arbitrary values of source impedance.

Fig. 3.5. (*a*) Simple transistor amplifier. (*b*) Middle- and high-frequency circuit model.

The choice of method for characterizing the amplifier is largely one of convenience for the particular problem at hand. For the circuit in Fig. 3.5, we will use the second approach, calculating the input impedance and the forward transfer ratio V_o/I_i. Again the decision concerning which forward transfer ratio to calculate is based largely on convenience. The various transfer ratios are related by the equations

$$V_o = I_o Z_L \qquad (3.10)$$

$$V_i = I_i Z_{\text{in}} \qquad (3.11)$$

where Z_L is the load impedance, and Z_{in} is the input impedance of the transistor-load combination. For example, we find by dividing Eq. 3.10 by Eq. 3.11 that the voltage gain is equal to the current gain times the ratio of load impedance to input impedance, a relation we will make use of in Chapter 6.

The appropriate circuit model for the calculation of V_o/I_i is shown in Fig. 3.5b, where again we have neglected the effects of the biasing resistor R_b. The node equations for this circuit are

$$(g_\pi + sC_\pi + sC_\mu)V - sC_\mu V_o = I_i \qquad (3.12a)$$

$$(g_m - sC_\mu)V + (g_o + G_L + sC_\mu)V_o = 0 \qquad (3.12b)$$

Again we can make approximations directly in Eqs. 3.12 because we see by inspection that the only negative term in the denominator of V_o/I_i is going to be $-(sC_\mu)^2$, a very small term. Thus no cancellation of the large terms in Eqs. 3.12 is going to occur. As we shall see in Chapter 8, if we have inductive loads, cancellation of large terms does indeed occur, and the above procedure would not be valid. On the basis that we have no important cancellation in the present case, however, we begin the simplification by neglecting g_o with respect to G_L.

The term sC_μ appears four times in this pair of equations, having analogous effects of loading and coupling as g_μ in the preceding discussion. In the first term of Eq. 3.12a, the C_μ term represents loading on the input node. There is no point in neglecting it, because it is easily lumped in with C_π here. The second term of Eq. 3.12a represents signal fed *back* from the second node to the first node, an important effect at higher frequencies. The $sC_\mu V$ term in the first term of Eq. 3.12b, representing signal fed *forward* from the input to the output, is almost always negligible compared with the signal fed forward by the dependent source $g_m V$. In the second term of Eq. 3.12b, the sC_μ term represents loading on the output node, an effect which is often negligible. Substitution of the numbers from Fig. 3.3 shows that for this example, the first sC_μ term in Eq. 3.12b is negligible over the entire range of validity of the hybrid-π model, whereas the second sC_μ term can be ignored below 15 mc. In actual fact, the second sC_μ term has negligible effect in the gain expression even at much higher frequencies, but the discussion must be carried considerably further before this will become apparent.

Our procedure will be to assume that the sC_μ terms in Eq. 3.12b are negligible, and then return later (Chapter 6) to show explicitly the range of validity of this assumption. On this basis, Eqs. 3.12 reduce to

$$[g_\pi + s(C_\pi + C_\mu)]V - sC_\mu V_o = I_i \qquad (3.13a)$$

$$g_m V + G_L V_o = 0 \qquad (3.13b)$$

Solving for V_o/I_i we get

$$\frac{V_o}{I_i} = \frac{-g_m}{g_\pi G_L + s[g_m C_\mu + G_L(C_\pi + C_\mu)]}$$

$$= \frac{-g_m R_L}{g_\pi + s(C_\pi + C_\mu[1 + g_m R_L])} \qquad (3.14)$$

Note that on the basis of the approximations implicit in Eqs. 3.13, the expression V_o/I_i reduces to a simple single-pole function [whereas inspection of the circuit (Fig. 3.5b) indicates two poles and a zero]. It is important to understand in terms of the *circuit*, as well as the equations, the consequences of these approximations. By so doing we can derive an *equivalent input circuit* which can be used to write down expressions such as Eq. 3.14 by inspection.

3.1.4 Derivation of Equivalent Input Circuit

One important way of simplifying circuit calculations with the hybrid-π model is to develop, on the basis of neglecting both of the C_μ terms in Eq. 3.12b, an equivalent input circuit which permits rapid calculation of the voltage V controlling the dependent source. To this end we calculate the admittance I_i/V from Eqs. 3.13:

$$\frac{I_i}{V} = g_\pi + s[C_\pi + C_\mu(1 + g_m R_L)] \qquad (3.15)$$

In circuit form, Eq. 3.15 can be represented by a resistor r_π in parallel with an equivalent single capacitance C_t of value

$$C_t = C_\pi + C_\mu(1 + g_m R_L) \qquad (3.16)$$

We can now form the complete equivalent input-circuit model by including the resistor r_x, as shown in Fig. 3.6a.

Equation 3.16 shows why the small feedback capacitor C_μ, in this case only 6 pf, can have such a profound influence on circuit performance. In our particular problem, $g_m R_L = 80$, and thus the 6 pf

$$C_t = C_\pi + C_\mu(1 + g_m R_L)$$

(a)

$$Y_{eq} = sC_\mu(1 + g_m Z_L)$$

(b)

Fig. 3.6. Equivalent input circuits for calculating V. (a) For resistive load R_L only. (b) For any load Z_L.

capacitor connected between input and output appears as a 486 pf capacitor in parallel with C_π.

There is another important restriction on Eq. 3.16 and Fig. 3.6a: the calculations were made on a circuit with a resistive load. *We obtain a pure capacitance C_t in the equivalent circuit only if the transistor load is a pure resistance.* In general, for a transistor with a load impedance Z_L, there is reflected back to the input circuit an admittance Y_{eq}, as defined in Fig. 3.6b. This equivalence is sometimes helpful in circuit analysis, although not nearly as useful as Fig. 3.6a.

To illustrate the usefulness of Fig. 3.6a, we rework by inspection the example of Sec. 3.1.3. In Fig. 3.6a, the voltage V across r_π resulting from the current source I_i applied at the input is

$$V = \frac{I_i}{g_\pi + sC_t} \qquad (3.17)$$

From Fig. 3.5, neglecting g_o and the loading effect of C_μ, we find

$$V_o = -g_m R_L V \tag{3.18}$$

Now, solving for V_o/I_i, we obtain

$$\frac{V_o}{I_i} = \frac{-g_m R_L}{g_\pi + sC_t}$$

which is identical with Eq. 3.14.

A plot of the frequency response of the transistor amplifier, as expressed mathematically in Eq. 3.14, is shown in Fig. 3.7. The numerical values used are from Figs. 3.1 and 3.5. The choice of log-log coordinates makes the plotting of $|V_o/I_i|$ versus ω particularly simple, because the curve then has two straight-line asymptotes. The low-frequency asymptote is a horizontal line, while the high-frequency asymptote has a slope of -1, because the magnitude varies as $1/\omega$ in this region. We recall that, as shown, the two asymptotes must intersect at the half-power frequency.

3.1.5 *High-Frequency Models*

For high-frequency calculations, in our example above 10 megacycles or so, the resistor r_π no longer plays an important role, and can be neglected, as shown in Fig. 3.2b. The calculations involved with this model are obviously very similar to those made for the middle- and high-frequency model in Sec. 3.1.3. Thus no further elaboration will be made at this point.

There are several other models which can be used to get a more accurate representation of transistor behavior in the high-frequency region, by accounting more carefully for the "extrinsic" circuit elements of the transistor. These models are discussed in detail in CLT.*

3.2 DETERMINATION OF ELEMENT VALUES FOR HYBRID-π MODEL

3.2.1 *The Small-Signal Measurement Problem*

Our next step is to develop a method for finding the element values of the hybrid-π model appropriate for a given transistor.

---

* *Characteristics and Limitations of Transistors*, by R. D. Thornton, D. DeWitt, E. R. Chenette, and P. E. Gray, hereafter referred to as CLT.

Fig. 3.7. Magnitude and phase of V_o/I_i from Eq. 3.14. Values are from Fig. 3.5: $\omega_\beta = 3.17 \times 10^7$ rad/sec, $\omega_T = 1.9 \times 10^9$ rad/sec.

There are seven circuit elements in the intrinsic hybrid-π model; therefore, it would at first appear that only seven independent measurements at the transistor terminals should suffice to specify the parameter values. Unfortunately, this is not so, because extrinsic elements associated with regions of the device other than where transistor action takes place make the measurement problem somewhat more complicated.

The specific terminal measurements must be selected with two things in mind. First, we should choose the measurement frequency so that only one (ideally), or at least a simple combination of a few elements, dominate an impedance or a transfer function. Second, the measurements must be relatively easy to make, yet reliable and repeatable. Thus the value of a circuit parameter should not depend critically on the making of terminal measurements with very high precision.

The various impedances, admittances, and transfer functions that can be measured directly on a three-terminal network (or the three two-port networks that can be made out of it) require some careful description. We must not only say *what* is being measured (impedance, transfer function, admittance), but also at *which* of the terminals it is being done, and what is the *load condition* on the other terminals. All of this terminal measurement description has been condensed into standard symbols which often appear on the transistor data sheets and in the literature. The language involved is that of two-port (or two terminal-pair) linear network theory. For transistors, the particular measurements which are usually most convenient to make are the hybrid or *h-parameter* measurements and the short-circuit-admittance or *y-parameter* measurements. In the following subsection these descriptions are reviewed briefly.

3.2.2 *Two-Port Network Descriptions*

For incremental signals, the transistor is a three-terminal *linear* network. We know from Kirchhoff's laws that for a three-terminal network there will be two independent terminal currents and two independent terminal-pair voltages. These variables, defined in Fig. 3.8, are related by two linear equations. There are actually six ways in which these equations can be written, corresponding to

Fig. 3.8. Definition of terminal variables for two-port networks.

the six ways of choosing two of the four variables as the independent ones. The two descriptions related directly to measurements convenient for transistors in the common-emitter connection are

$$V_i = h_{ie}I_i + h_{re}V_o$$
$$\qquad\qquad\qquad\qquad h\text{-parameter description} \qquad (3.19)$$
$$I_o = h_{fe}I_i + h_{oe}V_o$$

$$I_i = y_{ie}V_i + y_{re}V_o$$
$$\qquad\qquad\qquad\qquad y\text{-parameter description} \qquad (3.20)$$
$$I_o = y_{fe}V_i + y_{oe}V_o$$

The h-parameters may, of course, be related to the y-parameters by making the transformation of variables required to change Eqs. 3.20 to Eqs. 3.19.

The double subscript notation used in these equations requires some explanation. For the first subscript, i represents input, o output, f forward (i.e., from input toward output), and r reverse (i.e., from output back toward input). The second subscript on the h's and y's indicates the transistor connection being used, by referring to which terminal is "common" to both input and output loops. In this case the letter e indicates the *common-emitter* connection. Similarly, h_{ib} would be a *common-base* parameter and h_{ic} would be a *common-collector* parameter.

Circuit representations of the h- and y-parameter equations are shown in Fig. 3.9. Under certain conditions, for example the narrow-band calculations in Chapter 8, these can profitably be used directly as models for circuit calculations. However, for general use they have distinct drawbacks. Each of the h-parameters and y-parameters is a complex number varying in a more or less complicated way with frequency, ambient temperature, and operating point, and bearing no simple relation to the physics of the device.

(a) h-parameter

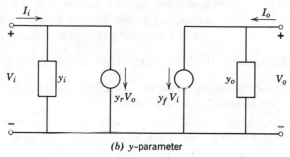

(b) y-parameter

Fig. 3.9. Circuit representations of two-port descriptions.

The immittances h_i, h_o, y_i, and y_o do not behave as single electrical elements, but rather as combinations of several such elements. The circuit designer must therefore either remember how each of the parameters varies as a function of frequency, temperature, and operating point, or else try to represent the elements as *RLC* combinations whose variation with temperature, etc., he can deduce from knowledge of transistor physics. The result of the latter representation is, of course, the hybrid-π model.

The guide to measurement of the parameters stems from Eqs. 3.19 and 3.20 (or Fig. 3.9). It is clear that for the *h*-parameters, for example,

$$h_i = \frac{V_i}{I_i}\bigg|_{V_o = 0} = \textit{short-circuit input impedance} = \text{input imped-}$$
ance with output terminals short-circuited.

$$h_r = \left.\frac{V_i}{V_o}\right|_{I_i=0} = \textit{open-circuit reverse voltage transfer ratio} = \text{volt-}$$
age developed at the open-circuited input terminals, per unit voltage applied at the output terminals.

$$h_f = \left.\frac{I_o}{I_i}\right|_{V_o=0} = \textit{short-circuit forward current transfer ratio}$$
(*or amplification*) = current developed in the short-circuited output terminals, per unit current applied at the input terminals.

$$h_o = \left.\frac{I_o}{V_o}\right|_{I_i=0} = \textit{open-circuit output admittance} = \text{admittance}$$
measured at the output terminals with the input terminals open-circuited.

In a similar manner, the *y*-parameters can be measured as follows:

y_i = *short-circuit input admittance* = input admittance with output terminals short-circuited.

y_r = *short-circuit reverse transfer admittance* = current developed in the short-circuited input terminals per unit voltage applied at the output terminals.

y_f = *short-circuit forward transfer admittance* = current developed in the short-circuited output terminals per unit voltage applied at the input terminals.

y_o = *short-circuit output admittance* = admittance measured at the output terminals with the input terminals short-circuited.

Various combinations of these measurements are often used by transistor manufacturers to specify small-signal transistor performance.

3.2.3 *Relations for Finding Hybrid-π Element Values*

The hybrid-π element values at a given operating point can be determined most accurately by using a combination of *h*- and *y*-parameter measurements taken at different frequencies. The intent is to make each measurement at a frequency where only one or two of the hybrid-π elements influence the measurement. Sometimes it is possible to measure one element in two ways: for example, first through y_{ie}, then through y_{re}. These two measurements should check. When they do not check (and sometimes they will not), it is usually because of model inaccuracies.

In any event, the following scheme for determining the hybrid-π elements works well and conforms closely with measurements quoted on many transistor data sheets. We start by determining an appropriate value for the dependent source parameter g_m. This is the one parameter which we will not measure either directly or indirectly. Instead, we will rely on the validity of the physical relation between g_m and I_C, discussed in Chapter 1.

$$g_m = \frac{q}{kT} |I_C| \qquad (3.21)$$

This method of determination is accurate, provided that I_C is much larger than I_{CO}, but small enough so that the condition of low-level injection applies (see Chapter 1).

The value of r_π can be determined by making a measurement of the short-circuit current gain, h_{fe} or β* at some convenient low frequency, say, 1000 cycles. The circuit model for this measurement is shown in Fig. 3.10. We have used the elementary low-frequency

---

* The short-circuit current gain is called h_{fe} in h-parameter notation, but for historical reasons, it is also called β. The low-frequency value of β or (h_{fe}) is designated as β_0. The quantity β_F, although closely related to β_0, is the parameter used in large-signal models, where by definition, it is not a function of voltage or current.

Fig. 3.10. Circuit model for h_{fe} and h_{ie} measurement to determine r_π and r_x, respectively.

hybrid-π model (Fig. 3.4) because clearly the requirement of low voltage-gain is met in this case! By inspection,

$$\frac{I_o}{I_i} = h_{fe}\bigg|_{1000\,\sim} \equiv \beta_0 = g_m r_\pi \qquad (3.22)$$

Thus, if we measure the short-circuit current gain β_0 at some low frequency, and calculate g_m from Eq. 3.21, we find

$$r_\pi = \frac{\beta_0}{g_m} \qquad (3.23)$$

The low-frequency value of the base resistance r_x can be determined by again using the circuit shown in Fig. 3.10, except in this case we measure the short-circuit input impedance h_{ie}. By inspection,

$$\frac{V_i}{I_i} = h_{ie}\bigg|_{1000\,\sim} = r_x + r_\pi \qquad (3.24)$$

Thus, if we measure h_{ie} and we know r_π from Eq. 3.23, we have

$$r_x = h_{ie}\big|_{1000\,\sim} - r_\pi \qquad (3.25)$$

A few words of caution are necessary, however. First, if the value of r_x is less than $r_\pi/10$, large errors in the determination of r_x may occur, resulting from the subtraction of two nearly equal numbers, h_{ie} and r_π. Fortunately in this case, because r_x is small anyway, its effect will be negligible, and sizeable errors in this determination will not appreciably affect circuit calculations. Second, r_x is unfortunately not independent of frequency. More precisely, the model element which represents transverse voltage drops in the base region should really be an RC transmission line (see Chapter 8 of PEM). Thus the value of base resistance obtained by the low-frequency method given here is not an appropriate value to use at higher frequencies, say, above 100 kc for this example. Later in the chapter we will discuss methods of measuring r_x at high frequencies.

One fairly direct way of finding the feedback resistor r_μ is to measure the open-circuit reverse voltage transfer ratio (h_{re}) at some low frequency, say, 1000 cycles. To show this, we must use the complete low-frequency hybrid-π model, Fig. 3.2a, and apply the appropriate terminal constraints, that is, an open circuit on

Fig. 3.11. Circuit model for h_{re} measurement to determine r_μ.

the input and a voltage-source drive at the output, as shown in Fig. 3.11. The appropriate equations are

$$\frac{V_i}{V_o} = h_{re}\bigg|_{1000\sim} = \frac{r_\pi}{r_\pi + r_\mu} \cong \frac{r_\pi}{r_\mu} \qquad (3.26)$$

$$\therefore\ r_\mu \cong \frac{r_\pi}{h_{re}\big|_{1000\sim}} \qquad (3.27)$$

The same circuit model of Fig. 3.11 with an input short added can be used to determine the output conductance g_o from a measurement of the low-frequency short-circuit output admittance y_{oe}. Under these conditions, the dependent source current $g_m V$ will equal*

$$g_m V = g_m \frac{r_\pi || r_x}{r_\pi || r_x + r_\mu} V_o \qquad (3.28)$$

To get the total current I_o, we add to this result the current flowing through r_o and through r_μ. Then, dividing by V_o, we obtain

$$\frac{I_o}{V_o} = y_{oe}\big|_{1000\sim} = \frac{g_m(r_\pi || r_x)}{r_\pi || r_x + r_\mu} + \frac{1}{r_\pi || r_x + r_\mu} + g_o \qquad (3.29)$$

We can often neglect the second term, and r_π in the denominator of the first term, as can readily be seen by substituting the typical values given in Fig. 3.1. Then g_o can be determined as follows:

$$g_o \cong y_{oe}\big|_{1000\sim} - \frac{g_m(r_\pi || r_x)}{r_\mu} \qquad (3.30)$$

$$\cong y_{oe}\big|_{1000\sim}$$

* Two vertical lines indicate "in parallel with." Hence for "$r_\pi || r_x$", read "r_π in parallel with r_x."

The value of the feedback capacitor C_μ can be determined by measuring the capacitance between base and collector leads of the transistor with the emitter incrementally open-circuited. Here we are in effect measuring the output capacitance of the transistor in the common-base connection, a quantity usually denoted as C_{ob}. Measurement of C_{ob} does not directly give the value of capacitor C_μ. For one thing, there is included in C_{ob} some of the *header capacitance*, the inherent capacitance associated with the transistor leads and the header. In addition, there exists substantial capacitance between collector and base associated with those regions of the collector-base junction outside the active region (see Fig. 1.7). These regions of the collector-base junction are often referred to as the *overlap diode**; the associated capacitance is thus called the *overlap-diode capacitance*. The overlap-diode capacitance and the header capacitance can be represented by a delta of capacitors connected to the terminals of the transistor model, as shown in Fig. 3.12. For low-power transistors, the approximate value of C_{be} and C_{ce} is $\frac{1}{2}$ pf, consisting mostly of header capacitance. On the

Fig. 3.12. Hybrid-π model with capacitors added to represent header capacitance and overlap-diode capacitance.

* See Chapter 4, and PEM, Sec. 8.4.

other hand, C_{bc} may be much larger because it consists mostly of overlap-diode capacitance. For low-power transistors it may be of the order of 2 pf, whereas for high-power units, it might be as large as 200 pf.

Even after the overlap-diode and header capacitances are taken into account, the measurement still seems to be indirect, because C_μ is buried in the middle of the hybrid-π model. However, it is a simple matter to choose a frequency such that the resistance r_x is much smaller than the reactance $1/\omega C_\mu$, thus making r_x negligible in a measurement. Direct circuit analysis will also show that the dependent source $g_m V$ and the resistor r_o can be replaced in this measurement by an additional resistor of value $\beta_0 r_o$ ($\cong r_\mu$) in parallel with C_μ. We conclude, therefore, that the value of C_μ can be determined by measuring the common-base output capacitance C_{ob} and subtracting from this the header and overlap-diode capacitances. The base-to-emitter voltage will be small in this measurement, so we can ignore capacitor C_{be}. Thus the appropriate amount of capacitance to subtract is $C_{bc} + C_{ce}$:

$$C_\mu = C_{ob} - C_{bc} - C_{ce} \tag{3.31}$$

Appropriate values for C_{bc}, C_{ce}, and C_{be} can be found from high-frequency y-parameter measurements, as we shall see in Sec. 3.3.

Capacitors C_π and C_μ are the elements which limit the high-frequency behavior of the transistor; therefore, it is reasonable to measure C_π at a frequency high enough so that it has a significant effect on circuit operation. Let us therefore determine the short-circuit forward current gain (h_{fe} or β) as a function of frequency, and from this expression determine C_π. We can calculate the required relationships by using the middle- and high-frequency hybrid-π model, Fig. 3.2c, with appropriate terminal constraints added, as shown in Fig. 3.13. Because of the short-circuit output constraint, the voltage V can be calculated directly as

$$V = \frac{I_i}{g_\pi + s(C_\pi + C_\mu)} \tag{3.32}$$

Thus the short-circuit current gain β is

$$\beta = \frac{I_o}{I_i} = h_{fe} \cong \frac{g_m}{g_\pi + s(C_\pi + C_\mu)} \tag{3.33}$$

Fig. 3.13. Circuit model for β or h_{fe} measurement to determine C_π.

Because we already know g_m, g_π, and C_μ, a measurement of β at any frequency where the capacitors have a significant effect will yield the required value for C_π. However, the calculation is simplified if we make the measurement at a frequency high enough so that g_π no longer has an appreciable effect on $|\beta|$. To show this graphically, and also to tie in several of the other parameters commonly given on data sheets which can be used to determine C_π, we plot in Fig. 3.14 the magnitude and phase of β as a function of frequency. The plot is based on Eq. 3.33, using the numerical values shown in Fig. 3.1. The low-frequency asymptote of the magnitude curve will be $g_m r_\pi$, and there will be a single break downward, occurring at a frequency

$$f_\beta = \frac{1}{2\pi r_\pi (C_\pi + C_\mu)} \tag{3.34}$$

That is, f_β *is the frequency where the magnitude of the common-emitter short-circuit current gain is down to 0.707 of its low-frequency value.* This frequency is sometimes called the β-cutoff frequency. At frequencies much above f_β, g_π is no longer important, and the magnitude curve becomes asymptotic to a line with a slope of -1 on log-log coordinates. Thus a measurement of the magnitude of beta at any frequency above approximately $3f_\beta$, that is, in the asymptotic region, will permit a relatively simple determination of C_π, as we can see by calculating $|\beta|$ from Eq. 3.33, neglecting g_π.

$$|\beta|_{\omega \gg \omega_\beta} = \frac{g_m}{\omega(C_\pi + C_\mu)} \tag{3.35}$$

Solving for C_π, we get

$$C_\pi = \frac{g_m}{\omega \, |\beta|_{\omega \gg \omega_\beta}} - C_\mu \tag{3.36}$$

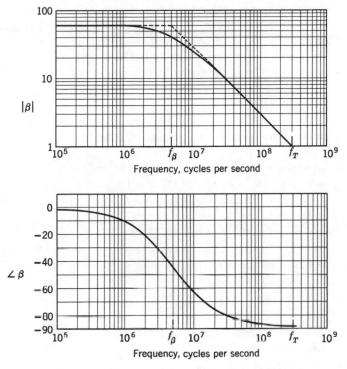

Fig. 3.14. Magnitude and phase of β versus frequency.

If the $|\beta|$ high-frequency asymptote is extrapolated, then at some frequency, the asymptotic value falls to one. This frequency is usually called f_T on transistor data sheets. If we substitute into Eq. 3.35 the two values $|\beta| = 1$ and $\omega = \omega_T$, (where $\omega_T \equiv 2\pi f_T$), we find

$$\omega_T = \frac{g_m}{C_\pi + C_\mu} \tag{3.37}$$

Now resubstituting into Eq. 3.35, we obtain the relations

$$|\beta|\,\omega = \omega_T \tag{3.38a}$$

$$|\beta|\,f = f_T \tag{3.38b}$$

which also could have been found by geometry from Fig. 3.14. In words, *the product of $|\beta|$ measured anywhere on the asymptote, and* *the frequency corresponding to that value of* $|\beta|$, *is equal to* f_T. On actual data, $|\beta|$ may not be unity at f_T, because other effects neglected here, such as header and overlap-diode capacitance, emitter lead inductance, and the inherent distributed nature of the device, make the model predictions inaccurate in this frequency range. Thus we define f_T as the frequency where $|\beta|$ extrapolated from the slope = -1 region falls to unity.

From Fig. 3.14, the two coordinates (β_0, f_β) also define a point on the $|\beta|$ asymptote, so they can be used in Eqs. 3.35 or 3.38. That is,

$$\beta_0 = \frac{g_m}{\omega_\beta (C_\pi + C_\mu)} \tag{3.39}$$

$$\beta_0 f_\beta = f_T \tag{3.40}$$

Thus we have two other ways of finding C_π, from Eq. 3.37 or 3.39.

$$C_\pi = \frac{g_m}{\omega_T} - C_\mu \tag{3.41}$$

$$C_\pi = \frac{g_m}{\beta_0 \omega_\beta} - C_\mu \tag{3.42}$$

3.2.4 *Relation between Hybrid-π Parameters and dc Volt-Ampere Characteristics*

The small-signal representations discussed in this chapter must be consistent with the large-signal low-frequency characterization discussed in Chapter 2 for, after all, they are both characterizations of the same device. Thus we must be able to check the low-frequency values of the small-signal parameters from the large-signal low-frequency characterization as represented by a complete set of input and output volt-ampere characteristics. Specifically, at any given operating point, the slopes of the individual input and output curves (or their reciprocals, depending on the way the curves are plotted) give h_{ie} and h_{oe}, respectively. The change in output current for unit change in input current, at constant output voltage, gives h_{fe}. The change in input voltage per unit change in output voltage, at constant input current, in principle gives h_{re}. But the results may be meaningless, because thermal effects may contribute an r_μ which is more important than the true space-charge-layer widening effect.

3.3 COMPARISON OF HYBRID-π CHARACTERIZATION WITH Y-PARAMETER DATA

3.3.1 *Comparison Neglecting Extrinsic Capacitance*

In most of the preceding sections of this chapter, we have assumed that the hybrid-π model alone, Fig. 3.1, without the addition of extrinsic elements, can be used to calculate the small-signal performance of a transistor. (The only place where this assumption was not used was in the determination of C_μ from a measurement of C_{ob}.) The validity of this assumption will now be checked by comparing measured transistor y-parameter data with the corresponding plots obtained from the hybrid-π model. A complete set of y-parameter data as a function of frequency, measured at $I_C \cong 1$ ma, is shown in Fig. 3.15. Also shown on these graphs are the same functions calculated from the hybrid-π model for the same transistor. In this figure we are, in effect, trying to fit the hybrid-π model to the measured y-parameters *without benefit of the extrinsic header and overlap-diode capacitance.*

The values of hybrid-π parameters used to obtain this fit are:

$$g_x = 3.7 \text{ mmhos} \qquad g_o = 0.026 \text{ mmho}$$

$$g_\pi = 0.35 \text{ mmho} \qquad C_\pi = 41 \text{ pf}$$

$$g_m = 36 \text{ mmhos} \qquad C_\mu = 3.3 \text{ pf}$$

$$g_\mu = 5.3 \times 10^{-5} \text{ mmho}$$

In order to establish a point of reference for further discussion of these results, it is necessary to find the value of f_T. In Sec. 3.2.3 we defined f_T in terms of the forward transfer characteristic β or h_{fe}. The value of f_T can also be found directly in terms of y_{fe}. Ignoring for the moment the extrinsic capacitance, that is, working only with the hybrid-π model of Fig. 3.2c, we find by direct circuit calculation

$$y_{fe} \cong \frac{g_x g_m}{g_x + g_\pi + s(C_\pi + C_\mu)} \tag{3.43}$$

At high frequencies, where C_π and C_μ dominate over g_x and g_π, $|y_{fe}|$ approaches an asymptote

$$|y_{fe}| \cong \frac{g_x g_m}{\omega(C_\pi + C_\mu)} \tag{3.44}$$

Fig. 3.15. Experimental data of y-parameters versus frequency. Calculated y-parameters for intrinsic hybrid-π model shown as dashed lines for comparison.

which is a line with a slope of -1 on log-log coordinates. By using Eq. 3.37 we find that for $\omega = \omega_T$,

$$|y_{fe}|_{\omega=\omega_T} = g_x \qquad (3.45)$$

When extrinsic elements are present, as they always are in the measured data, we cannot use Eq. 3.45 directly. Instead, we must

Fig. 3.15. (*Continued*)

work with $|y_{fe}|$ extrapolated from the region where the extrinsic capacitance has little effect. Thus, on the basis of Eq. 3.44, we can say that f_T is the frequency where $|y_{fe}|$ extrapolated from the region of unity negative slope equals g_x. From Fig. 3.15c we find that $f_T \cong 120$ mc for this transistor.

The comparison of the measured y-parameter data with the calculated curves based on the hybrid-π model *alone* (no extrinsic capacitance) shows that a reasonable fit can be obtained for this transistor *from low frequencies out to approximately 10 mc*, or in

Fig. 3.15. (*Continued*)

Fig. 3.15. (*Concluded*)

general out to about the break in the $|y_{fe}|$ curve at the *transverse cut-off frequency*

$$\omega_b \equiv \frac{g_x + g_\pi}{C_\pi + C_\mu} \qquad (3.46)$$

The y_{ie} and y_{fe} curves match within about 20% in magnitude and 5° in phase over this frequency range. The y_{re} and y_{oe} comparisons are somewhat poorer, as might be expected on the basis that the extrinsic capacitance, particularly the collector-base overlap capacitance, plays a dominant role in these parameters.

3.3.2 *Comparison Including Extrinsic Capacitance*

In Fig. 3.16 we have plotted the same measured y-parameter data as in Fig. 3.15. But this time we have attempted to fit the data by using a hybrid-π model augmented by extrinsic header

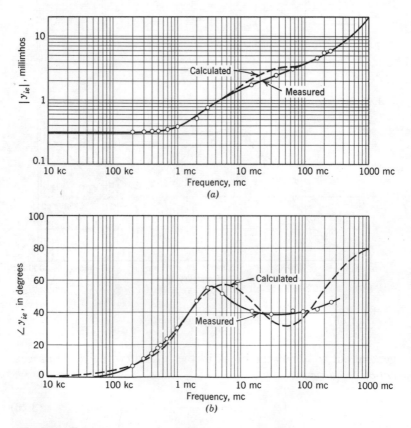

Fig. 3.16. Experimental data of y-parameters versus frequency, with calculated y-parameters for hybrid-π model with extrinsic elements added shown as dashed lines for comparison.

Fig. 3.16. (*Continued*)

and overlap-diode capacitance, as shown in Fig. 3.12. To aid in the understanding of this figure, we have plotted in Fig. 3.17 the behavior of the y-parameter magnitudes, and labeled the curves in terms of the hybrid-π parameters.

The values of the hybrid-π parameters used to obtain the fit in Fig. 3.16 are:

$$g_x = 3.3 \text{ mmhos} \qquad C_\mu = 2.3 \text{ pf}$$
$$g_\pi = 0.35 \text{ mmho} \qquad C_\pi = 33 \text{ pf}$$
$$g_\mu = 5.3 \times 10^{-5} \text{ mmho} \qquad C_{bc} = 1.7 \text{ pf}$$
$$g_o = 0.026 \text{ mmho} \qquad C_{be} = 1.5 \text{ pf}$$
$$g_m = 36 \text{ mmhos} \qquad C_{ce} = 1.1 \text{ pf}$$

Fig. 3.16. (*Continued*)

Fig. 3.16. (*Concluded*)

Note that the model parameter values are slightly different from those needed to make the fit in Fig. 3.15, particularly in regard to C_μ. There is an obvious improvement in the fit between the two sets of curves, particularly in the high-frequency region, between 10 and 120 mc. Thus, if we are willing to include extrinsic capacitance, we can achieve a good fit ($\pm 10\%$ in magnitude, $\pm 10°$ in phase) between the measured data and the hybrid-π model calculations for this transistor *all the way from dc to 120 mc*.

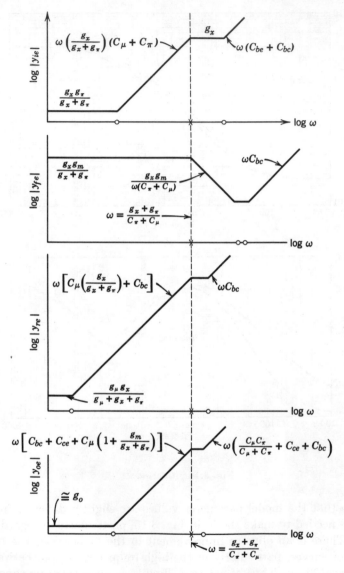

Fig. 3.17. Behavior of y-parameters (assuming $g_o \ll g_\pi$; C_{be}, $C_{bc} \ll C_\pi$).

It should be clear, however, that including extrinsic capacitance in all hybrid-π calculations would add considerably to the computational labor. However, we conclude from Figs. 3.15 and 3.16 that circuit calculations can be performed on the basis of the hybrid-π model *without extrinsic capacitance,* by making C_μ somewhat larger than it really ought to be to compensate for the omission of the extrinsic capacitor C_{bc}. The validity of this approximation below ω_b is borne out by the comparison presented in Fig. 3.15.

3.4 BASE RESISTANCE

Let us now return to the problem of measuring base resistance. It should be clear by now that using a single lumped resistance r_x to represent the transverse voltage drops in the base region of the transistor is the crudest approximation made in the development of the hybrid-π model. A much more accurate representation can be obtained by using a lossy RC transmission line with series resistance in the base lead, and shunt resistance and capacitance to the emitter. (PEM, Chapter 8.) Note, however, that we were able to obtain a rather good fit to measured y parameter data in Fig. 3.16 without recourse to any such distributed circuit. There are two reasons for this. First, we have in effect used parts of C_{be}, r_π and C_π, together with r_x, to form a single π-section approximation to the distributed RC line. Second, the y parameters are usually not particularly sensitive at low frequencies to the value of r_x, as can be seen from Fig. 3.17 together with the parameter values used in Fig. 3.16.

On the basis of the preceding discussion we must now formulate a method for finding r_x from terminal measurements. It should be clear that we cannot represent the truly distributed nature of the problem by a single value of r_x, even if we are willing to use the single π-section approximation incorporating C_{be}, r_π and C_π. Specifically r_x is going to have to be much larger at low frequencies than at high frequencies. Paradoxically, at low frequencies, where r_x may be fairly large, it also may be fairly difficult to measure. Fortunately, however, there is a close relationship between ease of measurement of r_x and its relative importance in circuit calculations. It is difficult to measure r_x at low frequencies because r_π

is usually much bigger than r_x, thus making r_x an insignificant part of the input impedance. By the same token, however, if r_π is much bigger than r_x, then r_x will not play an important role in circuit calculations. On the other hand, at high frequencies r_x may be small, but still represent an important part of the input impedance, and thus may well play an important role in circuit calculations. But under these same conditions it will also be relatively easy to measure.

We have already discussed ways of measuring r_x at low frequencies, although admittedly these measurements may be somewhat inaccurate. A method of finding the high-frequency value of r_x is suggested by Fig. 3.17. If there is a plateau in the high-frequency $|y_{ie}|$ data, then $|y_{ie}|$ in this region should equal g_x. Unfortunately, with many high-frequency transistors no such plateau exists, because the frequency response of the transistor has been improved to the point where overlap-diode and header capacitance effects take over before $|y_{ie}|$ can level off to the value g_x. This problem is evident in the $|y_{ie}|$ data of Fig. 3.16a. If there is no plateau in $|y_{ie}|$, then r_x can be found by measuring the real part of y_{ie} at a frequency high enough to make the impedance of $(C_\pi + C_\mu)$ much smaller than r_x. We can see by inspection of Fig. 3.12 that at these frequencies

$$g_x\big|_{\text{high frequency}} = \text{Re } [y_{ie}]_{\omega \gg g_x/(C_\pi + C_\mu)} \tag{3.47}$$

At high frequencies, the base resistance in most transistors tends to approach a small constant value, often called the *extrinsic base resistance*, which for many transistors can be as small as 25 ohms.

In many first-order calculations, the base resistance can be ignored completely. The circuit designer should remember, however, that there is always some base resistance present in every transistor, which if nothing else prevents direct access to the capacitor C_π.

3.5 SUMMARY OF MEASUREMENTS

All the measurements for determining the hybrid-π element values have been summarized in Table 3.1 for ready reference.

TABLE 3.1

Hybrid-π Element	Quantity to Measure	Relationship	
g_m	I_C	$g_m = \dfrac{q}{kT}\,|I_C|$	(3.21)
r_π	β_0	$r_\pi = \dfrac{\beta_0}{g_m}$	(3.23)
r_x (low frequency)	$h_{ie}|_{1000\sim}$	$r_x = h_{ie}|_{1000\sim} - r_\pi$	(3.25)
r_x (high frequency)	$y_{ie}|_{\omega \gg g_x/(C_\pi + C_\mu)}$	$g_x = \mathrm{Re}[y_{ie}]_{\omega \gg g_x/(C_\pi + C_\mu)}$	(3.47)
r_μ	$h_{re}|_{1000\sim}$	$r_\mu \simeq \dfrac{r_\pi}{h_{re}|_{1000\sim}}$	(3.27)
r_o	$y_{oe}|_{1000\sim}$	$g_o \simeq y_{oe}|_{1000\sim}$	(3.30)
C_μ	C_{ob}	$C_\mu \simeq C_{ob} - C_{bc} - C_{ce}$	(3.31)
C_π	$|\beta|$ on asymptote	$C_\pi = \dfrac{g_m}{\omega|\beta|} - C_\mu$	(3.36)
	f_T	$C_\pi = \dfrac{g_m}{\omega_T} - C_\mu$	(3.41)
	f_β	$C_\pi = \dfrac{g_m}{\beta_0 \omega_\beta} - C_\mu$	(3.42)
f_T		$f_T = \beta_o f_\beta$	(3.40)
		$= |\beta| f$	(3.38)

Other important relations:

$$f_T = \frac{g_m}{2\pi(C_\pi + C_\mu)} \tag{3.37}$$

$$f_\beta = \frac{1}{2\pi r_\pi (C_\pi + C_\mu)} \tag{3.34}$$

PROBLEMS

P3.1 A three-terminal device is known to have the linear incremental model shown within the dotted lines of Fig. 3.18. Element values are in ohms and farads.

   (a) Do you expect it to be easier to write a set of equilibrium equations on the loop basis or the node basis in this network?

Fig. 3.18.

(b) Write the set of equations of your choice and solve them for the voltage-transfer ratio $H = V_2/V_s$ as a function of g_m and s.

(c) What must be the value of g_m in order that $H(s) = 2$ for very low frequencies?

P3.2   For the circuit shown in Fig. 3.19, assume the following values:

$$R_s = 50 \ \Omega \qquad L_2 = \tfrac{1}{184} \text{ henry} \qquad g_m = 0.3 \text{ mhos}$$
$$r_1 = 50 \ \Omega \qquad L_3 = \tfrac{1}{8} \text{ henry} \qquad r_4 = 2.5 \times 10^4 \text{ ohms}$$
$$r_2 = 100 \ \Omega \qquad r_3 = 10^6 \ \Omega \qquad R_L = 10^3 \text{ ohms}$$

(a) Write the equations governing network equilibrium by the node method.

(b) By making appropriate approximations *within* these node equations, obtain a voltage-transfer ratio $H(s) = V_L/V_s$ which is

Fig. 3.19.

valid throughout the entire range of frequencies for which $H(s)$ has the form

$$H(s) = \frac{Ks}{s + a}$$

Keep track of your approximations and place a lower bound on the values of s for which your expression is valid.

P3.3 Given the following small-signal measurements on a transistor, find f_β, f_T and the intrinsic hybrid-π parameters at the operating point $I_C = 10$ ma, $V_{CE} = 10$ volts. All measurements were made at $I_C = 10$ ma, $V_{CE} = 10$ volts.

$$\begin{array}{ll} \beta_0 = 80 & C_{ce} = C_{bc} = 1 \text{ pf} \\ |\beta| = 3 \text{ at } 20 \text{ mc} & r_x = 50 \ \Omega \\ C_{ob} = 18 \text{ pf} & r_o = r_\mu = \infty \end{array}$$

P3.4 A high frequency incremental model of a transistor amplifier is shown in Fig. 3.20.

(a) If I_s is the complex amplitude of a sinusoidal excitation at a frequency ω, compute the input impedance V/I_s and the current gain I_o/I_s as functions of ω.

Fig. 3.20.

(b) If the input impedance found in part (a) for the circuit above has a real part, explain where the input signal power is going.

P3.5 At an operating point of $|I_C| = 5$ ma, $|V_{CE}| = 10$ volts, the small-signal parameters for the intrinsic hybrid-π model of a certain transistor are:

$$\begin{array}{ll} g_m = 0.2 \text{ mho} & r_x = 50 \text{ ohms} \\ r_o = 25 \ k & C_\pi = 500 \text{ pf} \\ r_\mu = 1.0 \text{ meg} & C_\mu = 10 \text{ pf} \\ r_\pi = 180 \text{ ohms} \end{array}$$

For low enough frequencies the small-signal behavior of the transistor
is represented adequately by the *resistive* model shown in Fig. 3.2a.

(a) What is the maximum frequency at which the use of this resistive
model is justified?

(b) The transistor is driven at the base-emitter terminals by a current
source I_b. Derive a Norton equivalent circuit for the output terminals. That is, find numerical values for A and R_o in the model
of Fig. 3.21.

(c) For a fixed value of I_b, what value of load resistance connected at
terminals c and e will maximize the power delivered to that load?
What is the input resistance V_{be}/I_b under this condition? Compare
with $(r_x + r_\pi)$.

(d) What condition must the load resistance R_L satisfy to justify the
use of the approximate model shown in Fig. 3.4a?

P3.6   The following measurements apply to a *pnp* transistor: At an operating
point of $|I_C| = 2$ ma, $|V_{CE}| = 5$ volts, and at a frequency of 1 kc,
the common emitter h-parameters are:

$$h_{ie} = 580 \text{ ohms} \qquad h_{re} = 1.5 \times 10^{-4}$$

$$h_{fe} = 37 \qquad h_{oe} = 2.8 \times 10^{-5} \text{ mho}$$

At the same operating point, $f_T = 29$ mc. At the same operating point
and at a frequency of 100 kc the common base output capacitance C_{ob}
is 5 pf.

Estimate the numerical values of the hybrid-π circuit parameters at an
operating point of $|I_C| = 2$ ma, $|V_{CE}| = 5$ volts.

Fig. 3.21.

4

Dependence of Small-Signal Model Parameters on Operating Conditions

4.0 INTRODUCTION

The small-signal characteristics and circuit performance of a transistor as observed at its terminals, depend in a complicated manner upon the operating conditions of the device. Particularly if we want to understand or, better still, predict the way in which the small-signal behavior of the device is influenced by variation of bias point or temperature, we must have a clear insight into the physical mechanisms involved in its operation. Understanding the effect of operating conditions is greatly assisted if the transistor is characterized by a model in which the basic internal physical mechanisms of the device are placed in evidence as directly as possible by corresponding circuit elements. The hybrid-π model has such properties and its great usefulness for the purpose of analyzing the performance of the transistor under small-signal conditions has already been stressed in Chapter 3.

Nevertheless, this model takes into account only those physical features which can be described in essentially a one-dimensional model of the device. In other words, the *transverse* flow of base current is assumed to produce negligible transverse voltage drop (which limits the validity of the model to moderate currents), and the effects of radical variations in cross section through the structure have been set aside (which either omits or mis-estimates some parameters of the model).

Moreover, the parameters of the hybrid-π model have been developed on the assumption that the relationship between stored minority charges and terminal currents is a linear one, for the bias conditions as well as for the small signals. This restricts the applicability of the quantitative results to the conditions referred to in semiconductor physics as *low-level injection*, in which added *minority*-carrier concentrations are everywhere kept small compared to total *majority*-carrier concentrations. Again, this implies a limitation to moderate total currents.

Similarly, at the collector junction the effect of incipient voltage breakdown, through the multiplication of current by the avalanche process that precedes it, has been omitted from the model thus far, thereby restricting the results to moderate collector voltages.

In addition, little has been said about the way in which recombination mechanisms change with temperature or current level, and these phenomena are important in connection with some of the circuit parameters.

Finally, the circuit effects of the transistor case and leads have not occupied much of our attention. These matters are often crucial at high frequencies, but because the package is really completely external to the transistor, we shall not deal further with its effects here.

In accordance with the foregoing remarks, we shall present first the way in which each of the hybrid-π model parameters would be expected to vary in the light of the simplified conditions under which the model has been developed. Then we shall add briefly to this description the effects of the other physical features mentioned above. The importance to circuit performance of these auxiliary features, however, should not be underestimated as a consequence of our relative depth of treatment. Some of these features are so complicated that we simply cannot treat them in detail here;* but, as might be expected, a few of them *dominate* almost completely the performance of high-power transistors, for example, in which operation at high currents and voltages is of special interest.

---

* Further discussion of these matters is given in CLT.

Fig. 4.1. Hybrid-π model of the transistor. Definition of capacitance components:

$$C_\pi - C_b + C_{je}$$
$$C_\mu = C_{jc} + C_d$$

where C_b = base charging capacitance

C_{je} = emitter-base space charge layer capacitance

C_d = collector diffusion capacitance

C_{jc}, C_{sc} = collector-base space charge layer capacitance components

With these precautionary comments in mind, we turn to the hybrid-π model (Fig. 4.1) for our immediate discussion.

The individual element values of this model as we have developed it depend, of course, on the conditions under which the device operates. However, each element, being identified primarily with a particular physical process, is governed by the operating conditions in a known and often simple manner. The change in the value of an element brought about by a change in operating point (viz., bias point I_C, V_C*) or temperature may be predicted, and its influence upon the electrical parameters of the device as measured at the terminals may then be assessed.

The model parameters may be divided into four main groups, each with a different characteristic dependence upon bias point.

* The notation V_C, V_E is used to signify generally "collector voltage" or "emitter voltage." Depending on context, V_C may be regarded as referring to terminal voltage V_{CE} or V_{CB}, or the actual voltage applied across the collector-base junction space-charger layer. Similarly, V_E may mean V_{EB} or the voltage across the emitter-base junction space-charge layer.

1. Those associated with current flow in the base as a result of minority carriers injected by the emitter-base pn junction: g_m, C_b, r_π; primarily dependent on I_C; little dependence on V_C (none for g_m).

2. Those representing the majority-carrier charging requirements of the junction space-charge layers: C_{je}, C_{jc}, C_{sc}; the first dependent only on V_E (which changes very little over the normal operating range), and the second two dependent only on V_C.

3. Those associated with *modification* of minority-carrier flow in the base as a consequence of base-width modulation: g_o, g_μ, C_d; dependent on both I_C and V_C.

4. Those associated with transverse flow of majority carriers in the base: r_x; this parameter is included in the simple hybrid-π model only as a "perturbation." That is, the effect on the external circuit of the voltage drops from this flow are included, but the further consequences of these transverse voltage drops with respect to the *internal* physics of the transistor have been omitted. On this basis, r_x depends only on V_C, and on that only weakly.

First, the parameters in group 1 above, which represent the fundamental transistor mechanism, are examined for bias point (I_C, V_C) dependence. After that, the operating-point dependence of the parameters in groups 2, 3, and 4 is discussed. Temperature dependence of parameters is then treated. Finally, effects that occur at either high collector current bias or high collector voltage bias are considered briefly.

4.1 PARAMETERS OF THE FUNDAMENTAL MODEL: g_m, C_b, r_π

The model parameters g_m, C_b and r_π are a representation of the basic internal mechanisms of the transistor; the injection of minority carriers into the base from the emitter, and their flow to the collector. The essential physical properties involved are summarized in Fig. 4.2 for a *pnp* transistor of uniform-base construction. The injected excess minority-carrier concentration $p_b'(0)$ corresponds to the forward-bias voltage V_{EB} applied across the emitter-base junction through the relation

$$p_b'(0) = p_{bo}(e^{qV_{EB}/kT} - 1) \qquad (4.1)$$

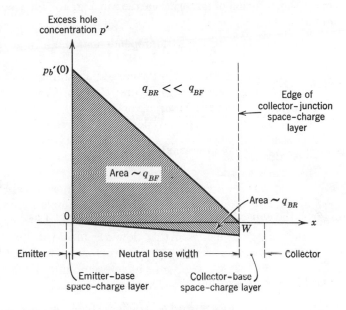

Fig. 4.2. Forward and reverse minority-carrier concentration distributions in the base of a *pnp* transistor with uniform base material.

as pointed out in Sec. 1.3.3, and the injected carriers are responsible for

(a) charging of the base by an excess charge q_{BF} of minority carriers (together with an excess neutralizing charge $(-q_{BF})$ of majority carriers, drawn in via the base lead);

(b) flow of current through the base to the collector by diffusion.

First we shall take up the effects of transport and storage, in terms of the model parameters g_m and C_b.

4.1.1 *Parameters* g_m *and* C_b

The parameter g_m is defined in Chapter 1 as

$$g_m \equiv -\frac{dI_{CF}}{dV_{EB}} \qquad (4.2)$$

In terms of the diffusion of minority carriers in Fig. 4.2, for a cross-sectional area A,

$$-I_{CF} = qD_bA\left(\frac{p_b{'}(0)}{W}\right) \tag{4.3}$$

or in view of Eq. 4.1

$$-I_{CF} = \frac{qD_bAp_{bo}}{W}\left(e^{qV_{EB}/kT} - 1\right)$$

Thus, because $q_{BF} \gg q_{BR}$ in normal operation,

$$g_m = \frac{q}{kT}\,|I_C| \tag{4.4}$$

Similarly, the capacitance C_b was defined in Chapter 1 as

$$C_b \equiv \frac{dq_{BF}}{dV_{EB}} \tag{4.5}$$

and from Fig. 4.2 we see that

$$q_{BF} = \tfrac{1}{2} qAp_b{'}(0)W \tag{4.6}$$

We also introduced in this connection the average charge replacement time in the base, τ_F, as

$$\tau_F \equiv -\frac{q_{BF}}{I_{CF}} = \frac{W^2}{2D_b} \tag{4.7}$$

in which we have used Eqs. 4.3 and 4.6 to obtain the last form. Thus, from Eqs. 4.5, 4.7, 4.2, and 4.4 we find for C_b the result

$$C_b = \left(-\frac{dq_{BF}}{dI_{CF}}\right)\left(-\frac{dI_{CF}}{dV_{EB}}\right) = \tau_F g_m = \tau_F \frac{q}{kT}\,|I_C| \tag{4.8}$$

Accordingly, as we have pointed out before, the transconductance g_m and base charging capacitance C_b are simply proportional to $|I_C|$, if the bias current is much greater than the reverse saturation current.

In the measured data presented in Fig. 4.3, $|I_C|$ is plotted against V_{EB} on a semi-logarithmic scale for a particular *npn* silicon transistor. A straight-line plot is to be expected on the basis of Eq. 4.4 (assuming that base current flow produces negligible dc transverse

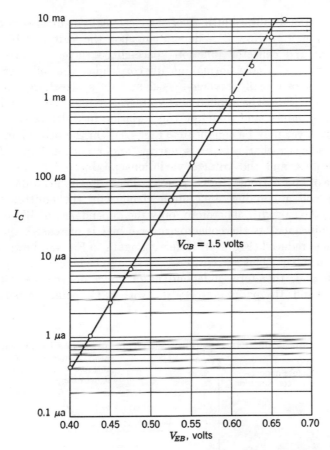

Fig. 4.3. Dependence of I_C on V_{EB} for a silicon *npn* diffused base transistor.

voltage drop in the base material). From Eq. 4.4, the proportionality of g_m to $|I_C|$ means that this straight line should have a constant slope q/kT. At sufficiently large collector current, deviation from the constant slope is observed. In the data presented here, this deviation is caused almost entirely by the effect of transverse base current, making the applied terminal voltage V_{EB} greater than that actually appearing across the emitter-base junction (see Sec. 4.4).

The expressions of Eqs. 4.6 or 4.3 for base charge or collector current, respectively, involve not only the injected hole concentration, but also the width W of the electrically neutral part of the base (Fig. 4.2). Now W is dependent upon the widths of both the emitter and collector junction space-charge layers; hence upon V_{EB} and V_{CB}. Under normal biasing conditions, the collector junction is substantially reverse-biased and its space-charge layer is relatively wide. The applied bias voltages are likely to cover a wide range of values, and therefore the variation in width of the space-charge layer may be significant (Fig. 4.4). On the other hand, the emitter space-charge layer is narrow under normal forward bias conditions, and the voltage variations produced by the normal range of bias currents are very small. These small variations in forward voltage produce but small changes in the emitter space-charge layer width. Therefore, only the dependence of W on V_C is of significance. As the collector reverse bias is increased, the base width is reduced (Fig. 4.4). Referring again to Eq. 4.4, however, at a given value of bias current $|I_C|$, g_m is seen to be independent of base width and, therefore, independent of collector voltage. On the other hand, the parameter τ_F, and with it C_b, being proportional

Fig. 4.4. The consequences of base-width modulation.

to W^2 (Eqs. 4.7 and 4.8), exhibit significant dependence on V_C at fixed $|I_C|$. Their values are, in fact, reduced as the collector reverse bias is increased. Experimental data bearing upon τ_F and C_b appear in Sec. 4.1.3.

4.1.2 *Parameter r_π*

The model parameter r_π ($\equiv 1/g_\pi$) also exhibits direct dependence on I_C. This is seen by writing from Eq. 3.23:

$$r_\pi = \frac{\beta_0}{g_m}$$

in which β_0 is the low-frequency current gain of the transistor in the common-emitter configuration, and we have neglected the effect of r_μ. Thus in view of Eq. 4.4,

$$r_\pi = \beta_0 \frac{kT}{q|I_C|} \tag{4.9}$$

Referring to the hybrid-π model of Fig. 4.1, the low-frequency input impedance in the common-emitter configuration with collector short-circuited to emitter, is found to be approximately

$$[h_{ie}]_{\text{low frequency}} \cong r_x + r_\pi \tag{4.10}$$

Figure 4.5 shows typical measurements of this impedance, and it is seen to fall rapidly with increase of $|I_C|$, owing primarily to the fall in r_π described by Eq. 4.9.

4.1.3 *Dependence of High-Frequency Current Gain on Operating Point*

The capacitance C_π of the hybrid-π model directly controls the common-emitter short-circuit current gain at high frequencies. Now C_π is defined as

$$C_\pi \equiv C_{je} + C_b$$

and from Eq. 4.8 may be rewritten as

$$C_\pi = C_{je} + \frac{q\tau_F}{kT}|I_C| \tag{4.11}$$

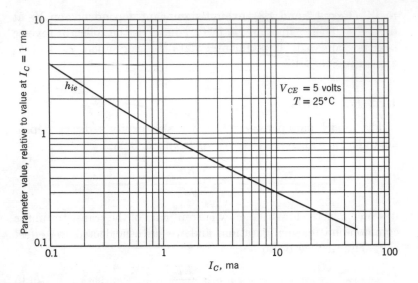

Fig. 4.5. Dependence of h_{ie} on collector current at low frequencies: silicon *npn* diffused-base transistor.

However, as we said before, the emitter junction voltage V_{EB} changes very little over a wide range of $|I_C|$, if $|I_C|$ is much greater than the saturation value. Thus, although the junction capacitance C_{je} is voltage dependent (Sec. 1.3.5), only small variation occurs for a wide range of I_C, and C_{je} can therefore be assumed to remain constant as I_C is varied in Eq. 4.11. This property may be verified by examining the common-emitter short-circuit current gain β at high enough frequencies so that $|\beta|$ is much less than the low-frequency value β_0, as follows.

From Eq. 3.33,

$$\beta = \frac{g_m}{g_\pi + j\omega(C_\pi + C_\mu)} = \frac{1}{1/\beta_0 + j\omega/\omega_T}$$

or provided $|\beta| \ll \beta_0$:

$$|\beta| \cong \frac{\omega_T}{\omega}$$

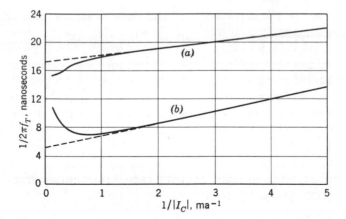

Fig. 4.6. Measured data for ω_T as a function of bias current. (a) Germanium uniform-base *pnp* transistor. (b) Germanium graded-base *pnp* transistor.

The parameter ω_T depends on operating point as follows:

$$\frac{1}{\omega_T} \equiv \frac{C_\pi + C_\mu}{g_m} = \frac{C_b + (C_{je} + C_\mu)}{g_m}$$

$$= \tau_F + (C_{je} + C_\mu)\frac{kT}{q|I_c|} \qquad (4.12)$$

in view of Eqs. 4.8 and 4.4.

Typical measured f_T ($-\omega_T/2\pi$) data are shown in Fig. 4.6, with $1/\omega_T$ plotted against $1/|I_c|$. The linear relationship, predicted from Eq. 4.12 by assuming that C_{je} and C_μ do not vary significantly with bias current, does exist, and extends over a wide range of current (it no longer holds at sufficiently high currents because of the current dependence of τ_F to be discussed in Sec. 4.4). Figure 4.6 shows data for both a uniform- and a graded-base transistor, and the expected variation is confirmed in both cases at low currents.*

* In a graded-base structure, the base impurity concentration is nonuniform; over a major fraction of the base width, the impurity concentration falls with increase of distance from emitter towards collector. This "grading" is responsible for an electric field which causes the diffusion of injected minority carriers through the base to be assisted by drift motion. Rapidity of flow of carriers through the base is thus increased when the base is graded, and the base charge q_{BF} corresponding to a given collector current (and hence the value of τ_F) is reduced below that of a comparable uniform-base device.

Because of the dependence of the time τ_F on the base width (Eq. 4.7), and the variation of C_μ with V_{CB}, the parameter f_T varies with collector bias voltage. As the reverse bias is increased, W and C_μ are reduced, and f_T is therefore increased. This property is illustrated in Fig. 4.7 which shows f_T versus I_C for a graded-base transistor at several values of V_{CE}. As in the previous figure, in such a device f_T exhibits a maximum value for a certain order of collector current, owing to the behavior of τ_F at high current levels (see Sec. 4.4).

4.2 MODEL PARAMETERS CONNECTED WITH PROPERTIES OF SPACE-CHARGE LAYERS

All the remaining parameters of the hybrid-π model, except r_x, depend for their very existence on the *modulation* by the small-signal voltages of the widths of the space-charge layers at the emitter-base and collector-base junctions (see Fig. 4.4). The numerical values of these parameters also depend on collector *bias* voltage, because the amount of width *modulation* produced by given signal voltages, and the effect of the modulation upon the rest of the device, depend on the absolute widths of the layers at the operating point. There is also a bias current dependence of

Fig. 4.7. Dependence of f_T on I_C and V_{CE} for a silicon graded-base *npn* transistor. The quantity plotted is $f \cdot |\beta|$ where $f = 20$ mc.

some of these parameters, arising from the dependence upon I_C of stored charge in the base region, Eq. 4.7, coupled with modulation of this stored charge by ac changes in base width with signal voltage (Fig. 4.4).

The parameters involved fall into two obvious groups: the junction capacitances C_{je} and C_{jc} (which are often very important in circuit applications); and the base-width modulation parameters g_o, g_μ, and C_d (which are seldom of any importance in circuit applications).

4.2.1 *Junction Capacitances*

The junction capacitance of a pn junction represents the incremental change in space charge within the space-charge layer, brought about by incremental change of junction voltage (Secs. 1.3.1 and 1.3.2, as well as Eqs. 1.7 and 1.10).

Physically, the junction capacitance decreases with increasing reverse-bias voltage because the dipole space-charge layer widens to sustain the larger voltage (see Fig. 1.2c and d), and the incremental capacitance is inversely proportional to this width. Conversely, C_j increases with increase of forward-bias voltage across the junction. However, for a wide range of forward current flowing through the junction, the junction voltage varies little because of the exponential nature of the junction volt-ampere relation. Accordingly, under forward-bias conditions the value of C_j varies little with junction *current*.

Figure 4.8a shows the results of measurement for both bias polarities of the emitter-junction capacitance for an alloy-junction transistor (step impurity transition) as a function of terminal voltage V_{EB}. The graph illustrates the properties discussed above.

Theory indicates that for such a step junction, $n = \frac{1}{2}$ in Eq. 1.10. Thus Eq. 1.10 suggests a plot of the capacitance data of Fig. 4.8a in the form $1/C_{je}^2$ against V_{EB}; this results in a straight-line relationship, as shown in Fig. 4.8b. For a linearly graded junction, theory predicts $n = \frac{1}{3}$, or that a linear relationship exists between $1/C_j^3$ and V. Figure 4.9 shows typical data of emitter-junction capacitance under conditions of reverse voltage bias for a graded-base silicon npn transistor, presented in the form $1/C_{je}^3$ versus V_{EB}. The straight line obtained shows that Eq. 1.10 is obeyed with $n = \frac{1}{3}$, so the junction approximates the property of linear impur-

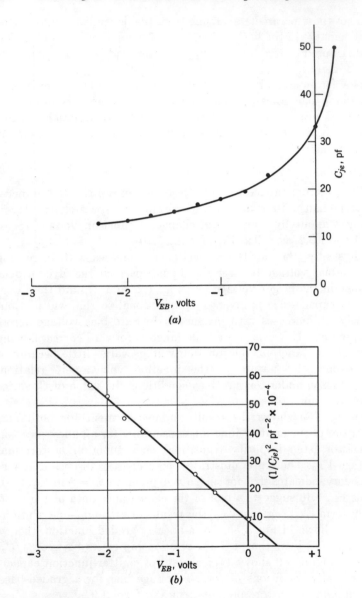

Fig. 4.8. Emitter-base junction capacitance: dependence on reverse bias voltage for a germanium *pnp* transistor of alloy junction construction (step junction transition at emitter).

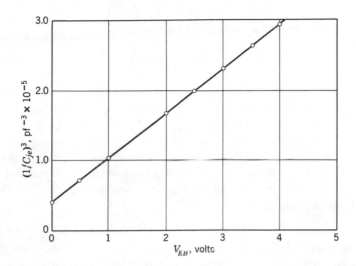

Fig. 4.9. Emitter-base junction capacitance: dependence on *reverse*-bias voltage for a silicon graded-base *npn* transistor.

ity grading. Similar results are obtained for the collector junction capacitance of this type of transistor at small reverse voltages (e.g., up to a few volts); for very large reverse-bias voltages, the *change* in capacitance with voltage approaches that of a step transition junction. In other cases of practical graded transistor junctions, the junction capacitance exhibits a voltage dependence for which n lies between limits of 0 and $\frac{1}{2}$.

4.2.2 *Base-Width Modulation Parameters*

As we have said, the base-width modulation parameters g_o, g_μ, and C_d (Fig. 4.1) are seldom of great importance in circuit applications. Therefore, the detailed derivation of their variation with operating bias is not worth reproducing from first principles here.* The results, expressed in the notation of Chapter 1, are

$$g_o \sim \frac{I_C}{W} \frac{d}{dV_{CB}} \left(\frac{1}{C_{jc}} \right) \tag{4.13a}$$

* The derivations appear in PEM, Chapter 8.

$$g_\mu \sim \frac{I_C}{W}\left(\frac{\tau_F}{\tau_{BF}}\right)\frac{d}{dV_{CB}}\left(\frac{1}{C_{jc}}\right) \tag{4.13b}$$

$$C_d \sim \frac{I_C}{W}\tau_F\frac{d}{dV_{CB}}\left(\frac{1}{C_{jc}}\right) \tag{4.13c}$$

The same characteristic properties of proportionality to I_C, and $1/W$ also apply in general for transistors of nonuniform base grading. We expect then that g_o, g_μ, and C_d should exhibit strong dependence on bias current I_C. This property is seen in Fig. 4.10a where the common-emitter output admittance h_{oe} (base open-circuited) at low frequencies is plotted against I_C for a particular transistor. From the model of Fig. 4.1, we may derive by the methods of Chapter 3,

$$h_{oe}|_{\text{low frequency}} \cong g_o + (\beta_0 + 1)g_\mu \tag{4.14}$$

The curve of Fig. 4.10a is not linear, but it does show major increases with current, especially at moderate and large currents. The differences from our expectations according to Eqs. 4.13 for the hybrid-π model, arise primarily from two effects. First, at low currents the conductances g_o and g_μ become very small. Accordingly, they are easily dominated by "external" conductances bridged across the high-voltage collector-junction region on the surface. Such conductances will almost certainly arise from electrical conduction through oxide layers or other chemical compounds on the junction surface, inasmuch as these layers are not perfect insulators. Thus h_{oe} will tend to a value independent of $|I_C|$ at low enough values of $|I_C|$. Second, at high currents β_0 and τ_F are no longer constant, as discussed further in Sec. 4.4.

In Fig. 4.10b is shown the dependence of h_{oe} on collector voltage V_{CE}. This behavior is caused by the combination of the effects of the factors $d(1/C_{jc})/dV_{CB}$ and $1/W$, each of which varies with collector voltage. Over the usual working range of moderate voltage, the first factor predominates and this causes g_o to fall with increase of reverse collector bias. Referring back to Eq. 1.10, we find that

$$\frac{d(1/C_{jc})}{dV_{CB}} \sim (\psi_0 - V)^{n-1} \tag{4.15}$$

where $V = -V_{CB}$ for a *pnp* transistor. Since $n < 1/2$, this factor is inevitably reduced as the reverse-bias value of V is increased.

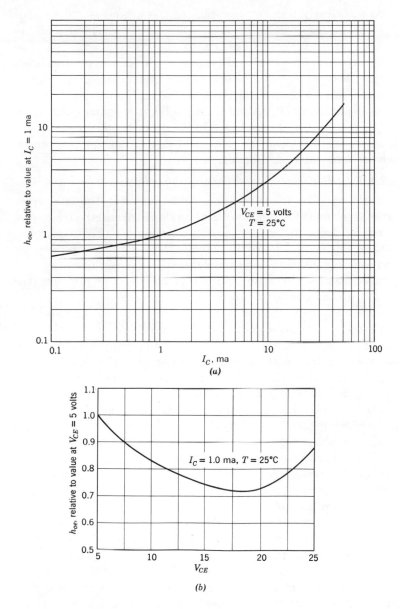

Fig. 4.10. Current and voltage dependence of output parameter h_{oe} at low frequency, for a silicon-graded base *npn* transistor.

At sufficiently large reverse-bias voltages, however, the factor $1/W$ in the expressions of Eqs. 4.13 exerts strong influence to increase the parameters, owing to the reduction of the base width to a very small value. It is even possible in some transistors for the base width to tend to zero at a certain collector-junction voltage. This is known as the "punch-through" condition.

As W approaches 0, g_o approaches ∞ because of the influence of the $1/W$ factor in Eq. 4.13a. On the other hand, the time τ_F is proportional to W^2, and thus we expect that g_μ and C_d will approach zero at large reverse voltages.

4.2.3 *Base Resistance r_x and Overlap Capacitance C_{sc}*

In the hybrid-π model as we have developed it, the base resistance r_x accounts for signal voltage developed across the transverse dimension from the emitter to the base contact (Fig. 4.11). The path of this current is partly through the region between emitter and collector junctions, and partly through a region from the base contact past the "overlap" portion of the collector junction (the area of which exceeds that of the emitter junction).

Evidently, the portion of base resistance between the two junctions can be increased significantly by constriction of the base layer owing to the widening of the collector space-charge region. Major increases in this portion of base resistance may therefore be expected at high collector voltages, especially in transistors for which punch-through can occur.

The rest of the base resistance, external to the emitter junction, is however relatively slightly affected by the widening of the collector space-charge layer. The relative contribution to r_x of this portion, versus the part described above, varies with the construction of the device and the bias current (discussed in the next section). In general, some increase of total base resistance r_x with increasing reverse collector voltage will occur.

Intimately connected with the base resistance problem is the portion of the collector junction which "overlaps" the emitter. The capacitance of this portion is observed in Fig. 4.11 to be relatively close to the base contact, physically, and there may or may not be a significant resistance to current which flows from that capacitance to the base contact. The circuit model of Fig. 4.1 suggests that there is not; it suggests that the "overlap capaci-

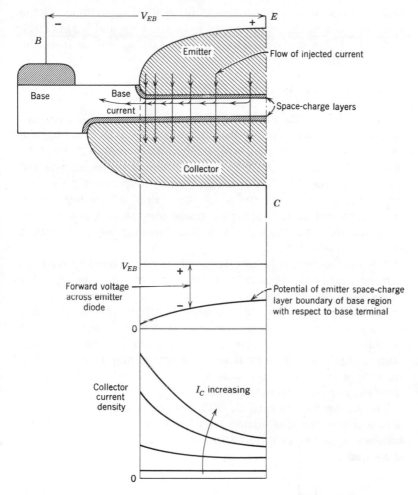

Fig. 4.11. Illustrating "collector overlap" and emitter "pinch-off" effects at high collector current level.

tance" C_{sc} shorts out the base resistance virtually entirely at high frequencies. In any event, the overlap capacitance C_{sc} would be expected to vary with collector voltage in the same way as the rest of the collector junction capacitance, represented in the model by C_{jc}. But this variation of C_{sc} may be difficult to measure in practice because of the presence of other fixed capacitance at the transistor terminals, which arises from the case and leads of the device itself (as we pointed out in Sec. 4.0), as well as from the external wiring.

4.3 DEPENDENCE ON TEMPERATURE

The model parameters most obviously affected by temperature are those connected with the injection of minority carriers from the emitter to the base. Thus g_m is inversely proportional to T (Eq. 4.4), whereas C_b varies as $(D_b T)^{-1}$ (Eqs. 4.8 and 4.7). Because of the variation of the diffusion coefficient with temperature,* we may expect C_b to vary as T^m, in which $0.3 \leq m \leq 0.7$ for *both* silicon transistors and germanium *pnp* transistors at and above room temperature. For germanium *npn* units, however, we would expect $C_b \sim T^{-0.3}$ instead.

The base resistance is also fairly obviously dependent on temperature, primarily because the resistivity of the semiconductor varies with temperature. For the usual resistivities employed, and at normal temperatures, this variation is attributable mainly to a decrease of majority-carrier mobility,* for reasons roughly similar to those which cause the resistance of metals to increase with temperature. Thus at normal temperatures r_x may be expected to increase with temperature according to a factor $T^{+1.5}$ to $T^{+2.7}$, depending on the material used in the base.

The strong variation of β_0 with temperature observed in Fig. 4.12 is characteristic of silicon transistors rather than germanium transistors, as we have noted in Chapter 2. It is not difficult to show that

$$\beta_0 \equiv \frac{dI_{CF}}{dI_{BF}} = \left(\frac{dI_{CF}}{dq_{BF}}\right)\left(\frac{dq_{BF}}{dI_{BF}}\right) = \frac{\tau_{BF}}{\tau_F} \qquad (4.16)$$

in view of Eq. 4.7 and the fact that τ_{BF} describes the minority carrier recombination rate in the base. We can see from Eq. 4.7 that τ_F varies with T only through D_b^{-1}, and we have pointed out

---

* See ISP, Table 1.2 and Eq. 3.69 (the Einstein relation). D_b varies as $T^{-(m+1)}$ with $1.3 \leq (m+1) \leq 1.7$ for Si and *p*-type Ge, but $(m+1) = 0.7$ for *n*-type Ge.

Fig. 4.12. Temperature dependence of parameters β_0 and h_{ie} (low frequency). Silicon graded-base *npn* transistor.

that D_b gets *smaller* at higher temperatures. Therefore, the *increase* of β_0 with T must arise from τ_{BF}, the minority-carrier lifetime. In silicon, most of the recombination of injected carriers takes place at imperfections or impurities (other than donors and acceptors) in the crystal structure, often located near surfaces within the emitter space-charge layer. At high temperatures, the rapid thermal motion of the carriers is thought to make their "capture" by such imperfections less probable, thus increasing τ_{BF} and β_0 with it.

Since $r_\pi = \beta_0(kT/q|I_C|)$ (Eq. 4.9), the temperature dependence of β_0 is combined with a direct proportionality with T, so that r_π undergoes a more rapid than proportional increase with temperature. This property is evident in the low-frequency data for $h_{ie}(\cong r_x + r_\pi)$, also shown in Fig. 4.12.

All other model parameters either exhibit very little dependence on temperature (C_{je}, C_{jc}, C_{sc}, g_o), or usually play a small enough role in the applications to make their variations less important ($g_\mu \sim \beta_0^{-1}$ and $C_d \sim D_b^{-1}$).

4.4 HIGH AND LOW CURRENT EFFECTS

In the foregoing discussion it was assumed that a linear relation between excess carrier concentrations and currents existed in the base region. At high current levels, however, significant departures from linearity occur, and two major physical processes are responsible for deviation from the properties previously established.

1. Flow of base current from the base region opposite the emitter area (viz., flow parallel to the plane of the emitter junction) sets up a corresponding potential distribution in the base. The emitter material itself is such a good conductor that no significant potential drops occur in it. Thus, as illustrated in Fig. 4.11, the effect of the transverse potential drops across the base is to cause the emitter-base junction to be progressively less forward-biased as the distance into the emitter area from its periphery increases. At high current levels this change in forward bias can cause the injection of current from the emitter to concentrate increasingly toward the emitter periphery when the current level (viz., I_C) is increased, as indicated in the figure. This effect is termed *emitter crowding or pinch-off*.

2. Associated with the injection of minority carriers into the base region is a concentration gradient of them from collector to emitter (Fig. 4.2). To maintain charge neutrality everywhere, a similar concentration gradient of *majority* carriers must also exist (Sec. 1.3.3). But in a good transistor there is almost no *longitudinal current* of *majority* carriers between emitter and collector; this is what makes it a good transistor and distinguishes the base region from any ordinary old piece of conducting material. So something must oppose the tendency of the *majority* carriers to diffuse away from the emitter, down their concentration gradient. A longitudinal electric field develops for this purpose; and because it *opposes* the diffusion current of majority carriers, it must *aid* the diffusion current of minority carriers (which are oppositely charged). To successfully oppose the majority-carrier concentration gradient, this field must increase in proportion to that gradient. Therefore, at low current levels this electric field is quite negligible; but when the injected concentration of minority carriers is comparable with the majority-carrier concentration, the electric field causes con-

siderable modification of the flow of minority carriers. Again, the effect is a nonlinear one because the *modification* produced by this field becomes greater as the current level is increased.

The above two nonlinear processes have a number of important consequences. The emitter pinch-off effect 1 reduces the mean distance of travel of base current in the base material, since injection of current from regions of the emitter most remote from the base contact is reduced. The base resistance r_x is therefore reduced in value as the dc bias $|I_C|$ is increased.

It is evident that effects 1 and 2 combine to exaggerate nonlinear current flow conditions in the base at high current levels. Effect 1 causes the current to concentrate toward the emitter periphery, and the injected current *density* therefore increases more rapidly than the total injected current, thus enhancing effect 2.

In a uniform-base device, the aiding drift field created by injection enhances the flow of injected minority carriers, and τ_F (the charge stored per unit current) is therefore reduced at high current levels. The frequency f_T therefore increases additionally at high currents, as illustrated by the data presented in Fig. 4.6a.

In a graded-base transistor, however, the nonuniform charged impurity concentration is designed to provide a "built-in" electric field under thermal equilibrium conditions. This field is arranged to aid minority-carrier progress across the base at *low* current levels. But at high current levels in such a device, the copious supply of both types of *mobile* carriers introduced by injection simply neutralizes the "built-in" charge distribution and removes the aiding effect of the original built-in field. Thus *more* minority charge is needed to supply a given current, by diffusion rather than by drift in a field, and τ_F increases. This effect causes a *reduction* of f_T (Eq. 4.12) and is responsible for the form of Figs. 4.6b and 4.7 at high currents.

At high currents, the transconductance g_m in the model deviates from the simple proportional dependence on $|I_C|$ which we have thus far predicted. This deviation may be caused by the effect of the *longitudinal* electric field set up in the base at high injection levels. Corresponding to this field, a *longitudinal* potential distribution is set up in the base material which would cause the voltage across the space-charge region of the emitter-base junction to be less than the applied forward voltage V_{EB}, even if there were no transverse effects due to flow of transverse base current in the base material. To represent this longitudinal effect, the value of g_m in the model must be made less than $q|I_C|/kT$. As pointed out in connection with Fig. 4.3, transverse crowding effects can also produce a similar result.*

The last effects to be discussed concern the dependence of the low-frequency current-gain parameter β_0 on bias current at both low and high current levels (Fig. 4.13).

This parameter increases somewhat with current at *low* current levels, because of nonlinear effects in the base. In silicon devices the reason for this increase is that the tendency of added minority and majority carriers to recombine is progressively reduced as the total carrier concentrations involved are increased from their equilibrium values. This occurs because, as we mentioned before,

* A detailed treatment of the high-current dependence of g_m is given in CLT.

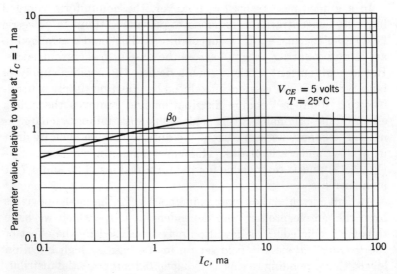

Fig. 4.13. Dependence of β_0 on collector current at low frequencies: silicon *npn* diffused-base transistor.

in silicon, recombination in the base material takes place for the most part at crystal imperfections or impurities located in the bulk, on the surfaces, and within the junction space-charge layers. As bias is applied, causing excess carrier concentration by injection, these imperfections get progressively filled up on the average, and fewer of them can accept new injected carriers for recombination. Thus the effective lifetime of *incrementally* added minority carriers in the base increases with bias current level, causing a corresponding increase in β_0.

In germanium devices, β_0 increases with current at very low currents from a very different effect. At very low currents, the incremental impedance of the emitter junction proper is very large. The shunting effect of surface "leakage" paths across the junction is then important and takes an appreciable fraction of the (very small) total emitter terminal current. This fraction does not contribute to minority-carrier injection in the base, and therefore does not change the collector current. Thus these leakage currents increase base current rather than collector current, and adversely affect β_0.

The current gain β_0 reaches a plateau after the low-current effects just discussed are overcome, and there is usually a reasonable range of bias current over which β_0 is substantially constant (Fig. 4.13). At high current levels, however, β_0 decreases with increasing current. The principal reason for this action (and several are actually involved) stems directly from the increase of *majority*-carrier concentration in the base at high injection levels. In the case of a *pnp* transistor, for example, the electron concentration in the base is *normally* much less than the hole concentration in the emitter— so that as much as possible of the emitter current shall be comprised of holes injected into the base (rather than electrons injected backwards from base into emitter). At high bias current levels, though, the increased concentration of majority electrons in the base results in the enhancement of "back" carrier injection *from* the base *to* the emitter region, thereby reducing the ratio of the incremental current injected into the base to the total incremental emitter current. This effect also increases base current rather than collector current, and causes β_0 to fall with increasing I_C at sufficiently high current level, as shown in Fig. 4.13.

4.5 HIGH-VOLTAGE EFFECTS

If the reverse-bias voltage of the collector-base junction is made sufficiently large, significant *avalanche multiplication* of the collector current carriers takes place as they traverse the space-charge layer. This is a collision process in which a hole or electron, moving in the electric field of the space-charge region, may undergo an impact-like interaction with the semiconductor crystal lattice, causing a bound electron to be freed. Such a process results in the creation of both a hole and a conduction electron, in addition to the incident charge carrier, and these subsequently drift (in opposite directions) in the space-charge-layer field, one of them adding to the collector current and the other subtracting from the normal base current. The strength of the effect depends on the intensity of the electric field in the space-charge layer: the larger the field (that is, the larger the collector reverse-bias voltage), the greater the kinetic energy acquired by charge carriers between collisions and the larger the number of collisions that liberate hole-electron pairs.

The dc effect of this multiplication (which is *not* a large factor on *collector* current) is nevertheless eventually to *reverse* the direction of the (small) base current, for a given value of collector current. The *incremental* effect of the multiplication is to increase the ratio of $\Delta i_C / \Delta i_B$ (that is, to increase β_0). Indeed it is possible that at some value of collector voltage the reduction in incremental base current produced by avalanche will just offset the normal increase associated with recombination in the base (and back-injection into the emitter), so that at this collector voltage β_0 will tend to infinity. This voltage is called the *sustaining voltage*.

Typical collector characteristics (I_C versus V_{CE}), illustrating both the reversal of dc base current, and the sustaining voltage, are shown in Fig. 4.14. The increase of current spacing between the characteristics above a certain collector voltage, but below the sustaining voltage, indicates the occurrence of the increase of β_0 already described.

Also seen in Fig. 4.14, *below* the sustaining voltage, is a strong increase in the slope of the characteristics. This increase occurs because the avalanche multiplication factor increases rapidly with voltage, but *the base current is constant along any particular curve*

Fig. 4.14. Collector characteristics: silicon graded-base *npn* transistor.

of the set. Therefore, to prevent the base current from changing with voltage on account of the increased avalanche effect, the base recombination current must increase by a cancelling amount. This requires a greatly increased injected current at the emitter, which produces a similar major increase of collector current. A corresponding argument explains the novel *decrease* of I_C with increase of V_{CE} *beyond* the sustaining voltage in Fig. 4.14. There, the total base current has already reversed direction and is dominated by the avalanche component. It is possible to operate the transistor for special high-speed switching purposes in the "avalanche mode," corresponding to operation beyond the sustaining voltage, provided the power dissipation is held within rated limits.

From the definition of the transconductance g_m as dI_C/dV_{BE}, at fixed V_{CE}, it is evident that this parameter is multiplied by the same factor as the injected current is multiplied by in the collector depletion layer. This is not very much larger than 1, as we have pointed out before. Thus the resistance r_π in the model must increase greatly with collector junction voltage in the same manner as β_0, in order to account for the major effects of avalanche multi-

FIG. 4.15. Summary of dependence of model parameters on operating condition. Except where in parentheses, statements refer to low-level injection conditions and voltages low enough for no avalanche multiplication effects.

Model Parameter	I_C	V_C	T
g_m	$\propto |I_C|$ (Increases less rapidly at high currents.)	(slight increase)	$\propto 1/T$
$\beta_0 = r_\pi g_m$	Constant at moderate currents. Falls at low currents. (Falls at high currents.)	Increases steadily. (Increases more rapidly at higher voltages; becomes infinite at sustaining voltage.)	Increases steadily.
$r_\pi = \beta_0/g_m$	Almost $\propto 1/|I_C|$ if β_0 shows little variation.	Increases steadily. (Becomes infinite at sustaining voltage.)	Increases more rapidly than $\propto T$.
r_μ	$\propto 1/|I_C|$ (Falls more rapidly at higher currents.)	Increases at low voltages. [Falls at higher voltages (main effect) due to onset of avalanche multiplication.]	Approximately same as β_0.
r_o	$\propto 1/|I_C|$	Increases at low voltages; at higher voltages (main effect) *falls* due to reduction of base width (and onset of avalanche multiplication).	Insensitive
r_x	Constant (falls at higher currents).	Increases steadily.	$\propto T^{m+2}$; for Si and Ge $-0.3 \leq m \leq +0.7$.

Important: All statements refer to effect of *increasing* $|I_C|$, $|V_C|$, or T.

FIG. 4.15. (*Continued*)

Model Parameter	I_C	V_C	T
C_b	$\propto |I_C|$ (At higher currents: uniform base, less rapid increase; graded base, more rapid increase.)	Reduces steadily.	$\propto 1/D_b T$ $\propto T^m$; where $+0.3 < m < +0.7$ for all Si and for Ge *pnp*. $m \approx -0.3$ for Ge *npn*.
C_{je}	Weak increase	Insensitive	Insensitive
C_{jc}	Insensitive	$\propto |V_{CB}|^{-n}$ approx. $n = \frac{1}{2}$ to $\frac{1}{3}$	Insensitive
C_d	$\propto |I_C|$	Decreases	$\propto T^{m+1}$ (see C_b)
$f_T = \dfrac{g_m}{2\pi(C_\pi + C_\mu)}$	Increases (steadily for uniform base; reaches peak and then falls at high currents for graded base).	Increases somewhat due to reduction in base width.	1. Reduces as T^{-1} if C_{je} and C_μ are comparable with C_b, as in graded base device (except at high currents). 2. Approximately $\propto D_b$ if $(C_{je} + C_\mu) \ll C_b$.

Important: All statements refer to effect of *increasing* $|I_C|$, $|V_C|$, or T.

plication upon the *base* current. The significance of this increase in r_π is that the supply of electrons to an n-type base, to replace those that recombine with injected holes, comes partly from the collector depletion layer as a result of avalanche multiplication of carriers, thus reducing the electron current that must enter the base via the base terminal. Indeed, beyond the sustaining voltage, r_π becomes negative.

Referring back to the discussion of base-width modulation effects in Sec. 4.2.2, a similarity is noted between the behavior of the parameter g_o as the *punch-through* condition is approached and its behavior when significant avalanche-multiplication effects are present: g_o can be increased rapidly as a result of either mechanism, as the collector reverse bias is increased.

It is possible for either avalanche-multiplication or punch-through effects to predominate at large collector voltage, depending on the particular design of the transistor.

4.6 SUMMARY

Many physical effects have been discussed above, and it is evident that if more than one of the basic conditions of operation (current, voltage, and temperature) changes simultaneously, the resulting change of a given model parameter may not be at all obvious. To facilitate the recollection of the various effects, the conclusions of the foregoing discussion are collected together and presented in summary form in Fig. 4.15.

PROBLEMS

P4.1   The approximate small-signal behavior of a pnp transistor biased in the normal region (active mode) can be represented by the hybrid-π model shown in Fig. 4.16. Assume that C_π is entirely the result of carrier storage in the neutral base region and C_μ is entirely the result of changes in the dipole layer of space charge at the collector junction.

(a) The quiescent collector current I_C is *doubled* while the quiescent collector-emitter voltage V_{CE} is held constant. Will the hole concentration $p_b'(0)$ at the emitter edge be doubled, halved, or stay nearly constant? Will the base width W be doubled, halved, or stay nearly constant?

(b) State, if possible, whether, as a consequence of these changes, the following parameters will double, stay nearly constant, or be reduced to half their former values: r_x, r_π, g_m, C_π, C_μ.

Fig. 4.16.

(c) The current I_C is held constant and the reverse bias voltage of the collector junction *increases* in magnitude enough to change the base width by a factor of two. Will $p_b'(0)$ be doubled, halved, or stay nearly constant? Will W be doubled, halved, or stay nearly constant?

(d) Repeat part (b) for the conditions of (c).

Transistor Bias Circuits:
Analysis and Design

5.0 INTRODUCTION

Biasing circuits must be carefully designed to overcome two deficiencies in transistors. First, transistors are temperature-sensitive (see, for example, Sec. 2.4). Second, substantial variations in β_F, β_R and the saturation currents occur among supposedly identical transistors bearing the same type number. We must design bias circuits so that these undesirable properties of the transistor do not cause circuit malfunction or failure.

In this chapter we first show that these deficiencies can be circumvented for many transistor-circuit applications by maintaining the operating point in the I_C, V_{CE} plane at some reasonably constant value. Then we develop a circuit configuration and a method of finding element values for a single-stage amplifier which will maintain the required reasonably constant operating point over a specified temperature range.

5.1 FACTORS INVOLVED IN SELECTION OF AN OPERATING POINT

5.1.1 The Safe Operating Region

There is a fairly definite area on the transistor output characteristics within which it is usually desirable to locate the transistor operating point. This area, which we call the "safe" operating region, is determined by the voltage, current, and power limitations of the transistor and by the gross nonlinearities in the transistor characteristics caused by the exponential nature of the emitter and collector diodes. The safe operating region on the output characteristics of a typical set of common-emitter curves has been indicated by shading in Fig. 5.1. A large part of the

Fig. 5.1. Common-emitter characteristics of a germanium-alloy transistor. (*a*) Input characteristics. (*b*) and (*c*) Output characteristics plotted on two different scales. Safe operating region indicated by shading.

boundary of this region is formed by the "maximum dissipation" curve, which marks the boundary between safe and unsafe operation, insofar as average power dissipation at the collector is concerned. The equation for the curve is $V_{CE}I_C = P_C$, forming a hyperbola when plotted in the I_C, V_{CE} plane. A maximum-power limit must be set on a transistor to prevent excessive junction temperatures from destroying the transistor or rendering it temporarily useless. Note that it is an *average* power rating. It is sometimes possible by careful design for the *peak* power to exceed this average rating for short periods of time, as long as internal peak temperatures are not excessive, but then a special investigation of the appropriate power ratings must be carried out if the manufacturer does not supply the needed information. This issue is discussed further in CLT.

The maximum voltage limitation appears on the figure as a vertical line. A maximum value of V_{CE} is usually specified to assure operation of the transistor below the *sustaining voltage*, the voltage at which the collector current becomes large regardless of value of applied base current (see Chapter 4, Sec. 4.5). The maximum I_C specification, on the other hand, is often not an absolute limit in the sense that the transistor will be destroyed, but it is a convenient way for the manufacturer to limit the region over which he must meet other specifications.

The remainder of the boundary of the safe operating region is set by the requirement of having the circuit biased in the normal region. For example, for the germanium *pnp* transistor characteristics shown in the figure, the collector voltage must always be more negative than -0.5 volt if the transistor is to stay out of saturation. Also, the collector current must be sufficiently negative to keep the transistor out of the cutoff region or, in other words, to insure that the emitter diode remains forward-biased.

For the particular transistor shown in Fig. 5.1, the maximum rating for the input voltage is $V_{BE} = +25$ volts (that is, reverse voltage on the emitter diode). It is clear that the maximum rating for the input voltage does not further restrict the choice of operating point for a linear amplifier. However, for other circuit applications, particularly pulse circuits, input ratings may be of considerable importance.

5.1.2 *Location and Control of Operating Point*

We have defined by Fig. 5.1 the safe operating region for a transistor linear amplifier. The operating point must be located somewhere within the shaded area. The next questions are: Precisely where within the shaded region do we locate the operating point? And how accurately do we have to maintain it? Three factors are important here. First, we must select and control the bias sufficiently to maintain linear operation, that is, prevent the amplifier from distorting at any temperature as a result of saturation of the collector diode or reverse-biasing of the emitter diode at the maximum or minimum of the voltage swings. Second, we must control the biasing in such a way that the transistor dissipation is always below the maximum allowable value. A third consideration arises from our discussions in Chapter 4, where we pointed out that the small-signal parameters in the hybrid-π model are functions of voltage, current, and temperature. We may wish to control the bias point in such a way that some of these parameters will remain reasonably constant. We will discuss these three considerations one at a time, with reference to the two undesirable properties of transistors mentioned above: (*a*) transistor characteristics are functions of temperature and (*b*) some characteristics and parameters of transistors vary widely from unit to unit among transistors of the same type number.

Maintenance of Linear Operation. To find the requirement for maintaining linear operation in spite of changes in ambient temperature, we must look at the variation of the transistor characteristics as a function of temperature, Fig. 5.2. For the germanium transistor, Fig. 5.2*a*, the dominant temperature effect on the output characteristic is a shift upward caused by the large increase in I_{CO}. However, as we pointed out in Sec. 2.4, the boundaries between the normal region and the saturation and cutoff regions do not change any substantial amount with temperature. Thus, in spite of the large change in the characteristics, the correct way to maintain linear operation is to *maintain the operating point at approximately the same value of I_C and V_{CE}*. Note that if we do this, I_B will have to change markedly with temperature, and in fact may very well have to reverse polarity.

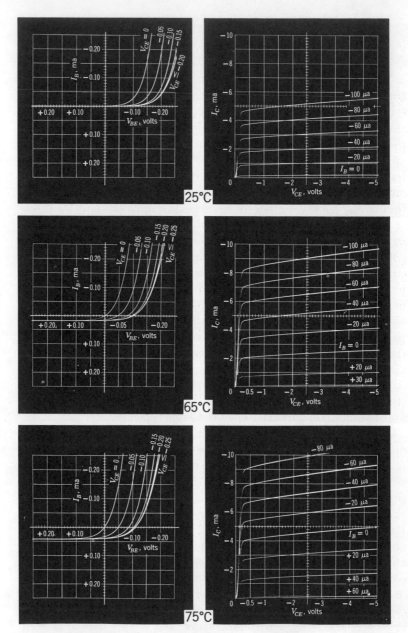

Fig. 5.2a. Common-emitter characteristics of a *pnp* germanium-alloy transistor, measured at 25°C, 65°C, and 75°C.

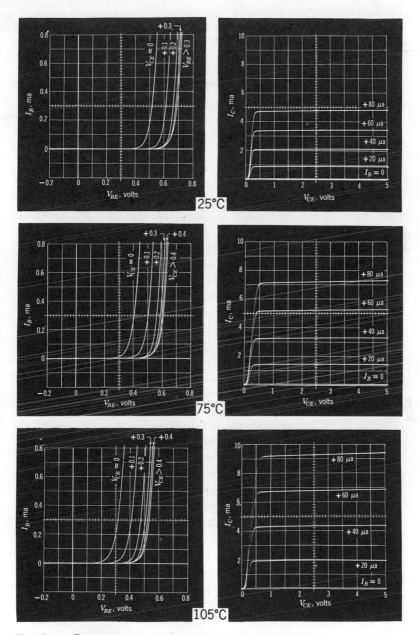

Fig. 5.2b. Common-emitter characteristics of an *npn* silicon transistor, measured at 25°C, 75°C, and 105°C

For silicon transistors, in which the dominant temperature effect on the output characteristics is an increase of β with increasing temperature, the normal region boundaries again change by only a very small amount (see Fig. 5.2b). Therefore, it is again best to maintain an approximately constant operating point.

Control of Transistor Dissipation. It is clear from the previous discussion that to control the biasing of the transistor in such a way as to keep the dissipation below its maximum value means keeping the operating point below the maximum-power-dissipation contour. In a transistor with a resistive load, this condition can be met by choosing the collector supply voltage and load resistor such that the load line always falls below the contour. This method cannot be used in amplifiers where the load resistor is specified at some low value because of other design considerations, or in amplifiers where the dc collector load is an inductor. In these cases, the dc load line will very likely intersect the maximum-power-dissipation contour, and it is entirely possible with improper bias design for the operating point to shift with temperature in such a way as to burn out the transistor. The situation is further aggravated by an effect called *thermal run-away,* which can be explained as follows.

The collector-to-base junction of the transistor, where essentially all of the dissipation occurs, is obviously not in perfect thermal contact with the transistor case, let alone with the surroundings. That is, there is some "thermal resistance" between the junction and the case, and between the case and ambient. Thus the power dissipated in the transistor will heat the junction to a temperature considerably above ambient. The internal increase in temperature will cause a change in the transistor characteristics as shown in Fig. 5.2. Under unfavorable conditions, this change in transistor characteristics may cause a still further increase in the internal temperature. This cyclic chain of events, which causes a rapid rise in transistor temperature and usually results in destruction of the transistor, is called thermal run-away.* It is clear that the power dissipation can be controlled, and hence thermal run-away prevented, if the biasing circuit is designed to *keep the operating point approximately fixed in the I_C, V_{CE} plane.*

* See CLT.

The situation is further complicated by the fact that the allowable transistor dissipation decreases with increasing temperature. The dissipation rating is based on the need to keep the junction below the temperature where transistor reliability and performance is impaired because of high I_{CO}, permanent changes in junction properties, or failure of soldered joints. This temperature is 85°C to 105°C for germanium, and 150°C to 250°C (usually about 200°C) for silicon. Because of the constant thermal resistance between the collector junction and the transistor case, the allowable dissipation decreases linearly to zero as the ambient temperature approaches the critical temperature given above.

There are two possible ways of handling this problem of changing allowable power dissipation. We can design for the "worst case," that is, keep the operating point fixed in the V_{CE}, I_C plane at a point below the smallest allowable dissipation which corresponds to the maximum temperature of operation required. Alternatively, we can design the bias circuit so that at room temperature the operating point is within the room-temperature maximum-dissipation curve, and at higher temperatures I_C is automatically reduced to keep the transistor within the dissipation rating. For simplicity in this chapter, we will use only the "worst-case" approach.

Control of Hybrid-π Parameters. It is a much more complicated problem to arrange the biasing so as to control some of the hybrid-π model parameters because, as we saw in Chapter 4 (Fig. 4.15), these parameters depend in a variety of ways on voltage, current, and temperature. It is possible to keep a single parameter fairly constant as a function of temperature: e.g., r_π in a silicon transistor can be held fairly constant by holding I_B fixed. (See Prob. P5.1.) But at the same time a fairly wide variation of some of the other parameters will occur. Thus, except in some special design problems, we may as well try here again to *keep I_C and V_{CE} approximately constant as the temperature changes.* In this way we at least avoid problems of variation of the hybrid-π parameters with current and voltage, if not with temperature.

We conclude that for all three reasons, maintenance of linear operation, control of power dissipation, and control of model parameters, often the best we can do is try to hold the operating point in the I_C, V_{CE} plane approximately constant. It should be clear that this conclusion, although reached by considering the problem of variation of parameters with temperature, also applies for variation of parameters for any other reason as well. For example, when any one of several transistors of the same type number but with different values of β must be used in a circuit, we can again insure satisfactory operation by trying to hold I_C and V_{CE} approximately constant.

5.1.3 *Choice of Terminal Variables to Control Operating Point*

The next question is: Which of the six terminal variables of the transistor do we wish to try to control in order to maintain a relatively fixed operating point on the output characteristics? The complete input and output characteristics shown in Fig. 5.2 are graphical representations of the two nonlinear equations required to specify the electrical behavior of the transistor. In functional form, these relations are

$$I_B = f_1(V_{BE}, V_{CE}) \tag{5.1a}$$

$$I_C = f_2(V_{CE}, I_B) \tag{5.1b}$$

Note that these are nonlinear, temperature-dependent equations involving the *total* current variables and *total* voltage variables. If we specify the value of any two of the transistor terminal variables, we can determine from Eqs. 5.1a and b and Kirchhoff's laws the values of all four remaining terminal variables. Biasing, therefore, essentially amounts to applying linear constraints to two of the six terminal variables of the transistor.

To start the discussion, suppose we first consider the possibility of using two *fixed*, independent sources as the two linear constraints. Although it is not apparent from Eq. 5.1, there are definite topological limitations in the selection of variables that we can fix or control in this manner. We cannot, for example, directly constrain with fixed sources both the current at a given terminal and the voltage between that terminal and either of the others. An example of this is shown in Fig. 5.3. In part (a), we have constrained V_{CE}, but the voltage source provides an alternate path for the current I to flow; hence we have not constrained I_C. In part b, on the other hand, we have constrained I_C, but not V_{CE}. Similar arguments hold at the other terminals.

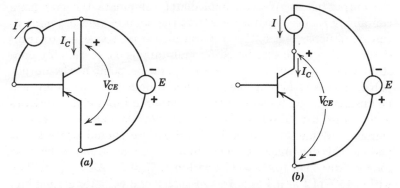

Fig. 5.3. Two futile attempts to control I_C and V_{CE} directly.

A little thought will show that adding resistors to the fixed sources only makes matters worse. As a matter of fact, the only way in which V_{CE} and I_C, for example, can be constrained is by using one fixed source, and one *dependent* source controlled by a sensing element. This type of biasing will be discussed in *Multistage Transistor Circuits*,* because it can be analyzed most readily from the point of view of feedback in multistage amplifiers.

In addition to these topological limitations, we know from Kirchhoff's laws that if we fix any two of the terminal currents, we have really fixed all three currents and, similarly, if we fix any two terminal-pair voltages, we have really fixed all three voltages. When the topological limitations and Kirchhoff's laws are applied, we find that there are only five possible choices of two variables left. These are:

1. V_{CE} and I_B.
2. Any two currents (meaning all three).
3. V_{BE} and I_C.
4. Any two voltages (meaning all three).
5. V_{CB} and I_E.

We must next decide which of these pairs of terminal variables we should try to control in order to control the operating point in

---

* *Multistage Transistor Circuits* (hereinafter referred to as MTC), by R. D. Thornton, D. O. Pederson, C. L. Searle, R. B. Adler, E. J. Angelo, Jr., and J. Willis.

the output plane. We can immediately eliminate the two pairs containing I_B, because it is clear from the point of view of temperature variations, Fig. 5.2, or β variations from transistor to transistor, that any biasing based on maintaining I_B reasonably constant will not maintain a constant operating point in the output plane. Also, any biasing based on maintaining V_{BE} constant will be unsatisfactory, because of the variation in input characteristics with temperature discussed in Sec. 2.4. We conclude by process of elimination that to control V_{CE} and I_C, we should control V_{CB} and I_E. This does indeed turn out to be a reasonable choice, because for β greater than 10, I_E will be within 10% of I_C. Also, V_{CB} will be within 10% of V_{CE} if V_{CE} is greater than 2 or 3 volts for germanium and 7 or 8 volts for silicon.

This same conclusion concerning the choice of terminal variables to control can be reached by plotting each pair of terminal constraints on the transistor characteristics of Fig. 5.2, and observing the variation in the operating point for the three different temperatures given in the figure. We can also see the relative merits of fixing I_E and fixing I_B by comparing Eq. 2.10 with Eq. 2.13. It is clear from these equations that I_C is much more sensitive to changes in I_{CO} and α_F when I_B is held fixed than when I_E is held fixed.

5.2 CIRCUITS WHICH STABILIZE I_E AND V_{CB}

5.2.1 *Circuit Configurations*

A transistor biasing circuit which keeps emitter current and base-to-collector voltage constant, yet allows the transistor to amplify ac signals, is shown in Fig. 5.4a. The dc emitter current is controlled by a current source, and the dc collector-to-base voltage is controlled by a battery through two inductors. A somewhat more "practical" version of the circuit is shown in Fig. 5.4b, where we have replaced the inductors with resistors and the current source by a battery in series with a resistor. The circuit in part b can be put into a more useful form by two linear network transformations. First, we find equivalent values of bias supplies needed when the batteries are placed in the base and collector leads, as shown in Fig. 5.4c. Then we replace the resistor and battery in the

Fig. 5.4. Progression from a biasing circuit using a battery, a current source, and inductors to a circuit using a single supply voltage and resistors.

base lead with a voltage divider from the collector-supply voltage, as shown in part d. The base-biasing circuit in c is actually the Thevenin equivalent of that in d.

An alternate bias-circuit configuration is shown in Fig. 5.5. In a, I_E is constrained by a current source connected from collector to emitter, and V_{CB} is constrained by a battery and inductor. In the circuit of Fig. 5.5b, the current source has been replaced by a battery and a load resistance, and the inductor has been replaced by an RC filter. It is not possible to move the battery in the base circuit to a location where one of its terminals can be grounded without somewhat compromising the bias stability. However, this battery can in many instances be replaced by a Zener diode as shown in c. For simplicity we will confine the remainder of the dis-

Fig. 5.5. Alternate progression to practical biasing circuit.

cussion to the circuit of Fig. 5.4, because the same issues are involved in both circuits.

It is perfectly clear that in going from the circuit in Fig. 5.4a to the more practical circuits of Fig. 5.4b, c, and d (or from Fig. 5.5a to 5.5c), we have compromised somewhat on our original intention to keep I_E and V_{CB} constant. The amount of compromise is, of course, closely related to the values of the resistors used in the circuit. In fact, this compromise is the essence of the bias design problem: How to choose R_e, V_B, R_b, and R_L to obtain adequate bias stability at the desired operating point, and at the same time adequate small-signal performance. By comparing Fig. 5.4a with 5.4b, we can establish some broad guidelines for design. For constant I_E and V_{CB}, make the drop across R_e as large as possible, consistent with obtaining the required size of output signal from the transistor. Then make R_b as small as possible, but at the same time much larger than $r_x + r_\pi$, to avoid shunting the input and thus lowering the ac gain.

For many noncritical applications where ambient temperature variations are small, we can postulate a first-order bias-design procedure on the basis of the preceding discussion. Having chosen an appropriate operating point, and V_{CC} and R_L, make the drop across R_e in Fig. 5.4c about 3 volts. Then calculate R_e based on the known I_C ($I_E \cong -I_C$). Now make R_b about ten or fifteen times R_e. This should give a value of R_b small enough for reasonable bias stability, but large enough to prevent excessive shunting of the input signal to ground. Next, calculate V_B by summing the voltage drops around the input loop:

$$V_B = -I_B R_b - V_{BE} + I_E R_e \tag{5.2}$$

Equation 5.2 can be solved to find the value of V_B by substituting the appropriate values for I_B, I_E, and V_{BE} at the operating point for $T = 25°C$. These values can be read directly off the transistor characteristics, if a complete set is available. Otherwise, they can be approximated by noting that $I_E \cong -I_C$, $V_{BE} \cong -0.2$ volts (for germanium), and $I_B \cong I_C/\beta_F$.

The last step is to convert R_b and V_B into the equivalent input network of Fig. 5.4d. To find R_1 and R_2, we note from Fig. 5.4c and d that

$$\frac{R_1 R_2}{R_1 + R_2} = R_b \tag{5.3}$$

$$\frac{R_2}{R_1 + R_2} V_{CC} = V_B \tag{5.4}$$

Solving these two equations, we get

$$R_1 = \frac{V_{CC}}{V_B} R_b \tag{5.5}$$

$$R_2 = \frac{R_1 R_b}{R_1 - R_b} \tag{5.6}$$

For many bias design problems, for example, those involving a large range of operating temperature, large variations in β, or large output signals, the simple design procedure given above will not yield satisfactory results. Under these conditions, we must analyse the bias-stability problem with considerably greater care. We must calculate exactly how much the bias point varies in the circuit,

Fig. 5.4, for a given set of resistor values; or conversely, we must carry out the design problem of finding the resistor values to achieve a certain specified stability of the operating point. This is the subject of the following section.

5.3 BIAS STABILITY CALCULATIONS

5.3.1 *Transistor Model (pnp)*

It is entirely possible to make the required bias stability calculations by using the Ebers-Moll model or equations (Fig. 2.4 or Eqs. 2.8 and 2.9), provided, of course, that we insert the appropriate values for the temperature dependence of the four basic parameters α_F, α_R, I_{CO}, and I_{EO}. However, it is usually much more convenient to use a model in which the temperature dependence is represented in a more explicit manner. One such representation for a *pnp* transistor is shown in Fig. 5.6. Here we have taken the temperature dependence which is implicit in the characteristics of the diodes used in the Ebers-Moll model and shown it explicitly by the use of four temperature-dependent sources. Typical values for these temperature-dependent sources are given in the figure for both silicon and germanium. By using ideal piecewise-linear diodes (square-box symbol) in this model, we are in effect ignoring the fact that the voltage V_{BE} is really current-dependent as well as temperature-dependent. To be more exact, we should thus include a resistor in series with $V_{BE}(T)$, but because of the presence of R_e, this resistor makes little difference in the final result.

Using the model of Fig. 5.6 for the transistor, let us calculate the change in operating point with temperature for the circuit in Fig. 5.4c. We are interested only in making calculations in the amplification region, so we can simplify the model by assuming that the collector diode is *off* and the emitter diode is *on*. The resulting circuit model is shown in Fig. 5.7.

5.3.2 *General Expression Relating I_C to I_{CO}, V_{BE}, and β*

The first step is to derive an equation which relates I_C to the temperature-dependent parameters $I_{CO}(T)$, $V_{BE}(T)$, and $\beta(T)$. Because the models in Fig. 5.6 and 5.7 are both for a *pnp* transistor, all expressions in this subsection apply only to *pnp* transistors. Suitable changes in sign must be made for *npn* transistors.

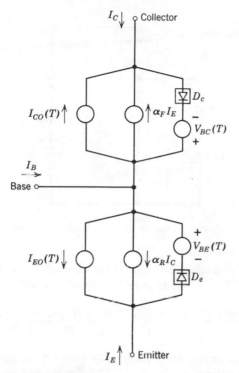

Fig. 5.6. Modification of *pnp* ideal-diode model to include temperature-dependence. Typical values for the temperature-dependent sources are:

Germanium: $I_{CO} = 10^{-6}$ amps at 25°C, doubling every 10°C

$\qquad I_{EO} \cong 0.75\ I_{CO}$

Silicon: $\qquad I_{CO} = 10^{-9}$ amps at 25°C, doubling every 7°C at high temperatures.

$\qquad I_{EO} \cong 0.75\ I_{CO}$

$$\frac{\Delta V_{BC}}{\Delta T} = \frac{\Delta V_{BE}}{\Delta T} = 2\ \text{mv/degree } C \text{ for both silicon and germanium } (\pm 50\%).$$

By summing the currents at the collector node in Fig. 5.7, we get

$$I_C = -I_{CO}(T) - \alpha_F I_E \qquad (5.7)$$

By summing the voltage drops around the input loop we relate $V_{BE}(T)$ to I_E:

$$V_B + I_B R_b + V_{BE}(T) - I_E R_e = 0 \qquad (5.8)$$

Fig. 5.7. Circuit model for bias calculations, *pnp* transistor.

Equations 5.7 and 5.8, together with the relations $I_C + I_E + I_B = 0$ and $\beta_F = \alpha_F/(1 - \alpha_F)$, can now be solved to yield

$$-I_C = \frac{\beta_F V_B + \beta_F V_{BE}(T) + (\beta_F + 1)(R_b + R_e)I_{CO}(T)}{(\beta_F + 1)R_e + R_b} \quad (5.9)$$

Because of the nonlinear relationship between β_F and I_C in this equation, we cannot evaluate $\Delta I_C/\Delta T$ by taking the derivative. However, if we make the assumption $\beta_F \gg 1$, and then collect the terms in β_F on the left-hand side of the equation, the analysis is greatly simplified:

$$R_b\left(-\frac{I_C}{\beta_F} - I_{CO}\right) \cong V_B + V_{BE}(T) + R_e(I_C + I_{CO}) \quad (5.10)$$

Writing Eq. 5.10 for two temperatures T_1 and T_2, and subtracting the equation for T_1 from the equation for T_2, we obtain

$$R_b\left[\frac{-I_{C2}}{\beta_{F2}} + \frac{I_{C1}}{\beta_{F1}} - \Delta I_{CO}\right] \cong \Delta V_{BE}(T) + R_e(\Delta I_C + \Delta I_{CO}) \quad (5.11)$$

where the subscript 1 denotes the values of I_C and β_F at temperature T_1, and subscript 2 denotes the values at T_2. Equation 5.11 can now be written in a form which gives the required value of R_b

in Fig. 5.4c explicitly in terms of R_e, the changes in $V_{BE}(T)$, I_{CO}, and β_F, and the permissible change in I_C,

$$R_b \cong \frac{\Delta V_{BE}(T) + R_e(\Delta I_C + \Delta I_{CO})}{-I_{C2}/\beta_{F2} + I_{C1}/\beta_{F1} - \Delta I_{CO}} \qquad (5.12)$$

where

$$\Delta V_{BE}(T) \equiv \frac{\partial V_{BE}}{\partial T}\bigg|_{I_E} (T_2 - T_1) \qquad (5.13)$$

$$\Delta I_{CO} \equiv I_{CO}(T_2) - I_{CO}(T_1) \qquad (5.14)$$

$$\Delta I_C \equiv I_{C2} - I_{C1} \qquad (5.15)$$

Note that everything on the right-hand side of Eq. 5.12 except R_e is a known constant, so the equation is no more complicated than

$$R_b = AR_e - B$$

The use of this equation can best be illustrated by the following design examples.

5.3.3 *Design Example for a Germanium Transistor*

Let us work through a specific design example, using the *pnp* transistor whose characteristics and maximum ratings are given in Fig. 5.1. Suppose we wish to design a transistor amplifier to develop a 5-volt peak-to-peak symmetric output swing across a 5-k load resistor without using a transformer. Other specifications and circuit parameters are:

> Temperature range: 25°C to 75°C
>
> I_{CO}: 2 μa at 25°C
>
> V_{CC}: −12 volts

The maximum possible power that the 5-k resistor and dc supply can deliver to *any* load, even a transistor, is

$$P_{\max} = V_{CC}^2/4R_L = 7.2 \text{ mw}$$

Thus, for this particular problem, the power dissipation in the transistor is small, so the most important consideration involved in locating the operating point will be the linearity of the amplifier. We therefore focus attention directly on the problem of obtaining linear operation for the required ±2.5-volt swing away from the operating point.

The minimum dc collector current needed to maintain linear operation is -2.5 volts/5 k or -0.5 ma. To find the maximum value of dc operating current, it is necessary to know the value of R_e. Unfortunately, R_e is one of the unknowns we are trying to solve for. For simplicity we solve the problem by iteration. We first assume a reasonable value for R_e, then work through the design to find R_b. If the resulting design is for some reason unsatisfactory, then the problem must be reworked for a new assumed value of R_e.

To aid in the choice of a reasonable initial value of R_e and the subsequent calculation of the maximum permissible value of I_C, it is helpful (but not essential) to draw on the output characteristics for 25°C and 75°C the dc and ac load lines of the circuit. This has been done in Fig. 5.8a and b for various assumed values of R_e. We are assuming in these figures that because $\alpha_F \cong 1$, I_E is approximately equal to $-I_C$, so the dc drop across R_e will be approximately $I_C R_e$. Thus the approximate dc load line has a slope of $1/(R_L + R_e)$. The ac load line with slope $1/R_L$ intersects the dc load line at the operating point. For the 25°C characteristic, we select the minimum operating point of -0.5 ma as calculated above. For the 75°C characteristic (obtained from Fig. 5.2a) we wish to choose the operating point at as high a current as possible,

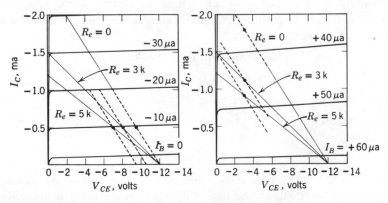

Fig. 5.8. Output characteristics with ac and dc load lines. *Left:* (25°C). *Right:* (75°C). Because the changes in I_{CO}, β, and V_{BE} with increasing temperature all tend to increase $|I_C|$, (see Fig. 5.6.), we associate the minimum operating point with the low temperature and the maximum operating point with the high temperature.

so that the tolerance on I_C can be as large as possible. (Recall that for this particular design, the sole requirement is maintenance of linear operation.) The curves of Fig. 5.8b show that we need a minimum $|v_{CE}|$ of about $\frac{1}{2}$ volt to stay out of saturation, so to get 2.5 volts peak output voltage, we need a minimum $|V_{CE}|$ of 3 volts. The three ac load lines are drawn to meet this condition.

We see from the figure that the maximum permissible value of I_C, and hence ΔI_C, goes down as R_e is increased, thereby making the stabilization problem more difficult. A reasonable compromise value for R_e therefore seems to be 3 k. From the figure we get $I_C|_{\max} = -1.1$ ma. Rather than design for operation at the very edges of the nonlinear regions, let us allow for component tolerances by setting I_{C1} at -0.7 ma and I_{C2} at -1.05 ma. Thus $\Delta I_C|_{\max} = -0.35$ ma.

We are given that $I_{CO} = 2\ \mu a$ at 25°C, and we know that it doubles for every 10 degrees centigrade rise in temperature, thus I_{CO} will be 64 μa at 75°C, or $\Delta I_{CO} \cong 60\ \mu a$. Also, we know that V_{BE} changes at most 3 mv per degree C, so $\Delta V_{BE} = 150$ mv. Also, from Fig. 5.8, $\beta_{F1} \cong 50$, and $\beta_{F2} \cong 75$. Substituting these values into Eq. 5.12, we obtain the following equation, in which the units are millivolts and milliamps:

$$R_b = \frac{150 + R_e(-0.35 + 0.06)}{(1.05/75 - 0.7/50 - 0.06)} \tag{5.16}$$

$$= -2500\ \Omega + 4.83 R_e$$

For our assumed value for R_e of 3000 ohms, R_b must be 12.1 k. Of course, any value of R_b less than 12.1 k will still yield the desired stability, so for this design a standard resistor value of 12 k would be chosen. On the other hand, if this calculation had led to a negative value of R_b, we might be forced to rework the design for a larger value of R_e (see Problem P5.12).

It is appropriate at this point to check the ac gain of the circuit to make sure that R_b is large enough compared to the transistor input resistance $r_x + r_\pi$ so that it is not shunting too much of the signal to ground. If R_b is too small, then the design should be reworked for a larger value of R_e. If R_e is already as large as it can possibly be, then some compromise must be made somewhere in the design between the stability requirement and the gain requirement for the stage. In fact, the biasing problem is always essentially a trade-off between bias stability and ac gain, although usually it is possible to achieve adequate temperature stability with only a ten or twenty percent loss in gain.

The last step in the design is to calculate the required value of V_B, and then complete the design of the input resistor network shown in Fig. 5.4d. The details at this point are identical to those presented on page 167. Specifically, we find V_B from Eq. 5.2, where V_{BE} in this equation is the true base-to-emitter voltage at 25°C. Then R_1 and R_2 can be found from Eqs. 5.5 and 5.6.

5.3.4 *Example of Bias Stability Calculations for Silicon Transistors*

Inspection of the output characteristics for silicon transistors, given in Fig. 5.2, confirms the fact that in silicon, changes in β as a function of temperature are much more serious than in germanium, but I_{CO} is not a serious problem because it is so small. Thus the biasing discussion for silicon, while similar in many respects to the example in Sec. 5.3.3 for germanium transistors, must reflect these two important differences. For completeness we will work this example for an *npn* transistor. For the *npn* case, we must modify Eq. 5.12 as follows:

$$R_b \cong \frac{\Delta V_{BE}(T) + R_e(\Delta I_C - \Delta I_{CO})}{-I_{C2}/\beta_{F2} + I_{C1}/\beta_{F1} + \Delta I_{CO}} \tag{5.17}$$

To keep the two examples as similar as possible, we will again try to design an amplifier to develop a 5-volt peak-to-peak symmetric voltage across a 5-k load resistor. Also, as before,

$$V_{CC}: 12 \text{ volts}$$

$$\text{Temperature range: } 25°C \text{ to } 75°C$$

However, this time we assume

$$I_{CO}: 10^{-9} \text{ amp at } 25°C$$

$$\beta_F: 30 \text{ at } 25°C$$

$$100 \text{ at } 75°C$$

For simplicity, we assume that after drawing the ac and dc load lines on the silicon output characteristics, we conclude again that $R_e \cong 3$ k, and $I_{C1} = 0.7$ ma, $I_{C2} = 1.05$ ma, so, as before,

$$\Delta I_C = 0.35 \text{ ma}$$

For silicon, I_{CO} doubles for every 15°C increase over this temperature range (see Fig. 1.6). Thus ΔI_{CO} can be neglected for this example.

We will use the same value of ΔV_{BE} as before:

$$\Delta V_{BE} = -150 \, \text{mv}$$

Now, substituting these values into the *npn* equation for R_b, Eq. 5.17, we obtain the following equation (units of millivolts and milliamps):

$$
\begin{aligned}
R_b &= \frac{-150 + R_e(0.35)}{(-1.05/100 + 0.7/30)} \\
&= -11{,}700 \, \Omega + 27.3 R_e
\end{aligned}
\tag{5.18}
$$

For our assumed value of 3000 ohms for R_e, R_b comes out in this case to about 70 k, a value which is obviously large enough to give no problems of input loading. In fact, it is so large that the design should probably be reworked for a smaller assumed value of R_e.

Knowing the value of R_b, we can now calculate V_B, and hence R_1 and R_2 from Eqs. 5.2, 5.5, and 5.6 as before, remembering, of course, to use $V_{BE} \cong 0.7$ volt for silicon.

The preceding discussion on biasing transistors was phrased in terms of variations of β_F and V_{BE} with temperature. However, Eqs. 5.12 and 5.17 are actually more general than this, because they can be applied to situations where β_F and V_{BE} vary for other reasons as well. Specifically, these same equations can be applied to both silicon and germanium transistors to study the problem of variation of operating point when transistors with different β's are plugged into the same circuit. This problem of the variation of β_F within a given transistor type is obviously of considerable importance in the design of any circuit which is going to be produced in quantity.

5.4 OTHER BIASING CIRCUITS

Three important general classes of biasing circuits will be discussed briefly in the following subsections: biasing with fixed resistors and batteries, multistage biasing, and biasing by temperature compensation.

5.4.1 *Single-Stage Biasing Circuits Composed of Resistors and Batteries*

One large class of biasing networks are those composed of fixed resistors and batteries, such as, for example, those discussed in Secs. 5.2 and 5.3. Fortunately, we do not have to study in detail every one of the many circuits which fall into this category. Any biasing circuit composed of one transistor, and any number of fixed resistors and batteries, can be reduced to the three-terminal Thevenin equivalent circuit shown in Fig. 5.9. And this Thevenin circuit is electrically equivalent to the network which we have been studying, Fig. 5.4c, insofar as the dc calculations are concerned. Thus the discussion in this chapter is widely applicable to other single-transistor biasing circuits not employing temperature compensation. A word of caution is necessary, however. The Thevenin equivalence applies only to *the dc circuit*, and really assures only that the corresponding dc voltages and currents *at the transistor terminals*, and hence the dc bias stability calculations, are the same in the two circuits. The circuits are *not* equivalent as regards power dissipation in the resistors, relative insensitivity to changes in resistor values, dynamic range, ac gain, etc.

5.4.2 *Multistage Biasing*

In multistage transistor circuits, a number of transistors are often directly coupled (without coupling capacitors), and the group of transistors biased as a unit. Multistage biasing network of this type are best handled from the point of view of negative feedback.

Fig. 5.9. Thevenin equivalent of any three-terminal biasing circuit composed of resistors and batteries.

Therefore, discussion of this issue has been postponed until after the feedback chapter in MTC.

5.4.3 *Bias Stabilization by Temperature Compensation*

An example of a somewhat different approach to the biasing problem is shown in Fig. 5.10. Here, instead of trying to minimize operating-point variations by manipulating the circuit, another temperature-dependent element such as a diode or a thermistor is added to the circuit in such a way that it tends to *compensate* for the temperature effects in the transistor.

In the particular configuration shown in Fig. 5.10, a reverse-biased germanium diode is used to compensate for I_{CO} effects in a germanium transistor. If we assume the collector supply voltage is much larger in magnitude than V_{BE}, then the current through R will be nearly constant

$$I_R \cong \frac{V_{CC}}{R} \qquad (5.19)$$

The diode is reverse-biased by an amount $|V_{BE}|$, which will usually be enough to insure that the diode current is reduced to its reverse saturation value of I_s. It follows that

$$I_B = -I_R + I_s \qquad (5.20)$$

Fig. 5.10. Bias stabilization of germanium transistor by compensation.

From Fig. 5.7 (or from Eq. 2.13),

$$I_C = \beta_F I_B - (\beta_F + 1)I_{CO} \qquad (5.21)$$

Substituting for I_B from Eq. 5.20, we obtain

$$I_C = -\beta_F I_R + \beta_F I_s - (\beta_F + 1)I_{CO} \qquad (5.22)$$

If the two reverse saturation currents I_s and I_{CO} are approximately equal at room temperature, and track fairly closely over the desired temperature range, then Eq. 5.22 shows that the dc collector current of the transistor will remain almost constant, independent of temperature.

The general approach of biasing by temperature compensation is particularly attractive when, for reasons of power economy, the power loss associated with the bias circuit of Fig. 5.4d cannot be tolerated. It is also a useful approach to the problem of biasing amplifiers in which the average collector current is not constant (pulse amplifiers and Class B amplifiers, for example).

PROBLEMS

P5.1   Prove that r_π in a silicon transistor can be held fairly constant as a function of temperature by biasing so as to keep I_B constant.

P5.2   A transistor amplifier and the periodic input signal with which it must operate are shown in Fig. 5.11. Assume that R_b can be adjusted to achieve any desired quiescent operating point between $I_C \cong 0$ and

(a)   (b)

Fig. 5.11.

$I_C = 20$ ma. Furthermore, V can be adjusted so that the ac output signal v_o has any desired "amplitude" (up to the limits set by cutoff or saturation of the transistor). Neglect variations of common-emitter current gain with collector current and assume low frequency operation. The objectives are to select the quiescent operating point (I_C, and therefore V_{CE}) *and* the output signal "amplitude" in such a way that the ac signal power developed in the load resistor is a maximum while the amplifier operates in a *linear* manner (i.e., without entering the cut-off or saturation regions).

(*a*) Determine I_C.

(*b*) Determine the maximum possible power developed in the load resistor, and the power supplied by the battery under idle conditions and with the maximum permissible signal.

P5.3 Using the circuit of Fig. 5.4*d*, design a biasing network for the germanium transistor shown in Fig. 5.1. Assume $V_{CC} = -10$ volts, $R_L = 500\ \Omega$, $r_x = 50\ \Omega$. The circuit must be capable of developing a 6-volt peak-to-peak sinusoidal output voltage across the 500 Ω load resistor. The current gain (current in R_L per unit input current) must be at least 30. The circuit must operate over a temperature range of 25°C to 65°C. Assume β_F is constant at 45 over the operating range of interest at 25°C, and constant at 65 for $T = 65$°C. $I_{CO} = 1\ \mu a$ at 25°C.

P5.4 Repeat P5.3 (if possible) for a 7-volt peak-to-peak swing. If impossible, explain which conditions cannot be satisfied, and why.

P5.5 Repeat P5.3 (if possible) for an 8-volt peak-to-peak swing. If impossible, explain which conditions cannot be satisfied, and why.

P5.6 Repeat Problem P5.3 with $R_L = 100\ \Omega$ and a peak-to-peak sinusoidal output swing of 1 volt.

P5.7 In the example of Sec. 5.3.3, which term would be dominant in determining temperature stability over the temperature range of 25°C to 35°C: $V_{BE}(T)$, $\beta_F(T)$, or $I_{CO}(T)$?

P5.8 Will the approximate design method of Sec. 5.2.1 work for the design specifications in the example of Sec. 5.3.3? The example of Sec. 5.3.4?

P5.9 At a temperature of 25°C the transistor in Fig. 5.12 has $\beta_F = 60$, $I_{CO} = 1\ \mu a$. Estimate the operating point (I_C, V_{CE}). Make reasonable approximations and state them.

P5.10 The I_{CO} of the germanium transistor in Fig. 5.12 doubles for every 10°C increase in temperature, and V_{EB} decreases at a rate of 2.3 mv per °C. Assume that the temperature dependence of β_F is negligible.

(*a*) Do the thermally induced changes of V_{EB} affect the operating point significantly in comparison with the changes of I_{CO} as the temperature increases above 25°C?

Fig. 5.12.

(b) Assuming that the amplifier must remain linear for a *sinusoidal* output signal (across R_L) of 2-volt peak-to-peak amplitude, what is the maximum temperature at which the circuit may be operated? Note that the emitter resistor is bypassed for signal frequencies.

P5.11 A *pnp* transistor is biased in the normal region by the circuit shown in Fig. 5.13a. At $T = 25°C$ the transistor has $\beta_F = 100$, $I_{CO} = 5$ μa, $V_{EB} = 0.4$ volt.

(a)   (b)

Fig. 5.13.

(a) What is the operating point (I_C, V_{CE}) at $T = 25°C$?

(b) An increase in temperature causes β_F to increase to 150, I_{CO} to increase to 20 μa, and V_{EB} to decrease to 0.35 volt. Estimate the change in I_C and V_{CE}.

The circuit is modified as shown in Fig. 5.13b.

(c) What is the operating point at $T = 25°C$?

(d) Will the change in operating point be greater or less than that of the first circuit for the same changes in transistor parameters?

P5.12 Rework Problem P5.3 for several different values of R_e and hence plot a graph of R_b versus R_e. There will be several ranges of values of R_e for which R_b is negative. Explain the significance of each of these ranges, and in particular indicate which represent satisfactory bias designs.

6

Frequency Response and Step Response Calculations

6.0 INTRODUCTION

In this chapter, we study the effects on the frequency response of the various capacitors in a single-stage transistor amplifier. Specifically, we calculate the voltage transmission function for the common-emitter amplifier shown in Fig. 6.1. Whereas all the discussion in this chapter is based on this common-emitter circuit, the method of approach for coupling and bypass calculations can

Fig. 6.1. Typical transistor stage with coupling capacitor C_1 and emitter bypass capacitor C_2.

equally well be applied to common-collector and common-base circuits (see Problems P7.7 and P7.8).

The functions of various resistors in the circuit of Fig. 6.1 have already been discussed in detail in Chapter 5. The capacitors, however, need some brief explanation. The coupling capacitor C_1 is needed to couple the ac signal from the source V_i to the base of the transistor, and at the same time to block the dc so that the source does not upset the bias conditions established by resistors R_{b1} and R_{b2}. The capacitor C_2 is called the emitter bypass capacitor, because its function is to provide an ac short circuit between the emitter and ground. If C_2 were not present, the ac signals would flow through R_e, and an appreciable reduction of voltage gain would result, as we shall see.

The incremental circuit model for the transistor amplifier is shown in Fig. 6.2. We will assume for simplicity that the voltage gain is moderate enough to justify the use of the simplified hybrid-π model which neglects r_μ and r_o. Also from here on in this chapter we will somewhat arbitrarily neglect the biasing resistor $R_b = R_{b1} \parallel R_{b2}$, on the basis that it is usually larger than either the source resistance R_s or the circuit input resistance. If this is not the case, it is a relatively simple matter to include R_b in the calculations, because it does not introduce any new poles or zeros in the expressions.

We can see, by inspection of Fig. 6.2, the general form of the voltage gain expression. There are four independent energy-storage elements in the network, so we would expect four complex natural frequencies, or poles of V_o/V_i. Thus the denominator of V_o/V_i

Fig. 6.2. Incremental circuit model for amplifier of Fig. 6.1, neglecting r_μ and r_o in the hybrid-π transistor model.

must be of fourth degree in s. Capacitor C_1 will be an open circuit at zero frequency, thereby introducing a transmission zero at zero frequency. In addition, we see from Fig. 6.2 that there will be a single zero at infinite frequency. Thus the numerator of the gain expression must be of third degree. We conclude that the general form of the gain expression is

$$\frac{V_o}{V_i} = K \left[\frac{s(s - s_1)}{(s - s_2)(s - s_3)} \right] \left[\frac{(s - s_4)}{(s - s_5)(s - s_6)} \right] \tag{6.1}$$

An exact analysis would show that the location of each finite pole and zero in Eq. 6.1 is dependent to some extent on the values of all of the capacitors in the circuit. Fortunately, however, in most designs the element values are such that approximations can be made which greatly simplify the calculations.

In a typical circuit, the several capacitors shown in the figure will have greatly different values. For example, C_μ will be of the order of 1 to 100 pf and C_π will be 10 to 1000 pf, whereas C_1 and C_2 will be 0.1 to 1000 μf. For these ranges of element values, there will be a mid-frequency range in the amplifier response where the gain will be essentially constant, a fall-off in gain at high frequencies caused primarily by C_π and C_μ, and a fall-off in gain at low frequencies caused primarily by C_1 and C_2. Thus the discussion is somewhat simplified if we break down Fig. 6.2 into three simpler circuits, one applicable in the low-frequency range, a second applicable at mid-frequencies, and a third applicable at high frequencies. The low-frequency circuit, Fig. 6.3a, we obtain by considering capacitors C_μ and C_π to be open circuits. The high-frequency circuit, Fig. 6.3b, we get by considering capacitors C_1 and C_2 to be short circuits. The mid-frequency circuit, Fig. 6.3c, contains no capacitors at all, that is we consider C_1 and C_2 to be shorted, and C_π and C_μ to be open.

The mid-frequency gain of the circuit can be calculated readily from Fig. 6.3c to be

$$\frac{V_o}{V_i} \text{ (mid-frequency)} = \frac{-\beta_0 R_L}{r_x + r_\pi + R_s} \equiv -A_0 \tag{6.2}$$

Even though we have now somewhat simplified the problem, it is clear that a certain amount of circuit analysis is still required to calculate the exact location of the natural frequencies for the low-

Fig. 6.3. Approximate circuit models for amplifier. (a) Low-frequency. (b) High-frequency. (c) Mid-frequency.

frequency circuit in Fig. 6.3a. So before proceeding further, let us calculate the low-frequency response of two simpler networks, one in which the only capacitor is a coupling capacitor, and the other containing only an emitter bypass capacitor. The appropriate low-frequency incremental circuit models are shown in Fig. 6.4.

6.1 CALCULATIONS INVOLVING THE COUPLING CAPACITOR

Let us first calculate the transmission function V_o/V_i for the network with the coupling capacitor, Fig. 6.4a. This function will

(a)

(b)

Fig. 6.4. Low-frequency circuit models for: (a) Circuit with only a coupling capacitor. (b) Circuit with only an emitter bypass capacitor.

have one zero at zero frequency and one pole, which is the natural frequency of the network. A convenient definition of a network natural frequency for this discussion is: that complex frequency s which will give rise to a zero of admittance measured across the terminals of nearly any element in the network.* Thus if we write the expression for the admittance appearing between the terminals of capacitor C_1 and set this admittance equal to zero, we obtain

$$s_a C_1 + \frac{1}{R_{1s}} = 0 \tag{6.3}$$

---

* At issue here is the problem of *separate parts* of a network. In Fig. 6.4a, for example, the generator $g_m V$ and R_L form a *separate part*, because in this simple model they are not coupled back to the input circuit. Thus the natural frequency arising from C_1 cannot be calculated by looking for a zero of admittance across R_L.

where R_{1s} is the Thevenin equivalent resistance of all of the rest of the network which appears in parallel with C_1. Solving for the natural frequency, we find

$$s_a = -\frac{1}{C_1 R_{1s}} \qquad (6.4)$$

We see from the network that the Thevenin equivalent resistance faced by C_1 is equal to

$$R_{1s} = R_s + r_x + r_\pi \qquad (6.5)$$

(The significance of the second subscript on R_{1s} will become clear in Sec. 6.3.)

To find the complete voltage transmission function, V_o/V_i, we now need to find the gain of the network at a frequency high enough so that capacitor C_1 appears as a short circuit, that is, in the midfrequency range. It is clear that Fig. 6.3c is an appropriate midfrequency model for this circuit as well, so the required midfrequency gain expression is given by Eq. 6.2. The complete voltage gain expression for the circuit of Fig. 6.4a is thus

$$\frac{V_o}{V_i} = \frac{-A_0 s}{s + 1/C_1 R_{1s}} \qquad (6.6)$$

The resulting pole-zero plot is shown in Fig. 6.5a, and the corresponding plots of magnitude and phase of V_o/V_i are shown in b. To illustrate the performance of the network in the time domain, we show in Fig. 6.5c the response of the circuit to a unit step of voltage. This response could be found by solving the differential equation for the network with a unit step applied at the input, or by applying Laplace transform methods to Eq. 6.6. However, for this simple single-pole problem, the response can be found by inspection. The capacitor will appear as a short circuit to the sudden step, so Eq. 6.2 can be used to calculate the size of the initial step in the output. The final value of the output response will be zero, and the time constant can be found from Eqs. 6.4 and 6.5.

6.2 CALCULATIONS INVOLVING THE EMITTER BYPASS CAPACITOR

Let us now make a similar calculation for the circuit of Fig. 6.4b, which contains only an emitter bypass capacitor. Following the

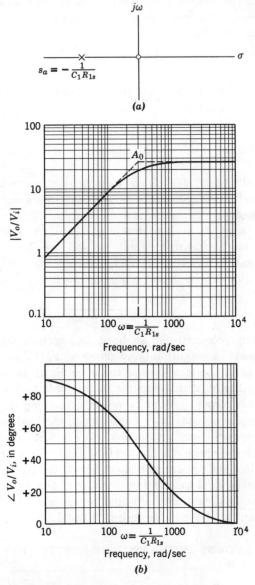

Fig. 6.5. Pole-zero pattern, frequency-response and unit-step response for circuit of Fig. 6.4(a).

(c)

Fig. 6.5 (*Continued*)

same procedure used in the previous section, we find the natural frequency of the network by finding the Thevenin equivalent resistance R_{2s} of all of the rest of the network which appears in parallel with C_2. A simple way of calculating this resistance from the circuit is to apply a voltage source V_e between emitter and ground, and calculate the resulting current I_e. The circuit for this measurement is shown in Fig. 6.6. This particular choice of driving source allows us to calculate by inspection the voltage V control-

Fig. 6.6. Circuit for calculating Thevenin equivalent resistance R_{2s} appearing in parallel with C_2.

ling the dependent source, thereby greatly simplifying the circuit calculations. Using the voltage-divider relation, we find

$$V = \frac{-r_\pi V_e}{r_x + r_\pi + R_s} \tag{6.7}$$

Therefore, the current I_e is

$$I_e = \frac{g_m r_\pi V_e}{r_x + r_\pi + R_s} + \frac{V_e}{R_e} + \frac{V_e}{r_x + r_\pi + R_s} \tag{6.8}$$

From this we find that the desired Thevenin equivalent resistance R_{2s} is

$$R_{2s} = \frac{V_e}{I_e} = R_e \left\| \left[\frac{r_x + r_\pi + R_s}{\beta_0 + 1} \right] \right. \tag{6.9}$$

where for convenience we have substituted β_0 for $g_m r_\pi$. Thus the network has a single pole at a frequency

$$s_b = -\frac{1}{C_2 R_{2s}} \tag{6.10}$$

There are several ways of showing that the network of Fig. 6.4*b* has a zero in the transmission function V_o/V_i. For example, we have just shown that the network has a pole which will cause the gain to fall off at low frequencies. But we see by inspection that the network has gain at dc, so there must be a transmission zero at some finite (nonzero) frequency.

Alternatively, we can say that a zero in the transmission function V_o/V_i will occur at a frequency where the admittance between emitter and ground goes to zero, because at that frequency it will no longer be possible to drive any signal into the base of the transistor. (Note that this is true only because we have neglected r_μ and C_μ in this model.) On this basis we can write the admittance equation

$$G_e + s_c C_2 = 0 \tag{6.11}$$

Thus the zero occurs at a frequency

$$s_c = -\frac{1}{R_e C_2} \tag{6.12}$$

(The reader can always resort to direct calculation of V_o/V_i to verify the presence and location of this zero.)

$$s_b = -\frac{1}{C_2 R_{2s}} \quad s_c = -\frac{1}{R_e C_2}$$

(a)

$$\omega = \frac{1}{C_2 R_e} \qquad \omega = \frac{1}{C_2 R_{2s}}$$

Frequency, rad/sec

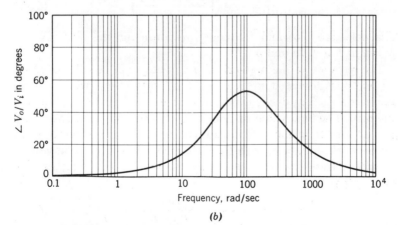

Frequency, rad/sec

(b)

Fig. 6.7. Pole-zero pattern, frequency response, and unit-step response of V_o/V_i for Fig. 6.4(b).

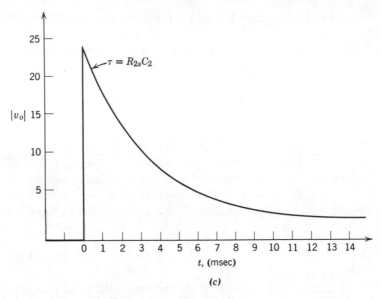

Fig. 6.7 (*Continued*)

The mid-frequency gain of this network is again given by Eq. 6.2, so the complete voltage gain expression is

$$\frac{V_o}{V_i} = -A_0 \left[\frac{s + 1/R_e C_2}{s + 1/R_{2s} C_2} \right] \qquad (6.13)$$

The pole-zero plot and frequency response for the network are shown in Fig. 6.7*a* and *b*.

The response of the network to a unit step can be calculated by the method discussed in Sec. 6.1. The initial step will have an amplitude A_0. The decay time constant can be found from Eqs. 6.9 and 6.10. The final value will not be zero, because the network has gain at zero frequency. This gain can be calculated directly from the network, Fig. 6.4*b*, with C_2 set to zero. Alternatively, it can be calculated from Eq. 6.13 by setting s equal to zero. In either case the result is

$$\left. \frac{V_o}{V_i} \right|_{dc} = - \frac{\beta_0 R_L}{r_x + r_\pi + R_e(1 + \beta_0) + R_s} \qquad (6.14)$$

The complete step response is shown in Fig. 6.7*c*.

We note in passing that Eq. 6.14 is the gain of an amplifier with an unbypassed emitter resistor ($C_2 = 0$). Comparison of Eq. 6.14 with Eq. 6.2 shows clearly the loss in gain which would result if the emitter resistor were left unbypassed.

6.3 INTERACTION BETWEEN COUPLING AND BYPASS CAPACITORS

6.3.1 *Determination of Transfer Function*

Let us return now to the problem of calculating the voltage transmission ratio V_o/V_i for the low-frequency equivalent circuit shown in Fig. 6.3a, repeated for convenience in Fig. 6.8. From the introductory discussion in Sec. 6.0, we know that the general form of V_o/V_i will be

$$\frac{V_o}{V_i} = -A_0 \frac{s(s - s_1)}{(s - s_2)(s - s_3)} \tag{6.15}$$

where s_1, s_2, and s_3 approximately correspond with s_1, s_2, and s_3 in Eq. 6.1. Because we have neglected both C_μ and r_μ, the zero at s_1 is caused only by capacitor C_1. The two poles, on the other hand, will each depend on both C_1 and C_2.

To derive the voltage gain expression in terms of the circuit parameters, we make use of the relation

$$\text{Voltage gain} = (\text{Current gain}) \left(\frac{\text{Load impedance}}{\text{Input impedance}}\right) \tag{6.16}$$

The current gain of the network in Fig. 6.8 is $-g_m r_\pi$, and the load impedance is R_L. To find the input impedance, we first find the

Fig. 6.8. Low-frequency circuit model for amplifier in Fig. 6.1.

input impedance of the transistor alone, then add on the impedance $(R_s + 1/sC_1)$. We do the problem in this manner to place emphasis on the transistor input impedance, a quantity which will be important in many circuit calculations.

To find the transistor input impedance, we perform a separate experiment in which we apply a current source I_1 to the input of the transistor and measure the resulting input voltage V_1 as shown in Fig. 6.9. We choose a current source drive here because in this way the voltage V controlling the dependent source is immediately known to be $I_1 r_\pi$. Thus the current through the emitter impedance Z_e (R_e in parallel with C_2) is $(1 + g_m r_\pi)I_1$ and the input voltage V_1 is

$$V_1 = I_1[r_x + r_\pi + (\beta_0 + 1)Z_e] \tag{6.17}$$

Therefore, the transistor input impedance is

$$Z_{\text{in}} = \frac{V_1}{I_1} = r_x + r_\pi + (\beta_0 + 1)\,\frac{R_e}{1 + R_e C_2 s} \tag{6.18}$$

It is interesting to note in passing the impedance-transforming properties of a transistor circuit which are exhibited in Eqs. 6.9 and 6.18. In Eq. 6.18 we see that the input impedance of the amplifier is equal to $(r_x + r_\pi)$ plus the external *emitter* impedance multiplied by the factor $(\beta_0 + 1)$. In Eq. 6.9, we find that the impedance seen between emitter and ground, other than the resistor R_e, is equal to $(r_x + r_\pi)$ plus the external impedance between *base* and ground, all divided by the same factor $(\beta_0 + 1)$. This property of transforming impedance by a factor of $(\beta_0 + 1)$ is an important characteristic of a transistor circuit. Calculations of this type occur

Fig. 6.9. Transistor input impedance calculation.

so frequently in circuit analysis that the reader is urged to remember the transformation property in detail.

Returning now to Fig. 6.8, the input impedance of the entire circuit is

$$Z = \frac{V_i}{I_i} = r_x + r_\pi + (\beta_0 + 1)\frac{R_e}{1 + R_e C_2 s} + R_s + \frac{1}{sC_1} \quad (6.19)$$

Substituting this value into Eq. 6.16, we find that the voltage gain of the circuit in Fig. 6.8 is

$$\frac{V_o}{V_i} = \frac{-g_m r_\pi R_L}{r_x + r_\pi + (\beta_0 + 1)\dfrac{R_e}{1 + R_e C_2 s} + R_s + \dfrac{1}{sC_1}}$$

$$= \frac{-A_0 s(s + 1/R_e C_2)}{s^2 + \dfrac{s}{C_1(r_x + r_\pi + R_s)} + \dfrac{s}{C_2\left(R_e\|\dfrac{r_x + r_\pi + R_s}{\beta_0 + 1}\right)} + \dfrac{1}{C_1 C_2 R_e(r_x + r_\pi + R_s)}}$$

$$(6.20)$$

6.3.2 *Network Natural Frequencies*

It is evident from Eq. 6.20 that the poles in the equation (the natural frequencies of the network) are not simple functions of one capacitor. To determine the values of the capacitors C_1 and C_2 to achieve a certain value of low-frequency response, we must find the roots of the denominator of Eq. 6.20. To simplify the equation somewhat, we note that the resistive parts of the s-term coefficients are in fact R_{1s} and R_{2s} from our previous derivations in Secs. 6.1 and 6.2. Also, the constant term contains R_{1s}. Thus Eq. 6.20 can be written as

$$\frac{V_o}{V_i} = \frac{-A_0 s(s + 1/R_e C_2)}{s^2 + \dfrac{s}{C_1 R_{1s}} + \dfrac{s}{C_2 R_{2s}} + \dfrac{1}{C_1 C_2 R_{1s} R_e}} \quad (6.21)$$

where, from before,

$$R_{1s} = R_s + r_x + r_\pi \quad (6.22)$$

$$R_{2s} = R_e \| \left[\frac{r_x + r_\pi + R_s}{\beta_0 + 1}\right] \quad (6.23)$$

If desired, R_{1s} can be identified as the resistance facing C_1 when C_2 is shorted. Similarly, R_{2s} is the resistance facing C_2 with C_1 shorted.

We wish now to solve for the poles of V_o/V_i by finding the roots of the denominator polynomial. This can be accomplished in several ways. For example, we could apply the standard equation for finding the roots of a quadratic, and then simplify the solution by using judicious approximations. Fortunately, however, in many active networks, the natural frequencies are widely split apart by the interaction of the various capacitors in the network. We can often take advantage of this fact in solving polynomials. To illustrate this, consider the polynomial

$$P(s) = k(s - s_a)(s - s_b) \equiv a_0 + a_1 s + a_2 s^2 \qquad (6.24)$$

We find by multiplying out the factors and comparing coefficients:

$$a_0 = k s_a s_b \qquad (6.25)$$

$$a_1 = -k(s_a + s_b) \qquad (6.26)$$

$$a_2 = k \qquad (6.27)$$

If the poles are widely separated, so that $s_a \ll s_b$, we see that

$$s_a \cong \frac{-a_0}{a_1} \qquad (6.28)$$

$$s_b \cong \frac{-a_1}{a_2} \qquad (6.29)$$

This method of approximate solution can be extended to higher-order polynomials: the approximate roots are always the ratios of adjacent coefficients of s.

Following the above procedure, we assume the poles of Eq. 6.21 are widely separated (by a factor of ten, say), and return later to establish the necessary conditions for this assumption. From Eqs. 6.28 and 6.29, the roots are then approximately

$$s_2 \cong \frac{-a_1}{a_2} = -\frac{1}{C_1 R_{1s}} - \frac{1}{C_2 R_{2s}} \qquad (6.30)$$

$$s_3 \cong -\frac{a_0}{a_1} = -\frac{1}{C_1 R_{1s}(R_e/R_{2s}) + C_2 R_e} \qquad (6.31)$$

The condition of $s_2 > 10 s_3$ can be written as

$$\left[\frac{C_1 R_{1s}}{C_2 R_{2s}} + 2 + \frac{C_2 R_{2s}}{C_1 R_{1s}} \right] \frac{R_e}{R_{2s}} > 10 \qquad (6.32)$$

The term in brackets, of the form $x + 2 + 1/x$, has a minimum value of 4, so assuming this minimum value (the most pessimistic value for this calculation), Eq. 6.32 reduces to

$$\frac{R_e}{R_{2s}} > 2.5 \qquad (6.33)$$

Substituting for R_{2s} from Eq. 6.23, we obtain

$$\frac{R_s + r_x + r_\pi + (\beta_0 + 1)R_e}{R_s + r_x + r_\pi} > 2.5 \qquad (6.34)$$

a condition which will usually be satisfied because of other conditions on the resistor values, unless of course R_s is large.

Subject to the condition of Eq. 6.33, we now know the location of the natural frequencies of the network. For $(R_e/R_{2s}) > 2.5$, Eq. 6.30 gives the correct value for the highest pole within 10%, as can be verified readily from Eqs. 6.26 and 6.27. Because this pole is the most important in determining the half-power frequency,* it is usually called the *dominant* natural frequency. Equation 6.31 gives the correct value for the low pole, the nondominant pole, again within 10% (see Eqs. 6.25 and 6.26).

6.3.3 *Determination of Capacitor Values for $R_e/R_{2s} > 2.5$*

We are now in a position to select coupling and bypass capacitor values to yield a given low-frequency response. If $(R_e/R_{2s}) > 2.5$, we know that the poles of V_0/V_i are separated by at least a factor of ten. Thus pole s_2 determines the low-frequency cutoff, and we therefore choose C_1 and C_2 in Eq. 6.30 to make $|s_2| \cong \omega_l$, where ω_l is the desired low-frequency 0.707 point* expressed in radians.

We are still free to choose arbitrarily either C_1 or C_2. To give some perspective on how best to choose these values, suppose we first choose C_1 and C_2 such that

$$C_1 R_{1s} = C_2 R_{2s} \qquad (6.35)$$

that is, the two short-circuit time constants are equal. Under these conditions, Eqs. 6.30 and 6.31 reduce to

---

* The frequency where the magnitude of a gain expression is down to 0.707 of its mid-frequency value is called the *0.707 frequency*, or the *half-power frequency*, or the *0.707 point*, or sometimes the *3 db frequency*.

$$s_2 \cong -\frac{2}{C_1 R_{1s}} = -\frac{2}{C_2 R_{2s}} \tag{6.36}$$

for the dominant pole, and

$$s_3 \cong -\frac{1}{2 C_2 R_e} \tag{6.37}$$

for the nondominant pole.

In contrast, we might choose to make one short-circuit time constant much larger than the other, by setting $C_2 = \infty$, for example. We see from Eq. 6.30 that under these conditions capacitor C_1 is reduced only by a factor of two from the value given by Eq. 6.36 for the "equal-time-constant" design.

6.3.4 *Example*

The trade-off between the two capacitor sizes can best be illustrated by a specific example. Suppose we wish to determine values of C_1 and C_2 so that the response of the amplifier in Fig. 6.1 is down to $0.707 A_0$ at 100 cps. We assume from gain and bias calculations we have the following values for g_m and the various resistors in the circuits:

$$R_L = 910 \text{ ohms} \qquad r_x = 100 \text{ ohms}$$
$$R_s = 1 \text{ k} \qquad r_\pi = 400 \text{ ohms}$$
$$R_e = 300 \text{ ohms} \qquad g_m = 0.1 \text{ mho}$$

From Eqs. 6.22, 6.23, and 6.33 we find

$$R_{1s} = 1.5 \text{ k} \qquad \frac{R_e}{R_{2s}} = \frac{300}{32.5} = 9.2$$
$$R_{2s} = 32.5 \text{ ohms}$$

Because $R_e/R_{2s} > 2.5$, we can determine the two capacitor values for the equal-time-constant design from Eq. 6.36, using

$$|s_2| \cong \omega_l = (2\pi)(100) = 628$$

The results are

$$C_1 = \frac{2}{\omega_l R_{1s}} = \frac{2}{(2\pi)(100)(1.5 \text{ k})} = 2.12 \ \mu\text{f}$$

$$C_2 = \frac{2}{\omega_l R_{2s}} = \frac{2}{(2\pi)(100)(32.5)} = 98 \ \mu\text{f}$$

If we use Eq. 6.30 rather than Eq. 6.36 to find C_1 and C_2, we obtain the following table of possible capacitor values:

Design	1	2	3	4	5
C_1	∞	4.2 μf	2.1 μf	1.5 μf	1.05 μf
C_2	49 μf	65 μf	98 μf	167 μf	∞

The final choice of values would depend on a number of factors, including the relative cost of capacitors with widely different voltage ratings, but certainly the equal time-constant design 3 is not an unreasonable choice.

On the basis of the equal time-constant design, the nondominant pole is, from Eq. 6.37,

$$s_3 = -\frac{1}{(2)(98 \times 10^{-6})(300)} \cong -17 \ sec^{-1}$$

The transmission zero due to the emitter bypass capacitor is at a frequency

$$s_1 = -\frac{1}{C_2 R_e} = -\frac{1}{(98 \times 10^{-6})(3 \times 10^2)} = -34 \ sec^{-1}$$

The pole-zero configuration, frequency response, and step response are shown in Fig. 6.10. The resulting frequency response is a little bit better than required, but not enough to warrant a redesign. Figures 6.5 and 6.7 were plotted for the same numerical values used in this example, to permit ready intercomparison of the three results, that is, coupling capacitor only, emitter bypass capacitor only, and both capacitors in the circuit.

The results of this section are much more general than the derivation might lead the reader to believe. What we have seen is that in an RC circuit with more than one capacitor, the natural frequencies of the network are often split widely apart by the interaction between the two capacitors, with the result that one natural frequency is strongly dominant. We have also seen that the frequency corresponding to $0.707 A_0$ can be approximated as the sum of the reciprocal short-circuit time constants. We will show in MTC that both of these statements apply to a wide class of RC networks.

Fig. 6.10. Results of design example. (*a*) Pole-zero pattern. (*b*) Magnitude and phase versus ω. (*c*) Unit-step response.

Fig. 6.10. (*Continued*)

6.3.5 *Determination of Capacitor Values for Source Resistance Large*

If the source resistance R_s becomes large, we can no longer neglect R_b in Fig. 6.2. However, making R_s large effectively "de-couples" the two capacitors, so that each may be treated separately. Thus we find by inspection of Fig. 6.2 (neglecting C_π and C_μ) that

$$s_3 \cong -\frac{1}{C_1 R_s} \tag{6.38}$$

$$s_2 \cong -\frac{1}{C_2 R_{2s}} \tag{6.39}$$

where

$$R_{2s} = R_e \,||\, \left[\frac{r_x + r_\pi + R_b}{\beta_0 + 1}\right] \tag{6.40}$$

Surprisingly enough, the same equation for determining C_1 and C_2, namely,

$$C_1 R_s = C_2 R_{2s} = 2/\omega_l \tag{6.41}$$

can still be used. In this case, the two natural frequencies will be identical, and the transmission function will have a second-order pole.

6.4 CALCULATION OF HIGH-FREQUENCY RESPONSE

We now turn to the problem of calculating the high-frequency response of the circuit in Fig. 6.1. The appropriate circuit model is shown in Fig. 6.11, repeated for convenience from Fig. 6.3b. We recall from the discussion in Sec. 6.0 that the complete voltage-gain expression for Fig. 6.11 is of the form

$$\frac{V_o}{V_i} = \frac{K(s - s_4)}{(s - s_5)(s - s_6)} \tag{6.42}$$

where s_4, $s_{,5}$ and s_6 correspond approximately with s_4, s_5 and s_6 in Eq. 6.1. We will first calculate V_o/V_i, using the approximate method outlined in Sec. 3.1.4, which will give us only the dominant pole of the high-frequency response. We will then make a more exact calculation which includes both poles and the zero. Finally, we will compare the results of both calculations to give some indication of the accuracy of the approximate calculation.

6.4.1 *Approximate High-Frequency Response Calculation*

Following the method of Sec. 3.1.4, we find the equivalent shunt capacitance from node V to ground, using Eq. 3.16:

$$C_t = C_\pi + C_\mu(1 + g_m R_L) \tag{6.43}$$

The resistance facing C_t is, by inspection of Fig. 6.11,

$$R_t = r_\pi \,||\, (r_x + R_s) \tag{6.44}$$

Fig. 6.11. High-frequency circuit model for circuit of Fig. 6.1.

so the approximate voltage-gain expression is

$$\frac{V_0}{V_i} = \frac{-A_0}{1 + sC_tR_t}$$

$$= \frac{-A_0}{1 + s[r_\pi \parallel (r_x + R_s)][C_\pi + C_\mu(1 + g_mR_L)]} \quad (6.45)$$

A plot of the magnitude and phase of Eq. 6.45 is shown in Fig. 6.12, using the numbers from Sec. 6.3.4, together with $C_\pi = 100$ pf, $C_\mu = 5$ pf. The frequencies ω_β and ω_T are marked on the graphs as reference points. For future reference we define the frequency when $|V_o/V_i|$ is down to $0.707A_0$ as ω_h, where

$$\omega_h = \frac{1}{R_tC_t} = \frac{1}{R_t[C_\pi + C_\mu(1 + g_mR_L)]} \quad (6.46)$$

6.4.2 *A More Accurate Calculation of High-Frequency Response*

To find a more accurate expression for V_o/V_i in Fig. 6.11, we write the node equations for the circuit in terms of nodes V and V_o. The algebra is simplified somewhat by first forming the Norton equivalent of V_i, R_s, r_x, and r_π, as shown in Fig. 6.13. The node equations now are

$$[G_t + s(C_\pi + C_\mu)]V - \qquad sC_\mu V_o = V_i/(R_s + r_x) \quad (6.47)$$

$$(g_m - sC_\mu)V + (G_L + sC_\mu)V_o = 0 \quad (6.48)$$

Solving for V_o/V_i, we obtain

$$\frac{V_o}{V_i} = \frac{-(g_m - sC_\mu)/(R_s + r_x)}{G_tG_L + s[G_tC_\mu + G_L(C_\pi + C_\mu) + g_mC_\mu] + s^2C_\mu C_\pi} \quad (6.49)$$

This equation has the basic form of Eq. 6.42. That is, it has a transmission zero resulting from signal fed forward by C_μ, cancelling that fed forward by the g_m generator, and two poles arising from the two independent energy storage elements. We shall show that Eq. 6.49 has one dominant pole, in the sense that the second pole and the zero occur at a much larger value of $|s|$, thus making the first pole the dominant factor in determining circuit performance over the frequency range of interest.

To solve for the poles of V_o/V_i, we set the denominator of Eq. 6.49 equal to zero, then multiply by R_tR_L:

$$1 + s[R_LC_\mu(1 + g_mR_t) + R_t(C_\pi + C_\mu)] + s^2R_tR_LC_\mu C_\pi = 0 \quad (6.50)$$

Fig. 6.12. Magnitude and phase of approximate V_o/V_i from Eq. 6.45, and more exact V_o/V_i from Eq. 6.49.

Fig. 6.13. High-frequency circuit model with Norton equivalent input circuit.

For most transistor circuits, $g_m R_t$ will be much greater than one, because from Eq. 6.44, R_t will be within a factor of two or three of r_π for source resistances of the order of r_π, and $g_m r_\pi \equiv \beta_0 \gg 1$. On this basis we neglect the 1 in the $s R_L C_\mu (1 + g_m R_t)$ term. Equation 6.50 then reduces to

$$1 + s R_t [C_\pi + C_\mu (1 + g_m R_L)] + s^2 R_t R_L C_\pi C_\mu = 0 \quad (6.51)$$

The coefficient of the s term in Eq. 6.51 is $1/\omega_h$ (see Eq. 6.46). Thus Eq. 6.51 simplifies to

$$1 + s/\omega_h + s^2 R_t R_L C_\pi C_\mu = 0 \quad (6.52)$$

To find the roots of Eq. 6.52, we will follow the procedure outlined in Sec. 6.3.2. We assume that the roots are widely separated and thus can be found from Eqs. 6.28 and 6.29.

$$s_5 \cong -\frac{a_0}{a_1} = -\omega_h = -\frac{1}{R_t [C_\pi + C_\mu (1 + g_m R_L)]} \quad (6.53)$$

$$s_6 \cong \frac{-a_1}{a_2} = \frac{-1}{\omega_h R_t R_L C_\pi C_\mu} \quad (6.54)$$

Note that the dominant natural frequency s_5 is the same as that calculated by the approximate method of Sec. 6.4.1.

The approximate location of s_6 can be found from Eq. 6.54 by substituting for ω_h from Eq. 6.46:

$$s_6 = -\frac{[C_\pi + C_\mu (1 + g_m R_L)]}{R_L C_\pi C_\mu} = -\frac{g_m + (C_\pi + C_\mu)/R_L C_\mu}{C_\pi} \quad (6.55)$$

Because $\omega_T = g_m/(C_\pi + C_\mu)$, we conclude that the non-dominant natural frequency s_6 is always larger in magnitude than ω_T.

By inspection of Eq. 6.49, we find that the value of the zero s_4 is

$$s_4 = \frac{g_m}{C_\mu} \tag{6.56}$$

a right-half-plane zero which is always much larger in magnitude than ω_T.

To check for consistency with the assumption of widely separated roots, we must compare s_6 with s_5. We showed above that the minimum magnitude for s_6 was $\omega_T = g_m/(C_\pi + C_\mu)$, occurring for R_L large. Under these same conditions, it is clear from Eq. 6.53 that s_5 will be small, in fact much smaller than ω_T. On the other hand, for a broad-band design we might want s_5 as large as possible. We see from Eq. 6.53 that the maximum magnitude of s_5 is

$$|s_5|_{(\text{max})} = \frac{g_x + g_\pi}{C_\pi + C_\mu} \tag{6.57}$$

which occurs for small R_L and small R_s. Under these same circumstances, s_6 will be very large, in fact, much above ω_T (see Eq. 6.55). A more detailed examination will show that because of the interrelated nature of the gain and bandwidth expressions, for most designs the nondominant pole s_6 will be larger in magnitude than the dominant pole s_5 by a factor of ten or more. (These matters are discussed in MTC). Thus our use of Eqs. 6.28 and 6.29 to find the roots is justified.

We conclude that the network of Fig. 6.11 has *one dominant natural frequency $s = -\omega_h$*, the same value we obtained from the simplified analysis in Sec. 6.4.1, and one nondominant natural frequency at a much higher frequency, in fact, above ω_T. The voltage transmission function for the network has one zero, which is much above ω_T. Thus the simplified analysis given in Secs. 3.1 and 6.4.1, which implicitly neglects the nondominant natural frequency and the transmission zero, should yield acceptable results up to approximately $\omega_T/5$. At this frequency, the nondominant pole will contribute insignificantly to the magnitude of the response, and add possibly 10° to the phase. At $\omega_T/5$ the zero will not contribute significantly to either the amplitude or phase. These facts are borne out by Fig. 6.12, where we have plotted the magnitude and phase of V_o/V_i, both from Eq. 6.45 and 6.49.

6.4.3 Effect of R_s and R_L on High-Frequency Response

The problem of designing a transistor amplifier to have a pre-scribed high-frequency response is not as clear-cut as in the case of the low-frequency design, because here many of the parameters in the equations are not under our direct control. It is clear, however, that half the battle is won if we first select a transistor with values of f_T and C_{ob} which are compatible with the desired high-frequency response. Having once picked the transistor, we see from Eq. 6.46 that the high-frequency response can be controlled to some extent by changing the source and load resistors R_s and R_L. Lowering R_s will improve the frequency response to a point, but when R_s gets down to a few hundred ohms, we see from Eqs. 6.46 and 6.44 that the bandwidth will become quite dependent on the value of r_x. Under these conditions, bandwidth calculations become quite un-reliable. As we pointed out in Chapter 3, using a single-lumped resistance r_x to represent the effects of transverse voltage drops in the base region is the crudest approximation made in the develop-ment of hybrid-π model. Thus reliable bandwidth calculations for R_s small can be obtained only by making a more accurate determi-nation of the input impedance (see CLT or MTC).

Lowering R_L will also improve the bandwidth to some extent by lowering the gain, and hence reducing the effect of C_μ. The reduc-tion in gain is unfortunately not accompanied by a proportional increase in bandwidth, except in extreme designs where the C_μ term is dominant in C_t. This is shown in Fig. 6.14, where the fre-quency response of an amplifier has been plotted for four values of R_L. If the gain is initially large, a reduction in R_L causes a reduc-tion in gain, but the bandwidth increases by nearly the same factor because of the reduction of the C_μ term in C_t. Thus the high-frequency asymptotes for $R_L = 10$ k and $R_L = 1$ k are fairly close together. However, if R_L is further reduced, the gain continues to go down, but little increase in bandwidth occurs. If we draw a curve through the four break frequencies in this figure, thus form-ing *the locus of break frequencies for varying R_L*, it is clear that a point is reached where further reduction in R_L yields no further increase in bandwidth. If the resulting bandwidth is still insuf-ficient, we must either select a new transistor with better proper-ties, or resort to somewhat more advanced circuit techniques which are discussed in MTC.

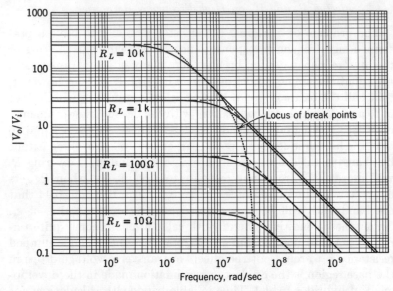

Fig. 6.14. High-frequency response for various values of load resistance R_L.

PROBLEMS

P6.1   The circuit of an elementary single-stage common-emitter amplifier is shown in Fig. 6.15. At the operating point, the parameters of the hybrid-π model are:

$$r_x = 100 \ \Omega \qquad C_\pi = 200 \ \text{pf}$$

$$r_\pi = 1 \ \text{k} \qquad C_\mu = 2 \ \text{pf}$$

$$g_m = 0.1 \ \text{mho}$$

$$r_o \to \infty \qquad r_\mu \to \infty$$

    (a) Draw the complete small-signal model of the amplifier.
    (b) What is the midband voltage gain $A_0 = V_o/V_i$?
    (c) What is the *upper* break frequency? That is, at what high frequency is the magnitude of the voltage gain reduced to $A_0/\sqrt{2}$?
    (d) What is the *lower* break frequency? That is, at what low frequency is the magnitude of the voltage gain reduced to $A_0/\sqrt{2}$?

P6.2   Assuming that the frequency is high enough so that the signal voltage across each capacitor in Fig. 6.16 is negligible, determine the small-signal voltage gain V_o/V_i if $R_L = 500$ ohms. Assume $T = 25°C$ and use $h_{ie} = 1000$ ohms and $h_{fe} = 60$.

Fig. 6.15.

P6.3 As the frequency drops, the small-signal gain of the circuit in Fig. 6.16 decreases because voltage drops across the two capacitors become important. If the amplifier is driven from a source resistance of 5000 ohms, and $C_2 = 50$ μf:

(a) Determine the frequency at which the gain is down by $1/\sqrt{2}$ as a consequence of the emitter bypass capacitor, assuming that the voltage drop across C_1 is negligible.

Fig. 6.16.

(*b*) Determine a value for C_1 so that the voltage drop across it is small enough at the frequency determined in (*a*) to justify neglecting it in calculating that break frequency.

P6.4   Find appropriate values for C_1 and C_2 in Fig. 6.16 to give a low-frequency 0.707 point of 35 cps.

P6.5   Design a single-stage transistor amplifier with the following specifications, using the configuration shown in Fig. 6.17.

Specifications

1. Available $V_{CC} = 12$ volts.
2. R_L must equal 4.7 k.
3. Operating temperature +25°C to +75°C.
4. Amplifier must remain linear over this temperature range with an output voltage (across R_L) of ±2.5 volts.
5. When driven by a current source, the small-signal transfer impedance ($V_{\text{out}}/I_{\text{in}}$) must be at least 150 k.
6. With a current-source drive, the low-frequency half-power point must be 100 cps.
7. DC power consumption must be as low as consistent with above requirements.
8. $I_{CO} = 1$ μa at 25°C (germanium).
9. $\beta_F = 60$, independent of operating point and temperature.

P6.6   Making reasonable approximations, complete the design of the transistor amplifier of Fig. 6.18. That is, determine the values of R_L, C_c, and V_B which cause the amplifier to meet the following specifications: (*a*) Undistorted output swing ±3 volts.

Fig. 6.17.

Fig. 6.18.

(b) Frequency response: the magnitude of the small-signal gain must not be less than 0.707 of its mid-frequency value at 130 cycles and at 50 kc.

The germanium transistor has the following parameters:

$$\beta_0 = 100 \qquad r_x \cong 0$$

$$C_\mu = 50 \text{ pf} \qquad \omega_T = 8 \times 10^7 \text{ radians/second}$$

For bias stabilization, design for a 10-volt drop across the emitter resistor, that is, $V_R = 10$ volts

Common-Base and Common-Collector Configurations: Models and Properties

7.1 COMMON-BASE CONFIGURATION

When a transistor is connected so that its *base* lead is common to both the input and output circuits, it is said to be in the *common-base* connection. Although historically this was the first transistor circuit configuration used, it is now not nearly as widely used as the common-emitter connection, for reasons which will become apparent when the properties of the circuit are discussed in detail.

The hybrid-π model is still an accurate representation of the incremental behavior of a transistor connected in the common-base configuration. However, this model is inconvenient for common-base applications because the $g_m V$ generator appears between the input and output terminals. For the important special case in which *base-width modulation effects are negligible*, we can transform the hybrid-π to an equivalent form which is more convenient for common-base calculations. The four steps in this transformation are shown in Fig. 7.1. Figure 7.1a shows the familiar hybrid-π, with r_o and r_μ, which arise from base-width modulation effects, omitted. In Fig. 7.1b we have replaced the $g_m V$ generator with two series-connected generators. This change has no effect on the currents or voltages. The left-hand $g_m V$ generator produces a current which is proportional to the voltage across it. Consequently, it can be re-

(a) Hybrid-π model arranged in common-base form

(b) Model with $g_m V$ generator replaced by two series-connected generators

(c) Model with one $g_m V$ generator replaced by a conductance

(d) Common-base T model.

Fig. 7.1. Development of the common-base T model from the hybrid-π model *without* base-width modulation effects.

213

placed by a conductance which can then be combined with r_π, as shown in Fig. 7.1c. The current produced by the right-hand $g_m V$ generator is obviously proportional to the current I in the equivalent conductance at the emitter. This proportionality is emphasized in Fig. 7.1d, where we have introduced the parameters

$$r_e = \frac{1}{g_m + 1/r_\pi} \cong \frac{1}{g_m} = \frac{kT}{q|I_C|} \qquad (7.1a)$$

$$\alpha_0 = \frac{g_m}{g_m + 1/r_\pi} \cong 1 \qquad (7.1b)$$

The resulting model, shown in Fig. 7.1d, is usually referred to as the *common-base T Model*.

7.1.1 *Interpretation of the T-Model*

Origin and interpretations of each of the elements in this model can be understood easily in terms of the physical mechanisms which occur in a transistor biased in the normal mode; that is, with a forward-biased emitter junction and a reverse-biased collector junction. The resistance r_e, usually referred to as the *emitter resistance*, describes the incremental relationship between the emitter-base junction voltage and the emitter current. The *base resistance* r_x represents the effects of transverse voltage drops in the base region caused by base current. The coefficient α_0, usually called the *low frequency common-base short-circuit current gain*, accounts for the fact that the incremental collector current is nearly as large as the incremental emitter current because of minority-carrier transport across the base. That is, the collector current results from the injection of minority carriers from the emitter into the base and their transport across the base region. Nearly all of the emitter current is associated with minority carrier injection into the base, and nearly all of the carriers injected into the base reach the collector junctions without annihilation by recombination along the way. Therefore, the coefficient α_0 is nearly unity. Most transistors have α_0 in the range from 0.9 to 0.995. Finally, the capacitance C_μ is the space-charge capacitance of the reverse-biased collector junction.

The T-model does *not* account for the effects of base-width changes caused by signal variations in the collector-base voltage.

Furthermore, it is *not* possible to modify the model to include base-width modulation effects in any simple way except for the relatively uninteresting low-frequency case ($\omega \ll \omega_\beta$). Consequently, the common-base T model is relatively inaccurate if the voltage gain is large enough to cause significant changes in the base width. For most transistors this limitation is reached for a voltage gain V_{cb}/V_{eb} in the neighborhood of 10^3.

7.1.2 *Common-Base Current Gain*

The incremental current gain I_c/I_e of the T model is equal to $-\alpha_0$ only at low frequencies. As the frequency increases, current in C_π causes the current I in r_e to be less than the terminal current I_e, and (I_c/I_e) falls in magnitude below $-\alpha_0$. In fact, analysis of the model given in Fig. 7.1d shows that the constant a in the dependent source aI_e is equal to

$$ a = \frac{\alpha_0}{1 + j(\omega/\omega_\alpha)} \tag{7.2} $$

where the break frequency ω_α is:

$$ \omega_\alpha = \frac{1}{r_e C_\pi} \tag{7.3} $$

Since $r_e \cong 1/g_m$, the frequency ω_α is approximately equal to the frequency ω_T (see Eq. 3.37):

$$ \omega_T = \frac{g_m}{C_\pi + C_\mu} \tag{7.4} $$

at which the magnitude of the common-emitter short-circuit current gain of the hybrid-π model has decreased to unity.

These results show clearly that the magnitude of a is not much less than α_0, even for frequencies approaching ω_T, at which neither model is accurate or useful. Nevertheless, it is necessary to include the frequency dependence of a in the T model because the base current, and thus the drop across r_x, is determined not by a but by $(1 - a)$. Although the magnitude of a may not change much as the frequencies increases, the fact that α_0 is almost unity and its phase does shift with frequency means that the corresponding fractional change in $|1 - a|$ may be enormous.

7.1.3 *An Alternate Form of the Common-Base Model*

The common-base T model of Fig. 7.1 can be modified to yield a model which is more convenient for circuit calculations in certain common-base applications. We can obtain this model by noting that the base current contains a component (the current in C_π) which is in quadrature with the emitter current. The corresponding component of the voltage drop across r_x is in quadrature with I_e and, consequently, can be represented by an inductor, as shown in Fig. 7.2. This is an approximate model because it does not correctly account for the voltage drop in r_x caused by current in C_μ. That is, C_μ appears between the collector and base terminals instead of between the collector and the inaccessible "internal" base terminal as in Fig. 7.1. Therefore, the model of Fig. 7.2 does not account for feedback through C_μ, although it does represent the loading of C_μ on the output (collector) terminal.

7.1.4 *Comparisons with the Common-Emitter Connection*

On the basis of either of the common-base models we can see that, for very low frequencies, the short-circuit input resistance of the common base connection is

$$h_{ib} = r_e + r_x(1 - \alpha_0) \tag{7.5}$$

The corresponding input resistance of the common-emitter connection is

$$h_{ie} = r_x + r_\pi = r_x + \beta_0/g_m \tag{7.6}$$

Fig. 7.2. Approximate common-base model, which neglects feedback effects caused by C_μ.

However, $1/g_m \cong r_e$. Therefore,

$$h_{ie} = r_x + \beta_0 r_e \cong \beta_0 h_{ib} \tag{7.7}$$

That is, the input resistance of the common-base configuration is approximately $1/\beta_0$ times the input resistance of the same transistor operated in the common-emitter configuration at the same quiescent operating point. Also, as evidenced by Eq. 7.2, the current gain of the common-base connection is always less than unity. Because the T model does not include base-width modulation effects, it is not possible to use it to make meaningful comparisons of reverse gain or output admittance.

The most significant drawback of the common-base circuit is that the voltage gain and the power gain of a series of cascaded common-base stages *cannot be greater than unity* unless transformers are used as coupling elements. The tremendous mismatch between the output impedance of one stage and the input impedance of the following stage is responsible for this limitation. However, common-base circuits are useful in certain applications which require either a large output voltage swing or a high output impedance.

7.2 COMMON-COLLECTOR CONFIGURATION

7.2.1 *Circuit Models*

In the common-collector connection, Fig. 7.3a, the input signal is applied at the base terminal of the transistor and the output signal is taken from the emitter terminal, the collector terminal being common to both input and output circuits. The hybrid-π model, appropriately redrawn in Fig. 7.3b, again provides a useful starting point for the discussion of models appropriate for this connection. Note that C_μ and r_μ now appear as shunt elements to ground at the input.

To start the discussion, let us calculate the properties of the simpler circuit shown in Fig. 7.4, then we can add in the effects of r_x, r_o, r_μ, and C_μ as needed. The voltage gain, current gain, input impedance, and output impedance of the amplifier can be readily calculated by writing the Kirchhoff voltage law equations and solving. However, these properties can also be found with greater ease and insight by following the methods introduced in Chapter 6.

(a)

(b)

Fig. 7.3. Common-collector circuit and model.

Fig. 7.4. Circuit model for calculating properties of common-collector connection.

Following the procedure of Sec. 6.3, we first calculate the current gain. By inspection:

$$I_2 = g_m V + I_1 = (g_m z_\pi + 1)I_1 \qquad (7.8)$$

where

$$z_\pi = \frac{1}{g_\pi + sC_\pi} \qquad (7.9)$$

We see from Eq. 3.33 that $g_m z_\pi$ is very nearly equal to β, the common-emitter short-circuit current gain, because C_π is usually much larger than C_μ. Thus the common-collector current gain is

$$A_i = \frac{I_2}{I_1} \cong \beta + 1 \qquad (7.10)$$

We can find the input impedance of the simplified circuit by noting the input voltage V_i resulting from the flow of input current I_1. This voltage will be

$$V_i = I_1 z_\pi + I_2 R_L$$
$$\cong I_1[z_\pi + R_L(\beta + 1)] \qquad (7.11)$$

Thus the input impedance is

$$Z_{\text{in}} = \frac{V_i}{I_1} \cong z_\pi + (\beta + 1)R_L \qquad (7.12)$$

It is clear from this equation that, at least at frequencies below f_β, the input impedance of the circuit will be high.

Knowing the current gain, input impedance and load impedance (R_L), we can calculate the voltage gain A_v

$$A_v \equiv \frac{V_2}{V_i} = A_i \frac{Z_L}{Z_{\text{in}}} \cong \frac{(\beta + 1)R_L}{z_\pi + (\beta + 1)R_L} \qquad (7.13)$$

We see from this equation that the voltage gain is usually a little less than one. We might have anticipated this result had we thought in terms of the transistor physics, for the input and output terminals of the circuit are connected together by the forward-biased emitter diode.

Using the method outlined in Chapter 6 (Fig. 6.6), we can readily calculate that the output impedance of the circuit (the equivalent impedance of the Thevenin source driving R_L) will be

$$Z_{\text{out}} \cong \frac{R_s + z_\pi}{\beta + 1} \qquad (7.14)$$

On the basis of the preceding calculations, we can now develop two simplified models for the common-collector circuit. Because the circuit has a high input impedance (Eq. 7.12), r_x can almost always be neglected. Also, r_o will usually be much larger than either R_L or the Thevenin output impedance of the circuit, Eq. 7.14, and thus can be neglected. The effects of r_μ and C_μ are important, in that they are the elements which limit the input impedance when R_L is large. We conclude that the model shown in Fig. 7.5a will adequately describe the behavior of the common-collector circuit. The voltage gain equation developed above (Eq. 7.13) applies equally well to the circuit of Fig. 7.5a. The output impedance expression, Eq. 7.14, will be correct within a few per cent for reasonable values of source resistance. The input-impedance and current-gain expressions must be modified to take into account the currents in r_μ and C_μ. The input impedance expression, for example, becomes

$$Z_{\text{in}} = [z_\pi + (\beta + 1)R_L] \parallel r_\mu \parallel \frac{1}{sC_\mu} \qquad (7.15)$$

Fig. 7.5. Simplified common-collector models.

The header and overlap-diode capacitances C_{bc}, C_{be}, and C_{ce} can be added to this model if desired, but they do not change the behavior in any important way.

For first-order calculations, it is possible to simplify the model even further. If we let r_μ become infinite, r_π become zero, and switch to a current-dependent current source, the model of Fig. 7.5b evolves. This can be shown either from the above equations or from the model of Fig. 7.5a.

7.2.2 *Properties of the Common Collector Circuit*

It is appropriate at this point to interpret the equations of Sec. 7.2.1 in terms of the properties of the common-collector circuit. Equation 7.15 shows that the input impedance of the circuit depends heavily on the value of the load resistance R_L. At low frequencies, the input resistance will be one or two orders of magnitude larger than R_L for typical values of β. Thus the common-collector circuit can be designed to have a very high input impedance at low frequencies. However, the input impedance will fall at high frequencies, because of the fall-off in β above f_β, approaching $R_L \parallel (1/sC_\mu)$ as the frequency approaches f_T

It is a simple matter to show from Eq. 7.15 that for certain values of *capacitive* load, the input impedance of the common-collector circuit has a negative real part (see Problem P7.6). Under these conditions, the circuit can be unstable for certain source impedances.

Equation 7.14 shows that the output impedance is a strong function of the source resistance, R_s. In fact, for R_s much larger than z_π, the output impedance is very nearly equal to R_s/β, and therefore is one or two orders of magnitude smaller than R_s at low frequencies.

Equations 7.14 and 7.15 represent an extension of the impedance-transforming concept discussed in Chapter 6. Specifically, we have calculated here a more general impedance-transformation ratio $(\beta + 1)$ between base and emitter, which is applicable over a broad frequency range.

To offset these rather convenient impedance-transforming properties, the common-collector circuit has a voltage gain which is at best only a little less than 1. The current gain, however, is approxi-

Fig. 7.6. Common-emitter circuit with unbypassed emitter resistor.

mately equal to that of the common-emitter connection, so fairly sizable power gain is still achieved.

We can often make use of the results of the previous paragraph to estimate the properties of other circuits. For example, let us find the voltage gain of the common-emitter circuit with an unbypassed emitter resistor, Fig. 7.6. Because the emitter and collector currents are very nearly equal, the incremental output voltage V_o will be related to the incremental emitter voltage V_e by the equation

$$\frac{V_o}{V_e} \cong \frac{-R_L}{R_e} \tag{7.16}$$

But from the preceding discussion, the voltage gain from input to emitter, V_e/V_i, will be approximately unity. Therefore, the over-all voltage gain of the circuit will be

$$\frac{V_o}{V_i} \cong \frac{-R_L}{R_e} \tag{7.17}$$

7.3 SUMMARY

In summary, the common-base circuit has voltage gain but no current gain, while the common-collector circuit has current gain but no voltage gain. Because the common-emitter circuit has *both* voltage gain and current gain, and because the input and output impedances for this connection are such that direct cascading of transistors results in reasonable impedance matching without transformers, the common-emitter connection is by far the most widely used transistor configuration today. Therefore, most of the discussion in this book is devoted to this connection.

PROBLEMS

P7.1 For the circuit of Fig. 7.7, find the quantities in the table below. Note that Z_{in} is defined with R_L connected, and Z_{out} is defined with R_s connected. Assume $C_\pi = C_\mu = 0$, $r_o = r_\mu = \infty$.

	Common Base	Common Emitter	Common Collector
$Z_{\text{in}} = V_{\text{in}}/I_{\text{in}}$			
$Z_{\text{out}} = V_{\text{out}}/I_{\text{out}}\vert_{V_s=0}$			
$A_v = V_{\text{out}}/V_{\text{in}}$			
$A_i = I_{\text{out}}/I_{\text{in}}$			

P7.2 (a) For the common-base, common-emitter and common-collector circuits, which has the highest input impedance? Which has the lowest output impedance?

(b) Under what condition does the common-emitter circuit have a voltage gain greater *in magnitude* than the other two circuits? Answer in terms of an inequality.

(c) Which of these circuits has a current gain of magnitude less than 1 and may also exhibit a small voltage gain if R_s is too large?

P7.3 The circuit in Fig. 7.8 can be used as a driver for a push-pull amplifier. Both transistors are type 2N1305. The frequencies of interest are low enough so that C_μ and C_π in each transistor have negligible effect, but high enough so that the coupling and bypass capacitor have negligible signal voltage across them.

Fig. 7.7.

Fig. 7.8.

(a) Show that with both outputs open-circuited, $V_o = -V_o'$ if the common-emitter short-circuit current gain h_{fe2} ($=\beta_{02}$) is large. Because the open-circuit output voltages are related in this way, the circuit of the output transistor is referred to as a *phase splitter*.

(b) Show that the open-circuit incremental voltage gains from the input terminals to the two output terminals are *approximately*:

$$\frac{V_o'}{V_i} \cong g_{m1}R_c \qquad \frac{V_o}{V_1} \cong -g_{m1}R_c$$

where g_{m1} refers to the input transistor. What inequalities involving the parameters of the two transistors and of the circuit must be satisfied to justify use of these approximate voltage gain expressions?

(c) Does $V_o = V_o'$ when arbitrary *identical* resistive loads are connected to the two outputs?

(d) This amplifier must provide sinusoidal output signals of 1 volt peak amplitude with a load of *1* k across each pair of output terminals. Select the dc load resistances R_L and the quiescent collector current I_{C2} of the output stage so that the output stage remains linear; that is, neither cuts off nor saturates with the maximum output signal. (The answers are not unique.)

(e) Using the value of R_L determined in part (*d*), specify the quiescent base-to-ground voltage required for the second stage in order to fix the quiescent collector current I_{C2} at the value specified in (*d*). A reasonable nominal value of V_{EB} for a 2N1305 with a collector current in the range of 1 ma is 0.2 volts (at 25°C).

(f) Estimate the range of quiescent base current of the output stage, using the following transistor parameters:

Parameter	Min.	Max.
β_F	50	150
I_{CO} (25°C)	0	10 μa

(g) Choose the quiescent collector current (I_{C1}) of the input stage so that the operating point of the output transistor will be insensitive to β_{F2} and I_{CO2}. Based on your choice of I_{C1}, select R_c.

(h) Estimate the peak signal voltage swing at the base of the output stage.

(i) What factors influence the selection of the quiescent emitter-to-ground voltage for the input stage? Select this voltage and determine R_e so that I_{E1} will develop the desired quiescent voltage.

(j) Specify the nominal quiescent base-to-ground voltage of the first stage and estimate the quiescent base current of this stage [use the parameters specified in (f)]. Specify R_{b1} and R_{b2} so that the input stage has the desired operating point and so that the operating point is insensitive to β_F and I_{CO}.

(k) Specify C_1, C_2, and C_3 so that the amplifier gain is at least 0.707 of its mid-frequency value at 20 cps. Assume that the amplifier is driven from a voltage source and *make reasonable approximations*. Also assume $\beta_0 \cong \beta_F$.

P7.4 Find the approximate values of the following low-frequency incremental parameters for the circuit in Fig. 7.9: input resistance V_i/I_i, output resistance (resistance seen by 1 k load with $V_s = 0$), voltage gain V_o/V_i, and current gain I_o/I_i. Each transistor has $\beta_0 = 30$.

Fig. 7.9.

Fig. 7.10.

P7.5 For the common-collector circuit, find the frequency at which the current gain is down to 0.707 of its low-frequency value. Compare with the 0.707 frequency of a common-emitter amplifier with the same R_s and R_L. Make a similar comparison on the voltage gain.

P7.6 (a) By starting with Eq. 7.12, find the range of values of capacitive load C_L which will cause the input impedance Z_{in} of the common-collector circuit to have a negative real part. This calculation applies to the model in Fig. 7.4.

(b) Will the inclusion of r_x, r_o, r_μ or C_μ materially change your answer to (a)?

P7.7 (a) For the common-base circuit of Fig. 7.10 find the mid-frequency voltage gain V_o/V_i. Assume for the transistor $r_x = 100$ Ω, $r_\pi = 400$ Ω, $g_m = 0.1$ mho.

(b) Find appropriate values for C_1 and C_2 to yield a low-frequency 0.707 point of 100 cps. Use the method discussed in Sec. 6.3.

P7.8 For the common-collector circuit of Fig. 7.11, find the value of C_1 required to give a low-frequency 0.707 point of V_o/V_i at 100 cps.

Fig. 7.11.

8

Tuned Amplifiers

8.0 INTRODUCTION

The preceding chapters have presented small-signal models of transistors and have shown how these models are used in the analysis and design of a number of important amplifier circuits. The objective of this chapter is to extend these techniques to the case of transistor amplifiers using tuned circuits.

Tuned amplifiers are used whenever it is necessary to amplify signals in some specified frequency range, and reject signals at all other frequencies. Thus the desired features of a tuned amplifier are that it provide as much gain as possible, constant over a specified bandwidth centered at a specified frequency, and as much signal rejection as possible outside this specified band. Additional detailed features of the frequency response are important, particularly when the signal to be amplified is a modulated signal (amplitude modulated or frequency modulated, for example) which consists of a carrier sinusoid and a number of other sinusoids which form a *symmetrical* frequency spectrum around this carrier. To preserve the form of the modulation signal, it is desirable that over the pass band, the gain be reasonably constant and the phase be a reasonably linear function of frequency. The small variations from this ideal that do occur in the gain and phase characteristics

227

should, like the signal spectrum, be symmetrical with respect to the center of the pass band. Fortunately, for sound theoretical reasons, designs that provide uniform gain also tend to provide linear phase shift.

The circuit diagram for a simple tuned transistor amplifier is shown in Fig. 8.1a. In the light of the preceding discussion, we wish to design this amplifier to have a frequency response of the general form shown in Fig. 8.1b. That is, we wish to have a symmetrical amplitude characteristic centered at a frequency ω_0. The phase characteristic shown in the figure is that associated with

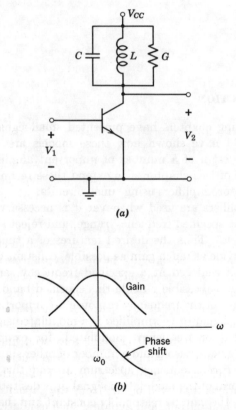

(a)

(b)

Fig. 8.1. Tuned transistor amplifier. (a) Circuit. (b) Desired gain and phase characteristic.

the tuned circuit alone. As we shall see, there will be some additional phase shift associated with the amplifier. In many designs it is possible to choose the center frequency ω_0 to be much larger than the required bandwidth. Such an amplifier is called a *narrow-band* amplifier, the only kind we shall consider in this chapter.

This narrow-band feature permits some simplification of the analysis and design problems for tuned amplifiers. But the presence of tuned circuits at the output, and ultimately also at the input, of such amplifiers presents some fundamental difficulties that we have had little occasion to consider before in single-stage problems. These difficulties concern the fact that a *single transistor stage may be unstable (that is, may oscillate) in the presence of certain combinations of ordinary passive source and load impedances.*

So far we have considered primarily low-pass amplifiers and, accordingly, only resistive (or at worst RC) load and source impedances. Moreover, we have also concentrated on the common-emitter connection of the transistor, and it turns out that this connection remains stable for all combinations of RC load and source impedances. That is, the coupling between output and input through g_μ, C_μ, and C_{sc} of the full hybrid-π model (Fig. 3.12) is simply not in the right phase to produce oscillations as long as the source and load impedances are of the RC type. Notice, however, that we did encounter briefly a difficulty in the common-collector connection with a capacitive load (see Sec. 7.2 or Prob. P7.6), and in fact a transistor in this connection *can* oscillate with RC loads if the source impedance happens to be inductive.

The significant new point about the tuned amplifier is the fact that narrow-band tuned circuits have susceptances that change from large *capacitive* to large *inductive* values over a very narrow frequency range. When the center frequency is high enough so that the coupling provided by C_μ or C_{sc} is important, and the center-frequency gain is high (because the amplifier is designed for that purpose), a common-emitter stage may well find itself with *inductive* source and load impedances at frequencies near band center, where the voltage gain is still high. Under these circumstances oscillations may well occur, from the capacitive coupling between input and output, and avoiding such oscillations becomes one important part of the tuned-amplifier design problem. It will not be surprising to learn that either a reduction of the input-output coupling or a reduction of the gain will be required to cope with these difficulties.

8.1 VOLTAGE GAIN FOR TUNED AMPLIFIER

To analyse the circuit of Fig. 8.1a, we must first decide on a suitable model for the transistor. We have pointed out above that in the preceding chapters our study of transistor amplifiers under small-signal operating conditions has been focused on the broadband, essentially low-pass case. The transistor has, accordingly, been characterized primarily by the hybrid-π model. For these purposes this model has a number of desirable features, including parameters that are closely related to the physical processes taking place in the transistor, and parameter values that are essentially independent of frequency. Among the less desirable features of the hybrid-π model, however, is the fact that the model containing "intrinsic" elements only is good up to about ω_b (see Eq. 3.46), and it is exactly in the range between ω_b and ω_T where we often wish to operate transistor tuned amplifiers. Thus to form a usable model in this range we must add to the intrinsic model "extrinsic" elements representing overlap diode capacitance, header capacitance, and in some cases emitter lead inductance as well, all of which complicate the model and the analysis problem considerably.

Because we are interested in analyzing circuit behavior only over a narrow band of frequency, it is possible to avoid some of the above difficulties by using the y-parameter model (Fig. 3.9) to represent the transistor. The y-parameter model, being a true π structure, is topologically somewhat simpler than the hybrid-π model, and over a narrow band the y-parameters are relatively simple functions of frequency. The disadvantage of this approach is that variation of the y-parameters as a function of operating point is not a simple matter, because the y-parameters are not simply related to the physical mechanisms in the transistor. On the basis of the y-parameter model, then, we arrive at the small-signal model of Fig. 8.2 for the tuned amplifier.

Figure 3.16 shows a representative set of common-emitter admittance parameters as a function of frequency. These curves indicate that the admittance parameters are slowly-varying functions of frequency. If the term "narrow-band amplifier" is taken

Fig. 8.2. Small-signal model for tuned amplifier.

to mean an amplifier in which the bandwidth is not more than about 10% of the center frequency, it is a satisfactory approximation to represent each admittance parameter by the first two terms in its Taylor series expansion about ω_0. In fact, adequate accuracy is achieved by keeping the first two terms in the imaginary part expansion, and only the constant term in the real part expansion. We have to retain two terms in the imaginary part because we are dealing with a resonant system in which the imaginary parts of the y-parameters may be cancelled out in the vicinity of the center frequency ω_0. Specifically, then, we approximate y_{ie} as follows:

$$y_{ie} = g_{ie} + j\omega_0 C_{ie} + j(\omega - \omega_0)C'_{ie} \qquad (8.1)$$

where g_{ie} and $\omega_0 C_{ie}$ are the real and imaginary parts of y_{ie} evaluated at the center frequency $\omega = \omega_0$, and

$$C'_{ie} = \frac{d}{d\omega} \operatorname{Im}[y_{ie}] \big|_{\omega=\omega_0} \qquad (8.2)$$

Similarly,

$$y_{fe} = g_{fe} + j\omega_0 C_{fe} + j(\omega - \omega_0)C'_{fe} \qquad (8.3)$$

$$y_{oe} = g_{oe} + j\omega_0 C_{oe} + j(\omega - \omega_0)C'_{oe} \qquad (8.4)$$

$$y_{re} = g_{re} + j\omega_0 C_{re} + j(\omega - \omega_0)C'_{re} \qquad (8.5)$$

For transistors in the common-emitter connection, the imaginary parts of the y-parameters are usually capacitive, increasing in magnitude with frequency (see Fig. 3.16). The parameters in Eqs. 8.1, 8.3, 8.4, and 8.5 are determined, either by the manufacturer or by the user, from measurements made on the transistor at the operating point of interest. Thus all of the annoying parasitic effects that were mentioned earlier are already included in the measured parameters.

To start the study of the tuned amplifier in Fig. 8.1a, we calculate the voltage gain V_2/V_1. In general, of course, two calculations are necessary to describe the behavior of the amplifier under arbitrary source and load conditions, as was pointed out in Chapter 3. If we calculate the voltage gain or current gain from the transistor input terminals to the output load, and the transistor input impedance, all for an arbitrary given load impedance, then we can readily find the gain for arbitrary source impedance. Alternatively, we can calculate the Thevenin or Norton equivalent of the transistor and source by calculating the open-circuit output voltage or short-circuit output current and the output impedance of the transistor, all with an arbitrary given source impedance. Then we can readily calculate the circuit response for an arbitrary load impedance. Because we have chosen the y-parameter representation for the transistor, it is easier to calculate the voltage gain V_2/V_1 than the current gain I_2/I_1 (in contrast to the discussion in Chapter 3 where, because of r_x in the hybrid-π model, it was easier to calculate the current gain). Partly for this reason, the calculation serves as useful introduction to the discussion. To complete the discussion we shall, of course, calculate in Sec. 8.3.2 in the input impedance of the circuit.

By inspection of Fig. 8.2 we find the voltage gain to be

$$A_v = \frac{V_2}{V_1} = \frac{-y_{fe}}{y_{oe} + j\omega C + G + 1/j\omega L} \tag{8.6}$$

Substituting from Eq. 8.4 for y_{oe}, we get

$$\frac{V_2}{V_1} = \frac{-y_{fe}}{j\omega(C + C'_{oe}) + j\omega_0(C_{oe} - C'_{oe}) + g_{oe} + G + 1/j\omega L} \tag{8.7}$$

It is clear now from Eq. 8.7 why we have chosen to retain more terms in the imaginary part of y_{oe} than in the real part. For center-frequency calculations the additional term will make no difference. But in bandwidth calculations, because we are interested in the *difference* between two nearly equal susceptances (that is, the capacitive and inductive terms in the denominator of Eq. 8.7), we are forced to employ a more accurate representation of $\text{Im}[y_{oe}]$. By the same token, because y_{fe} is *not* involved in the resonant part of the expression, we can neglect C'_{fe} and assume that y_{fe} is constant over the band. We note in passing that if $C'_{oe} = C_{oe}$, the imaginary part of y_{oe} can be represented simply by a constant capacitance, and if y_{fe} is constant, Eq. 8.7 reduces to the standard form for an *RLC* circuit.

In Eqs. 8.1 to 8.5, we chose the expansion on the basis that ω_0 would be the center frequency of the amplifier. In terms of a symmetrical voltage gain, the center frequency would naturally be defined as the frequency at which the magnitude is a maximum. But it is simpler, and very nearly the same for the narrow-band case, to take ω_0 as the frequency where the imaginary part of the denominator of the voltage gain expression goes to zero. In fact, these two conditions will be the same if the band is narrow enough so that y_{fe} can be considered to be constant. Thus from Eq. 8.7,

$$\omega_0(C + C_{oe}) = \frac{1}{\omega_0 L} \tag{8.8}$$

or

$$\omega_0 = \frac{1}{\sqrt{(C + C_{oe})L}} \tag{8.9}$$

The voltage gain at the center frequency, in accordance with the definition given above for center frequency, is from Eq. 8.7.

$$|A_v(\omega_0)| \equiv A_0 = \frac{|y_{fe}|}{g_{oe} + G} \tag{8.10}$$

The bandwidth of the amplifier between the half-power points can be found most readily by examining Eq. 8.7 in the vicinity of resonance. To this end we introduce a new frequency variable ω', defined by

$$\omega' = \omega - \omega_0 \tag{8.11}$$

which measures the frequency *deviation* from band center. By substituting for ω from this equation, we obtain from Eq. 8.7,

$$\frac{V_2}{V_1} = \frac{-y_{fe}}{j\omega'C + j\omega_0 C + j\omega_0 C_{oe} + j\omega'C'_{oe} + g_{oe} + G + 1/j(\omega_0 + \omega')L} \tag{8.12}$$

For a *narrow-band* amplifier we are interested only in values of ω' much smaller than ω_0. Under these conditions the inductive term in the denominator of Eq. 8.12 can be approximated as follows:

$$\frac{1}{j(\omega' + \omega_0)L} \cong \frac{1}{j\omega_0 L} - \frac{\omega'}{j\omega_0^2 L} \qquad (8.13a)$$

Now, substituting for $1/\omega_0 L$ from Eq. 8.8, we obtain

$$\frac{1}{j(\omega_0 + \omega')L} \cong -j\omega_0(C + C_{oe}) + j\omega'(C + C_{oe}) \qquad (8.13b)$$

Equation 8.12 then reduces to

$$\left.\frac{V_2}{V_1}\right|_{\omega \,\cong\, \omega_0} = \frac{-y_{fe}}{j\omega'(2C + C_{oe} + C'_{oe}) + g_{oe} + G} \qquad (8.14)$$

The half-power frequencies are, by definition, those frequencies where the real and imaginary parts of the denominator expression in Eq. 8.14 (or 8.7) are equal in magnitude. That is,

$$\omega'|_{\text{half power}} = \pm \frac{g_{oe} + G}{2C + C'_{oe} + C_{oe}} \qquad (8.15)$$

Therefore, the bandwidth between these two half-power frequencies, is

$$\text{Bandwidth} = \frac{g_{oe} + G}{C + (C_{oe} + C'_{oe})/2} \text{ rads/sec} \qquad (8.16)$$

Again, if $C_{oe} = C'_{oe}$, this formula reduces to a more familiar form.

If the transistor parameters are known, and if the center frequency and half-power bandwidth of the amplifier are specified, then Eqs. 8.9 and 8.16 fix two of the three parameters G, L, and C in the tuned circuit. Frequently the value of G is fixed by the load to which the amplifier must deliver its output signal or by additional considerations discussed in MTC in connection with multistage tuned amplifiers; in such cases the specifications listed above fix the parameters of the amplifier completely, as far as voltage gain requirements are concerned.

8.1.1 *Illustrative Example: Low Frequency*

Let us assume that a tuned amplifier, using a silicon planar transistor and having the form illustrated in Fig. 8.1*a*, is to be driven by a voltage source, and is to deliver its output to a resistive load of 1 kilohm. The circuit is to be designed for a center frequency $\omega_0 = 3 \times 10^6$ rad/sec (480 kc) and a half-power bandwidth of 6×10^4 rad/sec (9.6 kc). The y-parameters for the transistor in the vicinity of ω_0 are given in this table:

y-parameter	g	C	C'
y_{ie}	1 mmho	67 pf	50 pf
y_{fe}	50	0	0
y_{re}	0	−10	−10
y_{oe}	0.15	50	25

The conductance of the load is 1 mmho; if we neglect the small losses associated with the tuning inductor, the conductance G in Fig. 8.2 is the load conductance, 1 mmho.

The value of tuning capacitance that is required for the specified bandwidth is given by Eq. 8.16:

$$C + \frac{C_{oe} + C'_{oe}}{2} = \frac{g_{oe} + G}{\text{Bandwidth}}$$

$$= \frac{(0.15 + 1) \times 10^{-3}}{6 \times 10^4}$$

$$- 19,200 \text{ pf}$$

$$\therefore C = 19,200 - \tfrac{75}{2} \cong 19,160 \text{ pf}$$

Clearly the effects of C_{oe} and C'_{oe} are small in this example. The value of C which we have obtained is at the present time somewhat larger than is routinely available in stable low-loss capacitors of small physical size.

The value of tuning inductor required for the specified center frequency is given by Eq. 8.9:

$$L = \frac{1}{\omega_0^2(C + C_{oe})} = \frac{1}{(9 \times 10^{12})(19.2 \times 10^{-9})} \cong 5.8 \ \mu\text{h}$$

This value of inductance is rather small in the sense that a suitably high Q coil with this inductance value in this frequency range is not routinely available. The voltage gain $|V_2/V_1|$ at the resonant frequency is given by Eq. 8.10:

$$A_0 = \frac{|y_{fe}|}{y_{oe} + G} = \frac{50}{0.15 + 1} \cong 43$$

8.1.2 *Illustrative Example: High Frequency*

Let us repeat the above example, except this time design for a center frequency of 6×10^7 rad./sec. (9.55 mc) and a bandwidth of 2.4×10^6 rad./sec. (382 kc), using the transistor of Fig. 3.16. We find from the figure that in the vicinity of $\omega_0 = 6 \times 10^7$ rad/sec, the y-parameters can be approximated as follows:

y-parameter	g	C	C'
y_{ie}	1.15 mmhos	17.7 pf	6.9 pf
y_{fe}	19.1	-256	-13.2
y_{re}	-0.038	-2.6	-1.8
y_{oe}	0.69	15.6	5.3

Following the same procedure as before, we find,

$$C + \frac{C_{oe} + C'_{oe}}{2} = \frac{(1 + 0.69) \times 10^{-3}}{2.4 \times 10^6} = 702 \text{ pf}$$

$$\therefore C = 702 - \frac{15.6 + 5.3}{2} \cong 690 \text{ pf}$$

$$L = \frac{1}{36 \times 10^2 (690 + 15.6)} \cong 0.4 \ \mu\text{h}$$

$$A_0 = \frac{25}{0.69 + 1} \cong 15$$

8.2 IMPEDANCE TRANSFORMATION IN TUNED AMPLIFIERS

The specifications for the center frequency, the bandwidth, and the load conductance G in the first example, Sec. 8.1.1, which are typical of those encountered in low-frequency transistor amplifiers, lead to values of L and C that may be undesirable from a practical point of view. To avoid the problem of inconvenient element values, it is common practice to employ some form of impedance-transforming arrangement in tuned transistor amplifiers. One configuration often used for this purpose is shown in Fig. 8.3a. The coil used in this circuit is wound on a ferrite core, and the coefficient of coupling among the turns is very close to unity; that

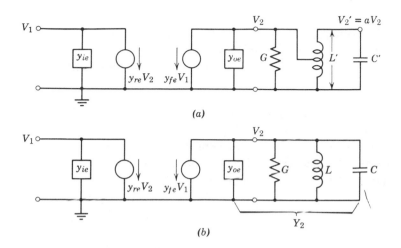

Fig. 8.3. Impedance transformation in tuned amplifiers. (*a*) Circuit. (*b*) Equivalent circuit, $L = L'/a^2$ and $C = a^2 C'$.

is, all the flux links all the turns of the coil. On this basis, if the voltage ratio of the transformer is

$$\frac{V_2'}{V_2} = a \tag{8.17}$$

as indicated in Fig. 8.3*a*, then the reflected capacitance appearing in parallel with G is

$$C = a^2 C' \tag{8.18}$$

Similarly, the equivalent inductance appearing in parallel with G is

$$L = \frac{L'}{a^2} \tag{8.19}$$

where L' is the total inductance of the coil. Figure 8.3*b* shows the amplifier with L' and C' referred to the primary side of the transformer. With the transformation ratio $a > 1$, reasonable values of L' and C' can be transformed into the inconvenient values required by the circuit. These facts are illustrated in the following example.

8.2.1 *Illustrative Example*

The tuned transistor amplifier in Sec. 8.1.1 is to be redesigned with a tapped coil (autotransformer) used to provide reasonable values for the tuning inductance and capacitance. Small-signal models for the circuit are shown in Fig. 8.3. As a matter of convenience, the tuning capacitance, C' in Fig. 8.3a, is chosen to be 220 pf. The problem is to determine the values of L' and a that are required to meet the original specifications.

The value of the apparent tuning capacitance appearing in parallel with the load conductance G was determined to be 19,160 pf. Thus with $C' = 220$ pf we obtain

$$a^2 = \frac{C}{C'} = \frac{19,160}{220} = 115 \qquad a = 10.7$$

The inductance required in parallel with G to meet the center-frequency specification is determined in Sec. 8.1.1 to be 5.8 μh. Thus

$$L' = a^2 L = (115)(5.8) = 666 \,\mu\text{h}$$

It should be possible to obtain a reasonable Q in a coil of this size at the specified operating frequency of 480 kc.

The voltage gain V_2/V_1 of this amplifier at resonance is the same as in the original design of Sec. 8.1.1, $A_0' = 43$.

The impedance-transforming property of the tapped coil in Fig. 8.3 offers an additional important feature. It turns out, for reasons developed in the following section and in MTC, that in designing tuned amplifiers it is usually necessary to control the conductance G presented to the amplifier by the load. When the actual load conductance G' is fixed and does not have a suitable value, the tapped coil can be used, as shown in Fig. 8.4, to trans-

Fig. 8.4. Impedance transforming in tuned amplifiers.

form this conductance to a suitable value. The conductance appearing on the collector side of the transformer in this circuit is

$$G = a^2G' \tag{8.20}$$

The desired value of G can thus be obtained by proper choice of the transformation ratio a.

When the transformation ratio in Fig. 8.4 is chosen to provide the desired value for G, it may or may not provide suitable values for L' and C' in the tuned circuit. When suitable element values do not result, it is common practice to connect the load conductance G' to a second tap on the coil. Thus two transformation ratios are provided, and the circuit can be adjusted simultaneously for the desired value of G and for suitable values of L' and C'.

The tapped coil in Fig. 8.4 is just one of a variety of configurations that can be used for impedance transformation. If the tuning capacitance in Fig. 8.4 is replaced by an equivalent series connection of two capacitors, then a tap at the junction of these capacitors provides a somewhat similar impedance transformation. There are many other types of impedance-transforming networks, and the selection of the circuit configuration to be used is based on a number of factors, including the band of frequencies in which the amplifier is to operate and the impedance levels involved.

8.3 GAIN, INPUT ADMITTANCE, AND INSTABILITY

In Sec. 8.1 we worked out the voltage gain V_2/V_1 of the tuned amplifier in Fig. 8.1a, thereby suppressing detailed consideration of the interaction between output and input circuits. Let us turn now to a somewhat more realistic calculation: the performance of the tuned amplifier when driven from a source with a purely conductive source admittance. The appropriate circuit model for such an amplifier is shown in Fig. 8.5a. We wish to find the overall transfer-gain expression V_2/I_s, and the input admittance of the amplifier. From these studies we will see how the interaction between input and output circuits affects the performance.

8.3.1 *Gain*

One of the simplest ways of evaluating the transfer-gain expression, V_2/I_s, and of seeing the effect of input-output interaction

(a)

(b)

Fig. 8.5. Tuned amplifier driven by a resistive source. (a) Small-signal model. (b) Model reduced by Norton's theorem.

on this expression, is to replace all of the circuit to the left of y_{oe} with its Norton equivalent circuit, I_n and Y_n, as shown in Fig. 8.5b. The current source I_n is evaluated by determining the short-circuit output current ($V_2 = 0$) from the $y_{fe}V_1$ source in Fig. 8.5a; thus

$$I_n = y_{fe}V_1 \Big|_{V_2 = 0} = \frac{y_{fe}}{G_s + y_{ie}} I_s \qquad (8.21)$$

The admittance Y_n is evaluated by applying 1 volt at V_2 with $I_s = 0$, and evaluating the current $y_{fe}V_1$; thus we have

$$y_{fe}V_1 \Big|_{I_s = 0} = y_{fe} \frac{-y_{re}V_2}{G_s + y_{ie}} \qquad (8.22)$$

Then the value of Y_n is

$$Y_n = \frac{y_{fe}V_1}{V_2} \Big|_{I_s = 0} = \frac{-y_{re}y_{fe}}{G_s + y_{ie}} \qquad (8.23)$$

This admittance can also be expressed in rectangular form as

$$Y_n = G_n + jB_n \qquad (8.23a)$$

The transfer gain can now be written by inspection of Fig. 8.5b; it is

$$V_2 = \frac{-I_n}{Y_n + y_{oe} + G + j\omega C + 1/j\omega L}$$

$$= \frac{-I_n}{G_n + jB_n + y_{oe} + G + j\omega C + 1/j\omega L}$$

(8.24)

It is shown below that I_n remains essentially constant for all frequencies in and near the narrow pass band of the amplifier; thus Eq. 8.24 has the same form as Eq. 8.6 for the voltage gain except for the term Y_n in the denominator. The interaction between the input and output circuits is accounted for by the Y_n term, and to see the effects of the interaction on the performance of the amplifier we must examine the nature of Y_n.

The admittance Y_n depends on the source conductance which is constant, and on the transistor parameters which are slowly varying functions of frequency. Further examination of Eq. 8.23 shows that Y_n, G_n, and B_n are also slowly varying functions of frequency and that G_n is positive (for the common-emitter connection). Thus Y_n can be treated as the transistor parameters were treated in Sec. 8.1, by expanding G_n and B_n in a power series. As in Sec. 8.1, for operation in the narrow pass band we retain only the constant term in the series for G_n, and the first two terms in the series for B_n, because the susceptances in Fig. 8.5b nearly cancel at frequencies near resonance. With these approximations Y_n has the same form as y_{oe}, and it is convenient to lump these two admittances together. With Y_n and y_{oe} combined, Eq. 8.24 has the same form as Eq. 8.6 for the voltage gain. It follows from these facts that in this case the effect of Y_n, and hence the effect of the input-output interaction, on V_2/I_s is to shift the center frequency and to alter the bandwidth from those given by Eqs. 8.9 and 8.16. It is shown in the following sections that these effects are small in a well-designed amplifier, so that the gain V_2/I_s and the voltage gain V_2/V_1 in fact have nearly the same center frequencies and bandwidths.

In connection with Eq. 8.24 it is stated that I_n is essentially constant in the pass band of the amplifier. To verify this statement, we note from Eq. 8.21 that I_n depends on the source conductance and on the transistor parameters; thus it is a slowly varying function of frequency. Furthermore, calculation of I_n does not involve the resonance phenomenon, nor any subtraction of terms. Therefore, for operation in the narrow pass band, neither the real nor the imaginary parts of I_n pass through zero; so both can be approximated by the constant terms in their power series expansions. That is, I_n is approximately constant in the pass band of the amplifier.

8.3.2 *Input Admittance*

The input admittance of this amplifier depends on the parameters in the output circuit as well as on those in the input circuit. This fact, accounted for by the current source $y_{re}V_2$, comes as a result of the internal feedback in the transistor, which may have a pronounced effect on the nature of the input admittance. To examine this matter further, the current in the source $y_{re}V_2$ can be expressed as

$$I = y_{re}V_2 = y_{re} \frac{-y_{fe}}{y_{oe} + Y_L} V_1 \qquad (8.25)$$

The current I can be accounted for by an admittance Y_1 connected across the input circuit from node V_1 to ground, as shown in Fig. 8.6. This admittance has a value

$$Y_1 = \frac{I}{V_1} = \frac{-y_{fe}y_{re}}{y_{oe} + Y_L} \qquad (8.26)$$

Let us start the discussion of the effect of Y_1 on circuit performance by examining Y_1 for some typical values of y_{fe} and y_{re}. Let us assume that y_{fe} is purely conductive, $y_{fe} = g_{fe}$, and y_{re} is

Fig. 8.6. An equivalent input circuit for the amplifier of Fig. 8.5.

purely capacitive, $y_{re} = -j\omega C_{re}$. By referring to Fig. 3.16, we see that these assumptions are in fact quite reasonable over a broad frequency range. Under these conditions,

$$Y_1 = \frac{j\omega C_{re} g_{fe}}{y_{oe} + Y_L} \tag{8.27}$$

Now at frequencies below the resonance of the *output tuned circuit*. $y_{oe} + Y_L$ will be inductive, and Y_1 *will have a negative real part*. As a result of this negative real part, the total admittance from node V_1 to ground is very likely to have a negative real part in some band of frequencies. For certain values of source impedance, self-sustaining oscillations can occur which will interfere with the proper operation of the transistor as an amplifier, as we shall see in more detail below.

Let us designate the total admittance from node V_1 to ground in Fig. 8.6 as Y_D. Thus

$$V_1 = \frac{I_s}{Y_D} = \frac{I_s}{G_s + y_{ie} + Y_1} \tag{8.28}$$

$$\equiv \frac{I_s}{G_D + jB_D}$$

If G_D is negative in some band of frequencies, then it is possible to make the following series of adjustments. At some frequency at which G_D is negative, a suitable susceptance (in this case, inductive) can be connected across the input terminals of the transistor to make $B_D = 0$. Then a suitable *positive resistance* can be connected across the input terminals to make $G_D = 0$. As a result of these adjustments, the total admittance at the input terminals is $Y_D = 0$. Now, with no input current applied, a sinusoidal voltage V_1 can exist at the frequency at which $Y_D = 0$. That is, the circuit will oscillate at this frequency.

The significance of the adjustment described above can also be interpreted in terms of poles and zeros. The adjustment makes $Y_D = 0$ for sinusoidal operation at some frequency ω_1; thus the admittance $Y_D(s)$ has a pair of zeros at $\pm j\omega_1$. It then follows from Eq. 8.28 that $V_1(s)$ has a pair of poles on the imaginary axis at $\pm j\omega_1$, so the circuit is unstable.

8.3.3 *Adjusting Amplifier Loading to Avoid Oscillation*

In spite of the fact that the real part of Y_D is negative over a band of frequencies, the circuit of Fig. 8.5 *as it stands* will operate in a satisfactory manner, without unwanted oscillations and with frequency characteristics of the desired form. This was shown in Sec. 8.3.1. In fact, we saw in Sec. 8.3.2 that to adjust this circuit for oscillations, an *inductive susceptance* of suitable value must be connected across the input terminals; such an inductance is not present in the circuit of Fig. 8.5.

The problem with the tuned amplifier is that, as we mentioned in Sec. 8.0, we often want to operate the amplifier not with a purely resistive input circuit, but with a *tuned input circuit*. Under these conditions, it is highly probable that at some frequency in the vicinity of the pass band, the condition for oscillation described above will be met, and the amplifier will be unstable. Therefore, we establish as a condition for a satisfactory design that the *real part of the impedance Y_D (I_s/V_1 in Fig. 8.5 or 8.6) must be positive* at all frequencies of interest:

$$\text{Re}[Y_D] = (G_s + g_{ie} + \text{Re}[Y_1]) > 0 \qquad (8.29)$$

Only by meeting this condition can we insure that the amplifier will be stable regardless of what passive elements we add at the input. Unfortunately, $\text{Re}[Y_1]$ is not a simple function. Therefore, we resort to a graphical interpretation to aid in the understanding of Inequality 8.29.

We begin by studying the admittance Y_1, Eq. 8.26. If we define $Y_2 = y_{oe} + Y_L$ as indicated in Fig. 8.5, then Eq. 8.26 can be written as

$$Y_1 = \frac{-y_{fe}y_{re}}{Y_2} \qquad (8.30)$$

Note from Eqs. 8.25 and 8.26 that Y_1 can also be written as

$$Y_1 = y_{re}\frac{V_2}{V_1} \qquad (8.31)$$

so Eqs. 8.7 and 8.14 can be converted from voltage gain expressions to Y_1 expressions by multiplying by y_{re}. Therefore, the denominator of these two equations is the expression we are now calling Y_2.

We see from Eq. 8.7 that the admittance Y_2 represents the parallel combination of G's, L's, and C's in the output circuit of the amplifier. For sinusoidal signals it is a complex number and a function of frequency. We can see from the denominator of Eq. 8.14 that, as the frequency of the sinusoidal signal is varied, the real part of this admittance remains constant at the value $g_{oe} + G$, while the imaginary part varies from large negative values to large positive values. Thus a plot of Y_2 as a function of frequency in the complex plane is a vertical straight line, as shown in Fig. 8.7. Each point on this locus corresponds to the complex value of Y_2 at some frequency; at $\omega' = 0$, (that is, $\omega = \omega_0$, the resonant frequency for Y_2), the admittance is real and is $G_2 = g_{oe} + G$. The frequencies where $|Y_2|$ is $\sqrt{2}G_2$, which are also approximately the frequencies where the magnitude of the voltage gain has dropped to 0.707 of $A_v(\omega_0)$, occur when the angle of Y_2 is $\pm 45°$. Thus the portion of the locus shown as a heavy line in Fig. 8.7 corresponds to the pass band of the amplifier.

In examining the admittance Y_1 in Eq. 8.30, it is profitable to focus attention on the impedance $Z_2 = 1/Y_2$. The locus of this impedance as a function of frequency in the complex plane is the inverse of the locus of Y_2, and it takes the form of a circle like the one shown in Fig. 8.8. The fact that the straight line in Fig. 8.7

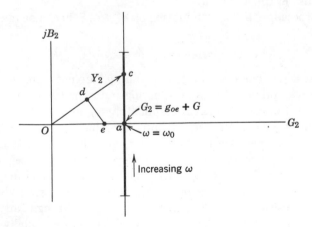

Fig. 8.7. Locus of $Y_2(\omega)$ in the complex plane.

inverts into a circle is established by a simple geometric proof as follows. The inverse of Y_2 can be written as

$$Z_2 = |Z_2|e^{j\theta_z} = \frac{1}{Y_2} = \frac{1}{|Y_2|} e^{-j\theta_y} \tag{8.32}$$

Thus the magnitudes of Z_2 and Y_2 are reciprocals, and the angles are equal but opposite in sign. Consider first the magnitudes, and make the following construction as shown in Fig. 8.7. Locate the point e such that $Oe = 1/Oa$. Choose point c anywhere on the locus of Y_2 (other than at point a), and locate point d such that $Oc = 1/Od$. It then follows that

$$\frac{Oe}{Oc} = \frac{Od}{Oa} \tag{8.33}$$

Thus triangles Oac and Ode are similar, and angle Ode is a right angle. From this fact it follows that triangle Ode is inscribed in a semicircle having Oe as its diameter. Since point c was chosen arbitrarily on the locus of Y_2, it is clear that all points on the locus of Y_2 invert into points on the circle having Oe as its diameter. Now, to satisfy the condition on the angles in Eq. 8.32, it is merely necessary to interchange the upper and lower semicircles; the result is the circular locus in Fig. 8.8. The radius of this circle is $1/2(g_{oe} + G)$. The portion of the circle shown as a heavy line corresponds to the pass band of the amplifier.

To proceed with the examination of Y_1, Eq. 8.30 can be rewritten as

$$Y_1 = -Z_2 y_{fe} y_{re} = -Z_2 |y_{fe} y_{re}| e^{j(\theta_{fe} + \theta_{re})} \tag{8.34}$$

Because the imaginary parts of y_{fe} and y_{re} are not being cancelled by the susceptance of some resonating inductor (this can best be seen from Eq. 8.30) we again assume that y_{fe} and y_{re} are constant over the frequency range of interest; that is, $C'_{fe} = C'_{re} \cong 0$. Therefore, the result of the multiplication in Eq. 8.34 is to change the magnitude and angle of Z_2 by a constant amount at frequencies in the vicinity of ω_0. It follows that the locus of Y_1 as a function of frequency is a circle like the one in Fig. 8.8 but with its size changed and its position rotated about the origin through an angle $\phi = \theta_{fe} + \theta_{re} + 180°$. For typical transistors we usually have $\theta_{re} \cong -90°$, and θ_{fe} usually lies between $0°$ and $-90°$. Thus the

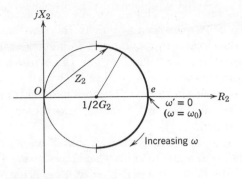

Fig. 8.8. Locus of $Z_2 = 1/Y_2$. $G_2 = g_{oe} + G$.

angle ϕ is usually between $0°$ and $+90°$, and the locus of Y_1 has the form shown in Fig. 8.9. It follows from Eq. 8.34 and from the method of construction that the radius of the circle in Fig. 8.9 is

$$b = \frac{|y_{fo}y_{re}|}{2(g_{oe} + G)} \tag{8.35}$$

The portion of the circle corresponding to the pass band is shown as a heavy line.

It should be noted that the complete circle corresponds to the entire range of frequencies between zero and infinity, whereas the

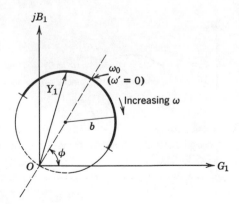

Fig. 8.9. Locus of $Y_1(\omega)$.

transistor parameters y_{fe} and y_{re} can be considered constant only in the range of frequencies in or near the pass band. Therefore, portions of the circle corresponding to frequencies remote from the pass band are shown dotted in Fig. 8.9. In narrow-band amplifiers, the tuned susceptance varies so rapidly with frequency that the range of frequencies in or near the pass band encompasses almost the entire circumference of the circle, and the circle yields much useful information.

The circular locus of Fig. 8.9 shows that Y_1 varies markedly over the pass band of the amplifier. It also shows that with the typical geometry of the figure, the real part of Y_1 is negative over a substantial range of frequencies. Thus there is a definite possibility that Inequality 8.29 may not be met, and that the amplifier may therefore oscillate when certain *passive* elements are added at the input as part of the source impedance.

To continue the graphical interpretation, we note from Fig. 8.6 and Eq. 8.1 that

$$Y_D = G_s + y_{ie} + Y_1$$
$$= G_s + g_{ie} + j\omega_0 C_{ie} + j(\omega - \omega_0)C'_{ie} + Y_1 \qquad (8.36)$$

For preliminary stability calculations, we can consider y_{ie} to be constant in the vicinity of the amplifier pass band. That is, in Eq. 8.36 we will assume $C'_{ie} = 0$. Then the locus of Y_D is obtained by simply adding the complex constant $g_{ie} + G_s + j\omega_0 C_{ie}$ to the locus of Y_1 shown in Fig. 8.9; the result is shown in Fig. 8.10. In

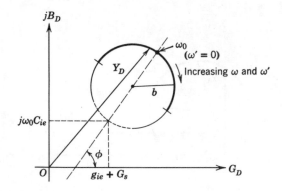

Fig. 8.10. Locus of $Y_D(\omega)$.

terms of this figure, the condition for stability is that the locus of Y_D must never enter the left half plane. From Fig. 8.9, we see that the maximum negative value of $\text{Re}[Y_1]$ is

$$\text{Re}[Y_1]_{\text{max neg}} = b \cos \phi - b \tag{8.37}$$

Therefore, the condition for stability, Inequality 8.29, can be rewritten as

$$(g_{ie} + G_s + b \cos \phi - b) > 0 \tag{8.38}$$

or, by substituting for b from Eq. 8.35,

$$\left(g_{ie} + G_s - \frac{\text{Re}[y_{fe}y_{re}]}{2(g_{oe} + G)} - \frac{|y_{fe}y_{re}|}{2(g_{oe} + G)} \right) > 0 \tag{8.39}$$

or

$$\{2(g_{ie} + G_s)(g_{oe} + G) - \text{Re}[y_{fe}y_{re}] - |y_{fe}y_{re}|\} > 0 \tag{8.39a}$$

It is important to note that the graphical constructions leading to this result tacitly assume $(g_{ie} + G_s) > 0$ and $(g_{oe} + G) > 0$; these conditions are obviously also necessary to insure that the amplifier is stable for all possible input conditions.

It is clear from Inequality 8.39 that the stability of the amplifier can be controlled by the choice of G_s and G (or by the choice of the transformation ratios of the transformers used to couple these elements to the amplifier). Increasing G reduces the radius of the circle as indicated by Fig. 8.11 and Eq. 8.35. Increasing G_s shifts

(b)

Fig. 8.11. The effect of changing G and $|y_{re}|$ on the size of the input admittance circle.

the circle of Fig. 8.11 to the right. Either of these changes can cause the circle to lie entirely in the right half of the complex plane and thereby insure that G_D is never negative.

Alternatively, it is possible to meet the condition of Inequality 8.39 by modifying the circuit of the tuned amplifier so that the apparent magnitude of y_{re} is reduced. Reducing y_{re} decreases the radius of the locus of Y_D as indicated in Fig. 8.11 and Eq. 8.35. If y_{re} is reduced to zero, the radius of the circular locus is zero, and Inequality 8.39 is clearly satisfied because Y_1 is zero. That is, when the magnitude of y_{re} is reduced or made zero, the interaction between the input and output circuits is reduced or eliminated.

8.3.4 *Transistor Stability*

The stability condition presented above (Inequality 8.39) depends on the source and load conductances as well as on the transistor parameters. It is also useful to have a stability condition for the transistor alone, apart from the source and load parameters. Specifically, we want a condition on the transistor parameters which indicates whether or not the transistor at a *given* frequency is stable *for arbitrary passive source and load admittances*. For this purpose we let $G_s = G = 0$ in Inequality 8.39 to obtain

$$\left(g_{ie} - \frac{\text{Re }[y_{fe}y_{re}]}{2g_{oe}} - \frac{|y_{fe}y_{re}|}{2g_{oe}} \right) > 0 \qquad (8.40)$$

Note that we are using the same criterion as before, that is, Inequality 8.39, with $G_s = G = 0$, to discuss the stability of the transistor, but this time at *one* frequency, and *arbitrary* input and output loads. This change of viewpoint is permissible because the tuned load in the previous discussion in effect subjected the transistor to all possible values of susceptance as the frequency changed by a small amount around ω_0. Thus the present condition of fixed frequency and arbitrary load is almost identical to the tuned load case previously discussed.

Inequality 8.40 provides a measure of the inherent instability of the transistor. If the transistor parameters at a given frequency make the quantity in parentheses negative, then the transistor itself is *potentially unstable*, that is, there are some source and load admittances for which self-sustaining oscillations will exist in the circuit. If the parameters are such that the quantity in parentheses is positive at a given frequency, then the transistor itself is *unconditionally stable at that frequency*. In this case the transistor will be stable regardless of the source and load admittances. Again, the geometric constructions leading to these results tacitly assume that g_{ie} and g_{oe} are positive; these conditions are necessary for unconditional stability.

It must be remembered that the transistor parameters are functions of frequency, and it turns out that almost all transistors are potentially unstable in some frequency ranges and unconditionally stable in others. For example, all transistors are unconditionally stable at low frequencies because y_{re} has a small magnitude and a favorable angle at these frequencies. It also turns out that all transistors are unconditionally stable at sufficiently high frequencies, principally because the magnitude of y_{fe} becomes small at these frequencies. Most transistors are potentially unstable, however, in some intermediate range of frequencies, and it is in this frequency range that many tuned amplifiers must operate. operate.

8.3.5 *Illustrative Example*

To illustrate these concepts, let us examine the stability of the amplifier discussed in Sec. 8.1.1. First, using Inequality 8.40, we find for the transistor alone

$$2g_{ie}g_{oe} - \mathrm{Re}\,[y_{fe}y_{re}] - |y_{fe}y_{re}| = (2)(1)(0.15) - 0 - (50)(0.03)$$
$$= -1.2 \text{ mmho}^2$$

Thus this transistor is potentially unstable in the vicinity of 480 kc. Let us now assume that the amplifier is driven by a source with a source admittance $G_s = 0.1$ mmho. From Inequality 8.39,

$$2(g_{ie} + G_s)(g_{oe} + G) - \mathrm{Re}\,[y_{fe}y_{re}] - |y_{fe}y_{re}|$$
$$= (2)(1.1)(1.15) - 0 - (50)(0.03) = 0.59 \text{ mmho}^2$$

Thus the amplifier is stable with these source and load conductances, even if we add an input tuned circuit.

The locus of the admittance Y_D appearing at the input of the amplifier is shown in Fig. 8.12. The numerical values used in con-

Fig. 8.12. Admittance locus for Example 8.3.5.

structing this locus are determined as follows. The radius of the circle is given by Eq. 8.35 as

$$b = \frac{|y_{fe}y_{re}|}{2(g_{oe} + G)} = \frac{(50)(0.03)}{(2)(1.15)} = 0.65 \text{ millimhos}$$

The angle ϕ, shown in Fig. 8.10, is

$$\phi = \theta_{fe} + \theta_{re} + 180° = 90°$$

And finally, since $\phi = 90°$, the bottom of the circle passes through the point

$$G_s + y_{ie} = 1.1 + j0.2 \text{ millimhos}$$

As shown in Fig. 8.12, the real part of the admittance at the input of the amplifier is positive at all frequencies, a fact that is consistent with the stability test above.

8.4 NEUTRALIZATION

The fact is established in Sec. 8.3 that, to obtain an amplifier which is stable for all values of input admittance, it is necessary either to make G_s and G suitably large or to make the apparent magnitude of y_{re} suitably small. The magnitudes of G_s and G can be controlled in a straightforward way by proper choice of the transformers connecting the source and load to the amplifier. Control of the apparent magnitude of y_{re} requires a special circuit configuration, however, and for this reason it needs further discussion.

The process by which circuit elements external to the transistor are used to reduce the apparent magnitude of y_{re} is called *neutralization;* the process has the effect of cancelling part or all of the internal feedback in the transistor. Neutralization thus reduces the radius of the input-admittance locus, as shown in Fig. 8.11, and it can be used to convert an amplifier which would be unstable for certain source admittances to one that is unconditionally stable for all source admittances. One circuit configuration used for neutralization is shown in Fig. 8.13; the neutralizing element is the admittance y_n connected between the input and output terminals external to the transistor. The feedback parameter y'_{re} for the neutralized transistor can be evaluated from Fig. 8.13 by applying a voltage at V_2 and determining the current I_1 that flows in a short circuit at the input terminals. With $V_1 = 0$ there is no current in y_{ie}, and Kirchhoff's current law at the input gives

$$I_1 = y_{re}V_2 - y_n V_2 \tag{8.41}$$

Thus

$$y'_{re} = \frac{I_1}{V_2}\bigg|_{V_1=0} = y_{ro} - y_n \tag{8.42}$$

Thus, to have complete neutralization with $y'_{re} = 0$ and no net feedback, it is necessary to have

$$y_n = y_{re} \tag{8.43}$$

With this adjustment the transistor is equivalent to an unneutralized transistor with $y_{re} = 0$; thus the voltages and currents in the input circuit are independent of the output circuit, no negative resistance is generated, and the transistor is unconditionally stable.

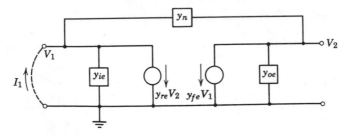

Fig. 8.13. The basic circuit configuration for neutralizing a transistor.

It must be remembered, however, that y_{re} is a function of frequency; thus to have $y'_{re} = 0$ for all frequencies, y_n must have a frequency characteristic that matches the characteristic of y_{re} exactly. Circuits adjusted in this way are said to be *unilateralized*, for there is no transmission of signals in the reverse direction under this condition. As a practical matter, however, it is impossible to match y_n with y_{re} exactly, and in practical circuits we merely try to cancel y_{re} approximately in a suitable band of frequencies encompassing the pass band of the amplifier. Circuits adjusted in this way are said to be *neutralized*.

In the usual case for sinusoidal signals, $y_{re} \cong j\omega C_{re}$ and Eq. 8.43 requires y_n to be a negative susceptance. The use of an inductor for y_n provides a negative susceptance; however, its frequency characteristic does not match that of y_{re} at all well. Thus an inductor cannot provide significant neutralization except in a very narrow band of frequencies, and it is seldom used for this purpose. Figure 8.14 shows a circuit configuration that permits a capacitor to be used as the neutralizing element. The sign reversal provided by the ferrite-core transformer contributes the minus sign needed in y_n. This circuit provides reasonably good neutralization over a suitably wide band of frequencies. If the transformation ratio of the transformer is $a = V_2'/V_2$, then the condition required for complete neutralization is

$$aC_n = C_{re} \tag{8.44}$$

In the analysis and design of neutralized tuned amplifiers it is convenient to lump the neutralizing element y_n in with the transistor and to determine a new set of y-parameters for the neutralized

Fig. 8.14. Practical tuned amplifier with neutralization.

transistor. This is easily done, and for the configuration shown in Fig. 8.13 the composite parameters referred to nodes V_1 and V_2 are

$$y'_{ie} = y_{ie} + y_n \qquad y'_{re} = y_{re} - y_n$$
$$y'_{fe} = y_{fe} - y_n \qquad y'_{oe} = y_{oe} + y_n \tag{8.45}$$

Composite parameters can be evaluated in a similar manner for other neutralizing configurations, and the results are similar in form to Eqs. 8.45. It is useful to note that if y_n is purely imaginary, as it often is in practice, it does not affect the real parts of the composite parameters.

Neutralization is not a completely satisfactory solution to the problem of stability in tuned amplifiers. For example, it requires a fairly careful adjustment of y_n if good performance is to be obtained, and this fact creates problems in assembly-line production. Moreover, the transistor parameters are functions of temperature and of the quiescent operating point. Thus, if the temperature changes or if the operating point is changed (to obtain automatic gain control, for example), the effectiveness of the neutralization may be destroyed. Therefore, in many cases it is desirable to leave the transistor unneutralized and to solve the stability problem by using suitably large values of load and source conductance, as discussed in Sec. 8.3, even though this latter procedure usually results in somewhat less gain than can be obtained with a neutralized amplifier having the same margin of stability. The usual engineering decision is to avoid neutralization unless the gain sacrificed in the alternative design is too great. A further study of the gain of the amplifier in Sec. 8.5 sheds additional light on these matters.

8.5 POWER GAIN OF TUNED AMPLIFIERS

We began this chapter by calculating the voltage gain of a tuned amplifier under the conditions of zero source resistance. Next, we calculated the transfer function V_2/I_s. Finally, we found the amount of added shunt input and output conductance or neutralization needed to insure stable operation. It is therefore reasonable to ask at this point: After these adjustments have been made, does the amplifier still have any gain?

The discussion of this question of gain is somewhat complicated by the transformers used in many tuned amplifier designs to couple the source and load to the transistor. These transformers change the current and voltage levels, and thus add annoying complications to the expressions for the current and voltage gains of the amplifier. On the other hand, lossless transformers do not change the power level. It is therefore usually simpler to work with the power gain when lossless transformers are present. We will now examine the power relations in the tuned amplifier and develop the expression for the power gain, in order to determine whether or not the amplifier is in fact increasing the signal power.

The small-signal model for a tuned amplifier is shown in Fig. 8.15. If the transistor is neutralized, the y-parameters shown are composite parameters including the effect of the neutralizing element as in Eqs. 8.45. If the actual load admittance is coupled to the amplifier through an impedance-transforming network, as is often the case, then Y_L is the load admittance referred to the primary side of the transformer.

To calculate the input power to the amplifier, we first recall that the current source $y_{re}V_2$ in Fig. 8.15 is equivalent to an admittance Y_1 shown in Fig. 8.6 and given by Eq. 8.26 as

$$Y_1 = - \frac{y_{fe}y_{re}}{y_{oe} + Y_L} \tag{8.46}$$

Thus, if V_1 is the rms value of the input voltage, the input power to the amplifier is

$$P_i = \text{Re}\,[y_{ie} + Y_1]\,|V_1|^2/2 \tag{8.47}$$

Fig. 8.15. Tuned amplifier.

Since the transformer (if any) coupling the load to the amplifier is assumed to be lossless, the power delivered to Y_L in Fig. 8.15 is the same as the power delivered to the load. Thus, if V_2 is the rms value of the voltage across Y_L, the output power delivered to the load is

$$P_o = \text{Re } [Y_L] \, |V_2|^2/2 \tag{8.48}$$

But also, from Fig. 8.15,

$$|V_2| = \frac{|y_{fe}| \, |V_1|}{|y_{oe} + Y_L|} \tag{8.49}$$

Thus

$$P_o = \frac{|y_{fe}|^2 \text{Re } [Y_L]}{|y_{oe} + Y_L|^2} \, |V_1|^2/2 \tag{8.50}$$

Therefore, the power gain of the amplifier is

$$\frac{P_o}{P_i} \equiv A_p = \frac{|y_{fe}|^2 \text{Re } [Y_L]}{|y_{oe} + Y_L|^2 \text{ Re } [y_{ie} + Y_1]} \tag{8.51}$$

It is helpful to note that the term under the "real-part" sign in the denominator is simply Y_D in Fig. 8.10 with $G_s = 0$.

The transistor parameters in Eq. 8.51 are slowly varying functions of frequency. However, the admittance Y_L, which appears three times in Eq. 8.51 (once implicitly in Y_1 through Eq. 8.46), represents in our particular example a high-Q tuned circuit, and it is not a constant; in fact, it is Y_L that gives the amplifier its band-pass characteristic. Thus the power gain is a function of frequency, and we shall show that for this case it has a maximum near the resonant frequency of the output circuit. The maximum value of the gain, and the frequency at which it occurs, can be determined from Eq. 8.51. However, the calculation is quite cumbersome for the general case, and we will not include it here; instead, we will consider some important special cases for which the calculation can be made easily.*

8.5.1 *Unilateral Case,* $(y_{re} = 0)$

Suppose first that the transistor is completely neutralized so that $y_{re} = 0$, and $Y_1 = 0$. Then, if we assume that the transistor

---

* For a more detailed treatment of the design of tuned-transistor amplifiers, see Linvill and Gibbons, *Transistors and Active Circuits*, Chapters 11 and 18, McGraw-Hill Book Co., New York, 1961.

parameters y_{fe} and y_{ie} are constant in the vicinity of ω_0 (that is, $C'_{fe} = C'_{ie} = 0$), it follows from Eqs. 8.51 and 8.46 that A_p is a maximum when $\omega = \omega_0$, the resonant frequency for $Y_2 = y_{oe} + Y_L$. Thus, for this case, the maximum power gain is

$$A_p(\omega_0)\,\big|_{y_{re}=0} = \frac{|y_{fe}|^2\,G}{g_{ie}(g_{oe} + G)^2} \qquad (8.52)$$

For $y_{re} = 0$, the output conductance of the transistor is simply g_{oe}, and maximum output power is obtained when the load conductance is matched to g_{oe}. Also, in this case, the input power is independent of the load conductance, and matched conductances yield the maximum available unilateral gain. From Eq. 8.52 with $G = g_{oe}$ this gain is

$$A_p(\omega_0)\,\Big|_{\substack{G=g_{oe}\\y_{re}=0}} = \frac{|y_{fe}|^2}{4g_{ie}g_{oe}} \qquad (8.53)$$

It is usually possible to obtain more gain than this from the transistor by leaving it partially or altogether unneutralized; however, the maximum available unilateralized power gain is a useful figure of merit for the transistor. Designs giving substantially greater gain than this usually have small margins of stability, and they are quite sensitive to variations in the circuit parameters; these facts are implied by the circle diagrams of Fig. 8.11. Thus Eq. 8.53 gives a useful indication of the power gain that can be obtained from the transistor in a practical tuned amplifier having reliable performance characteristics.

8.5.2 *Case Where Y_1 Is Small (G Large)*

It is pointed out at the end of Sec. 8.4 that there are some practical problems associated with neutralizing transistor amplifiers, and for that reason we often choose to insure amplifier stability by making G large. This choice precludes the possibility of matching conductances, and usually results in an amplifier giving somewhat less gain than the maximum that could be achieved with matched conductances. To examine the gain relations existing in this case it is convenient to define a *mismatch factor*

$$m = \frac{G}{g_{oe}} \qquad (8.54)$$

With this definition, the power gain at ω_0 is, from Eq. 8.51,

$$A_p(\omega_0) = \frac{m|y_{fe}|^2}{g_{ie}g_{oe}(1 + m)^2 - \text{Re}\,[y_{fe}y_{re}(1 + m)]} \qquad (8.55)$$

When the margin of stability in the amplifier is small, the two terms in the denominator of Eq. 8.55 nearly cancel at some frequency near ω_0, and the gain is large. It is clear, however, that small changes in the transistor parameters will cause large variations in the gain, and such a design is not suitable for most applications. When amplifier stability is provided by making y_{re} small, the "real-part" term in Eq. 8.55 is reduced, and if $y_{re} = 0$, the maximum unilateral gain (Eq. 8.53) can be obtained. When stability is obtained by making the load conductance large, the first term in the denominator of Eq. 8.55 becomes large compared to the second, and the entire denominator becomes fairly large, giving a relatively low gain. In a typical amplifier that is stabilized by mismatching, the gain obtained may be less than the maximum unilateral power gain by a substantial factor.

One of the first steps in the design of a tuned amplifier is to choose the mismatch factor m, and for this purpose it is useful to recall the admittance circle in Fig. 8.10. The radius of this circle is given by Eq. 8.35, and it can be expressed in terms of the mismatch factor as

$$b = \frac{|y_{fe}y_{re}|}{2g_{oe}(1 + m)} \qquad (8.56)$$

The value of m must be chosen to give a radius that makes the circle lie entirely in the right half of the complex plane with a suitable margin of safety. What constitutes a "suitable" margin of safety is a matter of engineering judgment to be decided for each different tuned-amplifier application. This matter is discussed further in connection with multistage amplifiers in MTC.

When an amplifier is to be designed with mismatched conductances to achieve a suitable margin of stability, it is important to have some estimate of how much gain is sacrificed in the process. If an amplifier is designed to have a gain significantly greater than the maximum unilateral gain, Eq. 8.53, then for reasons pointed out above the performance of the amplifier becomes rather sensitive to small changes in the circuit parameters. Therefore, we take Eq. 8.53, which depends only on the transistor parameters, as an indication of the maximum gain that can be obtained in a reliable amplifier. To estimate the gain sacrificed by mismatching, we thus form the ratio of Eq. 8.55 the gain with mismatching, to Eq. 8.53, the gain under matched unilateral conditions,

$$\frac{A_p(\omega_0)}{A_p(\omega_0)\Big|_{\substack{G=g_{oe} \\ y_{re}=0}}} = \frac{4m}{(1+m)^2 - \mathrm{Re}\left[\dfrac{y_{fe}y_{re}(1+m)}{g_{ie}g_{oe}}\right]} \tag{8.57}$$

8.5.3 *Illustrative Example*

Let us illustrate some of these ideas by calculating the power relations for the amplifier discussed in Sec. 8.1.1. Recall that at the center frequency of 480 kc, the transistor parameters in millimhos are

$$y_{ie} = 1.0 + j0.2 \qquad y_{re} = -j0.03$$

$$y_{fe} = 50 \qquad y_{oe} = 0.15 + j0.15$$

The maximum unilateral gain for this transistor is, from Eq. 8.53,

$$A_p(\omega_0)\Big|_{\substack{G=g_{oe} \\ y_{re}=0}} = \frac{50^2}{(4)(1.0)(0.15)} = 4170 = 36 \, \mathrm{db}$$

In principle, if the transistor were completely neutralized, and if the load conductance were matched to g_{oe}, the amplifier could provide this much gain.

The mismatch factor in this amplifier is

$$m = \frac{G}{g_{oe}} = \frac{1}{0.15} = 6.67$$

It can be seen from the example worked in Sec. 8.3.5 that if we match conductances to make $m = 1$, this amplifier will be unstable for certain source admittances. However, with $m = 6.67$ the amplifier is unconditionally stable with a fair margin of safety (see Fig. 8.12). We estimate the sacrifice in gain because of the mismatch to be, from Eq. 8.57

$$\frac{(4)(6.67)}{(7.67)^2} = 0.45$$

Thus the actual power gain at $\omega = \omega_0$ is

$$G_p(\omega_0) = (4170)(0.45) \cong 1900 \cong 33 \text{ db}$$

8.5.4 *Case Where Transistor Is Unconditionally Stable*

If the transistor is operating in a frequency range where it is unconditionally stable, (see Sec. 8.3.4), it is possible to adjust the load conductance for maximum power gain without ever obtaining an unstable amplifier. In this case, however, the gain is a complicated function of G (see Eq. 8.55) and to determine the value of G that maximizes the power gain is not a simple matter. It turns out, however, that $G = g_{oe}$ is within 3 db of the true maximum value,* and with this adjustment Eq. 8.55 yields

$$A_p(\omega_0)\,|_{G=g_{oe}} = \frac{|y_{fe}|^2}{4g_{ie}g_{oe} - 2\text{Re}\,[y_{fe}y_{re}]} \qquad (8.58)$$

8.5.5 *Maximum Frequency of Operation*

Although the admittance parameters of the transistor can be treated as constants in the narrow pass band of the tuned amplifier, in general they are functions of frequency. It turns out that as the center frequency of the pass band is increased, the parameters change in such a way that the gain that can be obtained decreases. It is of importance, therefore, to determine the maximum frequency at which it is possible to obtain any power gain at all. For this purpose we first find the y-parameters as a function of frequency from the hybrid-π model complete with extrinsic capacitance, Fig. 8.16. The data of Fig. 3.16 clearly justifies this procedure. The admittance parameters for the transistor under sinusoidal operating conditions at very high frequencies can be evaluated from this model by inspection if we assume that both r_x and r_π are much larger than $1/\omega C_\pi$. Then

$$g_{ie} \cong 1/r_x \qquad (8.59)$$

$$g_{oe} \cong g_m \frac{C_\mu}{C_\pi + C_\mu} = \omega_T C_\mu \qquad (8.60)$$

$$y_{re} = -\left[\frac{C_\mu g_x}{(C_\pi + C_\mu)} + j\omega C_{bc} \right] \qquad (8.61)$$

*Linvill: loc cit.

Fig. 8.16. Hybrid-π model. For ω near ω_T, r_π can be neglected.

Finally, neglecting the forward currents through C_μ and C_{bc} in comparison with $g_m V$,

$$y_{fe} \cong g_m \frac{1}{r_x} \frac{1}{j\omega(C_\pi + C_\mu)} = \frac{\omega_T}{j\omega r_x} \tag{8.62}$$

When the center frequency ω_0 of the pass band of the tuned amplifier is located at very high frequencies where Eqs. 8.59 to 8.62 apply, then Eq. 8.53 for the maximum unilateral gain yields

$$A_p(\omega_0) \Big|_{\substack{G=g_{oe} \\ y_{re}=0}} = \frac{(\omega_T/\omega_0 r_x)^2}{4\omega_T C_\mu/r_x}$$

$$= \frac{\omega_T}{4\omega_0^2 r_x C_\mu} \tag{8.63}$$

Next, we calculate the gain for $G = g_{oe}$, but without neutralization, using Eq. 8.58, on the basis that the transistor will be unconditionally stable in this frequency range. From Eqs. 8.61 and 8.62,

$$\text{Re } [y_{fe}y_{re}] = \frac{-\omega_T C_{bc}}{r_x} \tag{8.64}$$

Because this is negative, the power gain expression of Eq. 8.58 is bound to be less than the maximum unilateral gain, Eq. 8.63. Thus Eq. 8.63 represents the maximum gain obtainable at these frequencies. The center frequency at which the gain in Eq. 8.63 is unity, designated as ω_{max}, is therefore

$$\omega_{\text{max}} = \sqrt{\omega_T/4r_x C_\mu} \tag{8.65}$$

The frequency ω_{max} is sometimes used as a figure of merit for transistors; it is usually close to ω_T.

It follows from Eqs. 8.63 and 8.65 that the maximum unilateral gain can be written as $\omega^2_{max}/\omega_0^2$ for the range of high frequencies in which the model of Fig. 8.16 and our other approximations apply. Thus the maximum unilateral gain increases as $1/\omega_0^2$ as the center frequency ω_0 is reduced below ω_{max}, within the range of validity of our approximations.

PROBLEMS

P8.1 A narrow-band tuned amplifier having the form shown in Fig. 8.2 is to operate at a center frequency of 50 mc/sec with $V_{CE} = 10$ volts and $I_C = 1$ ma. The admittance parameters for the transistor are given by the curves of Fig. 3.16. The input signal is obtained from a low-impedance source that can be treated as a voltage source, and the output of the amplifier is to be delivered to a load resistor $R = 1/G$ = 250 ohms. The amplifier is to be designed for the center frequency specified above and for a half-power bandwidth of 5 mc.

(a) Obtain the y-parameters from the curves in Fig. 3.16 and determine the values of the capacitors C_{ie} and C_{oe} associated with them at a frequency of 50 mc. Also determine the values of C'_{ie} and C'_{oe}, defined as in Eqs. 8.2, and 8.4.

(b) Determine the values of tuning inductance and capacitance that must be connected across the output of the transistor to obtain the center frequency and bandwidth specified above, and determine the voltage gain at resonance, $| V_2/V_1 | = A_0$.

(c) Now suppose that a new source of signals, having an internal resistance $R_s = 1/G_s = 150$ ohms, is connected to the amplifier. Determine the new center frequency and half-power bandwidth in mc. *Suggestion:* Convert the signal source to a current source in parallel with G_s, lump G_s with g_{ie}, and find a Norton equivalent circuit at the output, as in Fig. 8.5b..

P8.2 At the frequency ω_1 the parameters of the transistor and load in Fig. 8.17 are:

$$y_{ie} = 1 \text{ millimho} \qquad y_{fe} = 5\underline{/-\pi/4} \text{ millimho}$$

$$-y_{re} = 0.1 \underline{/\pi/2} \text{ millimho} \qquad Y_L + y_{oe} = \frac{\sqrt{2}}{10}\underline{/-\pi/2} \text{ millimho}$$

(inductive load)

(a) Determine the input admittance of the amplifier $Y_1 = I_1/V_1$ at the frequency ω_1.

Fig. 8.17.

(b) State the condition on Y_s that will insure stability of the amplifier, and determine the range of values of Y_s for which this amplifier will be stable at ω_1.

P8.3   A certain tuned amplifier has its center frequency at 50 mc, and it uses the transistor for which the admittance parameters are given in Fig. 3.16 with $V_{CE} = 10$ volts and $I_C = 1$ ma. The load resistance is $R = 1/G = 250$ ohms, and the input signal is obtained from a high-impedance source that can be treated as a current source, $Y_s = 0$.

(a) Obtain the admittance parameters from Fig. 3.16, and check for possible stability problems, using Inequalities 8.39 and 8.40. Comment on the possibilities for instability.

(b) Determine the dimensions of the admittance diagram for Y_D (Fig. 8.10). Sketch the admittance diagram approximately to scale, and show the dimensions. Indicate the portion of the diagram corresponding to the pass band of the amplifier, and indicate the frequency ω_0.

(c) From the diagram part of (b) estimate the maximum and minimum $|Y_D|$ in the pass band.

P8.4   A neutralized tuned amplifier operating at a center frequency of 480 kc has the form shown in Fig. 8.14 with a = 2 and $G' = 0.25$ millimhos. The transistor parameters at the center frequency are given below.

y-parameter	g	C	C'
y_{ie}	1 mmho	67 pf	50 pf
y_{fe}	50	0	0
y_{re}	0	−10	−10
y_{oe}	0.15	50	25

(a) What value of C_n is required to neutralize the transistor completely?

(b) In mass production, C_{re} may vary as much as ±5 pf from the nominal value of −10 pf. Note that because y_{re} is essentially capacitive, C_{re} and C'_{re} are equal in value. Assuming that $G_s = 0$

and that C_n has the value of part (a), sketch the admittance diagram for Y_D (Fig. 8.11) for the two extreme cases and for the case in which C_{re} has the nominal value. Note that since y_{re} is purely imaginary, C_n does not affect the real parts of the y-parameters.

P8.5   The transistor of Problem P8.4 is to be used in an amplifier like the one shown in Fig. 8.15 with a center frequency of 480 kc. The parameters of the transistor at this frequency are given in P8.4. To provide a good margin of stability and to obtain small interaction between the input and output circuits, the load conductance G is to be chosen so that G_D (Fig. 8.10) does not vary more than plus or minus 20% over the pass band of the amplifier. The source of signals at the input can be treated as a current source.

(a) Determine the minimum value of G that can be used to meet the specification given above. *Suggestion:* Sketch the admittance locus for Y_D.

(b) For the conductance of part (a), find the mismatch factor m, the maximum unilateralized power gain, and the power gain, Eq. 8.55.

P8.6   In calculating the stability of the amplifier in Section 8.3.3, we assumed for convenience that $C_{ie}' = 0$. By means of Fig. 8.10 show the effect on the stability calculations of including C_{ie}'.

9

Dynamic Behavior
of Transistor Switches

9.0 INTRODUCTION

In this chapter we are concerned with the dynamic behavior of the transistor as it undergoes a transient process of transition from one dc steady state to another. The operation of the transistor as a switch was discussed in Chapter 2, where its properties in the *cutoff* and *saturation* states were examined. Here we shall be interested mainly in processes of switching between these extreme operating states, and especially in the conditions for rapid switching.

Dynamic analysis of the transistor in switching operation is based on the characterization of the device in terms of *stored charges*. The essential ideas behind such a characterization have been introduced in Chapter 1, and it will be assumed here that the fundamental definitions and relationships are understood. The discussion will, however, be simplified initially by considering only the stored minority-carrier charge in the base region; the stored charges associated with the junction space-charge regions are taken into consideration at a later stage after a number of important results have been established. A further simplification is to neglect small effects associated with transverse voltage drops. That is, throughout the discussion terminal and junction voltages are considered to be equal.

Throughout most of the chapter, simple forms of base drive in the form of step changes of base current, are considered. Although in practice close approximations to such conditions are often employed, they do not result in the most rapid processes of switching. More efficient forms of base drive, from the point of view of switching speed, are also indicated during the course of the chapter and are given particular consideration at the end.

A *pnp* transistor is used as a vehicle of discussion throughout, though with no implied restriction to this type of structure. Also, only the normal configuration is treated; the same approach is equally applicable to the inverted configuration with obvious modifications of notation.

The definitions of variables used are the same as in Chapter 1. Terminal voltages and currents are defined as in Fig. 1.8a, as far as polarities are concerned, while charge variables follow the notation developed in Sec. 1.4.2. Total instantaneous quantities are used throughout this discussion.

9.1 CHARGE CONTROL RELATIONSHIPS: NEUTRAL BASE REGION ONLY

To establish essential relationships it is simplest first to consider only forward injection from the emitter; viz., voltage v_{EB} across the emitter-base junction positive and collector-base junction voltage $v_{CB} = 0$. An excess "forward" minority-carrier charge (hole charge) q_F is set up in the neutral base region, as illustrated in Fig. 9.1a and is balanced by an equal charge $(-q_F)$ of excess majority carriers (electrons). Under dc steady-state conditions, flow of base current supplies the electrons to the base necessary to maintain the stored charge in presence of recombination processes. When the charge q_F in the base varies, during transient behavior, the base current also includes a charging component. These properties are expressed by the following *charge control* relation:

$$i_B = \frac{(-q_F)}{\tau_{BF}} + \frac{d(-q_F)}{dt} \qquad (9.1)$$

The stored forward charge defines the collector current via a second charge control relation:

$$i_C = \frac{-q_F}{\tau_F} \qquad (9.2)$$

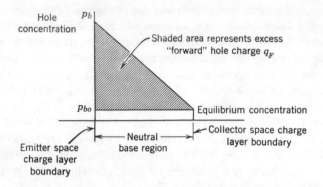

(a) Forward injection only
$$v_{EB} > 0, \ v_{CB} = 0$$

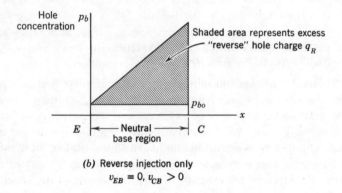

(b) Reverse injection only
$$v_{EB} = 0, \ v_{CB} > 0$$

Fig. 9.1. Components of excess minority-carrier charge set up in the base by forward and reverse injection. The case of a uniform-base *pnp* transistor is shown.

Expression in terms of the charge $(-q_F)$ is adopted in these equations to emphasize the connection between base current and *majority*-carrier charge in the base region. The parameter τ_{BF} is termed the *effective lifetime* of the excess stored charge. For practical transient switching processes, the dc steady-state relationship of Eq. 9.2 applies if the variation of q_F is sufficiently slow for the situation to be regarded effectively as one of a "progression of near-dc-steady-states." (See Chapter 1, Sec. 1.4.2, for further discussion of this property.*) In the dc steady state for *forward* operation of the transistor, the current gain is

$$\beta_F = \frac{i_C}{i_B}\bigg|_{v_{CB} = 0;\ i_B,\ i_C\ \text{constant}} = \frac{\tau_{BF}}{\tau_F} \qquad (9.3)$$

Similarly, as illustrated in Fig. 9.1*b*, for reverse operation of the transistor ($v_{CB} > 0$, $v_{EB} = 0$), the terminal base and emitter currents are defined in terms of a "reverse" excess minority-carrier charge q_R, injected by the collector, balanced by an equal excess majority carrier charge ($-q_R$):

$$i_B = \frac{(-q_R)}{\tau_{BR}} + \frac{d(-q_R)}{dt} \qquad (9.4)$$

$$i_E = \frac{(-q_R)}{\tau_R} \qquad (9.5)$$

The corresponding pairs of parameters τ_{BF}, τ_{BR}, and τ_F, τ_R are, in general, not equal. That is, τ_{BF} does not equal τ_{BR} and $\tau_F \neq \tau_R$, because of departure from structural symmetry of the device. Thus the reverse current gain in the dc steady state is

$$\beta_R = \frac{i_E}{i_B}\bigg|_{v_{EB} = 0;\ i_E,\ i_B\ \text{constant}} = \frac{\tau_{BR}}{\tau_R} \qquad (9.6)$$

which is not necessarily equal to β_F. As an illustration of the above properties, values of the various parameters for a representative alloy junction transistor are

$$\tau_F = 12 \times 10^{-9}\ \text{sec} \qquad \tau_{BF} = 1.2 \times 10^{-6}\ \text{sec} \qquad \beta_F = 100$$

$$\tau_R = 36 \times 10^{-9}\ \text{sec} \qquad \tau_{BR} = 0.36 \times 10^{-6}\ \text{sec} \qquad \beta_R = 10$$

In general, operation of the transistor with both junction voltages nonzero causes forward *and* reverse components of stored charge q_F, q_R to be set up. The total stored charge of excess minority carriers is the superposition of these two components.

$$q_B = q_F + q_R \qquad (9.7)$$

---

* A more detailed treatment of the concepts of charge control is given in PEM, Chapter 10.

The forward and reverse components of the terminal currents similarly add, giving

$$i_B = \frac{-q_F}{\tau_{BF}} - \frac{dq_F}{dt} \qquad\qquad - \frac{q_R}{\tau_{BR}} - \frac{dq_R}{dt}$$

$$i_C = \frac{-q_F}{\tau_F} \qquad\qquad + q_R\left(\frac{1}{\tau_R} + \frac{1}{\tau_{BR}}\right) + \frac{dq_R}{dt} \quad (9.8)$$

$$i_E = q_F\left(\frac{1}{\tau_F} + \frac{1}{\tau_{BF}}\right) + \frac{dq_F}{dt} \qquad\qquad - \frac{q_R}{\tau_R}$$

These are the complete *charge-control* relations of the transistor.

When operating in a switching role, the transistor is usually arranged in the common-emitter configuration and switched between the extremes of the *cut-off* and *saturation* states. In the cut-off state both the emitter and collector junctions are reverse-biased, and the corresponding components q_F, q_R of stored charge are *negative*. In the saturation state, both junctions are forward-biased; q_F, q_R are both positive.

To accomplish switching between these states, the *active* region of operation (emitter junction forward-biased, collector junction reverse-biased) must be traversed; q_F is therefore *positive* and q_R *negative* in this region. So great is the concentration of excess minority carriers corresponding to q_F, compared with the equilibrium concentration in the base (for v_{EB}, $v_{CB} = 0$), that $q_F \gg |q_R|$ in the active region, and thus the reverse charge may be neglected. At the most, q_R corresponds to a reduction of minority-carrier concentration from the equilibrium value to zero. For active-region operation, we therefore let $q_R = 0$ in Eqs. 9.8, effectively reducing the problem to one of forward operation only.

When analyzing transient behavior it is therefore necessary to consider both q_F and q_R when dealing with operation in the saturation state (when both v_{EB}, $v_{CB} > 0$), but only q_F during traverse of the active region. In the cut-off state, q_F and q_R are comparable in magnitude but are very small and are in fact negligible compared with the stored charges associated with the space-charge regions of the junctions (discussed in Sec. 9.4.)

9.2 TRANSIENT BEHAVIOR IN THE ACTIVE REGION

The transient response of the transistor in the active region of operation may be evaluated in terms of Eqs. 9.1 and 9.2. Only the forward charge q_F needs to be considered, as just explained. It will be seen later that the effects of stored charges in the junction space-charge layers may be included in an approximate fashion without changing the form of the charge-control equations, so that the following discussion is not as restricted as the initial limitation of the neglect of such charges might suggest. Two switching situations are examined. The first is the common situation of response to a step change of base current. The second concerns a technique for greatly increasing the transient switching speed and, of equal importance, for determining the values of the parameters τ_F, τ_{BF} by practical measurement.

9.2.1 Response to Step Change of Base Current

The circuit to be discussed is the simple common-emitter configuration shown in Fig. 9.2a. We will assume that the external base resistor R_B is so large that a change of input voltage v_s results in a step change $(-\Delta I)$ of base current, and that the transistor operates in the active region. If the initial values of currents and base charge are $i_B(0)$, $i_C(0)$, $q_F(0)$, solution of Eq. 9.1 gives the following result for the transient behavior of the stored charge:

$$q_F = q_F(0) + \Delta I \tau_{BF}(1 - e^{-t/\tau_{BF}}) \qquad (9.9)$$

Equation 9.2 gives a similar time dependence for i_C because of the simple proportionality between stored charge and collector current:

$$i_C = i_C(0) - \beta_F \Delta I(1 - e^{-t/\tau_{BF}}) \qquad (9.10)$$

These properties are illustrated in Fig. 9.2b; the exponential transients in the figure have a time constant equal to the "effective base lifetime" τ_{BF}.

The rise time t_r of the collector current, measured between the points of 10% and 90% of the total excursion, is found from Eq. 9.10 to be

$$t_r = 2.2\tau_{BF} \qquad (9.11)$$

Note that in a time $\tau_F = \tau_{BF}/\beta_F$, the collector current changes by such a small fraction of the exponential transient that its time

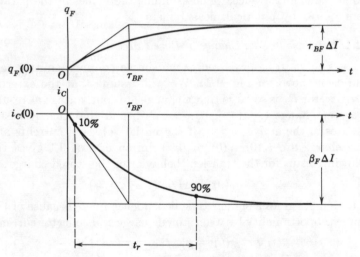

(a) Common-emitter switch.

(b) Response of q_F and i_C to step change $(-\Delta I)$ of base current.

Fig. 9.2. Response of common-emitter switch to step change of base current (active region operation).

dependence is almost linear (that is, follows closely an initial linear approximation to the exponential, as if to complete a total change $\beta_F \Delta I$ in the time τ_{BF}) as illustrated in Fig. 9.2b. Thus, after a time τ_F, the collector current changes by $(-\Delta I)$, equal to the applied change in base current.

By inserting the transistor parameters quoted earlier, we find that the response of q_F or i_C exhibits the relatively large time constant of 1.2 μsec., and the 10% to 90% rise time is 2.64 μsec. The collector current i_C changes by the amount of the applied base current step, however, in only 0.012 μsec.

We can obtain a shorter collector current rise time than the above by increasing the step change in base current, so that the transistor saturates before the collector current transient goes to completion. This is illustrated in Fig. 9.3, where the base current step has been adjusted so that $\beta_F \Delta I$ is greater than the maximum possible collector current excursion. Then when the transistor enters the saturation region, $v_{CE} \cong 0$ and the collector current is limited at the value $i_C \cong -V_{CC}/R_C$, a value defined entirely by the external circuit. In Fig. 9.3 $i_B(0)$, $i_C(0)$, $q_F(0) = 0$. Thus, if $\beta_F \Delta I > V_{CC}/R_C$, the collector current is "clamped" at $-V_{CC}/R_C$ before the exponential transient across the active region is completed. The 10% to 90% rise time can evidently be reduced to values much less than $2.2\tau_{BF}$ by this means. A more detailed dis-

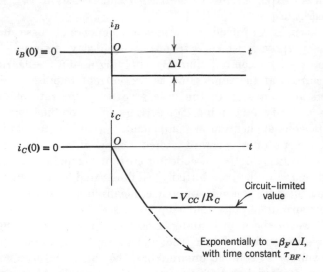

Fig. 9.3. Response of the common-emitter switch with a base current step sufficiently large for collector current to be limited by the external circuit before completing an exponential transient.

cussion of such switching operation of the transistor is given in Sec. 9.3.

9.2.2 *Response to Combined Step Changes of Base Charge and Current*

According to Eq. 9.2, if the base charge q_F is suddenly changed in value, the collector current also undergoes a step change. Although the charge-control relation is an oversimplification of the dynamic behavior of the transistor for such an input, the collector current does, in fact, change very rapidly (in a time appreciably less than τ_{BF}) to the new value. Figure 9.4 shows a transistor switch to which are applied simultaneously two components, i_{B1} and i_{B2}, of base current. Initially, let us consider the application of only i_{B1}, a current impulse of charge area $-\Delta Q$. Assuming the base to be initially uncharged, the collector current correspondingly undergoes a change from approximately zero to $-\Delta Q/\tau_F$. The collector current will not remain constant at this value, however. Because of recombination the stored charge, and hence the collector current, will decay exponentially to zero with time constant τ_{BF}, as expressed by Eq. 9.1.

At this point we introduce the second component of base current, i_{B2}, the purpose of which is to *prevent* the decay of stored charge in the base by recombination. By applying a step $(-\Delta Q/\tau_{BF})$ of base current at the same time as the current impulse, majority carriers are delivered to the base at exactly the rate of loss of excess majority (and minority) carriers by recombination. Thus simultaneous application of components i_{B1} and i_{B2} results in the establishment of a constant stored charge in the base, and a constant value $-\Delta Q/\tau_F$ of collector current (again, assuming zero stored charge in the base initially) as illustrated in the figure.

The above discussion is, of course, idealized in that we assumed perfect current impulse and step sources. These current sources can, however, be approximated closely in practice by using the circuit arrangement of Fig. 9.5a. If the step change $-\Delta V$ in the input voltage v_S is much greater than the change in base voltage between the initial and final dc states (for example, $\Delta V =$ several volts), then the charge on the capacitor C changes by $\Delta Q = C\Delta V$ and a charge $-\Delta Q$ of majority carriers is delivered to the base of the transistor. The base resistor R_B also supplies a step change of

Fig. 9.4. Collector current response of the transistor to simultaneous application of an impulse and step of base current.

base current, and the form of the collector current response depends on the relative magnitudes of the step changes of base charge and base current. Assuming the base region to be uncharged initially as in the preceding discussion (that is, v_S initially zero), to realize a step change in collector current it is necessary for the base current established to be equal to $-\Delta Q/\tau_{BF}$, or

$$-\frac{\Delta V}{R_B} = -\frac{(\Delta V)C}{\tau_{BF}}$$

giving

$$\tau_{BF} = R_B C$$

(9.12)

(a) Common-emitter switch with RC base drive circuit

(b) Collector current response waveforms

Fig. 9.5. Response of common-emitter switch to practical drive conditions capable of establishing a step change of base charge.

It is not actually necessary for the base to be uncharged initially. In general, if v_S changes from some initial value, the stored charge in the base is simply made to undergo a step change, with corresponding step changes of collector current—or voltage—if the condition of Eq. 9.12 is satisfied. The effect of departure from the condition of Eq. 9.12 is illustrated in the collector current waveforms of Fig. 9.5b: too large a value of the time constant R_BC corresponds to an insufficient steady flow of majority carriers to the base to supply the needs of recombination of charge established by the current impulse, and the increment of stored charge decays with time. Conversely, if R_BC is smaller than τ_{BF}, the stored charge increases with time until equilibrium is established.

By comparing the magnitude of the change in collector voltage with that in v_S, the value of the other "forward" charge control parameter, τ_F, may be determined: thus

$$\frac{|\text{Change in } v_{CE}|}{|\text{Change in } v_S|} = \frac{(C\Delta V/\tau_F)R_C}{\Delta V}$$

$$= \frac{CR_C}{\tau_F} = \left(\frac{R_C}{R_B}\right)\left(\frac{\tau_{BF}}{\tau_F}\right) \tag{9.13}$$

Measurements of this type, in which the time constant of a base drive circuit is adjusted for a step response of collector current or voltage, are commonly used for the determination of τ_{BF} and τ_F, or for corresponding parameters that include the effects of charge storage in the junction space-charge layers in an actual transistor.

9.3 SWITCHING INTO AND OUT OF THE SATURATION STATE

As pointed out in the discussion of Sec. 9.2.1 in connection with the simple transistor circuit of Fig. 9.2, the rise time of collector current or voltage in response to a step change of base current may be reduced if the transistor enters the saturation state before the full amplified base current is developed at the collector terminal. We shall now study this situation in more detail. Assume that the transistor is switched into saturation from an initial *cut-off* state of effectively zero collector current. Again, only the storage of charge in the base region will be considered at this time.

9.3.1 *Switching from Cut-Off to Saturation (Turn-On)*

As in the discussion of Sec. 9.2.1, the initial state of the common-emitter switch shown in Fig. 9.6a is v_S, i_B, $i_C \cong 0$ and $v_{CE} \cong -V_{cc}$. That is, we neglect the flow of reverse collector current in the cut-off state, a reasonable procedure because the collector current during the switching process will be of much greater value. At $t = 0$, the source voltage undergoes a step change $(-\Delta V)$, and the base current I_{B1} is established, where we assume

$$|I_{B1}| > \frac{V_{CC}}{R_C} \cdot \frac{1}{\beta_F} \tag{9.14}$$

(a) Common-emitter switch with step base circuit drive.

(b) Current response waveforms.

(c) Response waveforms of stored charges

Fig. 9.6. Response of common-emitter switch when driven from cut-off to saturation with a step drive of base current.

to insure saturation. While making the "turn-on" transition from cut-off to saturation, the collector current response is as given by Eq. 9.10 with $i_C(0) = 0$, namely

$$i_C = \beta_F I_{B1}(1 - e^{-t/\tau_{BF}}) \qquad (9.15)$$

The transistor enters the saturation region when $v_{CB} = 0$. At this instant, v_{CE} is small (for example, -0.3 volt for a germanium device), and almost immediately afterwards v_{CE} becomes the nearly zero value of the saturation state. It is reasonable, therefore, to regard the active region transient as terminating when $v_{CE} \cong 0$, or when

$$i_C = -V_{CC}/R_C = I_C \qquad (9.16)$$

That is, at a time t_1 (Fig. 9.6) the collector current is "clamped" at a *circuit-defined* value I_C given by Eq. 9.16, and Eq. 9.15 for the transient behavior of i_C when switching from cut-off to saturation is valid only for $t \leqq t_1$. Thus we find

$$t_1 = \tau_{BF} \ln \frac{1}{1 - (I_C/\beta_F I_{B1})} \qquad (9.17)$$

by substituting the conditions $t = t_1$, $i_C = I_C$ into Eq. 9.15.

It is worthwhile to express the "turn-on" switching performance of the transistor in terms of an *overdrive factor*. Thus, we define

$$n = \frac{I_{B1}}{(I_C/\beta_F)} = turn\text{-}on\ overdrive\ factor \qquad (9.18)$$

It is seen that, for the transistor to enter the saturation region, it is necessary that $n > 1$. If n is large, only a small portion of the exponential of Eq. 9.15 is used in traversing the active region, and the duration t_1 of the turn-on process is therefore short. From Eq. 9.17,

$$t_1 = \tau_{BF} \ln \frac{1}{1 - (1/n)} \qquad (9.19)$$

The 10% to 90% rise time of collector current or voltage (see Fig. 9.6b) during the turn-on transient is evaluated from Eq. 9.15 as

$$t_r = \tau_{BF} \ln \left[\frac{1 - (0.1/n)}{1 - (0.9/n)} \right] \qquad (9.20)$$

If the turn-on overdrive factor is large $(n \gg 1)$, Eq. 9.20 simplifies to

$$t_r \cong \tau_{BF} \, \frac{0.8}{n} \tag{9.21}$$

For example, with $n = 10$, the rise time given by Eq. 9.20 is $0.085 \, \tau_{BF}$ (Eq. 9.21 gives $t_r \cong 0.08 \, \tau_{BF}$). The advantages of applying an overdrive of base current $(n > 1)$ are quite apparent, and it is clear that rise times much less than τ_{BF} can be realized. In particular, if $n = \beta_F$, t_r is reduced to $0.8 \, \tau_F$.

9.3.2 *Analysis of Behavior in the Saturation Region*

When the transistor enters the saturation region, its transient behavior is not completed even though all terminal currents are effectively constant at circuit-defined values. At the instant of entry into saturation $(v_{CB} = 0)$, the collector junction begins to inject reverse charge q_R into the base, and subsequently both q_F and q_R build up until a steady state is reached, as shown in Fig. 9.6c. Correspondingly, both v_{EB} and v_{CB} increase slightly as the charge injected into the base region rises toward its steady-state value, while v_{CE} falls toward a very small final value (perhaps a few tens of millivolts). In the steady saturation state, the minority-carrier charge stored in the base is of such a value that the base current I_{B1} just replenishes carrier losses from recombination.

For analysis of dynamic behavior in the saturation region, it is convenient to consider the total base charge as comprising two components in the following manner:

$$q_B = q_{B0} + q_S \tag{9.22}$$

where q_{B0} is the charge stored in the base at the point of entry of the saturation region (boundary of active and saturation regions), and q_S is an additional "excess saturation charge." Figure 9.7 illustrates this subdivision of stored charge. Evidently

$$q_{B0} = |I_C| \tau_F \tag{9.23}$$

and is governed by the circuit-defined value of collector current, I_C. The excess stored charge q_S increases with the *excess base current*, defined as the additional I_B above the value I_C/β_F that corresponds to the boundary of the active and saturation regions.

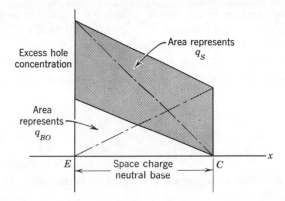

Fig. 9.7. Definition of excess saturation charge q_S. Uniform-base *pnp* transistor.

Of course, q_B also equals $q_F + q_R$ (Eq. 9.7). The subdivision of stored charge into $q_{B0} + q_S$ is more convenient here, however, because in the saturation region i_C is fixed at a constant value I_C by the external circuit, and only q_S varies. The component q_S is of great importance, for this is the *charge which must be removed from the base region* before the transistor can start to traverse the active region when switching back to the cut-off state is initiated. That is, if the base drive is reduced to zero in order to restore the initial state with $i_C \cong 0$ (see Fig. 9.6) the base charge must be reduced to the value q_{B0} before the collector current can change from the circuit-defined value I_C. A *storage delay*, t_s, thus elapses while the excess stored charge q_S is being removed from the base.

The storage delay time t_s depends on both the base drive conditions and the internal properties of the transistor. Both the turn-on current I_{B1}, and the "turn-off" value of base current, I_{B2}, during the process of discharging the base region, are of significance. In Fig. 9.6 we assumed $I_{B2} = 0$. However, more rapid removal of stored charge from the base is achieved if I_{B2} is made *positive*, corresponding to extraction of stored majority carriers from the base via the base terminal. Throughout the following discussion it will be assumed that, when switching the transistor from the saturation to the cutoff state, the base current is defined by the external circuit as having a constant value $I_{B2} \geqslant 0$.

We return now to discussion of behavior in the saturation region in response to turn-on base current I_{B1}. Ultimately, a steady state is reached, with a certain value of excess charge q_S stored in the base. We relate this charge to the excess base current, i_{BS}, by defining a saturation charge control parameter τ_S as:

$$\tau_S = [q_S/|i_{BS}|]_{\text{dc steady state}} \qquad (9.24)$$

where

$$i_{BS} = I_{B1} - I_C/\beta_F \qquad (9.25)$$

That is, in the steady state the total base current is given by

$$i_B = - \left[\frac{q_{B0}}{\tau_{BF}} + \frac{q_S}{\tau_S} \right] \qquad (9.26)$$

The reader may feel that assuming q_S proportional to i_{BS} is not obvious, although "reasonable." However, this property is readily established from the charge-control relations of Eqs. 9.8, by evaluating q_S (as $q_F + q_R - q_{B0}$) in terms of the circuit-defined currents I_C, I_{B1}, after setting the time derivatives equal to zero. Essentially, the definition of τ_S stems from the linearity of Eqs. 9.8; given that I_C and q_{B0} are defined as constant by the external circuit, the only variable quantities, q_S and i_{BS}, *must* be linearly related in the dc steady state. The relationships between the various charge components, and the evaluation of τ_S in terms of the basic charge-control parameters of Eqs. 9.8, are treated in detail in PEM, Chapter 10. It is shown there that

$$\tau_S = \frac{\alpha_F(\tau_F + \alpha_R \tau_R)}{1 - \alpha_F \alpha_R} \qquad (9.27)$$

The parameter τ_S thus expresses the net recombination tendency of the excess stored charge. The corresponding recombination current is furnished by the base current component i_S when the total base charge is maintained in the steady state. The parameter τ_S may be measured as the ratio of q_S to $|i_{BS}|$, as outlined Sec. 9.3.4.

Now, during transient changes in the saturation region, with a circuit-defined constant collector current $I_C = -V_{CC}/R_C$, the component q_{B0} of base charge may be regarded as remaining constant, while only q_S changes. Under transient conditions, we therefore express the base current as:

$$i_B = -\left(\frac{q_{B0}}{\tau_{BF}} + \frac{q_S}{\tau_S} + \frac{dq_S}{dt}\right) \qquad (9.28a)$$

since

$$\frac{dq_B}{dt} = \frac{dq_S}{dt}$$

The interpretation of Eq. 9.28a is that the base current has three components: recombination current associated with q_{B0}, recombination current associated with q_S, and a charging current which causes q_S (or q_B) to change.

Alternatively, we may express Eq. 9.28a as:

$$-\left(i_B - \frac{I_C}{\beta_F}\right) = \frac{q_S}{\tau_S} + \frac{dq_S}{dt} \qquad (9.28b)$$

Solution of this differential equation for the transient behavior of q_S is a simple matter *when i_B and I_C assume circuit-defined constant values*, as in the switching situation under consideration. Thus, if we set $i_B = I_{B1}$, corresponding to turn-on, the growth of q_S to the steady-state value of excess stored charge may be evaluated. Subsequently, if we set i_B to zero or $+I_{B2}$, in order to switch the transistor back to the cut-off state, Eqs. 9.28 express the fall of q_S to zero during the storage delay time interval t_s. This equation, of course, is valid only for $q_S \geq 0$.

Given the turn-on and turn-off values of base current, I_{B1} and I_{B2}, the storage delay t_s is readily determined if we assume that q_S reaches the steady-state value before turn-off drive is applied. Thus the initial value of q_S, prior to application of I_{B2}, is

$$q_S(0) = -(I_{B1} - I_C/\beta_F)\tau_S \qquad (9.29)$$

Taking the time origin at the point where i_B becomes I_{B2}, the solution for q_S is

$$q_S = q_S(0) - \tau_S(I_{B2} - I_{B1})(1 - e^{-t/\tau_S}) \qquad (9.30)$$

Thus q_S falls exponentially, with time constant τ_S, toward the negative value $-(I_{B2} - I_C/\beta_F)\tau_S$, but only the part of this behavior for $q_S \geq 0$ is meaningful (see Fig. 9.6c). At the instant when

$q_S = 0$, then $q_B = q_F$ and traverse of the active region to the cut-off state commences, with the behavior of the stored charge in the base expressed by Eq. 9.1.

The storage delay time t_s follows from Eq. 9.30. By setting $q_S = 0$, we obtain

$$t_s = \tau_S \ln \left[\frac{I_{B2} - I_{B1}}{I_{B2} - I_C/\beta_F} \right] \tag{9.31}$$

Alternatively, with a *turn-off overdrive factor* m defined as

$$m = \frac{-I_{B2}}{(I_C/\beta_F)} \tag{9.32}$$

and turn-on overdrive factor n defined in Eq. 9.18, we obtain from Eq. 9.31

$$t_s = \tau_S \ln \left[\frac{1 + n/m}{1 + 1/m} \right] \tag{9.33}$$

If both $n, m \gg 1$, as is often the case,

$$t_s \cong \tau_S \ln (1 + n/m) \tag{9.33a}$$

Over a wide range of base drive conditions, t_s is of the order of τ_S. For example, if $m = 0$ ($I_{B2} = 0$) and $n = 10$, Eq. 9.33 gives $t_s = 2.3\tau_S$. If I_{B2} is now given a positive value such that $n = m \gg 1$ then Eq. 9.33a is applicable, and the storage delay becomes $t_s \cong \tau_s \ln 2 = 0.69\tau_S$.

The above examples illustrate the property that a storage delay of the order of τ_S results under conditions of fairly large turn-on overdrive. This delay is the price paid for reduction of the rise time t_r; the larger the turn-on overdrive n, the smaller t_r but the larger t_s, for given circuit-defined I_C. A numerical illustration indicates the orders of magnitude involved. The transistor whose forward and reverse charge-control parameters are quoted in Sec. 9.1 has the "saturation parameter" $\tau_S = 0.44$ μsec.* With $n = 1$, $t_r = 2.64$ μsec, while $t_s = 0$. Making $n = 10$ reduces t_r to 0.102 μsec. If in this case the turn-off overdrive $m = 0$, $t_s = 1.02$ μsec, whereas if $m = 10$, t_s is reduced to 0.26 μsec.

---

* τ_s could be measured by the method indicated in Sec. 9.3.4, or calculated from the forward and reverse charge-control parameters by using Eq. 9.27.

9.3.3 *Switching Back to the Cut-off State (Turn-Off)*

The completion of the process of switching to the initial cut-off state is completed by i_C falling to zero exponentially as the active region of operation is traversed (see Eqs. 9.1, 9.2). Starting with time origin at the instant where q_S, q_R become zero,

$$i_C = -\frac{V_{CC}}{R_C} e^{-t/\tau_{BF}}$$ (9.34)

if $i_B = 0$ throughout the transient. The 10% to 90% fall time of this response is

$$t_f = 2.2\tau_{BF}$$ (9.35)

As discussed already, a large reduction in fall time is possible if the transistor is *turned off with overdrive* instead of simply reducing i_B to zero. When in the saturation state, both junctions are forward-biased, and the junction voltages are almost independent of the terminal currents, being defined only by the corresponding charges q_F, q_R stored in the base. Therefore, when switching the transistor to the OFF state, the direction of flow of i_B can actually be reversed (i_B made positive for a *pnp* transistor) in order to *remove* majority carriers from the base region and so effect rapid discharge of the base as considered above. Such a reverse base drive can also be maintained while the active region is being traversed, since the emitter-base junction is forward-biased throughout this process; so long as $q_F > 0$, the current flowing through the emitter-base junction can be controlled by the base drive circuit, provided that $|V_S| \gg |v_{BE}|$. For a rapid switch-off process, therefore, the base current is set at a positive value I_{B2} (that is, turn-off overdrive factor $m > 0$). The resulting waveform of collector current is illustrated in Fig. 9.8, and it is evident that much reduced values of t_f are achieved by employing turn-off overdrive. The exponential transient of i_C now traverses the active region as if to reach a positive final value; that is, during this phase

$$i_C = -\frac{V_{CC}}{R_C} + \beta_F\left(I_{B2} + \frac{V_{CC}}{\beta_F R_C}\right)\left(1 - e^{-t/\tau_{BF}}\right)$$ (9.36)

as may be verified from Eqs. 9.1, 9.2.

Fig. 9.8. Response waveforms for common-emitter switch of Fig. 9.6 with turn-off overdrive.

With the turn-off overdrive m defined as in Eq. 9.32, the 10% to 90% fall time t_f is found from Eq. 9.36 to be

$$t_f = \tau_{BF} \ln \left[\frac{1 + 0.9/m}{1 + 0.1/m} \right] \tag{9.37}$$

With large overdrive ($m \gg 1$),

$$t_f \cong \tau_{BF} \frac{0.8}{m} \tag{9.38}$$

This expression indicates the effectiveness of overdrive in reducing t_f to values much less than τ_{BF}.

9.3.4 *Measurement of the Saturation Charge-Control Parameter* τ_S

The parameter τ_S may be measured in a manner similar to that described in Sec. 9.2.2 for the forward parameters τ_F, τ_{BF}. The method is suggested by Eq. 9.28a, and involves the circuit arrangement of Fig. 9.9. Initially, the transistor is in the steady saturation state, defined by the values of the resistors R_C, R_B. Positive-going base drive is applied via the network v_S, R, C, the source voltage v_S undergoing a positive step ΔV much greater than $|v_{BE}|$. Simul-

(a) Circuit arrangement

(b) Response waveforms: with RC correct
$$\tau_S = RC$$

Fig. 9.9. Technique for measurement of saturation charge-control parameter τ_S.

taneously, therefore, a step of base current $\Delta V/R$ and a step of base charge $C\Delta V$ are applied to the transistor. The former is arranged just to drive the transistor to the boundary of the saturation and active regions; that is,

$$\frac{\Delta V}{R} = -i_{BS}$$

By suitable adjustment of the value of C, it is possible to arrange that

$$C\Delta V = q_S$$

The transistor then makes a step change to a new steady state at the boundary of the saturation region, q_S having been removed from the base and the steady base current changed correspondingly to maintain the smaller base charge at a constant value. Thus, with this adjustment of R and C,

$$\tau_S = RC$$

In practice, adjustment is made so that the collector current does not change on application of the positive base drive, as illustrated in Fig. 9.9. Reduction of R to too small a value causes the final value of i_C to change from $-V_{CC}/R_C$; too large a value of C causes a greater charge than q_S to be removed from the base and i_C to be reduced suddenly below $-V_{CC}/R_C$ at the onset of the base drive. When this measurement is carried out in practice, the value of RC obtained also includes the effects of charge storage in the junction space-charge layers. As discussed in the next section, such additional charge storage may be taken into account approximately in the above analysis of saturation region behavior simply by using the appropriate representative value of τ_S, as measured by the technique just described.

9.4 EFFECTS OF CHARGE STORAGE IN JUNCTION SPACE-CHARGE LAYERS

Associated with any change in junction voltage (v_{EB} or v_{CB}) is a change in charge stored in the space-charge layer of the corresponding junction. As the junction is forward-biased, the space-charge layer is reduced in width, and the amount of charge therein is also reduced. Consider the parts of the junction space-charge layers in the base of a *pnp* transistor: when a junction is forward-biased, a supply of electrons (majority carriers) has to enter the base to neutralize part of the junction space charge and so narrow the space-charge layer. This electron supply flows as base charging current. Thus, if both junctions are forward-biased, as in the saturation region, the total majority-carrier charge $(-q_{BT})$ supplied to the base has four components; that is,

$$(-q_{BT}) = -(q_F + q_{VE} + q_R + q_{VC}) \qquad (9.39)$$

as illustrated in Fig. 9.10 where $(-q_{VE})$ and $(-q_{VC})$ are the charges supplied to the space-charge layers in the process of reducing their width. It should be noted that all charge components are measured with respect to the equilibrium condition and become zero when the junction-applied voltage is zero.

Fig. 9.10. Definition of components of total excess majority-carrier charge in base material; n_{bo} is the equilibrium majority carrier concentration.

Under dynamic conditions, the base current now becomes, in general,

$$i_B = - \left[\frac{q_F}{\tau_{BF}} + \frac{q_R}{\tau_{BR}} + \frac{d}{dt} (q_F + q_{VE} + q_R + q_{VC}) \right] \quad (9.40)$$

The pair of charge components q_F, q_{VE} or q_R, q_{VC} associated with a junction always bear the same sign: positive for forward and negative for reverse voltage bias.

In the *cut-off* state, with both junctions reverse-biased, the charges q_{VE}, q_{VC} in the space-charge layer are negative and predominate over the corresponding charges q_F, q_R delivered to the charge-neutral base region; the latter may therefore be neglected. In the active region of operation, q_{VE}, q_F, and q_{VC} are significant, but q_R is quite negligible; the first two components are positive, while q_{VC} is negative. In the saturation region, all charge components are significant and are, of course, positive.

When the transistor is switched from the cutoff state, through the active region to saturation, it should be noted that all charge components make positive excursions. In particular, as the active region is traversed, the collector space-charge-layer component q_{VC} becomes less negative because the collector reverse bias is being reduced, until this charge becomes zero at the point of entry into the saturation region.

The charges q_F, q_R injected into the neutral base region are related by linear equations to the terminal currents due to these charges. No such simple relationships exist, however, for the space-charge-layer charges q_{VE}, q_{VC}—these are related in a *nonlinear* manner either to the junction voltage or to the current injected by the junction in the steady state. These nonlinear relationships are discussed in detail in PEM, Chapter 10. For example, the dependence of q_{VE} on the junction voltage v_{EB} of the emitter-base diode is as illustrated in Fig. 9.11; that of q_{VC} on v_{CB} is similar. As the junction voltage increases from negative bias values and becomes positive, the slope of the stored charge versus junction voltage characteristic increases. An exact analysis of the dynamic behavior of the transistor, taking into account the nonlinear nature of charge storage in the junction space-charge layers, would be very much more complicated than that of the previous sections where only the charges stored in the charge-neutral base region were considered.

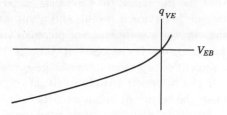

Fig. 9.11. Dependence of charge stored in space-charge layer (emitter-base junction) on junction voltage, with respect to the equilibrium condition.

Simplicity of analysis may be maintained, with some loss of accuracy, by *linearizing* the relationships between q_{VE}, q_{VC} and the terminal *currents* of the transistor. In this process we relate the total charges delivered to the base in the complete transient excursion (that is, between initial and final steady states) to the changes in terminal currents in the same manner as previously for q_F, q_R alone. In other words, the charge-storage properties of the transistor are represented by piecewise-linear relationships. For a given region of operation, for example the active region, a linear analysis is used, exactly as above, in terms of parameters that are defined in terms of the extreme endpoints of the region. We know that the linearized relationships are strictly correct only for the dc steady state at the *endpoints* of the region of operation concerned, but we *assume* that they apply with good approximation throughout the transient process of traversing this region.

As in all approximate methods of analyzing a physical situation, confidence in the approach to analysis is dependent upon the success with which observed practical behavior (of the transistor, operating in the switching role) can be predicted analytically. The linearized analysis described certainly has the virtue of simplicity, though it is known that the waveforms obtained will be somewhat in error owing to the omission of the nonlinear features of charge storage in the junction space-charge layers. This discrepancy is, however, small in practice unless the space-charge layer components of stored charge in the device are a major fraction of the whole. The endpoints of the predicted transient behavior are, of course, correct by definition.

It is found that the linearized (or piecewise linear) approach to analysis of switching behavior is useful, and gives good prediction of transient behavior, for a wide range of physical transistor types and of switching situations. Its success depends on the appropriate choice or measurement of representative charge-control parameters for the device in the intended switching situation; this choice is made simple when the transient behavior is between definite endpoints, set by circuit-defined base and collector currents, as in switching operations discussed in Sec. 9.3.

The new linearized parameters are distinguished from the previous ones by using T_F, T_{BF}, T_R, T_{BR} instead of the corresponding τ_F, τ_{BF}, τ_R, τ_{BR} in the basic charge-control Eqs. 9.8. Because of the additional charges supplied to the space-charge layers, $T_F > \tau_F$, $T_{BF} > \tau_{BF}$, and similarly for the reverse parameters. Of course, any measurement of charge-control parameters for an actual transistor, as a ratio of charge delivered to the base to the current established, gives these "total" parameters, T_{BF}, T_F, rather than those discussed in previous sections. Changes in charges stored in the space-charge layers are also involved when making measurement of the saturation charge-control parameter by the method described in Sec. 9.3.4, though usually the proportion of such charge involved is very small; therefore, this parameter should strictly also be represented by T_S to indicate that some degree of linearization of the true relationships has been made.

A more detailed discussion on the process of "linearizing" the charge-control relationships to include the nonlinear space-charge layer charging effects is given in PEM, Chapter 10.

9.5 TURN-ON DELAY

There is one particular respect in which the "linearizing" approach described in the previous section is inadequate for the explanation of observed effects. In a practical switching circuit, the transistor is often operated with the emitter-base junction somewhat reverse-biased in the cutoff state. Both q_{VE} and q_{VC} are thus negative. On the application of base drive current, entry of the active region of operation cannot take place until q_{VE} has been reduced to zero as the junction voltage v_{EB} rises from the initial negative value to zero. Now, in a common-emitter switch configuration (see Fig. 9.2), as v_{EB} is raised to zero, the voltage v_{BE} falls from an initially positive value to zero and, consequently, the collector-base junction voltage v_{CB} undergoes an equal *positive* increment (reverse bias reduced). Therefore, in the process of bringing the transistor to the boundary of the active region with $v_{EB} = 0$, q_{VE} has to be reduced to zero and the negative value of q_{VC} also has to be somewhat reduced. Before q_F or i_C can start to increase from zero values, a *turn-on delay* t_d elapses while the base current drive supplies the necessary charge to the space-charge layers. The majority-carrier charge delivered in time t_d can be written as:

$$-\Delta q_V = q_{VE} - \Delta q_{VC}$$

and if the base drive current is I_{B1}, then

$$t_d \cong -\Delta q_V / I_{B1} \tag{9.41}$$

In this estimation of the turn-on delay, it is assumed that the collector current, which flows while the collector junction space-charge is changing, causes very negligible change in collector voltage.

Figure 9.12 shows a typical collector voltage response waveform for a transistor operating under the conditions discussed. The collector current initially undergoes an excursion in the opposite direction to traverse of the active region, due to flow of charging current into the collector-base junction space-charge layer (viz.,

Fig. 9.12. Illustrating turn-on delay: *pnp* transistor.

initially *into* the collector for a *pnp* device). In the case shown, the emitter-base junction was initially reverse-biased by 1 volt, while the collector supply voltage (v_{CE} in the initial state) was -6 volts.

The turn-on delay is increased if appreciable stray or circuit capacitance is present between the base-emitter terminals of the transistor. Such an input capacitance (C_{in}) has to be charged while the initial reverse bias of the emitter-base junction is being reduced to zero. The charge required for this purpose is ($-v_{BE}(0)C_{\text{in}}$) where $v_{BE}(0)$ is the initial positive value of v_{BE}. The turn-on delay time now increases to

$$t_d \cong \frac{-\Delta q_V - v_{BE}(0)C_{\text{in}}}{I_{B1}} \tag{9.42}$$

It is possible to relate the charge Δq_V to the emitter and collector incremental junction capacitances C_{je}, C_{jc}; discussion of the relationships involved is given in PEM, Chapter 10.

In effect, the piecewise-linear approximation to the charge-storage properties of the transistor, for transient behavior between cut-off and the threshold of saturation, is now in two parts. The first part, which concerns the turn-on delay, is from the initial cut-off state up to where $v_{BE} = 0$, while the second is for the rest of the transient process of traversing the active region up to the instant where $v_{CB} = 0$ (or effectively, in an actual switching circuit, to where $v_{CE} \cong 0$).

9.6 BASE DRIVE FOR FAST SWITCHING RESPONSE

Switching by means of step changes of base drive current is frequently employed in practical applications. Using a large turn-on overdrive factor results in short rise time for the transition from the cut-off to the saturation state. However, large turn-on base current results in large excess stored charge in the base region in the saturation state, and correspondingly large storage delay time can be incurred when switching back to the cut-off state, unless large turn-off overdrive is employed.

The combination of a step drive of base current and base charge has been seen to result in very rapid change of state. If the source of excitation is of sufficiently low source impedance to approximate closely the conditions discussed in connection with the circuit of

Fig. 9.5, then switching across the active region can be accomplished in a time of the order of T_F. (The T parameters, representing the *total* charges stored in the base region, are employed throughout this section. The turn-on delay considerations of the previous section are neglected, but should be regarded as superimposed on the effects discussed here.) A close approximation to a step change of collector current between zero and the circuit-defined value I_C is achieved by delivering via C a charge of at least $I_C T_F$ where $I_C = -V_{CC}/R_C$ (assuming an initial cut-off state). To switch the transistor back to the OFF state with virtually no storage delay, C must extract a majority-carrier charge of at least $i_{BS} T_S$, where i_{BS} is the excess base current in the saturation state.

In practical circuits, a capacitor is very often used in the manner of Fig. 9.5 to achieve fast switching response; this element is then referred to as a "speed-up capacitor." Usually, however, the source impedance of the excitation source is not sufficiently low for true step-charge drive conditions to be realized, and the flow of current through the base drive capacitor is limited by this source impedance. Nevertheless, considerable improvement in switching speed is achieved in comparison with the situation with step base-current drive only.

In order to appreciate the limiting effect of source impedance in the base drive circuit, and at the same time to see the improvement in speed of response due to the speed-up capacitor, let us consider the switch circuit of Fig. 9.13 under conditions of turn-on drive. We shall assume that the source voltage undergoes a negative step change $(-\Delta V)$ from zero, where ΔV is much greater than the change of base voltage v_{BE} between the initial cut-off and final saturation state. On application of the base drive step, the base current is initially $-\Delta V/R_S$, decaying exponentially to the value $-\Delta V/(R_S + R_B)$ as shown in Fig. 9.13. Neglecting the effect of v_{BE}, we obtain

$$i_B = I_{B1} + (I_{B0} - I_{B1})e^{-t/CR'}$$

where $\qquad I_{B0} = \dfrac{-\Delta V}{R_S}$

$$I_{B1} = \dfrac{-\Delta V}{(R_S + R_B)}$$

$$(9.43)$$

Fig. 9.13. Response of a transistor switch with "speed-up" capacitor in the base drive circuit, and excitation from a source of finite internal resistance.

and

$$\frac{1}{R'} = \frac{1}{R_S} + \frac{1}{R_B} \cong \frac{1}{R_S} \qquad (9.44)$$

if $R_S \ll R_B$.

While traversing the active region, the response of stored base charge and collector current to this base current waveform has two exponential components; one component is of time constant CR' (time constant of base drive circuit) and the other of time constant T_{BF}. Clearly, the speed of response is increased as a result of the inclusion of the element C in the base circuit; if $R_B \gg R_S$, this improvement can be large. Alternatively, a desired value of rise time can be achieved with a smaller value of steady-state turn-on base current I_{B1} than without C, so that the excess stored charge in the saturation state (and therefore the storage delay t_s when switching off) is reduced.

A simple approximate expression for the collector current response during the turn-on process may be derived if the rise time t_r is quite small compared with the time constant CR' of the base drive current. In this case, i_B does not vary much during the rise time and may be assumed to be constant at a suitable average value KI_{B0}, where K is somewhat less than unity, as illustrated in Fig. 9.13. Thus,

$$i_C \cong \beta_F K I_{B0}(1 - e^{-t/T_{BF}}) \qquad (9.45)$$

during the transition to the saturation state. If $|KI_{B0}| \gg |I_{B1}|$, inclusion of C in the circuit results in major decrease of turn-on time.

Figure 9.13 illustrates the collector-current response (and also the response of total base charge) for switching from cut-off to saturation and back again. Initially, the transistor enters deeply into saturation owing to the large base-current drive delivered via C, but subsequently "relaxes" to a very reduced degree of saturation. Switching back to the cut-off state is similarly speeded up by the influence of the large turn-off overdrive current that flows through C.

PROBLEMS

P9.1 A transistor switch is shown in Fig. 9.14. The charge-control parameters of the transistor are:

$$\tau_F = \tau_R = 2 \times 10^{-9} \text{ sec} \qquad \tau_{BF} = \tau_{BR} = 10^{-7} \text{ sec}$$

Fig. 9.14.

At $t = 0$, $v_1(t)$ changes to $+10$ volts, thereby initiating a change in the switch from the OFF state to the ON state. *The current in the switch terminals (i) is zero.*

(a) Sketch and dimension the base current $i_B(t)$. Make reasonable approximations.

(b) How much time must elapse before the switch can sustain a current of 10 ma magnitude ($i = \pm 10$ ma) without being pulled out of the ON condition ($v \cong 0$)?

(c) After the excess charge in the base has reached a steady state, the base-emitter circuit is opened ($i_B = 0$). Sketch and dimension the resulting time dependence of the total excess charge in the base $q_B(t)$.

P9.2   A transistor has the following charge control parameter values (assumed to be independent of bias currents):

$$\tau_F = 12 \times 10^{-9} \text{ sec}$$
$$\beta_F = 100$$
$$\tau_R = 36 \times 10^{-9} \text{ sec}$$
$$\beta_R = 10$$

(a) Evaluate the forward stored charge q_F if the collector current $I_C = -2$ ma and the transistor operates just on the boundary of the saturation region with $v_{CB} = 0$.

(b) Determine the base charge components q_F, q_R if the base current is now made $I_B = -0.5$ ma with I_C still equal to -2 ma. Compare the total charge stored in the base in (a) and (b).

P9.3   The transistor of Problem P9.2 is operated in the simple switching circuit of Fig. 9.15. Initially, the device is in the cut-off state. Switching to the saturation region is effected in rise time t_r by applying a constant input base-current drive I_{B1} (negative for *pnp* device). While in the saturation region, the collector current is constant at the circuit-

Fig. 9.15.

defined value I_C. Switching back to the original cut-off state follows when base current is changed to the value I_{B2} (positive for *pnp* device). If

$$I_{B1} = -0.5 \text{ ma}$$
$$I_C = -2 \text{ ma}$$
$$I_{B2} = +0.5 \text{ ma}$$

calculate the rise time t_r, storage delay-time t_s, and fall-time t_f of the resulting collector-current response. (Note that the influence of charges stored in the space-charge layers is neglected throughout this problem. A "linearized" calculation of fall time, taking into account such charge storage would yield the above result but with the effective parameter T_{BF} replacing τ_{BF}; T_{BF} is defined in terms of the *total* charge removed from base material in traversing the active region, including the effects of the space-charge layers.)

Index